Revival of Piety Through an Islamic Theodicy

Tallal M. Zeni

Revival of Piety Through an Islamic Theodicy

This edition published 2020 by
Kindle Direct Publishing

ISBN: 978-1-7346362-7-7 paper
ISBN: 978-1-7346362-1-5 ebook

Front cover Arabic calligraphy by Arabiccalligraphy4you.
The inner verse is: *O ye who believe! Fear God as He should be feared, and die not except in a state of Islam. And hold fast, all together, by the rope of God.* See Q.III.102-103.
The outer verse is: *Whoso obeyeth God and the Messenger, they are with those unto whom God hath shown favour, of the prophets and the saints and the martyrs and the righteous.* See Q.IV.69.

Table Of Contents

Acknowledgements v
Introduction vii

PART ONE

Chapter One: God's Providence for Humankind 3
Chapter Two: God's Beautiful Names and His Infallibility from any Evil 18
Chapter Three: The Wisdom of God's Creation and Commandments 28
Chapter Four: The Greatness of the Prophets 46
Chapter Five: The Greatness of Muḥammad: the Seal of the Prophets 75
Chapter Six: The Excellence of Abū Bakr, ʿUmar, ʿUthmān and ʿAlī 104
Chapter Seven: Piety 125

PART TWO

Chapter Eight: Muslim Approaches to the Problems of Evil and Hellfire 147
Chapter nine: Non-Muslim Approaches to the Problems of Evil and Hellfire 177
Chapter Ten: The Wisdom in Allowing Suffering 218
Chapter Eleven: An Exposition on Evil 264
Chapter Twelve: The Wisdom in Allowing Evil 333
Chapter Thirteen: Hypocrisy 396

PART THREE

Chapter Fourteen: Hellfire 447
Chapter Fifteen: Paradise 467

Epilogue 489
Bibliography 495
Index 515

Acknowledgements

All praise and gratitude is due to God (Glorious is He), Who has facilitated the completion of this work by virtue of His grace. We cannot thank the Holy Lord enough for all of His innumerable blessings.

Second, I would like to thank Andrew Booso for his support throughout the editing process, his excellent advice, as well as his meticulous editing. He has made many significant contributions, which improved the fluency and readability of the text. I would like to acknowledge again that it has been a great joy to work with Andrew and Fatima Azzam, whom I thank for their enduring patience and endless support on the two prior books: *Ibn Qayyim al-Jawziyya on Divine Wisdom and the Problem of Evil* and *Ibn Qayyim al-Jawziyya on Knowledge*.

I ask God (Glorious and Exalted is He) to accept this work and make it a means to reduce the evil in this world and increase the piety and righteousness of myself and others. May the Almighty Lord grant His providence, mercy and grace to myself, my family and relatives, and to all the believers in this world and in the Hereafter!

Introduction

In the Name of God the Most Beneficent Most Merciful

All praise and gratitude is due to God (Glorious is He). We rely on our Holy Lord, for He is Most Loving, Most Wise and Most Generous, and He is Omniscient and Omnipotent. We seek His guidance to all goodness in this world and the Hereafter. We seek refuge in Him from the evil of Satan and the wicked, as well as the evilness of ourselves and our actions. And we trustfully depend on God (Glorious and Exalted is He) for His assistance so that we may strive to reduce suffering and evil in this world.

The problem of evil has consumed the thoughts of innumerable sages over many millennia. A multitude of theodicies, some by Muslim scholars and others from non-Muslims, will be discussed here—particularly in Chapters Eight and Nine—in order to shed light upon their various approaches to this critical topic. From a traditional Islamic foundation, Ibn Qayyim al-Jawziyya has provided one of the most in-depth articulations of theodicy. His most significant thoughts on the subject were translated in *Ibn Qayyim al-Jawziyya on Divine Wisdom and the Problem of Evil*. This book seeks to go beyond that work by providing more comprehensive solutions to the problems of evil, hypocrisy and Hellfire, by God's grace and guidance.

A few *sūra*s of the Qur'ān, as will be discussed in Chapter One, provide a straightforward theodicy sufficient to protect the vast majority of Muslims from attributing evil to our Holy Lord or disbelieving in Him. But in order to develop a far-reaching theodicy, the entire Qur'ān as well as the Sunna of the Prophet Muḥammad (may God bless him and grant him peace) must be utilized—this will be pursued throughout the remainder of the book. A few key points will be made here.

First of all, God (Glorious is He) expounds upon His Beautiful Names and Glorious Attributes throughout the Qur'ān. The manifestation of the consequences of a great number of His Names and Attributes in this world represents the principle reason for its creation. Specifically, the Holy Lord may limit the manifestation of some of His Names, for instance that He is the Omnipotent and Most Generous, in order to allow the manifestation of a greater number of other Beautiful Names of His.

Moreover, it can be stated that the emergence of the prophets and messengers, who are the best of humankind, as well as the higher ranks of believers, i.e. the pious, devout, righteous and truly faithful—all of these being beloved to our Holy Lord—can be thought of as the second most important reason for the creation of this world. These ranks could not have been demonstrated nor attained by those human beings in a world wherein evil was non-existent. The characteristics and differences of each of these groups will be developed in Chapter Seven, as well as throughout the book, due to their centrality to the issues of theodicy.

Many books, while advancing a theodicy, fail to discuss or adequately appreciate the importance of piety and righteousness or their role in minimizing evil. Certainly, the Scriptures (including the Qur'ān) and the traditions of His prophets (including Muḥammad) do elaborate on these traits. Therefore, eight chapters will expound upon that which is good, as well as discussing Paradise, while seven chapters will delve into evil, hypocrisy, suffering and the Hellfire. All chapters, including the former, will provide numerous solutions to the problem of evil. The central point is that God's love of the goodness exhibited by these ranks of pious and righteous believers preponderates over the evil that exists, even though the former represent a small percentage of humankind.

Now, the Holy Lord has commanded all of His prophets—from Adam to Muḥammad (the Seal of His Prophets) and inclusive of Jesus—to worship Him alone and to convey His Oneness to humanity. The prophets are our role models, and a detailed discussion of the ways by which they strove against evil will therefore be discussed. The characteristics, actions, prophecies and miracles of the Prophet Muḥammad in particular are discussed at length so that it becomes clear that he (may God bless him and grant him peace) is a Prophet and Messenger of the Holy Lord. Moreover, this book seeks to prove that the characteristics and actions of Muḥammad are consistent with those of other prophets mentioned in the Bible, and resemble most closely those of the Prophet David (may God bless and grant peace to them both).

Suffering will be differentiated from evil, and many of the wise purposes for the presence of both will be discussed in depth. Those who are able to endure suffering and overcome evil for the sake of God come to possess and display devout characteristics that could not have otherwise become manifest. Actions of the heart (such as patience, reliance and dependence), as well as those of the body and intellect (such as striving and fighting against evil and repudiating it), could not have occurred in the absence of evil. A discussion regarding the importance of fulfilling His commandments by enjoining good and forbidding evil will also provide a practical theodicy.

Furthermore, it is only due to the construct of this world that the believers (who represent a minority of humanity) can be differentiated from the disbelievers (who are the majority) and from the hypocrites (who are less in number than the believers). This differentiation could not have been achieved had the world only contained good, without any suffering or evil. Finally, dysteleological or gratuitous evils and examples thereof will also be discussed at length, together with solutions to that problem.

The ultimate objective of this book is to provide sufficient proof that only Islam, with its true revelation and provision of knowledge, adequately addresses the problems of evil (including gratuitous types), hypocrisy and Hellfire. In this fashion, the strength and goodness of Islam will become evident to a far greater degree. The attainment of this certainty along with the performance of righteous actions and striving against evil are the only means towards a revival of piety and resurgence of righteousness, by the grace of God.

Many years were spent contemplating and researching this book. All praise and gratitude is due to God (Glory be to Him). I have sought to follow the revelation (i.e. the Qur'ān and Sunna along with some references to the Bible) throughout, and it is my hope that everything is concordant to it.[1] If anything is not, I seek forgiveness from the

[1] The methodology for referencing the Qur'ān and Sunna in this work is similar to that used in Tallal M. Zeni (tr.), *Ibn Qayyim al-Jawziyya on Divine Wisdom and the Problem of Evil* (Cambridge: Islamic Texts Society, 2017). For instance, translations of the Qur'ān are derived from Pickthall's classic, even if slightly amended, unless attributed to another famous translation. In regards to the Sunna, references to *Ṣaḥīḥ Muslim* have first the number for the Arabic print and then the number for the English translation.

Holy Lord.[2] I hope that any controversial issue, while seeking to leave no stone unturned, will not turn readers away from the great goodness of Islam or other benefits within this book. In that light, I have only sought to pursue the truth hoping that the True One (*al-Ḥaqq*) accepts it. Moreover, I hope that the length will not turn away readers—some may want to read the first three chapters and then skip to Part Two, returning only to Chapters Four through Seven once referenced in the latter.

When I commenced this journey, I never envisioned that the solutions would become as expansive or complex as they have. That said, the wise purposes that God (Glorious is He) possesses are vast, and humanity cannot know or recount them in their entirety. Nonetheless, a critical threshold was reached and it was necessary to conclude the book. Certainly, in this regard, we recall the statement of the Exalted: *Ye are to expound it to mankind and not to hide it.*[3] However, this book should be more than sufficient in expounding a comprehensive and satisfactory theodicy, God willing.

It is my hope that God (Glorious is He) will accept this and allow it to lead to goodness, piety and righteousness. We ask God (Exalted is He) to include us among the followers of His Prophet Muḥammad (may God bless him and grant him peace). May the Holy Lord bestow His mercy upon us in Paradise, and protect us from hypocrisy and the punishment of Hellfire!

---

[2] The Prophet Muḥammad (may God bless him and grant him peace) said: "If a judge (*ḥākim*) gives a verdict and his verdict is correct [i.e. in agreement with God and His Messenger], he will receive double the reward. And if he gives a verdict [to the best of his knowledge] yet his verdict is wrong, he will still receive a reward." Bukhārī 7352; Muslim 1716/4487; Tirmidhī 1326; Abū Dāwūd 3574; Ibn Māja 2314; Nasā'ī 5381; Aḥmad 17,774.

[3] Q.III.187.

PART ONE

Chapter One

God's Providence for Humankind

God (Glorious and Exalted is He) has revealed the Qur'ān (as well as the prior Scriptures) to guide humankind so that they may worship Him alone, follow His prophets, attain piety and perform righteous actions. The problem of evil is addressed throughout the Qur'ān. This chapter will provide a straightforward theodicy based on solely four *sūras* of the Qur'ān as well as a few other verses therein.

This clear theodicy is provided in the beginning of the Qur'ān with the opening chapter, Sūrat al-Fātiḥa, in the middle with Sūrat al-Kahf, and finally at the end with Sūrat al-Falaq and Sūrat al-Nās. Sūrat al-Fātiḥa is recited at least 117 times per week assuming that only the obligatory (*farḍ*) prayers are performed;[1] al-Kahf is recommended for recital at least once per week;[2] and the Prophetic practice was to recite al-Falaq and al-Nās at least 21 times per week.[3] God thus constantly reminds humankind of His providence, mercy and beneficence in these chapters and by prescribing such practices.

Sūrat al-Fātiḥa

The objective of Sūrat al-Fātiḥa in terms of the problem of evil is to preempt it—and God knows best. God (Exalted is He) is well aware that the existence of evil will seduce and delude many people away from His Straight Path, and therefore He revealed this chapter (*sūra*)

---

[1] The Prophet Muḥammad mentioned that Sūrat al-Fātiḥa is the greatest chapter in the Qur'ān (see Bukhārī 4474; Nasā'ī 913), and that one's prayer is not accepted if it is not read in each unit of prayer (see Bukhārī 756; Muslim 394/874; Tirmidhī 247; Abū Dāwūd 822; Ibn Māja 837; Nasā'ī 910; Aḥmad 7291).

[2] The Prophet Muḥammad advised: "Whoever reads Sūrat al-Kahf on Friday is granted a light from then to the next Friday." Al-Ḥākim 3392; Bayhaqī (*Sunan*) 5996. It is "sound" according to Albānī (*Ṣaḥīḥ al-Jāmiʿ al-ṣaghīr* 6470).

[3] The Prophet Muḥammad used to read Sūrat al-Falaq and Sūrat al-Nās along with Sūrat al-Ikhlāṣ three times every night before going to bed. See Bukhārī 5017; Tirmidhī 3402; Abū Dāwūd 5056; Aḥmad 24,853.

to provide the believers with a "preventative medicine" to avoid going astray.

Before reading this *sūra* one must first seek refuge with God (Glorious is He) from Satan: *And when thou recitest the Qur'ān, seek refuge in God from Satan the outcast.*[4] The Devil is the source of evil in this world; and by seeking refuge with God, one acknowledges the need for God's assistance and protection. This represents the first step to avoiding evil.

Next, the Holy Lord introduces Himself as the Most Beneficent (*al-Raḥmān*) and Most Merciful (*al-Raḥīm*) in the first verse of Sūrat al-Fātiḥa. Furthermore, God emphasizes His beneficence and mercy as He repeats these two Attributes of His in the third verse.[5] One opinion regarding those two Names of His is that *al-Raḥmān* represents His mercy that encompasses all of humankind, while *al-Raḥīm* represents His mercy that is specific to the believers.[6]

God (Exalted is He) is certainly the Most Beneficent, as He states in another chapter: *Those who bear the Throne, and all who are round about it, hymn the praises of their Lord and believe in Him and ask forgiveness for those who believe (saying): Our Lord! Thou comprehendest all things in mercy and knowledge, therefore forgive those who repent and follow Thy way.*[7] Note here that although the angels are affirming that God's mercy encompasses all things, they are only supplicating on behalf of those who repent and follow God's Path—not all of humanity.

Now, if one is certain that God is beneficent and merciful, as indicated in Sūrat al-Fātiḥa, then one will also be benevolent to others (whether believers or disbelievers) and treat them with compassion. This mercy leads to a decrease in harm, injustice and evil on a societal level.

---

[4] Q.XVI.98.

[5] Q.I.1–3: *In the Name of God, the Beneficent, the Merciful. Praise be to God, Lord of the Worlds, the Beneficent, the Merciful.*

[6] See Scott Lucas (tr.), *Ṭabarī Selections from The Comprehensive Exposition of the Interpretation of the Verses of the Qur'ān* (Cambridge: The Royal Aal Al-Bayt Institute for Islamic Thought and Islamic Texts Society, 2017), vol. I, pp. 103–106. Another viewpoint is that *al-Raḥmān* describes God's mercy for both this world and the Hereafter, while *al-Raḥīm* depicts the Holy Lord's mercy in the Hereafter alone.

[7] Q.XL.7. This verse follows Q.XL.6: *Thus was the word of thy Lord concerning those who disbelieve fulfilled: That they are owners of the Fire.*

Then in the next verse of Sūrat al-Fātiḥa one praises God alone for He is the Creator and Lord of the Worlds, and He alone is the Sovereign Owner of the Day of Judgment.[8] His sovereignty and lordship indicate His might, power and justice. This verse is recited more than seventeen times each day in the obligatory prayers alone. Praising God (Glorious is He) has a remarkable effect on a believer—if one deeply affirms that the Holy Lord is praiseworthy and the sovereign King,[9] then one will be inoculated from attributing any evil to Him. Notice that this only applies to those who pray to the Lord in accordance with His commandments. They are recompensed for their prayer in that they are much less likely to attribute evil to the Holy Lord. On the other hand, those who do not pray, as well as those who are disbelievers, are susceptible to harbouring ill thoughts of the Lord as their remembrance of these Attributes of His are not repeated nor contemplated by them with the necessary frequency.[10]

God is praiseworthy in all times, whether during moments of ease or hardship. Thankfulness is especially needed in times of ease and is done to show gratitude for His blessings. Most people, however, are not thankful to God (Exalted is He) at all: *Thy Lord is full of bounty for humankind, but most of them do not give thanks.*[11] In contrast, the believers praise God (Glorious is He) in all circumstances, and acknowledge that He is beneficent, merciful, magnanimous and wise.

Next, one states in Sūrat al-Fātiḥa: *Thee (alone) we worship; Thee (alone) we ask for help.*[12] Although worshipping the Holy Lord can be

---

[8] Q.II.2–4: *Praise be to God, Lord of the Worlds, the Beneficent, the Merciful. Master of the Day of Judgment.*

[9] Ibn al-Qayyim states: "The point is that for His sovereignty to be universal and absolute it is necessary to affirm His determination such that nothing occurs within His kingdom in the absence of His will...In addition, for His praiseworthiness to be universal and absolute it is necessary that nothing in His creation or commandments be devoid of wisdom or praiseworthy ends. God is greater and more glorious [than to allow anything to exist within it in the absence of His will or wisdom, or devoid of praiseworthy ends]." See Tallal Zeni (tr.), *Ibn Qayyim al-Jawziyya on Divine Wisdom and the Problem of Evil* (Cambridge: Islamic Texts Society, 2017), p. 186.

[10] The Lord is holy and absolutely good; but since the disbeliever was heedless and did not follow God's commandments, he became forsaken and was left to harbor such evil thoughts.

[11] Q.XXVII.73. See also Q.II.243, Q.X.60, Q.XII.38 and Q.XL.61.

[12] Q.I.5.

performed in a world devoid of evil, seeking His help and depending (*istiʿāna*) on Him can only be carried out by the righteous when striving against evils. Trustful dependence is a characteristic of righteousness, which represents a higher level than piety (*taqwā*) since, in the former case, one is striving against evil and trying to change it to good, whereas in the latter, the pious individual is only avoiding that which is evil.

One also relies on God (Glorious is He) to guide him or her to the Straight Path, which entails faith and good deeds as well as avoidance of evil. The last two verses of Sūrat al-Fātiḥa are: *Show us the Straight Path, the path of those whom Thou hast favoured; not the (path) of those who earn Thine anger nor of those who go astray.*[13] Those whom the Holy Lord has truly favoured, from a religious standpoint, are indicated in the verse: *Whoso obeyeth God and the Messenger, they are with those unto whom God hath shown favour, of the prophets and the saints and the martyrs and the righteous.*[14] Therefore, the believers, by virtue of their faith and obedience to God and His Messenger Muḥammad, become associated with and tread the same Straight Path as the righteous and higher ranks who are upon it.

As regards those who are not on the Straight Path, there are a number of possibilities regarding their identities. One group that has deserved His wrath—and is relevant to the problem of evil—is mentioned in the following verse: *All who entertain evil thoughts about God, evil encompasses them from all sides, and God's condemnation (ghaḍab) rests upon them; and He has rejected (laʿana) them [from His grace], and has readied Hell for them: and how evil a journey's end!*[15] Therefore, those who attribute evil to the Holy Lord are deserving of His wrath (*ghaḍab*). Since they attributed evil to Him (Glorious and Exalted is He) they were deserving of an evil turn of fortune. Hence one must only attribute good to the Holy Lord.

The second possibility is well known and is based on the Prophet Muḥammad's statement: "The Jews have deserved His wrath, while the Christians have gone astray."[16] Many verses of the Old Testament

---

[13] Q.I.6–7.

[14] Q.IV.69.

[15] Q.XLVIII.6 (Muḥammad Asad translation).

[16] Tirmidhī 2954. It is "authentic" according to Albānī (*Ṣaḥīḥ al-Jāmiʿ al-ṣaghīr* 8202).

also affirm that the Israelites or Jews have deserved the Almighty Lord's wrath.[17] In the case of the Christians, as with similar groups, those who worship others besides the Holy Lord alone have gone astray. The final possibility regarding those who have earned His wrath will be discussed later in this book.

By way of summation, Sūrat al-Fātiḥa inoculates one against many aspects of the problem of evil without a believer possibly even recognizing it. It also encourages us to depend on Him and strive against evil. The Prophet Muḥammad (may God bless him and grant him peace) also advised the Muslims to recite it when suffering from a disease and at the time of a calamity like death.[18]

Finally, immediately after Sūrat al-Fātiḥa, God (Glorious is He) states in Sūrat al-Baqara: *This is the Scripture whereof there is no doubt, a guidance unto those who are pious.*[19] Here and throughout the Qur'ān, the Holy Lord mentions the pious so as to emphasize the importance of becoming one of them, and to advise us to avoid sinfulness and evilness.

Sūrat al-Kahf

When turning to consider Sūrat al-Kahf one must contemplate it in its entirety—not just the story of Moses and Khiḍr. Sūrat al-Kahf, like Sūrat al-Fātiha, begins by praising the Holy Lord.[20] This, again, is important as a means of inoculating one from any ill thoughts of the Holy Lord. One thus avoids attributing any evil to Him (Glorious is He) and affirms that He acts righteously in accordance with His wisdom. Furthermore, while one praises God in Sūrat al-Fātiḥa as the Lord and King of the Day of Religious Recompense (*Malik yawm al-dīn*), in Sūrat al-Kahf one praises Him for revealing His Scripture

---

[17] See Deuteronomy 9.7–8; 2 Chronicles 34.21-25; Psalms 106.40; Ezra 5.12. This will be discussed further in Chapter Eleven.

[18] See Bukhārī 1335 and 5736; Muslim 2201/5733; Tirmidhī 1026; Abū Dāwūd 3198 and 3896; Ibn Māja 1495; Nasā'ī 1987; Aḥmad 10,985.

[19] Q.II.2. Pickthall translates *al-muttaqīn* as "those who ward off (evil)".

[20] There are four other chapters that begin by praising God: al-Anʿām (VI), Ibrāhīm (XIV), Saba' (XXXIV) and Fāṭir (XXXV).

unto His devoted and elite servant Muḥammad,[21] who is the Seal of His prophets and messengers. The Holy Lord also, in this *sūra*, affirms His perfect justice: *Thy Lord wrongeth no one.*[22]

The Qur'ān affirms His Oneness throughout—He alone should be worshipped—and in this manner Sūrat al-Fātiḥa and Sūrat al-Kahf affirm His Oneness from the standpoints of Him being the One Lord, the Deity, and the Holy King of this multiverse.[23] By way of emphasizing this Oneness, Sūrat al-Kahf moves to absolutely deny that God (Glorious and Exalted is He) has any offspring and warns those who claim such: *No knowledge have they of such a thing, nor had their fathers. It is a grievous thing that issues from their mouths as a saying—what they say is nothing but falsehood!*[24] The most widespread claim of a son is obviously that of the Christians regarding Jesus the son of Mary, and it has led many people astray, as mentioned above. The claim of the Trinity will be discussed further in Chapter Eleven.

Again, God (Exalted is He) has declared throughout the Qur'ān that He alone should be worshipped, and that all of the offspring of Adam, including Jesus, are servants of His.[25] Near the conclusion of Sūrat al-Kahf, the Holy Lord states: *Do the disbelievers reckon that they can choose My bondmen as protecting friends? Say: Shall We inform you who will be the greatest losers by their works? Those whose effort goeth astray in the life of the world, and yet they reckon that they do good work.*[26] The actions of those who worship others besides God—whether it be Jesus or

---

[21] Fakhr al-Dīn al-Rāzī also mentions another secret when he states that God began Sūrat al-Isrā' (the chapter preceding Sūrat al-Kahf) by glorifying Himself: "Whenever glorifying [the Holy Lord] is mentioned, it precedes praising Him…Therefore, [God] glorified Himself when He notified us that He raised Muḥammad (may God bless him and grant him peace): *Glorified be He Who carried His servant by night [from the Inviolable Place of Worship to the Far distant place of worship the neighbourhood whereof We have blessed, that We might show him of Our tokens!]*. Then He praised Himself when mentioning that He revealed His Scripture upon Muḥammad…That is because glorifying Him deems Him to be infallible above anything which is not appropriate [and therefore He is perfect], whereas praising Him connotes that He perfects others." See Fakhr al-Dīn al-Rāzī, *Tafsīr al-Rāzī* (Beirut: Dār Iḥyā' al-Turāth al-ʿArabī, 1999), vol. XXI, p. 421.

[22] Q.XVIII.49.

[23] This is similar to what is mentioned in Sūrat al-Nās, which will be discussed below.

[24] Q.XVIII.4–5 (Yusuf Ali translation).

[25] This will be discussed in detail in Chapters Four and Eleven.

[26] Q.XVIII.102–104.

other humans, the angels or idols—will be obliterated on the Day of Judgment, even if those actions are beneficial or "good".[27]

Next, it is of note that Sūrat al-Kahf also mentions Satan specifically: *And (remember) when We said unto the angels: Fall prostrate before Adam, and they fell prostrate, all save Iblīs. He was of the jinn, so he rebelled against his Lord's command. Will ye choose him and his seed for your protecting friends instead of Me, when they are an enemy unto you? Calamitous is the exchange for evildoers.*[28] This verse confirms that Satan was a jinn—not an angel. Iblīs[29] was a jinn amongst the angels worshipping the Lord, but harboured pride, arrogance and hatred hidden to all except God Who is omniscient and omnipotent. God (Exalted is He) manifested Satan's true evilness by creating Adam and commanding all to prostrate to the father of mankind. This verse also confirms that the disbelievers have freely chosen to follow Satan, perpetrate evil, and disobey God's commandments and prohibitions.

Next, Sūrat al-Kahf mentions that everything present on this earth is here in order to test us: *We have placed all that is on the earth as an ornament thereof that We may try them: which of them is best in conduct.*[30] This alludes to the fact that this world is a trial and tribulation to distinguish people and separate them according to their ranks, whether to bliss or punishment. God (Exalted is He) subsequently commands Muḥammad (may God bless him and grant him peace) and the believers to avoid the *pomp and glitter of this life*.[31] Ultimately all of the beauty of this world will end: *And coin for them the similitude of the life of the world as water which We send down from the sky, and the vegetation of the earth mingleth with it and then becometh dry twigs that the winds scatter.*[32] Therefore, one should instead concern oneself with belief and righteous conduct seeking to attain everlasting bliss in the Hereafter. God (Glorious is He) states at the end of Sūrat al-Kahf:

---

[27] See Q.XXV.23: *We shall have turned towards all the [supposedly good] deeds they ever wrought, and shall have transformed them into scattered dust* (Muḥammad Asad translation).

[28] Q.XVIII.50.

[29] Iblīs is one of the names of the Devil or Satan (*Shayṭān*). It is derived from the word *ablasa*, which means "to despair of all hope or goodness".

[30] Q.XVIII.7.

[31] See Q.XVIII.28 (Yusuf Ali translation).

[32] Q.XVIII.45.

Whoever hopeth for the meeting with his Lord, let him do righteous work, and make none sharer of the worship due unto his Lord.[33]

Sūrat al-Kahf emphasizes the importance of the righteous, and this is wise and appropriate. Since this *sūra* discusses the problem of evil, it emphasizes those who strive against it and seek to transform evil to good, i.e. the righteous.[34] Yet the mention of piety (*taqwā*) is notably absent within this *sūra*, which indicates that it is not sufficient to be solely pious when confronting evil. This will be discussed further in Chapter Seven.

Now, Sūrat al-Kahf includes four main stories within it, and they will be considered in regards to the problem of evil. The first two stories address the manner by which the believers should approach the evildoers and disbelievers if the faithful are weak, whereas the last two stories advise the righteous how to act in general. All of the wisdoms and morals will be considered together below.

The first story regarding the seven believers[35] illustrates that avoiding or fleeing from the disbelievers should only occur if one is fearful that remaining amongst them will result in one becoming a disbeliever or being persecuted and killed. The king and people, who were disbelievers, were going to stone these believers to death if they did not become polytheists again, and it was for this reason that the latter escaped. The believers stated: *If they should come to know of you, [they] will stone you or turn you back to their religion.*[36] The believers were thus justified in fleeing and escaping due to this persecution.

God (Exalted is He) preserved those believers as they "slept" in the cave for 300 years. As to their identity, one opinion is that these seven believers were monotheists who followed the uncorrupted teachings of Jesus, and were persecuted by their people on account of their faith[37]. It was only after Christianity, according to this opinion, was

---

[33] Q.XVIII.110.

[34] The righteous believers are mentioned towards the beginning and end of Sūrat al-Kahf, as well as throughout in verses 2, 30, 46, 82, 88 and 107. Their righteous deeds are accepted by the Holy Lord, and therefore they will be granted eternal life in Paradise.

[35] See Q.XVIII.9–26.

[36] Q.XVIII.20.

[37] See Muḥammad b. Jarīr al-Ṭabarī, *Tafsīr al-Ṭabarī*, ed. Aḥmad Shākir (Beirut: Mu'assasat al-Risāla, 2000), vol. XVII, pp. 605–612.

adopted many centuries later that they were awakened to serve as a miracle and testament to their belief. They also represented a sign that God (Glorious is He) will similarly resurrect all of humanity on the Day of Judgment.

This period of 300 years may also indicate the maximum time period which God (Exalted is He) allows for the religion to remain strange and then resurge. In this case, resurgence did not occur as a result of the efforts of those seven believers, but rather by the grace of God and the efforts of others. On the other hand, if striving and fighting are carried out by the believers, resurgence of the religion of God may occur within a generation, such as happened during the time of the Prophets David and Muḥammad (may God bless them both).

The point is that in order to avoid persecution by the disbelievers, the believers must strive or fight against the disbelievers in a pious and righteous manner and uphold the legal limits of the Holy Lord. This is certainly the methodology of the Prophets Moses, David and Muḥammad (may God bless them all).

The approach to evil, if a believer is weak, is also illustrated in the second story of Sūrat al-Kahf.[38] The believer in the story advised his disbelieving friend to worship God alone and appreciate His blessings saying: *If only, when thou enteredst thy garden, thou hadst said: That which God willeth (will come to pass)! There is no strength save in God!*[39] Therefore, at a minimum, a believer should advise others to worship God alone and acknowledge His blessings. This believer was able to advise the other without fear of persecution.

Another benefit in the story is that the disbeliever, after his garden was destroyed, regretted his disbelief and said: *Would that I had ascribed no partner to my Lord!*[40] Therefore, this verse seems to imply—and God knows best—that he later became a believer and worshipped God alone. Thus the suffering that one endures—represented in this story by the loss of one's harvest—may occur in order for the individual to return to the Holy Lord, attain belief and do good deeds. The events of the first two stories also allowed the believers therein to become

---

38 See Q.XVIII.32–44.

39 Q.XVIII.39–40.

40 Q.XVIII.42.

more certain of the Lord's providence and promise. They ultimately attained higher levels of faith as a result. And God knows best.

The fourth story in Sūrat al-Kahf involves Dhū al-Qarnayn, who was a righteous ruler empowered by the Holy Lord.[41] He journeyed to many nations in accordance with God's will and wisdom. God (Exalted is He) commanded him in regards to the first nation he met: *Either punish [the wrongdoers] or show the [righteous] kindness.*[42] Dhū al-Qarnayn followed the commandment of the Lord and stated: *As for him who doeth wrong, we shall punish him, and then he will be brought back unto his Lord, Who will punish him with awful punishment! But as for him who believeth and doeth right, good will be his reward, and We shall speak unto him a mild command.*[43]

Dhū al-Qarnayn was told on another journey by the respective nation: *Gog and Magog do great mischief on earth: shall we then render thee tribute in order that thou mightest erect a barrier between us and them? He said: (The power) in which my Lord has established me is better (than tribute): Help me therefore with strength (and labour): I will erect a strong barrier between you and them.*[44] Therefore, Dhū al-Qarnayn isolated and prevented, in essence, the wicked disbelievers from spreading corruption. It seems—and God knows best—that had Dhū al-Qarnayn and his army been able to fight against Gog and Magog they would have done so, but since they were unable he pursued a lesser good, which was to contain those evildoers. Consequently, if the believers are strong, yet not to the degree of the disbelievers, they should seek to contain and prevent the latter from perpetrating wickedness and corruption.

In addition, this story of Dhū al-Qarnayn shows that even greater evils could have been allowed to occur in this world, but the Holy Lord has prevented them through various means. The evils that do occur indirectly lead to types of good beloved to Him like striving and fighting for His sake, which could not have otherwise occurred.

The third story of Moses and Khiḍr illustrates a few key principles in regards to the problem of evil.[45] First, Moses and Joshua encountered

---

41 See Q.XVIII.83–99.
42 Q.XVIII.86.
43 Q.XVIII.87–88.
44 Q.XVIII.94–95 (Yusuf Ali translation).
45 See Q.XVII.60–82.

hunger and fatigue before they were guided to find Khiḍr, and suffered forgetfulness. Joshua said: *I forgot the fish—and none but Satan caused me to forget to mention it.*[46] The devil prods people to perpetrate evil and also makes them forget to do what is good or right and neglect the remembrance of the Holy Lord. The point is that one should anticipate having to suffer in order to attain knowledge, particularly theodicean knowledge.

Their first encounter illustrates that a lesser harm is allowed to occur in order to prevent a greater one. Khiḍr's action to mar the ship represented a lesser harm to those poor sailors and prevented it from being seized.[47] Had it been seized, the sailors would have suffered greater loss and harm. Events in this world could have been more harmful or evil (as illustrated above), but have been limited. The preponderant goods that have occurred outweigh the harms.

In addition, Khiḍr told Moses, while on the ship: "God has taught me knowledge from His knowledge, which you do not have; and you have been taught by God of His knowledge, which I do not possess...The knowledge, which you and I have, compared to God's knowledge is only like [a drop of water that] a bird drinks compared to the ocean."[48]

Khiḍr's killing of an innocent (*zakiyya*) child[49] in the next encounter prevented the latter from thereafter rebelling against his parents and disbelieving in the Holy Lord; hence such greater evils were averted. In addition, the child will probably be substituted with Paradise

---

[46] Q.XVIII.63. This concept is also illustrated in the story of Joseph whereby he remained in prison longer because of the winemaker's forgetfulness: *And [Joseph] said unto him of the twain who he knew would be released [i.e. the winemaker]: Mention me in the presence of thy lord. But Satan caused him to forget to mention it to his lord, so he (Joseph) stayed in prison for some years* (Q.XII.42).

[47] See Q.XVIII.71: *So they twain set out till, when they were in the ship, he made a hole therein. (Moses) said: Hast thou made a hole therein to drown the folk thereof? Thou verily hast done a dreadful thing*; and Q. XVIII.79: *As for the ship, it belonged to poor people working on the river, and I wished to mar it, for there was a king behind them who is taking every ship by force.*

[48] Bukhārī 122; Muslim 2380/6163; Tirmidhī 3149; Aḥmad 21,114.

[49] See Q.XVIII.74: *So they twain journeyed on till, when they met a lad, he slew him. (Moses) said: What! Hast thou slain an innocent soul who hath slain no man? Verily thou hast done a horrid thing*; and Q.XVIII.80–81: *And as for the lad, his parents were believers and we feared lest he should oppress them by rebellion and disbelief. And we intended that their Lord should change him for them for one better in purity and nearer to mercy.*

rather than Hellfire[50] as many contend that he died before reaching puberty—and God knows best. Thus this child's death, although a calamity, represented a blessing for his parents and probably a greater good for himself. Finally, this encounter affirms that God (Exalted is He) knows all that will occur in the future (*ᶜĀlim al-ghayb*) as well as being Omniscient.

In addition, believing parents should not despair or blame the Holy Lord if their child dies, but should instead submit themselves to the decree of the Holy Lord for only He knows where the greater good resides. The true believers, according to the Prophet Muḥammad (may God bless him and grant him peace), must have faith (*īmān*) "in His [ontological] predestination, both good and evil (*sharr*)".[51]

Khiḍr affirmed that God commanded his actions: *I did it not upon my own command.*[52] Many scholars, such as Ibn Kathīr, contend that Khiḍr was a prophet[53]—not just a righteous or truly faithful believer. Certainly it would be unjust for any person, even a truly faithful believer (*ṣiddīq*), to harm another innocent individual, and there is no evidence that Abū Bakr al-Ṣiddīq ever did anything akin to that. Dhū al-Qarnayn likewise did not carry out anything beyond what is conventional and concordant to the Divine Law. Therefore, Khiḍr was most likely a prophet. And God knows best.

The third encounter of Moses and Khiḍr illustrates that God's blessings may be withheld because an individual is not ready for them.[54] The two orphans' buried treasure remained as such until they reached approximately forty years of age—had it been exposed

---

50 The child would have disbelieved had he reached adulthood. Therefore, the fact that he died before reaching puberty meant that he was allowed to die in a state of sinlessness.

51 Muslim 8/93; Tirmidhī 2610; Abū Dāwūd 4695; Ibn Māja 63; Nasā'ī 4993; Aḥmad 191.

52 Q.XVIII.82.

53 See Rashad Azami (tr.), *Stories of the Prophets* (Riyadh: Darussalam, 2003), pp. 435 and 465–466.

54 See Q.XVIII.77: *And they found therein a wall upon the point of falling into ruin, and he repaired it. (Moses) said: If thou hadst wished, thou couldst have taken payment for it*; and Q.XVIII.82: *And as for the wall, it belonged to two orphan boys in the city, and there was beneath it a treasure belonging to them, and their father had been righteous, and thy Lord intended that they should come to their full strength and should bring forth their treasure as a mercy from their Lord; and I did it not upon my own command.*

beforehand they would not have been able to protect it. This episode also demonstrates that suffering may occur due to one's inadequacy or due to the rule of law not being upheld by a society. Certainly had the town, in which these two orphans lived, been a pious and law-abiding one, there would have been no need for Khiḍr to reinforce the wall overlying the treasure, and the length of privation endured by the orphans (due to being deprived from that treasure) would have been shorter. This encounter also emphasizes that one must do good without expecting any reward or compensation from others (even if the latter are disbelievers). One should place one's hope in God and seek His reward in Paradise alone.

One final lesson derived from the story of Moses and Khiḍr concerns Moses (may God bless him) not awaiting Khiḍr's mentioning of the wise purposes behind his actions (which were commanded by the Holy Lord Who is the Most Wise).[55] Humankind unfortunately is much more impatient in this regard. Instead of believing that God (Most Blessed and Exalted is He) has wise purposes in His creation and commandments, many instead resort to harbouring ill thoughts of Him, attributing evil to Him, or disbelieving altogether.

People should instead remain patient, tranquil and unflappable although it can be very trying at times. Events may appear to be paradoxical and counterintuitive but what is beloved by the Holy Lord cannot be achieved without indirect necessary concomitants. We should worship Him alone, follow His prophets, attempt to understand that which we can of His wise purposes and await the elucidation of the remainder at the appropriate time God (Glorious is He) has dictated. God's wisdom is infinite. Patience is necessary to understand the problem of evil. In conclusion, Sūrat al-Kahf mentions many approaches and solutions to the problem of evil.

---

[55] The Prophet Muḥammad (may God bless him and grant him peace) said: "May God have mercy upon us and upon Moses—had he been more patient, he would have seen [Khiḍr carry out] more wonders." See Muslim 2380/6163; Abū Dāwūd 3984. It should be noted that in another situation the Prophet Muḥammad said about Moses (may God bless them both): "May God have mercy upon Moses, he was harmed more than this and yet he remained patient." See Bukhārī 3150. This statement of the Prophet was likely said during the Meccan phase of his message as Surāt al-Kahf was revealed in Mecca.

Sūrat al-Falaq and Sūrat al-Nās

Sūrat al-Falaq and Sūrat al-Nās are the last two chapters in the Qur'ān. The Prophet Muḥammad (may God bless him and grant him peace) used to read Sūrat al-Falaq and al-Nās along with Sūrat al-Ikhlāṣ[56] three times every night before going to bed.[57] We are advised to read them in order to seek God's protection and refuge from the wickedness perpetrated by creatures, whether humankind or Satan.

Sūrat al-Falaq is: *Say: I seek refuge in the Lord of the Daybreak (falaq) from the evil of that which He created: from the evil of the darkness when it is intense, and from the evil of malignant witchcraft, and from the evil of the envier when he envieth.*[58] Of note, *falaq* can also be translated as anything that God (Glorious is He) has parted or split. In that manner this entire universe, which was split apart from one point, can be considered. Therefore, the first verse can be rendered as: "I seek refuge in the Lord of the Universe" or "all that the Lord has created into existence". This is the viewpoint of Ṭabarī.[59] Ibn al-Qayyim also states: "know that *falaq* entails all of creation (*al-khalq kulluhu falaq*)...In this manner, the wisdom of seeking refuge in the Lord of all that was split apart (*falaq*) becomes evident. In addition, through this, the miraculous, great and glorious nature of the Qur'ān becomes clear."[60] Thus the Holy Lord "commands His Prophet to seek refuge [with God] from the evil of every single thing, since everything other than Him is something He created".[61] The consensus of Sunni scholars affirms that the Holy Lord is the Creator of everything, both good and evil.

---

56 Sūrat al-Ikhlāṣ is: *Say: He is God, the One! God, the eternally Besought of all! He begetteth not nor was begotten. And there is none comparable unto Him.* Q.CXII.1–4.

57 See Bukhārī 5017; Tirmidhī 3402; Abū Dāwūd 5056; Aḥmad 24,853.

58 Q.CXIII.1–5

59 See Lucas (tr.), *Ṭabarī Selections*, vol. II, pp. 439–440, wherein Ṭabarī states that "since God (Majestic is His praise) did not provide any indicators that He intended *Lord of the falaq* to refer to some things which are called *falaq* to the exclusion of others, and since God (Exalted is His remembrance) is the Lord of everything He created, it is necessary for the meaning [of this verse] to include everything that is called *falaq*, as He is Lord of all that".

60 Ibn al-Qayyim, *Badā'ʿ al-fawā'id* (Beirut: Dār al-Kutub al-ʿArabī, 2010), vol. II, p. 220. See also *Tafsīr al-Rāzī*, vol. XXXII, pp. 371–372.

61 See Lucas (tr.), *Ṭabarī Selections*, vol. II, p. 440.

Sūrat al-Nās is: *Say: I seek refuge in the Lord of humankind, the King of humankind, the God of humankind, from the evil of the sneaking whisperer [i.e. Satan], who whispereth in the hearts of humankind, of the jinn and of humankind.*[62] This chapter emphasizes that refuge should be sought in God because He is the Lord, King and Deity—it is only befitting that refuge be sought in Him alone. Satan is the initial prompt for evil, and this will be discussed further in Chapter Eleven.

In summation, these *sūra*s acknowledge evil as an entity and address it. Sūrat al-Fātiḥa inoculates one against the problem of evil, by making one affirm the Holy Lord's mercy, praiseworthiness, lordship, sovereignty and providence. Sūrat al-Kahf, in its entirety, provides a straightforward theodicy, which affirms His wisdom and emphasizes the importance of righteousness and striving against evil. Finally, Sūrat al-Falaq and Sūrat al-Nās advise the believers to seek refuge in the Holy Lord alone from evil. Nonetheless, the problem of evil is addressed in the Qur'ān from beginning to end, as well as in the Sunna of the Prophet Muḥammad. This book will expound upon this complex, sophisticated and stunning theodicy, by the grace of God.

---

62 Q.CXIV.1–5.

Chapter Two

God's Beautiful Names and His Infallibility from any Evil

God! There is no deity save Him. His are the most Beautiful Names.[1] As this verse indicates, after affirming God's Oneness and His right to be worshipped alone, the servant must attest that His Names and Attributes are beautiful, glorious and exalted. Each of the Beautiful Names of God indicate His Essence as well as what that Name indicates, whether an Attribute or a specific action of His.[2]

Many of God's Beautiful Names are mentioned in the following verses: *He is God, Whom there is no other deity, the Knower of the invisible and the visible. He is the Beneficent, Merciful. He is God, Whom there is no other deity, the Sovereign Lord, the Holy One, Peace, the Keeper of Faith, the Guardian, the Majestic, the Irresistible, the Superb. Glorified be God from all that they ascribe as partner (unto Him). He is God, the Creator, the Shaper out of naught, the Fashioner. His are the most Beautiful Names. All that is in the heavens and the earth glorifieth Him, and He is the Almighty, the Wise.*[3] God is the Most Beneficent, the Ever-Living (*al-Ḥayy*) and the Self-Sustaining (*al-Qayyūm*); and He is the Doer of Good (*al-Barr*) and the Bestower (*al-Wahhāb*).

Affirming God's Beautiful Names, Glorious Attributes and Holy Essence is a requisite of testifying to His absolute Oneness and being knowledgeable: *There is no god but He: That is the witness of God, His angels, and those endued with knowledge, standing firm on justice. There is no god but He, the Exalted in Power, the Wise.*[4] Thus the Holy Lord has

---

[1] Q.XX.8. Pickthall translates *ilāh* as "god" and others render it as "deity".

[2] See Ibn Taymiyya, *Majmūʿ al-fatāwā* (Medina: Mujammaʿ al-Malik Fahd li-Ṭibāʿat al-Muṣḥaf al-Sharīf, 1995), vol. XIII, p. 334.

[3] Q.LIX.22–24. Pickthall translates *al-Jabbār* as "the Compeller". To avoid any misunderstanding that it could indicate divine compulsion, it is translated as "the Irresistible".

[4] Q.III.18 (Yusuf Ali translation).

confirmed the loftiness of those who have knowledge in witnessing the greatest truth and reality, namely that there is no deity save God.[5]

The Holy Lord is the Most Wise (*al-Ḥakīm*), and the juxtaposition of this along with His Name the Almighty is present in forty-seven verses of the Qur'ān. Thus, "the Almighty Most Wise" is one of the most common combinations of His Beautiful Names at the end of the Qur'ānic verses. Therefore, although God is Almighty (*al-ʿAzīz*) and Omnipotent, His actions proceed from His wisdom as well, and He limits the manifestation of His power to achieve the wise purposes that He loves. God's love has led to the origination of creation, His wisdom has shaped it, and His mercy has allowed it to continue to exist (in spite of the sins of humanity). A Biblical verse also affirms that He is the only true deity and that this world was created in accordance with His wisdom: "But the Lord is the true God, he is the living God...He hath made the earth by his power, he hath established the world by his wisdom, and hath stretched out the heavens by his discretion."[6]

Other juxtapositions with the Most Wise in the Qur'ān include the Omniscient (*al-ʿAlīm*) in thirty-eight verses and the All Cognizant (*al-Khabīr*) in three verses.[7] The Lord's knowledge extends to everything whereas humankind *encompass nothing of His knowledge save what He will.*[8] Even before creating everything, God (Glorious is He) knew what would happen for eternity.[9] God's actions proceed from His wisdom and manifest His omnipotence, omniscience, awareness,

---

[5] Ibn al-Qayyim expands significantly on the meaning and implications of this verse. See Tallal Zeni (tr.), *Ibn Qayyim al-Jawziyya on Knowledge* (Cambridge: Islamic Texts Society, 2016), pp. 6–8.

[6] Jeremiah 10.10–12.

[7] Other juxtapositions with the "Most Wise" are present in one verse each: the One Who grants repentance (*al-Tawwāb*), the One to Whom all praise is due (*al-Ḥamīd*), the Vast (*al-Wāsiʿ*) and the Most High (*al-ʿAliy*).

[8] Q.II.255.

[9] The Prophet Muḥammad (may God bless him and grant him peace) said that God (Glorious is He) first created the pen and then commanded it to "write everything decreed for eternity" (Tirmidhī 2155); or "until the Day of Judgment" (Abū Dāwūd 4700; Aḥmad 22,707; al-Ḥākim 3840; Bayhaqī (*Sunan*) 17,703). Both of these narrations are "authentic" according to Albānī (*Ṣaḥīḥ al-Jāmiʿ al-ṣaghīr* 2017 and 2018, respectively).

praiseworthiness, forgiveness and mercy accordingly. God (Glorious and Exalted is He) states: *Is not God the wisest of judges?*[10]

Some schools of thought within Islam, primarily the Ashᶜarīs,[11] state that God's actions do not have to be always concordant with His wisdom, but can occur solely due to His will.[12] The Ashᶜarīs use verses in the Qur'ān that return matters to God's will as proof for their position. However, it will be contended here that if a matter mentioned within a verse is straightforward, then God may give the justification and wisdom for His commandment or statement;[13] but if an issue is highly complex He instead ascribes it to His will—and God knows best. Indeed, God is glorious and exalted above being arbitrary.

The first example to consider is the verse: *The guiding of them is not thy duty* (*O Muḥammad*), *but God guideth whom He will.*[14] It is well known that even the messengers do not know what is in the hearts of people (aside from what God has inspired them with) nor do they know who is deserving of being guided by God. The Qur'ān and Sunna are very clear that God loves goodness and belief, and that He (Glory be to Him) dislikes evilness and disbelief. And God only guides those who are good—He does not guide those who are evil. Due to the matter of guidance being so complex, God ascribes the matter to His will—it is not arbitrary. God (Glorious is He) is the Most Wise and is not unjust.

Likewise only God knows those who are suitable for conveying His message: *The Exalter of Ranks, the Lord of the Throne. He causeth*

---

10 Q.XCV.8 (Yusuf Ali translation).

11 The Ashᶜarīs represent a school of thought founded by Abū al-Ḥasan ᶜAlī b. Ismāᶜīl b. Abū Bishr Isḥāq al-Ashᶜarī (d. 324/936). This theology upheld God's absolute will, while giving less importance to His wisdom or benevolence, in justifying His creation and commandments. They also adhered to a theory of divine command ethics, which states that God's command of something renders it good, regardless. Moreover, they upheld a doctrine of occasionalism, wherein causes are just occasions for God to bring about intended effects. Ashᶜarī thought will be discussed more in-depth in Chapter Eight.

12 See Zeni (tr.), *Ibn Qayyim al-Jawziyya on Divine Wisdom and the Problem of Evil*, pp. X–XII.

13 Ibid., pp. 43–54.

14 Q.II.272.

the Spirit of His command upon whom He will of His servants, that He may warn of the Day of Meeting.[15] Only God knows what each person would have done had he been sent to convey the message, and therefore God chooses those most suitable for it: *God knoweth best with whom to place His message.*[16]

God (Exalted is He) also states: *Knowest thou not that unto God belongeth the sovereignty of the heavens and the earth? He punisheth whom He will, and forgiveth whom He will. God is able to do all things.*[17] The Holy Lord's punishment and forgiveness are predicated upon the Divine Laws and commandments, which He has informed us of in the Qur'ān, as well as the Sunna of His Messenger Muḥammad. But the matter is so highly complex that only God knows the reality of whom He will forgive and whom is deserving of punishment; only He knows what is in the hearts of people and is able to bring that out; and only God (Glorious is He) knows who will die as a disbeliever and who will die as a believer. These matters are all in accordance with God's wisdom, omniscience, justice and mercy.

God (Glorious is He) also states: *Had God willed He could have made you (all) one nation, but He sendeth whom He will astray and guideth whom He will, and ye will indeed be asked of what ye used to do.*[18] Here the Holy Lord's wise purposes behind the creation of both the blissful and the wretched, which results in many praiseworthy outcomes, are so complex that it cannot even be described; thus He (Glorious and Exalted is He) ascribes the matter to His will. Although this book may elucidate some wise purposes which are in accordance with the Qur'ān and Sunna, only God knows His far-reaching wisdom in total.

God (Most Blessed and Exalted is He) also states: *Thy Lord does create and choose as He pleases: no choice have they (in the matter): Glory to God! and far is He above the partners they ascribe (to Him)!*[19] Humankind has no choice regarding His creation—that is self-evident. Who knows all of the complexity behind the Lord's creation of this universe? Since it is

---

15 Q.XL.15.

16 Q.VI.124.

17 Q.V.40.

18 Q.XVI.93.

19 Q.XXVIII.68 (Yusuf Ali translation).

highly complex He ascribes the matter of His creation to His will (*mā yashā'*).

God (Exalted is He) withholds much of His knowledge: *And of knowledge ye have been vouchsafed but little,*[20] and *they encompass nothing of His knowledge save what He will.*[21] God grants His knowledge for certain wise purposes, but either withholds it or does not permit a deeper understanding of it for other wise reasons. This will be expanded upon later. In conclusion, God's will is concordant with His wisdom.

In explanation of the position of Ibn Taymiyya (which was also adopted by his student Ibn al-Qayyim), Jon Hoover states: "God does create things that He hates, but He does this only for the sake of a wise purpose that He loves...Ibn Taymiyya [thus] subordinates God's will to God's love."[22] In this manner, it is maintained that God's will is concordant with both His wisdom and love.

In particular, God loves manifesting the consequences of His Beautiful Names. That said, God does not attain any greater perfection by manifesting them—His Beautiful Names exist in His Essence whether or not He manifests their consequences to His creation. The Holy Lord also loves the pious and righteous, and loves the many complex wise purposes He has created this world for.

Ibn al-Qayyim's discussion of many of God's Beautiful Names illustrates that He is infallible above evil. Amongst these Names are: the Holy (*al-Quddūs*); the One Who is faultless and bestows peace (*al-Salām*); the Almighty (*al-ʿAzīz*); and the Most High (*al-ʿAliy*), which connotes that He is high above any fault, evil or deficiency.[23] Ibn al-Qayyim adds regarding His Name, the One Deserving of All Praise (*al-Ḥamīd*): "His perfect praiseworthiness necessitates that no evil, misconduct or deficiency be attributed to Him—neither in His Names, actions or Attributes. His Beautiful Names preclude any attribution of evil, misconduct or injustice to Him."[24]

---

20 Q.XVII.85.

21 Q.II.255.

22 Jon Hoover, *Ibn Taymiyya's Theodicy of Perpetual Optimism* (Leiden: Brill, 2007), p. 73.

23 See Zeni (tr.), *Ibn Qayyim al-Jawziyya on Divine Wisdom and the Problem of Evil*, pp. 20–22.

24 Ibid., p. 22.

Those who attribute evil to the Holy Lord will be recompensed accordingly—this includes those who attribute evil to Allāh, which is the Arabic word for God and the Name of the Creator for Arab Christians as well. God (Glorious is He) has stated: *And God's [alone] are the Attributes of perfection; invoke Him, then, by these, and stand aloof from all who distort the meaning of His Attributes: they shall be requited for all that they were wont to do!*[25] God is the Judge (*al-Ḥakam*) and the Reckoner (*al-Ḥasīb*). We should only characterize God as He has Himself done or in the manner of His prophets and messengers: *Glory to thy Lord, the Lord of Honour and Power! (He is free) from what they ascribe (to Him)! And peace on the messengers! And Praise to God, the Lord and Cherisher of the Worlds.*[26]

The Holy Lord states: *Glorified be He and High Exalted above (all) that they ascribe (unto Him);*[27] *Praised be He and High Exalted above all that ye associate (with Him)!*[28] God is glorious (*subḥāna*[hu]) and exalted (*taʿāla*) above any inadequacy, imperfection or deficiency. The Holy Lord is glorious and exalted above any false attributions which the disbelievers characterize Him by.

God (Glorious is He) is the Most Just (*al-ʿAdl*)—He does not commit any injustice: *Verily, God does not wrong [anyone] by as much as an atom's weight;*[29] and *God willeth no injustice for (His) servants.*[30] The Prophet Muḥammad related in a *ḥadīth qudsī* that God (Most Blessed and Exalted is He) has said: "I have forbidden Myself from carrying out injustice, so do not be unjust to one another."[31] His justice can only be truly manifested in a world wherein good and evil are present.

God is also the Truth (*al-Ḥaqq*) and the Guide (*al-Hādī*). The Most Glorious guides to the truth and the Straight Path, as mentioned in many Qur'ānic verses.[32] The Holy Lord also states: *God is the Light of the*

---

25 Q.VII.180.

26 Q.XXXVII.180–182.

27 Q.VI.100.

28 Q.X.18, Q.XVI.1, Q.XXVIII.6, and Q.XXXIX.67.

29 Q.IV.40 (Muḥammad Asad translation).

30 Q.XL.31.

31 Muslim 2577/6572; Aḥmad 21,420.

32 See Q.II.142 and 213; Q.IV.68 and 175; Q.VI.39, 87 and 161; Q.X.25 and 35; Q.XVI.121; Q.XXII.54; Q.XXIV.46.

heavens and the earth;[33] *God is the Protecting Guardian of those who believe. He bringeth them out of darkness into light. As for those who disbelieve, their patrons are false deities. They bring them out of light into darkness;*[34] *And he for whom God hath not appointed light, for him there is no light.*[35] God creates what He wills and then selects those whom He deems appropriate for His guidance and spiritual light.

God is the Most Merciful (*al-Raḥīm*), the Most Forgiving (*al-Ghafūr*), the Ever-Forgiving (*al-Ghaffār*), the Effacer [of sins] (*al-ʿAfū*), the Ever-Relenting (*al-Tawwāb*), the Forbearing (*al-Ḥalīm*) and the Subtly Kind (*al-Laṭīf*)—and God loves to manifest these Attributes of His. Had it not been for His love, mercy, generosity and forgiveness this world would not even have been brought into existence by Him nor remained—*and He is the Forgiving, the Loving* (*al-Wadūd*).[36]

We must affirm His Names and Attributes without anthropomorphizing, distorting or denying them (*bilā takyīf, tashbīh, tamthīl, taḥrīf, aw taʿṭīl*).[37] The Holy Lord is Eternal and Self-Subsisting. The Holy Lord's Essence is divine and uncreated. He states: *Naught is as His likeness.*[38] It is self-evident that the nature and quiddity of creatures is completely unlike the Almighty Lord's Essence. The characteristics of humanity are infinitesimal in comparison to the Glorious Attributes of the Almighty Lord, just like our power in comparison to His omnipotence, or how our knowledge is like a drop of water within an ocean in comparison to the omniscience of God,[39] and our senses in comparison to His hearing and seeing everything in the multiverse. Therefore, God (Exalted is He) continues the verse by stating: *Naught is as His likeness; and He is the Hearer, the Seer.*[40]

---

33 Q.XXIV.35.

34 Q.II.257.

35 Q.XXIV.40.

36 Q.LXXXV.14. See also the statement of the Prophet Shuʿayb in verse Q.XI.90: *My Lord is Merciful, Loving.*

37 See Ibn Taymiyya, *Minhāj al-Sunna al-Nabawiyya fī naqd kalām al-Shīʿa wa'l-Qadariyya* (Riyadh: Jāmiʿat al-Imām Muḥammad b. Saʿūd al-Islāmiyya, 1986), vol. II, p. 111.

38 Q.XLII.11.

39 See Bukhārī 122, Muslim 2380/6163, Tirmidhī 3149 and Aḥmad 21,114, where Khiḍr draws this parallel.

40 Q.XLII.11.

The ontologic characteristics of humanity are far more limited than their religious ones. God (Glorious is He) has granted humanity far greater degrees of religious knowledge than that of the sciences. That is because the former knowledge is clearly more beloved to the Holy Lord, as well as being essential to their success in this world and their bliss in the Hereafter. Since the understanding of wisdom is more dependent upon religious knowledge, it is maintained that the Holy Lord has enabled us to understand significant aspects of His wisdom if we follow the revelation, particularly the Qur'ān and Sunna (which are far more complete than prior Scriptures).

Next, it should be mentioned that the Qur'ān balances between God's Transcendence and His Immanence. God (Exalted is He) states: *He is the First and the Last, the Evident (al-Ẓāhir) and the Immanent (al-Bāṭin): and He has full knowledge of all things. He it is Who created the heavens and the earth in six days, and is moreover firmly established on the Throne...And He is with you wheresoever ye may be. And God sees well all that ye do.*[41] The Holy Lord is the Most High and is above His Throne, but He is with us in regards to His knowledge, sight and hearing. God (Exalted is He) states: *And when My servants question thee concerning Me, then surely I am nigh. I answer the prayer of the suppliant when he crieth unto Me. So let them hear My call and let them trust in Me, in order that they may be led aright.*[42] God is the One Who is near (*al-Qarīb*) and the One Who answers supplications (*al-Mujīb*).

God is Most Wise and Most Merciful; had He created us to live on this earth in a state in which He and His angels were apparent to us, then it is contended that our inevitable sinfulness would have had immediate consequences. Human beings, because of their weak nature, would not be able to fulfill the duties and direct commandments of the Almighty Lord, and would thus all be deserving of punishment.[43] Therefore, the fact that we do not encounter God in this world where

---

41 Q.LVII.3.

42 Q.II.186.

43 When Adam disobeyed the Lord's prohibition (of eating from the tree), he was sent down from the Garden to this earth, despite having repented. See Q.II.35–39. On the other hand, when Satan disobeyed a clear command from God to prostrate to Adam and remained stubbornly proud and obstinate, the devil became damned. See Q.XXXVIII.71–85.

we are tested is appropriate for our characteristics as human beings. In this construct, God (Glorious is He) forgives us for our sins if we repent and return to Him, although we may suffer other consequences—may God forgive us! More importantly, Divine hiddenness is an infinite mercy from God to those who will ultimately become believers as they will be rewarded in Paradise. On the other hand, the angels—who do not sin but instead follow all of God's orders—do encounter God and this is appropriate for their characteristics.

Now, some Beautiful Names of God indicate a specific action of His; and all of His actions are just, wise and good. Examples of such Beautiful Names are: The One Who bestows honour (*al-Muʿizz*) and the One Who dishonours (*al-Mudhill*); the Benefactor (*al-Munʿim*) and the One Who harms (*al-Ḍārr*); the One Who exalts (*al-Rāfiʿ*) and the One Who abases (*al-Khāfiḍ*); the One Who bestows (*al-Bāsiṭ*) and the One Who constricts (*al-Qābiḍ*); the One Who enriches (*al-Mughnī*) and the One Who bars (*al-Māniʿ*). Had creatures with free will to choose obedience or disobedience not existed, the manifestation of these latter Names by God, Who is the Most Just (*al-ʿAdl*), would not have occurred. These latter Names of God are only manifested congruent to His wisdom and justice.

The Holy Lord is the Trustee (*al-Wakīl*) and the Protector (*al-Walī*). These Beautiful Names can only be manifested in a world wherein good and evil exist, and individuals are allowed to freely choose between the two opposites. How can all these aforementioned Beautiful Names be manifested in a wise manner if evil does not exist?

Nonetheless, we know that the Holy Lord has not manifested all of His Names for the Prophet Muḥammad has stated within one of his supplications: "I ask You by every Name that You have named Yourself with, or have revealed in Your Book, or have taught any of Your creation, or have kept hidden within Your knowledge of the Unseen..."[44] In addition, the Prophet (may God bless him and grant him peace) mentioned that on the Day of Judgment: "God will inspire me with many manners by which to praise and glorify Him that He

---

[44] Aḥmad 3712; Ibn Ḥibbān 972; al-Ḥākim 1877. It is "authentic" according to Albānī (*Silsilat al-aḥādīth al-ṣaḥīḥa* 199).

has not inspired to anyone else before."[45] This will enable the Prophet Muḥammad to supplicate to God (Glorious is He), glorify and praise Him using Names of His that we do not currently know. God has not dictated the manifestation of those particular Names in this world for reasons known to Him alone.

If God (Exalted is He) had only willed to manifest His Beautiful Names of the Holy, the Omnipotent and the Most Generous, then He would have created this world completely absent of evil. However, creating the world in the manner that it exists allows the manifestation of His Beautiful Names: the One Who accepts repentance and the One Who forgives, the One Who exalts and the One Who abases, the One Who bestows honour and the One Who dishonours, in addition to many other Attributes to be discussed later. Therefore, the nature of this world manifests certain Beautiful Names in a manner concordant with His love, wisdom, will and justice.

We do not know—nor can we speculate—whether God (Most Blessed and Exalted is He) has created other worlds anterior to ours or will create them posteriorly in order to manifest other Names of His. This is within the realm of God's infinite knowledge, and only if He informs us of that in the Hereafter can we know. As regards this world, we can only say as the angels said before us to the Holy Lord: *Be glorified! We have no knowledge saving that which Thou hast taught us. Lo! Thou, only Thou, art the Knower, the Wise.*[46]

---

45 Bukhārī 4712; Muslim 194/480; Tirmidhī 2434; Aḥmad 9633.

46 Q.II.32.

Chapter Three

The Wisdom of God's Creation and Commandments

God (Glorious is He) states: *His verily is all creation and commandment. Blessed be God, the Lord of the Worlds!*[1] God has created all that exists and then sent the prophets and messengers to convey His noble commandments. This verse illustrates the differentiation of the ontological (*kawnī*) from the deontological (*dīnī*), respectively.[2]

The prophets said to their peoples: *Can there be doubt concerning God, the Creator of the heavens and the earth? He calleth you that He may forgive you your sins and reprieve you unto an appointed term.*[3] God (Exalted is He) is the Creator (*al-Khāliq*), the Originator (*al-Bāri'*) and the Fashioner (*al-Muṣawwir*). Everything is created by God alone, while He is: *the Eternal, the Uncaused Cause of all being.*[4] God is the Creator, and it is self-evident that this world, which consists of the same atomic elements, is created by Him alone (Exalted is He). Humankind cannot create nor can they truly fathom how something can be brought into existence from non-existence.

God (Glorious and Exalted is He) states: *Do not the unbelievers see that the heavens and the earth were joined together (as one unit of creation), before We*

---

[1] Q.VII.54. See also Q.LXV.12.

[2] See Ibn al-Qayyim's distinction between God's ontological (*kawnī*) and religious (*dīnī*) will in Zeni (tr.), *Ibn Qayyim al-Jawziyya on Divine Wisdom and the Problem of Evil*, pp. 229–236.

[3] Q.XIV.10.

[4] Q.CXII.2. Of note, God (Exalted is He) has been eternally creating. This was the position of Ibn Taymiyya, as explained by Jon Hoover: "God's willing of something to happen [is not eternal but rather] occurs at the time that it happens...[yet] God has been willing and acting from eternity." See Hoover, *Ibn Taymiyya's Theodicy of Perpetual Optimism*, pp. 85–87. That said, God (Exalted is He) "has been qualified with attributes of perfection from eternity and He is still thus. He has not changed". See Jon Hoover, "God Acts by His Will and Power: Ibn Taymiyya's Theology of a Personal God in his Treatise on the Voluntary Attributes", in Yossef Rapoport and Shahab Ahmed (eds.), *Ibn Taymiyya and his Times* (Karachi: Oxford University Press, 2010), p. 69. See Ibn Taymiyya, *Majmūʿ al-fatāwā*, vol. VI, p. 250.

clove them asunder? We made from water every living thing. Will they not then believe?[5] This verse affirms that this world, in its entirety, was created as one entity[6] before being split apart. The views of Ṭabarī and Ibn al-Qayyim in this regard were already mentioned in Chapter One. The origination of the creation in this manner makes it even more evident that the Holy Lord is the Originator of everything, for He created this world from one point in space and time. The universe has not existed pre-eternally, which was claimed by many philosophers (including Aristotle and Avicenna/Ibn Sīnā) and refuted by the scholars of Islam.[7]

Furthermore, the Lord has created everything in pairs: *Glory to God, Who created in pairs all things that the earth produces, as well as their own (human) kind and (other) things of which they have no knowledge.*[8] The Holy Lord is One, whereas everything else He has created is originated from fundamental elements having paired opposites. This is amazingly evident at the subatomic as well as the macroscopic level.

This pairing in the material ontological creation is continued in a religious sense. It should not therefore be surprising that God (Glorious is He) has created good and evil (or Paradise and Hellfire) nor should this lead one to question the existence of God. At the deepest level, this pairing in the deontological realm (i.e. good and evil) is allowed only so as to manifest the consequences of the paired Beautiful Names of the Holy Lord (for instance the One Who exalts and the One Who abases)—God being sublime and infallible above any evil. The Holy Lord will exalt those who piously obey His commandments, and will abase and forsake those who disbelieve in Him.

The Holy Lord has fine-tuned the creation of this universe, and it could not have existed otherwise. This is alluded to in the Qur'ān when God (Exalted is He) states: *We have created everything by measure,*[9]

---

[5] Q.XXI.30 (Yusuf Ali translation).

[6] Muḥammad Asad translates this part of the verse as: *The heavens and the earth were [once] one single entity, which We then parted asunder.*

[7] See, for example, Ghazālī's refutation in Michael E. Marmura (tr.), *The Incoherence of the Philosophers* (Provo: Brigham Young University Press, 2000), pp. 2–46.

[8] Q.XXXVI.36 (Yusuf Ali translation). See also Q.LI.49: *And all things We have created by pairs, that haply ye may reflect.*

[9] Q.LIX.49. See also Q.XV.91: *And there is not a thing but with Us are the stores thereof. And We send it not down save in appointed measure.*

and *He hath created everything and hath meted out for it a measure.*[10] The determined measure (*qadr*) relates to the precise measurement of each entity and its characteristics. The existence of this world and life through fine-tuning is, in itself, evidence of God's omniscience and omnipotence. The arguments for fine-tuning are nearly infinite, as they apply to every created thing. God (Glorious is He) states: *If ye would count up the favours of God, never would ye be able to number them.*[11] The fine-tuning of this universe nullifies the claim that it emanated, whether by necessity or by accident.[12]

Examples of fine-tuning arguments include: had the strong nuclear force been slightly stronger only hydrogen would have ever formed in this universe, and if slightly weaker this universe would not have formed at all. Next, the balance of matter to antimatter had to be accurate to one part in ten billion for the universe even to arise. Also, had the universe contained much more matter, additional gravity would have made it collapse upon itself; and if less, the universe would have expanded too quickly for galaxies to form. In addition, had the cosmological constant, which is on the order of 10^{-122} and is only relevant for galaxies and structures billions of light years across, not been so extremely minute, stars would not have formed. Finally, had the values of other constants, masses of elemental particles, amounts of dark energy or matter been only slightly different the universe would either not have existed at all or not supported life.[13]

It should be mentioned that although all of these fine-tuning arguments are beneficial, they only lead to deism and do not guide a person further than that. If an individual states that he or she believes in the One Lord because of His fine-tuning or the "almost unbelievable complexity"[14] of human DNA, for example, he or she

---

[10] Q.XXV.2.

[11] Q.XVI.18 (Yusuf Ali translation).

[12] The argument of necessity is claimed by philosophers like Ibn Sīnā, and the argument by accident is asserted by atheists.

[13] See, for example, Martin Rees, *Just Six Numbers: The Deep Forces That Shape the Universe* (New York: Basic Books, 2001). Note that the above only discuss the presence of the basic building blocks—they do not get into further complexities of the universe.

[14] Antony Flew and Roy Abraham Varhese, *There is a God: How the World's Most Notorious Atheist Changed his Mind* (New York: Harper One, 2007), p. 75.

must then worship Him alone and follow the revelation as conveyed by His prophets (including Muḥammad). It is only by following the Holy Lord's revelation that we can become truly guided. Deism does not avail an individual if unaccompanied by the following of His prophets and messengers.

This world is also endowed with symmetry.[15] Despite this fine-tuning and symmetry, many systems in this world can be scientifically classified as chaotic. Although a chaotic system appears random, due to its sensitive dependence on initial conditions, the system is actually deterministic.[16] Had the initial conditions been specified with infinite precision, making long-term predictions within that system would be possible. On the subatomic scale, quantum mechanics represents, from our viewpoint, another indeterministic system; but it is also determined by the One Who is omniscient. Both of these examples—chaos and quantum mechanics—reveal to us that our scientific knowledge is limited and incomplete, whereas God's knowledge is perfect for He has fined-tuned everything in existence. It is only because of God's omnipotence and omniscience of all the Unseen and future events that this universe and humanity exist in reality and part of His design. The more one contemplates upon His fine-tuning of everything in this universe, the more one's mind is dazzled, astonished and boggled.

Now, it will be contended in this book that fine-tuning has occurred in both the physical world and in the religious realm for the Creator and Deity is One. If God (Almighty and Most Glorious is He) can fine-tune the physical world, why could He not the religious one? Indeed, the latter religious fine-tuning is clearly more important to the Holy

---

[15] Brian Greene states: "Special relativity is based on the symmetry embodied in the principle of relativity—the symmetry between all constant-velocity vantage points. The gravitational force, as embodied in the general theory of relativity is based on the equivalence principle—the extension of the principle of relativity to embrace all vantage points regardless of the complexity of their states of motion. And the strong, weak, and electromagnetic forces are based on the more abstract gauge symmetry principles… String theory takes us down another notch on the scale of explanatory depth because all of these symmetry principles, as well as another, supersymmetry—emerge from its structure." Brian Greene, *The Elegant Universe* (New York: W. W. Norton, 2010), pp. 374–375.

[16] James Gleick, *Chaos: Making a New Science* (New York: Penguin Books, 1987), p. 23.

Lord than the ontological since the purpose of humanity is a religious one, i.e. to worship Him alone and obey His commandments—this will be addressed later. This fine-tuning does not negate the free will of humankind—God (Glorious is He) has accounted for that also.

God (Glorious is He) ontologically creates many entities within this world that He does not like, however He loves and commands only that which is good. This is the position of Ibn al-Qayyim and others, and what will be maintained herein, in contrast to those who hold a position of divine command ethics.[17] God (Exalted is He), being the Creator of everything and being the One Who established the nature and essence of any particular entity, can certainly make that which He commands concordant with what He has created as good. The question of whether a commandment is good solely because God commands it is therefore an inappropriate one, for the Creator and Deity is One. On the other hand, claiming that God (Glorious is He) would command something sinful is incompatible with His statement: *God never commands what is shameful: do ye say of God what ye know not?*[18] This claim also attributes faultiness to Him for commanding something other than good—Glorious is He above doing so—and attributes inadequacy to Him for not being able to make good that which He commands—Exalted is He above such a thing. The Holy Lord does no injustice nor does He command anything inappropriate or evil—He is the Most Just and the Most Wise.

God (Glorious is He) has also commanded us to right any wrongs and change things for the better. We should not be content with evil just because the Holy Lord has ontologically created it—we should always strive against evil. We should also work to resolve suffering, such as poverty, in accordance with God's commandments. God (Exalted is He) has stated: *And when it is said unto them: spend of that wherewith God hath provided you, those who disbelieve say unto those who believe: Shall we feed those whom God, if He willed, would feed? Ye are in naught*

---

17 See Ayman Shihadeh, "Theories of Ethical Value in Kalām: A New Interpretation", in Sabine Schmidtke (ed.), *The Oxford Handbook of Islamic Theology* (Oxford: Oxford University Press, 2016), pp. 384–407. See also Zeni (tr), *Ibn Qayyim al-Jawziyya on Knowledge*, pp. XX–XXII.

18 Q.VII.28 (Yusuf Ali translation).

else than error manifest.[19] These disbelievers thus use the ontological creation of God as an excuse to avoid following His deontological commandments. Instead, God (Exalted is He) has created conditions and causes to differentiate those who will freely chose to follow His commandments—here represented by giving alms and spending in charity—and also strive against evil and perform actions beloved to Him.

God (Exalted is He) has empowered His creation to be a cause for good. This demonstrates His omnipotence to a greater degree than if He had been the direct cause of all events (i.e. that posited by the theory of occasionalism[20]). One who can empower others is more powerful and more perfect than one who cannot. To deny causality is to deny revelation, reason and reality.[21] It is precisely because of God's wisdom and justice, as well as the absence of divine compulsion, that causality exists. That said, nothing happens without His allowance: *Ye will not, unless God willeth. God is Knower, Wise,*[22] and *ye will not, unless (it be) that God willeth, the Lord of creation.*[23] There is no creator other than the Holy Lord.

Now, God (Exalted is He) created the angels before human beings—the time of their creation being otherwise unspecified. The angels are created from light (in accordance with the *ḥadīth*[24] of the Prophet Muḥammad), which signifies that they are purely good. This purity is demonstrated by the fact that the angels worship God alone. An angel worshipping God occupies every handbreadth in this universe.[25] The Holy Lord states: *Those who dwell in His presence are not too proud to worship Him, nor do they weary; they glorify (Him) night and day; they flag*

---

19 Q.XXXVI.47.

20 Occasionalism is the idea that causes are themselves ineffectual, and are just occasions for God to directly bring about resultant effects. God, in this thinking, is solely and directly responsible for all effects that occur.

21 See Ibn al-Qayyim's repudiation of occasionalism in Zeni (tr.), *Ibn Qayyim al-Jawziyya on Divine Wisdom and the Problem of Evil,* pp. X, 39–42 and 87–91.

22 Q.LXXVI.30.

23 Q.LXXXI.29.

24 Muslim 2996/7495; Aḥmad 25,194.

25 See the *ḥadīth* of the Prophet in Tirmidhī 2312; Ibn Māja 4190; Aḥmad 21,516; al-Ḥākim 3883; Bayhaqī (*Sunan*) 13,337; *Ḥilya*, vol. II, p. 236. It is "sound" according to Albānī (*Ṣaḥīḥ al-Jāmiʿ al-ṣaghīr* 2449).

not.[26] *Never did the Christ feel too proud to be God's servant, nor do the angels who are near unto Him.*[27] Those who recognize even a small portion of the glory of the Holy Lord appreciate the opportunity to be sincere servants of His. Also, if the angels' worship of God (for what is likely billions of years) is considered relative to all the evil perpetrated by humanity, one will recognize that the latter is miniscule compared to the former good.

Belief in the angels is essential to faith. The Prophet Muḥammad (may God bless him and grant him peace) defined faith as: "To believe in God, His angels, His Scriptures, His messengers, and meeting Him on the Day of Resurrection."[28] The Holy Lord states: *The Messenger believeth in that which hath been revealed unto him from his Lord and (so do) the believers. Each one believeth in God and His angels and His Scriptures and His messengers—We make no distinction between any of His messengers—and they say: We hear, and we obey. (Grant us) Thy forgiveness our Lord. Unto Thee is the journeying.*[29]

Gabriel is the greatest angel created by God (Glorious is He). One of Gabriel's names is the Holy Spirit (*al-rūḥ al-qudus*) because he is pure and devoid of any faults.[30] The Holy Lord sent Gabriel to relay the revelation to the Prophet Muḥammad, as he relayed it to previous prophets. God (Glorious is He) states: *It is not fitting for a man that God should speak to him except by inspiration, or from behind a veil, or by the sending of a messenger to reveal, with God's permission, what God wills: for He is Most High, Most Wise.*[31] The *messenger* is Gabriel.

God also revealed Paradise and Hellfire to Gabriel before creating humanity. The Prophet (may God bless him and grant him peace) said:

---

[26] Q.XXI.19–20.

[27] Q.IV.172 (Muḥammad Asad translation).

[28] Bukhārī 4777; Muslim 9/97; Ibn Māja 64; Aḥmad 9501. Of note, there is another narration which includes as a part of faith the belief in "His [ontologic] decree and determination: both good and bad." See Muslim 8/93; Tirmidhī 2610; Abū Dāwūd 4695; Ibn Māja 63; Nasā'ī 4993; Aḥmad 191.

[29] Q.II.285.

[30] See Zeni (tr.), *Ibn Qayyim al-Jawziyya on Divine Wisdom and the Problem of Evil*, p. 20.

[31] Q.XLII.51 (Yusuf Ali translation).

> After God created Paradise and Hellfire, He sent Gabriel to Paradise saying: "View it and what I have prepared for its inhabitants." [Gabriel] saw it and returned saying: "By Your might, no one will hear of it except that they will [want to] enter it." Then [God] commanded that [Paradise] be surrounded by hardships and said: "Return to it and view it and what I have prepared for its inhabitants." [Gabriel] then said: "By Your might, I fear that no one will enter it." Then [God] said: "Go and view Hellfire and what I have prepared for its denizens." [Gabriel] saw its [flames] rising up and said: "By Your might, no one will [want to] enter it." Then [God] commanded [Hellfire] to be surrounded by temptations and told [Gabriel]: "Return and view it." When Gabriel saw that it was surrounded by temptations, he returned and said: "By Your might, I fear that no one will be saved from [Hellfire], but instead all will enter it."[32]

Therefore, the combination of temptations (leading to impiety) and hardships (leading to disbelief) have made it much more likely for humankind to go to Hellfire (whether or not they are ultimately entered into Paradise).

God (Glorious is He) also informed the angels that He would be creating humanity, who will perpetrate evil and corruption:

> *And when thy Lord said unto the angels: I am about to place a viceroy in the earth, they said: Wilt thou place therein one who will do harm therein and will shed blood, while we hymn Thy praise and sanctify Thee? He said: Surely I know that which ye know not. And He taught Adam all the names, then showed them to the angels, saying: Inform Me of the names of these, if ye are truthful. They said: Be glorified! We have no knowledge saving that which Thou hast taught us. Lo! Thou, only Thou, art the Knower, the Wise.*[33]

So God's creation of humanity is for wise purposes that He (Glory be to Him) withheld even from the angels. That said, humanity has been granted knowledge (both religious and otherwise) which the angels do not possess. Although humankind may know the names, which are superficial and partial representations of entities, we are fundamentally limited in the ability to know the absolute realities of them. Nonetheless, this knowledge represents one of the greatest

---

[32] Tirmidhī 2560; Abū Dāwūd 4744; Nasā'ī 3794; Ibn Ḥibbān 7394. It is "authentic" according to Albānī (*Ṣaḥīḥ al-Jāmiʿ al-ṣaghīr* 5210).

[33] Q.II.30–32.

means for the offspring of Adam to attain the Holy Lord's favour. Furthermore, it is only by freely choosing to worship God alone, obeying His commandments, and avoiding evil or striving against it for His sake that one may be rewarded by Him, in accordance with His grace and mercy. Since the angels do not possess a free will they are not *rewarded* with Paradise, although they do enter it.

Everything that God creates is congruous with its role as relatively good or evil. Thus the nature of every creature is appropriate to its actions. Therefore, the angels, who have no sins or inadequacies (as they worship God continuously and obey all of His commandments), will never be placed in a situation where they will have to suffer—they must be secure.

Whereas the angels were created from light, humankind, in being granted the free will to do good and/or evil, could not congruently be created from pure light. Humankind is made from the earth, which is good for the most part. One proof of this is the verse of the Holy Lord: *O ye who believe! Render not vain your almsgiving by reproach and injury, like him who spendeth his wealth only to be seen of men and believeth not in God and the Last Day. His likeness is as the likeness of a rock whereon is dust of earth; a rainstorm smiteth it, leaving it smooth and bare.*[34] Here the goodness of almsgiving is represented as the earth (*turāb*). Although the individual giving it in this instance is either a hypocrite or disbeliever—whose heart is represented as a hard rock, and whose actions will be obliterated and not be rewarded by the Holy Lord because of his insincerity or disbelief—the almsgiving is nevertheless deemed good just as the earth is considered to be good. This is a truly beautiful similitude and parable drawn by the Holy Lord. The earth also leads to the growth of fruitful trees, which ties in to the discussion below.

A brief discussion of both spiritual and material light will now ensue. If people freely choose to be good then they will be granted an inner spiritual light in their hearts in this life and a material light

[34] Q.II.264.

in the Hereafter.[35] This inner spiritual light is represented by God's statement: *The similitude of His light is as a niche wherein is a lamp. The lamp is in a glass. The glass is as it were a shining star. (This lamp is) kindled from a blessed tree, an olive neither of the East nor of the West, whose oil would almost glow forth (of itself) though no fire touched it. Light upon light. God guideth unto His light whom He will. And God speaketh to humankind in allegories, for God is Knower of all things.*[36]

According to Ubayy b. Kaᶜb:[37] "God began by mentioning His light and then depicted the light [present within the heart] of the faithful."[38] The light within the heart purely shines outwardly as there is only transparent glass dividing the inner from the outer aspect. Therefore, the outer self of a truly faithful individual is no different than his or her inner self. Ibn al-Qayyim mentions:

> The niche (*mishkāt*) is the chest of a believer, whereas the glass symbolizes his heart due to its fineness (*riqqa^tiha*), purity and strength. Due to his gentleness (*riqqa^tihi*), the believer encompasses three traits: he is merciful (*yarḥam*), benevolent (*yuḥsin*) and compassionate (*yataḥannan wa yashfiq*) with people. Due to his purity, knowledge of matters is elucidated to him clearly, and he is therefore also able to distance himself from impurity, filth and foulness. Due to his strength, he is firm in following [and carrying out] the commandments of God (Exalted is He), and is tough against the enemies of God (Exalted is He)...The lamp represents

---

35 See Q.LVII.12: *On the day when thou (Muḥammad) wilt see the believers, men and women, their light shining forth before them and on their right hands, (and wilt hear it said unto them): Glad news for you this day: Gardens underneath which rivers flow, wherein ye are immortal. That is the supreme triumph.* See also Q.LXVI.8: *O ye who believe! Turn unto God in sincere repentance! It may be that your Lord will remit from you your evil deeds and bring you into Gardens underneath which rivers flow, on the day when God will not abase the Prophet and those who believe with him. Their light will run before them and on their right hands; they will say: Our Lord! Perfect our light for us, and forgive us! Lo! Thou art Able to do all things.*

36 Q.XXIV.35.

37 Abū Mundhir Ubayy b. Kaᶜb (d. 29/649) was a pre-eminent Companion who witnessed the Battle of Badr. The Prophet (may God bless him and grant him peace) mentioned him as one of the four that his contemporaries should learn the exegesis of the Qur'ān from (the others being Ibn Masᶜūd, Sālim mawlā Abī Ḥudhayfa and Muᶜādh b. Jabal). See Muslim 2464/6334; Aḥmad 6523.

38 See Lucas (tr.), *Ṭabarī Selections*, vol. I, pp. 317–331, for Ṭabarī's full discussion of this verse. Alternatively, the lamp may be interpreted as the Prophet Muḥammad (much like in verse Q.XXXIII.45–46) or the Qur'ān itself.

> the light of faith within his heart, while the blessed tree symbolizes revelation, which encompasses guidance and the true religion. The latter provides fuel for the lamp. *Light upon light* represents the light of the sound innate disposition accompanied by true perception [superimposed by] the light of revelation as well as the Scripture...For this reason, the [truly faithful believer] is almost able to articulate the truth and wisdom before hearing it from the traditions [i.e. from the Qur'ān and Sunna]...In this manner, he recognizes that reason, the Divine Law, innate disposition and revelation are all concordant. His reason, innate disposition and experience all therefore affirm that what the Messenger (may God bless him and grant him peace) conveyed is the truth and that it does not conflict with reason—they are in agreement and congruent. This is the sign of *light upon light*.[39]

This faith within the hearts of the believers results in actions or fruits—in this verse that fruit is the olive. That olive fruit then provides further oil, which in turn originates greater light, and therefore a perpetual cycle of goodness arises. True faith results in righteous deeds, which then cycle back to increase one's faith even further, by the grace of the Holy Lord.

The part of the verse that reads, *whose oil would almost glow forth (of itself) though no fire touched it*, illustrates that the truly faithful are almost guided to the religious truth, even in the absence of revelation. Then, once a prophet and revelation arrive to such good-hearted and truly faithful individuals, they believe immediately. The fire herein represents the religion (as evidenced by other verses[40]), because some hardships as well as purification will occur as a result of truly following the religion. This will be discussed further in Chapter Ten.

---

[39] Ibn al-Qayyim, *Ijtimāʿ al-juyūsh al-Islāmiyya ʿalā ḥarb al-Muʿaṭṭila wa'l-Jahmiyya*, ed. Zā'id b. Aḥmad al-Nushayrī (Mecca: Dār ʿĀlam al-Fawā'id, 2009), pp. 25–27.

[40] For instance, see the similitude in Q.II.17: *Their likeness is as the likeness of one who kindleth fire, and when it sheddeth its light around him God taketh away their light and leaveth them in darkness, where they cannot see.* One interpretation of this verse is that the fire represents the message and religion of Islam, which results in great light and goodness, but also indirectly leads to hardships that will be suffered by the believers. Those who see the light and yet *God taketh away their light and leaveth them in darkness* are the hypocrites. The hypocrites, therefore, are only left with heat that ultimately burns them in Hellfire. See *Tafsīr al-Ṭabarī*, vol. I, pp. 318–329, for other interpretations.

God is the Light of this universe and He has elucidated the reality of this universe, this life and the Hereafter. The Holy Lord has termed His Scriptures "light", and He has created light to elucidate the reality and nature of what is in existence. Consider the following verses in regards to the former: *So believe in God and His Messenger and the light which We have revealed.*[41] *And if they deny thee, even so did they deny messengers who were before thee, who came with miracles and with the Psalms and with the Scripture giving light.*[42] *Lo! We did reveal the Torah, wherein is guidance and a light;*[43] *And We caused Jesus the son of Mary, to follow in their footsteps, confirming that which was (revealed) before him in the Torah, and We bestowed on him the Gospel wherein is guidance and a light, confirming that which was (revealed) before it in the Torah—a guidance and an admonition unto those who ward off (evil).*[44]

In all of the above instances, as well as others, the revelation is termed *nūr* ("light"). But in one instance it is termed *ḍiyā'*: *And We verily gave Moses and Aaron the Criterion (of right and wrong) and a light (ḍiyā') and a Reminder for those who keep from evil.*[45] There are many opinions as to the difference between *nūr* and *ḍiyā'*, but it will be contended that the former represents light alone, whereas the latter is light associated with heat.[46] Therefore, the *ḍiyā'* in this verse most likely represents the Tablets, upon which God wrote the Ten Commandments, whereas the *Criterion* is the Torah (which was already described as a light (*nūr*) in verse 44 of Sūrat al-Mā'ida)—and God knows best. All glory and praise is due to God, the Light of this world and the Hereafter.

God (Exalted is He) also named the Prophet Muḥammad (may God bless him and grant him peace) an illuminating lamp (in a spiritual sense): *O Prophet! We have sent thee as a witness and a bringer of good tidings and a warner. And as a summoner unto God by His permission, and as a lamp that giveth light.*[47] God (Glorious is He) also stated: *O People of the Book!*

---

41 Q.LXIV.8. Thus the Qur'ān here is described as a light.

42 Q.III.184. See also Q.XXXV.25 for a similar verse.

43 Q.V.44.

44 Q.V.46.

45 Q.XXI.48.

46 The light reflected by the moon is termed *nūr* in the Qur'ān, while the light emanating from the sun is called *ḍiyā'*.

47 Q.XXXIII.45–46.

Now hath Our Messenger come unto you, expounding unto you much of that which ye used to hide in the Scripture, and forgiving much. Now hath come unto you light from God and plain Scripture.[48] May God (Exalted is He) bless the Prophet Muḥammad who has guided much of humanity to what is beloved to the Holy Lord, so that they may love Him and be loved by Him! The Holy Lord, Who is the Light of the heavens and the earth, has granted His messengers and prophets the greatest degrees of His spiritual light, allowing them to guide to His religious light.

Light is the closest thing to pure good in this world. Light is timeless and massless, but still created. Light elucidates the nature of objects. It would not be possible to carry out anything good in our lives without material light. Indeed, nothing harmful is attributed to light itself—it cannot cause pain nor does it cause suffering.[49] Light instead is the source of all goodness. The spiritual path is also similar to a material ray of light in that both are straight (*mustaqīm*).

Furthermore, light is involved in the origination of matter and then elucidates it. If one considers $E = mc^2$ as $m = E/c^2$ instead, then one can recognize that mass is one manifestation of energy just like light, heat or radiation. Thus matter is a very selective manifestation of energy; the selection factor being technically the speed of light not once but squared. Matter is good. Thus God (Exalted is He) creates energy and then through a property of light selects out matter. Light is therefore the key to everything both in the ontological universal sense and the religious deontological sense. God is the Creator of light; His veil is light; and He is the Spiritual Light of the heavens and the earth Who guides to His light.

---

[48] Q.V.15. The light in this verse refers to the Prophet Muḥammad—see *Tafsīr al-Ṭabarī*, vol. X, p. 143.

[49] One exception is a similitude regarding the hypocrites, and it involves being blinded from lightening as per verse Q.II.20: *The lightning almost snatcheth away their sight from them. As often as it flasheth forth for them they walk therein, and when it darkeneth against them they stand still.* The Holy Lord blinds them in a spiritual sense because of their betrayal and failure to follow His guidance. The disbelievers, on the other hand, are immersed in God's blessings yet can barely see the light or not at all as per the similitude in verse Q.XXIV.40: *Or as darkness on a vast, abysmal sea. There covereth him a wave, above which is a wave, above which is a cloud. Layer upon layer of darkness. When he holdeth out his hand he scarce can see it. And he for whom God hath not appointed light, for him there is no light.*

A PRELIMINARY DISCUSSION ON WHETHER THIS IS THE BEST OF ALL POSSIBLE WORLDS

Now, some contend that this world is "the best of all possible worlds" in a general sense based upon the statement of the Holy Lord: *Who makes most excellent (aḥsana) everything that He creates.*[50] Ṭabarī stated that the best interpretation of this verse is that "God perfected His handiwork".[51] Saᶜdī states that this indicates how God (Exalted is He) has created everything "in a manner appropriate and concordant to its [function]".[52] Ibn al-Qayyim stated that everything God has created fulfills "praiseworthy objectives and intended wise purposes".[53] Ibn Taymiyya stated that the Holy Lord "only created good and evil for wise purposes, which ultimately indicate that His actions and [creative ability] are good and perfect".[54]

It will be contended that every constitutive element has the capacity to achieve perfection, but in reality only some entities, whether ontological or religious, have been allowed by the Almighty Lord to achieve perfection (insofar as a created thing is able to be described as such). God has perfected (*aḥsana* or *atqana* or *aḥkama*)[55] and fine-tuned creation, but in many cases it becomes corrupt, particularly those who are free-willed creatures. Had every creature attained perfection, though, many of His wise purposes would not have occurred. Ultimately, only the believers will be perfected by the Holy Lord in Paradise.

It has been already affirmed that the Almighty Lord is a perfect Creator, Originator and Fashioner. However, this does not indicate that everything, which He has created, fully displays His generosity and magnanimity nor can any creature or world do so. The Holy Lord can always create something better in accordance with His grace and wisdom. God's creative ability is perfect and infinite, whereas

---

50 Q.XXXII.7 (Muḥammad Asad translation). Yusuf Ali translates the first part as: *He Who has made everything which He has created most good.* Pickthall translates it as: *Who made all things good which He created.* Of note, the continuation of verse 7 into verse 8 is: *And He began the creation of man from clay. Then He made his seed from a draught of despised fluid.*

51 See Lucas (tr.), *Ṭabarī Selections*, vol. I, p. 356.

52 See ᶜAbd al-Raḥmān al-Saᶜdī, *Taysīr al-Karīm al-Raḥmān fī tafsīr kalām al-Mannān* (Cairo: Dār Ibn Ḥazm, 2012), p. 634.

53 Zeni (tr.), *Ibn Qayyim al-Jawziyya on Divine Wisdom and the Problem of Evil*, p. 33.

54 Ibn Taymiyya, *Minhāj al-Sunna an-Nabawiyya*, vol. III, p. 142.

55 See *Tafsīr al-Ṭabarī*, vol. XIX, p. 506.

each individual creature is finite. Ultimately, God (Exalted is He) has fine-tuned His creation, both from an ontological and deontological perspective, to fulfill His wise purposes.[56]

As regards God's creation (Exalted is He), He says: *Have they not then observed the sky above them, how We have constructed it and beautified it, and how there are no rifts therein (furūj)?*[57] The Sublime has also said: *He Who created the seven heavens one above another: No want of proportion wilt thou see in the Creation of (God) Most Gracious. So turn thy vision again: seest thou any flaw (fuṭūr)?* [58] Ṭabarī states that *no want of proportion* (*tafāwut*) indicates that there is no inconsistency; rather, God's creation is continuous without gaps (*fuṭūr*).[59] Thus, when one considers the sky and heavens above, no faultiness or rifts can be observed therein. They are continuous and harmonious, which is not the case with other creatures—the lack of gaps is specific to the heavens. However, on the Day of Judgment, even the heavens will be split apart.[60] Therefore, God (Glory be to Him) has created the heavens in continuity, but can and will then split them up.

---

[56] See also *Tafsīr al-Rāzī*, vol. XXIV, p. 574, where Rāzī states that God has created "everything concordant to wisdom (*ḥikma*), and has made it proper (*ṣawāb*)". He also refutes the Muʿtazilī ʿAbd al-Jabbār—who claims that this verse indicates that God (Glorious is He) is not the creator of everything, including that which is evil or repugnant (*qabā'iḥ*)—by affirming that the consensus of scholars has also refuted his stance. Indeed, the Almighty Lord is the creator of both good and evil. But later Rāzī claims divine voluntarism when interpreting verse Q.LXVII.3—see *Tafsīr al-Rāzī*, vol. XXX, p. 582. Both positions of Rāzī are consistent with the fact that he is an Ashʿarī. It should be mentioned that although Rāzī is a neo-Ashʿarī and argued in favour of divine voluntarism, his exegesis includes many insightful comments, and therefore it is referenced often throughout the text.

[57] Q.L.6. Yusuf Ali translates it as: *Do they not look at the sky above them?– How We have made it and adorned it, and there are no flaws in it?* Muḥammad Asad translates it as: *Do they not look at the sky above them—how We have built it and made it beautiful and free of all faults?*

[58] Q.LXVII.3 (Yusuf Ali translation). Pickthall translates it as: *Who hath created seven heavens in harmony. Thou [Muḥammad] canst see no fault (tafāwut) in the Beneficent One's creation; then look again: Canst thou see any rifts (fuṭūr)?* Muḥammad Asad translates it as: *[Hallowed be] He who has created seven heavens in full harmony with one another: no fault will thou see in the creation of the Most Gracious. And turn thy vision [upon it] once more: canst though see any flaw?*

[59] See Lucas (tr.), *Ṭabarī Selections*, vol. II, pp. 273–274. The word *fuṭūr* is similar in meaning to *furūj*, which indicates rifts (*shuqūq* or *futūq*).

[60] The Holy Lord states: *When the heaven is cleft asunder* (*infaṭarat*) (Q.LXXVII.9 (Yusuf Ali translation)) and *when the heaven is split asunder* (Q.LXXXIV.1). See also Q.LV.37 and Q.LXIX.16 for similar verses.

God (Glorious is He) states also: *Thou seest the mountains and thinkest them firmly fixed: but they shall pass away as the clouds pass away: (such is) the artistry of God, Who disposes of all things in perfect order (atqana): for He is well acquainted with all that ye do.*[61] Thus God has perfected (*atqana*) His creation. There is no doubt that His scientific laws, by which He has created the heavens, earth and mountains, and allowed all of the technological advancements of the modern age, lead to harmony therein. If one contemplates the beauty of all that God (Exalted is He) has created including: the sun and the glorious colours in the sky at its rising and setting, the blue sky with white clouds, the stars and the moon bright in the dark night sky with the latter waxing and waning, and the hundreds of billions of galaxies (each with hundreds of billions of stars); tropical islands with white sandy beaches and turquoise lagoons, beautifully coloured fish and sea life, fjords jutting out from the sea, and snow-capped mountains; the complex ecosystem with its array of animals, insects, trees and plants; and finally the complexity of the human body with its trillions of neurons within the brain, and complex macroscopic and microscopic physiologic processes conducted by the heart, lungs, liver, spleen and bone etc.—it is self-evident that God (Exalted and Glorious is He) is the perfect Creator! *So blessed be God, the best to create!*[62]

Now, all of the aforementioned must be reconciled with His statement: *the evil of that which He created.*[63] This verse describes both the evil perpetrated by free-willed creatures whom He has originated, as well as the evil existent within them since He is the only Creator. Those who claim that God (Glorious is He) considers the evil that He has created to be either ontologically or religiously good have greatly erred. Instead, the evil they perpetrate may indirectly lead to

---

[61] Q.XXVII.88 (Yusuf Ali translation). Pickthall translates it as: *And thou seest the hills thou deemest solid flying with the flight of clouds: the doing of God Who perfecteth (atqana) all things. Lo! He is Informed of what ye do.* Muḥammad Asad translates it as: *And thou wilt see the mountains, which [now] thou deemest so firm, pass away as the clouds pass away: a work of God, who has ordered all things to perfection! Verily, He is fully aware of all that you do!*

[62] Q.XXIII.14 (Yusuf Ali translation).

[63] Q.CXIII.2. Yusuf Ali translates it as: *From the mischief of created things.* Muḥammad Asad translates it as: *From the evil of aught that He has created.*

the occurrence of good, which could not otherwise have occurred, and therefore the Holy Lord has wisely created them.

God has perfectly fine-tuned creation to form a system leading to the wise purposes He has dictated for it. Function fits form and vice versa. God (Exalted is He) states that: *Verily, We create man in the best conformation*;[64] and yet the Almighty Lord also states: *man was created weak*,[65] and *God is He Who shaped you out of weakness, then appointed after weakness strength, then, after strength, appointed weakness and grey hair. He createth what He will. He is the Knower, the Mighty*.[66] With these verses, it becomes clear that the Almighty Lord has created humankind to fulfill a purpose, which can only be accomplished with varying levels of strengths and weaknesses as well as perfections and inadequacies. God (Exalted is He) also states: *Verily, We have created man into toil and struggle*.[67] Humankind has been created weak, but then strengthened; ignorant, but then granted knowledge; and within an environment characterized by hardships in order to achieve the many wise purposes that God (Exalted is He) has dictated.

In addition, that this world is characterized by decay, inadequacy and deficiencies as well as hardships and evil should not be surprising, since the vast majority of its human inhabitants are disbelievers. It would not be appropriate to have higher levels of beauty and blessings when the majority of people are disbelievers. The Holy Lord is omniscient and He has allowed and predestined all that. Thus God (Glorious is He) has created this world in a concordant manner.

Hence this book will contend that this is the best possible world only insofar as it allows the manifestation of the Beautiful Names of God, as well as allowing the occurrence of many wise purposes dictated by Him. Among these wise purposes is the manifestation of the elevated ranks of prophets, the truly faithful, the righteous and pious believers and their actions. But it cannot be said in general absolutist terms that this is the best possible world—this will be discussed further in Chapter Eight of Part Two. God's creative power though is perfect and flawless, just as His wisdom is dazzling.

---

64 Q.XCV.4 (Muḥammad Asad translation).

65 Q.IV.28.

66 Q.XXX.54.

67 Q.XC.4 (Yusuf Ali translation).

God's power is truly unfathomable, and He is omnipotent. On the Day of Judgment He will fold up this universe with all of its hundreds of billions of galaxies (each containing hundreds of billions of stars) and its black holes. God (Glorious and Exalted is He) states: *And they esteem not God as He hath the right to be esteemed, when the whole earth is His handful on the Day of Resurrection, and the heavens are rolled in His right hand. Glorified is He and High Exalted from all that they ascribe as partner (unto Him).*[68]

[68] Q.XXXIX.67.

Chapter Four

The Greatness of the Prophets

God (Glorious is He) sent His messengers and prophets to convey His message to humankind. The religion that the prophets have called to is one: *He hath ordained for you that religion which He commended unto Noah, and that which We inspire in thee* (*Muḥammad*), *and that which We commended unto Abraham and Moses and Jesus, saying: Establish the religion, and be not divided therein.*[1]

The Prophet Muḥammad (may God bless him and grant him peace) said: "The religion [of all of the prophets] is one [and the same]."[2] The prophets are intermediaries between God and humanity only in that they elucidate God's Names and Attributes, His commandments and prohibitions.

The identifying characteristics of the prophets may be considered as follows: first, they universally call people to worship God alone and obey His commandments. Second, the prophets are either granted miracles, the ability to prophesize into the future or given knowledge of the past. The ability to prophesize is contained in the verses: (*He is*) *the Knower of the Unseen, and He revealeth unto none His secret, save unto every messenger whom He hath chosen.*[3]

Third, everything the prophets convey is the truth. Moses said: *O Pharaoh! I am a Messenger from the Lord of the Worlds, approved upon condition that I speak concerning God nothing but the truth.*[4] Therefore, the prophets are protected (*maʿṣūm*) from any falsehood.[5]

It is incumbent upon people to believe in all of the prophets: *Those who disbelieve in God and His messengers, and seek to make distinction between God and His messengers, and say: We believe in some and disbelieve in others, and seek to choose a way in between—such are disbelievers in truth; and for*

---

[1] Q.XLII.13.

[2] Bukhārī 3443; Muslim 2365/6132; Aḥmad 9270.

[3] Q.LXXII.26–27.

[4] Q.VII.104–105.

[5] See also Q.LXIX.43–47.

disbelievers We prepare a shameful doom. But those who believe in God and His messengers and make no distinction between any of them, unto them God will give their wages; and God was ever Forgiving, Merciful.[6] Thus those who reject even one prophet are considered to be disbelievers.[7] Furthermore, neglecting God's message and ignoring the prophets leads individuals to feel lost and abandoned. This is in accordance with His wisdom; for it is only by following the prophets that one may become guided by the Holy Lord.

Now, there are various opinions regarding the difference between a messenger (*rasūl*) and a prophet (*nabī*). Some have opined that the messenger brings forth the Divine Law in a manner that supersedes a former prophet or prophets.[8] It would appear that this definition would be too restrictive. Others have opined that the prophets were allowed freedom to administer their worldly affairs in a manner they wished, whereas the messengers must follow the commandments of the Holy Lord in all matters and are rewarded accordingly.

It appears though that the main difference between the messengers and the prophets is that the messengers are always granted victory ultimately, whereas the prophets are not necessarily made triumphant over the disbelievers. The Qur'ān states: *God hath decreed: I verily shall conquer, I and My messengers. God is Strong, Almighty.*[9] The Almighty Lord thus specified that victory was granted to the messengers (*rusul*). Furthermore, the Qur'ān states: *When God made* (*His*) *covenant with the prophets,* (*He said*)*: Behold that which I have given you of the Scripture and knowledge. And afterward there will come unto you a messenger, confirming that which ye possess. Ye shall believe in him and ye shall help him* (*tanṣurunna*[hu]). *He said: Do ye agree, and will ye take up My burden* (*which I lay upon you*) *in*

---

6 Q.IV.150–152.

7 See Q.II.136: *Say* (*O Muslims*)*: We believe in God and that which is revealed unto us and that which was revealed unto Abraham, and Ishmael, and Isaac, and Jacob, and the tribes, and that which Moses and Jesus received, and that which the prophets received from their Lord. We make no distinction between any of them, and unto Him we have surrendered.*

8 See Ṣadr al-Dīn Muḥammad b. Abī al-ʿIzz, *Sharḥ al-ʿAqīda al-Ṭaḥāwiyya* (Beirut: al-Maktab al-Islāmī, 1984), p. 158. For instance, Jesus (may God bless him), who was without a doubt the Messenger of God—not just a prophet—did not come with a new Divine Law, but rather affirmed the commandments within the Torah, while allowing some things that were previously forbidden. See Q.III.50.

9 Q.LVIII.21.

this (matter)? They answered: We agree. He said: Then bear ye witness. I will be a witness with you.[10] Therefore, the prophets are obligated to assist and aid the messengers towards the victory that God has promised the latter. God (Exalted is He) also states: *Till when the messengers despaired and thought that they were denied, then came unto them Our help, and whom We would was saved.*[11] Hence the messengers and believers following them are ultimately saved and granted victory.[12]

In addition, the prophets may be killed by the disbelievers, whereas the messengers are always granted victory before their death. The Sublime states: *Those who disbelieve the revelations of God, and slay the prophets wrongfully, and slay those of mankind who enjoin equity: promise them a painful doom.*[13] On the other hand, God (Exalted is He) states: *And because of their saying: We slew the Messiah, Jesus the son of Mary, God's Messenger—they slew him not nor crucified him, but it appeared so unto them. And those who disagree concerning it are in doubt thereof; they have no knowledge thereof save pursuit of a conjecture; they slew him not for certain.*[14] Therefore, one of the reasons why Jesus could never have been killed by the disbelievers is that he was a Messenger of God, and so he must attain victory prior to his death. This is one of the reasons why he will be brought back before the Day of Judgment—this will be discussed later.

Now, most of those whom the Holy Lord has inspired and sent forth to guide humankind were prophets. The Messenger Muḥammad (may God bless him and grant him peace) stated that the number of prophets was "124,000" and the number of the messengers was only "315".[15]

---

10 Q.III.81. Muḥammad Asad translates *tanṣurunna*[hu] as "succor him".

11 Q.XII.110. In this case, the messengers despaired of the disbelievers becoming believers—not of God's victory for them and their followers.

12 The verse Q.V.70 appears to negate this argument. However, the contention is that victory is attained by the messengers before their death, whereas the prophets are not granted victory over the disbelievers in accordance with the wisdom of God (Glorious is He). The Messenger Muḥammad, along with other Companions, ate poisoned goat meat whereby at least one of the latter died immediately. The Messenger Muḥammad lived four years afterwards and was granted ultimate victory, but he said while dying: "I have continued to suffer pain from the [poisoned] meal at the time of Khaybar, but it is only at this time that it has killed me." See Bukhārī 4428; Abū Dāwūd 4512.

13 Q.III.21. See also Q.II.61 and Q.III.112.

14 Q.IV.157.

15 Aḥmad 22,288; Ibn Ḥibbān 361. It is "authentic" according to Albānī (*Silsilat al-aḥādīth al-ṣaḥīḥa* 2668 and *Mishkāt al-maṣābīḥ* 5737).

Therefore, the percentage of the messengers was less than 1% (~0.25%), and thus most of those whom were sent by the Holy Lord were not granted victory in a worldly sense. This is concordant with reality, and the wise purposes for this will be discussed in Chapter Twelve.

A survey of many of the twenty-five messengers and prophets mentioned in the Qur'ān will now follow. The manner by which the prophets strove against evil will be kept in focus, but other objectives will also be pursued. These include affirming that Islam is God's religion—a Western religion like Judaism and Christianity, not an Eastern one. It is also hoped that those who ascribe evil to Islam and the Muslims will desist from doing so after recognizing that Islam affirms the Oneness of God, the importance of following His good commandments and the central role of His prophets. Islam is not an innovation of Muḥammad (may God bless him and grant him peace), but rather the revelation of the Holy Lord to him concordant with what He inspired to prior messengers.

God (Exalted is He) mentions eighteen of the prophets in Sūrat al-Anᶜām:

> *That is Our argument. We gave it unto Abraham against his folk. We raise unto degrees of wisdom whom We will. Lo! Thy Lord is Wise, Aware. And We bestowed upon him Isaac and Jacob; each of them We guided; and Noah did We guide aforetime; and of his seed (We guided) David and Solomon and Job and Joseph and Moses and Aaron. Thus do We reward the good. And Zachariah and John and Jesus and Elias. Each one (of them) was of the righteous. And Ishmael and Elisha and Jonah and Lot. Each one (of them) did We prefer above (Our) creatures, with some of their forefathers and their offspring and their brethren; and We chose them and guided them unto a Straight Path. Such is the guidance of God wherewith He guideth whom He will of His bondmen. But if they had set up (for worship) aught beside Him, (all) that they did would have been vain.*[16]

The other seven prophets specifically mentioned in the Qur'ān are Adam, Enoch (Idrīs), Hūd, Ṣāliḥ, Shuᶜayb, Isaiah (Dhū al-Kifl) and Muḥammad (may God bless them all). As mentioned before, we must believe in all of these prophets—disbelief or failure to follow one prophet represents disbelief in them all.

---

[16] Q.VI.83–89.

Now, Adam had many honours bestowed upon him by God according to the *ḥadīth* stating that he is "the father of mankind, and the one whom God has created with His Hand", and "the one into whom God breathed of His spirit (*rūḥi*[hi]), taught the names of all things and commanded His angels to prostrate to".[17] The fact that God *taught Adam all the names*[18] establishes that knowledge is one of the most eminent things that humans can possess.[19]

God (Glorious is He) created humankind to be viceroys on this earth,[20] and He had destined Adam to live on this earth even before He created him. The Holy Lord placed Adam and Eve (who were sinless) in the Garden beforehand to teach humanity the consequences of sins, and to reveal the enmity of Satan towards them.[21] After their lapse, *Their Lord called them, (saying): Did I not forbid you from that tree and*

---

[17] Abū Dāwūd 4702. It is "sound" according to Albānī (*Silsilat al-aḥādīth al-ṣaḥīḥa* 1702). See also Bukhārī 4712; Muslim 194/480; Tirmidhī 2434; Aḥmad 2692.

[18] See Q.II.31. This knowledge likely includes the names of the angels and offspring of Adam as well as the names of other animate and inanimate creatures. See *Tafsīr al-Ṭabarī*, vol. I, pp. 480–486. Of note, these entities could be seen, since the entire verse states: *And He taught Adam all the names, then showed them to the angels, saying: Inform Me of the names of these, if ye are truthful.* Thus these names were not names of entities that were invisible to the eye, or names of characteristics that were not manifest.

[19] Ibn al-Qayyim discusses this at length in *Miftāḥ dār al-saʿāda*—see Zeni (tr.), *Ibn Qayyim al-Jawziyya on Knowledge.*

[20] See Q.II.30–31: *And when thy Lord said unto the angels: Lo! I am about to place a viceroy in the earth, they said: Wilt thou place therein one who will do harm therein and will shed blood, while we hymn Thy praise and sanctify Thee? He said: Surely, I know that which ye know not. And He taught Adam all the names, then showed them to the angels, saying: Inform Me of the names of these, if ye are truthful.* Contrast that to Genesis 3.22–23: "And the LORD God said, Behold, the man is become as one of us, to know good and evil: and now, lest he put forth his hand, and take also of the tree of life, and eat, and live for ever: Therefore the LORD God sent him forth from the garden of Eden, to till the ground from whence he was taken."

[21] See Q.XX.117: *Then We said: O Adam! Verily, this [Satan] is an enemy to thee and thy wife: so let him not get you both out of the Garden, so that thou art landed in misery*, and Q.XX.120: *But Satan whispered evil to him: he said, "O Adam! shall I lead thee to the Tree of Eternity and to a kingdom that never decays?"* (Yusuf Ali translation). Some classical sources explain how Adam's having *rebelled* and *erred* in Q.XX.121 means "he made a mistake" because of being "beguiled" by the devil, in light of Q.XX.115: *We had already, beforehand, taken the covenant of Adam, but he forgot: and We found on his part no firm resolve* (Yusuf Ali translation). See Aisha Abdarrahman Bewley (tr.), *Muhammad Messenger of Allah: Ash-Shifa of Qadi 'Iyad*, 2nd edition (Granada: Madinah Press, 1992), pp. 329–330.

tell you: Lo! Satan is an open enemy to you? They said: Our Lord! We have wronged ourselves. If Thou forgive us not and have not mercy on us, surely we are of the lost![22] God is omniscient, and there is nothing in existence—both past and future—that is hidden from Him (Glorious and Exalted is He). Then, God accepted Adam's repentance: *Then his Lord chose him, and relented toward him, and guided him.*[23] Although Adam and Eve repented and they were forgiven for their sins, they still had to suffer the consequences of their disobedience, i.e. they had to fall from heaven to earth. This descent to earth was ontologically decreed by the Holy Lord in accordance with His wisdom.[24] God's determination thus occurs through causes, and in the presence of human free choice.

We likewise need to admit to any of our wrongdoings and ask for God's forgiveness. Although a lapse or sin may be forgiven, its negative consequences may continue; therefore one must try to avoid sins as much as possible. The Holy Lord states: *So fear God as much as ye can; listen and obey and spend in charity for the benefit of your own soul.*[25]

After many generations humans forgot the Holy Lord's commandments and were seduced by the Devil into worshipping idols. God sent Noah to bring them back to worshipping Him alone: *We sent Noah unto his people (saying): Warn thy people ere the painful doom come unto them. He said: O my people! I am a plain warner unto you. (Bidding you): Serve God and keep your duty unto Him and obey me.*[26] Noah continued to call them for 950 years, but the vast majority disbelieved and ridiculed him.[27]

---

[22] Q.VII.22–23. Contrast this to the text of Genesis 3.9–11 in the Old Testament: "And the LORD God called unto Adam, and said unto him, Where art thou? And he said, I heard thy voice in the garden, and I was afraid, because I was naked; and I hid myself. And he said, Who told thee that thou wast naked? Hast thou eaten of the tree, whereof I commanded thee that thou shouldest not eat?"

[23] Q.XX.121–122. God mentions in Q.XX.115 the forgetfulness of Adam as one of the reasons for his sin: *And verily We made a covenant of old with Adam, but he forgot, and We found no constancy in him.*

[24] Ibn al-Qayyim lists twenty-six wise purposes in *Miftāḥ dār al-saʿāda*—see Zeni (tr.), *Ibn Qayyim al-Jawziyya on Divine Wisdom and the Problem of Evil*, pp. 1–18.

[25] Q.LXIV.16 (Yusuf Ali translation).

[26] Q.LXXI.1–3.

[27] See verses Q.XI.36–39.

God (Exalted is He) flooded all of the disbelievers, while Noah and the few who believed were saved on the ship.[28] It is clear that the Almighty Lord could have continued to destroy disbelievers of later nations, just as He did with the disbelievers amongst Noah's people; however, He allowed them to remain in accordance with certain wise purposes. The Holy Lord states: *And We sent Noah and Abraham, and established in their line prophethood and Revelation: and some of them were on right guidance. But many of them became rebellious transgressors.*[29]

God (Glorious is He) commends Abraham in many verses: *When his Lord said unto him: Surrender! he said: I have surrendered to the Lord of the Worlds;*[30] *Who is better in religion than he who surrendereth his purpose to God while doing good (to men) and followeth the tradition of Abraham, the upright? God (Himself) chose Abraham for a friend;*[31] and *Abraham was a nation obedient to God, by nature upright, and he was not of the idolaters; thankful for His bounties; He chose him and He guided him unto a Straight Path.*[32] The Holy Lord also told Abraham: *I have appointed thee a leader for mankind. (Abraham) said: And of my offspring (will there be leaders)? He said: My covenant includeth not wrongdoers.*[33]

Abraham (may God bless him) advised his people: *Serve God, and keep your duty unto Him; that is better for you if ye did but know...But if ye deny, then nations have denied before you. The messenger is only to convey (the message) plainly.*[34] But Abraham's people disbelieved and rejected his message:

---

[28] See verses Q.XI.40–43. These verses also allude to one of Noah's sons being a disbeliever and thus drowned with them. Contrast this to Genesis 9.20–25: "And Noah began to be an husbandman, and he planted a vineyard: And he drank of the wine, and was drunken; and he was uncovered within his tent. And Ham, the father of Canaan, saw the nakedness of his father, and told his two brethren without. And Shem and Japheth took a garment, and laid it upon both their shoulders, and went backward, and covered the nakedness of their father; and their faces were backward, and they saw not their father's nakedness. And Noah awoke from his wine, and knew what his younger son had done unto him. And he said, Cursed be Canaan; a servant of servants shall he be unto his brethren."

[29] Q.LVII.26.

[30] Q.II.130.

[31] Q.IV.125.

[32] Q.XVI.120–121.

[33] Q.II.124.

[34] Q.XXIX.16–18.

> *So naught was the answer of (Abraham's) people except that they said: Slay him or burn him. But God did save him from the Fire. Verily in this are Signs for people who believe. And he said: For you, ye have taken (for worship) idols besides God, out of mutual love and regard between yourselves in this life; but on the Day of Judgment ye shall disown each other and curse each other: and your abode will be the Fire, and ye shall have none to help.*[35]

Thus God (Exalted is He) saved Abraham and Lot, his nephew: *And We rescued him and Lot (and brought them) to the land which We have blessed for (all) peoples.*[36]

God (Glorious is He) dictated that the prophets would arise from Abraham's lineage. Abraham was first bestowed Ishmael, and he was commanded to take and leave him and his mother Hagar in Mecca. Hagar asked Abraham: "Has God commanded you to do so?" After he replied in the affirmative, she stated: "Then, He will not neglect us." Subsequently, "she saw an angel at the place of Zamzam, digging the earth with his heel (or his wing), till water flowed from that place."[37] A tribe later settled there—"the wilderness of Paran" in the terminology of the Old Testament.[38] The Old Testament affirms the greatness of Ishmael and his nation: "And as for Ishmael, I have heard thee: Behold, I have blessed him, and will make him fruitful, and will multiply him exceedingly; twelve princes shall he beget, and I will make him a great nation."[39]

---

35 Q.XXIX.24–25 (Yusuf Ali translation).

36 Q.XXI.71.

37 See the Prophetic *ḥadīth* in Bukhārī 3364.

38 See also Genesis 21.14–21: "And Abraham rose up early in the morning, and took bread, and a bottle of water, and gave it unto Hagar, putting it on her shoulder, and the child, and sent her away: and she departed, and wandered in the wilderness of Beersheba. And the water was spent in the bottle, and she cast the child under one of the shrubs. And she went, and sat her down over against him a good way off, as it were a bowshot: for she said, Let me not see the death of the child. And she sat over against him, and lift up her voice, and wept. And God heard the voice of the lad; and the angel of God called to Hagar out of heaven, and said unto her, What aileth thee, Hagar? Fear not; for God hath heard the voice of the lad where he is. Arise, lift up the lad, and hold him in thine hand; for I will make him a great nation. And God opened her eyes, and she saw a well of water; and she went, and filled the bottle with water, and gave the lad drink. And God was with the lad; and he grew, and dwelt in the wilderness, and became an archer. And he dwelt in the wilderness of Paran." See also Genesis 16.10–12.

39 Genesis 17.20.

Abraham would return on multiple occasions to Hagar and Ishmael, in accordance with God's commandments. God (Exalted is He) states:

> *So We gave him tidings of a gentle son. And when (his son) was old enough to walk with him, (Abraham) said: O my dear son, I have seen in a dream that I must sacrifice thee. So look, what thinkest thou? He said: O my father! Do that which thou art commanded. God willing, thou shalt find me of the steadfast. Then, when they had both surrendered (to God), and he had flung him down upon his face, We called unto him: O Abraham! Thou hast already fulfilled the vision. Thus do We reward the good. Lo! that verily was a clear test.*[40]

God also states: *And We ransomed him with a momentous sacrifice. And We left (this blessing) for him among generations (to come) in later times: Peace and salutation to Abraham! Thus indeed do We reward those who do right. For he was one of our believing servants. And We gave him the good news of Isaac—a prophet—one of the righteous.*[41]

Ibn al-Qayyim stated regarding Abraham being commanded to sacrifice Ishmael:

> God honoured and rewarded Abraham for his submission to the commandment of God in this regard, and He blessed his offspring and made them immensely numerous, filling all corners of the earth. There is no one more generous than God (Most Blessed and Exalted is He), and He is the Most Beneficent. Thus, God will grant whoever leaves something for His sake, or does something for His sake, many times more than what he has forgone and reward him manifold for what he has done.
>
> A person's fear is especially heightened to the utmost degree when asked to sacrifice his son due to the concern that his lineage will become cut-off. But when Abraham offered his son up to God and Ishmael likewise offered himself up, God multiplied his lineage and blessed them until they filled this earth[42]. Furthermore, God

---

[40] Q.XXXVII.101–105.

[41] Q.XXXVII.106–112 (Yusuf Ali translation).

[42] See Genesis 22.17–18: "That in blessing I will bless thee, and in multiplying I will multiply thy seed as the stars of the heaven, and as the sand which is upon the sea shore; and thy seed shall possess the gate of his enemies; And in thy seed shall all the nations of the earth be blessed; because thou hast obeyed my voice." See also Genesis 17.8: "And I will give unto thee, and to thy seed after thee, the land wherein thou art a stranger, all the land of Canaan, for an everlasting possession; and I will be their God."

brought forth the prophets, including Muḥammad (may God bless him and grant him peace), from amongst Abraham's lineage specifically.[43]

Abraham returned later to build the Kaᶜba along with Ishmael:

> *And when Abraham and Ishmael were raising the foundations of the House, (Abraham prayed): Our Lord! Accept from us (this duty). Lo! Thou, only Thou, art the Hearer, the Knower. Our Lord! And make us submissive unto Thee and of our seed a nation submissive unto Thee, and show us our ways of worship, and relent toward us. Lo! Thou, only Thou, art the Relenting, the Merciful. Our Lord! And raise up in their midst a messenger from among them who shall recite unto them Thy revelations, and shall instruct them in the Scripture and in wisdom and shall make them grow. Lo! Thou, only Thou, art the Mighty, Wise.*[44]

According to the *ḥadīth* of the Prophet Muḥammad, the Holy Kaᶜba was built forty years before the Aqṣā Mosque in Jerusalem.[45] Finally, Abraham advised his sons as well as Jacob, his grandson:

> *O my sons! God hath chosen for you the (true) religion; therefore die not save as men who have surrendered (unto Him). Or were ye present when death came to Jacob, when he said unto his sons: What will ye worship after me? They said: We shall worship thy god, the god of thy fathers, Abraham and Ishmael and Isaac, One God, and unto Him we have surrendered.*[46]

The story of Joseph and his brothers[47] is well documented in the Qur'ān and the Old Testament. One point will be mentioned here—namely that the Prophet Jacob had knowledge and gnosis, which his

---

43 See Zeni (tr.), *Ibn Qayyim al-Jawziyya on Divine Wisdom and the Problem of Evil*, p. 258.

44 Q.II.127–129.

45 Bukhārī 3366; Muslim 520/1161; Ibn Māja 753; Nasā'ī 753; Aḥmad 21,333. The Prophet also said regarding Mecca: "This city has been made sacred by God the day He created the heavens and the earth, and it will remain so until the Day of Judgment." See Bukhārī 3189; Muslim 1353/3302; Nasā'ī 2875; Aḥmad 2353.

46 Q.II.131–133.

47 Jacob's sons were born according to Genesis 29 and 30 by: his wives Leah (6 children) and Rachel (2—Joseph and Benjamin), who were both daughters of his maternal uncle, i.e. his cousins, and sisters to each other; and the respective handmaids of his wives, namely Zilpah and Bilhah, who gave birth to two boys each after being given in marriage to Jacob. Of note, Genesis 29.23–30 depicts Laban, Jacob's maternal uncle, as deceiving Jacob by marrying him to his oldest daughter Leah, rather than the younger Rachel, whom Jacob had sought to marry in return for seven years of service. It was only thereafter that Laban consented to give Rachel in marriage to him.

sons were unaware of, while further wisdoms regarding the story will be discussed later. Jacob was granted knowledge of those future events by the Almighty Lord, whereas Joseph's brothers were not. The Qur'ān confirms Jacob's understanding and recognition, whereas the Old Testament denies it.

Jacob was aware of the implications of Joseph's dream and the jealousy that would arise from his brothers.[48] Jacob also knew that Joseph had not been killed and that his brothers were lying in that regard.[49] And many years later after Joseph was reunited with Benjamin, Jacob said: *(My course is) comely patience! It may be that God will bring them all unto me. Lo! He, only He, is the Knower, the Wise...I know from God that which ye know not. Go, O my sons, and ascertain concerning Joseph and his brother, and despair not of the Spirit of God.*[50] Jacob also told them once they gave him the glad tidings of Joseph being alive: *Said I not unto you that I know from God that which ye know not?*[51] The point is that although the messengers and prophets (including

---

[48] Joseph said: *O my father! I saw in a dream eleven planets and the sun and the moon, and I saw them prostrating themselves unto me. He said: O my dear son! Tell not thy brethren of thy vision, lest they plot a plot against thee. Satan is for man an open foe. Thus thy Lord will prefer thee and will teach thee the interpretation of events, and will perfect His grace upon thee and upon the family of Jacob as He perfected it upon thy forefathers, Abraham and Isaac. Thy Lord is Knower, Wise.* Q.XII.4–6. Contrast the Qur'ānic verses to Genesis 37.9–10: "Behold, I have dreamed a dream more; and, behold, the sun and the moon and the eleven stars made obeisance to me. And he told it to his father, and to his brethren: and his father rebuked him, and said unto him, What is this dream that thou hast dreamed? Shall I and thy mother and thy brethren indeed come to bow down ourselves to thee to the earth?"

[49] Jacob said: *Nay, but your minds have beguiled you into something. (My course is) comely patience. And God it is Whose help is to be sought in that (predicament) which ye describe.* Q.XII.18. Contrast this to Genesis 37.33–35: "And he knew it, and said, It is my son's coat; an evil beast hath devoured him; Joseph is without doubt rent in pieces. And Jacob rent his clothes, and put sackcloth upon his loins, and mourned for his son many days. And all his sons and all his daughters rose up to comfort him; but he refused to be comforted; and he said, For I will go down into the grave unto my son mourning. Thus his father wept for him."

[50] Q.XII.83–87. See Genesis 42.38: "And he said, My son [Benjamin] shall not go down with you; for his brother [Joseph] is dead, and he is left alone: if mischief befall him by the way in the which ye go, then shall ye bring down my gray hairs with sorrow to the grave."

[51] Q.XII.96. Contrast this to Genesis 45.26: "And told him, saying, Joseph is yet alive, and he is governor over all the land of Egypt. And Jacob's heart fainted, for he believed them not."

Jacob) are granted much knowledge by the Holy Lord, they may withhold the details of that knowledge from others (according to the commandment of God to achieve the wise purposes He has dictated).

As mentioned previously, Lot believed along with his uncle, Abraham, and accompanied him. God (Glorious is He) subsequently sent Lot to a wicked nation: *And Lot! (Remember) when he said unto his folk: Will ye commit abomination such as no creature ever did before you? Lo! ye come with lust unto men instead of women. Nay, but ye are wanton folk. And his people gave no answer but this: they said: Drive them out of your city: these are indeed men who want to be clean and pure! And We rescued him and his household, save his wife.*[52] In this manner, Lot forbade those people from homosexuality and sexual indecency.

God (Exalted is He) punished those disbelievers with three different punishments: *But the (mighty) Blast overtook them before morning, and We turned (the cities) upside down, and rained down on them brimstones hard as baked clay.*[53] The Old Testament similarly documents their punishment; however, the conclusion of Lot's story in the Bible is blasphemous.[54]

Finally, if one looks closely at this story in the Qur'ān one notes that there is no mention of whether the people of Lot worshipped God alone or were polytheists. All the other nations that God (Exalted is He) destroyed were polytheist—no nation was ever completely destroyed because of their perpetration of a destructive major sin (*al-mūbiqāt*). It can therefore be concluded that the Holy Lord will destroy (whether directly or indirectly) a society in which homosexuality is present (at a defined level) regardless of whether they worship Him

---

[52] Q.VII.80–83.

[53] Q.XV.73–74 (Yusuf Ali translation).

[54] See Genesis 19.31–36: "And the firstborn said unto the younger, Our father is old, and there is not a man in the earth to come in unto us after the manner of all the earth: Come, let us make our father drink wine, and we will lie with him, that we may preserve seed of our father. And they made their father drink wine that night: and the firstborn went in, and lay with her father; and he perceived not when she lay down, nor when she arose. And it came to pass on the morrow, that the firstborn said unto the younger, Behold, I lay yesternight with my father: let us make him drink wine this night also; and go thou in, and lie with him, that we may preserve seed of our father. And they made their father drink wine that night also: and the younger arose, and lay with him; and he perceived not when she lay down, nor when she arose. Thus were both the daughters of Lot with child by their father."

alone or not. Those individuals who continue to perpetrate sodomy and do not repent, even if they are monotheistic, should be concerned of the probability they may never exit Hellfire. And God knows best.

Many centuries elapsed after Joseph and his brothers moved to Egypt, and the Israelites were subsequently enslaved by Pharaoh and the Egyptians. The story of Moses (may God bless him) is well documented in the Old Testament and Qur'ān, and he is one of the greatest messengers. God (Exalted is He) spoke directly to Moses saying:

> *Verily, I am thy Lord! Therefore (in My presence) put off thy shoes: thou art in the sacred valley Ṭuwā. I have chosen thee: listen, then, to the inspiration (sent to thee). Verily, I am God: There is no god but I: So serve thou Me (only), and establish regular prayer for celebrating My praise. Verily, the Hour is coming—My design is to keep it hidden for every soul to receive its reward by the measure of its endeavour. Therefore, let not such as believe not therein, but follow their own lusts, divert thee therefrom, lest thou perish!*[55]

After God informed Moses that his brother Aaron would be granted prophethood so as to assist him, He said: "*Go, both of you, to Pharaoh, for he has indeed transgressed all bounds; But speak to him mildly; perchance he may take warning or fear (God)... So go ye both to him, and say, 'Verily we are messengers sent by thy Lord: Send forth, therefore, the Children of Israel with us, and afflict them not: with a Sign, indeed, have we come from thy Lord! And peace to all who follow guidance!'*"[56]

The Holy Lord also informed Moses that he will ultimately be victorious over Pharaoh: "*We will certainly strengthen thy arm through thy brother, and invest you both with authority, so they shall not be able to touch you: with Our Sign shall ye triumph—you two as well as those who follow you.*"[57] God (Exalted is He) states: *And verily We gave unto Moses nine tokens, clear proofs (of God's Sovereignty)... [Moses] said [to Pharaoh]: In truth thou knowest that none sent down these (portents) save the Lord of the heavens and the earth as proofs.*[58] But Pharaoh and the Egyptians obstinately rejected saying:

> *"Whatever be the Signs thou bringest, to work therewith thy sorcery on us, we shall never believe in thee." So We sent (plagues) on them: wholesale death, locusts, lice,*

---

55 Q.XX.12–16.

56 Q.XX.43–47 (Yusuf Ali translation).

57 Q.XXVIII.35 (Yusuf Ali translation).

58 Q.XVII.101–102.

frogs, and blood: signs openly self-explained: but they were steeped in arrogance, a people given to sin. Every time the penalty fell on them, they said: "O Moses! On your behalf call on thy Lord in virtue of his promise to thee: If thou wilt remove the penalty from us, we shall truly believe in thee, and we shall send away the Children of Israel with thee." But every time We removed the penalty from them according to a fixed term which they had to fulfill, behold! They broke their word! So We exacted retribution from them: We drowned them in the sea, because they rejected Our Signs and failed to take warning from them.[59]

God (Glorious is He) also stated that Pharaoh and the Egyptians *rejected those Signs in iniquity and arrogance, though their souls were convinced thereof.*[60]

The Holy Lord states:

We inspired Moses and his brother with this message: "Provide dwellings for your people in Egypt, make your dwellings into places of worship, and establish regular prayers: and give glad tidings to those who believe!" Moses prayed: "Our Lord! Thou hast indeed bestowed on Pharaoh and his chiefs splendour and wealth in the life of the present, and so, Our Lord, they mislead (men) from Thy Path. Deface, our Lord, the features of their wealth, and send hardness to their hearts, so they will not believe until they see the grievous penalty." God said: "Accepted is your prayer (O Moses and Aaron)! So stand ye straight, and follow not the path of those who know not."[61]

By inspiration we told Moses: "Travel by night with my servants; for surely ye shall be pursued."[62] *So [Pharaoh and his army] pursued them at sunrise. And when the two bodies saw each other, the people of Moses said:*[63] *"We are sure to be overtaken." (Moses) said: "By no means! my Lord is with me! Soon will He guide*

[59] Q.VII.132–136 (Yusuf Ali translation).
[60] Q.XXVII.14 (Yusuf Ali translation).
[61] Q.X.87–89 (Yusuf Ali translation).
[62] Q.XXVI.52–56 (Yusuf Ali translation).
[63] See Exodus 14.10–12: "And when Pharaoh drew nigh, the children of Israel lifted up their eyes, and, behold, the Egyptians marched after them; and they were sore afraid: and the children of Israel cried out unto the LORD. And they said unto Moses, Because there were no graves in Egypt, hast thou taken us away to die in the wilderness? wherefore hast thou dealt thus with us, to carry us forth out of Egypt? Is not this the word that we did tell thee in Egypt, saying, Let us alone, that we may serve the Egyptians? For it had been better for us to serve the Egyptians, than that we should die in the wilderness." See also Exodus 16.3: "And the children of Israel said unto them, Would to God we had died by the hand of the LORD in the land of Egypt, when we sat by the flesh pots, and when we did eat bread to the full; for ye have brought us forth into this wilderness, to kill this whole assembly with hunger."

> *me!" Then We told Moses by inspiration: "Strike the sea with thy rod." So it divided, and each separate part became like the huge, firm mass of a mountain. And We made the other party approach thither. We delivered Moses and all who were with him; but We drowned the others. Verily in this is a Sign: but most of them do not believe. And verily thy Lord is He, the Exalted in Might, Most Merciful.*[64]

Thus, God (Glorious is He) manifested nine signs to Pharaoh and the Egyptians, although He knew that they would not believe. It only increased them in their arrogance such that they could not even recognize the miraculous parting of the sea. Their disbelief, oppression and stubborn obstinacy justified them being drowned. Another important objective of these nine signs—and God knows best—was so that the Israelites would attain greater faith and know that the Holy Lord is omnipotent. This would then enable them to recognize that God (Exalted is He) would save them. Yet their faith remained lacking, as illustrated in both the Qur'ān and Old Testament.

The Almighty Lord saved the Israelites with such a great miracle: "For I am the Lord that bringeth you up out of the land of Egypt, to be your God: ye shall therefore be holy, for I am holy."[65] Moreover, despite seeing their enemies drowned by the Almighty Lord, once the Israelites were commanded to fight against the disbelievers they refused:

> All the children of Israel murmured against Moses and against Aaron: and the whole congregation said unto them, Would God that we had died in the land of Egypt! or would God we had died in this wilderness! And wherefore hath the LORD brought us unto this land, to fall by the sword, that our wives and our children should be a prey? were it not better for us to return into Egypt? And they said one to another, Let us make a captain, and let us return into Egypt. Then Moses and Aaron fell on their faces before all the assembly of the congregation of the children of Israel. And Joshua the son of Nun, and Caleb the son of Jephunneh, which were of them that searched the land, rent their clothes: And they spake unto all the company of the children of Israel, saying, The land, which we passed through to search it, is an exceeding good land. If the LORD delight in us, then he will bring us into this land, and give it us; a land which floweth with milk and honey. Only rebel not ye against the

---

64 Q.XXVI.60–68 (Yusuf Ali translation).

65 Leviticus 11.45.

> LORD, neither fear ye the people of the land; for they are bread for us: their defence is departed from them, and the LORD is with us: fear them not. But all the congregation bade stone them with stones. And the glory of the LORD appeared in the tabernacle of the congregation before all the children of Israel. And the LORD said unto Moses, How long will this people provoke me? and how long will it be ere they believe me, for all the signs which I have shewed among them?[66]

It was only after wandering forty years in the wilderness—whereby those generations of Israelites who had worshipped the golden calf and/or refused to fight had passed away—that the Holy Lord allowed the younger Israelites to conquer the disbelievers under the leadership of Joshua[67]:

> So Joshua arose, and all the people of war, to go up against Ai: and Joshua chose out thirty thousand mighty men of valour, and sent them away by night.[68] And the king of Ai they took alive, and brought him to Joshua. And it came to pass, when Israel had made an end of slaying all the inhabitants of Ai in the field, in the wilderness wherein they chased them, and when they were all fallen on the edge of the sword, until they were consumed, that all the Israelites returned unto Ai, and smote it with the edge of the sword. And so it was, that all that fell that day, both of men and women, were twelve thousand, even all the men of Ai. For Joshua drew not his hand back, wherewith he stretched out the spear, until he had utterly destroyed all the inhabitants of Ai. Only the cattle and the spoil of that city Israel took for a prey unto themselves, according unto the word of the LORD which he commanded Joshua. And Joshua burnt Ai, and made it an heap for ever, even a desolation unto this day. And the king of Ai he hanged on a tree until eventide.[69]
>
> And the LORD said unto Joshua, Fear them not: for I have delivered them into thine hand; there shall not a man of them stand before thee. Joshua therefore came unto them suddenly, and went up from Gilgal all night. And the LORD discomfited them before Israel, and slew them with a great slaughter at Gibeon, and chased them along the way that goeth up to Bethhoron, and smote them to Azekah, and unto Makkedah.

---

66 Numbers 14.2–12. See also Deuteronomy 1.34–45.

67 See the Prophetic *ḥadīth* in Bukhārī 122; Muslim 2380/6163; Tirmidhī 3149; Aḥmad 21, 119.

68 Joshua 8.3.

69 Joshua 8.23–29.

> And it came to pass, as they fled from before Israel, and were in the going down to Bethhoron, that the LORD cast down great stones from heaven upon them unto Azekah, and they died: they were more which died with hailstones than they whom the children of Israel slew with the sword. Then spake Joshua to the LORD in the day when the LORD delivered up the Amorites before the children of Israel, and he said in the sight of Israel, Sun, stand thou still upon Gibeon; and thou, Moon, in the valley of Ajalon. And the sun stood still, and the moon stayed, until the people had avenged themselves upon their enemies. Is not this written in the book of Jasher? So the sun stood still in the midst of heaven, and hasted not to go down about a whole day. And there was no day like that before it or after it, that the LORD hearkened unto the voice of a man: for the LORD fought for Israel.[70]

The Old Testament then documents Joshua's battles against many other cities.[71] And Joshua, according to the Old Testament, defeated many kings.[72] Thus the Almighty Lord had commanded the Israelites to completely destroy many polytheistic nations, and Joshua carried that out faithfully.

After the victories of Joshua, the Israelites settled—by the grace of God (Exalted is He)—the promised land, as Moses had previously told them: *O my people! Go into the holy land which God hath ordained for you.*[73] Thus God (Glorious is He) fulfilled His promise to them, and they occupied a land that had been previously held by the polytheists.

---

[70] Joshua 10.8–14. Of note, the Prophet Muḥammad (may God bless him and grant him peace) said: "The sun has never been held [from setting] for a human except for Joshua b. Nūn on his path to Jerusalem." Aḥmad 8315. It is "sound" according to Albānī (*Silsilat al-aḥādīth al-ṣaḥīḥa* 202—see also 2226). Also, see al-Ḥākim 2618.

[71] See Joshua 10.29–40: "So Joshua smote all the country of the hills, and of the south, and of the vale, and of the springs, and all their kings: he left none remaining, but utterly destroyed all that breathed, as the LORD God of Israel commanded." These cities included: Makkedah, Libnah, Lachish, Eglon, Hebron and Debir.

[72] See Joshua 11.1–17: "And they smote all the souls that were therein with the edge of the sword, utterly destroying them: there was not any left to breathe: and he burnt Hazor with fire. And all the cities of those kings, and all the kings of them, did Joshua take, and smote them with the edge of the sword, and he utterly destroyed them, as Moses the servant of the LORD commanded." They were the kings of Hazor, Madon, Shimron and Achshaph.

[73] Q.V.21.

Finally, it should be noted that there exist verses within the Old Testament addressed to the Israelites regarding making peace and declaring war:

> When thou comest nigh unto a city to fight against it, then proclaim peace unto it. And it shall be, if it make thee answer of peace, and open unto thee, then it shall be, that all the people that is found therein shall be tributaries unto thee, and they shall serve thee. And if it will make no peace with thee, but will make war against thee, then thou shalt besiege it: And when the LORD thy God hath delivered it into thine hands, thou shalt smite every male thereof with the edge of the sword: But the women, and the little ones, and the cattle, and all that is in the city, even all the spoil thereof, shalt thou take unto thyself; and thou shalt eat the spoil of thine enemies, which the LORD thy God hath given thee. Thus shalt thou do unto all the cities which are very far off from thee.[74]

Now, after being established in the land, the Israelites became impious again and many were displaced from their homes until the time of David (may God bless him). David is one of the greatest messengers of the Holy Lord. It is narrated in a *ḥadīth* that God showed Adam all of humanity: "[Adam] saw a man who had such a great light between his eyes that he was amazed by it. [Adam] asked: 'O my Lord, who is that?' [God] replied: 'A man from a later nation of your offspring named David.'"[75] This *ḥadīth* is interesting in that David (may God bless him) was portrayed as such despite not being one of the top five

---

[74] Deuteronomy 20.10–15. Of note, the verses which follow the above, i.e. Deuteronomy 20.16–20, state: "But of the cities of these people, which the LORD thy God doth give thee for an inheritance, thou shalt save alive nothing that breatheth: But thou shalt utterly destroy them; namely, the Hittites, and the Amorites, the Canaanites, and the Perizzites, the Hivites, and the Jebusites; as the LORD thy God hath commanded thee: That they teach you not to do after all their abominations, which they have done unto their gods; so should ye sin against the LORD your God. When thou shalt besiege a city a long time, in making war against it to take it, thou shalt not destroy the trees thereof by forcing an axe against them: for thou mayest eat of them, and thou shalt not cut them down (for the tree of the field is man's life) to employ them in the siege: Only the trees which thou knowest that they be not trees for meat, thou shalt destroy and cut them down; and thou shalt build bulwarks against the city that maketh war with thee, until it be subdued."

[75] Tirmidhī 3076; al-Ḥākim 3257; Bayhaqī (*Sunan*) 20,518. It is "authentic" according to Albānī (*Ṣaḥiḥ al-Jāmiʿ al-ṣaghīr* 5208).

messengers, i.e. Noah, Abraham, Moses, Jesus and Muḥammad (may God bless them all).

That said, David was, according to a *ḥadīth* of the Prophet Muḥammad (may God bless them both), "the greatest worshipper of humankind".[76] The Prophet Muḥammad described David's devotion by saying: "The most beloved fasts to God are the fasts of David, as he would fast on alternating days. Also, the most beloved prayers to God are the prayers of David, as he would sleep half of the night, then pray for one third of it, and [finally] sleep for [the remaining] sixth."[77]

Indeed, of all of the prophets, the one who appears to most resemble the Messenger Muḥammad in his actions is David (may God bless them both)—and God knows best. They both received Scripture, both had to emigrate from their native city only to later return victorious, both fought against the disbelievers, and later generations have been tested due to the marriages of David and Muḥammad. The first three points will be discussed herein, whereas the fourth will be discussed in the next chapter.

The Holy Lord states: *And we preferred some of the prophets above others, and unto David We gave the Psalms.*[78] Note in this verse that God (Glorious is He) did not mention that He favoured David because He had granted him a kingdom or wealth, but rather because He revealed to him the Psalms.

David (may God bless him) fought for the sake of the Holy Lord. God (Exalted is He) states:

> *And when they went into the field against Goliath and his hosts they said: Our Lord! Bestow on us endurance, make our foothold sure, and give us help against the disbelieving folk. So they routed them by God's leave and David slew Goliath; and God gave him the kingdom and wisdom, and taught him of that which He willeth. And if God had not repelled some men by others the earth would have been corrupted. But God is a Lord of Kindness to (His) creatures.*[79]

---

[76] Muslim 1159/2729. See also Tirmidhī 2490 and al-Ḥākim 3621 where the statement of the Prophet Muḥammad that David was the "greatest worshipper of humanity" is "authentic" according to Albānī (*Ṣaḥiḥ al-Jāmiʿ al-ṣaghīr* 4453).

[77] Bukhārī 3420; Muslim 1159/2729; Abū Dāwūd 2448; Ibn Māja 1712; Nasā'ī 1630; Aḥmad 6491.

[78] Q.XVII.55.

[79] Q.II.250–251.

The Prophet Muḥammad also said that David "would never flee [from battle] after encountering [the disbelievers]".[80] These verses and *ḥadīths* all illustrate the eminent status of David (may God bless him).

Next, similar to the Prophet Muḥammad who emigrated from Mecca to Medina, David's life was put in danger and therefore he emigrated along with Samuel[81]. In addition, the Prophet Muḥammad ultimately returned to Mecca victorious, and David ultimately defeated the enemies of God and was granted sovereignty over the Israelites.

Thereafter David (may God bless him) fought for the sake of God against many more enemies, including the Amelikites,[82] the Philistines,[83] the Moabites and the polytheists within Syria at that time,[84] among many others. Similarly, the Prophet Muḥammad (may God bless him and grant him peace) fought against the polytheists in many battles.

God (Glorious is He) stated: *And We verily gave knowledge unto David and Solomon, and they said: Praise be to God, Who hath preferred us above many of His believing servants! And Solomon was David's heir.*[85] Solomon was devoted to his Lord; and he would say: *My Lord, arouse me to be thankful for Thy favour wherewith Thou hast favoured me and my parents, and to do good that shall be pleasing unto Thee, and include me in (the number of) Thy righteous servants.*[86]

The Prophet Muḥammad (may God bless him and grant him peace) said of Solomon:

> When Solomon the son of David built the temple in Jerusalem he asked God (Almighty and Most Glorious is He) for three things. [First] he asked [God] to grant him wisdom in his rulings, so that they may be in agreement with [His] rulings—he was granted such. He also asked God to bestow upon him a kingdom unlike any other granted to anyone else—he was granted such. And he asked God, once he completed the

80 Bukhārī 1977; Muslim 1159/2736; Tirmidhī 770; Nasā'ī 2393; Aḥmad 6534.
81 See 1 Samuel 22.1–5.
82 See 1 Samuel 30.
83 See 2 Samuel 5.
84 See 2 Samuel 8.
85 Q.XXVII.15–16.
86 Q.XXVII.19.

> construction of the temple (*al-masjid*), that anyone who only travelled to pray therein be forgiven [and become sinless] as if he was just born by his mother. He was granted the first two and I hope that he was granted the third.[87]

Likewise, the Old Testament affirms Solomon's wisdom and sovereignty. Solomon asked for "an understanding heart to judge thy people, that I may discern between good and bad" whereupon the Old Testament states:

> And the speech pleased the LORD, that Solomon had asked this thing. And God said unto him, Because thou hast asked this thing, and hast not asked for thyself long life; neither hast asked riches for thyself, nor hast asked the life of thine enemies; but hast asked for thyself understanding to discern judgment; Behold, I have done according to thy words: lo, I have given thee a wise and an understanding heart; so that there was none like thee before thee, neither after thee shall any arise like unto thee. And I have also given thee that which thou hast not asked, both riches, and honour: so that there shall not be any among the kings like unto thee all thy days.[88]

Whilst both David and Solomon (may God bless them both) were granted much wisdom, Solomon was granted greater degrees by the grace of God, Who is the Most Wise. A matter was brought before David and Solomon and they: *gave judgment concerning the field, when people's sheep had strayed and browsed therein by night; and We were witnesses to their judgment. And We made Solomon to understand (the case); and unto each of them We gave judgment and knowledge.*[89] The judgment of Solomon[90] represented a higher degree of wisdom over the long term.

---

87 Ibn Māja 1408; Nasā'ī 693; Aḥmad 6644; al-Ḥākim 3624; Bayhaqī (*Shuʿab*) 3877. It is "authentic" according to Albānī (*Ṣaḥīḥ al-Jamiʿ al-ṣaghīr* 2090).

88 1 Kings 3.6–13. See also 1 Kings 4.29–32.

89 Q.XXI.78–79.

90 According to *Tafsīr al-Ṭabarī*, David ruled that the shepherd must compensate the farmer with a number of sheep equivalent to the value of the damaged crop. On the other hand, Solomon ruled that the shepherd must compensate the farmer with an equivalent amount of wool and milk, as well as any sheep that were born until the next year (when the crop was to be restored). See *Tafsīr al-Ṭabarī*, vol. XVIII, pp. 475–479. Ibn al-Qayyim discusses this in *Iʿlām al-muwaqqiʿīn ʿan-Rabb al-ʿālamīn* (Beirut: Dār al-Kitāb al-ʿArabī, 2006), pp. 244–245. Thus Solomon's judgment maintained the base capital in the hands of each owner. Since the benefit of the farm was no longer accrued by the farmer (for that season),

Although both judgments were fair it was God, the Most Wise, Who taught Solomon and gave him greater wisdom than David to rule in the most equitable manner.

Another matter in which both David and Solomon judged is represented in the *ḥadīth* of the Prophet Muḥammad (may God bless him and grant him peace):

> Two women went out together with their infants, whereupon a wolf dragged one of the infants away. One [mother] said to other: "It took your infant." While the other said: "It dragged yours away instead!" They therefore went to David whereupon he judged in favour of the older [woman]. They then went to Solomon the son of David and informed him [of the story and judgment of David]. He said: "Bring me a knife to divide the infant between the two of you." The younger said: "Do not do that—may God have mercy on you—he is her infant." Solomon thus judged in favour of the younger [mother].[91]

Solomon (may God bless him) also stated in the Qur'ān: "*O my Sustainer! Inspire me so that I may forever be grateful for those blessings of Thine with which Thou hast graced me and my parents, and that I may do what is right [in a manner] that will please Thee; and include me, by Thy grace, among Thy righteous servants.*"[92] Solomon acknowledged the blessings of the Holy Lord stating: *This is of the bounty of my Lord, that He may try me whether I give thanks or am ungrateful. Whosoever giveth thanks he only giveth thanks*

Solomon similarly ruled that the benefit of the flock no longer be enjoyed by the shepherd, but instead by the farmer, for that same duration. But after the crops ripen during the next season, and the farmer reaps from them, then likewise the shepherd will also derive full benefit of his flock—each having retained his capital. In conclusion, when damages occur efforts should be made to preserve the capital of the stakeholders, while the compensation is pulled from the yield of the one who directly or indirectly led to the damage.

[91] Bukhārī 3427; Muslim 1720/4495; Nasā'ī 5402; Aḥmad 8480. The Old Testament narrates a similar story about two mothers who disputed in regards to an infant after the other died, but does not mention David ruling on the matter. See 1 Kings 3.25–27: "And the king [Solomon] said, Divide the living child in two, and give half to the one, and half to the other. Then spake the woman whose the living child was unto the king, for her bowels yearned upon her son, and she said, O my lord, give her the living child, and in no wise slay it. But the other said, Let it be neither mine nor thine, but divide it. Then the king answered and said, Give her the living child, and in no wise slay it: she is the mother thereof."

[92] Q.XXVII.19 (Muḥammad Asad translation).

for (*the good of*) *his own soul; and whosoever is ungrateful* (*is ungrateful only to his own soul's hurt*). *For lo! my Lord is Absolute in independence, Bountiful.*[93]

Solomon fought against the disbelievers just as David and Joshua did before him (may God bless them all). Solomon mobilized an army against the disbelievers of Sheba who worshipped the sun.[94] Solomon was intent on spreading the message of God to the people of Sheba or conquering them, thus he stated: *We verily shall come unto them with hosts that they cannot resist, and we shall drive them out from thence with shame, and they will be abased.*[95] Ultimately, the Queen of Sheba surrendered to the Holy Lord.[96] In conclusion, Solomon has only been commended by the Holy Lord in the Qur'ān—Solomon never disbelieved nor did he practice magic nor did he worship others.[97] This will be discussed further in the next chapter.

Now, Isaiah and Jeremiah are discussed in the Bible as prophets. The former is likely to be the Qur'ānic Dhū al-Kifl.[98] The latter is discussed by Ibn Kathīr in his book *al-Bidāya wa'l-nihāya* whereby his name in Arabic is Armiyā'. Jeremiah was informed by the Holy Lord regarding the Israelites:

> Then said the LORD unto me, Though Moses and Samuel stood before me, yet my mind could not be toward this people: cast them out of my sight, and let them go forth. And it shall come to pass, if they say unto thee, Whither shall we go forth? then thou shalt tell them, Thus saith the LORD; Such as are for death, to death; and such as are for the sword, to the sword; and such as are for the famine, to the famine; and such as are for the captivity, to the captivity.[99] For thus saith the LORD, Enter not into the house of mourning, neither go to lament nor bemoan them: for I have taken away my peace from this people, saith the LORD, even lovingkindness and mercies.[100] I will give all Judah into the hand of the

93 Q.XXVII.40.
94 See Q.XXVII.24–26.
95 Q.XXVII.37.
96 See Q.XXVII.44.
97 See Q.II.102.
98 See Q.XXI.85–86.
99 Jeremiah 15.1–2.
100 Jeremiah 16.5.

> king of Babylon, and he shall carry them captive into Babylon, and shall slay them with the sword.[101]

The destruction of Jerusalem thereafter ensued at the hands of the armies of Nebuchadnezzar. God (Exalted is He) states: *And We decreed for the Children of Israel in the Scripture: Ye verily will work corruption in the earth twice, and ye will become great tyrants. So when the time for the first of the two came, We roused against you servants of Ours of great might who ravaged (your) country, and it was a threat performed.*[102]

This represents the beginning of the scattering of the Israelites, with some subsequently settling in the Arabian Peninsula. Of note, the Almighty thereafter determined and promised them: *Dwell in the land; but when the promise of the Hereafter cometh to pass We shall bring you as a crowd gathered out of various nations.*[103]

Later generations of Israelites returned to Jerusalem, and the prophet Zachariah (or Zacharias) was sent to them. God (Exalted is He) states:

> *(Remember) when the wife of ʿImran said: My Lord! I have vowed unto Thee that which is in my belly as a consecrated (offering). Accept it from me. Lo! Thou, only Thou, art the Hearer, the Knower! And when she was delivered she said: My Lord! Lo! I am delivered of a female—God knew best of what she was delivered—the male is not as the female; and lo! I have named her Mary, and I crave Thy protection for her and for her offspring from Satan the outcast. And her Lord accepted her with full acceptance and vouchsafed to her a goodly growth; and made Zachariah her guardian. Whenever Zachariah went into the sanctuary where she was, he found that she had food. He said: O Mary! Whence cometh unto thee this (food)? She answered: It is from God. God giveth without stint to whom He will. Then Zachariah prayed unto his Lord and said: My Lord! Bestow upon me of Thy bounty goodly offspring. Thou art the Hearer of Prayer. And the angels called to him as he stood praying in the sanctuary: God giveth thee glad tidings of (a son*

---

101 Jeremiah 20.4. See also Jeremiah 11.1–14.

102 Q.XVII.4–5. "Servants" here connotes the ontologic, not deontologic, sense of the word. See also Jeremiah 25.9: "Behold, I will send and take all the families of the north, saith the LORD, and Nebuchadnezzar the king of Babylon, my servant, and will bring them against this land, and against the inhabitants thereof, and against all these nations round about, and will utterly destroy them, and make them an astonishment, and an hissing, and perpetual desolations."

103 Q.XVII.104.

> *whose name is) John, (who cometh) to confirm a word from God, lordly, chaste, a prophet of the righteous.*[104]

Zachariah asked the Holy Lord for a son so that the latter could inherit the prophethood and guide the Israelites. John (*Yaḥyā*) was commanded: *O John! Hold fast the Scripture. And we gave him wisdom when a child, and compassion from Our presence, and purity; and he was devout, and dutiful toward his parents. And he was not arrogant, rebellious. Peace on him the day he was born, and the day he dieth and the day he shall be raised alive!*[105]

Mary was a truly faithful woman (*ṣiddīqa*).[106] God (Exalted is He) states:

> *And when the angels said: O Mary! God hath chosen thee and made thee pure, and hath preferred thee above (all) the women of creation. O Mary! Be obedient to thy Lord, prostrate thyself and bow with those who bow (in worship)...(And remember) when the angels said: O Mary! God giveth thee glad tidings of a Word from Him, whose name is the Messiah, Jesus the son of Mary, illustrious in the world and the Hereafter, and one of those brought near (unto God). He will speak unto humankind in his cradle and in his manhood, and he is of the righteous. She said: My Lord! How can I have a child when no mortal hath touched me? He said: So (it will be). God createth what He will. If He decreeth a thing, He saith unto it only: Be! and it is.*[107]

When Mary carried and presented Jesus to her people, he miraculously spoke to them as a baby saying:

> *Lo! I am the servant of God. He hath given me the Scripture and hath appointed me a prophet, and hath made me blessed wheresoever I may be, and hath enjoined upon me prayer and zakat so long as I remain alive, and (hath made me) dutiful toward her who bore me, and hath not made me arrogant, unblest. Peace on me the day I was born, and the day I die, and the day I shall be raised alive!*[108]

---

104 Q.III.35–39.
105 Q.XIX.12–15.
106 See Q.V.75.
107 Q.III.42–47.
108 Q.XIX.30–33.

God (Exalted is He) also stated in regards to Jesus:

> *And He will teach him the Scripture and wisdom, and the Torah and the Gospel, and He will make him a messenger unto the Children of Israel, (saying): I come unto you with a sign from your Lord. Lo! I fashion for you out of clay the likeness of a bird, and I breathe into it and it is a bird, by God's leave. I heal him who was born blind, and the leper, and I raise the dead, by God's leave. And I announce unto you what ye eat and what ye store up in your houses. Lo! herein verily is a portent for you, if ye are to be believers. And (I come) confirming that which was before me of the Torah, and to make lawful some of that which was forbidden unto you. I come unto you with a sign from your Lord, so keep your duty to God and obey me. God is my Lord and your Lord, so worship Him. That is a Straight Path.*[109]

Instead of the people following Jesus (may God bless him), who brought forth all of the aforementioned miracles (some of which were similar to those performed by Elijah[110]) and religious knowledge, most disbelieved and some attempted to kill him. God (the Almighty and Most Glorious) states:

> *O Jesus! Lo! I am gathering thee and causing thee to ascend unto Me, and am cleansing thee of those who disbelieve and am setting those who follow thee above those who disbelieve until the Day of Resurrection*[111]*...As for those who disbelieve I shall chastise them with a heavy chastisement in the world and the Hereafter; and they will have no helpers. And as for those who believe and do good works, He will pay them their wages in full. God loveth not wrongdoers. This (which) We recite unto thee is a revelation and a wise reminder. Lo! the likeness of Jesus [in the sight*

---

[109] Q.III.48–51. See also Q.XIX.16–28 and Q.V.110.

[110] According to the Old Testament, Elijah supplicated to God and through His grace blessed the food of a woman and brought her child back to life (1 Kings 17.1–24), consumed many disbelievers with a fire from heaven (2 Kings 1.8–14), parted the Jordan river and walked across on dry land, and was raised up in a whirlwind (2 Kings 2.1–15). Elisha also brought a child back to life, by the grace of God, according to 2 Kings 4.32–37. Elisha also accompanied Elijah after the latter parted the Jordan river, by God's grace.

[111] See also Q.IV.157–159 (Yusuf Ali translation) where God (Exalted is He) rejects those who falsely boasted: *"We killed Christ Jesus the son of Mary, the Messenger of God"; but they killed him not, nor crucified him, but so it was made to appear to them, and those who differ therein are full of doubts, with no (certain) knowledge, but only conjecture to follow, for of a surety they killed him not. Nay, God raised him up unto Himself; and God is Exalted in Power, Wise. And there is none of the People of the Book but must believe in him before his death; and on the Day of Judgment he will be a witness against them.*

> *of] God is as the likeness of Adam. He created him of dust, then He said unto him: Be! and he is.*[112]

God (Glorious and Exalted is He) also states: *Such was Jesus the son of Mary: (this is) a statement of the truth concerning which they doubt. It befitteth not (the Majesty of) God that He should take unto Himself a son. Glory be to Him! When He decreeth a thing, He saith unto it only: Be! and it is.*[113] The Holy Lord affirms that: *They surely disbelieve who say: God is the Messiah, son of Mary. The Messiah (himself) said: O Children of Israel! Worship God, my Lord and your Lord. Lo! whoso ascribeth partners unto God, for him God hath forbidden Paradise. His abode is the Fire. For evildoers there will be no helpers;*[114] and: *They do blaspheme who say: God is one of three in a Trinity: for there is no god except One God. If they desist not from their word (of blasphemy), verily a grievous penalty will befall the blasphemers among them. Why turn they not to God, and seek His forgiveness? For God is Oft-forgiving, Most Merciful.*[115]

On the Day of Resurrection the Almighty Lord will say:

> *"O Jesus the son of Mary! Didst thou say unto men, 'worship me and my mother as gods in derogation of God'?" He will say: "Glory to Thee! never could I say what I had no right (to say). Had I said such a thing, Thou wouldst indeed have known it. Thou knowest what is in my heart, [yet] I know not what is in Thine. For Thou knowest in full all that is hidden. Never said I to them aught except what Thou didst command me to say, to wit, 'worship God, my Lord and your Lord'; and I was a witness over them whilst I dwelt amongst them; when Thou didst take me up Thou wast the Watcher over them, and Thou art a witness to all things. If Thou dost punish them, they are Thy servant[s]: If Thou dost forgive them, Thou art the Exalted in power, the Wise."*[116]

Jesus (may God bless him) will thus affirm on the Day of Judgment (as well as in this world) that he was a servant and messenger.

Worshipping God (Glorious and Exalted is He) alone is repeated over and over by the prophets in the Qur'ān. If their people believe then further knowledge and commandments are prescribed. If, however,

---

112 Q.III.55–59.

113 Q.XIX.34–35. The concept of the Trinity is also rejected in Q.IV.171.

114 Q.V.72.

115 Q.V.73–74 (Yusuf Ali translation).

116 Q.V.116–117 (Yusuf Ali translation).

such people do not worship God alone, their religion is not accepted. The later Christian faith, as influenced by Paul[117] and the author of the Gospel of John in the first century, deviated from affirming God's Oneness and worshipping Him alone. Therefore, the Holy Lord does not discuss further aspects of Christianity other than repudiating their associationism, Trinity, etc.—and God knows best. The Holy Lord has forbidden those who worship other than Him from entry into Paradise, as stated in numerous Qur'ānic verses.

Now there are some prophets who are only mentioned in the Qur'ān and not in the Bible, namely Hūd,[118] Ṣāliḥ and Shuᶜayb. They all advised their people to worship God alone. God (Exalted is He) states: *To the ᶜĀd people, (We sent) Hūd, one of their (own) brethren; he said: "O my people! worship God! Ye have no other god but Him. Will ye not fear (God)?"*[119] But his people rejected monotheism and were thus destroyed.[120] God (Exalted is He) states regarding the Prophet Ṣāliḥ: *To the Thamūd people (We sent) Ṣāliḥ, one of their own brethren. He said: "O my people! Worship God: ye have no other god but Him. It is He Who hath produced you from the earth and settled you therein: then ask forgiveness of Him, and turn to Him (in repentance): for my Lord is (always) near, ready to answer."*[121] God (Glorious is He) also states: *And as for Thamūd, We gave them guidance, but they preferred blindness to the guidance.*[122] Thus Thamūd were destroyed also. Finally, regarding Shuᶜayb, God (Exalted is He) states:

> *To the Madyan People (We sent) Shuᶜayb, one of their own brethren: he said: "O my people! worship God: Ye have no other god but Him...And O my people! give*

---

[117] Michael Hart states that Christianity "was not founded by a single person but by two people—Jesus and St. Paul...Jesus formulated the basic ethical ideas of Christianity, as well as its basic spiritual outlook and its main ideas concerning human conduct. Christian theology, however, was shaped principally by the work of St. Paul. Jesus presented a spiritual message; Paul added to that the worship of Christ." Michael Hart, *The 100: A Ranking of the Most Influential Persons in History* (New York: Citadel Press, 1978), p. 31.

[118] Ibn Kathīr states that Hūd is the son of Salah b. Arphaxad b. Shem b. Noah. Ibn Kathīr also states that the tribe of ᶜĀd was the first to worship idols after the flood. See Azami (tr.), *Stories of the Prophets*, p. 90–91.

[119] See Q.VII.65–71.

[120] Q.XI.53–58. See also Q.XXIII.35–38 and Q.XLI.15–16.

[121] Q.XI.61–67 (Yusuf Ali translation).

[122] Q.XLI.17.

> *just measure and weight, nor withhold from the people the things that are their due: commit not evil in the land with intent to do mischief...I only desire (your) betterment to the best of my power; and my success (in my task) can only come from God. In Him I trust."*[123]

But they also disbelieved and were thus destroyed. In the end, Shuᶜayb said: *O my people! I delivered my Lord's messages unto you and gave you good advice; then how can I sorrow for a people that rejected [the truth]?*[124]

Finally, according to the Qur'ān, many of the prophets advised their people: *Fear (itaqqū) God, and obey me.*[125] This phrase was repeated by the prophets Noah, Hūd, Ṣāliḥ, Lot and Shuᶜayb in Sūrat al-Shuᶜarā', and said by Jesus in Sūrat Āl-ᶜImrān and Sūrat al-Zukhruf.[126] Abraham also advised his people to worship God alone and be pious in Sūrat al-ᶜAnkabūt,[127] while Elias advised the Israelites of the same in Sūrat al-Ṣāffāt.[128] Advising people to be pious as well as to worship God alone is from God's providence.

As is apt for the final revelation to humanity, there are many verses of the Qur'ān in which God (Glorious is He) affirms His Oneness, advises piety and faith in the Final Messenger: *So fear God...Obey God and His Messenger, if ye do believe.*[129] The Prophet Muḥammad (may God bless him and grant him peace) said: "We [i.e. the Muslims] are the last to come but we will be the foremost on the Day of Resurrection (even though the past nations were given the Scripture before us)."[130] The truthfulness and greatness of the Messenger Muḥammad will be discussed next.

---

123 Q.XI.84–88 (Yusuf Ali translation). See also Q.XXVI.176–189.

124 Q.VII.93. See also Q.VII.85–92.

125 See eight verses in Sūrat al-Shuᶜarā': Q.XXVI.108 and 110 were said by Noah, 126 and 131 by Hūd, 144 and 150 by Ṣāliḥ, 163 by Lot, and 179 by Shuᶜayb.

126 See Q.III.50 and Q.XLIII.63.

127 See Q.XXIX.16.

128 See Q.XXXVII.123–130.

129 Q.VIII.1 (Yusuf Ali translation).

130 Bukhārī 876; Muslim 855/1978; Nasā'ī 1367; Aḥmad 7401.

Chapter Five

The Greatness of Muḥammad: the Seal of the Prophets

God (Glorious is He) states: *Muḥammad is not the father of any man among you, but he is the Messenger of God and the Seal of the Prophets.*[1] The Prophet Muḥammad (may God bless him and grant him peace) was distinguished in many aspects—being the Seal of the Prophets (*khātam al-nabiyyīn*) is one.[2] He was sent to all of humankind, including the Jews and Christians, for the Holy Lord states: *O People of the Book! Now hath Our Messenger come unto you to make things plain unto you after an interval (of cessation) of the messengers, lest ye should say: There came not unto us a messenger of cheer nor any warner. Now hath a Messenger of cheer and a warner come unto you.*[3]

God (Glorious is He) also states:

> *Say (O Muḥammad): O humankind! I am the Messenger of God to you all—(the Messenger of) Him unto Whom belongeth the Sovereignty of the heavens and the earth. There is no deity save Him. He quickeneth and He giveth death. So believe in God and His Messenger, the Prophet who can neither read nor write, who believeth in God and in His Words, and follow him that haply ye may be led aright.*[4] *And We have not sent thee (O Muḥammad) save as a bringer of good tidings and a warner unto all humankind; but most of humankind know not.*[5]

---

1 Q.XXXIII.40. See also verses 19–23 in Sūrat Āl-ʿImrān.

2 The Prophet Muḥammad said, "I have been distinguished from other prophets in six ways: I have been granted encompassing [eloquent] speech, granted victory by [God striking] fear [in the hearts of the disbelievers], and permitted the spoils [of war]. The earth has been purified for me so as to permit prayer therein. I have been sent to all of humankind, and I am the Seal of the Prophets." See Muslim 523/1167; Tirmidhī 1553; Aḥmad 9337.

3 Q.V.19.

4 Q.VII.158. The fact that the Messenger Muḥammad was illiterate proves that he had not derived his knowledge from reading prior Scripture, but rather from the Holy Lord Himself Who revealed it to him.

5 Q.XXXIV.28. God (Glorious is He) also stated in Q.V.67: *O Messenger! Make known that which hath been revealed unto thee from thy Lord, for if thou do it not, thou wilt not have conveyed His message. God will protect thee from humankind.*

The Prophet said: "A prophet used to be sent to only his people, but I have been sent to the entirety of humankind."[6]

God's love of an individual is predicated upon the person following His Prophet and Messenger: *Say (O Muḥammad, to humankind): If ye love God, follow me; God will love you and forgive you your sins. God is Forgiving, Merciful. Say: Obey God and the Messenger. But if they turn away, lo! God loveth not the disbelievers.*[7] Therefore, one must obey and follow Muḥammad, the Messenger of God, in order to prove that he or she truly loves the Holy Lord. In addition, God (Exalted is He) stated: *If anyone desires a religion other than Islam [i.e. submission to God], never will it be accepted of him; and in the Hereafter he will be in the ranks of those who have lost [all spiritual good].*[8]

God (Glorious and Exalted is He) also stated that the Prophet Muḥammad was mentioned in prior Scriptures and that his message is true and righteous:

> *Those who follow the Messenger, the Prophet who can neither read nor write, whom they will find described in the Torah and the Gospel (which are) with them. He will enjoin on them that which is right and forbid them that which is wrong. He will make lawful for them all good things and prohibit for them only the foul; and he will relieve them of their burden and the fetters that they used to wear. Then those who believe in him, and honour him, and help him, and follow the light which is sent down with him: they are the successful.*[9]

ʿAbd Allāh b. Salām, formerly a Jewish rabbi living in Medina, believed in the Prophet Muḥammad and converted to Islam.[10] He narrated that the first thing he heard the Messenger say in Medina was: "O people! If you spread peace [or the greeting of *salām* to all],

---

6 Bukhārī 335; Aḥmad 14,264.

7 Q.III.31–32.

8 Q.III.85 (Yusuf Ali translation).

9 Q.VII.157.

10 See Bukhārī 3329; Aḥmad 12,057. ʿAbd Allāh b. Salām asked the Prophet Muḥammad not to tell the Jews of Medina that he had converted until after the Prophet had asked them about him, otherwise they would slander him (*bahat*[ūn]) from the beginning. The Jews first said that ʿAbd Allāh was "the best of them...one of their leaders...and one of the most knowledgeable scholars amongst them". But after the Prophet told them that ʿAbd Allāh b. Salām had converted and he came before them and declared that "there is no deity but God and Muḥammad is the Messenger of God", they said "he [i.e. ʿAbd Allāh b. Salām] is the most evil amongst us".

feed [the needy], establish the ties of kinship, and pray at night while others are asleep—you will enter Paradise in peace."[11]

Ibn al-Qayyim states—in agreement with the aforementioned verses—that the Holy Lord sent His prophets to convey the message and now "has closed all of the paths to Him except that of [the Prophet Muḥammad]".[12] Therefore, the only way now to achieve religious success and Paradise is to follow the Prophet Muḥammad and the Qur'ān which he conveyed.

PROOFS OF MUḤAMMAD'S PROPHETHOOD

The proofs for Muḥammad's prophethood are better documented than those of Moses and Jesus.[13] This is maintained by Ibn Taymiyya who states that "the signs and evidences which prove the prophethood of Muḥammad (may God bless him and grant him peace) are many and diverse—certainly greater and more numerous than those of other prophets".[14] The Prophet Muḥammad's many Companions reported the events of his life, his actions and his statements, and then transmitted his Sunna generation after generation until it was

[11] Tirmidhī 2485; Ibn Māja 1334; Aḥmad 23,784; al-Ḥākim 7277. It is "authentic" according to Albānī (*Silsilat al-aḥādīth al-ṣaḥīḥa* 569). In addition, a Jewish boy living in Medina also became Muslim whereupon the Prophet said: "All praise is due to God Who rescued him from Hellfire." Bukhārī 1356; Abū Dāwūd 3095; Aḥmad 13,375. That said, unfortunately the majority of the Jews living in Medina at the time of the Prophet Muḥammad rejected him and failed to follow him—this will be discussed in Chapter Eleven.

[12] See Zeni (tr.), *Ibn Qayyim al-Jawziyya on Divine Wisdom and the Problem of Evil*, p. 2.

[13] Saiyad Khan states: "Can any other religion even remotely come close to possessing tens of thousands of detailed sayings and actions of their Prophet or founder, let alone with complete chains of narration? It is no wonder that the renowned historian, A. Toynbee, declared: 'The sources for the study of Islamic history from Muḥammad's lifetime onwards are copious and many of them are first-rate value from a historians point of view. Muḥammad's career, unlike Jesus', can be followed point by point—and, in some chapters, almost day by day—in the full light of history.'" See Saiyad Fareed Khan and Saiyad Salahuddin Ahmad, *God, Islam, and the Skeptic Mind* (Kuala Lampur: Blue Nile Publishing, 2004), p. 162; Arnold Toynbee, *A Study of History* (London: Oxford University Press, 1962), vol. XII, p. 463.

[14] Ibn Taymiyya, *al-Jawāb al-ṣaḥīḥ li-man baddala dīn al-Masīḥ*, ed. Safar b. ᶜAbd al-Raḥmān al-Ḥawālī (Riyadh: Maktabat al-Malik Fahd al-Waṭaniyya, 2011), vol. I, p. 263 and vol. II, p. 500.

compiled by Bukhārī,[15] Muslim[16] and other *Ḥadīth* scholars such that there should be no doubt as to his historicity and veracity. In this fashion, the Prophet's Sunna regarding prayer, fasting, zakat and pilgrimage along with his jurisprudence (in all its complexity) was preserved and promulgated.

Next, the Holy Lord revealed the Qur'ān unto the Prophet Muḥammad (may God bless him and grant him peace) who faithfully conveyed it[17]: *It is We Who have sent down the Qur'ān to thee by stages,*[18] and: *We have, without doubt, sent down the Message; and We will assuredly guard it.*[19] The greatest evidence of the truthfulness of the Prophet Muḥammad is the Qur'ān itself.

God (Glorious is He) states: *If the whole of humankind and jinns were to gather together to produce the like of this Qur'ān, they could not produce the like thereof, even if they backed up each other with help and support.*[20] Thus humanity was challenged to produce something similar to the Qur'ān. Since they could not do so, they were then challenged to produce an equivalent of only 10 *sūras*,[21] and then finally only one *sūra*.[22] Ibn Taymiyya states that the Qur'ān is a "sign, evidence and miracle in many ways, including the wording (*lafẓ*), prose (*nuẓum*) and eloquence (*balāgha*). This is in addition to the meanings themselves in which God (Exalted is He) informs us of His Names and Attributes, His angels, the past and future Unseen, and the Resurrection [or Hereafter]. God also provided many proofs that lead to [intellectual] certainty, as well as rational analogies contained within the similitudes".[23] If anyone

---

[15] Abū ʿAbd Allāh Muḥammad b. Ismāʿīl b. Ibrāhīm b. al-Mughīrāh al-Bukhārī (d. 256/870) was born in the city of Bukhara. Imām Bukhārī went on to collect the most authentic book of *ḥadīths* known as *Ṣaḥīḥ al-Bukhārī*, which is comprised of 7275 *ḥadīths* with repetition or 2230 without repetition.

[16] Abū al-Ḥusayn Muslim b. al-Ḥajjāj b. Muslim b. Ward al-Naysābūrī (d. 261/875) was a student of Imām Aḥmad and Imām Bukhārī. His *Ṣaḥīḥ Muslim* is comprised of 7563 *ḥadīths* with repetition or 3033 without repetition.

[17] See Q.X.15.

[18] Q.LXXVI.23.

[19] Q.XV.9 (Yusuf Ali translation).

[20] Q.XVII.88 (Yusuf Ali translation). Sūrat al-Isrā' (Q.XVII) was revealed in Mecca before Sūrat Yūnus (Q.XI) and Sūrat Hūd (Q.X).

[21] See Q.XI.13 (revealed in Mecca).

[22] See Q.X.38 (revealed in Mecca) and Q.II.23 (revealed later in Medina).

[23] Ibn Taymiyya, *al-Jawāb al-ṣaḥīḥ*, vol. II, p. 508.

contemplates the knowledge encompassed within the Qur'ān and Sunna and compares it to that contained within the Torah, Psalms and Gospel, one will recognize that Islam is far more complete. The Holy Lord withholds His knowledge for certain wise purposes and then reveals it in consideration of others.

The Qur'ān commands only goodness and forbids all evilness. God (Glorious is He) states: *God enjoineth justice and kindness, and giving to kinsfolk, and forbiddeth lewdness and abomination and wickedness.*[24] No knowledge or commandment to goodness exists in the former Scriptures except that the Qur'ān contains them in either a similar or more beneficial fashion.[25]

The Qur'ān and Sunna have also informed us of many matters concerning the Day of Judgment, which the prior revelations—i.e. Torah, Psalms and Gospel—did not.[26] The Prophet Muḥammad (may God bless him and grant him peace) also explained Paradise and Hellfire in a manner greatly exceeding that which Jesus and Moses notified their companions. This will be elaborated upon in Chapters Fourteen and Fifteen.

THE MESSENGER'S CALL TO GOD

The Prophet Muḥammad was first bestowed the inspired revelation while worshipping God in seclusion in a cave. It was after this that his wife, Khadīja, took him to her cousin Waraqa b. Nawfal who said: "This is the same as what was revealed [by Gabriel] upon Moses. I wish that I was [alive and] strong when your people will expel you [from Mecca]." The Prophet asked: "Will they truly expel me?" Waraqa said: "Yes. Everyone who conveyed what you will has been opposed. If I were to live to that time I would assist you to become triumphant."[27]

---

[24] Q.XVI.90.

[25] See Ibn Taymiyya, *al-Jawāb al-ṣaḥīḥ*, vol. I, p. 263.

[26] Ibn Taymiyya states: "Since Muḥammad (may God bless him and grant him peace) is the Seal of the Prophets and has been sent close to the Hour, he described the Resurrection in a manner which no prior [prophet] had ever done." Ibn Taymiyya, *al-Jawāb al-ṣaḥīḥ*, vol. II, p. 537.

[27] Bukhārī 3; Muslim 160/403; Aḥmad 25,865.

The Messenger Muḥammad (may God bless him and grant him peace) then called to Islam in secrecy as God (Exalted is He) commanded him. After three years he publicly called those living in Mecca and the surrounding towns.[28] He remained in Mecca for thirteen years, and many of the Companions were persecuted during the Meccan phase. A good number of Companions (approximately 102) even had to migrate to Ethiopia due to this persecution. During the last three of the Meccan years the Muslims were completely boycotted by the disbelievers; and at one point they were starved until all they could eat was the leaves of trees.[29] Therefore, the proportion of those Companions who suffered persecution, torture and starvation (as well as those who emigrated) was very high in the early phases of Islam.

Following all of those hardships a delegation from Medina, headed by Saᶜd b. Muᶜādh, came to meet the Prophet Muḥammad. Saᶜd and most of the Medinans subsequently embraced Islam.[30] The next year

---

[28] See Q.VI.91–92: *And this is a blessed Scripture which We have revealed, confirming that which (was revealed) before it, that thou mayst warn the Mother of Villages and those around her. Those who believe in the Hereafter believe herein, and they are careful of their worship.*

[29] Banū Muṭṭalib and Banū Hāshim made a pact to protect the Prophet Muḥammad (out of tribal loyalty since many of them remained polytheists). The rest of Quraysh decided to boycott those two clans and the Muslims. For three years they lived under extremely harsh conditions of hunger; it reached the point where they were eating the leaves of trees. The boycott was finally annulled after five of the Qurayshīs came to oppose the pact. Six months later the Prophet's uncle and guardian Abū Ṭālib, the leader of Banū Hāshim, died and only two months later the Prophet's wife Khadījah died. Consequently, the Qurayshīs began to again engage in acts of oppression. The Prophet went to Ṭā'if (a town east of Mecca) and stayed there for ten days to preach Islam; but the people rejected him in a violent manner. It was only afterwards that many of the inhabitants of Medina accepted Islam and the Prophet Muḥammad was finally commanded to emigrate there.

[30] Of note, there were three major Jewish tribes living within Medina, who were awaiting a prophet and would repetitively warn the Medinans that they would conquer them afterwards. Therefore, the polytheist Medinans were prepared for the coming of a prophet. However, it was the latter who ultimately converted to Islam and followed the Prophet Muḥammad, while the Jews disbelieved. God (Exalted is He) states in Q.II.89 regarding those Jews: *And when there cometh unto them a Scripture from God, confirming that in their possession, though before that they were asking for a signal triumph over those who disbelieved, and when there cometh unto them that which they know (to be the truth) they disbelieve therein. The curse of God is on the disbelievers.*

they pledged the second ʿAqaba Pledge to support the Prophet and the Meccan Companions. The Meccan Companions then began to emigrate to Medina, leaving behind much of their wealth and possessions in Mecca. The Prophet Muḥammad was then commanded to emigrate to Medina[31] along with Abū Bakr.[32]

In Medina the Prophet Muḥammad (may God bless him and grant him peace) created a brotherhood between the emigrants from Mecca (*Muhājirīn*) and the supporters of Medina (*Anṣār*). This provided definitive terms of responsibility for all that were both wise and sustainable. The Prophet Muḥammad said: "None of you truly believes until he loves for his brother what he loves for himself."[33] The Prophet also quickly built a mosque in Medina.

After the emigration to Medina, God (Exalted is He) promised the Prophet Muḥammad that He would protect him: *O Messenger! Make known that which hath been revealed unto thee from thy Lord, for if thou do it not, thou wilt not have conveyed His message. God will protect thee from humankind.*[34] One small example exemplifies this: a disbeliever came upon the Prophet while he was sleeping during one of his journeys and took his sword. The Prophet (may God bless him and grant him peace) then awoke to find that man standing in front of him with the sword in his hand. The man then said: "Who will protect you from me now?" The Prophet Muḥammad said: "God." The sword then

---

31 See Bukhārī (3902) and Aḥmad (3517) wherein Ibn ʿAbbās states: "God's Messenger started receiving the Divine Revelation at the age of forty. Then he stayed in Mecca for thirteen years, receiving the Divine Revelation. Then he was ordered to emigrate and he lived as an emigrant for ten years [in Medina]. He died at the age of sixty-three." Abū Bakr accompanied the Prophet Muḥammad in his emigration to Medina. The Quraysh had agreed among themselves to assassinate Muḥammad; but when they entered his dwelling in order to kill him they found ʿAlī (may God be pleased with him) in the Prophet's bed, as the Prophet Muḥammad had already departed.

32 The Prophet Muḥammad and Abū Bakr first paradoxically traveled south towards Yemen and stayed in a cave at Thawr. They stayed there for three days and then followed a difficult untrodden path along the coast north towards Medina in order to avoid the disbelievers tracking them. Their journey lasted a total of eleven days.

33 Bukhārī 13; Muslim 45/170; Tirmidhī 2515; Nasā'ī 5016; Aḥmad 13,963.

34 Q.V.67. It was previously revealed in a Meccan *sūra*: *We defend thee from the scoffers.* Q.XV.95.

fell out of the man's hands and he sat down. The Prophet then let the man go.[35]

God (Exalted is He) also informed the Prophet Muḥammad and his Companions that they would ultimately be granted victory over the disbelievers.[36] This victory came after continued aggression from the Quraysh, who marched from Mecca to Medina to fight three wars against the Muslims at Badr, Uḥud and the Trench—these will be discussed later in the book. It was not until the treaty of Ḥudaybiya, in the sixth year after the emigration (after *hijra* or AH), that no further wars were carried out by Quraysh against the Muslims.

The Ḥudaybiya Treaty occurred after the Prophet (may God bless him and grant him peace) and approximately 1400 Companions—all unarmed—journeyed to perform ʿUmra at the Kaʿba in Mecca. The Prophet Muḥammad had dreamed that he would enter Mecca and perform circumambulation (*ṭawāf*) around the Kaʿba with his Companions. Although it was the custom of Quraysh to allow anyone to perform ʿUmra, they blocked the Muslims. Ultimately, it was agreed to allow them to come back the following year to perform ʿUmra.[37] Indeed, God promised the believers that they would return: *Ye shall indeed enter the Inviolable Place of Worship, if God will, secure, (having your hair) shaven and cut, not fearing. He knoweth that which ye know not, and hath given you a near victory beforehand.*[38] Some Companions felt that they were humiliated by these terms;[39] however, the Prophet Muḥammad replied: "I am the Messenger of God, and He will not

---

35 Bukhārī 2913; Muslim 843/1949; Aḥmad 14,929.

36 See Q.III.12. See also Q.LIV.45 and Q.II.137.

37 The Prophet Muḥammad and 2000 of the Companions thus performed ʿUmra in the following year. Of note, the treaty also stipulated a ten-year suspension of war during which each side was free to conclude treaties with any other third party.

38 Q.XLVIII.27.

39 This was not only due to the fact that the Muslims were prevented from performing ʿUmra after they had journeyed and nearly reached Mecca; but also because of the stipulation that if any individual from Quraysh tried to escape to Medina, then that person must be returned to Quraysh. Also, it was stipulated, on the other hand, that if a Muslim or individual from Medina tried to escape to Mecca, then he or she would not be returned.

abandon me."[40] The Holy Lord then revealed Sūrat al-Fatḥ which began: *Lo! We have given thee [O Muḥammad] a signal victory*.[41]

In reality, the Treaty of Ḥudaybiya led to the marginalization of the political and religious impact of Quraysh within Arabia. The Muslims were now recognized by Quraysh as a political and religious entity, and thus Quraysh essentially relinquished their claim to religious leadership of Arabia. It also allowed many Arabs of the peninsula to freely seek out the Prophet Muḥammad and become Muslim; thus the number of the Companions exponentially increased multiplying seven fold over the next two years to become approximately 10,000. The Prophet (may God bless him and grant him peace) was also able to send emissaries and invitations out to the rulers of the Byzantine Empire, the Persian Empire, Ethiopia, Egypt, among others to accept Islam.[42] The Treaty of Ḥudaybiya was indeed paradoxically a victory. Finally, it was only two years later that the Prophet Muḥammad and his Companions peacefully entered Mecca victorious and the majority of Quraysh converted to Islam. The majority of those living in the Arabian Peninsula converted to Islam thereafter by the grace of God.

Throughout the period before victory, the Prophet Muḥammad (may God bless him and grant him peace) had remained perseverant despite all of the evil opposition he encountered, which included being slandered, ridiculed, boycotted, starved and fought against. In the end, with the majority of those living in the Arabian Peninsula converting to Islam, the Prophet Muḥammad and his Companions numbered 140,000 in his Farewell Pilgrimage, after only numbering 100 in the early phase of his mission in Mecca. This is a reminder that although the messengers and their followers endured suffering and evil initially, they were ultimately granted victory.

THE MESSENGER'S CHARACTERISTICS AND LEGACY

God commended the Prophet Muḥammad saying: *Verily in the Messenger of God ye have a good example for him who looketh unto God and the Last Day, and remembereth God much*,[43] and that the Prophet possessed

---

40 Bukhārī 3182; Muslim 1765/4633; Aḥmad 15,975.

41 Q.XLVIII.1.

42 Muslim 1774/4609; Tirmidhī 2716.

43 Q.XXXIII.21.

an *exalted standard of character*.[44] God (Glorious and Exalted is He) also states: *God and His angels shower blessings on the Prophet. O ye who believe! Ask blessings on him and salute him with a worthy salutation*.[45]

The Prophet Muḥammad was well known to be characterized by the following attributes, as described by Ibn Taymiyya:

> [He was characterised by] truthfulness, piety, justice and noble traits, as well as being devoid of wickedness, injustice, or any abominable attribute. This all was affirmed by those who knew him before he became a prophet, by those who believed in him, as well as those who disbelieved after he became a prophet. There was nothing that he could be criticized for, neither in his speech, actions or characteristics, nor did he ever lie, oppress, nor perpetrate wickedness...He remained truthful and just, carrying out his oaths throughout all of his varied circumstances, whether war or peace, security or fear, wealth or poverty, whether he had few Companions or many, whether he was victorious over his opponents or whether the [disbelievers temporarily] had the upper hand...until [Islam] became triumphant [during his lifetime] in all Arab lands. Beforehand it was filled with idol worship, the following of sorcerers and [astrologers], and service to others instead of the Creator. Those [disbelievers] killed others unjustly, cut the ties of kinship, and were unaware of the Hereafter or the Resurrection. But after [his prophethood] the [Muslim Arabs] became the most knowledgeable of all people on earth, the most religious, the most just and the most distinguished. Some Christians—upon seeing [the Companions when they came to Syria]—even said that the [apostles] who accompanied the Messiah were not superior to them...[46] Moreover, all that has been recounted regarding his perfect knowledge and religion invalidate [any attribution of] evilness, wickedness or ignorance to him.[47]

The Prophet Muḥammad's character was "completely derived from the Qur'ān",[48] and he lived his life according to the Qur'ān so as to attain the Holy Lord's pleasure through the implementation of His

44 Q.LXVIII.4 (Yusuf Ali translation).

45 Q.XXXIII.56.

46 Ibn Taymiyya, *al-Jawāb al-ṣaḥīḥ*, vol. II, pp. 514–516.

47 Ibn Taymiyya, *al-Jawāb al-ṣaḥīḥ*, vol. II, p. 519.

48 Muslim 746/1739; Abū Dāwūd 1342; Ibn Māja 2333; Nasā'ī 1601; Aḥmad 24,269.

Divine Law. The Messenger was "the most distinguished, most generous and most courageous".[49]

The Prophet Muḥammad (may God bless him and grant him peace) would also pray at night until his feet became swollen. It was said to him: "O Messenger of God! Has not God forgiven you for your past and future sins (*dhanb^ika^*)?" The Prophet replied: "Should I not be a thankful servant?"[50] And during the last ten nights of Ramadan the Prophet would pray all night and require the same of his family.[51] The Prophet Muḥammad was "the most generous in doing good, particularly during Ramadan".[52]

The Prophet "did not curse or use bad words, nor did he damn people".[53] When asked to condemn the disbelievers the Prophet Muḥammad said: "I have not been sent to curse people; rather, I have been sent as a mercy [to humankind]."[54] The Prophet Muḥammad moreover "would not requite an evil [done against him] with an evil, but rather he would forgive and overlook."[55] He would never take revenge against anyone for his sake but would only take retribution if God's legal limits were transgressed.[56]

The Prophet Muḥammad also encouraged his followers to be kind and treat their families well: "The best of you is the best to his family, and I am the best to my family."[57] He (may God bless him and grant

---

49 Bukhārī 2820; Muslim 2307/6006; Tirmidhī 1687; Aḥmad 12,922. Of note, one of the Companions said about the Prophet: "If a war intensified we—even the most courageous of us—would protect ourselves by the side of [the Messenger of God]." Muslim 1776/4616. This was narrated by al-Barāʾ b. ʿĀzib. The Prophet's courage, certainty, patience and strength for the sake of God were exemplified during the Battles of Uḥud and Ḥunayn.

50 Bukhārī 1130; Muslim 2819/7124; Tirmidhī 412; Ibn Māja 1419; Nasāʾī 1644; Aḥmad 18,198.

51 See Bukhārī 2024; Muslim 1174/2787; Aḥmad 1105.

52 Bukhārī 6; Muslim 2308/6009; Nasāʾī 2095; Aḥmad 2616.

53 Bukhārī 6031; Aḥmad 12,463.

54 Muslim 2599/6613.

55 Tirmidhī 2016; Aḥmad 25,417. It is "authentic" according to Albānī (*Silsilat al-aḥādīth al-ṣaḥīḥa* 2458). See also Bukhārī 4838 for a similar narration.

56 See Bukhārī 3560; Muslim 2327/6045; Abū Dāwūd 4785; Aḥmad 24,830.

57 Tirmidhī 3895; Ibn Māja 1977; Bayhaqī (*Sunan*) 15,699. It is "authentic" according to Albānī (*Silsilat al-aḥādīth al-ṣaḥīḥa* 285).

him peace) possessed a "beautiful face"[58] and "if he was pleased his face became bright like the moon".[59] ᶜAbd Allāh b. Salām mentioned that he knew that the face of the Messenger was not that of a false prophet. God (Exalted is He) states regarding the hypocrites: *Had We so willed, We could have shown them up to thee, and thou shouldst have known them by their marks: but surely thou wilt know them by the tone of their speech.*[60] In contrast, the Holy Lord states in regards to the believers: *Thou wilt see them bow and prostrate themselves (in prayer), seeking grace from God and [His] good pleasure. On their faces are their marks, (being) the traces of their prostration.*[61]

Michael Hart, who ranked the Prophet Muḥammad as the most influential person in history, states: "Of many important historical events, one might say that they were inevitable and would have occurred even without the particular political leader who guided them...But this cannot be said of the Arab conquests. Nothing similar had occurred before Muhammad, and there is no reason to believe that the conquests could have been achieved without him."[62] The Prophet's Companions Abū Bakr, ᶜUmar, ᶜUthmān and ᶜAlī went on to be righteous leaders who enjoined good, forbade evil and fought against it. During their caliphates (as well as during those who followed them) Islam spread throughout the Middle East, parts of Asia and northern Africa.

The triumph and spread of the Muslims is also proof of Muḥammad's prophethood for the followers of a false prophet have never been granted such success. Instead all of the false prophets who arose after Muḥammad, whether in the Arabian Peninsula or otherwise, were all defeated and conquered. As for the argument that many disbelieving kings and rulers were victorious, none of them ever claimed that they were prophets of God. The Almighty Lord has many wise purposes in allowing the disbelieving kings to overcome the believers, which will be discussed later. The point here is that no *false prophet* has ever been allowed to become triumphant, instead God (Exalted is He) ultimately

58 Bukhārī 3549; Muslim 2337/6066.

59 Bukhārī 3556, Muslim 2769/7016; Aḥmad 15,789.

60 Q.XLVII.30.

61 Q.XLVIII.29 (Yusuf Ali translation).

62 Hart, *The 100: A Ranking of the Most Influential Persons in History*, pp. 9–10.

brings about his demise. The most powerful false prophet will be the Antichrist, yet Jesus (may God bless him) will come back to this earth and along with the Muslims will defeat and kill the Antichrist.

In addition, the claim of the disbelievers that Muḥammad was a false prophet is addressed by the Holy Lord: *Shall I inform you, (O people!), on whom it is that the evil ones descend? They descend on every lying, wicked person.*[63] The Holy Lord also states regarding false prophets:

> *Who can be more wicked than one who inventeth a lie against God, or saith, I have received inspiration, when he hath received none, or (again) who saith, I can reveal the like of what God hath revealed? If thou couldst but see how the wicked (do fare) in the flood of confusion at death! The angels stretch forth their hands, (saying): Yield up your souls: this day shall ye receive your reward, a penalty of shame, for that ye used to tell lies against God, and scornfully to reject of His signs!*[64]

False prophets are perpetrators of wickedness and lies. On the other hand, the Prophet Muḥammad (may God bless him and grant him peace) truthfully conveyed and affirmed the Oneness of God and belief in His Scriptures, and he commanded humanity to love, obey and serve the Holy Lord alone. He enjoined prayers, fasting, zakat and pilgrimage, as well as all good character traits (like truthfulness, justice, beneficence, chastity, fulfilling one's promises and oaths etc.), and forbade all wickedness and evil traits. The Holy Lord has greatly differentiated between the true prophets and the false ones, the pious and the wicked, and the angels and the devils.[65] Muḥammad is a true Messenger and Prophet of the Almighty Lord.

THE MESSENGER MUḤAMMAD'S PROPHESIES AND MIRACLES

The Messenger Muḥammad (may God bless him and grant him peace) made many prophesies and their fulfillment prove his truthfulness and prophethood. True predictions of the future can only be consistently be made by the truthful prophets sent by the Holy Lord Who is the Absolute Truth and Knower of the future and Unseen. Making a prediction involves specifics and details—not a prediction regarding some future anticipated cyclical event. It is not surprising to note that

---

63 Q.XXVI.221–222 (Yusuf Ali translation).

64 Q.VI.93.

65 See Ibn Taymiyya, *al-Jawāb al-ṣaḥīḥ*, vol. II, pp. 663–664.

no specific or significant predictions are made in the Tao Te Ching, Analects or the Dhammapada. When a prediction is paradoxical and yet comes true, it provides an even greater proof that it is indeed prophetic. The Old Testament states and affirms the above regarding prophetic predictions:

> I will raise them up a Prophet from among their brethren, like unto thee, and will put my words in his mouth; and he shall speak unto them all that I shall command him. And it shall come to pass, that whosoever will not hearken unto my words which he shall speak in my name, I will require it of him. But the prophet, which shall presume to speak a word in my name, which I have not commanded him to speak, or that shall speak in the name of other gods, even that prophet shall die. And if thou say in thine heart, How shall we know the word which the LORD hath not spoken? When a prophet speaketh in the name of the LORD, if the thing follow not, nor come to pass, that is the thing which the LORD hath not spoken, but the prophet hath spoken it presumptuously: thou shalt not be afraid of him.[66]

More than ten of his prophesies will be discussed here, while others will be discussed later in the book. First, the Qur'ān, which the Prophet Muḥammad conveyed, foretold the victory of the Romans over the Persians: *The Romans have been defeated in the nearer land, and they, after their defeat, will be victorious within ten years. God's is the command in the former case and in the latter, and on that day believers will rejoice in God's help to victory. He helpeth to victory whom He will. He is the Mighty, the Merciful. It is a promise of God. God faileth not His promise, but most of humankind know not.*[67]

The Prophet Muḥammad also foretold that the Muslims "would fight against the [disbelievers] of the Arabian Peninsula and be granted victory by God, then against the Persians and God would grant them victory, then they will fight against the Romans and God will grant them victory. Finally, they will fight against the Antichrist and be granted victory by God".[68] The first three have already occurred. The Prophet Muḥammad also told the Companions that they would attain

---

66 Deuteronomy 5.18–22. "From among their brethren" is considered by some to be proof of the prophethood of a descendent of Ishmael, i.e. Muḥammad.

67 Q.XXX.2–6.

68 Muslim 2900/7284; Aḥmad 18,973.

the treasures of the Persians and the Romans and use them for the sake of God; and it happened as it was predicted.[69] One can only imagine the confidence and firm resolve that these prophecies imparted in the Companions, as these mighty empires were defeated! With regards to the fourth prophecy just mentioned, it will come true in the future when the Muslims will be the believers who fight along with Jesus against the Antichrist and the disbelievers.

The Messenger Muḥammad conveyed, by virtue of what was revealed to him in the Qur'ān, that some like Abū Lahab[70] and al-Walīd b. al-Mughīra[71] would never become believers, and would instead die as disbelievers and be punished in Hellfire. The Prophet was also permitted by the Holy Lord to supplicate against Abū Jahl (ᶜAmr b. Hishām), ᶜUtba b. Rabīᶜa, Shayba b. Rabīᶜa, al-Walīd b. ᶜUtba, Umayya b. Khalaf, ᶜUqba b. Abī Muᶜayṭ and ᶜUmāra b. al-Walīd—all of them were killed by the Muslims in the Battle of Badr.[72] The Prophet even foretold the exact spots on which Abū Jahl, ᶜUtba, Shayba and Umayya would die on the battlefield[73]—this was only possible because God (Glorious is He) revealed that to the Prophet Muḥammad.

The Prophet told his Companions of the death of al-Najāshī, the ruler of the Ethiopians, and the Chosroes, the king of the Persians, at the time they died. The miraculous nature of such disclosures is emphasized by the fact that it would usually take weeks in the seventh century CE for news to travel such vast distances. He then prayed

---

69 Bukhārī 3120; Muslim 2918/7327; Tirmidhī 2216; Aḥmad 7184.

70 See verses Q.CXI.1–3: *The power of Abū Lahab will perish, and he will perish. His wealth and gains will not exempt him. He will be plunged in flaming Fire.* Of note, Abū Lahab did not die until twelve years after this was revealed, and yet he remained and died as a disbeliever accordingly.

71 See verse Q.LXXIV.26: *Soon will I cast him into Hell-Fire!* See also *Tafsīr al-Ṭabarī*, vol. XXIII, pp. 19–26.

72 ᶜAbd Allāh b. Masᶜūd narrated that the Prophet was once praying in prostration to God in the Kaᶜba when Abū Jahl ordered ᶜUqba b. Abī Muᶜayṭ place the intestines of a camel on the Prophet's back. The Prophet remained in prostration to the Holy Lord until his daughter Fāṭima removed them. Afterwards the Prophet supplicated to the Almighty Lord to destroy those mentioned disbelievers (as well as a seventh that Ibn Masᶜūd forgot). See Bukhārī 240 and 520; Muslim 1794/4649; Aḥmad 3722.

73 See Muslim 1779/4621; Tirmidhī 2681; Abū Dāwūd 2681; Aḥmad 13,703.

for al-Najāshī (who had become a Muslim) saying: "Your brother has died, so pray for him."[74]

Similarly, the Prophet Muḥammad notified his Companions in Medina regarding those who were martyred in the Battle of Mu'tah at the same time of its occurrence. Mu'tah was more than 600 miles away from Medina, yet the Prophet informed his Companions that "Zayd led but was martyred; Jaʿfar then led but was martyred; and [ʿAbd Allāh] ibn Rawāḥa then led but was martyred." The Messenger of God (may God bless him and grant him peace) wept at this point and said: "Then Khālid b. al-Walīd, who is one of the swords of God, led until God granted them victory."[75]

The Prophet Muḥammad also gave his Companions glad tidings after many of them had been martyred in the Battle of Uḥud.[76] The Companions would later achieve victory and amass much wealth as prophesized.

The Prophet Muḥammad used an allegory to foretell of the caliphates of Abū Bakr and ʿUmar b. al-Khaṭṭāb, and how the latter would achieve great victories and power.[77] The Prophet foretold that the "Caliphate [according the Sunna of] the Prophet would last thirty years. Then those whom God grants His kingdom [would rule]."[78]

The caliphates of Abū Bakr, ʿUmar, ʿUthmān, ʿAlī and al-Ḥasan indeed lasted thirty lunar years from 11–40 AH. The Prophet Muḥammad also prophesized that tyrannical dictators would oppress the Muslims after those Caliphates and subsequent dynasties ended.

---

[74] Bukhārī 1245; Muslim 953/2210; Tirmidhī 1039; Abū Dāwūd 3204; Ibn Māja 1535; Nasā'ī 1970; Aḥmad 19,867.

[75] Bukhārī 1246 and 3757; Aḥmad 12,114.

[76] See Bukhārī 1344; Muslim 2296/5976; Aḥmad 17,344.

[77] The Prophet Muḥammad said: "While I was sleeping, I saw myself standing next to a well with a bucket. I drew as much water from the well as God willed. Then Ibn Abī Quḥāfa [i.e. Abū Bakr] took the bucket from me and brought out one or two buckets [of water] and there was weakness in his drawing the water. May God forgive him for his weakness! Then the bucket turned into a very big one, and Ibn al-Khaṭṭāb took over. I have never seen a person as strong as ʿUmar in carrying out such hard work—all of the people were able to drink to their satisfaction." Bukhārī 3664; Muslim 2392/6192.

[78] Tirmidhī 2226; Abū Dāwūd 4646; Aḥmad 21,919; al-Ḥākim 4438. It is "authentic" according to Albānī (*Silsilat al-aḥādīth al-ṣaḥīḥa* 459).

A return to leaders completely following the prophetic guidance will only occur after all the aforementioned has happened.[79]

The Prophet also foretold the following: "The east and west of the earth have been drawn together for me, and my Community will spread to what has been drawn together for me."[80] Ibn Taymiyya states: "The matter occurred as he had foretold for his Community spread to the east and west much more than to the northern and southern regions [of this earth]."[81]

The Prophet Muḥammad also said: "I asked my Lord for three things, and he granted me two and denied one of them: [1] I asked Him to not allow an enemy of my Community to overcome them (*yajtāḥ*[ahum]), and He granted me that. I then asked Him [2] to not overtake them all with a famine, and He granted me that. I finally asked Him [3] to not allow infighting, but He denied me that."[82] Unfortunately, infighting has occurred and enmity has been displayed by various sects against the truthful followers of the Prophet Muḥammad over the centuries.

The Prophet Muḥammad predicted the apostasy of many of the Arabs in the Arabian Peninsula after his death. The Prophet said: "I will be standing [on the Day of Judgment] at the Pool (*ḥawḍ*) and I will see some amongst you who will come to me, but other people will be taken away from me. I will say: 'O Lord! They are from me and from my followers.' Then it will be said: 'Do you know what they did after you? By God, they kept on turning on their heels [i.e. became apostates].'"[83] In this regard, the Prophet Muḥammad (may God bless him and grant him peace) said: "Whoever turns away from my Sunna (tradition) is not a follower of mine."[84]

---

79 See Aḥmad 18,406. It is "sound" according to Albānī (*Silsilat al-aḥādīth al-ṣaḥīḥa* 5).

80 Muslim 2889/7258; Tirmidhī 2176; Abū Dāwūd 4252; Ibn Māja 3952; Aḥmad 17,115.

81 Ibn Taymiyya, *al-Jawāb al-ṣaḥīḥ*, vol. II, p. 582.

82 Muslim 2890/7260 and Ibn Māja 3951 (both include 2 and 3, but not 1, as their narrations instead have a prophecy about his Community not all being drowned to death); Tirmidhī 2175; Aḥmad 22,125.

83 Bukhārī 6593; Muslim 2293/5972.

84 Bukhārī 5063; Muslim 1401/3403; Nasā'ī 3217; Aḥmad 13,534.

Ḥudhayfa[85] narrated that the Prophet Muḥammad informed them of the major events that will occur until the Day of Judgment.[86] Another narration reports that the Prophet dedicated the time from *fajr* prayer until sunset to doing such.[87] Thus the Prophet Muḥammad has foretold many other future events, including occurrences in the Hereafter, and many of these prophecies will be discussed later in this book.

The Prophet Muḥammad also foretold of his impending death: "God has given one of His servants the choice to either receive the splendour and luxury of the worldly life or to accept the goodness [of the Hereafter] with Him. So, he has chosen that goodness with God." Abū Bakr wept upon hearing that, and the other Companions became surprised. Abū Saʿīd al-Khudrī said that it was only afterwards that they came to recognize that it was the Prophet who was given that option, whereas Abū Bakr recognized the meaning immediately.[88]

The Prophet told his daughter Fāṭima that she would be the first of his relatives to die after him, and that she would be the leader (*sayyida*) of women in Paradise.[89] He (may God bless him and grant him peace) also foretold that his grandson al-Ḥasan would be a "master, and God would allow reconciliation to occur because of him between two massive assemblies of Muslims".[90] This all occurred accordingly.

As for some of the miracles of the Prophet, they include the splitting of the moon. God (Exalted is He) said: *The Hour (of Judgment) is nigh, and the moon is cleft asunder.*[91] ʿAbd Allāh b. Masʿūd[92] narrated that: "The moon split into two while we were with the Prophet (may God bless him and grant him peace). Thereupon [the Prophet] said: 'Bear

[85] Ḥudhayfa b. al-Yamān (d. 35/656) was a Companion of the Prophet. He participated in all the battles after Uḥud. He was known as the "Keeper of the Secret of the Messenger of God", as the Prophet Muḥammad told him the identities of the Hypocrites.

[86] See Bukhārī 6604; Muslim 2891/7263; Abū Dāwūd 4240.

[87] Muslim 2892/7267; Aḥmad 22,888.

[88] See Bukhārī 3904; Muslim 2382/6170.

[89] See Bukhārī 3624 and 4433; Muslim 2450/6314; Ibn Māja 1621; Aḥmad 26,032.

[90] Bukhārī 2704; Tirmidhī 3773; Abū Dāwūd 4662; Nasāʾī 1410; Aḥmad 20,448.

[91] Q.LIV.1.

[92] ʿAbd Allāh b. Masʿūd (d. 29/650) was a pre-eminent Companion as he was the sixth man to accept Islam. He was considered to be the foremost reciter of the Qurʾān. He also narrated 848 *ḥadīths*.

witness! Bear witness [to this miracle]!'"[93] Ibn Taymiyya mentioned that the Prophet used to read this *sūra* during the Friday prayer as well as during the *ʿEīd* prayers, and all of the Muslims affirmed this sign and none denied it. Thus the splitting of the moon was well known to the people living at that time.[94] Ibn Taymiyya also stated that "God (Exalted is He) juxtaposed His mention of the Day of Judgment with the splitting of the moon because the coming of Muḥammad (may God bless him and grant him peace) is one of the signs of the Hour," whereby it serves as a proof "of the possibility of the heavens being split, which will be a precursor to the Day of Judgment".[95]

The Prophet Muḥammad was taken to Jerusalem on the Night Journey (*Isrā'*)[96] for God (Exalted is He) said: *Glorified be He Who carried His servant by night from the Inviolable Place of Worship (al-masjid al-ḥarām) to the Far distant place of worship (al-masjid al-aqṣā) the neighbourhood whereof We have blessed, that We might show him of Our tokens!*[97] In the associated Ascension (*Miʿrāj*) he saw many signs of the Holy Lord, and he reached a higher level than all the other prophets. The Prophet also received God's commandment of five daily prayers—each of which is rewarded tenfold.[98] Thus the Prophet was raised just as Jesus[99] and Elijah[100] were. Elijah did not return, whereas the Messenger Muḥammad returned that same night and Jesus will return before the Day of Judgment. It is also noteworthy that the Prophet Muḥammad

---

93 Bukhārī 3869, 4863 and 4865; Tirmidhī 3287; Aḥmad 4270. See also Bukhārī 4868; Muslim 2802/7076; Tirmidhī 3289; Aḥmad 16,750.

94 See Ibn Taymiyya, *al-Jawāb al-ṣaḥīḥ*, vol. II, pp. 604–605. God (Exalted is He) states: *When the heaven is split asunder.* Q.LXXXIV.1. See also Q.LV.37 and Q.LXIX.16.

95 See Ibn Taymiyya, *al-Jawāb al-ṣaḥīḥ*, vol. I, pp. 244–245.

96 See Bukhārī 4710; Muslim 162/411 and 170/428; Aḥmad 23332; al-Ḥākim 4407. See also Albānī (*Silsilat al-aḥādīth al-ṣaḥīḥa* 306 and 874). The Night Journey and the Ascension occurred in the 12th Meccan year (about 12–16 months before the Migration to Medina).

97 Q.XVII.1.

98 See Bukhārī 349; Muslim 162/411; Aḥmad 12,505.

99 See Q.IV.157–158: *They said (in boast): We killed Christ Jesus the son of Mary, the Messenger of God. But they killed him not, nor crucified him, but so it was made to appear to them, and those who differ therein are full of doubts, with no (certain) knowledge, but only conjecture to follow, for of a surety they killed him not. Nay, God raised him up unto Himself; and God is Exalted in Power, Wise.*

100 See 2 Kings 2.11–15.

(may God bless him and grant him peace) peacefully entered all three holy cities of Islam: Medina and Mecca (along with his Companions), and Jerusalem (on the Night Journey).

Another miracle occurred when a blind man came to the Prophet (may God bless him and grant him peace) and said: "Supplicate to God (Exalted is He) to cure me." The Prophet said: "If you would be patient it would be better for you. But if you prefer I will supplicate for you to God." The man again asked the Prophet to supplicate. The Prophet told him to make ablution well, pray two units of prayer, and then supplicate in the following manner: "O God! I ask you, and turn myself towards You by virtue of Your Prophet Muḥammad, who is a prophet of mercy…" Before the Companions left the gathering this man could see.[101]

The Prophet was once asked by a Bedouin to pray for rain and so he supplicated to God (Exalted is He) from the pulpit. It started raining before he came down from it, and it rained continuously for one week. Thereafter, another person asked him to supplicate for the rain to stop—he did so, and it ceased.[102]

One of the miraculous means that the Almighty Lord used to defend the Prophet was through the angels whom He sent to assist the believers during the Battle of Badr as well as other wars. In the first instance at Badr, this occurred after the Prophet supplicated to the Lord: "O God! Fulfill and grant what You have promised me. O God! If You allow this group of Muslims to die, You will not be worshipped on this earth." The Prophet Muḥammad continued to supplicate in this manner until his cloak fell from his shoulders, whereupon Abū Bakr put it back and said: "O Prophet of God! Your beseeching is sufficient for He will fulfill what He has promised you." At this point, God (Glorious and Exalted) revealed: *When ye sought help of your Lord and He answered you (saying): I will help you with a thousand of the angels, rank on rank.*[103] Some of Companions then saw the disbelievers being killed in front of them—not by sword or spear, but by the angels.[104]

---

[101] See Tirmidhī 3578; Ibn Māja 1385; Aḥmad 17,240; al-Ḥākim 1930. It is "authentic" according to Albānī (*Mishkāt* 2495).

[102] Bukhārī 1033; Muslim 897/2078; Nasā'ī 1518.

[103] Q.VIII.9.

[104] See Muslim 1763/4588; Tirmidhī 3081; Aḥmad 208.

During the digging of the Trench, hunger afflicted the Prophet Muḥammad and the Companions. Jābir b. ᶜAbd Allāh saw the Prophet in such a state, and so after slaughtering a sheep and grinding up some barley, he asked the Prophet along with a few of the Companions to come to his house. The Prophet (may God bless him and grant him peace) called instead all of the Companions who then followed him. The Prophet then blessed the meat and the barley; and then all of the Companions, who numbered approximately 1000, were able to eat.[105]

On the day of Ḥudaybiya there was no water to drink or make ablution. After the Companions informed the Prophet of that, he (may God bless him and grant him peace) put his hand in a pitcher and the water started to spring forth between his fingers. Then approximately 1400 Companions were able to quench their thirst and make ablution.[106] During the Battle of Tabuk the Prophet also blessed a well such that it gushed forth,[107] and blessed the food so that it multiplied.[108]

In conclusion, the Prophet Muḥammad was bestowed the Qur'ān, conveyed his Sunna (both of which were preserved), foretold many prophecies, and was granted many miracles. All these authentically illustrate and prove his veracity, by the grace of God (Glorious and Exalted is He). On the Day of Judgment, the Prophet Muḥammad will be recognized as being the "best of humanity (*sayyid walad Ādam*)",[109] and he will be granted the highest and "most blessed station (*al-maqām al-maḥmūd*)",[110] which entails interceding on behalf of a vast number of believers.[111]

---

105 Bukhārī 4102; Muslim 2039/5315. In another event, a Bedouin woman along with her people also believed in the Prophet Muḥammad after witnessing him blessing the little water and food she possessed so as to allow forty to drink and eat. Bukhārī 3571; Muslim 682/1563.

106 Bukhārī 3576; Aḥmad 14,933.

107 Muslim 706/5947; Aḥmad 22,070.

108 Muslim 27/139; Aḥmad 11,080.

109 Muslim 2278/5940; Tirmidhī 3148; Abū Dāwūd 4673; Ibn Māja 4308; Aḥmad 10,972.

110 See Bukhārī 4718; Tirmidhī 3148; Aḥmad 13,562.

111 See Bukhārī 4476; Muslim 193/475; Tirmidhī 2434; Ibn Māja 4312; Aḥmad 15.

TESTING THROUGH THE MARRIAGE OF SOME OF THE PROPHETS

One of the final objectives of this chapter is to prove that people may be tested through the marriage of some of the prophets. Specifically, the marriages of Moses, David, Solomon and Muḥammad (may God bless them all) will be investigated. First, there was testing in the marriage of Moses as depicted in the Bible:

> And Miriam and Aaron spake against Moses because of the Ethiopian woman whom he had married: for he had married an Ethiopian woman. And they said, Hath the LORD indeed spoken only by Moses? Hath he not spoken also by us? And the LORD heard it. (Now the man Moses was very meek, above all the men which were upon the face of the earth.) And the LORD spake suddenly unto Moses, and unto Aaron, and unto Miriam, Come out ye three unto the tabernacle of the congregation. And they three came out. And the LORD came down in the pillar of the cloud, and stood in the door of the tabernacle, and called Aaron and Miriam: and they both came forth. And he said, Hear now my words: If there be a prophet among you, I the LORD will make myself known unto him in a vision, and will speak unto him in a dream. My servant Moses is not so, who is faithful in all mine house. With him will I speak mouth to mouth, even apparently, and not in dark speeches; and the similitude of the LORD shall he behold: wherefore then were ye not afraid to speak against my servant Moses? And the anger of the LORD was kindled against them; and he departed. And the cloud departed from off the tabernacle; and, behold, Miriam became leprous, white as snow: and Aaron looked upon Miriam, and, behold, she was leprous. And Aaron said unto Moses, Alas, my lord, I beseech thee, lay not the sin upon us, wherein we have done foolishly, and wherein we have sinned. Let her not be as one dead, of whom the flesh is half consumed when he cometh out of his mother's womb. And Moses cried unto the LORD, saying, Heal her now, O God, I beseech thee. And the LORD said unto Moses, If her father had but spit in her face, should she not be ashamed seven days? Let her be shut out from the camp seven days, and after that let her be received in again. And Miriam was shut out from the camp seven days: and the people journeyed not till Miriam was brought in again. And afterward the people removed from Hazeroth, and pitched in the wilderness of Paran.[112]

[112] Numbers 12.1–16.

Although the above criticism of Miriam against Moses is possible, it was not mentioned in Islamic sources. Nonetheless, as a general rule, those who speak out against the prophets and messengers will face the consequences of their words. The point here though is that, according to the Old Testament, this marriage of Moses served as a test.

The Bible also narrates statements against David and Solomon as a result of their marriages. As regards David, God (Exalted is He) states in the Qur'ān that two litigants approached him directly:

> *This my brother hath ninety nine ewes while I had one ewe; and he said: Entrust it to me, and he conquered me in speech. (David) said: He hath wronged thee in demanding thine ewe in addition to his ewes, and many partners oppress one another, save such as believe and do good works, and they are few. And David guessed that We had tried him, and he sought forgiveness of his Lord, and he bowed himself and fell down prostrate and repented. So We forgave him that; and lo! he had access to Our presence and a happy journey's end. (And it was said unto him): O David! We have set thee as a viceroy in the earth; therefor judge aright between humankind, and follow not desire that it beguile thee from the way of God.*[113]

The writers of the Bible, on the other hand, attribute a major sin, i.e. adultery, to David (which he is innocent of):

> And it came to pass in an eveningtide, that David arose from off his bed, and walked upon the roof of the king's house: and from the roof he saw a woman washing herself; and the woman was very beautiful to look upon. And David sent and inquired after the woman. And one said, Is not this Bath-sheba, the daughter of Eliam, the wife of Uriah the Hittite? And David sent messengers, and took her; and she came in unto him, and he lay with her; for she was purified from her uncleanness: and she returned unto her house.[114]

Now it may be possible that David asked for Bath-sheba, but any speculation beyond that is impermissible. It is also not permissible

---

[113] See Q.XXXVIII.21–26. See 2 Samuel 12.1–24 for a similar analogy—in the Biblical version it was related by Nathan.

[114] 2 Samuel 11.2–4. The Biblical version then states that Uriah was killed in battle, and therefore David married her after the period of mourning had concluded. 2 Samuel 12.24 later states: "And David comforted Bath-sheba his wife, and went in unto her, and lay with her: and she bare a son, and he called his name Solomon: and the LORD loved him."

for Muslims to state that David (may God bless him) sent Uriah the Hittite (Bath-Sheba's prior husband according to the Bible) into the front line of battle so as to increase his chance of being killed[115] since there is no basis for that in the Qur'ān or Sunna. Most importantly, it is blasphemous to attribute adultery to David, a prophet and messenger of God, who is above committing such a major sin and is forgiven for other lesser sins.

The point, though, is that many Jews and Christians attribute to David (may God bless him) evilness and adultery due to this story of his marriage. The greatness of David (may God bless him) is self-evident, and it has been discussed already. Even worse though is the claim that Saul is better than David, and that David "fits the profile of a classic hypocrite better than Saul"[116]—this will be repudiated later in Chapter Thirteen.

Regarding Solomon, the Biblical writers attribute polytheism to him, which he is infallible of, due to his marriages:

> But king Solomon loved many strange women, together with the daughter of Pharaoh, women of the Moabites, Ammonites, Edomites, Zidonians, and Hittites; Of the nations concerning which the LORD said unto the children of Israel, Ye shall not go in to them, neither shall they come in unto you: for surely they will turn away your heart after their gods: Solomon clave unto these in love. And he had seven hundred wives, princesses, and three hundred concubines: and his wives turned away his heart. For it came to pass, when Solomon was old, that his wives turned away his heart after other gods: and his heart was not perfect with the LORD his God, as was the heart of David his father.

---

[115] See 2 Samuel 11.14–17: "David wrote a letter to Joab, and sent it by the hand of Uriah. And he wrote in the letter, saying, Set ye Uriah in the forefront of the hottest battle, and retire ye from him, that he may be smitten, and die. And it came to pass, when Joab observed the city, that he assigned Uriah unto a place where he knew that valiant men were. And the men of the city went out, and fought with Joab: and there fell some of the people of the servants of David; and Uriah the Hittite died also."

[116] See James S. Spiegel, *Hypocrisy: Moral Fraud and other Vices* (Grand Rapids: Baker Books, 1999), p. 18. He states: "Saul's successor, David, is a more likely candidate for hypocrisy...David fits the profile of the classic hypocrite better than Saul, for his action does not seem to be motivated by fear or any other overwhelming passion. Yet...David is not aware of his duplicity, that is until he is confronted by Nathan. Moreover, and most significant, when David's sin is plainly exposed to him, he does repent."

> For Solomon went after Ashtoreth the goddess of the Zidonians, and after Milcom the abomination of the Ammonites. And Solomon did evil in the sight of the LORD, and went not fully after the LORD, as did David his father. Then did Solomon build an high place for Chemosh, the abomination of Moab, in the hill that is before Jerusalem, and for Molech, the abomination of the children of Ammon. And likewise did he for all his strange wives, which burnt incense and sacrificed unto their gods. And the LORD was angry with Solomon, because his heart was turned from the LORD God of Israel, which had appeared unto him twice, and had commanded him concerning this thing, that he should not go after other gods: but he kept not that which the LORD commanded. Wherefore the LORD said unto Solomon, Forasmuch as this is done of thee, and thou hast not kept my covenant and my statutes, which I have commanded thee, I will surely rend the kingdom from thee, and will give it to thy servant. Notwithstanding in thy days I will not do it for David thy father's sake: but I will rend it out of the hand of thy son.[117]

However, the Qur'ān states explicitly: *Solomon disbelieved not.*[118] Solomon is infallible above worshipping others: he worshipped God alone and followed His commandments. It is a significant irony that Solomon, who wielded the greatest kingdom and power for the Israelites, was accused of disbelief in the Bible.

The point, again, is that the marriages of David and Solomon (may God bless them both) led some to ascribe evilness to these two prophets—whether a major sin or disbelief—and this is blasphemous. Instead the Holy Lord renders the marriage of some prophets, particularly those who have been granted much success and triumph, to be a test for people. We should also note that although the Old Testament mentioned that David married a hundred women and Solomon married 700, the characteristics of the vast majority of these women—whether their age or otherwise—was not alluded to.

Similarly, the marriages of the Prophet Muḥammad are a test for people in the face of the overwhelming knowledge and triumph that characterized his message. The most controversial of the marriages of the Prophet Muḥammad was to ᶜĀ'isha (may God be pleased with her) due to the narrations conveying that she was married at a young

---

117 1 Kings 11.1–12.

118 Q.II.102.

age. ʿĀ'isha narrated that the Prophet told her: "You were shown to me twice in my dreams. I saw an angel carrying you wrapped within a piece of silk and saying: 'This is your wife.' [...] I said: 'If this is from God then He will bring it to pass.'"[119] This illustrates that the Prophet Muḥammad did not immediately implement the first dream, but rather verified the commandment with the second.

There are many wise purposes in the Holy Lord commanding the Prophet to marry her. Much good has resulted from the Prophet's marriage to ʿĀ'isha, which could not have otherwise occurred. All of these goods outweigh the controversy. First, the fact that he (may God bless him and grant him peace) married her at such a young age ensured that she would live a long life beyond his passing. The Prophet died eight years after marrying her and so she lived that period with the Prophet and then approximately forty-six years afterwards. This allowed ʿĀ'isha (may God be pleased with her) a long period of time to pass on the teachings of the Prophet Muḥammad. In fact, she narrated 2,210 *ḥadīth*s—only to be preceded by Abū Hurayra,[120] ʿAbd Allāh b. ʿUmar[121] and Anas b. Mālik[122] in this regard. Her narration of *ḥadīth*s led to much religious knowledge being conveyed, and that has been critical to completely understanding the Prophet's Sunna. Indeed, the wives of the Prophet and his Companions conveyed and taught his teachings fully (may God be pleased with them all).

Next, a very significant proof indicating the truthfulness of the Prophet resulted from an event surrounding ʿĀ'isha. Upon the return from the Battle of Banū Muṣṭaliq in the year 6 AH, ʿĀ'isha left the Prophet and the army to answer the call of nature, but then realized that she had lost her necklace. As she began to search for it the encamped army began to leave. One of the believers in the rear of the army noticed her and took her back to Medina on his camel while he

---

119 Bukhārī 7012; Muslim 2438/6283.

120 ʿAbd al-Raḥmān b. Ṣakhr al-Azdī, known as Abū Hurayra (d. 61/681), was a pre-eminent Companion. He narrated 5374 *ḥadīth*s with repetition (or about 1500 without repetition).

121 Abū ʿAbd al-Raḥmān ʿAbd Allāh b. ʿUmar (d. 74/693) was a prominent Companion and son of ʿUmar b. al-Khaṭṭāb. He narrated more than 2600 *ḥadīth*s.

122 Anas b. Mālik b. Naḍar al-Khazrajī al-Anṣārī (d. 93/711) was a Companion who served the Prophet Muḥammad. He narrated 2286 *ḥadīth*s.

walked. The Hypocrites, prodded by their leader ʿAbd Allāh b. Ubayy b. Salūl, subsequently spread malicious rumours of an illicit affair. For an entire month these rumours spread amongst the Muslims[123]. Yet the Prophet Muḥammad never claimed to know the truth in this matter, and he even consulted some of his Companions on the best course of action.[124] The Messenger never claimed a verse of revelation or a tradition in order to protect ʿĀ'isha's dignity, or by extension his. God (Most Blessed and Exalted is He) thereafter revealed her innocence in Sūrat al-Nūr.[125] The point is that the Prophet Muḥammad never did or said anything beyond what was revealed to him by the Holy Lord. Of note, Zaynab bint Jaḥsh, another wife of the Prophet, avoided getting dragged into that calumny and instead would say: "I only know good [regarding ʿĀ'isha]."[126]

There were many other contributions of ʿĀ'isha. The permission to perform dry ablution (*tayammum*) was indirectly due to ʿĀ'isha.[127] She was involved in politics and consulted by ʿUmar b. al-Khaṭṭāb during his caliphate. ʿĀ'isha rejected the claim of some that ʿAlī was appointed by the Prophet Muḥammad to be his successor.[128] She was also involved in the Battle of al-Jamal—this will be alluded to later—but subsequently retired to teaching (both women and men) until her death. May God be pleased with ʿĀ'isha, the mother of the believers (*umm al-mu'minīn*)!

The other controversial marriage of the Prophet Muḥammad (may God bless him and grant him peace) was to Zaynab bint Jaḥsh (may God be pleased with her). Muḥammad's adopted son Zayd had previously married Zaynab, but both were very unhappy therein and ultimately divorced. God (Exalted is He) states:

> *And when thou saidst unto him on whom God hath conferred favour and thou hast conferred favour* [i.e. Zayd]*: Keep thy wife* [i.e. Zaynab] *to thyself, and fear God.*

---

123 Of note, ʿĀ'isha was sick for much of that month and was unaware of the slander. When she did become aware she only became more ill, and wept until she had no more tears to shed.

124 See Bukhārī 2661; Muslim 2770/7020; Aḥmad 25,623.

125 See Q.XXIV.11–17.

126 Bukhārī 4141; Muslim 2770/7020; Aḥmad 25,623.

127 Bukhārī 334; Muslim 367/816; Nasā'ī 310; Aḥmad 25,455.

128 See Bukhārī 2741; Muslim 1636/4231; Ibn Māja 1636; Aḥmad 24,039.

> *And thou didst hide in thy mind that which God was to bring to light, and thou didst fear humankind whereas God hath a better right that thou shouldst fear Him. So when Zayd had performed that necessary formality (of divorce) from her, We gave her unto thee in marriage, so that (henceforth) there may be no sin for believers in respect of wives of their adopted sons, when the latter have performed the necessary formality (of release) from them. The commandment of God must be fulfilled.*[129]

Zaynab used to say to the other wives of the Prophet: "Your parents married you [to the Messenger], while God Himself (Exalted is He) from above seven heavens married me to him."[130] Anas b. Mālik said in this regard: "Were the Messenger of God (may God bless him and grant him peace) to hide something, he would have hidden [verse 37 of Sūrat al-Aḥzāb]."[131] Therefore, the Prophet's marriage to Zaynab represents another proof for the Qur'ān being the Word of the Holy Lord, and not that of Muḥammad.

Now some criticize the Prophet Muḥammad (may God bless him and grant him peace) for this marriage to Zaynab.[132] But one must note that Muḥammad did not mention his thoughts, but rather kept them hidden. Not only that, after Zayd informed the Prophet that he intended to divorce Zaynab, the Messenger advised him to remain married and not divorce her. If you compare this to the discussion attributed to the Prophet David (may God bless him) in relation to him asking for Bath-Sheba, as mentioned in the Qur'ān and Bible, then one should recognize that both instances were to test people, and that those who criticize Muḥammad must criticize David to a greater degree (and therefore bear the sin of doing so in both cases).

Now although Zaynab did not relate anywhere near the number of *ḥadīths* narrated by ʿĀ'isha, she did alone relate the following statement of the Prophet: "There is no deity but God. Woe unto the Arabs from an impending evil. Today two fingerbreadths of the barrier of Gog and Magog have come undone." Zaynab then asked: "O Messenger of God! Will we become ruined even if the righteous are alive amongst

---

129 Q.XXXIII.37. See also the *ḥadīth* in Bukhārī 4787.

130 Bukhārī 7420; Tirmidhī 3213.

131 Bukhārī 7420.

132 See Robert Spencer, *The Truth about Muhammad: Founder of the World's Most Intolerant Religion* (Washington DC: Regnery, 2006), pp. 59–61, 67 and 171.

us?" He replied: "Yes, if wickedness (*khabath*) is widespread."[133] No other Companion related this *ḥadīth* in this fashion. This will be discussed later in Chapter Twelve.

Finally, some of the wives of the Prophet Muḥammad asked before he died: "Which of us will be the first to follow you [and die]?" The Messenger responded: "The most generous of you (*aṭwal*^ukunna^ *yad*^an^)."[134] The most generous of them was Zaynab and she was the first to pass away. This represents another prophecy of the Messenger Muḥammad.

In conclusion, the marriages of the Prophet to both ʿĀ'isha and Zaynab were ordained by the Holy Lord for particular wise purposes, including proving further the veracity of the prophethood of Muḥammad, preserving the religion of Islam and his Sunna, and testing humanity as to who will follow the Prophet Muḥammad versus those who will turn away from Islam and ignore all of the evidences of his prophethood. And God knows best.

---

133 Bukhārī 3598; Muslim 2880/7235; Tirmidhī 2187; Ibn Māja 3953; Aḥmad 27,413.

134 Bukhārī 1420; Muslim 2452/6316.

Chapter Six

The Excellence of Abū Bakr, ᶜUmar, ᶜUthmān and ᶜAlī

God's Messenger Muḥammad (may God bless him and grant him peace) said, as narrated by Saᶜīd b. Zayd: "Ten are [guaranteed] Paradise: the Prophet is in Paradise, Abū Bakr is in Paradise, ᶜUmar is in Paradise, ᶜUthmān is in Paradise, ᶜAlī is in Paradise, Ṭalḥa is in Paradise, al-Zubayr b. al-ᶜAwwām is in Paradise, Saᶜd b. Mālik is in Paradise, and ᶜAbd al-Raḥmān b. ᶜAwf is in Paradise." [Saᶜīd b. Zayd added:] "And if you want I can name the tenth." The Companions then asked him: "Who is it?" He remained quiet. They asked him again: "Who is it?" He said: "It is Saᶜīd b. Zayd."[1] In another narration, the tenth Companion is Abū ᶜUbayda b. al-Jarrāḥ.[2]

The Prophet Muḥammad stated that the Companions represent "the best generation of Adam's offspring".[3] He also said: "The best of humankind is my generation [i.e. the Companions], then those who follow them [i.e. the Successors], then those who follow them."[4] As regards the aforementioned ten Companions, the Prophet Muḥammad may have specifically mentioned them because they represent the best of all of the Muslims, whether Companions or the last of this Community.

It is sufficient that God (Glorious is He) stated in the Qur'ān: *Ye are the best community that hath been raised up for humankind. Ye enjoin right conduct and forbid indecency; and ye believe in God.*[5] The Holy Lord also said

---

[1] Abū Dāwūd 4649; Ibn Māja 134; Aḥmad 1638. It is "authentic" according to Albānī (*Ṣaḥīḥ al-Jāmiᶜ al-ṣaghīr* 4010). Of note, Saᶜd b. Mālik b. Wuhayb is Saᶜd b. Abī Waqqāṣ.

[2] Tirmidhī 3747; Aḥmad 1675; Ibn Ḥibbān 7002. It is "authentic" according to Albānī (*Ṣaḥīḥ al-Jāmiᶜ al-ṣaghīr* 50).

[3] Bukhārī 3557; Aḥmad 8857.

[4] Bukhārī 2652; Muslim 2533/6469; Tirmidhī 2221; Ibn Māja 2362; Nasā'ī 3809; Aḥmad 4173.

[5] Q.III.110. Some interpretations state that this verse refers specifically to the Companions of the Prophet Muḥammad, i.e. that they are the best of humanity, while other interpretations state that the Community of Muḥammad in general is the best

regarding the emigrants from Mecca (*Muhājirīn*) and the supporters of Medina (*Anṣār*): *God is well pleased with them and they are well pleased with Him, and He hath made ready for them Gardens underneath which rivers flow, wherein they will abide for ever. That is the supreme triumph.*[6]

Moreover, the Holy Lord said regarding the 1400 Companions who accompanied the Prophet Muḥammad to the Treaty of Ḥudaybiya: *God was well pleased with the believers when they swore allegiance unto thee beneath the tree, and He knew what was in their hearts, and He sent down peace of reassurance on them, and hath rewarded them with a near victory.*[7] In this regard, the Prophet Muḥammad said: "No one who pledged allegiance beneath the tree, by God's grace, will enter Hellfire."[8]

God (Glorious is He) has also promised Paradise for those Companions who believed after the Treaty of Ḥudaybiya: *Those who spent and fought before the victory are not upon a level (with the rest of you). Such are greater in rank than those who spent and fought afterwards. Unto each hath God promised good (ḥusnā).*[9] Therefore, all of the Companions, including those who believed after the Treaty of Ḥudaybiya or the liberation of Mecca, have been promised Paradise—each rewarded in accordance with his or her righteous actions.

It is notable that there is no similar statement in the Old or New Testament regarding the respective Jewish or Christian forefathers. In addition, Ibn Taymiyya goes further: "Abū Bakr, ᶜUmar, ᶜUthmān and ᶜAlī are superior to the disciples [of Jesus] (*al-ḥawāriyyīn*) by the consensus of the Muslims scholars."[10] The deeds and acts of these

---

when compared to past nations. See *Tafsīr al-Ṭabarī*, vol. VII, pp. 100–106; *Tafsīr al-Rāzī*, vol. VIII, pp. 323–326.

6 Q.IX.100.

7 Q.XLVIII.18.

8 Muslim 2496/6404; Tirmidhī 3860; Abū Dāwūd 4653; Aḥmad 14,778.

9 Q.LVII.10. See also Q.IV.95 and Q.XXI.101; *Tafsīr al-Ṭabarī*, vol. XXIII, pp. 174–177; *Tafsīr al-Rāzī*, vol. XXIX, pp. 452–453.

10 Ibn Taymiyya, *al-Jawāb al-ṣaḥīḥ*, vol. I, pp. 413–414. Ibn Taymiyya also states something similar when comparing the Muslims to the Jews or Christians: "It is well known that the Community of Muḥammad (may God bless him and grant him peace) is more perfect and more just than the People of the Book (whether Jewish or Christian). This [Community] possesses all of the noble traits mentioned in the Torah and Gospel. The People of the Book do not possess any religious knowledge or act except that the Community of Muḥammad more perfectly exhibits it." Ibn Taymiyya, *al-Jawāb al-ṣaḥīḥ*, vol. II, p. 544.

Rightly-Guided Caliphs were great indeed. Moreover, they all achieved victory in the absence of a messenger, i.e. after the Prophet Muḥammad's death, whereas the disciples of Jesus were unable to achieve such immediate victory.

It is beyond the scope of this book to describe, in elaborate detail, the good deeds and actions of the Companions; however, some of the noble characteristics and righteous acts of the four Rightly-Guided Caliphs will be alluded to in this chapter and briefly elsewhere.

THE TYPES OF RULERS

Before discussing the Rightly-Guided Caliphs, it is important to mention that the Prophet Muḥammad (may God bless him and grant him peace) said: "Follow my Sunna as well as the methodology (*sunna*) of the Rightly-Guided Caliphs after me."[11] The Prophet Muḥammad also said: "The Caliphs would last for thirty years, then God will grant the kingdom (or His kingdom) to those whom He wills".[12] It is of note that the Prophet did not say in either *ḥadīth* "king" (*malik*) or "kings" (*mulūk*) or something akin to that. Herein follows a discussion to prove that when the word "king" is mentioned in the Qur'ān it has a negative connotation upon those kings it is referring to.

First, consider the statement of the Queen of Sheba that is narrated in the Qur'ān: *Verily, whenever kings enter a country they corrupt it, and turn the noblest of its people into the most abject.*[13] Therefore, those who are named "kings" in the Qur'ān perpetrate corruption (*fasād*)

---

[11] Tirmidhī 2676; Abū Dāwūd 4607; Ibn Māja 42; Aḥmad 17,142; Ibn Ḥibbān 5; al-Ḥākim 329; Bayhaqī (*Sunan*) 20,338. It is "authentic" according to Albānī (*Silsilat al-aḥādīth al-ṣaḥīḥa* 2735). Of note, the Prophet Muḥammad began the *ḥadīth* by stating: "Whoever lives will see after [my death] much discord." Therefore, he foretold of many calamities that would afflict the Companions, Successors and so on.

[12] Tirmidhī 2226; Abū Dāwūd 4646; Aḥmad 21,919; al-Ḥākim 4697; Ibn Ḥibbān 6943. It is "sound" according to Albānī (*Silsilat al-aḥādīth al-ṣaḥīḥa* 459 and *Ṣaḥīḥ al-Jāmiʿ al-ṣaghīr* 3257). The wording of Abū Dāwūd was used here. Of note, the caliphates of Abū Bakr, ʿUmar, ʿUthmān, ʿAlī and al-Ḥasan lasted thirty lunar years: 11–40 AH / 632–661 CE.

[13] Q.XXVII.34 (Muḥammad Asad translation). Of note, Sheba was a disbeliever at that point and her statement does not reflect negatively on Solomon. One can consider it like the statement of Pharaoh against Moses: *Behold I fear lest he cause you to change your religion, or lest he cause corruption to prevail in the land!* Q.XL.28 (Muḥammad Asad translation).

by definition. It is well known that the Holy Lord is critical of corruption: *As for that abode of the Hereafter We assign it unto those who seek not oppression in the earth, nor yet corruption.*[14] Those who are corrupt will have no place in Paradise.

Another characteristic of kings is that they legislate their own laws and follow their own desires rather than following the Divine Law. Therefore, God (Exalted is He) states regarding the king of Egypt during the time of Joseph: *He could not have taken his brother according to the king's law unless God willed.*[15] The law (*dīn*) was attributed specifically to the king here, and this reveals that he turned away from the Divine Law. Of note, the difference between a king and a Pharaoh is that the former corrupt (*fasada*) whereas the latter transgress (*ṭaghā*), oppress (*ʿalā*) and corrupt.[16] Nonetheless, both have turned away from the Divine Law—for this and the aforementioned reasons both types are disbelievers.

On the other hand, whenever God (Glorious is He) wants to refer positively to someone given sovereignty, He states that "He has bestowed the kingdom upon him" (*ātā*^hu^ *Allāh al-mulk*), or He refers to that individual as an owner or possessor rather than being a "king". Examples include God's reference to David (may God bless him): *David slew Goliath; and God gave him the kingdom and wisdom, and taught him of that which He willeth.*[17] Furthermore, the Holy Lord refers to the *kingdom* (*mulk*) of Solomon, and did not refer to him as being a *king* (*malik*).[18] Likewise, consider the reference to the Queen of Sheba (as she ultimately became a believer) as: *a woman ruling over them (tamlik*^uhum^*), and she hath been given (abundance) of all things, and hers is a mighty throne.*[19]

A third possibility is represented by the juxtaposition of *prophet* with *king*. In this case, the king-prophet is righteous and beloved to the Holy Lord, and not just solely named as a "king" who causes

---

14 Q.XXVIII.83.

15 Q.XII.76.

16 See verses Q.LXXXIX.10–12 and Q. XLIV.31.

17 Q.II.251.

18 See Q.II.102.

19 Q.XXVII.23.

corruption. It should be recalled that David was a king-prophet[20] and Caliph as God (Exalted is He) said to him: *O David! We have set thee as a viceroy* (*khalīfa*) *in the earth; therefore judge aright between humankind, and follow not desire that it beguile thee from the way of God.*[21] Thus one who is named by God (Glorious is He) as a Caliph judges with justice, in contrast to those named as "kings" who perpetrate corruption and follow their desires. Likewise, the fact that the Prophet Muḥammad named his successors as *Caliphs* and not *kings* indicates that they were righteous and just, that they followed the Prophetic Sunna completely, and were dearly beloved to him and the Holy Lord.

Finally, it should be mentioned that even when God (Glorious and Exalted is He) refers to Himself—and He is the True King—it is never as a King alone, but rather it is juxtaposed either as the Righteous King (*al-Malik al-Ḥaqq*) or the Holy King (*al-Malik al-Quddūs*). The former is represented in the verse: *Now God be Exalted, the Righteous King! There is no God save Him, the Lord of the Throne of Grace,*[22] whereas the latter is present in: *He is God, Whom there is no other deity, the King, the Holy One,* [*the One Who is faultless and bestows*] *Peace, the Keeper of Faith, the Guardian, the Majestic, the Irresistible, the Proud. Glorified be God from all that they ascribe as partner* (*unto Him*).[23] Therefore, all of God's actions in administering His kingdom, whether ontologic or religious, are just, righteous and holy.

If one considers verse four of Sūrat al-Fātiḥa as *King of the Day of Religious Recompense* (*Malik Yawm al-Dīn*), this also attributes holiness and righteousness to Him for it juxtaposes the religion to His being the King. All other verses include the term "sovereignty" (*mulk*) to

---

[20] That said, God (Glory be to Him) sent Gabriel to the Prophet Muḥammad giving him the choice of being either a king-Prophet or a servant-Prophet. The Prophet Muḥammad sought Gabriel's advice, whereupon Gabriel advised the Messenger to humble himself. Therefore, Muḥammad (may God bless him and grant him peace) said: "I will be a servant-Prophet." Aḥmad 7160; Bayhaqī (*Sunan*) 13,327; Ibn Ḥibbān 6365; *Ḥilya*, vol. III, 256. It is "authentic" according to Albānī (*Silsilat al-aḥādīth al-ṣaḥīḥa* 1002).

[21] Q.XXXVIII.26.

[22] Q.XXIII.116. Of note, Pickthall translates *al-Ḥaqq* as "The True". See also Q.XX.114.

[23] See verse Q.LIX.23 (adapted from Pickthall). Pickthall translates *al-Malik* as "the Sovereign Lord", *al-Jabbār* as "the Compeller", and *al-Mutakabbir* as "the Superb".

denote His Sovereignty and Ownership. Consider, for example: *Blessed is He in Whose hand is the Sovereignty, and He is Able to do all things,*[24] *Say: O God! Owner of Sovereignty! Thou givest sovereignty unto whom Thou wilt, and Thou withdrawest sovereignty from whom Thou wilt. Thou exaltest whom Thou wilt, and Thou abasest whom Thou wilt. In Thy hand is the good. Thou art Able to do all things.*[25]

Now, as regards the Caliphs following the Prophet Muḥammad, the first of them was Abū Bakr followed by ᶜUmar, ᶜUthmān and ᶜAlī.[26] All four of them were promised Paradise, as indicated in the *ḥadīth* narrated by Saᶜīd b. Zayd at the beginning of this chapter. They are the best of this Community, for they were righteous and spread the establishment of prayer and zakat throughout the land, while fighting against evil and corruption. Therefore, may God bless those who commend them and may God hold accountable those who criticize them! Herein follows a brief exposition of their goodness and righteousness.

ABŪ BAKR

Abū Bakr was the first man to believe and follow the Prophet Muḥammad (may God bless him and grant him peace). His proselytizing efforts were a significant factor in many becoming Muslim at the hands of the Prophet Muḥammad, such as ᶜUthmān, Ṭalḥa, al-Zubayr, ᶜAbd al-Raḥmān b. ᶜAwf and Saᶜd b. Abī Waqqās. It was also through the striving and wealth of Abū Bakr that seven oppressed slaves who desired to become Muslim were set free. Abū Bakr would ultimately spend all of his money for Islam in the lead up to Tabuk.[27]

Abū Bakr also defended the Prophet Muḥammad when ᶜUqba b. Abī Muᶜayṭ tried to strangle the Prophet while he was prostrating in prayer in front of the Kaᶜba. Abū Bakr pushed ᶜUqba aside and said:

---

24 Q.LXVII.1.

25 Q.III.28.

26 Of note, al-Ḥasan b. ᶜAlī followed ᶜAlī as the fifth Caliph.

27 Tirmidhī 3675; Abū Dāwūd 1678; al-Ḥākim 1510. It is "sound" according to Albānī (*Mishkāt* 6030). Of note, in this *ḥadīth* ᶜUmar gave half of his wealth in charity; but once he saw that Abū Bakr gave all of his wealth, he said: "I will never be able to supercede him in anything."

Would ye kill a man because he saith: My Lord is Allāh, and hath brought you clear proofs from your Lord?[28] Abū Bakr subsequently accompanied the Prophet on his emigration from Mecca to Medina, and God (Exalted is He) honoured and distinguished him by naming him as the Prophet's Companion: *If you do not succour the Messenger, then [know that God will do so—just as] God succoured him at the time when those who were bent on denying the truth drove him away, [and he was but] one of two: when these two were [hiding] in the cave, [and] the Messenger said to his companion, "Grieve not: verily, God is with us."*[29] God (Almighty is He) then granted Abū Bakr, the second of the two, peace and tranquility, and preserved and assisted them both to reach Medina unharmed.

The exegetes also maintain that Abū Bakr is the one being referred to in the following verses: *Far removed from [Hellfire] will be the righteous. Who giveth his wealth that he may grow (in goodness). And none hath with him any favour for reward, except as seeking (to fulfil) the purpose of his Lord Most High. He verily will be content.*[30]

Two years after the emigration to Medina Abū Bakr fought alongside the Prophet in the Battle of Badr, as well as all of the subsequent battles. At the Battle of Uḥud, Abū Bakr remained with the Prophet Muḥammad to the end. On the Day of Ḥudaybiya, when other Companions had yet to understand the wisdom in their delayed entry into Mecca for another year, Abū Bakr followed the Prophet (may God bless him and grant him peace) completely. It is beyond the scope of this chapter or book to detail all of Abū Bakr's great actions; however, it is sufficient to state that the Prophet Muḥammad (may God bless him and grant him peace) said that he hoped that Abū Bakr

---

28 See Bukhārī 3678; Aḥmad 6908. The Qur'ānic verse therein is Q.XL.28. Note, it was mentioned in another episode that ʿUqba b. Abī Muʿayṭ placed the intestines of a camel on the Prophet Muḥammad when he was praying. Fāṭima removed them off of him. See Bukhārī 240 and 520; Muslim 1794/4649; Aḥmad 3722.

29 Q.IX.40 (Muḥammad Asad translation). Of note, Asad uses "Apostle" rather than "Messenger". Abū Bakr was grieved due to his concern that they would be found. He said to the Prophet Muḥammad while they were in the cave: "If they would have looked down they would have seen us." It was at that point that the Prophet said: "What do you think about two who are supported by a third, Who is God." Bukhārī 3653; Muslim 2381/6169; Tirmidhī 3096; Aḥmad 11.

30 Q.XCII.17–21. See *Tafsīr al-Ṭabarī*, vol. XXIV, pp. 479–480; *Tafsīr al-Rāzī*, vol. XXXI, pp. 187–189.

would be able to enter from each and every one of the eight gates of Paradise.[31] The Prophet Muḥammad also said: "God (Exalted is He) has taken me as a close friend (*khalīl*) like He took Abraham as a close friend. But if I was to take from amongst my Community a close friend it would be Abū Bakr."[32]

ᶜAmr b. al-ᶜĀṣ (may God be pleased with him) narrated that he asked the Prophet (may God bless him and grant him peace): "Who is the most beloved person to you?" He replied: "ᶜĀ'isha." I inquired: 'Who among the men?' He answered: "Her father [i.e. Abū Bakr]." I asked: 'Then who?' He replied: "ᶜUmar b. al-Khaṭṭāb.' He then named other men."[33] In another tradition, ᶜĀ'isha was asked regarding the most beloved Companions of the Messenger of God to him and she replied: "Abū Bakr", then "ᶜUmar", and then "Abū ᶜUbayda b. al-Jarrāḥ".[34]

The Prophet Muḥammad also said: "Follow the example of my two companions who will come after me: Abū Bakr and ᶜUmar."[35] Yet on one occasion a slight dispute arose between Abū Bakr and ᶜUmar (may God be pleased with them both). Afterwards, Abū Bakr asked for ᶜUmar's forgiveness, but the latter refused. Thereupon, Abū Bakr hastened to the Prophet Muḥammad (may God bless him and grant him peace) and told him the story whereupon the Prophet repeated three times: "May God forgive you, Abū Bakr!" ᶜUmar then came to that gathering and the signs of anger showed on the Prophet Muḥammad's face. Thereupon the Messenger said: "God sent me to you all whereupon you all said [at that time]: 'You have lied.' On the other hand, Abū Bakr said [I was] truthful and he himself, as well as through his wealth, consoled me. Will you all then leave my companion alone? Will you all then leave my companion alone?" Thereafter Abū Bakr was never harmed again.[36] This episode no doubt reinforced Abū Bakr's eminent status in the minds of ᶜUmar

---

[31] See Bukhārī 1897; Muslim 1027/2371; Tirmidhī 3674; Nasā'ī 2238; Aḥmad 7633.

[32] Muslim 532/1188.

[33] Bukhārī 3662; Muslim 2384/6177; Aḥmad 17,811.

[34] Tirmidhī 3657; Ibn Māja 102; Aḥmad 25,829; al-Ḥākim 4446. It is "authentic" according to Albānī in *Ṣaḥīḥ wa ḍaᶜīf Sunan al-Tirmidhī*, vol. VIII, p. 157.

[35] Tirmidhī 3805; Aḥmad 23,245; al-Ḥākim 4451; Bayhaqī (*Sunan*) 10,056. It is "authentic" according to Albānī (*Silsilat al-aḥādīth al-ṣaḥīḥa* 1233).

[36] Bukhārī 3661.

and the other Companions. It also emphasizes, going forward from this episode, that those who harm or criticize Abū Bakr in any fashion have disobeyed a commandment of the Prophet Muḥammad.

There is one other episode wherein a disagreement arose between Rabīʿa al-Aslamī and Abū Bakr. Abū Bakr regretted something he said and asked Rabīʿa to reciprocate, but the latter refused. They both went to the Prophet Muḥammad wherein he (may God bless him and grant him peace) approved of Rabīʿa's refusal and taught him to say: "May God forgive you, Abū Bakr."[37] This should be the approach of the Muslims towards Abū Bakr and all of the Companions, i.e. to desist from criticizing them.

Next, consider the statement of the Holy Lord: *O ye who believe! Whoso of you becometh a renegade from his religion, (know that in his stead) God will bring a people whom He loveth and who love Him, humble toward believers, stern toward disbelievers, striving in the way of God, and fearing not the blame of any blamer. Such is the grace of God which He giveth unto whom He will. God is All-Embracing, All-Knowing.*[38] Although this verse was revealed during the lifetime of the Prophet Muḥammad, widespread apostasy did not happen in Arabia until after his death. Ṭabarī, as well as other exegetes, maintain that this verse refers to Abū Bakr and the Companions who fought against the apostates;[39] therefore, God (Glory be to Him) has bestowed His grace and love upon Abū Bakr and the Muslims who upheld the purity of Islam and its pillars.

There are many evidences establishing that Abū Bakr was to be the leader after the Prophet Muḥammad. A Companion asked the Messenger of God (may God bless him and grant him peace): "What should I do if I come looking for you but cannot find you?" The Prophet replied: "If you cannot find me, then go to Abū Bakr."[40] The Prophet Muḥammad also appointed Abū Bakr to lead all of the Companions, including ʿAlī, in pilgrimage to the Holy Kaʿba in the ninth year AH—this was after the Battles of Khaybar (7 AH) and Tabuk (8 AH). Abū Bakr was ordered to declare that the polytheists (many of whom circumambulated the Kaʿba naked) would no longer

---

37 Aḥmad 16,577. It is "sound" according to Albānī (*Silsilat al-aḥādīth al-ṣaḥīḥa* 3145).

38 Q.V.54.

39 See *Tafsīr al-Ṭabarī*, vol. X, pp. 411–414.

40 Bukhārī 3659; Muslim 2386/6179; Aḥmad 16,755.

be able to do so the next year. The Prophet Muḥammad subsequently led the Farewell Pilgrimage in the tenth year AH.

In addition, when the Prophet Muḥammad became weak during his final illness, he (may God bless him and grant him peace) ordered that Abū Bakr lead the Companions in prayer—this was obviously the last appointment the Prophet Muḥammad made in his life.[41] Abū Bakr, at a minimum, led seventeen prayers.[42] When the Prophet felt better after a few days, he joined the prayer after Abū Bakr had already begun to lead it: "When Abū Bakr saw [the Prophet] he wanted to retreat but the Prophet beckoned him not to do so, and asked [some Companions] to seat him beside Abū Bakr, and so they did. Abū Bakr was following the Prophet, and the people were following Abū Bakr."[43]

In addition, the Prophet Muḥammad told ʿĀ'isha during his final illness: "Bring me your father [i.e. Abū Bakr] and your brother, so that I may write a declaration in regards to Abū Bakr such that no one else will desire [to become Caliph] or think that he is more deserving." Thereafter, the Prophet decided not to do so and said: "God and the believers refuse that there be any disagreement regarding Abū Bakr."[44] Here it becomes clear that God (Glorious is He) has willed in both a religious and ontologic manner that Abū Bakr follow the Prophet in leading the Companions and Successors; that the Prophet Muḥammad made a proclamation for Abū Bakr to follow him, but did not have it written down; and that all those who are believers necessarily accept Abū Bakr as the Caliph to follow the Prophet Muḥammad (may God bless him and grant him peace). Note that the Prophet did not say "my Companions" but instead said "believers"; thus anyone from this Community, whether from the beginning or the end, who would

---

41 See Bukhārī 664; Muslim 418/936; Tirmidhī 3672; Ibn Māja 1232; Nasā'ī 833; Aḥmad 19,700.

42 Ibn Taymiyya, *Minhāj al-Sunna al-Nabawiyya*, vol. V, p. 486.

43 See Bukhārī 687; Muslim 418/936; Tirmidhī 362; Nasā'ī 797; Aḥmad 25,876.

44 Muslim 2387/6181; Ibn Ḥibbān 6598. In another wording the Prophet said the reason was so that "people will not become divided after my [death]", but he concluded with the phrase: "God and the believers refuse that there be any disagreement regarding Abū Bakr." Aḥmad 24,199. It is "authentic" according to Albānī (*Silsilat al-aḥādīth al-ṣaḥīḥa* 690).

like to be classified as a believer (*mu'min*)—not just as a Muslim—should be pleased with Abū Bakr as the first Caliph[45] after the Prophet Muḥammad (may God bless him and grant him peace). The difference between the rank of a believer and that of a Muslim will be discussed in the next chapter as well as later in the book.

Moreover, the Prophet Muḥammad said: "Follow my Sunna as well as the methodology of the Rightly-Guided Caliphs after me."[46] The actions of the Rightly-Guided Caliphs, i.e. Abū Bakr, ʿUmar, ʿUthmān and ʿAlī, are model examples to following the Prophetic tradition. Abū Bakr was a truly faithful servant (*ṣiddīq*), which is the highest level after the prophets, while ʿUmar was one inspired with divine guidance (*muḥaddath*). It will be contended in this book that a *muḥaddath* represents a subset of the *ṣiddīq* rank—that said, Abū Bakr's rank is above that of ʿUmar (may God be pleased with them both). This will be discussed further in the next chapter.

Now, in the immediate aftermath of the Prophet's death, the Companions were in shock. Abū Bakr, though, strengthened them by saying: "Whoever used to worship Muḥammad (may God bless him and grant him peace) should know that Muḥammad has died. And whoever worships God should know that God is Ever-Living, and He will never die."[47] Then Abū Bakr recited the verse: *Muḥammad is but a messenger, messengers (the like of whom) have passed away before him. Will it be that, when he dieth or is slain, ye will turn back on your heels? He who turneth back on his heels doth no hurt to God, and God will reward the thankful.*[48] The Companions began to wail as they now recognized that the Messenger Muḥammad had truly died.

The Companions then congregated at Saqīfat banī Sāʿida wherein the Medinites had initially nominated Saʿd b. ʿUbāda to be the new leader and then proposed—after some resistance from the Meccan

---

[45] The very few Companions who did not ultimately accept Abū Bakr as the first Caliph may be exempt from this general rule as God (Glorious is He) has declared His pleasure with them in the Qur'ān.

[46] Tirmidhī 2676; Abū Dāwūd 4607; Ibn Māja 42; Aḥmad 17,144; al-Ḥākim 329; Bayhaqī (*Sunan*) 20,338. It is "authentic" according to Albānī (*Ṣaḥīḥ al-Jāmiʿ al-ṣaghīr* 2549).

[47] Bukhārī 3668; Ibn Māja 1627; Aḥmad 25,841.

[48] Q.III.144. This verse was revealed seven years earlier, after the Battle of Uḥud.

Companions—that two rulers would be nominated: one from the Medinites and one from the Meccans. ᶜUmar b. al-Khaṭṭāb then acknowledged that the best of the Companions and the most beloved of them to the Prophet was Abū Bakr. Finally, after Abū Bakr spoke to the congregation and ᶜUmar pledged to him, all of the Meccans and all of the Medinites (except for Saᶜd) pledged allegiance to Abū Bakr as the Caliph.[49] It is interesting to note that no sound evidence exists for any of the Companions in that congregation mentioning or nominating ᶜAlī b. Abī Ṭālib. In addition, it is significant that Abū Bakr did nothing much less say anything to Saᶜd (who never pledged[50]) nor to ᶜAlī[51] (who delayed in pledging allegiance to him for six months[52]).

Indeed, Abū Bakr followed the Prophet Muḥammad completely in his caliphate as he upheld the pillars of Islam and sent out the army led by Usāma b. Zayd (as planned by the Prophet Muḥammad). The two most prominent actions of Abū Bakr's short caliphate (which lasted only two years) were that he fought against the false prophets and apostates and that he collected all of the parchments upon which were written the verses of the Qur'ān. Of note, the latter occurred after ᶜUmar became concerned that the Qur'ān was at risk of being incompletely preserved with the death of many of the Companions who had fought against the apostates. Thus out of this evilness (of apostasy) and death (of many of the Companions who had memorized the Qur'ān) came something good (i.e. the collection of the written Qur'ān in one standardized form). This manuscript stayed with Abū Bakr until he died. Subsequently, ᶜUmar kept it until he was martyred; and finally, it remained with Ḥafṣa, who was ᶜUmar's daughter and

---

[49] Bukhārī 3668.

[50] It is noteworthy that Saᶜd b. ᶜUbāda remained alive throughout Abū Bakr's caliphate and into ᶜUmar's.

[51] The Shiites state that others (up to 10 individuals) did not pledge as well. See Abbas Muhajirani, "Twelve-Imām Shi'ite theological and philosophical thought", in Seyyed Hossein Nasr and Oliver Leaman (eds.), *History of Islamic Philosophy* (London and New York: Routledge, 1996), p. 120. Even if that was the case they still represent less than 0.1% of the more than ten thousand Companions. Certainly, nowadays it is quite difficult to obtain a two-thirds majority approving any particular leader never mind more than 99%.

[52] See Bukhārī 4240; Muslim 1759/4580.

the Prophet's wife.[53] It is also noteworthy to mention that both Abū Bakr and ʿUmar were the only ones buried alongside the Prophet Muḥammad (as ʿĀ'isha had given her intended burial site to ʿUmar).

Next, there are numerous *ḥadīths* that show the eminence of ʿUmar above all others (except Abū Bakr); hence, Abū Bakr selected ʿUmar to follow him as Caliph. For example, there is the aforementioned *ḥadīth* and prophetic directive: "Follow the example of my two companions who will come after me: Abū Bakr and ʿUmar."[54] ʿAlī himself also acknowledged that the best individuals of this Community after the Prophet himself were Abū Bakr and ʿUmar, according to many narrations from him.[55]

ʿUmar b. al-Khaṭṭāb

ʿUmar b. al-Khaṭṭāb converted to Islam in the eighth year after the Prophet began preaching Islam. Thereafter, the Companions became stronger, more confident, and were able to pray openly in the Kaʿba; thus, ʿUmar became known as "he who distinguishes between truth and falsehood" (*al-fārūq*). Ibn Masʿūd, one of the pre-eminent Companions, said: "We were given victory from the time ʿUmar became a Muslim."[56]

The Prophet Muḥammad said: "Among the nations which preceded you (including the Israelites) were men who used to be inspired with guidance although they were not prophets. If there is any such individual amongst my followers it is ʿUmar."[57] It is noteworthy that the Prophet Muḥammad mentioned that ʿUmar would be divinely

---

[53] See Bukhārī 4986.

[54] Tirmidhī 3805; Aḥmad 23,245; al-Ḥākim 4451; Bayhaqī (*Sunan*) 10,056. It is "authentic" according to Albānī (*Silsilat al-aḥādīth al-ṣaḥīḥa* 1233). In another *ḥadīth* the Prophet Muḥammad states: "If they follow Abū Bakr and ʿUmar they will remain righteous (*yarshudū*)." Muslim 681/1562; Aḥmad 22,546.

[55] See Bukhārī 3671; Abū Dāwūd 4629; Ibn Māja 106; Aḥmad 834, 837, 879, 909 and 1051; *Ḥilya*, vol. VII, pp. 198–201. ʿAlī acknowledged this to his son Muḥammad b. al-Ḥanafiyya (in Bukhārī 3671 and Abū Dāwūd 4629) and while delivering sermons in Kufa (Aḥmad 837, 909 and 1051).

[56] Bukhārī 3863.

[57] Bukhārī 3689; Muslim 2398/6204; Tirmidhī 3693; Aḥmad 24,285. These narrations mention the preceding nations (*umam*) in general, except that of Bukhārī where the Israelites are specified.

inspired—not that he would be infallible. Indeed, the Prophet (may God bless him and grant him peace) never mentioned that infallible individuals would exist within his Community. The Prophet Muḥammad also said: "God has endowed ᶜUmar with truthfulness in his speech and in his heart."[58]

ᶜAbd Allāh b. ᶜUmar reported that his father said: "I correctly agreed with my Lord on three occasions: [regarding] the Station of Abraham [as a place of prayer], the woman's veil/scarf [as a religious requirement], and the [way in which to treat the non-Muslim] prisoners of Badr."[59] ᶜUmar's opinion was also confirmed by the Holy Lord when he opined that the Hypocrites[60] should not be prayed upon by the believers. The Prophet Muḥammad (may God bless him and grant him peace) also informed us on at least two occasions that ᶜUmar b. al-Khaṭṭāb was granted and would be bestowed vast religious knowledge.[61]

ᶜUmar also fought alongside the Prophet Muḥammad in all of the battles. The eminence of ᶜUmar b. al-Khaṭṭāb is self-evident and well-recognized.[62] ᶜUmar remained at Abū Bakr's side during the latter's caliphate. And during ᶜUmar's caliphate, Islam spread far and wide. It had been limited to the Arabian Peninsula during the time of Abū Bakr, but after ᶜUmar it extended to all of Syria, Iraq, and much of

---

58 Tirmidhī 3682; Aḥmad 5145; al-Ḥākim 4501; Ibn Ḥibbān 6889. It is "authentic" according to Albānī (*Ṣaḥīḥ al-Jāmiᶜ al-ṣaghīr* 1736).

59 Muslim 2399/6206. Another narration includes the first two, but the third is regarding the matter represented in verses Q.LXVI.3–5. See Bukhārī 402; Aḥmad 157.

60 Bukhārī 1366; Tirmidhī 3097; Ibn Māja 1523; Nasā'ī 1966; Aḥmad 95. This regards the Prophet Muḥammad praying upon the leader of the Hypocrites, ᶜAbd Allāh b. Ubayy b. Salūl, based on the verse: *Ask forgiveness for them (O Muḥammad), or ask not forgiveness for them; though thou ask forgiveness for them seventy times God will not forgive them.* Q.IX.80. The Prophet said: "I was given a choice, and I have chosen. If I knew that exceeding seventy times would result in them being forgiven, I would do so." ᶜUmar, however, objected and a verse was later revealed: *And never (O Muḥammad) pray for one of them who dieth, nor stand by his grave. Lo! they disbelieved in God and His Messenger, and they died while they were evildoers.* Q.IX.84

61 See Bukhārī 23; Muslim 2390/6189; Tirmidhī 2285; Nasā'ī 5011; Aḥmad 11,814. See also Bukhārī 82; Muslim 2391/6190.

62 Indeed, Michael Hart places ᶜUmar within the top one hundred most influential people in history. See Hart, *The 100: A Ranking of the Most Influential Persons in History*, pp. 261–265. Recall that Hart regarded Muḥammad as the most influential individual in history.

Egypt and Iran. Indeed, the Prophet Muḥammad prophesized that the Muslims would ultimately conquer the Persian and the Byzantine empires and "use their treasures for the sake of God."[63] This began during the caliphate of ʿUmar with the destruction of the Persian empire.

On one occasion, during his caliphate, ʿUmar set out with the Companions towards Syria, but then realized that a plague had broken out there. ʿUmar sought their advice about whether to continue or to return, and one of the Companions opined that they should continue as it would be inappropriate "to run away from the Divine decree". ʿUmar then replied: "Yes, we are running from the Divine decree to the Divine decree." Then ʿAbd al-Raḥmān b. ʿAwf said: "I heard God's Messenger say: 'If you hear of the presence [of a plague] in a land, do not enter it; but if it spreads in the land where you are, do not flee from it.'" Thereupon ʿUmar b. Khaṭṭāb praised God and returned.[64] This represents an important tradition that illustrates the manner by which the Divine decree should be approached.

In another instance, Ḥudhayfa narrated that ʿUmar b. al-Khaṭṭāb asked him about the major tribulations that were to come. Ḥudhayfa replied: "Do not be concerned about them, O Caliph of the Believers. There is a closed door between you and them." ʿUmar asked: "Will that door be broken or just opened?" Ḥudhayfa replied: "Broken." Thereupon ʿUmar said: "Then it will never be closed again." Masrūq later asked Ḥudhayfa: "Who is the door?" Ḥudhayfa replied: "ʿUmar."[65] This tradition illustrates that major tribulations would only begin to occur after the martyrdom of ʿUmar. These tribulations intensified greatly after the martyrdom of ʿUthmān and led to great divisions that persist to this day—this will be discussed in Chapter Twelve.

The Prophet Muḥammad (may God bless him and grant him peace) foretold that both ʿUmar b. al-Khaṭṭāb and ʿUthmān would be martyred.[66] At the end of his caliphate, ʿUmar b. al-Khaṭṭāb appointed a board consisting of six of the pre-eminent Companions—ʿUthmān,

---

63 Bukhārī 3120; Muslim 2918/7327; Tirmidhī 2216; Aḥmad 7184.

64 Bukhārī 5729; Muslim 2219/5784.

65 Bukhārī 525; Muslim 144/369; Tirmidhī 2258; Ibn Māja 3955; Aḥmad 23,412.

66 See Bukhārī 3675; Tirmidhī 3697; Abū Dāwūd 4651; Aḥmad 22,811.

ʿAlī, ʿAbd al-Raḥmān b. ʿAwf, Ṭalḥa, al-Zubayr and Saʿd b. Mālik, all of whom had been promised Paradise by the Prophet Muḥammad—to determine amongst themselves the next Caliph. The latter three had no interest in becoming Caliph; thus Ṭalḥa voted for ʿUthmān, al-Zubayr voted for ʿAlī, while Sāʿd voted for ʿAbd al-Raḥmān. ʿAbd al-Raḥmān (who also did not desire the caliphate) asked ʿUthmān and ʿAlī whether they would agree to abide by his decision if he removed himself from consideration—they both agreed. ʿAbd al-Raḥmān then consulted the Companions throughout Medina for three days, sleeping but little. It was only after taking into account all of their opinions that he nominated ʿUthmān[67]. It is noteworthy that the nomination of ʿUthman occurred while there was peace in Medina without dissension, and that all of the Muslims, including ʿAlī, pledged to him without exception. It is also clear that in nominating those six, ʿUmar ensured that the Caliphs who would succeed him would be from amongst the ten promised Paradise. Four dropped out by their own free will, thus leaving ʿAlī to be the obvious successor to ʿUthmān in accordance with the majority opinion of the Companions and Successors at that time.

ʿUthmān b. ʿAffān

ʿUthmān b. ʿAffān was one of the earliest men to become Muslim, doing so only after Abū Bakr, ʿAlī and Zayd b. Ḥāritha. ʿUthmān subsequently married Ruqayya, the Prophet Muḥammad's daughter. They emigrated to Ethiopia due to the persecution suffered by the early Muslims. They later returned and emigrated to Medina. Ruqayya died during the Battle of Badr, with ʿUthmān at her side. Nevertheless, the Prophet Muḥammad told him: "You will be rewarded like those who participated in Badr."[68] A year later ʿUthmān married Umm Kulthūm, a second daughter of the Prophet. Since ʿUthmān had married two daughters of the Prophet Muḥammad, he was named the "possessor of two lights" (*dhū al-nūrayn*).

The Prophet Muḥammad praised ʿUthmān for his modesty and said: "Should I not feel shy before a man [i.e. ʿUthmān] whom the

[67] See Bukhārī 1392 and 7207.

[68] Bukhārī 3130 and 3698; Tirmidhī 3706; Aḥmad 5772.

angels feel shy of?"[69] The Prophet Muḥammad also said: "The most merciful of my Community with my Community is Abū Bakr, the most firm upon the path of God is ʿUmar, the most sincere in modesty is ʿUthmān, the best judge is ʿAlī…"[70] ʿAbd Allāh b. ʿUmar said: "During the lifetime of the Prophet (may God bless him and grant him peace) we would not consider anyone equal to [i.e. the best were] Abū Bakr followed by ʿUmar followed by Uthmān."[71]

The Prophet Muḥammad appointed ʿUthmān in charge of Medina during the campaign of Dhāt al-Riqāʿ. And during Ḥudaybiya, ʿUthmān was sent to Mecca by the Prophet Muḥammad to let the Meccans know that the Muslims came in peace to perform ʿUmra and to negotiate with them. But during that occasion it was rumored that ʿUthmān was killed, so the Prophet Muḥammad asked the Companions with him to give a pledge under the tree. The Prophet Muḥammad himself pledged on behalf of ʿUthmān.

One of ʿUthmān's greatest acts during the lifetime of the Prophet was that he equipped the army of Tabuk, and so the Prophet Muḥammad (may God bless him and grant him peace) promised him Paradise.[72] The Prophet also said thereafter: "ʿUthmān will not be held accountable for anything after today."[73]

After the Prophet Muḥammad's death and during the caliphates of Abū Bakr and ʿUmar, ʿUthmān remained in Medina. He was part of the council that ʿUmar would consult during his caliphate. During the caliphate of ʿUthmān, the Islamic empire expanded to encompass much of North Africa, Cyprus, Azerbaijan and Armenia, the rest of Iran and much of Afghanistan.

---

69 Muslim 2401/6209; Aḥmad 514.

70 Ibn Māja 154; al-Ḥākim 6281. It is "authentic" according to Albānī (*Ṣaḥīḥ al-Jāmiʿ al-ṣaghīr* 868). See also Tirmidhī 3790; Aḥmad 12,904; Ibn Ḥibbān 7131; al-Ḥākim 5784; Bayhaqī (*Sunan*) 12,186—it is "authentic" according to Albānī (*Silsilat al-aḥādīth al-ṣaḥīḥa* 1224).

71 Bukhārī 3697; Abū Dāwūd 4627.

72 See Bukhārī 2778. The Prophet said something similar after ʿUthmān purchased and donated all of the water that came out of Rūmah's well. See Bukhārī 2778; Tirmidhī 3703; Nasāʾī 3608; Aḥmad 555.

73 Tirmidhī 3701; Aḥmad 20,630; al-Ḥākim 4553. It is "sound" according to Albānī (*Mishkāt* 6073).

As mentioned previously, a manuscript of the Qur'ān was collected during Abū Bakr's caliphate through his directive of Zayd b. Thābit. At the time of ʿUthmān's caliphate, this same manuscript was with Ḥafṣa. ʿUthmān again tasked Zayd b. Thābit (as well as others) to copy the manuscript and send copies to the various regions and provinces.[74] The greatness of ʿUthmān's action here should not be underestimated—had it not occurred during ʿUthmān's caliphate, it would have been extremely difficult to later accomplish it in consideration of the divisions and discord that occurred thereafter. Again, the Qur'ān remained preserved as promised by God (Exalted is He).[75]

The Prophet informed ʿUthmān of the calamity that would afflict him[76] and that he would be martyred (being killed unjustly).[77] But the Prophet affirmed that ʿUthmān and those who followed him would be upon the true guidance.[78] The Prophet Muḥammad spoke of this confidentially to ʿUthmān nearly twenty-four years prior to the event, and advised him how to act when he would be martyred. Therefore ʿUthmān refused to defend himself and instead said: "I will remain patient upon [that oath I took with the Prophet]."[79] ʿUthmān also refused to command others to kill those who sought to assassinate him, saying: "I will not be the first to shed the blood of the Community of the Messenger Muḥammad (may God bless him and grant him peace)."[80] This is another proof of the greatness of ʿUthmān (may God be pleased with him) and his care for this Community. It

---

74 See Bukhārī 4987; Tirmidhī 3104. The others who assisted Zayd b. Thābit included: ʿAbd Allāh b. al-Zubayr, Saʿīd b. al-ʿĀṣ and ʿAbd al-Raḥmān b. al-Ḥārith b. Hishām.

75 See Q.XV.9: *We have, without doubt, sent down the Message; and We will assuredly guard it (from corruption)* (Yusuf Ali translation).

76 See Bukhārī 3674; Muslim 2403/6212; Tirmidhī 3710; Aḥmad 19,509. Abū Musā al-Ashʿarī narrated that the Prophet Muḥammad gave Abū Bakr, ʿUmar b. al-Khaṭṭāb and ʿUthmān b. ʿAffān the glad tidings of entering Paradise, although ʿUthmān was also informed that a calamity (*balwā*) would befall him.

77 See Tirmidhī 3708; Aḥmad 5953. It is "sound" according to Albānī (see the discussion within *Silsilat al-aḥādīth al-ṣaḥīḥa* 3118).

78 See Ibn Māja 111; Aḥmad 18,129; al-Ḥākim 4552. It is "authentic" according to Albānī (*Silsilat al-aḥādīth al-ṣaḥīḥa* 3119).

79 Ibn Māja 113; Aḥmad 24,253 and 25,797; Ibn Ḥibbān 6918. It is "authentic" according to Albānī (*Mishkāt* 6079).

80 Aḥmad 481.

also represents another prophesy of the Messenger (may God bless him and grant him peace) that was fulfilled.

ᶜAlī b. Abī Ṭālib

ᶜAlī b. Abī Ṭālib was the first cousin of the Prophet Muḥammad. During ᶜAlī's childhood there was great dearth and hardship. Since his father Abū Ṭālib was poor, Muḥammad offered to take care of and bring up ᶜAlī, and he accepted. ᶜAlī became Muslim at the age of ten shortly after being invited to do so by the Prophet Muḥammad; thus ᶜAlī was the first child to accept Islam.

When the Quraysh finally decided to attempt to assassinate the Prophet Muḥammad, he (may God bless him and grant him peace) was permitted by God (Exalted is He) to emigrate to Medina. It was at that time that the Prophet Muḥammad asked ᶜAlī to remain at his home in his bed, so as to allow the Prophet and Abū Bakr to leave Mecca and emigrate undetected. ᶜAlī took up this heroic task and was ready to sacrifice himself. Upon realizing that it was ᶜAlī, and not the Prophet, in bed, the Quraysh interrogated him, but ultimately set him free. ᶜAlī (may God bless him) then emigrated alone to Medina on foot, and joined up with the other Companions.

ᶜAlī married Fāṭima, the Prophet's daughter, in the second year after the hijra, and they had al-Ḥasan and al-Ḥusayn in the third and fourth year AH, respectively. During the ninth year AH, the Prophet Muḥammad assembled his family members including his daughter Fāṭima, ᶜAlī and their young children in the context of an invocation (*mubāhala*) with the Christians of Najrān. In this regard, God (Exalted is He) commanded the Prophet Muḥammad to say: *Come! We will summon our sons and your sons, and our women and your women, and ourselves and yourselves, then we will pray humbly (to our Lord) and (solemnly) invoke the curse of God upon those who lie.*[81] That said, the Christians of Najrān did not show up.

ᶜAlī fought in all of the battles alongside the Prophet Muḥammad and other Companions except for Tabuk (due to a Prophetic directive). He was the flag bearer during the Battle of Khaybar, after the Prophet Muḥammad had said: "I will give the flag to a man who

---

81 Q.III.61.

loves God and His Messenger, and who is beloved by God and His Messenger."[82] Thus the Prophet Muḥammad affirmed that both he and God (Glorious is He) loved ʿAlī b. Abī Ṭālib.[83] Hence it is clearly established from all of the above that the believers must love Abū Bakr, ʿUmar, ʿUthmān, ʿAlī and the other Companions who were promised Paradise, as the Prophet loved them. Love of the Medinite supporters (and by extension the Meccan emigrants who preceded them in faith) is incumbent as the Prophet Muḥammad said: "A sign of faith is love of the Medinite supporters (*Anṣār*), while a sign of hypocrisy is hatred of the supporters."[84]

As for the Battle of Tabuk, the Prophet Muḥammad ordered ʿAlī to stay behind in Medina while he (may God bless him and grant him peace) marched along with Abū Bakr, ʿUmar, ʿUthmān and the other Companions to Tabuk. This will be discussed later in Chapter Eleven.

After the Prophet Muḥammad's death, ʿAlī remained in Medina and was part of the council that ʿUmar would consult (along with ʿUthmān) during his caliphate. He supported ʿUthmān during his caliphate. After ʿUthmān's martyrdom, ʿAlī became the obvious choice to become the leader of the Muslims, as mentioned above. As for the Shiite claim that ʿAlī should have been appointed the leader to follow the Prophet Muḥammad, this will be discussed in detail in Chapter Eleven along with other matters regarding Shiite doctrine, including the imamate.

The caliphate of ʿAlī though was beset by many divisions and discord occurring primarily due to the martyrdom of ʿUthmān. The internecine wars occurred between two groups of believers during the caliphate of ʿAlī: first, at the Battle of al-Jamal and the second at Ṣiffīn. These will be discussed in Chapter Twelve. After the Battle of Ṣiffīn, the Khārijīs seceded from ʿAlī's camp, and deemed him to be a disbeliever. ʿAlī did not fight them, though, until after they refused to hand over the individual(s) who killed the son of Khabbāb b. al-Aratt.[85] ʿAlī (may God be pleased with him) defeated the Khārijīs

---

82 Bukhārī 2942; Muslim 2404/6220; Tirmidhī 3724; Aḥmad 1608.

83 See also Bukhārī 4209; Muslim 2407/6224; Aḥmad 22,993.

84 Bukhārī 17; Muslim 74/235; Nasāʾī 5019; Aḥmad 12,316.

85 See Aḥmad 21,064; Bayhaqī (*Sunan*) 16,767.

as prophesized by the Messenger Muḥammad[86] in the Battle of Nahrawān.

It is an unfortunate fact that the spread of Islam halted during the caliphate of ᶜAlī due to the infighting, regardless of where the blame resides. ᶜAlī was later martyred, as per another prophesy,[87] by a Khārijī who had survived the Battle of Nahrawān. ᶜAlī's son al-Ḥasan assumed the caliphate after him but he subsequently stepped down from the caliphate in favour of Muᶜāwiya after six months. This is concordant with the prophesy of the Messenger Muḥammad who foretold that al-Ḥasan would become "a master [or leader] (*sayyid*), and that through him God would make reconciliation between two groups of Muslims".[88] Thus the Prophet Muḥammad praised al-Ḥasan and his action—he did not attribute any weakness or incapacity to al-Ḥasan. The Prophet Muḥammad also mentioned in that *ḥadīth* that the two groups were Muslims. Al-Ḥasan's action is concordant with verse nine of Sūrat al-Ḥujurāt wherein reconciliation and making peace between the believers is advised. Again, all of these events, which will be discussed later in detail, occurred as per Muḥammad's prophesies, and are further proofs of his truthfulness and verify his being a prophet.

In the end, following the Sunna of the Prophet Muḥammad and all of the Rightly-Guided Caliphs who followed him is necessary to remain upon the straight and true path. One should also love the Companions of the Prophet Muḥammad who enjoined good and forbade evil, and spread the religion of Islam. One should not harbour any rancour towards them but should instead recite the following verse of the Qur'ān: *And those who came (into the faith) after them say: Our Lord! Forgive us and our brethren who were before us in the faith, and place not in our hearts any rancour toward those who believe. Our Lord! Thou art Full of Pity, Merciful.*[89]

---

86 See Muslim 1064/2456; Aḥmad 11,018.

87 See Aḥmad 18,321; al-Ḥākim 4590; Bayhaqī (*Sunan*) 16,069. It is "sound" according to Albānī (*Silsilat al-aḥādīth al-ṣaḥīḥa* 1743).

88 See Bukhārī 3746; Tirmidhī 3773; Abū Dāwūd 4662; Nasā'ī 1410; Aḥmad 20,392.

89 Q.LIX.10.

Chapter Seven

Piety

God (Glorious and Exalted is He) has advised and encouraged the believers throughout the Qur'ān to have piety and fear Him. The Holy Lord states: *O ye who believe! Fear God as He should be feared, and die not except in a state of Islam.*[1] God (Exalted is He) has also encouraged us to be God-conscious and pious in the following verse: *Verily, the noblest of you in the sight of God is the one who is most deeply conscious of Him* (*atqā*^kum^).[2] An exposition of those who are pious, and how they differ with those above and below their rank, will now be given.

The Pious (muttaqūn) and the Devout (muḥsinūn)

An important set of verses that describe the pious and differentiate the devout from them is present in Sūrat Āl-ʿImrān:

> *And vie one with another for forgiveness from your Lord, and for a Paradise as wide as are the heavens and the earth, prepared for those who ward off (evil) (muttaqīn): those who spend (of that which God hath given them) in ease and in adversity; those who control their wrath and are forgiving toward humankind—God loveth the devout (muḥsinīn)*[3]*—and those who, when they do an evil thing (fāḥisha) or wrong themselves, remember God and implore forgiveness for their sins—Who forgiveth sins save God only?—and will not knowingly repeat (the wrong) they did. The reward of such will be forgiveness from their Lord, and Gardens underneath which rivers flow, wherein they will abide forever—a bountiful reward for workers!*[4]

---

1 Q.III.102 (Yusuf Ali translation).

2 Q.XLIX.13. See Q.II.278; Q.III.200; Q.V.35; Q.IX.119; Q.XXXIII.70; Q.XXXIX.10; and Q.LVII.28 for other verses where God (Glorious is He) encourages the believers to be pious.

3 Of note, Pickthall translated *al-muḥsinīn* as "the good".

4 Q.III.133–136.

Firstly, it will be contended here that the *fāḥisha*[5] mentioned in the above verses represent intermediate sins (defined as those sins in-between major sins (*kabā'ir*) and minor sins (*lamam*)) and that they are incurred by the pious (*muttaqūn*). The devout, on the other hand, do not perpetrate intermediate sins. The Holy Lord states: *To God belongs all that is in the heavens and on earth: so that He [recompenses] those who do evil, according to their deeds, and He rewards those who do good (aḥsanū) with what is best. Those who avoid great sins (kabā'ir) and shameful deeds (fawāḥish), only (falling into) small faults (lamam)—verily, thy Lord is ample in forgiveness.*[6]

The devout are a higher rank than the pious as the former fear God, avoid both major and intermediate sins, control their anger and have mercy on humankind. The pious likewise fear God and avoid major sins, but they may incur intermediate sins. That said, when the pious do perpetrate those intermediate sins, they regret those disobediences, repent to God and seek His forgiveness.

God (Exalted is He) also states: *Lo! he who wardeth off (evil) and endureth (findeth favour), for God loseth not the wages of the devout.*[7] Thus the devout go one step beyond the pious by being patient in obeying God's commandments. This is achieved by avoiding sins that the pious may incur; namely the intermediate evil sins (*fawāḥish*).

The devout also put their trust in and rely on the Almighty Lord to avoid sinfulness: *Now whatever ye have been given is but a passing comfort for the life of the world, and that which God hath is better and more lasting for those who believe and put their trust in their Lord, and those who shun the worst of sins (kabā'ir) and indecencies (fawāḥish) and, when they are wroth, forgive.*[8] Since the devout only commit minor sins, the devil has no control over them: *He [Satan] hath no power over those who believe and put their*

---

[5] This contention only regards the word *fāḥisha*; but when the definite article precedes it, i.e. *al-fāḥisha*, it specifically indicates a major sexual indecency, such as fornication, adultery or sodomy.

[6] Q.LIII.31–32 (adapted from the Yusuf Ali translation).

[7] Q.XII.90. Of note, here Pickthall translates *al-muḥsinīn* as "the kindly".

[8] Q.XLII.36–37. Of note, the end of Q.XLII.37 is similar to Q.III.134: *Those who control their wrath and are forgiving toward humankind; God loveth the good (muḥsinīn)*. Hence these verses most likely describe the devout, as well as the fact that they avoid both the major and intermediate sins.

trust in their Lord.[9] Taking the former verse into account substantiates that the latter verse refers to the devout.

The Prophet Muḥammad (may God bless him and grant him peace) defined the devout in the *ḥadīth* that also mentions submission (*islām*) and faith: "Devotion (*iḥsān*) is to worship God as if you can see Him. Although you cannot see Him [in this world], He sees you."[10] A person will only feel that the Holy Lord is watching over him if love for God permeates his heart. Avoidance of the intermediate, as well as the major, sins is therefore necessary to achieve that love. Moreover, although God (Exalted is He) loves both the pious and the devout, the Prophet Muḥammad mentioned *iḥsān*, which is the higher rank of the two, so as to encourage people to pursue that level. And God knows best.

The Prophet Muḥammad also said: "God has prescribed (*kataba*) skilled proficiency (*iḥsān*) in all things."[11] Therefore, *iḥsān* can be thought of as being a perfectionist, and it includes both religious and worldly matters. Perfection in religious affairs can be achieved if one first avoids intermediate as well as major sins.

To return to an exposition of the characteristics of the pious, God (Glorious is He) also describes them in the following manner: *the steadfast, and the truthful, and the obedient, those who spend (and hoard not), those who pray for pardon in the watches of the night.*[12] The pious seek forgiveness for their sins and supplicate to God, night and day, to protect them from Hellfire. They follow the commandments of the Holy Lord and His Messenger, remain steadfast upon them, and only speak the truth.

The pious also fear God when bequeathing their inheritance and follow God's commandments completely in that regard: *It is prescribed for you, when death approacheth one of you, if he leave wealth, that he bequeath unto parents and near relatives in kindness. (This is) a duty for all those who*

---

9 Q.XVI.99.

10 Bukhārī 50; Muslim 8/93; Tirmidhī 2610; Abū Dāwūd 4695; Ibn Māja 63; Nasā'ī 4990; Aḥmad 367.

11 Muslim 1955/5055; Tirmidhī 1409; Abū Dāwūd 2815; Ibn Māja 3170; Nasā'ī 4416; Aḥmad 17,113.

12 Q.III.17.

ward off (evil).[13] They do not favour some over others in a manner inconsistent with God's commandments.

Now, the term *muttaqūn* alludes to the fact that the pious avoid (*tark*) the major sins and regret their acquisition of intermediate ones. But there is another name for a pious individual that indicates the good actions which he or she carry out, and it is *birr* (plural *abrār*). The Exalted states: *The [pious] man (birr) is he who wardeth off (evil)*.[14] Thus *birr* refers to the pious individual or to the actions which the pious carry out, while *taqwā* refers to those actions which they avoid.

God (Glorious is He) also states that the

> *Pious (birr) is he who believeth in God and the Last Day and the angels and the Scripture and the prophets; and giveth wealth, for love of Him, to kinsfolk and to orphans and the needy and the wayfarer and to those who ask, and to set slaves free; and observeth the prayer and payeth zakat; and those who keep their treaty when they make one; and the patient in tribulation and adversity and time of stress. Such are they who are sincere. Such are the God-fearing*.[15]

God (Exalted is He) also states: *Help ye one another unto righteousness (birr) and pious duty (taqwā)*,[16] and *Ye will not attain unto piety until ye spend of that which ye love*.[17] The Holy Lord also states regarding the pious (*abrār*): *They perform (their) vows, and they fear a day whose evil flies far and wide. And they feed, for the love of God, the indigent, the orphan and the captive, (saying): We feed you for the sake of God alone: no reward do we desire from you, nor thanks. We only fear a day of distressful wrath from the side of our Lord*.[18]

Being just (*ʿadl*) is also a characteristic of the pious (*abrār*). The Holy Lord states: *O ye who believe! stand out firmly for God, as witnesses to fair dealing, and let not the hatred of others to you make you swerve to wrong and depart from justice. Be just: that is next to piety: and fear God. For God is well-acquainted with all that ye do*.[19] God (Exalted is He) commands an unwavering adherence to justice: *O ye who believe! Be ye staunch in*

---

[13] Q.II.180.

[14] Q.II.189. Pickthall translates *birr* as "righteous".

[15] Q.II.177.

[16] Q.V.2.

[17] Q.III.92.

[18] Q.LXXVI.7–10.

[19] Q.V.8 (Yusuf Ali translation).

justice, witnesses for God, even though it be against yourselves or (your) parents or (your) kindred.[20]

Next, the pious fulfill their pledges: (*The chosen of God is*) *he who fulfilleth his pledge and wardeth off (evil), for God loveth those who ward off (evil).*[21] Keeping one's pledge includes doing so during both war and peace: *Fulfil their treaty to them till their term. God loveth those who keep their duty (unto Him).*[22] *So long as they are true to you, be true to them. God loveth those who keep their duty (muttaqīn).*[23]

The Prophet Muḥammad (may God bless him and grant him peace) said: "The best amongst [my Community] are those with the best character,"[24] and "I was sent to promote righteous character."[25] Ibn al-Qayyim has listed many pious and righteous traits:

> Every characteristic that God has commended the servants with in the Qur'ān is due to knowledge and its consequences, while every one that He has criticized is a result of ignorance and its consequences. He commended them for their faith, which is the apex of knowledge and its core, and for their good deeds, which are the fruits of beneficial knowledge. He has commended them for: having gratitude and patience, hastening to do good deeds, loving Him and fearing Him, having hope and repenting to Him, forbearance, dignity, intelligence, reason, chastity, generosity, and preferring [God and His Messenger's commandments] over their desires, advising His servants and showing mercy, kindness and humility to them, forgiving those who harm them and pardoning the perpetrators, expending benevolence to all of them, doing good after making a mistake, enjoining good and forbidding evil, being patient in those circumstances that require patience, being content with their destiny, being gentle with the loyal supporters and showing strength against their enemies, being true to their promises, fulfilling their oaths, avoiding the ignorant ones, and accepting advice from those giving it. [God also commended them] for certainty, reliance [on Him], tranquility, calmness, perseverance, empathy; being just in statements, actions and characteristics; strength

---

20 Q.IV.135.

21 Q.III.76.

22 Q.IX.4.

23 Q.IX.7.

24 Bukhārī 6035; Tirmidhī 1975; Aḥmad 6504.

25 Aḥmad 8952; al-Ḥākim 4221; Bayhaqī (*Sunan*) 20,783. It is "sound" according to Albānī (*Silsilat al-aḥādīth al-ṣaḥīḥa* 45).

> in carrying out His commandments, enlightenment in His religion, carrying out and accomplishing His rights, removing those who bar His cause, calling [others] to Him and His pleasure and to His Paradise, warning others of the inroads of those who are astray, elucidating the paths of seduction and the state of those who follow [to prevent others from falling into it], exhorting others to the truth and to patience, urging others to feed the poor, having reverence for their parents, bonding with their relatives, expending salutations to all the believers, in addition to all the other praiseworthy characteristics and pleasing actions that God (Glory be to Him) has bore witness to.[26]

The sooner one works and adopts these pious and righteous characteristics the better, as one can then attain an ever-increasing rank with the Holy Lord. If one waits until one's forties or later, one will be more limited in attaining many of those praiseworthy characteristics. Moreover, they will have perpetrated in the interim many sins, whether intermediate or major, which will form barriers that prevent them from attaining higher levels. Therefore, one should become religious, follow the Holy Lord's commandments, and do good from one's youth. Finally, those who worshipped the Holy Lord from their youth will be one of seven types of people who will be shaded under the Throne of God on the Day of Judgment.[27]

The Holy Lord will reward the pious in this world and the Hereafter: *The earth is God's. He giveth it for an inheritance to whom He will. And the sequel is for those who keep their duty (unto Him) (muttaqīn).*[28] *Have patience! The sequel is for those who ward off (evil).*[29]

The Righteous (Ṣāliḥūn) and the Truly Faithful (Ṣiddīqūn)

Now, the rank above the pious and the devout is that of the righteous (*ṣāliḥūn*). They possess the traits of the pious and they go further in that they *enjoin right conduct and forbid indecency, and vie one with another in*

---

[26] See Zeni (tr.), *Ibn Qayyim al-Jawziyya on Knowledge*, pp. 148–149.

[27] See Bukhārī 660; Muslim 1031/2380; Tirmidhī 2391; Nasā'ī 5380; Aḥmad 9665. See also Ibn Ḥajar al-ʿAsqalānī, *Fatḥ al-Bārī sharḥ Ṣaḥīḥ al-Bukhārī*, ed. Muḥibb al-Dīn al-Khaṭīb (Beirut: Dār al-Maʿrifa, 1960), vol. II, p. 144.

[28] Q.VII.128.

[29] Q.XI.49.

good works. These are of the righteous.[30] Therefore, they enjoin others to righteousness and forbid evil. A righteous person works to right the wrong and change things for the better (*aṣlaḥa*): *Whosoever refraineth from evil and amendeth—there shall no fear come upon them neither shall they grieve.*[31]

In addition, the Holy Lord states: *Before this We wrote in the Psalms, after the message [given to Moses]: "My servants, the righteous, shall inherit the earth."*[32] When this verse is juxtaposed to: *Those who, if We establish them in the land, establish regular prayer and give zakat, enjoin the right and forbid wrong,*[33] it proves that the latter verse is referring to the righteous who forbid evil.

The Holy Lord also states: *And as for those who believe and do good works, We verily shall make them enter in among the righteous.*[34] Thus it is contended that every instance in the Qur'ān which states the phrase *believe and do good works* (*āmanū wa ʿamilū al-ṣāliḥāt*) is a reference to the righteous (*ṣāliḥūn*).[35] The Sublime states: *It is not your wealth nor your sons, that will bring you nearer to Us in degree: but only those who believe and work righteousness—these are the ones for whom there is a multiplied reward for their deeds, while secure they (reside) in the dwellings on high!*[36] God (Exalted is He) commends the righteous by stating: *Those who have faith and do*

---

30 Q.III.114.

31 Q.VII.35.

32 Q.XXI.105 (Yusuf Ali translation). See Psalms 33.12: "Blessed is the nation whose God is the LORD: and the people whom he hath chosen for his own inheritance"; and Psalms 34.17–19: "The righteous cry, and the LORD heareth, and delivereth them out of all their troubles. The LORD is nigh unto them that are of a broken heart; and saveth such as be of a contrite spirit. Many are the afflictions of the righteous: but the LORD delivereth him out of them all"; and Psalms 37.9–11: "For evildoers shall be cut off: but those that wait upon the LORD, they shall inherit the earth. For yet a little while, and the wicked shall not be: yea, thou shalt diligently consider his place, and it shall not be. But the meek shall inherit the earth; and shall delight themselves in the abundance of peace"; and Psalms 37.28–29: "For the LORD loveth judgment, and forsaketh not his saints; they are preserved for ever: but the seed of the wicked shall be cut off. The righteous shall inherit the land, and dwell therein for ever."

33 Q.XXII.41.

34 Q.XXIX.9.

35 Also compare the previously mentioned verses Q.XXI.105 and Q.XXIV.55.

36 Q.XXXIV.37 (Yusuf Ali translation).

righteous deeds, they are the best of creatures.[37] Therefore, the religion of Islam advises and obliges us to enjoin good and forbid evil, and to improve upon the status quo. It does not encourage humankind to acquiesce to sorrow or dearth. Righteousness represents the opposite of quietism or passivity.

One of the righteous subtypes are the scholars of the Lord who have attained much religious knowledge and have then instructed and taught it to others.[38] The Exalted said: *Be ye faithful [scholars] of the Lord (rabbāniyyīn) by virtue of your constant teaching of the Book and of your constant study thereof.*[39] A righteous individual reforms in order to achieve goodness, and therefore he must correct the errors of others (*aṣlaḥa*). This is portrayed in many verses of the Qur'ān. For instance, the Prophet Shuᶜayb (may God bless him) stated: *I wish not, in opposition to you, to do that which I forbid you to do. I only desire (your) betterment (iṣlāḥ) to the best of my power; and my success (in my task) can only come from God. In Him I trust, and unto Him I look.*[40] Likewise, God (Exalted is He) states: *And when We did appoint for Moses thirty nights (of solitude), and added to them ten, and he completed the whole time appointed by his Lord of forty nights; and Moses said unto his brother: Aaron, take my place among the people. Do right (aṣliḥ), and follow not the way of mischief-makers.*[41] Therefore, Aaron (may God bless him) was bid to enjoin the Israelites to do good and forbid them from evil[42] while Moses was away preparing to speak to the Holy Lord (Glorious is He) and receive the Tablets.

Many of the verses of the Qur'ān allude to those who repent and then do good (*tāb wa aṣlaḥa*). Repentance is the first step an individual takes in returning to the Holy Lord. It not only indicates that he will avoid evil, but it also implies that he will by necessity make amends and do good himself. Some may limit the meaning of *aṣlaḥa* to

---

37 Q.XCVIII.7 (Yusuf Ali translation).

38 See Zeni (tr.), *Ibn Qayyim al-Jawziyya on Knowledge*, pp. 171–172.

39 Q.III.79.

40 Q.XI.88.

41 Q.VII.142.

42 Ṭabarī narrates that Aaron was charged to "assist the [Israelites] in obeying God and worshipping Him" and "prevent them from worshipping [the golden] calf", i.e. enjoining them to do good and forbidding them from doing evil. See *Ṭafsīr al-Ṭabarī*, vol. XIII, p. 88.

making amends[43] or doing right for only one's own benefit. Instead this book will contend that *aṣlaḥa* refers to that individual reforming and correcting the actions of society around him (as well as those carried out by himself). The word *aṣlaḥa* therefore adds an additional meaning in that the individual works to better others and rid them of their evil acts and words.

It should be mentioned here that it can now be recognized that those who are worshippers or ascetics, but do not strive against evil in their society, may be considered at best to be pious or devout, and that their rank is below that of the righteous. It is precisely righteous deeds, including forbidding and striving against evil, which permit one to be elevated to a higher rank than those who may be devout and/or display an ascetic character (*zuhd* or *wara*ʿ).

Some devout believers will seek to avoid uncertain (or even permissible matters) if they feel that these may possibly lead to intermediate sins. This is a praiseworthy form of asceticism if the intent is to avoid the possibility of sinfulness, and it is termed *wara*ʿ. The Prophet Muḥammad (may God bless him and grant him peace) said: "The highest religious [trait] (*khayr dīn*^{ikum}) is devout asceticism (*wara*ʿ)."[44] The meaning of this—and God knows best—is that devout asceticism (*wara*ʿ) is higher than piety (*taqwā*) and devotion (*iḥsān*), not that it is better than prayer and other actions that the Prophet has praised in other *ḥadīth*s.

The objective of this book is to emphasize the importance of avoiding all major sins and minimizing intermediate sins (and deeply regretting those latter that one does perpetrate) so as block oneself from the possibility of perpetrating a major sin. In that fashion a society can achieve piety and then work towards righteousness if enough members resolve to undertake this path. Instead of avoiding what is good or adhering to poverty, one should strive against evil and be willing to sacrifice whatever is necessary for God's sake. It is better to be righteous than a devout ascetic. Indeed, if one ponders upon the Qur'ān one will find that the pious and righteous are emphasized,

---

43 See verses Q.III.89, Q.V.39, Q.VI.54 and Q.XXIV.5.

44 Al-Ḥākim 317; Bayhaqī (*Shuʿab*) 1578. It is "authentic" according to Albānī (*Saḥīḥ al-Jāmiʿ al-ṣaghīr* 1727 and 3308).

whereas the devout are mentioned rarely, and the devout ascetics not at all. Had devout asceticism (*wara*ʿ) been emphasized in the Qur'ān, the number of righteous and higher ranks may have even been less. Since the righteous are those who best strive against evil, a further decrease in their number would have allowed evils to be perpetrated unopposed to a greater degree within society. And God knows best.

Regarding other characteristics of the righteous, it appears that being just in an exemplary fashion (*qisṭ*) is one of their characteristics, as the Holy Lord states: *Make peace* (*aṣliḥū*) *between them justly, and act equitably. God loveth the equitable.*[45] The exemplary nature of the justice carried out by the righteous is a higher level than that carried out by the pious, as the former entails giving more than that which is fairly due. The Prophet Muḥammad (may God bless him and grant him peace) stated: "The dispensers of exemplary justice (*muqsiṭīn*) will be seated on pulpits of light in proximity to God."[46]

One should always remain virtuous and adopt the high moral ground even when one confronts the most wicked types of people. God (Glorious is He) commanded Moses and Aaron (may God bless them both): *And speak unto* [*Pharaoh*] *a gentle word, that peradventure he may heed or fear,*[47] although Pharaoh had claimed that he was a deity and had *transgressed all bounds.*[48] Even in such circumstances, one must be just and equitable—not one who recompenses an evil with another.

Now, the Prophet Muḥammad (may God bless him and grant him peace) said: "This knowledge [inherited from the Prophet] will be conveyed by the successors [of this Community] who are upright and trustworthy (*ʿudūl*). They will repudiate the distortions of the extremists (*taḥrīf al-ghālīn*), those who attempt to break-up [the religion] by negating [its precepts] (*intiḥāl al-mubṭilīn*), and the misinterpretations of those who are ignorant (*ta'wīl al-jāhilīn*)."[49] Whilst commenting on these characteristics, Ibn al-Qayyim states that "some may make a mistake regarding this term 'upright and

---

45 Q.XLIX.9.

46 Muslim 1827/4721; Nasā'ī 5381.

47 Q.XX.44.

48 See Q.XX.43.

49 Bayhaqī (*Sunan*) 20,911; Ibn Kathīr, *al-Bidāya wa'l-nihāya*, vol. X, p. 337. It is "authentic" according to Albānī (*Mishkāt* 248).

trustworthy' by assuming that this uprightness alludes only to those who have no sins; but that is not the case. Instead, it refers to those who can be entrusted with this religion, even if they do some things which they must repent to God for. These [sins] do not negate them being upright and trustworthy, just like their presence does not negate one being a believer or being supported [by Him]."[50] It will be contended that the righteous will incur evil sins (*sayyi'āt*), which include intermediate and minor sins based on the verse: *Save him who repenteth and believeth and doth righteous work; as for such, God will change their evil deeds (sayyi'āt) to good deeds. God is ever Forgiving, Merciful.*[51] Thus the righteous believers are not exempt from incurring intermediate sins. Therefore, the avoidance of the righteous is like that of the pious: both groups avoid major sins but may incur intermediate and minor sins.

As to the aforementioned *ḥadīth*, it illustrates that the upright and righteous scholars must work to repudiate falsehood. In fact, this may be one of their most important characteristics. Ibn al-Qayyim states in his book *Madārij al-sālikīn*: "Whoever worships God by striving against His enemy has attained a great share of [the characteristic of] being truly faithful. The greater the servant's love and loyal support for his Lord, as well as his enmity towards His enemy, the greater his participation in striving... This form of servitude [to God] is only realized by a few. Whoever has tasted its sweetness will lament the time he spent beforehand [in heedlessness of it]."[52] Striving against the disbelievers is a characteristic of both the righteous and the truly faithful.

The Prophet Muḥammad said: "A person will continue to be truthful (*yaṣduq*) until he becomes one who is truly faithful."[53] It

---

[50] See Zeni (tr.), *Ibn Qayyim al-Jawziyya on Knowledge*, p. 238. Ibn Taymiyya also states that it is not incumbent that the saints be perfect or not make mistakes. It is instead possible that some religious knowledge is hidden from them or that some matters appear to them other than they are. See Ibn Taymiyya, *al-Furqān bayn awliyā' al-Raḥmān wa awliyā' al-Shayṭān*, ed. ʿAbd al-Qādir Arna'ūṭ (Damascus: Maktabat Dār al-Bayān, 1985), pp. 62–65.

[51] Q.XXV.70. See also Q.XXIX.7.

[52] Ibn al-Qayyim, *Madārij al-sālikīn bayn manāzil iyyāka naʿbudu wa-iyyāka nastaʿīn* (Beirut: Dār al-Kitāb al-ʿArabī, 1996), vol. I, p. 241.

[53] Bukhārī 6094; Muslim 2607/6638; Tirmidhī 1971; Aḥmad 3638.

will be contended that this truthfulness encompasses all of one's intentions and actions—not just one's speech. Ibn al-Qayyim relayed that Ibn Taymiyya opined that the truly faithful individual is one whose "entire heart and spirit as well as his outward have completely submitted and followed the Messenger" and therefore he is not in need of "inspiration (*taḥdīth* or *ilhām*) or mystical unveiling (*kashf*)".[54] Therefore, a truly faithful believer's speech and actions are all good—they mirror and faithfully represent his heart and spirit. His apparent self is the same as his hidden self. Although the truly faithful individual has followed the Qur'ān and Sunna completely, he is in need of wisdom to reconcile between all of the proofs and evidences encompassed within the revelation. God, the Most Wise, states: *He giveth wisdom unto whom He will, and he unto whom wisdom is given, he truly hath received abundant good.*[55]

Although no one can reach the faith of Abū Bakr al-Ṣiddīq, Ibn al-Qayyim maintained that some scholars can attain the level of the truly faithful.[56] In similar fashion, this book will maintain that many of the Companions and those following them were truly faithful. Consider that the Prophet Muḥammad (may God bless him and grant him peace) said: "Many men have attained perfection, whereas only Mary the daughter of ʿImrān [i.e. the mother of Jesus] and Āsiya, the wife of Pharaoh, did so."[57] Since God (Exalted is He) mentions that Mary, the mother of Jesus, was a truly faithful woman (*ṣiddīqa*) in verse 75 of Sūrat Āl-ʿImrān, it follows then that those who have attained perfection are those who are truly faithful (in addition to the prophets). Thus, although Abū Bakr's rank is higher than that of one who is inspired such as ʿUmar b. al-Khaṭṭāb, both ranks are within true faith.

---

[54] Ibn al-Qayyim, *Madārij al-sālikīn*, vol. I, p. 64. Ibn Taymiyya argues that the *ṣiddīq* absolutely and completely follows everything from the Prophet while the *muḥaddath* takes some things from his heart. See Ibn Taymiyya, *al-Radd ʿalā al-manṭiqiyyīn* (Beirut: Dār al-Maʿrifa, 2010), p. 514.

[55] Q.II.269.

[56] Ibn al-Qayyim states: "Thus if the scholar's writings reach the level of true faith then his ink becomes better than the blood of a martyr, as long as the latter is not considered to be one of the truly faithful." See Zeni (tr.), *Ibn Qayyim al-Jawziyya on Knowledge*, p. 78.

[57] Bukhārī 3433; Muslim 2431/6272; Tirmidhī 1834; Ibn Māja 3280; Aḥmad 19,668.

Ghazālī mentions that the rank of the truly faithful is occupied by those "whose existence [in this world is devoted] to their Lord, not to themselves",[58] and that they "love what the Lord uses [them] for".[59] Ibn al-Qayyim also stated: "Whoever pursues knowledge so that he may revive Islam is one of the truly faithful."[60]

Reviving Islam occurs, in part, by fully repudiating "the extremists", "those who attempt to break-up [the religion] by negating [its precepts]" and "those who are ignorant". But in order to do so one's heart must be completely pure, thus allowing it to recognize all types of evil. The truly faithful are better able to recognize evil than the righteous.

Therefore, it will be contended that the avoidance of the truly faithful reaches the level of devotion (*iḥsān*), i.e. avoidance of all sins except minor ones (*lamam*). In this fashion, their hearts recognize all that is evil or sinful, and they are then able to repudiate it fully or strive against it. Repudiating evil, fighting and striving against it, and forbidding it, as well as being devout, are all characteristics of the truly faithful. Moreover, since the hearts of the truly faithful are the purest, they are able to love the Holy Lord the most. And God knows best.

Love of the Holy Lord and Obedience to His commandments

Loving the Holy and Almighty Lord (Glorious is He) is part of Judaism, Christianity and Islam. Consider the following verses of the Old Testament: "And now, Israel, what doth the Lord thy God require of thee, but to fear the Lord thy God, to walk in all his ways, and to love him, and to serve the Lord thy God with all thy heart and with all thy soul, to keep the commandments of the Lord, and his statutes, which I command thee this day for thy good?"[61] "And thou shalt love

---

58 Ghazālī, *Iḥyā' ʿulūm al-dīn* (Beirut: Dār Ṣāder, 2010), vol. IV, p. 389.

59 Ibid., vol. IV, p. 69.

60 See Zeni (tr.), *Ibn Qayyim al-Jawziyya on Knowledge*, p. 161. It should be mentioned that Ibn al-Qayyim based this thought on a "weak" *ḥadīth*: "Whoever dies while pursuing knowledge so as to revive Islam will only be separated from the prophets due to the latter's status of prophethood." Ibn ʿAbd al-Barr 219; al-Muttaqī al-Hindī 28,829; Dārimī 336. It is again "weak" according to Albānī (*Mishkāt* 249).

61 Deuteronomy 10.12–13.

the Lord thy God with all thine heart, and with all thy soul, and with all thy might."[62] Also consider verses of the Synoptic Gospels where Jesus (may God bless him) affirmed that all love should be for the Holy Lord and God.[63] In the Gospel of Mark it affirms: "Jesus answered [one of the scribes], The first of all commandments, Hear, O Israel; The Lord our God is one Lord: And thou shalt love the Lord thy God with all thy heart, and with all thy soul, and with all thy strength: this is the first commandment. And the second is like, *namely* this, Thou shalt love thy neighbor as thyself. There is none other commandment greater than these."[64] In the Gospel of Matthew, Jesus states: "On these two commandments hang all the law and the prophets."[65]

In the traditions, a man came to the Prophet Muḥammad (may God bless him and grant him peace) asking the timing of the Hour and the Day of Judgment, whereupon the Prophet replied: "What have you prepared for it?" The man replied: "Love of God and His Messenger." The Prophet replied: "You are with those you love." The Companion Anas b. Mālik, who narrated this *ḥadīth*, states: "After the advent of Islam, we were never happier with anything more than this statement of the Prophet (may God bless him and grant him peace). I love God, His Messenger, Abū Bakr and ʿUmar, and I hope that I will be with them, even though I have not done the deeds they have."[66] In the Qur'ān, the Holy Lord states: *Say (O Muḥammad, to humankind): If ye love God, follow me; God will love you and forgive you your sins. God is Forgiving, Merciful.*[67] True love for the Holy Lord can only be possessed and displayed by those who follow His commandments and prohibitions and fulfill His covenant.

---

62 Deuteronomy 6.5.

63 See Luke 10.27–28.

64 Mark 12.29–31. See also Matthew 22.37–40.

65 Matthew 22.40.

66 Bukhārī 3688; Muslim 2639/6713; Tirmidhī 2385; Aḥmad 12,715.

67 Q.III.31.

Furthermore, Ibn al-Qayyim states:

> Since true love is only achieved when one prefers the Beloved more than anything else, it is only through enduring great difficulties in His path and seeking His contentment that this love is achieved and known to be truly established within their hearts...On the other hand, a love that is contingent upon well being, blessings, pleasure, and attaining one's desires from the beloved is not a true love, and it will not hold up in the face of difficulties and obstacles...Thus, there is an immense difference between one who worships God in times of joy, ease, and well-being only, and one who worships Him in times of joy and hardship, ease and difficulty, well-being and tribulation.[68]

True love for the Holy Lord can only be displayed in a world in which suffering and evil exist.

Now the Prophet Muḥammad (may God bless him and grant him peace) has said: "If an individual possesses these three [characteristics] then he has experienced (*wajada*) the sweetness of faith: [1] he finds nothing more beloved to him than God and His Messenger; [2] he only loves another person for the sake of God; and [3] he hates to return back to disbelief—after God has saved him from that—just as he would hate to be thrown in Hellfire."[69] Thus having love for God (Most Blessed and Exalted is He), His Messenger Muḥammad (may God bless him and grant him peace) and one's fellow believers—for the sake of God alone—is necessary to truly experience the pleasure contained within this faith of Islam.

The love of a believer for the Holy Lord may continue to increase until it permeates his or her entire heart. Perfect love of God and knowing His Names and Attributes are specifically intended. Perfect worship occurs as a result of perfect love and humility to the Holy Lord. God is the True Beloved and He is deserving of devoted worship and servitude. If one truly understands this world and the Hereafter,

---

68 See Zeni (tr.), *Ibn Qayyim al-Jawziyya on Divine Wisdom and the Problem of Evil*, pp. 9–10.

69 Bukhārī 21; Muslim 43/165; Tirmidhī 2624; Ibn Māja 4032; Nasā'ī 4988; Aḥmad 12,002. See Ibn al-Qayyim, *Madārij al-sālikīn*, vol. II, p. 67, for a discussion thereof. The Prophet also said: "One who is content with God as his Lord, Islam as his religion, and Muḥammad as his Prophet has tasted (*dhāq*) the sweetness of faith." Muslim 34/151; Tirmidhī 2623; Aḥmad 1778.

as well as the glory and praiseworthiness of the Holy Lord, one will only desire the pleasure and contentment of God (Glorious is He). Even if one encounters hardship in this world, one feels delight and pleasure in one's heart due to the hope that the Lord will be pleased with one's sincere servitude to Him and striving against evil. One must ultimately love God for His Essence, Beautiful Names and Glorious Attributes—not for any worldly benefits that may be bestowed by Him due to following His commandments and doing good deeds.

Loving the Holy Lord is not reduced by loving one's wife, children, or others. Instead, since humankind cannot essentially or independently attain any trait, one is in need of loving and being beloved by others in order to then achieve, extrapolate and experience higher levels of love for God (Glorious is He). One must completely submit one's religious will to God's religious will and one's love to God's love—this represents a pure expression of one's love for the Holy Lord. Indeed, the life of the Prophet Muḥammad (may God bless him and grant him peace) substantiates and exemplifies this principle.

If one truly loves the Holy Lord one will search out and pursue the religion and what is pleasing to Him. Those who have contemplated upon all of the various religious beliefs, and then become or remain Muslim possess much higher levels of faith, love and sincerity to the Holy Lord. But this can only occur in a world wherein the Almighty Lord is immanent. Divine hiddenness thus allows the elucidation of those who truly love Him.

True love for God is only proven if one continues to do good despite the rejection and opposition of others, or the loss of that which one possesses. God (Exalted is He) states: *Behold, God has bought from the believers their lives and their possessions, promising them Paradise in return...Rejoice then in the bargain which you have made with Him: for this, this is the triumph supreme.*[70] These believers are willing to sacrifice whatever they possess, whether extrinsic or intrinsic, for the sake of God (Glorious is He). Some will have to sacrifice everything and some little; some will do so out of their free choice and upon some it will be forced. Regardless, this represents a great sacrifice because they have

70 Q.IX.111.

turned away from this world and sought only His pleasure. Is there any greater love than this?

In conclusion, the loyal supporters of God or His saints (*awliyā'*) include the pious and those of higher ranks. The Holy Lord states: *Behold! Verily on the saints (awliyā') of God there is no fear, nor shall they grieve; those who believe and (constantly) guard against evil (yattaqūn).*[71] So long as there remain pious and righteous individuals on this earth, then by definition the loyal supporters and saints of the Holy Lord will remain. God (Exalted is He) also states: *Friends on that day will be foes one to another, save those who kept their duty [to God] (muttaqīn), O My servants! For you there is no fear this day, nor is it ye who grieve.*[72] The pious are His true servants, and they follow His guidance, as He (Exalted is He) states: *This is the Book; in it is guidance sure, without doubt, to those who fear God... They are on (true) guidance, from their Lord, and it is these who will prosper.*[73] Such people have fulfilled His covenant in a manner that He loves.

The Believers (mu'minūn) and Believing Muslims (muslimūn)

In regards to the ranks below those of the pious, there are two: the believers (*mu'minūn*) and the believing Muslims (*muslimūn*). The believers carry out the pillars of Islam: testifying that God alone (Glorious and Exalted is He) should be worshipped and that Muḥammad is His Prophet and Messenger, performing the five obligatory prayers, giving zakat, fasting during the month of Ramaḍān, and performing the pilgrimage—this was outlined in the *ḥadīth* mentioned earlier. The goodness and benefit of these pillars are self-evident. They have been discussed in Islamic literature at length and will not be recounted here. Needless to say, in addition to promoting goodness and piety, these pillars reduce suffering, decrease evil, and prevent or delay a society's devolvement into sinfulness and disorder.

Nonetheless, these obligatory pillars should be exceeded so that one may attain a higher rank than solely being considered a general

---

71 Q.X.62–63. Of note, Pickthall translates *awliyā'* as "friends".

72 See Q.XLIII.67–68.

73 Q.II.2–5 (Yusuf Ali translation). See also Q.II.38: *Verily, there cometh unto you from Me a guidance; and whoso followeth My guidance, there shall no fear come upon them neither shall they grieve.*

believing Muslim. The purpose of this worldly life is to worship the Holy Lord and to perform good deeds which will bring one closer to Him. The Messenger of God (may God bless him and grant him peace) said: "The nearest a servant comes to his Lord is when he is prostration; so supplicate more often therein."[74] One's rank in Paradise becomes higher and more proximate to God (Exalted is He) predicated on the prayers and pious deeds that one has performed in this life. Prayer also decreases the chance that one will perpetrate intermediate or major sins: *Recite that which hath been inspired in thee of the Scripture, and establish prayer. Verily, prayer preserveth from lewdness (faḥshā') and iniquity (munkar).*[75] Furthermore, recitation of the Qur'ān within prayers or outside of them allows humans to repeat the Words of God (Exalted is He), whereby the immeasurable spiritual benefit of so doing can be experienced.

In addition, the pursuit of religious knowledge, which includes learning the Qur'ān and Sunna, the performance of supererogatory prayers and fasting, giving charity, and performing ʿUmra[76] enable one to attain greater reward and preserve one from many evil sins by the grace of God. Other good deeds that the believers and believing Muslims may perform were discussed previously.

The believers avoid many of the major sins for the Holy Lord states: *O ye who believe! Observe your duty to God, and give up what remaineth (due to you) from usury, if ye are (in truth) believers.*[77] Therefore, those who are believers do not engage in the major sin of usury or interest (*ribā*). The Prophet Muḥammad (may God bless him and grant him peace) likewise said: "An adulterer is not a believer (*mu'min*) after he commits adultery. A thief is not a believer after he steals. The drinker of alcohol is not a believer after he drinks."[78] Hence anyone who engages in

---

74 Muslim 482/1083; Abū Dāwūd 875; Nasā'ī 1137; Aḥmad 9461.

75 Q.XXIX.45. It has already been discussed that *faḥshā'* are intermediate sins, and it will be argued in Chapter Eleven that both *munkar* and *kabā'ir* refer to major sins.

76 The Prophet Muḥammad (may God bless him and grant him peace) said: "ʿUmra expiates sins committed between it and the previous one. And the reward of a Ḥajj accepted [by God] (*mabrūr*) is Paradise." Bukhārī 1773; Muslim 1349/3289; Ibn Māja 2888; Nasā'ī 2629; Aḥmad 15,701.

77 Q.II.278.

78 Bukhārī 2475; Muslim 57/208; Abū Dāwūd 4689; Ibn Māja 3936; Nasā'ī 4871; Aḥmad 8895.

these most wicked major sins is not a believer—that individual is only considered to be a believing Muslim (assuming he or she performs the pillars of Islam). This will be discussed further in Chapter Eleven. The main objective of this chapter is again to highlight the characteristics and deeds of the pious and higher ranks.

In conclusion, one should accumulate all the good, pious and righteous deeds possible for there is no return after death. The Prophet Muḥammad (may God bless him and grant him peace) said: "When a person dies his deeds cease except in three cases: continuous charity, knowledge that is benefitted from, and a benevolent child who supplicates [to God] for him."[79] There is no second chance—no rebirth back into this world—there is only the Hereafter: Hellfire or Paradise. The worth of humankind is not intrinsic but is predicated on their proximity to the Holy Lord, the Ever-Living and Self-Subsisting, and on His acceptance of their good deeds.

---

79 Muslim 1631/4223; Abū Dāwūd 2880; Ibn Māja 241; Aḥmad 8844.

PART TWO

Chapter Eight

Muslim Approaches to the Problems of Evil and Hellfire

The Muslim theologians dedicated much effort in putting forward many theodicies. The most elaborate and detailed theodicy is that of Ibn Qayyim al-Jawziyya, and it has been translated in *Ibn Qayyim al-Jawziyya on Divine Wisdom and the Problem of Evil*. This theodicy can be classified as "traditional" as it is concordant with the Qur'ān, the Sunna and the knowledge transmitted by the Predecessors (*salaf*). Some elements of this theodicy will be discussed first due to its breadth and coherence, and because it sets a foundation on which to consider other less detailed Muslim theodicies.

The traditional theodicy of Ibn Qayyim al-Jawziyya

Ibn al-Qayyim does not treat the lapse of Adam and Eve as a catastrophe or something that could have been avoided, but instead argues that there are many wise purposes associated with humankind being sent down from Paradise to this earth. These wise purposes include manifesting God's Beautiful Names and favouring the prophets, truly faithful, martyrs and righteous from amongst all of humanity. The sincere faith of the believers can also be elucidated since they may worship the Holy Lord by their free choice, truly love Him, and carry out His commandments in a wide variety of manners for His sake. The believers will then be returned to Paradise in a more perfect state—having performed the necessary good deeds and crossed the bridge of trials and tribulations—and be rewarded accordingly. By experiencing the hardships of this world first, they will appreciate the eternal bliss of Paradise to a far greater degree.[1]

Ibn al-Qayyim maintains that one of the greatest reasons for the Almighty Lord creating both good and evil in this world is to manifest the effects of His Names, Attributes and actions in a manner concordant

---

[1] See Zeni (tr.), *Ibn Qayyim al-Jawziyya on Divine Wisdom and the Problem of Evil*, pp. 3–18.

to His wisdom: "If the effects of His Names and Attributes cannot become manifest, except by [creating] opposing [entities], then His wisdom deems it to be inevitable that He bring them into existence. Had they not been created, then His Attributes would not have become manifested, and this is implausible."[2] At the same time, Ibn al-Qayyim rejects any attribution of evilness to the Holy Lord, whether in regards to His Names, Attributes or actions. He thus affirms God's holiness, omniscience, omnipotence, praiseworthiness, beneficence and justice.

His theodicy then differentiates between God's acts (*afʿāli*[hi]) and what He enacts (*mafʿūlāti*[hi]) or ontologically wills: "God's actions themselves (Glory be to Him) are not divided [into beloved or not], since all of His actions are beloved and pleasing to Him. Therefore, one must differentiate between His actions and what He enacts. His actions are all pure good, just, advantageous and wise—there is no evil within them from any aspect whatsoever. As for what He enacts it is subject to division [into good or not].'[3]

The innate disposition (*fiṭra*)[4] of humankind is also explained by Ibn al-Qayyim as being good and pure, in keeping with the *ḥadīth* of the Prophet Muḥammad (may God bless him and grant him peace): "Every infant is born with a sound innate disposition (*fiṭra*)."[5] The Holy Lord also states within a *ḥadīth qudsī*: "I have created all of My servants on the true belief (*ḥunafā'*), but the devils came upon them and preoccupied them away from My religion, and commanded them—without authority—to worship others along with Me."[6] The perpetration of evil by humankind therefore first occurred due to Satan whispering to Adam and Eve, and continues to occur due to promptings of Satan as well as other devils. In addition, the human ego or lower self (*nafs*) also incites one to perpetrate evil.[7] In this fashion there exists the extrinsic instigation of the devils to evil as well as intrinsic motivators, i.e. the innate disposition to good and the lower self's inclination to evil.

---

[2] Ibid., p. 103.

[3] Ibid., pp. 204–207.

[4] See Bukhārī 1358; Muslim 2658/6755; Tirmidhī 2138; Abū Dāwūd 4716; Aḥmad 7181.

[5] Bukhārī 1385; Abū Dāwūd 4714; Aḥmad 7181.

[6] Muslim 2865/7207; Aḥmad 17,484.

[7] See Q.XII.53: *Lo! the (human) soul enjoineth unto evil, save that whereon my Lord hath mercy.*

Ibn al-Qayyim goes on to state that evil can be considered as (1) privation—principally ignorance and injustice, (2) anything disassociated from the Holy Lord,[8] (3) the perpetration of what the Holy Lord has prohibited, or (4) the abandonment of what He has commanded.[9] Ibn al-Qayyim then begins to reconcile the existence of evil by stating: "Although the existence [of a particular good] may be better than its non-existence, its existence [in all situations] may result in forgoing (*fawāt*) something that is more beloved to God. Likewise, although the non-existence of something evil may be preferable to its existence [in one aspect] it may be that its existence is a means or a cause that leads [indirectly] to something more beloved to Him."[10] Thus the existence of evil may indirectly lead to greater goods, which are carried out by the believers in response to those evils—these deeds would not have otherwise been possible. Moreover, the existence of suffering or evil, according to Ibn al-Qayyim, may occur in order to result in the reformation of society or to prepare it for some subsequent good.[11]

Within his theodicy, Ibn al-Qayyim also includes many aspects of God's wisdom in permitting the existence of Satan, who is the "basis and root [element] of all [wickedness]".[12] For instance, he writes: "The creation of Iblīs and his army has [indirectly] led to the establishment of [waging battle and striving in His path] and their consequences,"[13] and "Had those who were faithful and righteous been the overwhelming majority, then the possibility of waging battle [in His path]—which is one of the most eminent types of worship—would have eluded us."[14] He also states in *Ṭarīq al-hijratayn*: "Complete servitude cannot occur except through true love. True love itself cannot be manifested unless the lover sacrifices all that he [or she] possesses of wealth, ruling position or power for the sake of the Beloved and to gain proximity to Him. Indeed, the highest degree

8 See Zeni (tr.), *Ibn Qayyim al-Jawziyya on Divine Wisdom and the Problem of Evil*, pp. 24–27
9 Ibid., p. 98.
10 Ibid., p. 23.
11 Ibid., p. 159.
12 Ibid., p. 114.
13 Ibid., p. 132.
14 Ibid., p. 193.

of love is manifested by sacrificing one's life for His sake."[15] Thus Ibn al-Qayyim begins to provide a justification for gratuitous evils.

Finally, whilst the Holy Lord is angry with Satan, the devils and the disbelievers, Ibn al-Qayyim maintains that His pleasure with His prophets and saints is comparatively greater.[16] Further aspects of Ibn al-Qayyim's theodicy will be discussed later in this chapter as well as in subsequent ones.

Qadarīs and Muᶜtazilīs

Now, the first major break from the Predecessors came from the Qadarīs.[17] The Qadarīs put forth their doctrine so as to absolve the Lord of creating evil. Thus the Qadarīs claimed that evil is created by humans.[18]

The Muᶜtazilīs then followed in the footsteps of the Qadarīs by claiming that humans are the creators of their acts, both evil and good. Jon Hoover states: "Muᶜtazilī Kalām theology provides the primary instance of an Islamic free-will theodicy...Humans for their part have free will and create their own good and bad deeds apart from God's control."[19] The Muᶜtazilīs also obligated God to do what is beneficial and most advantageous (*al-ṣalāḥ wa'l-aṣlaḥ*) for humanity and to be omnibenevolent,[20] thus denying His freedom of action.

---

[15] Ibn al-Qayyim, *Ṭarīq al-hijratayn wa bāb al-saᶜādatayn*, ed. Muḥammad Ajmal al-Iṣlāḥī (Mecca: Dār ᶜĀlam al-Fawā'id, 2008), p. 254.

[16] Zeni (tr.), *Ibn Qayyim al-Jawziyya on Divine Wisdom and the Problem of Evil*, p. 137.

[17] The Prophet Muḥammad (may God bless him and grant him peace) said: "The Qadarīs are the Zoroastrians of this Community" (Abū Dāwūd 4691; Ibn Māja 92; Aḥmad 5584; al-Ḥākim 286; Bayhaqī (*Sunan*) 20,869). It is "sound" according to Albānī (*Ṣaḥīḥ al-Jāmiᶜ al-ṣaghīr* 4442). The Zoroastrians believe in the existence of two deities: one was the creator of good and the other the creator of evil. Therefore, the Qadarīs who believed that humans are the creators of evil have resembled the Zoroastrians who believe in another deity to create evil.

[18] See Zeni (tr.), *Ibn Qayyim al-Jawziyya on Divine Wisdom and the Problem of Evil*, p. 203.

[19] Hoover, *Ibn Taymiyya's Theodicy of Perpetual Optimism*, pp. 1–2.

[20] Ibn al-Qayyim responds to this with eighteen points that illustrate how that claim is inconsistent with the Qur'ān, the Sunna, experience and reality. Ibn al-Qayyim ultimately maintains that God's actions are consistent with His wisdom, mercy, beneficence and justice. See Ibn al-Qayyim, *Miftāḥ dār al-saᶜāda wa manshūr wilāyat al-ᶜilm wa'l irāda*, ed. ᶜAbd al-Raḥmān b. Ḥasan b. Qā'id (Mecca: Dār ᶜĀlam al-Fawā'id, 2015), pp. 991–999. See also Zeni (tr.), *Ibn Qayyim al-Jawziyya on Divine Wisdom and the Problem of Evil*, pp. 283–284 (footnote 16).

They claimed that if God were to act in a contrary manner then He would be deemed unjust. Of note, the Qadarīs and Muʿtazilīs (as distinct groups) are now extinct, and thus will not be elaborated upon in further detail.

ASHʿARĪS

The Ashʿarī doctrine then followed in response to the Muʿtazilīs. It began with its eponymous founder, Abū al-Ḥasan al-Ashʿarī, who rejected the Muʿtazilī doctrine after initially adhering to it. In contrast to the Muʿtazilī position of divine omnibenevolence, the Ashʿarīs uphold God's absolute will—not His benevolence or wisdom—in justifying His creation and commandments.

Many Ashʿarīs denied that His actions necessarily had wise purposes (*ghayr muʿallala*), motives or objectives, because they claimed that these would suggest He gained perfection through the accomplishment of them, which would then suggest that He was deficient before their attainment[21]. That said, Ghazālī affirmed that God "is wise in His acts and just in His decrees".[22] Therefore, some Ashʿarīs did not discount altogether the principle that there was divine wisdom behind God's acts.

Indeed, late-Ashʿarī doctrine seeks to defend itself against being misunderstood as denying God's acting with wisdom, as evidenced in the words of Ibrāhīm al-Bājūrī in his commentary on *Umm al-barāhīn*: "You should know that although His actions and judgments are transcendent and exalted beyond motives, they still contain wisdom [*ḥikma*], even if it does not reach our rational minds. If His actions were without wisdom, they would be futile, and that is impossible for Him, the Exalted."[23]

The Ashʿarīs also put forth a theory of divine command ethics which held that whatever God commands is good; and if God commanded the opposite, it would still be deemed to be good by virtue of His

---

[21] See Ibn al-Qayyim's refutation of Fakhr al-Dīn al-Rāzī's arguments in Zeni (tr.), *Ibn Qayyim al-Jawziyya on Divine Wisdom and the Problem of Evil*, pp. 72–93.

[22] Ghazālī, *Iḥyā'*, cited in Nuh Ha Mim Keller (tr.), *The Reliance of the Traveller: A Classic Manual of Islamic Sacred Law* (Evanston: Sunna Books, 1994), p. 821.

[23] See Suraqah Abdul Aziz (tr.), *A Refined Explanation of the Sanusi Creed The Foundational Proofs* (Rotterdam: Sunni Publications, 2013), p. 111.

command of it. The Ashʿarīs also denied causality because they claimed that the presence of intermediaries would signify that God is in need of them. When all of the aforementioned Ashʿarī positions are considered—i.e. that events are due to His will alone, their divine command ethics and denial of causality—it is difficult to escape the conclusion that Ashʿarīs give less importance to His wisdom in shaping this world.

Hoover summarizes the Ashʿarī approach to theodicy in the following manner: "The voluntarism of Ashʿarī Kalām theology rejects the question of theodicy as meaningless. God's unfettered will, sufficiency apart from the world, and exclusive power preclude asking why God does this or that. God is not limited by any necessity of reason, and His acts require no deliberation, rational motive or external cause. Thus God's creation of injustice, unbelief and other evils is not susceptible to any explanation except that God wills it."[24]

One also reads with interest the words of Timothy Winter, who conceded that Ashʿarism adopted a

> thoroughgoing anti-theodicy...For Ashʿarism, a school often linked to a Sufi devotional tradition nervous about the shaping of a theory choice by hubris, it was arrogant as well as philosophically difficult to claim that one's mind could authoritatively identify natural facts of a moral nature and still more arrogant to claim that the Creator must be observed or considered to be constrained by those natural facts. God is not subject to moral necessity, for He is its ground...In this system no theodicy is meaningful, since God is just and merciful according to a canon of wisdom which need not coincide at all with humanly detected aesthetic or revealed conceptions. Indeed, for Ashʿarism, every attempt at a theodicy is likely to be hubristic, demanding divine submission to prior natural facts and compliance with humanly fallible intuitions...[But Ashʿarī doctrine] insisted that wisdom was in effect simply a synonym for divine agency."[25]

In response to this, it will be maintained that so long as theodicy (as will be discussed later) follows the Qur'ān and Sunna, then it is neither

---

[24] Hoover, *Ibn Taymiyya's Theodicy of Perpetual Optimism*, pp. 1–2.

[25] Timothy Winter, "Islam and the Problem of Evil", in Chad Meister and Paul Moser (eds.), *The Cambridge Companion to the Problem of Evil* (New York: Cambridge University Press, 2017), pp. 240–43.

"hubristic" nor "arrogant" to advance it; rather, it is praiseworthy and beneficial. In fact, it has the potential to even lead one to a deeper religious experience of knowledge and a greater love for the Holy Sublime Lord.

Is not attempting to understand the Divine wisdom and what He loves the highest scholarly pursuit? A theodicy based upon revelation leads to a greater understanding of the Holy Lord's Beautiful Names and Glorious Attributes, which He has manifested in this world, as well as His praiseworthiness—this understanding then leads to a greater love for Him (Most Blessed and Glorious is He). Furthermore, the Ashʿarī doctrine upholding divine command ethics[26]—i.e. that God could have commanded either of two opposites, and it is only His will which led to a particular commandment—ascribes arbitrariness to the Holy Lord and minimizes His praiseworthiness. This then hinders one from feeling true love for the Holy Lord, based upon religious understanding (*fiqh*) and reason, which is the ultimate aim of existence. In reality, the Ashʿarī anti-theodicy stance hindered deeper religious understanding and insights. And God knows best.

Some may feel that a theodicy should not be pursued because it may entail delving into the Divine secret of predestination (*qadar*). The Prophet Muḥammad (may God bless him and grant him peace) said: "If my Companions are mentioned then abstain [from saying anything negative]...And if the [Divine] predestination is mentioned, then refrain [from delving into it]."[27] It will be contended that this *ḥadīth* does not prohibit the pursuit of a theodicy, but rather prohibits delving into why a particular individual must suffer afflictions or evil, as only God knows the particulars. Stated differently, avoiding the pursuit of the reasons underlying divine predestination prohibits us

---

[26] Shihadeh also explains in regards to Rāzī and Ashʿarī doctrine that the "definition of 'good' and 'bad' works at two levels. In the sphere of human action, it underpins a theory of divine command ethics by establishing that revelation is the sole legitimate source for norms that govern human action and behavior. At the same time it supports a broader theological voluntarism: since God's command applies only to His creatures, His own will and acts are unconstrained by any duties or prohibitions." See Ayman Shihadeh, "Theories of Ethical Value in Kalām: A New Interpretation", p. 402.

[27] Ṭabarānī (*al-Muʿjam al-kabīr*) 1427; Ibn ʿAbd al-Barr 1481; Abū Nuʿaym, *Ḥilya*, vol. IV, p. 108. It is "authentic" according to Albānī (*Silsilat al-aḥādīth al-ṣaḥīḥa* 34). Of note, the Prophet, in this *ḥadīth*, made it impermissible to criticize his Companions.

from delving into the local problem of evil—not a general theodicy based on the Qur'ān and Sunna. Pursuit of a local or personal justification for all occurrences is unknowable to us, nor is it beneficial. Ibn al-Qayyim affirmed that we cannot know the "particulars", i.e. local matters, but rather "God provides insight to those whom He wishes of His creation to what He wills" [28] in regards to a general theodicy. A further theodicy will thus be advanced from Chapter Ten onward based on revelation.

Regardless, the Ashʿarī creed has been adopted by a majority of Sunni theologians. In addition, as a result of Ashʿarī doctrine being widespread in Muslim lands, many non-Muslims equate Ashʿarī doctrine with Islam itself, rather than viewing the Traditionalist doctrine of Ibn al-Qayyim as a more (or at least equally) authoritative articulation on the matter. Some non-Muslims thus claim that Islam deems God's acts to be "arbitrary"[29]—not rational—or that God in Islam is not bound to act in accordance with His Word, wisdom, or promises:

> But for Muslim teaching, God is absolutely transcendent. His will is not bound up with any of our categories, even that of rationality. Here [Theodore] Khoury quotes a work of the noted French Islamist R. Arnaldez, who points out that Ibn Hazm went so far as to state that God is not bound even by his own word, and that nothing would oblige him to reveal the truth to us. Were it God's will, we would even have to practise idolatry.[30]

Such an irrational statement of Ibn Ḥazm contradicts all that is present in the Scriptures (whether the Torah, Gospel or Qur'ān) and

---

[28] See Zeni (tr.), *Ibn Qayyim al-Jawziyya on Divine Wisdom and the Problem of Evil*, p. 263.

[29] For instance, Alvin Plantiga states: "The Christian tradition, for example, emphasizes God's love and benevolence; in the Moslem view, on the other hand, God has a somewhat more arbitrary character." See Alvin Plantiga, *God, Freedom, and Evil* (Grand Rapids: William B. Eerdmans Publishing, 1974), p. 1.

[30] Pope Benedict, "Faith, Reason and the University: Memories and Reflections", Aula Magna of the University of Regensburg, 12 September 2006. Of note, Ibn Ḥazm is not an Ashʿarī, but rather of the Literalist school (*Ẓāhirī*). This school held that analogical reasoning could not be utilized in jurisprudential matters. Of note, 38 Muslim scholars penned an "Open Letter to His Holiness Pope Benedict XVI" stating that Ibn Ḥazm's Ẓāhiri school of thought "is followed by no one in the Islamic world today", and therefore does not represent Islam.

the traditions of all of His prophets. Ibn Ḥazm's[31] claim should not be used as a proof against Islam, just as the Ashᶜarī position should not be seen as the final theological articulation of Islam on theodicy.

Indeed, God (Glorious is He) is the Most Wise and He loves and commands that which is good (worshipping Him alone being the greatest good). God (Glorious is He) will punish all of those who practised idolatry or disbelieved in Him or His prophets. The Holy Lord speaks only the truth, and He will fulfill His Word and all of His promises (which were conveyed by His prophets): *God! There is no god but He: of a surety He will gather you together against the Day of Judgment, about which there is no doubt. And whose word can be truer than God's?*[32]

Māturīdīs

Now the Māturīdī school of theology, named after its eponymous founder Abū Manṣūr Muḥammad al-Māturīdī (d. 333/944), affirmed God's wisdom like the traditionalists. He defined wisdom as "putting everything in its proper place" (*waḍᶜu kulli shay'in mawḍiᶜa[hu]*).[33] Sherman Jackson's study of the Muᶜtazilī, Ashᶜarī, Māturīdī and Traditionalist doctrines in relation to the problem of black suffering concluded that divine omnibenevolence and omnipotence for the first two groups "serve to exonerate God of evil", while the Māturīdīs contended that

---

[31] Abū Muḥammad ᶜAlī b. Aḥmad b. Saᶜīd b. Ḥazm (d. 438/1064) was a scholar and prolific writer of Muslim Spain. He codified literalist Ẓāhirī thought (founded by Dāwūd al-Ẓāhirī (d. 270/884)) and was its most well-known adherent. Unfortunately, Ibn Ḥazm held some irrational views, such as: "If God had willed He could punish the righteous and reward the wretched." See James Pavlin, "Sunni *Kalām* and Theological Controversies", in Nasr and Leaman (eds.), *History of Islamic Philosophy*, p. 109. Ibn Ḥazm held other beliefs which would render God to be unwise—God is infallible and holy above that. That said, Ibn Ḥazm wrote over 400 volumes, including *al-Faṣl fī al-milal wa'l-niḥal* and *al-Īṣāl ilā fahm kitāb al-khiṣāl*. See Dhahabī, *Siyar aᶜlām al-nubalā'*, vol. XVIII, pp. 184–212.

[32] Q.IV.87 (Yusuf Ali translation).

[33] Rodrigo Adem (tr.), *Al-Māturīdī and the Development of Sunnī Theology in Samarqand* (Leiden: Brill, 2015), p. 299. Of note, Ibn Taymiyya similarly states: "Injustice is to put something into an improper place, while justice is to put everything into its proper place. God (Glory be to Him) is Wise and Just, and He puts all things into their proper places... [This is in agreement with the definition put forth by the grammarian] Abū Bakr b. al-Anbārī [d. 328/940]." Ibn Taymiyya, *Risāla fī maᶜnā kawn al-Rabb ᶜādilan wa-fī tanzīhihi ᶜan al-ẓulm*, in *Jāmiᶜ al-rasā'il li-Ibn Taymiyya* (Riyadh: Dār al-ᶜAṭā', 2001), pp. 123–124.

God allows evil only if it can "serve a wise end".[34] Therefore, the Māturīdīs affirmed that God creates everything, including evil, but that He only allows evil for certain wise purposes. In this regard, the Māturīdī doctrine is similar to that of the Traditionalists.

Sufism

In regards to Sufism—which has come to be associated with asceticism, ritualistic remembrance of God and pursuit of mystical unveiling—Timothy Winter states:

> although suffering may seem entirely unmerited, it can be the enigmatic, perhaps entirely incomprehensible anticipation of God's miraculous work of deliverance. Perhaps this led to the frequent idea that distress is a sign of divine favor, an ascetical view which became widespread in Sufi mysticism, which often identified the highest degrees of spiritual accomplishment with the virtue of *riḍā*, satisfaction with the divine decree...life with all its hardships is a divine gift itself.[35]

Jalāl al-Dīn al-Rūmī also emphasized contentment (*riḍā*) with God's decree, as well as trust in and love of God in order to "overcome the anguish and move up the spiritual ladder to reach nearness with God".[36] The Sufi wayfarer thus seeks, through annihilation of his desires as well as through love of Him, to achieve contentment and proximity to the Lord. Ibn ᶜAṭā' Allāh al-Iskandarī (d. 1309), a Sufi of the Shādhilī order, felt that being veiled from God, whether due to His veil or the veils of creation, is the cause of suffering.[37]

Although important, the Sufi approach does not provide a true theodicy, as no justification or explanation for the spectrum of evil aside from the aforementioned is sought. The modern and popular

---

34 Sherman Jackson, *Islam and the Problem of Black Suffering* (Oxford: Oxford University Press, 2009), pp. 110–111. Of note, Ibn al-Qayyim mentioned that "slavery is a by-product of disbelief." Zeni (tr), *Ibn Qayyim al-Jawziyya on Divine Wisdom and the Problem of Evil*, p. 110.

35 Winter, "Islam and the Problem of Evil", p. 232.

36 Nasrin Rouzati, "Evil and Human Suffering in Islamic Thought—Towards a Mystical Theodicy", *Religions*, 2018, pp. 9 and 47.

37 Aḥmad b. Muḥammad b. ᶜAṭā'illāh al-Iskandarī and ᶜAbdullāh Gangohī, *The Book of Wisdoms: Kitāb al-Ḥikam, A Collection of Sufi Aphorisms*, tr. Victor Danner (London: White Thread Press, 2014), pp. 285–288.

form of Sufism, in contrast to some of its original and historical forms, has also minimized the role of righteous deeds to alleviate the real suffering and evil endured by others. Mystical unveiling, granted more worth than its due by some Sufis,[38] also distances their theodicy from transmitted or rational evidence. Nonetheless, Sufism has, according to Montgomery Watt, "enabled countless men and women to lead tolerable lives in conditions of incredible hardship".[39]

THE THEODICY OF SAᶜĪD NURSĪ

The theodicy of Saᶜīd Nursī, the highly-influential Turkish scholar of the modern period, has been investigated in two recent books. The immensity of his legacy and popularity in modern Turkey also compels mentioning him here.

Tubanur Ozkan investigates Nursī's theology of the Divine Names[40] in which he links "literally everything and every event with the Names and Attributes of God".[41] Ozkan adds:

> Nursi points out that the realities and attributes of all beings and of the universe are each based on one or more divine names. True natural science, he explains, is based on the name of All-Wise (*Ḥakīm*), true medicine on the name of Healer (*Shāfī*), and geometry on the name of

---

[38] For example, Ghazālī states: "The way of moderation…[is only found by] those granted success [from God], those who perceive things with illumination [from God] rather than only by transmitted reports. Then, when the mysteries of things as they truly are, are unveiled to them, they go back to the traditions and narrations, and affirm what accords with what they have witnessed with the light of certitude, and figuratively interpret what does not accord with it. As for the one who takes the cognition of these things from transmitted reports alone, he will not be able to secure a firm foothold in them or find a solid position." See Khalid Williams (tr.), *The Principles of the Creed: Book 2 of The Revival of the Religious Sciences* (Louisville: Fons Vitae, 2016), pp. 55–56. Of note, Ibn al-Qayyim rejected that mystical unveiling (or reason) could take precedence over sound traditions, and he affirmed that reason and revelation are always concordant.

[39] Montgomery Watt, "Suffering in Sunnite Islam", *Studia Islamica*, No. 50, 1979, pp. 5–19. Watt considers Ashᶜarī and Sufi thinking to formulate this conclusion to his article.

[40] See Izzet Coban, "Nursi on Theodicy: A New Theological Perspective", in Anna-Teresa Tymieniecka and Nazif Muhtaroglu (eds.), *Classical Issues in Islamic Philosophy and Theology Today* (New York: Springer, 2010), p. 116.

[41] Tubanur Ozkan, *A Muslim Response to Evil: Said Nursi on the Theodicy* (Farnham: Ashgate, 2015), p. 71.

> Determiner (*Muqaddir*), etc. Just as all the sciences are based on and come to an end in a name, the realities of all human attainments are based on the divine names. Thus, the fact that human beings go through different kinds of hardships and *ashrār* (pl. *sharr*) may be to reflect and be a mirror of the numerous Names and Attributes of his Creator. These apparent *ashrār* may help [the human being] to develop and reach perfection... [Also] vital for the understanding of the problem of [evil] *sharr* is that God is known for having qualities that are apparently contradictory. These are most commonly categorized into two groups, being called Glorious (*Jalālī*) and Beauteous (*Jamālī*) names such as His Wrath and Mercy respectively... Not only does He interrelate with each creation in a different way, the forms of this interrelation change over time. For instance God is the giver of life (*muḥyī*) and at the same time the taker of life (*mumīt*). [42]

Ozkan states that "Nursi partially shares the theory of privation boni, and employs the theory of 'the best of all possible worlds,' 'world of duality' and the 'principle of plenitude' in his own way. Nursi discussed the necessity of minor *ashrār* [lit. evils] as a test [and in order for the greater good (*khayr*) to happen]...Nursi would agree that there is an infinite wisdom behind the creation of *sharr* ['evil'] and we can know only as much of it as our wisdom allows."[43] Ozkan further writes: "Nursi shares the idea of al-Maturidī that the combination, confrontation, and interpenetration of opposites in creation, such as *khayr* ["good"] and *sharr*, pain and pleasure, light and darkness, heat and cold, beauty and ugliness and guidance and misguidance manifests God's divine wisdom and indicates God's Unity."[44] Finally, Ozkan states that "according to Nursi, underneath every veil of apparent ugliness, there is hidden most shining instances of beauty and order".[45]

Nursī also discussed natural disasters. Thomas Michel outlines Nursī's response to queries posed to him after an earthquake in Turkey led to the death of more than 30,000 people. When asked why everyone including the innocent are punished for the sins of relatively few evildoers, Nursī's answer according to Michel was:

---

[42] Ibid., pp. 73–74.
[43] Ibid., pp. 93–94.
[44] Ibid., p. 109.
[45] Ibid., p. 115.

> It is not correct to say about any human society that only a few people have sinned. In every society, most people are in one way or another involved in the general wrongdoing. Whether it be the injustices visited upon the poor, the corruption of politicians and businessmen, public promiscuity, or general disbelief, many people cooperate silently in such misdeeds in various ways. Whether by complacently ignoring the wrong, by profiting from the wrongdoing in one way or another, by passively putting up with it and doing nothing to stop it, or by defending the rights of miscreants to carry out their offences, guilt is more widespread than that for which a relatively small number of perpetrators is responsible...Nursi interprets this verse [*And guard yourselves against a chastisement which cannot fall exclusively on those of you who are wrongdoers*[46]] to mean this world is like a proving ground or examination hall in which each person's level of responsibility and accountability is being tested. If in the case of disaster the [truly] innocent were spared while the guilty were being punished, then evildoers would do what is right, not because they wanted to obey and believe in God, but simply out of self-interest, to avoid worldly destruction.[47]

Bilal Kuspinar states regarding Nursī's approach to explaining the existence of Satan:

> In the existence of Satan, [Nursi] proclaims, there are numerous purposes. First of all man's attainment of perfection and happiness is possible through his struggle against the temptations of Satan... Were it not for his striving, man would have been just like the angels... [Therefore] the very creation of Satan, according to Nursi, is for the moral progress and spiritual perfection of man and therefore its creation in this particular respect is not only good and just but beautiful, too... [Regarding the existence of particular evils and calamities] Nursi suggests... [that] He creates them occasionally out of His Will in order to preserve and maintain the universal laws all of which in fact serve for universal purposes and benefits.[48]

Regarding the Hereafter, Nursī maintains: "There must in addition be a realm of punishment appropriate to God's glory and dignity. For

---

46 Q.VIII.25.

47 S. J. Thomas Michel, "God's Justice in Relation to Natural Disasters", in Ibrahim M. Abu Rabiᶜ (ed.), *Theodicy and Justice in Modern Islamic Thought: The Case of Said Nursi* (Farnham: Ashgate, 2010), pp. 221–22.

48 Bilal Kuspinar, "Justice and Balance in Creation: Said Nursi's Analysis," in ibid., pp. 233–34.

generally the oppressor leaves the world while still in possession of his might, and the oppressed while still subjected to humiliation. These matters are therefore deferred for the attention of a supreme tribunal; it is not that they are neglected."[49]

THE BEST OF ALL POSSIBLE WORLDS

Abū Ḥāmid Muḥammad al-Ghazālī[50] proposed a best of all possible worlds theodicy in the eleventh century CE: "Nothing in possibility is more wonderful (*abdaʿ*) than what it is," and "There is not in possibility anything whatever more excellent, more perfect, and more complete than it. For if there were and He had withheld it, having power to create it but not deigning to do so, this would be miserliness contrary to the divine generosity and injustice contrary to the divine justice. But if He were not able, it would be incapability contrary to divinity".[51]

Eric Ormsby investigated the various positions held by the Islamic scholars on this statement for it "engendered a controversy that lasted from [Ghazālī's] own lifetime until well into the 19th century".[52] Suyūṭī responded to those who felt that the dictum contradicted God's omnipotence by saying:

---

49 Bediuzzaman Said Nursi, *The Words*, tr. Sukran Vahide (Suzler Nesriyat Ticaret ve Sanayi, A.S. 1992), p. 76, quoted in Ian Markham, "Living Life in the Light of Death: A Conversation with Bediuzzaman Said Nursi", in Ibrahim M. Abu-Rabiʿ (ed.), *Theodicy and Justice in Modern Islamic Thought*, p. 24.

50 Abū Ḥāmid Muḥammad b. Muḥammad al-Ghazālī (d. 504/1111) is considered by many to be the "Renewer'"(*mujaddid*) of his century and "the Proof (*ḥujja*) of Islam". His theology was Ashʿarī and Sufi, while his jurisprudence was Shāfiʿī. He wrote many significant books, including the *Iḥyāʾ ʿulūm al-dīn* [The Revival of the Religious Sciences], which bridged the gap between orthopraxy and Sufism, and is considered to be his greatest work. He also wrote *Tahāfut al-falāsifa* [The Incoherence of the Philosophers], which successfully refuted Greek philosophy and its supporters amongst the Arab philosophers, such as Fārābī and Ibn Sīnā. He also provided the Islamic creed for the schools built by Niẓām al-Mulk, which led to a "Sunni revival". See Abdul Rahman Azzam, *Saladin: The Triumph of the Sunni Revival* (Cambridge: Islamic Texts Society, 2014), pp. 8 and 12.

51 Eric Ormsby, *Theodicy in Islamic Thought: The Dispute over al-Ghazālī's "Best of All Possible Worlds"* (Princeton: Princeton University Press, 1984), p. 39. For the Arabic, see Ghazālī, *Iḥyāʾ ʿulūm al-dīn*, vol. IV, pp. 319–320. This dictum is within Book 35, which is titled "His Oneness and Reliance upon Him" (*al-tawḥīd wa'l-tawakkul*).

52 Ormsby, *Theodicy in Islamic Thought*, p. 32.

> It does not contradict [the belief] that God can create into existence something other than what exists, rather [it refutes the notion] that the alternative be more wonderful than what exists. The "Proof of Islam" [i.e. Ghazālī] rejected that there could exist something more wonderful than what exists, despite affirming that He has the power to [create otherwise]. We also affirm that [God] is capable [of creating something better]. God (Exalted is He) has said, *And if thy Lord willed, all who are in the earth would have believed together* [Q.X.99]. But what [Ghazālī] has rejected is this possibility being more wonderful than what currently exists.[53]

That said, it was contended in the introduction to *Ibn Qayyim al-Jawziyya on Divine Wisdom and the Problem of Evil* that Ibn al-Qayyim disagreed with that dictum. He never used the word "dazzling/wonderful" (*badīᶜa*) to describe this world; rather, Ibn al-Qayyim utilized it fifteen times in reference to God's wisdom (*ḥikmatu*[hu] *al-badīᶜa*). For instance, he affirmed the "complete nature of His dazzling wisdom and overwhelming omnipotence";[54] and that the creation of "opposites is in order to manifest His dazzling wisdom, vanquishing power, accomplished will, and perfect and complete sovereignty".[55]

Consequently, it was clear for Ibn al-Qayyim that God's wisdom—which is an Attribute of His for He is the Most Wise—as well as His good actions are dazzling, whereas that which He enacts, i.e. this world and what it contains, may be divided into aspects that are wonderful or not: "God (Glory be to Him) created three abodes: one that is purely dedicated to bliss, pleasure, delight and joy; one that is purely dedicated to pain, suffering, calamities and evils; and one that is mixed having both good and evil, bliss and wretchedness, pleasure and pain."[56]

As for Paradise, God (Exalted is He) created it with progressively higher levels, and He will populate the believers within those according to their deeds. But God (Glorious is He) could have created an even better Paradise, whereby all the believers occupied an

---

53 See Jalāl al-Dīn al-Suyūṭī, *Tashyīd al-arkān fī laysa fi'l-imkān abdaᶜ mimmā kān*, addendum to Ghazālī, *Iḥyā' ᶜulūm al-dīn*, vol. V, p. 371.

54 Zeni (tr.), *Ibn Qayyim al-Jawziyya on Divine Wisdom and the Problem of Evil*, p. 97.

55 Ibid., p. 101.

56 Ibid., p. 145.

equivalent most exalted rank with the same bliss; yet even such a case of bliss could itself be extended to a higher degree, as God's ability to keep raising the bliss therein is endless. Therefore, characterizing this world or even Paradise as being the "best" is only congruent in some aspects—neither can be generally deemed as such.[57] Ibn al-Qayyim thus maintains that God (Exalted is He) has structured both this world and Paradise concordant with His divine wisdom, and that the Holy Lord created this world in order to achieve the wise purposes He has dictated.

In general terms, how could this world be considered the best of all possible worlds when the Prophet Muḥammad said: "Had this world been worth a mosquito's wing in the sight of God, He would not have allowed a disbeliever to have a sip of water"[58]? Had this world been the best possibility, then it would not have been characterized in such an insignificant fashion. Ibn al-Qayyim states:

> The Sublime only created [this world] as a bridge to the Hereafter so that His [believing] servants could equip themselves [with good deeds]. They could not have become proximate to Him except by establishing His remembrance and doing what He loves, which includes attaining knowledge. Such actions allow one to know God and worship, remember, praise and glorify Him. It is only for these reasons that He created it and its inhabitants. The Exalted says: *I created the jinn and humankind only that they might worship Me.*[59] He also said: *God it is Who hath created seven heavens, and of the earth the like thereof. The commandment cometh down among them slowly, that ye may know that God is Able to do all things, and that God surroundeth all things in knowledge.*[60] Thus the two verses imply that the Sublime only created the heavens and the earth so that He may be known through His Names and Attributes. In this manner we can better worship Him alone, for that is our obligation. God (Glory be to Him) loves that His servants remember, worship, know and love Him. [He also loves] whatever leads to these or is a necessary concomitant of them. On the

---

57 Ibid., pp. XXI–XXII.

58 Tirmidhī 2320; Ibn Māja 4110; al-Ḥākim 7847; Bayhaqī (*Shuʿab*) 9981. It is "authentic" according to Albānī (*Silsilat al-aḥādīth al-ṣaḥīḥa* 943).

59 Q.LI.56.

60 Q.LXV.12.

other hand, everything else is hated and blameworthy in His sight and is, therefore, deserving of censure.[61]

Moreover, the Messenger of God (may God bless him and grant him peace) said: "Indeed, the world is cursed; everything in it is cursed except for the remembrance of God and what is conducive to it, the scholar and the student."[62] In addition, we can affirm that this world contains the most evil of any world because the Prophet Muḥammad (may God bless him and grant him peace) said regarding the Day of Judgment: "My Lord is angry [that] Day in a way that He has never been before. He will never be as angry as that again."[63] The Holy Lord's anger is due to the evilness perpetrated by humankind and jinn in this world. Therefore, even if we assume that God has created or will create worlds in which He allows His creation to freely do either good or evil, the evil anterior or posterior to this world will necessarily be less.

In summary, characterizing existence, i.e. what God has enacted or willed, as being wonderful is ambiguous, for there is much suffering, evil and disbelief in this world. Ibn al-Qayyim avoids all that by maintaining that it is God's wisdom, which is dazzling/wonderful. It seems that the best way to reconcile Ghazālī's dictum and Ibn al-Qayyim's position is to hold that what is good in this world is more wonderful than if good had existed alone, and that God has many dazzling wise purposes in mixing good and evil herein.

Some other Muslim theodicies

There are other philosophical theodicies that emerged in the Muslim lands, which are inconsistent with revelation from one standpoint or another; yet they are worthy of consideration here.

To begin with, we have Avicenna (Ibn Sīnā) who incorporated Neoplatonic elements into his philosophy, and did put forward his notion of a theodicy. He claimed a "triadic emanative scheme" regarding this world, as explained by Michael Marmura: "Accordingly

---

61 Zeni (tr.), *Ibn Qayyim al-Jawziyya on Knowledge*, pp. 56–57.

62 Tirmidhī 2322; Ibn Māja 4112; Bayhaqī (*Shuʿab*) 1580. It is "sound" according to Albānī (*Silsilat al-aḥādīth al-ṣaḥīḥa* 2797).

63 Bukhārī 4712; Muslim 194/480; Tirmidhī 2434; Aḥmad 9623.

after the emanation of the first intellect from God, the series that ensues is a series of celestial triads. Each triad consists of an intellect, a soul, and a sphere."[64] This emanative scheme claims that God's creation necessarily emanates from Him, without His free will or choice (*mūjib*[an] *bi'l-dhāt*)—God is infallible above that.

According to Shams Inati, Avicenna's "solution" to the problem of evil can be summarized as follows: 1) God is good and providential, but precisely because of His goodness, God cannot intend any good or evil in the world; 2) there is more good than evil in the universe—essential evil is rare, only non-essential evil is encountered; 3) evil is a necessary consequence of good, and to wish the removal of evil is to wish the removal of good; 4) evil is a necessary means for the good; 5) God is not omnipotent—that is, God cannot free the world from evil; 6) essential evil is privation of being, and therefore cannot be caused by God, Who is the cause of being only; and 7) human evil is due to human free will.[65]

The most problematic aspects of Avicenna's "solution" are the first, fifth and sixth positions, which limit God's power and creative ability. Denying God's omnipotence is heretical and contradicts the Qur'ān, which states in thirty-five verses that God is able to do all things. Inati states that Avicenna "must have adhered to this thesis… [but he did not explicitly deny God's omnipotence] for fear of the theologians".[66] Inati also mentioned that Avicenna claimed that God acts out of necessity[67]—again, God is infallible above all these claims.

For these reasons, as well as many others, Ibn al-Qayyim characterizes Avicenna as "the leader of the heretics" (*shaykh al-*

---

64 Michael E. Marmura, *The Metaphysics of the Healing* (Provo: Brigham Young University Press, 2005), p. xxi.

65 Shams Inati, *The Problem of Evil: Ibn Sīnā's Theodicy* (Binghamton: Global Publications, 2000), pp. 169–173.

66 Ibid., pp. 172–173.

67 Ibid., p. 169. Of note, Ayman Shihadeh discusses how Rāzī argued that "theodicy has no place in [Avicennan] philosophy" since Avicenna claimed that God is necessitating through His Essence (*mūjib*[an] *bi'l-dhāt*). Shihadeh also discusses "the plenitude of evil in Rāzī's world" and his "anti-theodicean stance", the latter of which is consistent with his neo-Ashᶜarite theology. See Ayman Shihadeh, "Avicenna's Theodicy and Rāzī's Anti-Theodicy", *Intellectual History of the Islamicate World*, vol. VII, 2019 (Jan.), pp. 61–84.

mulḥidīn).[68] Likewise, Ghazālī deemed Avicenna to be a disbeliever, as the latter claimed that the world is pre-eternal, denied God's knowledge of particulars, and denied bodily resurrection.[69]

We then have Ibn Rushd (Averroes) who attributed the existence of evil to "the necessity of matter" and "the natural elements…and the composition" of humanity,[70] as well as the free will of the agent's mind.[71] But Ibn Rushd claims that God only "knows those aspects of particulars which reflect the divine consciousness, the rational aspects, but not those aspects of them which are outside that consciousness"[72] and that "He is unresponsive in this matter [concerning evil]".[73] Thus Ibn Rushd also attributes deficiency to the Holy Lord's omniscience and omnipotence.

Ibn ᶜArabī, born in Muslim Spain, met Ibn Rushd but did not adopt his philosophy.[74] Instead, Ibn ᶜArabī developed a mystical philosophy[75] entailing monism. Only some salient aspects, including his monism and his thoughts regarding mystical unveiling, will be discussed as delving more deeply into Ibn ᶜArabī's notions would only distract us from the task at hand, and would require a book of its own. It is only after mentioning these salient aspects that Ibn ᶜArabī's theodicy can be better understood.

---

68 Ibn al-Qayyim, *Shifāʾ al-ᶜalīl fī masāʾil al-qaḍāʾ waʾl-qadar waʾl-ḥikma waʾl-taᶜlīl*, eds. Aḥmad b. Ṣāliḥ b. ᶜAlī al-Ṣamᶜānī and ᶜAlī b. Muḥammad b. ᶜAbd Allāh al-ᶜAjlān (Riyadh: Dār al-Ṣamayᶜī, 2013), p. 213.

69 See the first, thirteenth and twentieth discussions, respectively, in Michael E. Marmura (tr.), *The Incoherence of the Philosophers*. See also Aladdin M. Yaqub (tr.), *Al-Ghazālī's Moderation in Belief* (Chicago: The University of Chicago Press, 2013), p. 244.

70 George Hourani, "Averroes on Good and Evil", in *Studia Islamica*, vol. XVI, 1962, pp. 21–28.

71 Ozkan, *A Muslim Response to Evil*, p. 58

72 Leaman, *Evil and Suffering in Jewish Philosophy*, p. 111.

73 Ozkan, *A Muslim Response to Evil*, p. 59.

74 Ibn ᶜArabī's reception up to the 16th century has been discussed in Alexander D. Knysh, *Ibn ᶜArabi in the Later Islamic Tradition: The Making of a Polemical Image in Medieval Islam* (New York: SUNY Press, 1998). That said, his position in relation to Islamic Law is largely uncontested; see Omar Ebaidat, "Muḥyī l-Dīn Ibn ᶜArabī's Personalist Theory of the *Sharīᶜa*: *An Examination of His Legal Doctrine*", *Journal of Sufi Studies*, vol. VI, 2017, pp. 1–46.

75 See Binyamin Abrahamov (tr.), *Ibn al-ᶜArabī's Fuṣūṣ al-Ḥikam: An Annotated Translation of 'The Bezels of Wisdom'* (London and New York: Routledge, 2015), p. 5.

Monism pervades Ibn ʿArabī's writings, as seen in *al-Futūḥāt al-Makkiyya* and *Fuṣūṣ al-ḥikam*. He claims that the cosmos represents the self-disclosure of God and His Names. Ibn ʿArabī often makes an analogy of this world as being a "mirror"[76] or image of God and a manifestation of the Divine Names. For instance, Ibn ʿArabī stated:

> There is nothing in *wujūd* [i.e. existence] but God. In the same way, if you were to say, "There is nothing in the mirror except the one who is disclosing himself to it," you would be speaking the truth. Nevertheless, you know that there is nothing at all "in the mirror," nor is there anything of the mirror in the viewer. But within the very form of the mirror, the display of variations and traces is perceived...No entity of any existent thing becomes manifest except through His self-disclosure. So the mirror is the Presence of Possibility, the Real is the one who looks within it, and the form is you in keeping with the mode of your possibility.[77]

William Chittick explains that Ibn ʿArabī claims: "everything other than God is nonexistent in itself...[S]ince the entities have no existence of their own, nothing is perceived but the *wujūd* of God imbued with the properties (*aḥkām*) of the entities".[78] Although Ibn ʿArabī himself, according to Chittick, never proclaimed "Oneness of

[76] For instance, Ibn ʿArabī states: "God is your mirror, through which you see yourself, and you are His mirror through which He sees His names and the manifestation of their rules, and these names are nothing other than Himself." He also says: "In the substrates, God's manifestations and all their aspects are diversified, and the substrate can receive every aspect." He also says: "The mirror is a single essence, yet the beholder sees many forms in the mirror." Abrahamov (tr.), *Ibn al-ʿArabī's Fuṣūṣ al-Ḥikam*, pp. 30, 48 and 145, respectively. Abrahamov summarizes by saying: "In Ibn ʿArabī's view, not only the cosmos as a whole serves as a mirror of Him, but also the Perfect Human Being, Adam, contains in himself all of the forms of God's names...just as the human being serves as God's mirror, so God is the human being's mirror through which he sees his own soul. God is reflected in the cosmos and the cosmos is reflected in God." Ibid., p. 8.

[77] William Chittick, *The Self-Disclosure of God: Principles of Ibn al-ʿArabī's Cosmology* (Albany: State University of New York Press, 1998), p. 15.

[78] William Chittick, "Rūmī and *waḥdat al-wujūd*", in Amin Banani, Richard Hovannisian and Georges Sabagh (eds.), *The Heritage of Rumi* (New York: Cambridge University Press, 1994), p. 75.

existence (*waḥdat al-wujūd*)... the term gradually came to be adopted by his followers[79] to designate his position". [80]

In reality, Ibn ᶜArabī often misinterpreted ambiguous verses and traditions (and sometimes even verses which are categorical-in-meaning) in order to give credence to his monism. This was despite the fact that monism contradicted "[all of the] Scriptures, the Sunna of the Prophet Muḥammad, the consensus of the Predecessors and Imams...and sound reason."[81] That said, a detailed exposition of his misinterpretations is beyond the scope of this book.

Moreover, in some cases Ibn ᶜArabī attributes statements to the Prophet, which are fabricated and have no basis in the *Ḥadīth* collections, to give credence to his philosophy. For example, he repeats more than thirty times in *al-Futūḥāt al-Makkiyya*[82] and three times in *Fuṣūṣ al-ḥikam*[83] the statement: "Whoever knows himself knows his Lord,"[84] and attributes it to the Prophet Muḥammad in each of those instances even though it is fabricated. Ibn ᶜArabī again does this to support his monism; for instance, he states: "Thus, whoever knows himself (or his soul) through this knowledge knows his Lord, because He created him in His image; moreover, he is the very ipseity and

---

79 Ibn ᶜArabī's followers include Ṣadr al-Dīn Qūnawī (d. 673/1274), who then taught Saᶜīd al-Dīn Farghānī (d. 690/1291). Another proponent was Saᶜd al-Dīn Hammūya (d. 649/1252). See Chittick, "Rūmī and *waḥdat al-wujūd*", pp. 70–109.

80 William Chittick, "Ibn ᶜArabī", in Nasr and Leaman (eds.), *History of Islamic Philosophy*, p. 504.

81 Ibn Taymiyya, *Majmūᶜ al-fatāwā*, vol. V, p. 230.

82 Chittick translates this statement as: "He who knows himself knows his Lord." It is attributed to the Prophet throughout *al-Futūḥāt al-Makkiyya*, ed. Aḥmad Shams al-Dīn (Beirut: Dār al-Kutub al-ᶜIlmiyya, 1999), including volumes: I, pp. 103, 173, 496, 499, 532; II, pp. 33, 122, 140, 157, 314; III, pp. 53, 339, 365–66, 385, 449; IV, pp. 87, 148, 161, 175, 205; V, pp. 65, 106, 149, 281, 427; VI, pp. 156–57, 236, 301, 362, 374–75; VII, pp. 80, 211, 217, 255, 336, 389; and VIII, pp. 193, 217, 248. Chittick has translated many of these passages—see Chittick, *The Self-Disclosure of God*, p. 436, for an index of those instances.

83 Abrahamov (tr.), *Ibn al-ᶜArabī's Fuṣūṣ al-Ḥikam*, pp. 37, 51 and 172.

84 It is "fabricated" according to Albānī (*Silsilat al-aḥādīth al-ḍaᶜīfa wa'l-mawḍūᶜa* 66). Again, this statement is not present in any of the Ḥadīth collections. One should instead know himself in order to [1] rid himself of any inadequacy or evilness, which is in opposition to God's religious commandments, and [2] to attain all goodness in accordance with His religious commandments.

reality of God."[85] Again, the aforementioned statement is not present in any *Ḥadīth* collection.[86]

Ibn ʿArabī also claimed that mystical unveiling could attribute statements to the Prophet Muḥammad that he never said to others in person, and that unveiling could supercede the opinion of *Ḥadīth* scholars. Regarding the latter, Ibn ʿArabī states:

> There is many a weak hadith which is not put into practice because of the weakness of its line of transmission...yet which is sound in fact... But this friend may have heard the Spirit casting this very ḥadīth upon the reality of Muḥammad...[thus] he is like the Companion who heard it from the mouth of God's Messenger...There is also many a hadith which is sound by way of transmission...Then he asks the Prophet about this sound hadith, and he denies it and says, "I did not say it." Thereby the friend comes to know of its weakness, so he ceases putting it into practice.[87]

Thus Ibn ʿArabī claims here that mystical unveiling can lead to new true knowledge, which may contradict established laws. Ibn Arabī

---

85 Abrahamov (tr.), *Ibn al-ʿArabī's Fuṣūṣ al-Ḥikam*, p. 90. See also ibid., p. 51, where he states: "the cosmos is nothing but His self disclosure in the forms of fixed entities...and that He is manifest through various forms according to the realities of these entities and their states." Whoever has read Ibn ʿArabī's *Fuṣūṣ al-ḥikam* may perceive some wisdom within it, but each bezel, i.e. chapter, contains so much that is either inconsistent with traditional Islam, has false claims about the prophets, or is outright heretical such that any wisdom therein is lost. It is, however, beyond the scope of this book to detail all of that incoherence. Although some defenders of Ibn ʿArabī stress that his works suffered from corruption by copyists, in particular *Fuṣūṣ al-ḥikam* (but not the *Futuḥāt al-Makkiyya*)—see Keller, *Reliance*, pp. 1080–1—one would have to claim that the vast majority of *Fuṣūṣ al-ḥikam* was altered or not attributable to him. Regardless, Ibn ʿArabī's monism and his view of mystical unveiling are present in both works, and are the focus of the limited discussion here.

86 Another example of Ibn ʿArabī attributing a statement to the Prophet Muḥammad and to God is: "I [i.e. God] was a hidden and unknown treasure and (therefore) I loved (or wanted) to be known." This is "fabricated" according to Albānī (*Silsilat al-aḥādīth al-ḍaʿīfa wa'l-mawḍūʿa* 6023). Abrahamov states that this "tradition is considered spurious by the experts of *Ḥadīth*; hence, Ibn ʿArabī ascribed its authenticity to unveiling". Abrahamov (tr.), *Ibn al-ʿArabī's Fuṣūṣ al-Ḥikam*, pp. 160 and 169. See also William C. Chittick, *The Sufi Path of Knowledge* (Albany: State University of New York, 1989), p. 391, n. 14. For examples of Ibn ʿArabī's use of this tradition in *al-Futuḥāt al-Makkiyya*, see vol. III, p. 167, 350, 484; IV, p. 43; V, p. 394; VIII, pp. 210–211.

87 Chittick, *The Sufi Path of Knowledge*, p. 251.

claims elsewhere that he was able to receive and access divine dictation: "If not for the Intellect's *wujūd* I would not know Him, if not for the Tablet's *wujūd*, I would not take His dictation."[88]

One should recall that ʿUmar b. al-Khaṭṭāb, who was divinely inspired (*muḥaddath*), would always consult with the other Companions to seek out the Prophet's statements, and he would never claim that a notion brought on from a dream or through mystical unveiling took precedence over other Companions' knowledge of the Sunna. ʿAlī b. Abī Ṭālib would make others swear that they truly heard a *ḥadīth* from the Prophet Muḥammad—he would only believe them if they swore to hearing it.[89] The Companions were also well aware of the Prophet Muḥammad saying: "Whoever intentionally attributes a false statement to me should prepare himself for Hellfire."[90] Therefore, they were cautious in transmitting *ḥadīths* they heard from the Prophet for fear of misrepresenting them or being incorrect.

Ibn ʿArabī went even further claiming that he inherited "all the works, states, and stations of Muhammad"[91] but unlike the "Seal of the Prophets", i.e. the Prophet Muḥammad who was only able to receive the law-giving revelation from Gabriel, he, as "the Seal of the Saints", was able to access the principal source (*al-maʿdan*) and Tablet from which the angel Gabriel took for his true knowledge of the real (*ʿilm al-ḥaqīqa*).[92] Ibn ʿArabī again acknowledged Muḥammad as the Seal of the Prophets and "the [final] (missing) brick",[93] but that he is the:

---

[88] Chittick, *The Self-Disclosure of God*, p. 122.

[89] See Tirmidhī 406; Abū Dāwūd 1521; Ibn Māja 1395; Aḥmad 2. It is "sound" according to Albānī (*al-Taʿlīqāt al-ḥisān ʿalā Ṣaḥīḥ Ibn Ḥibbān* 622).

[90] Bukhārī 110; Muslim 3; Tirmidhī 2659; Abū Dāwūd 3651; Ibn Māja 30; Aḥmad 9316. Of note, the *ḥadīth* in Bukhārī 110 and Aḥmad 9316 also includes the Prophet Muḥammad saying: "Whoever sees me in a dream has truly seen me, since the Devil cannot picture himself in my form..." It is almost as if the Prophet Muḥammad is saying that some will falsely claim that they have seen him in their dreams, in addition to falsely attributing statements to him. And God knows best.

[91] William C. Chittick, *Ibn ʿArabi: Heir to the Prophets* (Oxford: OneWorld, 2009), p. 126.

[92] See Ibn Taymiyya, *al-Furqān bayna awliyāʾ al-Raḥmān wa awliyāʾ al-shayṭān*, p. 103 as well as Ibn al-Qayyim, *Ighāthat al-lahfān min maṣāyid al-Shayṭān*, ed. Muḥammad ʿUzayr Shams and Muṣṭafā b. Saʿīd Ītīm (Mecca: Dār ʿĀlam al-Fawāʾid, 2011), vol. II, p. 1012.

[93] The Prophet Muḥammad indicates that he is the final brick (*labina*) in the *ḥadīth* within Bukhārī 3535; Muslim 2286/5959; Tirmidhī 3613; Aḥmad 7485.

> Seal of God's Friends... [who] saw two missing bricks, one made of gold and the other of silver[94]...He necessarily regarded himself as the two missing bricks needed to complete the wall. The reason that entails his seeing two bricks is his following outwardly the Law of the Seal of the Messengers, and this is the place of the silver brick. It is the outward aspect, (meaning) the rules that he follows. In like manner he learns from God inwardly that which he follows outwardly, for he necessarily contemplates things as they really are. Regarding the inward aspect, this is the place of the golden brick. He [i.e. the Seal of the Saints] and the angel, who reveals (messages) to the Messenger, acquire their knowledge from the same source.[95]

In this fashion, Ibn ʿArabī also disbelieved in the verse of the Qur'ān wherein God (Glorious is He) states: *This day have I perfected your religion for you, completed My favour upon you, and have chosen for you Islam as your religion.*[96] Unveiling or divine inspiration does not lead to new revelation or some truer knowledge inaccessible to the prophets, but rather it is one means by which one can attain a deeper understanding and insight into the Qur'ān and Sunna, greater wisdom and/or a deeper experience of divine providence.

Finally, it will be contended that Ibn ʿArabī's incorporation of confusion or bewilderment (*ḥayra*) into his philosophy[97] may represent an implicit recognition on his part of the incoherence of monism with Scripture and revelation. Ibn ʿArabī states: "There is nothing but He and bewilderment."[98] Ibn ʿArabī also falsely attributed a statement to the Prophet Muḥammad in this regard: "O God, increase my

94 See Ibn ʿArabī, *al-Futūḥāt al-Makkiyya*, vol I. pp. 480–81, for Ibn ʿArabī's account of himself seeing this dream and being the gold and silver bricks.

95 Abrahamov (tr.), *Ibn al-ʿArabī's Fuṣūṣ al-Ḥikam*, pp. 30–31.

96 Q.V.3 (Yusuf Ali translation).

97 See Chittick, *The Sufi Path of Knowledge*, pp. 3–4 and 380–381 as well as Chittick, *The Self-Disclosure of God*, pp. 86–90. Of note, the Qur'ān alludes to the state of being bewildered (*ḥayrān*) in a negative fashion—see Q.VI.71 (Yusuf Ali translation).

98 See Chittick, *The Self-Disclosure of God*, pp. 90.

bewilderment (*zidnī taḥayyur*[an]) in Thee."[99] Ibn ʿArabī then adds: "For this [i.e the station of bewilderment] is the highest station, the clearest vision, the nearest rank, the most brilliant locus of manifestation, and the most exemplary path."[100] In contrast, the Prophet Muḥammad (as well as the other prophets) elucidated the Straight Path and provided guidance and religious knowledge, which allowed his Companions to attain certainty (*ʿilm al-yaqīn*) and God's pleasure—that is what all the seekers should pursue.

As regards the problem of evil, since Ibn ʿArabī and his followers claim that everything other than God is non-existent, they assert that evil is either non-existent or represents privation.[101] Ibn ʿArabī stated that "there cannot be a world more wonderful than the present world (*laysa fi'l-imkān abdaʿ min hādha al-ʿālam*), for it is in the image of the Merciful...We are His external form, while His Ipseity is the spirit which governs the form."[102] Ibn ʿArabī's explanation for evil, according to Hoover, is that:

> Evil and imperfection, which are paradoxically no more than privation and otherness from the sole reality of God and yet real in that they thwart God's Law and human purposes, are necessary in order to afford God the

99 See Ibn ʿArabī, *al-Futūḥāt al-Makkiyya*, vol. I, pp. 408–409; vol. IV, p. 261 and 343. See also Chittick, *The Sufi Path of Knowledge*, p. 381. Of note, Nāṣir al-Dīn al-Albānī did not comment on this statement, but it is not present in any *Ḥadīth* collection and Ibn Taymiyya states that all of the *Ḥadīth* scholars consider it to be fabricated. See Ibn Taymiyya, *Majmūʿ al-fatāwā*, vol. II, p. 202; vol. V, p. 179; vol. XI, pp. 383–387. Ibn Taymiyya also stated that it "is impermissible for anyone asking or supplicating to become more confused (or bewildered). Instead, if one is confused one should ask for guidance and knowledge". See Ibn Taymiyya, *Majmūʿat al-rasā'il wa'l-masā'il li-Ibn Taymiyya*, ed. Rashīd Riḍā (Cairo: Lajnat al-Turāth al-ʿArabī, 1976), vol. I, pp. 205–206. See also ibid., vol IV, p. 45

100 See Chittick, *The Sufi Path of Knowledge*, p. 381, as well as Ibn ʿArabī, *al-Futūḥāt al-Makkiyya*, vol. IV, p. 343.

101 See Jon Hoover, "A Typology of Responses to the Philosophical Problem of Evil in the Islamic and Christian Traditions", *The Conrad Grebel Review*, vol. XXI, no. 3, 2003, p. 86.

102 Abrahamov (tr.), *Ibn al-ʿArabī's Fuṣūṣ al-Ḥikam*, p. 133. Note that the reason that Ibn ʿArabī comes to this conclusion is completely different to that which led theists like Ghazālī and others to believe that this is the best possible world.

> possibility to manifest the infinite diversity, the great plenitude,[103] of His names. Everything in existence reflects a divine name...Nonetheless, Ibn ʿArabī maintains that, out of courtesy for God, we should address God only with names that He has revealed. We should not, for example, call God Liar or Ignorant.[104]

Thus imperfections, deficiencies or evils in this world are claimed by Ibn ʿArabī and other monists to be due to privation from God Himself—not privation from the good that He has created (as maintained by many theists). In the end, monism (*waḥdat al-wujūd*) is heretical and is completely incompatible with the Qur'ān and Sunna as well as all of the prior Scriptures. God is glorious and exalted above the heretical views of the monists. God (Glorious and Exalted is He) is transcendent and distinct from what He has created and enacted: *God—He is the Reality (al-Ḥaqq); and those besides Him whom they invoke, they are but vain falsehood: verily God is He, Most High, Most Great.*[105]

Thereafter Ibn Sabʿīn adopted *waḥdat al-wujūd* in purely pantheistic terms by claiming that "only God really exists [and] there is no real basis to the distinction between the existence of God and of everything else". This contrasts with Ibn ʿArabī who, according to Chittick, "admits the existence of contingent things".[106] Yet, unsurprisingly, Ibn Sabʿīn extends the same viewpoint to deny the existence of evil: "Since existence is One and is absolute Good, how can evil come about?"[107]

---

[103] The principle of plenitude is a Neoplatonic concept. Ibn ʿArabī relied to some degree on Avicennean concepts—this being one of them.

[104] Hoover, *Ibn Taymiyya's Theodicy of Perpetual Optimism*, p. 178.

[105] Q.XXII.62 and Q.XXXI.30. Also note that the Holy Lord states: *God is the Reality: it is He Who gives life to the dead, and it is He Who has power over all things. And verily the Hour will come: there can be no doubt about it, or about (the fact) that God will raise up all who are in the graves.* Q.XXII.5–6 (Yusuf Ali translation).

[106] Abu'l-Wafa al-Taftazani and Oliver Leaman, "Ibn Sabʿīn", in Nasr and Leaman (eds.), *History of Islamic Philosophy*, p. 347. Chittick states: "One has to agree with Michel Chodkiewicz that Ibn Sabʿīn was thoroughly influenced by the perspective of Ibn ʿArabī, even if he does not acknowledge this fact in his works." Chittick, "Rūmī and *waḥdat al-wujūd*", p. 82.

[107] Abu'l-Wafa al-Taftazani and Leaman, "Ibn Sabʿīn", p. 348.

Then there is the modern Muhammad Iqbal who is considered by some to be a panentheist.[108] However, Iqbal was not a consistent panentheist, much like how Ibn ʿArabī was not a pure monist. Iqbal adopted a free will theodicy wherein "man is the author of his own actions"[109] being "co-partner" and "co-worker of God" in order to advance "ego making"[110]. This egocentric view is in opposition to most religions and spiritual endeavours—whether it be Sufism, traditional Islam, Christianity, or even Eastern religions—for devotion can only occur through the avoidance of pride. Iqbal at times also denied the "existence of evil or non-holy or Satanic" and denied "any real significance to sin".[111] His panentheism also led him to claim that God is not omnipotent, but rather interdependent with His creation: "God will overcome all evil that it is possible to defeat with our cooperation."[112] God is sublime and exalted above all these heresies.

Of course, pantheism and its permutations, like monism, are antithetical to Islam and heretical. Pantheism leads some to worship everything; others to make heretical statements such as claiming that Pharaoh is better than Moses since the former claimed that he was a deity (thus acknowledging pantheism in part) or that Christians are disbelievers only because they limited godhood to Jesus;[113] or

---

[108] See Muhammad Maroof Shah, *Problem of Evil in Muslim Philosophy: A Case Study of Iqbal* (Delhi: Indian Publishers' Distributors, 2007), p. 173. Panentheism entails belief that "God is interdependent with the world...and God attains perfections successively", and that "creation is out of something eternally at the other pole (ex hulas)." Ibid., p. 174.

[109] Ibid., p. 31. Shah also states: "Iqbal conceives man as copartner of God in creation and advocates spiritual pluralism... He makes man co-worker of God." Ibid., pp. 172–173.

[110] Shah states: "Iqbal too is not happy with the orthodox attitude to prayer, as expressing our humility and repentance and seeking God's help, letting God possess our soul... Iqbal's philosophy of religion is, by and large, man centered rather than God centered... Iqbal has great faith in man and his goodness—in ego's triumphant march, defeating evil and catching hold of the infinite... God, in Iqbal's scheme, does not actively help the finite egos to reach perfection." Ibid., pp. 100–104. See also pp. 112, 134 and 154.

[111] Ibid., pp. 62 and 80.

[112] Ibid., p. 174.

[113] See Ibn Taymiyya, *al-Furqān bayna awliyā' al-Raḥmān wa awliyā' al-Shayṭān*, pp. 114–115.

to others deeming nothing to be illicit or forbidden[114]—all of these represent further forms of disbelief and wickedness.

In summation, it is affirmed here that God Himself exists in His Essence above His Throne (Glorious and Exalted is He) for He is the Most High (*al-ʿAliy*); that the manifestations of His Names, Attributes and actions exist; and what He has created and enacted (*mafʿūlāti[hi]*) exist—His creation being separate and distinct from Him, and *there is nothing whatever like unto Him.*[115] No evil is attributable to the Holy Lord, although everything existent in this world has been created by the Holy Lord, both good and evil.

Now that various Muslim theodicies, including the philosophical and heretical types, have been discussed, this chapter will conclude with a brief discussion on the Hellfire.

Hellfire

Numerous Sunni scholars contend that there is scholarly consensus (*ijmāʿ*) that the disbelievers will be eternally punished in Hellfire.[116] Now, since the Prophetic *ḥadīth*s maintain that God's mercy (Glorious is He) precedes and prevails over His wrath,[117] but the majority of humankind are disbelievers[118] (and therefore deserving of eternal punishment according to the mainstream orthodox position), it may be argued that the scholarly consensus does not appear to have reconciled the Holy Lord's preponderant mercy with the presence of the eternal punishment of Hellfire for all disbelievers.

A few contrasting views to the scholarly consensus will now be mentioned. Mohammad Khalil opined that Ghazālī may have been a

---

114 This was claimed by one of the pantheists, al-Tilmasānī, as well as others. See Ibn Taymiyya, *al-Furqān bayna awliyā' al-Raḥmān wa awliyā' al-Shayṭān*, p. 112–113.

115 Q.XLII.11 (Yusuf Ali translation).

116 Numerous references are given for such Sunni authorities by Jon Hoover, including the statement of Ījī in *Kitāb al-mawāqif*: "The Muslims have reached a consensus that the unbelievers will abide in the Fire forever; their chastisement will not be cut off." See Jon Hoover, "Islamic Universalism: Ibn Qayyim al-Jawziyya's Salafī Deliberations on the Duration of Hell-fire", *The Muslim World*, vol. XCIX, 2009, pp. 197–8.

117 See Bukhārī 3194 and 7422; Muslim 2751/6970; Tirmidhī 3543; Ibn Māja 189; Aḥmad 7500 and 9159.

118 See Q.XII.103.

universalist in reality: "Like other Ashʿarites, Ghazālī maintains that true unbelievers will remain in Hell 'forever' (*ʿalā al-taʾbīd*)," but then adds:

> Yet I would be remiss not to mention Ghazālī's cryptic conclusion to his exposition of the divine names, the Compassionate and the Caring: "Never doubt that [God] is 'the most merciful of the merciful' [Q. 7:151], or that 'His mercy outstrips His wrath,' and never doubt that the one who intends evil for the sake of evil and not for the sake of good is undeserving of the name of mercy. Beneath all this lies a secret whose divulgence the revealed law [*al-sharʿ*] prohibits, so be content with prayer and do not expect that it be divulged." Ghazālī goes on to state that this "secret" is not discernable to most people. One can only wonder what it is. Given the available evidence, however, it would be difficult to aver that this is a sign of his being a closet universalist.[119]

Ibn ʿArabī held that "although certain types of unbelievers will remain forever in hell, even they will cease to suffer after a period of time...in the end, the chastisement will become 'sweet' (*ʿadhib*) for those who suffer it".[120] Ibn ʿArabī claimed this so as to maintain God's preponderant mercy, but in doing so he denied the meaning and true nature of Hellfire as described by God (Glorious and Exalted is He) in the Qurʾān and the Prophet Muḥammad in the Sunna.

Traditionalists like Ibn Taymiyya and Ibn al-Qayyim maintained, on the other hand, that many of the Predecessors held the opinion that the punishment of Hellfire will eventually end for the disbelievers. Ibn al-Qayyim argued at the end of his *Shifāʾ al-ʿalīl* that the punishment of the disbelievers will ultimately come to an end.[121] But he subsequently chose a position of universal salvation in a later

---

119 Mohammad Khalil, *Islam and the Fate of Others: The Salvation Question* (Oxford: Oxford University Press, 2012), pp. 46–48.

120 See Chittick, *Ibn ʿArabī: Heir to the Prophets*, pp. 128–139. Ibn ʿArabī states: "As for the people of the Fire, they finally attain felicity, but [remain] in Hell, for the form of the Fire will become necessarily cool and safe for those who dwell in it at the end of their punishment period...The felicity of the people of the Fire after exhausting the (sufferings) they deserve is like the felicity of God's friend (Abraham) when he was thrown into the fire." See Abrahamov (tr.), *Ibn ʿArabī's Fuṣūṣ al-Ḥikam*, p. 130.

121 See Zeni (tr.), *Ibn Qayyim al-Jawziyya on Divine Wisdom and the Problem of Evil*, pp. 192–193

work of his, *al-Ṣawāʿiq al-mursala*, stating that once the punishment of Hellfire purifies the disbelievers from their wickedness, then all that remains is their pure innate disposition, by which God, in His vast mercy, allows the individual to enter Paradise. That said, Ibn al-Qayyim later abandoned universal salvation in his final work, *Zād al-maʿād*,[122] stating: "Since those who worship others [besides God] have a nature and essence which is wicked, they will never be purified through [the punishment of] Hellfire...For this reason, God (Exalted is He) has prohibited those who have worshipped others from entering Paradise."[123] Nevertheless, it is contended that Ibn al-Qayyim still held to the view that the punishment of *all* of the disbelievers will end.[124] Muslim claims of universal salvation will not be discussed further here as they are inconsistent with categorical verses of the Qur'ān as well as the Sunna.

This author will contend that the punishment of Hellfire will end for *most*—not all—of the disbelievers. This viewpoint is not inconsistent with revelation—it will be reconciled with all of the transmitted evidences of the Qur'ān and Sunna along with reason in Chapter Fourteen.

---

[122] *Zād al-maʿād* was written after both *Shifā' al-ʿalīl* and *al-Ṣawāʿiq al-mursala*, and was likely his last work; see Livnat Holtzman, "Ibn Qayyim al-Jawziyyah", in Joseph E. Lowery and Devin Stewart (eds.), *Essays in Arabic Literary Biography II:* 1350–1850 (Wiesbaden: Harrassowitz Verlag, 2009), p. 217.

[123] Ibn al-Qayyim, *Zād al-maʿād fī hady khayr al-ʿibād* (Beirut: Mu'assasat al-Risāla, 1994), vol. I, p. 68.

[124] See Zeni (tr.), *Ibn Qayyim al-Jawziyya on Divine Wisdom and the Problem of Evil*, pp. XXIV–XXVIII, for a more in-depth discussion.

Chapter Nine

Non-Muslim Approaches to the Problems of Evil and Hellfire

The objective of this chapter is to touch on a vast array of non-Muslim religious theodicies and defenses. There is much that can be gleaned from these. That said, brief comments regarding significant errors will be mentioned as needed. This chapter will conclude, as did the last, with eschatological considerations.

The following quotations from Michael Peterson and John Hick will set the scene for the specific discussions. Peterson states: "What a religious system says about evil reveals a great deal about what it takes ultimate reality and humanity's relation to it to be. Hence the credibility of a religion is closely linked to its ability to give its adherents categories for thinking about the presence of evil."[1] He also added: "All three great theistic religions—Judaism, Christianity, and Islam—face the challenge of addressing this issue."[2] Hick states: "The two demands upon a theodicy hypothesis are (1) that it be internally coherent, and (2) that it be consistent with the data both of the religious tradition on which it is based, and of the world, in respect both of the latter's general character as revealed by scientific inquiry and of the specific facts of moral and natural evil."[3]

---

[1] Michael Peterson, *God and Evil: An Introduction to the Issues* (Boulder: Westview Press, 1998), p. 7.

[2] Michael Peterson, *The Problem of Evil* (Notre Dame: University of Notre Dame Press, 2017), p. 1.

[3] John Hick, "An Irenaean Theodicy", in Stephen T. David (ed.), *Encountering Evil: Live Options in Theodicy* (Louisville: Westminster John Knox Press, 2001), p. 38. Martin Scott mentions five criteria: "1. Fidelity: Does it utilize the sources of theology, especially scripture and tradition? 2. Coherence: Does it make sense logically? Is it internally consistent? 3. Relevance: Does it speak to contemporary experiences of evil? 4. Creativity: Does it creatively engage the problem of evil? 5. Humility: Does it recognize and respect the limits of theodicy?" Martin Scott, *Pathways in Theodicy: An Introduction to the Problem of Evil* (Minneapolis: Fortress Press, 2015), p. 66.

AUGUSTINE AND THE FREE WILL THEODICY

The Christian approach to the problem of evil often begins with the work of Augustine of Hippo. He proposed a free will theodicy aimed, in part, to rebut the dualism inherent within Manichaeism. Augustine maintained that God is omnipotent, omniscient and holy. He also viewed the human will itself, as well as the freedom to act, as good. Thus he maintained that evil arises only when the will is misused and chooses to turn away from God.[4] Evil was therefore defined as the absence or privation of good.[5]

Though this free will often leads to evil, Augustine maintained that its occurrence was valuable, as God "judged it better to bring good out of evil than not to permit any evil to exist".[6] Augustine also argued that the "opposition of contraries" is necessary to achieve the "beauty of the course of this world",[7] and that "the whole of creation, even including those aspects we call evil, is good when seen from God's perspective".[8] With regards to this last point, it is important to highlight that traditional Islam maintains that evil is evil from God's perspective and that He has forbidden it and dislikes it.

Augustine maintained that even though wicked souls "make ill use of good natures, [God] makes a good use of evil wills".[9] He also maintained that it was only through divine grace and mercy that the elect will attain salvation.[10] These arguments are correct and akin to that of many Islamic scholars such as Ibn al-Qayyim[11] for God (Exalted is He) places everything in its appropriate place and uses it concordantly.

---

4 Gillian R. Evans, *Augustine on Evil* (Cambridge: Cambridge University Press, 1982), pp. 116–117 and 136.

5 Ibid., p. 166.

6 Albert C. Outler (tr.), *Augustine: Confessions and Enchiridion* (Philadelphia: The Westminster Press, 1955), Chapter VIII, no. 27, p. 355.

7 Augustine, *The City of God*, tr. Marcus Dods (Peabody: Hendrickson, 2014), Book XI, Chapter 17, p. 325.

8 Peterson, *God and Evil*, p. 91.

9 Augustine, *The City of God*, Book XI, Chapter 18, p. 325.

10 See Evans, *Augustine on Evil*, pp. 126–135.

11 See Zeni (tr.), *Ibn Qayyim al-Jawziyya on Divine Wisdom and the Problem of Evil*, Chapter Two, pp. 22–23.

As for how sin arose in a world in which nothing can occur outside of God's will, Griffin states that Augustine "overcome[s] this contradiction by making a distinction between two 'wills' in God. Whereas we go against God's will in one sense when we sin, Augustine says, we nevertheless fulfill God's *eternal* will".[12] Augustine stated: "In a strange and ineffable fashion even that which is done against his will is not done without his will".[13] This statement can be understood from an Islamic standpoint if the first will is His religious will and the second is His ontologic will[14] (or God's eternal will, in the words of Augustine). But Augustine is not able to account for how "unqualifiedly good creatures" can perpetrate sins: "Unable to find a satisfactory logical solution to this difficulty...Augustine subsumes the mystery of free will under the mystery of predestination."[15]

Archbishop William King agreed with the importance of free will stating that "the Divine Wisdom seems to have set apart the Government of Free Agents as its peculiar Province."[16] King also elaborates that God created the world as such in order "to have something wherein to exercise [H]is Attributes externally"[17] and it is for "the Glory of God [such] that the Divine Attributes namely Power, Goodness and Wisdom, shine forth as clearly as His Works."[18]

John Hick's soul-making theodicy

John Hick takes issue with the above free-will theodicy stating: "Now this doctrine of God's creation of beings whom He knows will fall and whom, having fallen, He does not intend to raise up again, is directly at variance with the thought that He permits sin only in order to bring

---

12 Griffin, *God, Power, and Evil: A Process Theodicy*, p. 66.

13 Outler (tr.), *Augustine: Confessions and Enchiridion*, Chapter XXVI, no.100, p. 399.

14 See Zeni (tr.), *Ibn Qayyim al-Jawziyya on Divine Wisdom and the Problem of Evil*, pp. 229–36.

15 Peterson, *God and Evil*, pp. 90–91.

16 William King, *Essay on the Origin of Evil* (New York: Garland Publishing, 1978), p. 249.

17 Ibid., p. 249.

18 King stated in full: "When therefore the Scripture teaches us that the World was created for the Glory of God, 'tis to be understood that the Divine Attributes namely Power, Goodness and Wisdom shine forth as clearly as His Works, as if he had no other intent in making them beside the Ostentation of these Attributes; nor could they have answer'd that end more fitly, if they had been design'd for Glory." Ibid., p. 54.

out of it the greater and more glorious good of redemption."[19] Hick also finds the "privation of good" explanation of evil to be inadequate: "To describe, for example, the dynamic malevolence behind the Nazi attempt to exterminate the European Jews as merely the absence of some good, is utterly insufficient...Cruelty is not merely an absence of kindness, but is something with a demonic power of its own."[20] Hick states instead:

> There is thus to be found in Irenaeus the outline of an approach[21] to the problem of evil which stands in important respects in contrast to the Augustinian type of theodicy. Instead of the doctrine that man was created finitely perfect and then incomprehensibly destroyed his own perfection and plunged into sin and misery, Irenaeus suggests that man was created as an imperfect, immature creature who was to undergo moral development and growth and finally be brought to the perfection intended for him by his Maker. Instead of the fall of Adam being presented, as in the Augustinian tradition, as an utterly malignant and catastrophic event, completely disrupting God's plan, Irenaeus pictures it as something that occurred in the childhood of the race, an understandable lapse due to weakness and immaturity rather than an adult crime full of malice and pregnant with perpetual guilt.[22] And instead of the Augustinian view of life's trials as divine punishment for Adam's sin, Irenaeus sees our world of mingled good and evil as a divinely appointed environment for man's development towards the perfection that represents the fulfillment of God's good purpose for him. Irenaeus was the first great Christian theologian to think at all systemically along these lines, and although he was far from working out a comprehensive theodicy his

---

[19] John Hick, *Evil and the God of Love* (New York: Palgrave Macmillan, 1966, Reissued 2010), p. 177.

[20] Ibid., pp. 56–57.

[21] Hick follows the Protestant theologian Friedrich Schleiermacher (1768–1834), who independently added to the Irenaean theodicy "carrying some of the same themes much further and in a more systematic form". Ibid., p. 219.

[22] Hick states in another section: "In the Augustinian tradition the doctrine of the fall plays a central role, whereas in the Irenaean type of theodicy, whilst it is not necessarily denied in all its forms, the doctrine becomes much less important. The accompanying notions of an original but lost righteousness of man and perfection of his world, and of inherited sinfulness as a universal consequence of the fall, which jointly render that event so catastrophic and therefore so crucial for the Augustinian theodicy, are both rejected." Ibid., p. 237.

> hints are sufficiently explicit to justify his name being associated with the approach.[23]

Hick also points out that:

> The Augustinian tradition embodies the philosophy of evil as non-being, with its Neo-Platonic accompaniments of the principle of plenitude, the conception of the great chain of being, and the aesthetic vision of the perfection of the universe as a complex harmony. In contrast, the Irenaean type of theodicy is more purely theological in character and is not committed to the Platonic or to any other philosophical framework. The Augustinian theodicy, especially in Thomist thought and in the Protestantism of the eighteenth-century "optimists"...sees God's relation to His creation in predominately non-personal terms. God's goodness is His overflowing plenitude of being...[while] evil is traceable to the necessary finitude and contingency of a dependent world which however exhibits an aesthetic perfection when seen from the divine standpoint; and the existence of moral evil is harmonized within this perfect whole by the balancing effect of just punishment. These are all ideas to which the category of the personal is peripheral. According to the Irenaean type of theodicy, on the other hand, man has been created for fellowship with his Maker and is valued by the personal divine love as an end in himself. The world exists to be an environment for man's life, and its imperfections are integral to its fitness as a place of soul-making.[24]

Hick thus develops the thought, following the Irenaean tradition, that "this world must be a place of soul-making".[25] Had suffering been non-existent this world would be "without need for the virtues of self-sacrifice, care for others, devotion to the public good, courage, perseverance, skill, or honesty...Perhaps most important of all, the capacity to love would never be developed, except in a very limited sense of the word."[26]

---

[23] Ibid., pp. 214–15.
[24] Ibid., pp. 236–37.
[25] Ibid., p. 259.
[26] John Hick, "Soul-Making and Suffering", in Marilyn McCord Adams and Robert Merrihew Adams (eds.), *The Problem of Evil* (Oxford: Oxford University Press, 1990), p. 179.

Hick further states:

> [H]umanity is created at an epistemic distance from God in order to come freely to know[27] and love the Maker; and that one is at the same time created as a morally immature and imperfect being in order to attain through freedom the most valuable quality of good...The development of human personality—moral, spiritual, and intellectual—is a product of challenge and response. It does not occur in a static situation demanding no exertion and no choices... [It] requires that their environment, instead of being a pain-free and stress-free paradise...be an environment which offers challenges to be met, problems to be solved, dangers to be faced, and which accordingly involves real possibilities of hardship, disaster, failure, defeat, and misery as well as of delight and happiness, success, triumph, and achievement. [It is only in this manner] that they can develop the higher values of mutual love and care, of self-sacrifice for others, and of commitment to a common good.[28]

So Hick emphasized soul-making to achieve moral and spiritual perfection in order to subsequently enjoy proximity, love and fellowship with God. Nonetheless, Hick acknowledged that soul-making cannot be the only reason: "The mystery of dysteleological suffering is a real mystery, impenetrable to the rationalizing human mind...If the soul-making purpose fails, there can surely be no justification for 'the heavy and the weary weight of all this unintelligible world'. And yet, so far as we can see, the soul-making process does in fact fail in our own world at least as often as it succeeds."[29] Hick's failure to understand dysteleological suffering led him to notions inconsistent with Scripture in regards to life after death. This will be discussed at the end of this chapter, but for now Hick concludes:

> I find that the realities of human goodness and human happiness make it a credible possibility that this life, with its baffling mixture of good and evil, and including both its dark miseries and its shining joys, including both man's malevolence and his self-forgetting love, is indeed part of

[27] Richard Swinburne states likewise that: "God has reason to ensure that we only get to [proximity to Him] as a result of our own choice (e.g., in another world as a result of our conduct in this one)." Richard Swinburne, "Natural Evils and Moral Choice", in *American Philosophical Quarterly*, vol. XV, no. 4, 1978, pp. 295–301.

[28] John Hick, "An Irenaean Theodicy", pp. 44–47.

[29] Hick, *Evil and the God of Love*, pp. 335–36.

a long and slow pilgrim's progress toward the Celestial City. If so, the journey must have many stages beyond our present one; and the end must be good beyond our present imagining.[30]

SUFFERING AS A MEANS TOWARDS LOVE AND MORAL GOODNESS

Kevin Tewes adds another wisdom that he feels is more important than the "free will" or "soul-making", and it is that suffering occurs so that God may manifest His love for us. He states: "God, in His wisdom, ranks love above all other considerations" and that love is an "objective that is *infinitely* more important" than "spiritual growth and positive character development" as well as "retribution or free will".[31] Ultimately, Tewes states that "God does not want us to experience merely a tepid, mediocre love with Him. God wants us to experience an extreme love, and extreme love is only possible when both parties have extreme faith in one another. For this reason we should expect that our faith will be stretched and pulled to its outermost limit during the course of our lives... [and that this] will be difficult and painful."[32]

Daniel Speak states that it might be a great good for human beings to seek out the Lord "as a result of real cognitive and volitional effort...to have a kind of relationship with God that is not the result of an imposed presence of God... [and] to choose to act *freely* rather than as a result of divine coercion".[33]

Philip Quinn adds that this world provides an avenue in which some of humanity may achieve "unsurpassable moral goodness".[34] Therefore, the objective is to create beings who may revere, adore and worship the perfect and Holy Lord as well as display unsurpassable moral goodness in manners that otherwise would not have been possible if this world did not contain the types of evil it does.

---

30 Ibid., p. 386.

31 Kevin Tewes, *Answering Christianity's Most Difficult Question—Why God Allows Us to Suffer* (Chapel Hill: Triune Publishing, 2015), pp. iv, 9 and 18–19.

32 Ibid., pp. 108–109.

33 Daniel Speak, *The Problem of Evil* (Cambridge: Polity Press, 2015), p. 81.

34 Philip L. Quinn, "God, Moral Perfection, and Possible Worlds", in Frederick Sontag and M. Darrol Bryant (eds.), *God: A Contemporary Discussion* (New York: Rose of Sharon Press, 1982), p. 213.

CHRISTIAN OPENNESS THEISM

The Christian theodicy of openness theism contends that the world enables us to "enter into reciprocal relations of love with God... [that] God is 'open' to creation... [and that] God's purpose in creating was to bring forth beings who could respond to his love by loving God in return as well as by establishing loving relationships and social structures among creatures".[35] The open theists, however, claim that:

> God's plan is not a detailed script or blueprint, but a broad intention... The future actions of genuinely free creatures can only be known as probabilities, not certainties, and they deny that God has "middle knowledge," that is, the knowledge of what every individual will do or would have done in all possible sets of circumstances... God did not want moral evil to arise—it was not part of his plan... There is no "happy fall" (*O felix culpa*) into sin. Evil is not part of a divine blueprint ordained by God. Though a soul-making theodicy can have a limited role in an open theist theodicy, it is the free will defense and God's work to redeem evil that takes center stage... [Moreover, this] "logic-of-love defense" is thus framed in terms of God's purposes in creation rather than merely in terms of the supposed intrinsic worth of human freedom.[36]

Thus open theists deny that God is truly omniscient, in order to avoid attributing the existence of evil to God and so as to explain the presence of gratuitous evil. They believe that "God is doing all he can, short of overriding his project, to prevent what evil he can, and, for that evil that does occur, God works to bring good out of those situations... Gratuitous [evils are truly] pointless, for they were not intended with the purpose of attaining a greater good."[37] Paul Helm responds: "The openness view, because of what it believes about God's ignorance of the future, cannot offer an adequate interpretation."[38]

---

[35] John Sanders, "God, Evil, and Relational Risk", in Peterson (ed.), *The Problem of Evil*, pp. 327–330.

[36] Ibid., pp. 329–333.

[37] Ibid., p. 335

[38] Paul Helm, "God's Providence Takes No Risks", in Peterson (ed.), *The Problem of Evil*, p. 359.

GOTTFRIED LEIBNIZ AND HIS RESPONDENTS

Gottfried Leibniz[39] proposed a "best of all possible worlds" theodicy much like Ghazālī, as mentioned in the last chapter. Leibniz followed Augustine in maintaining that God has allowed evil to bring about greater good or more good for the universe.[40] Leibniz stated: "It is sufficient to show that a world with evil might be better than a world without evil; but I have gone even farther in the work, and have even proved that this universe must be in reality better than every other possible universe."[41]

Leibniz's contention was discussed by many including Nicholas Malebranche, Antoine Arnauld, as well as others. Many of those debates are discussed by Steven Nadler in his book *The Best of All Possible*

---

[39] Gottfried Wilhelm Leibniz (1646–1716) was born in Leipzig, Germany. He studied Law and eventually became the counselor of justice to the Elector of Mainz. Facing the prospect of a French war against Germany, Leibniz developed "A Plan for a New Holy War" and he was sent to convince the French to institute "a new crusade against the infidel. This time, however, the target would not be Jerusalem but Egypt. A conquest of that ancient land would benefit not only France, Leibniz intended to argue, but all of Europe. It would bring intramural peace among the Western powers and allow the Christian states to band together and strengthen their defenses against the ever-present Muslim threat from the east, especially the Turks." See Steven Nadler, *The Best of All Possible Worlds: A Story of Philosophers, God, and Evil in the Age of Reason* (Princeton: Princeton University Press, 2010), pp. 13–14. That said, Leibniz in his later years did develop "a positive view of Islam as a theology"—although he accuses some Muslims of "indulging in the 'sophism' of 'Lazy Reason', that is, fatalism"—and acknowledged Islam "for the destruction of paganism in many parts of the world". See Daniel J. Cook, "Leibniz and 'Orientalism'," in *Studia Leibnitiana*, vol. XL, no. 2, 2008, pp. 168–190 (specifically pp. 183–184).

[40] See Gottfried Leibniz, *The Theodicy*, in *The Philosophical Works of Leibniz*, tr. George Duncan (New Haven: Tuttle, Morehouse, & Taylor, 1890), p. 195.

[41] Ibid., p. 195. In reality, Leibniz did not *prove* that this universe is better than others from all aspects. Rather, his argument is: "If the will of God did have for a rule the principle of the best, it would either tend toward evil, which would be the worst; or it would be in some way indifferent to good and to evil, and would be guided by chance… [E]ven if God should abandon himself to chance only in some cases and in a certain way (as he would do, if he did not always work entirely for the best and if he were capable of preferring a lesser work to a greater, that is, an evil to a good, since that which prevents a greater good is an evil), he would be imperfect, as well as the object of his choice; he would not merit confidence; he would act without reason in such a case, and the government of the universe would be like certain games, equally divided between reason and chance." Ibid., pp. 203–204.

Worlds. Malebranche claimed that God was determined to create this world utilizing the simplest of laws, and that this principle takes precedence over all other considerations. Therefore, Malebranche "says that God does not create the best of all possible worlds; there are many other possible worlds that are more perfect than the actual world because they contain fewer evils, but God does not create them because to do so He would have to violate the simplicity and generality of His ways".[42] Leibniz countered that God acts in a wise and intelligible manner to achieve what is good, and it is because of God's wisdom and goodness that He inevitably chooses and creates the best. Both Leibniz and Malebranche agreed that God does not act arbitrarily.[43]

Antoine Arnauld agreed that this is the best of all possible worlds, and that evil is a kind of good, "a dissonance in the harmony of the universe [which] makes a contribution to this harmony".[44] This type of theodicy reflects a "consider the whole" approach. Arnauld goes further "emphasizing the infinite distance between God and human beings and ultimate inscrutability of His wisdom", thus stating: "We believe that God's providence extends to all things...But to know how this happens and in what way everything that happens in the world is directed, regulated, and governed by the secret orders of this infinite providence is something that infinitely surpasses our intelligence."[45] For Arnauld, God's will reigns supreme, as he stated in the following terms: "If we are asked why God created the world, we should reply only that is because He wanted to...we should not say, as [Malebranche] does, that 'He wanted to obtain an honor worthy of Himself'...We ought rather to say that He wanted to because He

---

[42] Nadler, *The Best of All Possible Worlds*, pp. 129–130. Arnauld objected to this simplicity argument by maintaining that for God, Who is Omnipotent, all means are equally easy and available. Ibid., p. 179.

[43] Ibid., p. 136.

[44] Nadler, *The Best of All Possible Worlds*, pp. 152–153. Alexander Pope stated in his "Essay on Man" something similar: "All chance, direction, which thou canst see; All disorder, harmony not understood; All partial evil, universal good; And, spite of pride erring reason's spite; One truth is clear, whatever is, is right." See *Alexander Pope: The Major Works*, ed. Pat Rogers (Oxford: Oxford University Press, 2006), p. 280.

[45] Ibid., p. 158.

wanted to, that is, that we ought not to seek a cause of that which cannot have one."[46]

Nadler states: "Despite appearance, Arnauld does not really offer a theodicy at all. In fact, he regards the whole project of theodicy as misguided and grounded in human presumption, and not just because he believes the wisdom that guides God's activity to be inaccessible to us. Rather, for Arnauld, a rationalist theodicy is based on an altogether improper conception of God's nature and a thorough misunderstanding of the structure of divine agency."[47] Nadler also adds:

> Arnauld consistently denies that God acts "arbitrarily" or "capriciously" and he insists in several contexts that whatever God does is done "reasonably." But these are ambiguous claims... Given everything Arnauld says about the relationship between wisdom and will in God, and in light of the kinds of criticisms he levels against Malebranche's conception of divine agency, it is not clear how he can avoid the conclusion that God *is* capricious or arbitrary in this sense... [Arnauld in essence holds instead that] God's performing some action or causing some event is what makes that action or event a reasonable thing to do. These are ex post facto reasons... God's volitions and actions are reasonable not because they are guided by reasons, as would be the case were He an agent whose actions were governed by practical rationality, but because they make reasons... [I]f whatever God does is necessarily just and wise only because God does it, then all theodicean claims are trivial.[48]

Again, the arguments of Arnauld most closely parallel those of the Ashᶜarīs in that they both insist that God's will reigns supreme and that there not need be any reason or wisdom for His actions. That said, Arnauld rejected occasionalism. Yet Malebranche did hold the doctrine of occasionalism, but denied divine voluntarism and instead maintained that God wills and acts in a wise and intelligible manner accessible to humankind. Thus occasionalism and divine voluntarism are not associated with one another in the thinking of Arnauld and Malebranche, unlike the Ashᶜarīs who link them both together.

---

46 Ibid., p. 163.
47 Ibid., p. 159.
48 Ibid., pp. 209–211.

Leibniz also rejected divine voluntarism and maintained that God's acts are done by Him because they are good—not that they are good solely because they are done by Him or as a result of His will.[49] Leibniz argued that:

> In saying, therefore, that things are not good according to any standard of goodness, but simply by the will of God, it seems to me that one destroys, without realizing it, all the love of God and all His glory; for why praise Him for what He has done if He would be equally praiseworthy in doing the contrary? Where will be His justice and His wisdom if He has only a certain despotic power, if arbitrary will takes the place of reasonableness, and if in accord with the definition of tyrants, justice consists in that which is pleasing to the most powerful?[50]

This is eloquently stated, and agrees with some of the objections that Ibn al-Qayyim and others advanced against the Ashᶜarī position.[51]

DENIAL OF LEIBNIZ'S OPTIMISM

Some Christian theologians disagreed with the optimism of Leibniz. For instance, Charles Journet states: "The notion of the best of all possible worlds is by definition unrealizable...for 'whatever things he has made, God could make a better one', and so on indefinitely. To demand that God, to be above reproach, must make the best of all possible worlds is to demand him to make what is not feasible, and to give existence to something absurd."[52] Robert M. Adams similarly argued: "Why can't it be that for every possible world there is another that is better? And if there is no maximum degree of perfection among

---

[49] Ibid., pp. 186 and 198.

[50] See Gottfried Leibniz, *Discourse on Metaphysics: Correspondence with Arnauld and Monadology*, tr. George Montgomery (Chicago: The Open Court Publishing Company, 1902), pp. 4–5. This passage is present in Leibniz, *Discourse on Metaphysics*, section 2. See also Nadler's discussion in *The Best of All Possible Worlds*, pp. 198–201, where he adds that if those who hold divine voluntarism are "right, then claims about God's moral nature are empty and there is no point in praising God for what He has done, because He would be equally praiseworthy had He done just the opposite".

[51] Ibn al-Qayyim rejected divine voluntarism and affirmed God's praiseworthiness, wisdom and justice. See Zeni (tr.), *Ibn Qayyim al-Jawziyya on Divine Wisdom and the Problem of Evil*, pp. XV, 10–11, 133–134.

[52] Charles Journet, *The Meaning of Evil*, tr. Michael Barry (London: Geoffrey Chapman, 1963), pp. 117–18.

possible worlds, it would be unreasonable to blame God, or think less highly of His goodness, because He created a world less excellent than He could have created."[53]

Earlier, the Lisbon earthquake of 1755, which killed more than 60,000 on All-Saints Day (many of whom were churchgoers), led many writers to openly question optimism or mock it. Prominent among them were Voltaire who rebuked Leibniz through his poem concerning the earthquake[54] as well as through his book *Candide*. Nadler though states:

> Leibniz does *not* have in mind what Voltaire accuses him of claiming. Candide believes that to say that this is the best of all possible worlds means that everything in this world turns out for the best *for him*, and, presumably for any other creature. One may suffer through pain and misfortune, but only because they lead to felicity. This is not Leibniz's view... Rather, Leibniz claims that any other possible world is worse

---

[53] See Robert M. Adams, "Must God Create the Best?" *The Philosophical Review*, vol. LXXXI, no. 3, 1972, p. 317. Adams continues in a footnote: "Leibniz held (in his *Theodicy*, pt. I, sec. 8) that if there were no best among possible worlds, a perfectly good God would have created nothing at all. But Leibniz is mistaken if he supposes in this way God could avoid choosing an alternative less excellent than others He could have chosen. For the existence of no created world at all would surely be a less excellent state of affairs than the existence of some of the worlds that God could have created."

[54] Part of Voltaire's poem states:

Leibnitz can't tell me from what secret cause
In a world governed by the wisest laws,
Lasting disorders, woes that never end
With our vain pleasures real sufferings blend;
Why ill the virtuous with the vicious shares?
Why neither good nor bad misfortunes spares?
I can't conceive that "what is, out to be,"
In this each doctor knows as much as me...
A caliph once when his last hour drew nigh,
Prayed in such terms as these to the most high:
"Being supreme, whose greatness knows no bound,
I bring thee all that can't in Thee be found;
Defects and sorrows, ignorance and woe."
Hope he omitted, man's sole bliss below.

See Voltaire, "The Lisbon Earthquake: An Inquiry into the Maxim, 'Whatever Is, Is Right.'" This is included in Voltaire, *From the Works of Voltaire: A Contemporary Version*, tr. William Fleming (New York: E. R. DuMont, 1901), Volume X, Part II, pp. 16–18.

> *overall* than this one, regardless of any single person's fortunes in it... [T]he evil, like the good, makes a positive contribution to the overall optimality of the world by constituting a part of its contents. It belongs to the conception of the best of all possible worlds that it involves a large number of wonderful, good things... [I]t is metaphysically superior... [and] contains the highest degree of perfection, insofar as it realizes the maximum level of created being or reality.[55]

David Hume was also critical of the optimism of Leibniz, speaking through his character Philo: "Leibniz has denied [human misery], and is perhaps the first who ventured upon so bold and paradoxical an opinion; at least, the first who made it essential to his philosophical system."[56] Hume then writes:

> The whole earth...is cursed and polluted. A perpetual war is kindled amongst all living creatures...The stronger prey upon the weaker and keep them in perpetual terror and anxiety...And thus on each hand, before and behind, above and below, every animal is surrounded with enemies which incessantly seek his misery and destruction...Man, it is true, can, by combination, surmount all his *real* enemies and become master of the whole animal creation...Man is the greatest enemy of man. Oppression, injustice, contempt, contumely, violence, sedition, war, calumny, treachery, fraud—by these they mutually torment each other...[Also consider] the lingering torment of diseases...the disorders of the mind...though more secret, are not perhaps less dismal and vexatious. Remorse, shame, anguish, rage, disappointment, anxiety, fear, dejection, despair—who has ever passed through life without cruel inroads from these tormentors? [...] Labor and poverty, so abhorred by everyone, are the certain lot of the far greater number; and those few privileged persons who enjoy ease and opulence never reach contentment or true felicity. All the goods of life united would not make a very happy man, but all the ills united would make a wretch indeed...Charles V... publicly avowed *that the greatest prosperities which he had ever enjoyed, had been*

---

[55] Nadler, *The Best of All Possible Worlds*, pp. 98–103. Nadler also states: "The harmony characteristic of the best of all possible worlds is accessible only to those who, given to metaphysical speculation, can 'look more deeply' and see beyond the hodgepodge of appearances in order to grasp the invisible order that unifies them." Ibid., p. 105.

[56] David Hume, *Dialogues Concerning Natural Religion*, ed. Richard H. Popkin (Indianapolis and Cambridge: Hackett Publishing Company, 1980), p. 59. It was originally published in London in 1779.

mixed with so many adversities that he might truly say he had never enjoyed any satisfaction or contentment.[57]

Hume also wrote: "Epicurus' old questions are yet unanswered. Is [God] willing to prevent evil, but not able? Then he is impotent. Is he able, but not willing? Then he is malevolent. Is he both able and willing? Whence then is evil?"[58] Hume ends by writing: "The true conclusion is that the original Source of all things is entirely indifferent…and has no more regard to good above ill than to heat above cold, or to drought above moisture, or to light above heavy."[59]

Certainly, Hume's detailing of all ills, while ignoring the predominant goods, has led to many incorrect conclusions. The underlying reasons and wise purposes for the construct of the world as we know it—beyond what was already mentioned in prior chapters—will be discussed in Chapters Ten through Thirteen. May God protect us from attributing indifference, faults or evil to Him (Glorious and Exalted is He above such blasphemies)! For now, Hick's response to Hume (and others) will be mentioned:

> Hume, Mill, and Russell, for example, assume that the purpose that an infinitely good and powerful deity must have in creating an environment for finite persons is to produce for them a maximum of pleasure and a minimum of pain. The alternative view, which is found in many Christian works, particularly outside the Augustinian tradition, is that the world is a "vale of soul-making", designed as an environment in which finite persons may develop the more valuable qualities of moral personality.[60]

---

57 Ibid., pp. 175–184.

58 Ibid., p. 186.

59 Ibid., p. 221. Paul Draper discusses a similar "Indifferent Deity Hypothesis" whereby the Creator, although omnipotent and omniscient, "has no intrinsic concern about the pain or pleasure of other beings". He also states: "If God exists, then for centuries He has been allowing his children to torment, torture, and kill each other. Thus, even if they were once worthy of great responsibility, they no longer are, and hence are not benefitted by having such responsibility." See Paul Draper, "The Distribution of Pain and Pleasure as Evidence for Atheism", in Peterson (ed.), *The Problem of Evil*, pp. 569–571.

60 Hick, *Evil and the God of Love*, p. 166.

FYODOR DOSTOEVSKY ON EVIL

Fyodor Dostoevsky addressed the existence of evil in his book *The Brothers Karamazov*. His character Ivan protests the existence of evil that leads, in particular, to the suffering of children. Ivan tells of an eight-year old child who, after inadvertently hurting the paw of a general's favourite hound, was locked up, then stripped naked, and finally chased down by the general's hounds to be torn to pieces before his mother's eyes.

The suffering of children leads Ivan to object to the divine plan claiming that the "whole of truth is not worth such a price. I do not, finally, want the mother to embrace the tormentor who let his dogs tear her son to pieces! [...] And if that is so, if they dare not forgive, then where is the harmony? [...] they have put too high a price on harmony; we can't afford to pay so much for admission. And therefore I hasten to return my ticket...It's not that I don't accept God, Alyosha, I just most respectfully return him the ticket." Alyosha, his young brother who is a monk, responds: "That is rebellion."[61]

Ivan concludes by asking Alyosha: "Tell me yourself, I challenge you—answer. Imagine that you are creating a fabric of human destiny with the object of making men happy in the end, giving them peace and rest at last, but that it was essential and inevitable to torture to death only one tiny...little child...would you consent to be the architect on those conditions?" Alyosha responds initially in the negative,[62] but at the end of the story states: "Ah, children, ah, dear friends, do not be afraid of life! How good life is when you do something good and rightful! [...] Certainly we shall rise, certainly we shall see and gladly, joyfully tell one another all that has been."[63]

The reality is that "Ivan's" query was proposed by one who has not been placed in a position of responsibility. For instance, surgeries

---

[61] Fyodor Dostoevsky, *The Brothers Karamazov*, trs. Richard Pevear and Larissa Volokhonsky (New York: Farrar, Straus and Giroux, 1990), p. 245. Ivan thus "would return his ticket to paradise on judgment day, because he cannot accept the price of universal happiness, even if it is only a single baby which must be tortured to death." See Carol Kates, "A Nietzschean Theodicy", *International Journal for Philosophy of Religion*, vol. LV, 2004 (March), p. 75.

[62] Fyodor Dostoevsky, *The Brothers Karamazov*, p. 245.

[63] Ibid., p. 776.

may result in morbidity or even mortality, but their benefit is preponderant to their harm, and therefore patients seek them, while surgeons inform patients about those risks and perform them. To not perform a surgery, which could have a 0.1% mortality rate, in order to avoid one patient in a thousand from death, would deprive 99.9% the opportunity to benefit from that surgery.

Furthermore, God (Glorious is He) has created this world to manifest the effects of many of His Beautiful Names, Glorious Attributes and good actions, in addition to His many wise purposes. Ultimately, "Ivan" and humanity do not have a choice regarding their existence. God (Exalted is He) states: *Thy Lord does create and choose as He pleases: no choice have they (in the matter).*[64] God (Glorious is He) is not in need of anyone's worship and He has given humankind the free choice to worship whom they please, but those who worship other than the Holy Lord will be punished: *Whoso is rebellious to God and His Messenger, he verily goeth astray in error manifest.*[65] So one can choose whether to believe or disbelieve, follow His commandments or disobey them—no one is compelled: *There is no compulsion in religion.*[66]

That said, Dostoevsky—through Ivan—correctly points out that often times the suffering of the innocent is neglected by those in power despite them having the ability to remedy affairs. Consider, for example, Anthony Lake who was critical of that neglect early in his career but acknowledged it stating: "Policy—good, steady policy—is made by the 'tough-minded.' [...] To talk of suffering is to 'lose effectiveness,' almost to lose one's grip. It is seen as a sign that one's rational arguments are weak."[67] The point is that government officials

---

64 Q.XXVIII.68 (Yusuf Ali translation).

65 Q.XXXIII.36.

66 Q.II.256. John Stuart Mill says: "Whatever power such a being may have over me there is one thing which he shall not do: he shall not compel me to worship him." See John Stuart Mill, "The Philosophy of the Conditioned as Applied by Mr. Mansel to the Limits of Religious Thought", in *Collected Works of John Stuart Mill*, ed. J. M. Robson (Toronto: University of Toronto Press, 1979), vol. IX, p. 103. Mill goes on to state that "if a such being can sentence me to hell for not so calling him [good like my fellow creatures], to hell I will go".

67 See Samantha Power, *"A Problem from Hell": America and the Age of Genocide* (New York: Harper Perennial, 2002), p. 315. This is quoted from his *Foreign Policy* article in 1971, entitled "The Human Reality of Realpolitik." Although Anthony Lake, at that

often neglect the suffering of the weak and innocent—whereby much evil lies in that neglect—but we should still work to reduce or eliminate the latter's suffering and change things for the better, as much as we are able.

Finally, it should be mentioned that Ivan also attributes all sorts of evils to the Muslims. He claims that the Turks and Circassians "burn, kill, rape women and children, they nail prisoners by their ears to fences and leave them like that until morning, and in the morning they hang them... [They] have also taken delight in torturing children, starting with cutting them out of their mothers' wombs with a dagger, and ending up tossing nursing infants up in the air and catching them on their bayonets before their mothers' eyes".[68] If these instances are true, and not fabrications, they are done in direct contradiction to the teachings of Islam, the Qur'ān and the Sunna of the Prophet Muḥammad. Those who perpetrate wickedness, evil, injustice, oppression or terrorism will be held responsible in the Hereafter (if not earlier in this world), regardless of whether they are Muslim or non-Muslim.

The opposition of J. L. Mackie to theodicy

The atheist J. L. Mackie objects to the free will theodicies by arguing that if the wills of mankind are "really free this must mean that even God cannot control them, that is, God is no longer omnipotent".[69] Mackie goes on to state that God could have created mankind with

---

time, urged policymakers to take human suffering into consideration, he neglected to take his own advice, according to Samantha Power, during the 1990s when he was the National Security Adviser at the time of the Bosnian genocide. Power adds that "at the State Department, officials say, to talk of human suffering remained something that was 'not done.' Those who complained about the human consequences of American decisions (or here, nondecisions) were still branded emotional, soft, and irrational. The language of national interest was Washington's lingua franca, and so it would remain." See Ibid., pp. 315–316.

[68] Fyodor Dostoevsky, *The Brothers Karamazov*, p. 238.

[69] J. L. Mackie, "Evil and Omnipotence", *Mind*, vol. LXIV, no. 254, 1955 (April), p. 210. The Jesuits of the 16th century felt that God caused "circumstances in which He knew that we would *freely* act in accordance with His plans". See Robert Merrihew Adams, "Middle Knowledge and the Problem of Evil", in *The Problem of Evil*, p. 110.

a free will "such that they always freely choose the good[70]...[God's] failure to avail [H]imself of this possibility is inconsistent with [H]is being both omnipotent and wholly good".[71] Therefore, Mackie claims that the presence of evil in this world negates that God is omnipotent and omnibenevolent. Traditional Islam, in contrast, maintains that our wills are free but within the power of the Holy and Omnipotent Lord: *And ye will not, unless (it be) that God willeth, the Lord of Creation.*[72] And God is infallible above any deficiency or evil.

Mackie also claims that religious beliefs not only "lack rational support, but that they are positively irrational".[73] Mackie, though, does not *prove* religious beliefs or theodicies are irrational;[74] rather, his specious claim only reveals that his knowledge (as well as that of others) has theretofore been inadequate in understanding God's wise purposes or in reconciling God's omnipotence, omniscience and holiness with the existence of evil. In reality, no human is in "an epistemic position to make such a judgment".[75] Furthermore, for something to be described as irrational in this matter it must result in harm or evil occurring to the One Who is Omnipotent—but that is

70 Peter von Inwagen states a corollary of this: "If there had been a peal of thunder at the moment Eve was trying to decide whether to eat the apple, she would freely have decided not to eat it." See Peter von Inwagen, *The Problem of Evil: The Gifford Lectures delivered in the University of St. Andrews in* 2003 (Oxford: Clarendon Press, 2006), p. 79. He states that this has been "accepted by a wide range of theists, among them most (if not all) Dominicans and Thomists, the sixteenth-century Spanish Jesuits, and Alvin Plantiga". Ibid., p. 79. Finally, von Inwagen raises the related issue of the "hiddenness" of God in Chapter 8.

71 J. L. Mackie, "Evil and Omnipotence", p. 209.

72 Q.LXXXI.29. See also Q.LXXVI.30: *Yet ye will not, unless God willeth. Lo! God is Knower, Wise.*

73 J. L. Mackie, "Evil and Omnipotence", p. 200.

74 Alvin Plantiga states similarly that Mackie and others fail to *show* that there is an explicit contradiction; they only *assert* such. Plantiga states that Mackie "makes scarcely a beginning towards finding some additional premises that are necessarily true and that together with members of set A [i.e. God is omnipotent and wholly good, yet evil exists] formally entail an explicit contradiction...[In fact,] set A has not been shown to be [even] implicitly inconsistent." Alvin Plantiga, *God, Freedom, and Evil* (Grand Rapids: William B. Eerdmans Publishing, 1974), pp. 23–24.

75 See Michael Peterson, "Christian Theism and the Evidential Argument from Evil", in Peterson (ed.), *The Problem of Evil*, pp. 170–71.

impossible. It is not irrational for God (Exalted is He) to allow evil to exist amongst His creation for wise purposes they may be unaware of.

In accordance with traditional Islamic theology, it will be maintained that the Holy Lord is omnipotent and omniscient, but that God (Exalted is He) in His wisdom has dictated to restrict the manifestation of His power in order to attain greater goods beloved to Him, which could not have justly been otherwise achieved. It should not be surprising that God (Exalted is He) has restricted manifesting His omnipotence for, in reality, no Attribute of God (Glorious is He) is fully manifested—that would be impossible, as they are all infinite and perfect.

Plantiga's free will defense

Now, defenses, in contrast to theodicies, are limited in that they only try to "rebut particular objections to theism"[76] or provide "what God's reason *might possibly* be".[77] Alvin Plantiga states that a "theist would rather know what God's reason *is* for permitting evil than simply that it's possible that He has a good one…[but a Free Will Defense] is all that's needed".[78]

Plantiga states: "The Free Will Defender disagrees with both Leibniz and Mackie…[by asking] what is the reason for supposing that *there is* such a thing as the best of all possible worlds? No matter how marvelous a world is…isn't it possible that there be an even better world containing even more persons enjoying even more unalloyed bliss?"[79] Plantiga continues: "What is really characteristic and central to the Free Will Defense is the claim that God, though omnipotent, could not have actualized just any possible world He pleased."[80] Plantiga introduces a concept of "transworld depravity" indicating that individuals will inevitably perpetrate evil in every possible world and that "it was beyond the power of God Himself

---

76 Marilyn McCord Adams and Robert Merrihew Adams, *The Problem of Evil* (Oxford: Oxford University Press, 1990), p. 3.

77 Alvin Plantiga, *God, Freedom, and Evil* (Grand Rapids: William B. Eerdsman Publishing, 1974), p. 28.

78 Ibid., p. 28.

79 Ibid., p. 34.

80 Plantiga, *God, Freedom, and Evil*, p. 34.

to create a world containing moral good but no moral evil...and this despite the fact that He is omnipotent. Under these conditions God could have created a world containing no moral evil only by creating one without significantly free persons."[81]

It will be argued later that, from an Islamic perspective, God (Glorious is He) can actualize any world if it is concordant with His justice and wisdom. So He could have created a world in which there were only believers: *Had He willed He could indeed have guided all of you*,[82] and no evil would have existed. This would have led to the lapse, however, of many of the wise purposes that He has intended to demonstrate.

Although many philosophers do feel that Plantiga's Free Will Defense adequately refutes Mackie's arguments, the free will defense (and theodicy) is "unable to deal with either the amount of evil that actually exists or with one of the kinds of evil that actually exists: evil that is not a consequence of human acts."[83] Marilyn McCord Adams felt that it was "hopeless" to try to find reasons for horrendous evils, and agreed with Plantiga that "not only do we not know God's *actual* reason for permitting them; we cannot even *conceive* of any plausible candidate point of reason consistent with worthwhile lives for human participation in them."[84] Thus the Free Will Defense is ultimately

---

[81] Ibid., p. 53. Plantiga states that "a being properly eliminates an evil state of affairs if it eliminates that evil without either eliminating an outweighing good or bringing about a greater evil". Ibid., p. 20.

[82] See Q.VI.149. See also Q.X.99: *If it had been thy Lord's will, they would all have believed—all who are on earth!* (Yusuf Ali translation). Therefore, this rejects Plantiga's transworld depravity, i.e. the notion that evil individuals would be such in each and every possibly world that God could create. On the other hand, God (Exalted is He) also states in Q.XXIV.21: *Had it not been for the grace of God and His mercy unto you, not one of you would ever have grown pure.*

[83] Peter von Inwagen, *The Problem of Evil*, p. 84.

[84] Marilyn McCord Adams, "Horrendous Evils and the Goodness of God", in *The Problem of Evil*, pp. 215–216. Plantiga specifically states: "The Christian must concede he doesn't know [why horrifying kinds of evil exist]. That is, he doesn't know in any detail. On a quite general level, he may know that God permits evil because he can achieve a world he sees as better by permitting evil than by preventing it; and what God sees as better is, of course, better. But we cannot see *why* our world, with all its ills, would be better than others we think we can imagine, or *what*, in any detail, is God's reason for permitting a given specific and appalling evil. Not only can we not

inadequate regarding gratuitous or dysteleological evil. Interestingly, nearly thirty years after Plantiga's initial Free Will Defense, he adopts a Felix Culpa Theodicy[85] thus stating this is the best possible world—this will be discussed later in Chapter Eleven.

THE PROBLEM OF GRATUITOUS EVIL

William Rowe advances an "evidential" argument, which highlights the existence of gratuitous evils—i.e. horrendous evils for which no greater good can be postulated—and states that God "could have prevented them without losing some greater good or permitting some evil equally bad or worse".[86] Rowe also discusses why *any* or *all* the evil, the *various kinds* of evil, the *amount* of evil, and some *particular* evils exist.[87] In so doing, Rowe concedes that although Hick "has provided a reasonable answer to the permission of *any* and the various *kinds* of evil",[88] the latter has failed in other respects. Rowe states:

> What seems obvious to Hick and to us is (1) that the amount and intensity of evil in our world far exceeds what is needed for soul-making, and (2) that the evils in our world are distributed in a haphazard fashion, apparently unrelated to anyone's stage of development in soul-making.

---

see this, we can't think of any very good possibilities. And here I must say that most attempts to explain *why* God permits evil—theodicies, as we may call them—strike me as tepid, shallow, and ultimately frivolous." See Alvin Plantiga, "Self Profile", in James E. Tomberlin and Peter van Inwagen (eds.), *Profiles: Alvin Plantiga* (Dordrecht: D. Reidel Publishing, 1985), p. 35.

[85] Plantiga, "Supralapsarianism, or 'O Felix Culpa'", in Peter van Inwagen (ed.), *Christian Faith and the Problem of Evil* (Grand Rapids: Eerdmans, 2004), pp. 1–25. Felix Culpa is literally translated as "a happy sin". It refers to the fall of Adam and how that (as well as other evils) led to what many Christians claim were necessary components of the incarnation and atonement. See also Kevin Diller, "Are Sin and Evil Necessary for a Really Good World? Questions for Alvin Plantiga's Felix Culpa Theodicy", *Faith and Philosophy*, vol. XXV, no. 1, 2008, pp. 87–101. Diller states: "In Christian Scripture evil is not explained; instead we find that it is permitted, confounded, and finally eradicated. In a *Felix Culpa* theodicy, evil is made a *necessary* component of achieving a higher good. This imbues evil with purpose and makes evil finally reasonable."

[86] William Rowe, "Paradox and Promise: Hick's Solution to the Problem of Evil", in Harold Hewitt, Jr (ed.), *Problems in the Philosophy of Religion: Critical Studies of the Work of John Hick* (New York: St. Martin's Press, 1991), pp. 111–124.

[87] Ibid., p. 112.

[88] Ibid., p. 117.

> In light of this, how can anyone seriously propose the good of soul-making as the reason for God's permission of *all* the pain and suffering in our world? [...] [Thus] Hick's argument does not solve the problem of the amount, intensity, and distribution of evil in our world.[89]

He concludes that Hick's soul-making theodicy and the free-will theodicy are inadequate to explain the existence of massive amounts of evil, including those which are gratuitous, as these often thwart "moral and spiritual growth".[90]

Rowe finally claims that atheism explains the amount and degree of intrinsic evils as well as particular evils better than theism.[91] Peter von Inwagen rejects such a notion by drawing up parallel arguments and then rebutting them (which will not be discussed here). He concludes that the pattern of suffering in this world does not provide enough evidence to favour the hypothesis of indifference or atheism over theism.[92]

Now, William Hasker agrees that although God would "prevent the occurrence of an evil state of affairs...unless [He] could not do so without thereby losing some greater good, or permitting some evil equally bad or worse", i.e. no gratuitous evil (or NGE) would be allowed, but "it is an extremely important part of God's intention for human persons that they should place a high priority on fulfilling moral obligations, and should assume major responsibility for the welfare of their fellow human beings".[93] Hasker then poses a "thought experiment" based on the above stating:

> Consider, then, the situation of a moral agent who is contemplating some morally objectionable but nevertheless tempting course of action. The agent in question, we will assume, is astute enough to realize that God is governing the world in accordance with NGE. The agent, perhaps,

---

89 Ibid., pp. 118–119.

90 Ibid., pp. 121–122. As noted previously, Hick did recognize the inadequacy of his "soul-making theodicy" to explain the existence of gratuitous evil.

91 Ibid., p. 122.

92 See Peter von Inwagen, "The Problem of Evil, the Problem of Air, and the Problem of Silence", in James E. Tomberlin (ed.), *Philosophical Perspectives: vol. 5, Philosophy of Religion* (Atascadero: Ridgeview, 1991), pp. 135–65.

93 William Hasker, "God and Gratuitous Evil", in Peterson (ed.), *The Problem of Evil*, p. 476.

> reflects that if she takes the morally reprehensible course, others may suffer as a result. But then it occurs to her that the consequences of her action will not be "all bad" by any means. She recognizes, in fact, that the following principle of Offsetting Good (OG) is true: Any harm resulting from a morally wrong action will be offset by a "greater good" that God could not have obtained without permitting the evil in question...Does this mean that the world overall will be no worse off (and possibly better off) if the agent commits the wrong action, than if she refrains from it... [Taking all of the above into consideration] the agent's inclination to take moral requirements seriously is likely to be very significantly lessened [if NGE is operative].[94]

Hasker thus concludes:

> If we know that God will permit a morally wrong action only if it results in a compensating good, then our motivation to take morality seriously as a guide to life is likely to be seriously impaired...[So gratuitous evil] serves a very important purpose—namely, to convince human beings of the importance of fulfilling our moral obligations...The evils that seem gratuitous to us may really be so; there may be no greater good resulting from them that could not be achieved otherwise. That this is so gives us reason to battle against these evils and their consequences; it does not give us reason to give up our faith in the God who fights the battle along with us.[95]

Thus, the allowance of gratuitous evil should indirectly result in humankind avoiding evil and striving to a greater degree against all types of evil, so as to minimize the occurrence of the gratuitous types. It will be contended in Chapters Eleven and Twelve that gratuitous evils can be considered dysteleological from most aspects, but not all. Indeed, there are some wise purposes and goods that would have lapsed had they not occurred.

One other response comes from what is known as "skeptical theism", which is the "view that there exists a great epistemic gulf between God and humanity, so that various aspects of God—such as his will, intentions, and goals—are bound to strike us as mysterious. This view has its roots in traditional forms of theism as expressed within Judeo-

---

[94] Ibid., pp. 477–79.

[95] Ibid., pp. 479–86.

Christian and Islamic religions".[96] The skeptical theists therefore object to Rowe's argument by stating: "We have no good reason for thinking that the possible goods we know of are representative of the possible goods that there are...Furthermore, it wouldn't be at all surprising if our powers for comprehending and appreciating goods are currently but *contingently* limited—perhaps even extremely so."[97]

Rowe responds: "Since understanding the goods for the sake of which [He] permits terrible evils to befall us would itself enable us to better bear our suffering, God has a strong reason to help us understand those goods."[98] Therefore, he argues that human suffering in such a case is not accompanied by any direct comforting communication from God, i.e. it is met with divine silence. In this regard, the analogy of parents who let their children know the good reasons for their suffering, and that they are beloved, is also drawn by Rowe and others. Regardless, we can see that skeptical theists cannot provide a convincing response to divine hiddenness beyond alluding to the mysterious nature of God's ways.

God (Glorious is He) is not silent: He has revealed what He loves and what He dislikes through His messengers, and commanded us to obey His commandments and prohibitions. As for the 'hypothesis of indifference', God (Exalted is He) states: *Is not He (best) Who answereth the wronged one when he crieth unto Him and removeth the evil, and hath made you viceroys of the earth? Is there any deity beside God? Little do they reflect!*[99] Claiming divine indifference would attribute deficiency to Him, and would deny many of His Beautiful Names, including the Holy, the Most Beneficent, the Kind, the All-Hearing, among many others. Finally, the Almighty Lord will grant victory to the righteous (if they reach a critical mass) and fulfill His promises to them—is that not congruent with what is wise?

---

96 Nick Trakakis, "What No Eye Has Seen: The Skeptical Theist Response to Rowe's Evidential Argument", *Philo*, vol. VI, no. 2, 2003, p. 267.

97 Michael Bergmann, "Skeptical Theism and Rowe's New Evidential Argument from Evil", *Nous*, vol. XXXV, no. 2, 2001, pp. 279–285.

98 See Michael L. Peterson and Raymond J. VanArragon (eds.), *Contemporary Debates in the Philosophy of Religion* (Malden: Blackwell Publishing, 2004), p. 26.

99 Q.XXVII.62.

SOME JEWISH PHILOSOPHERS ON THE PROBLEM OF EVIL

The thoughts of a few Jewish philosophers will now be considered including those of Saadya,[100] Maimonides and Spinoza, as well as some modern philosophers.

Regarding Saadya, Oliver Leaman writes:

> For Saadya there are three purposes resulting from the phenomenon of human suffering—education, punishment, and testing[101]...There are a variety of reasons for allowing the evil people in the world to continue with their impious behavior. They may eventually repent, they may produce virtuous children, they may have produced some virtuous deeds, they may be employed to punish those even worse than themselves and they may be there to benefit the virtuous. Finally they may be allowed to linger in order to make their punishment even harsher.[102]

These wise purposes are consistent with a traditional Islamic theodicy.

As regards Maimonides,[103] he tried to reconcile Scripture with Aristotelian thought. Maimonides employed the "principle of plenitude"[104] and adopted a "consider the whole" approach, i.e. the quantity of good in this universe far outweighs the evil. Even if the latter is greater at some points in time, when considered over the long history of humankind, evil is lesser than the good we have experienced.[105]

However, Maimonides also, in accordance with Aristotelian thought, argued in the following terms, according to Leaman:

> Divine providence is limited in its scope to the heavenly spheres and species, with the individuals falling under these influential bodies and

---

100 Saadya ben Joseph or Saadya Gaon (d. 942 CE) was a Jewish philosopher who lived in Iraq during the Abbasid caliphate. Interestingly, he was "firmly on the side of the Muᶜtazilites...although he incorporated [some aspects of Ashᶜarism] in his approach to theology". See Oliver Leaman, *Evil and Suffering in Jewish Philosophy* (Cambridge: Cambridge University Press, 1995), pp. 48–63.

101 Ibid., p. 53.

102 Ibid., p. 56.

103 Moses Maimonides (d. 1204) was born in Cordoba. He wrote two very lengthy books: *Guide of the Perplexed* and *Mishneh Torah*. The first was a philosophical reference and the latter a book of orthodox jurisprudence. See Lenn E. Goodman, "Judaism and the Problem of Evil", in *The Cambridge Companion to the Problem of Evil*, pp. 193–209, and Leaman, *Evil and Suffering in Jewish Philosophy*, pp. 64–101.

104 Leaman, *Evil and Suffering in Jewish Philosophy*, p. 70.

105 See Nadler, *The Best of All Possible Worlds*, p. 87–88.

> universal groups being governed by chance. The only exception here is the case of human beings, and then only some human beings, who are able to key in to high levels of abstract thought...Maimonides' concept of God [is that] God seems to have very little grasp, if any, of what is going on in the world, so that the traditional idea of God's providence has to be abandoned. God appears to be lacking in knowledge...It is no good complaining to God, as Job does initially, when things go wrong. God cannot do anything about it, but we can.[106]

Again, God is exalted and infallible above the claims of those who deny His omniscience and omnipotence.

With regards to Spinoza, it should be noted that he was ostracized by the Jewish community of Amsterdam.[107] This was because he brought forth many heresies, including: God is nothing but nature itself; God is not wise or good; and God does not freely choose, will, command or judge. God is glorious and exalted above such blasphemies. Indeed, these thoughts of Spinoza most closely resemble those who stripped God (Glorious is He) of His Attributes, like the Jahmīs or Muʿaṭṭilīs. Nadler adds: "For Spinoza, this is not the best of all possible worlds; it is the only possible world."[108]

In addition, Oliver Leaman has discussed the difficulty that the Holocaust, in which the Nazi Germans killed six million Jews, poses for Jewish theodicy. Eliezer Berkovitz and Ignaz Maybaum adopted traditional approaches by arguing that the Holocaust corresponds to other anti-Jewish events such as the destruction of the First and Second Temples or that carried out by Nebuchadnezzar. They held that the latter helped humankind "by dispersing the Jews to disseminate God's message among the nations", and therefore the Holocaust survivors should likewise "persist in their attempt at the progressive transformation of society".[109]

Elie Wiesel, on the other hand, put forward the following argument, according to Leaman:

---

[106] See Leaman, *Evil and Suffering in Jewish Philosophy*, pp. 72, 81, and 89.

[107] See Nadler, *The Best of All Possible Worlds*, pp. 220–21.

[108] Ibid., p. 232.

[109] Leaman, *Evil and Suffering in Jewish Philosophy*, pp. 190–192 and 206–207.

> God let down the Jews through allowing the Holocaust to occur, and yet the Jews should continue to adhere to their faith...They should continue with their Jewish lifestyle, and if their practical action to help others does not end up redeeming God, at least it will redeem themselves. Wiesel sees the relationship between God and the Jews as an eternal process of interrogation. In it "there are quarrels and reconciliations, more quarrels and more reconciliations...yet neither God nor the Jews ever gave up on the other...[Through this] endless engagement with God we proved to Him that we are more patient than He, more compassionate too".[110]

Furthermore, Arthur Cohen argued that God was benevolent by creating this world and humanity, but that "the events of the Holocaust imply that God does not participate in history...God's involvement in the world now is through his Law, not through direct action...[in order to leave] scope for human freedom".[111]

Then there is Richard Rubinstein who believes in God in "a mystical and immanent sense" whereby he claims that God "does not have the ordinary divine characteristics, such as power to influence the world...[T]here is no effort on the part of the maker of the universe to balance good and evil, and so there is no point in wondering why God does not prevent harm to the innocent...the whole business of theodicy is futile".[112]

Leaman then discusses the notion that the Holocaust provided "valuable emotional ammunition" and laid the foundations for the establishment of Israel. But he adds:

> If God does act in history one might have expected him to produce a Jewish state in a less chaotic and bloodthirsty manner. In any case, the existence of the State does indeed put the responsibility for their future in the hands of its citizens, yet it is far from obvious that the future will be secure, or that it will not be secular as opposed to religious. The creation of the State is an event of immense importance in Jewish history, and yet

---

110 Ibid., pp. 186 and 210. For the quote of Wiesel, see Elie Wiesel, *A Jew Today*, tr. Marion Wiesel (New York: Random House, 1978), pp. 193–194. This type of Jewish thinking will be addressed in Chapter Eleven. God is sublime and exalted above the statements of those who claim they exhibit some praiseworthy attributes in a manner better than Him.

111 Leaman, *Evil and Suffering in Jewish Philosophy*, pp. 190 and 205.

112 Ibid., pp. 187 and 203–204.

> one might wonder how it relates to the slaughter of millions of people in another part of the world. One might even wonder how to reconcile the creation of the State with the inevitable injustice to the non-Jewish inhabitants of the region. Justifying the Holocaust in terms of its role in the creation of the State of Israel just will not do. It raises far more questions that it settles.[113]

In the final analysis, the demonic types of evil leading to the Holocaust and its massive number of deaths have confounded Jewish efforts, among others, at arriving at a theodicy. It should be mentioned that the number of Muslims that have been killed over the last 100 years—whether by genocide, unjust wars, occupation, or economic sanctions—is likewise great and approaches six million. Although the death and destruction that the Muslims have suffered represents a much smaller percentage and is over a longer period of time in comparison to that of Jews, it is, nonetheless, a greater tragedy in one sense: the evil perpetrated against the Muslims has been executed by many more nations and religious groups. This will be discussed later in Chapter Twelve.

EASTERN PHILOSOPHIES

In the first instance, Taoism can be considered either as a form of pantheism or deism if one assumes that the Great Infinity is the Holy Lord. This philosophy, however, strips the Lord of commanding: "Although the Great Infinity is infinite and therefore undefined it is silent in it Primal Simplicity,"[114] and "It is the very wellspring of life, always outpouring never commanding. Although the source for every need, it is never demanding."[115] According to this philosophy, there are no Divine commandments (and no prophets)—only humans can determine what is good or evil in this philosophy.

Moreover, evil exists, for Taoists, so as to allow us to know what is good,[116] but: "When evil ceases to exist, neither will good exist. Without good and evil, we simply will live totally in our human

[113] Ibid., pp. 207–208.

[114] Lao Tzu, *The Tao Te Ching*, tr. Ralph Alan Dale (London: Watkins Publishing, 2006), verse 32, p. 95.

[115] Ibid., verse 34, p. 101.

[116] Ibid., see verse 2, p. 11.

natures."[117] It is self-evident that there has never existed a time in history where evil has ceased to exist, instead it is only increasing. But if evil becomes non-existent, it would only be due to the fact that good would become widespread. Regardless, humankind is left to its own devices and rationality to confront this world. So for the Taoist there is no theodicy and no eschatology.[118]

Confucianism, likewise, represents a moral system according to human reason. Confucius emphasized benevolence, in particular: "If a man sets his heart on benevolence, he will be free from evil."[119] But Confucius did not speak much about evil: "The topics the Master did not speak of were prodigies, force, disorder and gods."[120] That said, Confucianism represents a form of polytheism as prayers are offered to "the gods above and below".[121] Furthermore, there is no formal theodicy and no eschatology in Confucianism. As regards the latter, D. C. Lau states: "While giving men no assurances of an after life, Confucius, nevertheless, made great moral demands on them...Since in being moral one can neither be assured of reward nor guaranteed success, morality must be pursued for its own sake."[122]

Hinduism represents an extreme form of polytheism, with its vast assortment of idols and deities. It also considers the world to be pre-eternal—having no beginning or end. The Hindu notions of karma and reincarnation were developed in a sense to account for evil and pain. But its notion of reincarnation is scientifically unverifiable and unsubstantiated—followers (except for in extremely rare and isolated cases) do not even claim to remember past lives nor can they do so in detail. Moreover, due to this ignorance, reincarnation will not even help them avoid repeating or perpetrating worse evils—there is no

---

[117] Ibid., see verse 60, pp. 169–170. Dale states: "Therefore, when we finally re-establish the Great Integrity, we human beings will live without good and evil, just as every other species in our planet."

[118] See verse 73, which in part states: "But the Great Integrity never judges you for whatever path you happen to take." Ibid., p. 201.

[119] Confucius, *The Analects*, tr. D.C. Lau (London: Penguin Books, 1979), Book IV, verse 4, p. 72. See Book IV and XII for further statements on benevolence.

[120] Ibid., Book VII, verse 21, p. 88.

[121] Ibid., see Book VII, verse 35, p. 91. Confucius also praises one of his students for "making offerings to ancestral spirits and gods". See ibid., Book VIII, verse 21, p. 95.

[122] See the Introduction to *The Analects* by D. C. Lau, pp. 12–13.

providence in this system of thought. Furthermore, karma does not provide a first cause but instead only indefinitely postpones explaining the origin of evil[123]. It is thus characterized by infinite regress. The claim of karma can never provide a reason or justification for the evils that exist.

A skewed understanding of justice may also occur in Hinduism, as a victim is thought to deserve evil due to bad karma, and the oppressor becomes "merely the instrumental means for meting out the justice".[124] In this instance, injustice becomes justice in this system of thought. Karma and reincarnation also cannot account for the ever-increasing levels of evils, especially the gratuitous types. Since more creatures exist now than in the past, the degree of evil each experiences should be distributed more and thus become less for each individual; but that is obviously not the case.

Finally, since reincarnation and karma are (1) unverifiable and thus based upon dogma, (2) only claimed by those who either practise extreme polytheism (Hindus and some Buddhists) or atheism (Buddhists)—both of which are clearly false, and (3) contradict all of the Scriptures and traditions of the prophets; it follows that the notions of reincarnation and karma are clearly false. The fear of karma by many of its followers, though, has provided a moral backbone to Hinduism, preventing them from perpetrating greater evils against others.

Of note, the Advaita Vendanta branch of Hinduism also claims that once ultimate enlightenment (i.e. nirvana) is achieved, those attaining it will realize that the reality is one (i.e. monism) and that evil and suffering were only illusions.[125] This was rejected previously. In the end, Hinduism of any variety does not provide a theodicy.

On the other hand, there are two forms of Buddhism which represent an atheistic system of thought. K. N. Jayatilleke states that "the Buddha is an atheist and Buddhism in both its Therevāda and Mahāyāna forms is atheism...In denying that the universe is a product

---

[123] See Arthur L. Herman, *The Problem of Evil and Indian Thought* (Delhi: Motilal Banarsidass, 1976), pp. 261–264.

[124] Chad Meister, *Evil: A Guide for the Perplexed* (New York: Bloomsbury, 2018), pp. 153–159.

[125] Ibid., see pp. 137–148.

of a Personal God, who creates it in time and plans a consummation at the end of time, Buddhism is a form of atheism."[126] The *Dhammapada* states: "Self is the lord of self. Who else could be the lord? With self well subdued a man finds a lord such as few can find."[127]

Buddhists also claim that the universe is pre-eternal "in a state of oscillation, continually expanding and contracting without beginning or end in time".[128] As for pain and suffering, the *Dhammapada* states: "He who takes refuge with Buddha the Law and the Church; he who with clear understanding sees the four holy truths: viz. pain, the origin of pain, the destruction of pain, and the eightfold holy way that leads to the quieting of pain. That is the safe refuge, that is the best refuge; having gone to that refuge, a man is delivered from all pain."[129] Therefore, refuge is taken in the Buddha and his teachings, as well as one's reason and acts, rather than taking refuge in the Holy Lord, as is advised in Western religions.

---

[126] K. N. Jayatilleke, *The Message of the Buddha*, ed. Ninian Smart (New York: The Free Press, 1975), p. 105. Jayatilleke adds: "Buddhist atheism is not the same as materialistic atheism in that Buddhism speaks of the objectivity of moral and spiritual values and of a transcendent reality beyond space, time, and causation." Ibid., p. 36. Of note, D'Alwis states that orthodox Buddhists "do not consider the worship of devas as being sanctioned by him who disclaimed for himself and all the devas any power over man's soul. Yet the Buddhists are everywhere idol-worshippers. Buddhism, however, acknowledges the existence of some of the Hindu deities, and from the various friendly offices which those devas are said to have rendered to Gotama. Buddhists evince a respect for their idols." See "Notes" to *The Dhammapada*, tr. Friedrich Max Muller (London: Watkins Publishing, 2006), p.126.

[127] Guatama Buddha, *The Dhammapada*, tr. Friedrich Max Muller (London: Watkins Publishing, 2006), Chapter XII, verse 160, p. 39. Also, consider the verse: "All that we are is the result of what we have thought. It is founded on our thoughts, it is made up of our thoughts." Ibid., Chapter I, verse 1 or 2, p. 7.

[128] Jayatilleke, *The Message of the Buddha*, p. 105.

[129] Buddha, *The Dhammapada*, Chapter XIV, verses 190–192, p. 46. Stated differently the four noble truths are (1) that pain and suffering exist, (2) their causes are attachments and desires, (3) it is only by avoiding attachments and selfish desires that one can eliminate pain and suffering, and (4) the pathway to achieve #3 is the noble eightfold path, which consists of right views, right resolve, right speech, right conduct, right livelihood, right effort, right mindfulness, and right meditation. See also Meister, *Evil: A Guide for the Perplexed*, pp. 150–151.

In addition, these Buddhists assert that the elimination of suffering and pain occurs through the avoidance of evil[130] and annihilation of all desires: "No sufferings befall the man who is not attached to name and form and who calls nothing his own."[131] Although minimizing one's desires is important, it is self-evident that one cannot eliminate all suffering—that is not possible even for a monk.

Buddhism does affirm an evil invisible entity: "one should attack Mara (the tempter) with the weapon of knowledge, one should watch him when conquered and should never rest."[132] Buddhists therefore do affirm the presence of evil and a supernatural form of it, but claim that those who have annihilated their desires and "have reached the highest are no longer themselves and are outside the domain of good and evil and beyond the reach of guilt".[133] This is akin to antinomianism, and it denies evil at that stage of enlightenment.

Now, since Buddhism denies the Holy Creator and Deity, there is no theodicy per se in their doctrine.[134] Jayatilleke states that "the Buddhist attitude to evil is not to deny its presence or try to reconcile its existence with the creation of the world by a good God, but to observe its presence and, by studying its nature and causes, to eliminate it".[135] Therefore, the pursuit of the noble eightfold path in Buddhism is to eliminate suffering, while avoidance of evil in Hinduism is to avoid bad karma, and the pursuit of benevolence in Confucianism is for the sake of morality itself. Finally, there is likewise no true eschatology in Buddhism.[136]

---

130 See Buddha, *The Dhammapada*, Chapter I, verse 1, p. 7: "If a man speaks or acts with an evil thought, pain follows him." Also, consider: "If a man commits a sin let, him not do it again; let him not delight in sin: the accumulation of evil is painful." Ibid., Chapter IX verse 117, p. 31. See also Chapter X, verses 137–140, p. 35.

131 Ibid., Chapter XVII, verse 221, p. 54.

132 Ibid., Chapter III, verse 40, p. 15. See also Jayatilleke, *The Message of the Buddha*, pp. 256–259.

133 See "Notes" to *The Dhammapada*, p. 161.

134 See Jayatilleke, *The Message of the Buddha*, p. 151.

135 Ibid., p. 259.

136 See Jan Nattier, "Buddhist Eschatology", in *Oxford Handbook of Eschatology*, ed. Jeremy Walls (Oxford: Oxford University Press, 2008), pp. 151–171. Nattier states: "Buddhists share with members of other Indian religions (notably the Hindus and the Jains) the idea that the universe passes through an unending series of cycles of manifestation and nonmanifestation." Ibid., p. 151.

In essence, Eastern thought tends to focus on wisdom—that is the ornament they pursue—albeit only attaining it in a limited fashion. Although wisdom is beneficial and beautiful, even in a limited amount, it will not benefit those who turn their back on the Holy Lord and His prophets, nor those who have worshipped other deities alongside the One True God. Moreover, since these systems do not address the problem of evil as traditionally framed or provide a theodicy, they will not be mentioned further.

The objective of Judaism, Christianity and Islam (as well as the prior prophets) was to rid the world of polytheism and to turn people to the worship of the One Holy Lord. Unreasonably, Ibn Warraq states in his book: "One of the great achievements of Muhammad, we are told, was ridding Arabia of polytheism. But this, I have tried to argue, is monotheistic arrogance. There are no compelling arguments in favor of monotheism, as opposed to polytheism. Indeed, as Hume showed, there is nothing inherently absurd in polytheism."[137] God (Exalted is He) warns those who think similarly: *Hast thou not seen those unto whom a portion of the Scripture had been given, how they believe in idols and false deities, and how they say of those (idolaters) who disbelieve: These are more rightly guided than those who believe? Those are they whom God hath cursed, and he whom God hath cursed, thou wilt find for him no helper.*[138]

ATHEISM

On the other end of the spectrum that has been discussed thus far exists amoral atheism. Atheists reject the Holy Lord and the Divine commandments—they follow instead their own desires, considering their own wisdom to be greater than that of any Scripture or prophet.

Now, the reality is that there is nothing constructive about atheism in its pure form. Some atheists frankly speak in terms of destruction, like "end of faith",[139] "deconstruction",[140] etc., and this is consistent

---

137 Ibn Warraq, *Why I am not a Muslim* (Amherst: Prometheus Books, 2003), p. 119.

138 Q.IV.51–52.

139 See Sam Harris, *The End of Faith: Religion, Terror, and the Future of Reason* (New York: W. W. Norton & Company, 2004).

140 Michel Onfray states: "The book sets out to accomplish 3 objectives: deconstruction of the three monotheisms, deconstruction of Christianity in particular and deconstruction of theocracy." See Michel Onfray, *Atheist Manifesto: The Case Against Christianity, Judaism, and Islam*, tr. Jeremy Leggatt (New York: Arcade Publishing, 2007), p. 59.

with their overall approach and effect. Alister McGrath also explains: "The historical origins of modern atheism lie primarily in an extended criticism of the power and status of the church, rather than in any asserted attractions of a godless world."[141] The statement of Thomas Paine[142] exemplifies that criticism: "All national institutions of religion, whether Jewish, Christian, or Turkish, appear to me no other than human invention set up to terrify and enslave mankind, and monopolize power and profit."[143] Whatever those criticisms may be they are outweighed by the goodness of Judaism, Christianity and Islam as social institutions. It will be maintained that if the commandments of the Holy Lord and teachings of the prophets are followed then justice and freedom will endure to a greater degree, mercy and peace will spread, and citizens will be more likely able to share in the success of the society.

Again, atheism itself has a deconstructive effect upon societies, although some atheists may come to possess characteristics or abilities by which they can act constructively. Atheism, when systematically empowered, leads to greater disorder, chaos and evils than the historical forms of institutionalized religion. These logical consequences of atheism were anticipated in an 1878 letter written by Dostoevsky: "Now suppose that there is no God, and no personal immortality... Tell me then: Why am I to live decently and do good, if I die here below? [...] And if that's really so (and if I am clever enough not to let myself be caught by the standing laws), why should

---

[141] See Alister McGrath, *The Twilight of Atheism: The Rise and Fall of Disbelief in the Modern World* (New York: Galilee and Doubleday, 2006), p. 11. Likewise McGrath states: "Atheism, for Voltaire, remains an excessive reaction against a corrupt church, not a positive philosophy in its own right...His argument is simple: the attractiveness of atheism is directly dependent upon the corruption of Christian institutions." Ibid., p. 27.

[142] Thomas Paine was not an atheist but rather a deist. He states: "I believe in God, and no more, and I hope for happiness beyond this life. I believe in the equality of man; and I believe that religious duties consist in doing justice, loving mercy, and endeavoring to make our fellow creatures happy...My own mind is my own church." See Thomas Paine, *The Age of Reason* (London: Freethought Publishing, 1880), pp. 1–2.

[143] Ibid., p. 2.

I not kill, rob, steal, or at any rate live at the expense of others?"[144] McGrath states: "While Dostoyevsky's writings give little hint of the horrendous evils to come in the Stalinist era there can be little doubt that he was trying to draw the attention of his readers to the darker side of atheism. Atheism, it has often been argued, was the necessary precondition for the Stalinist era...Dostoyevsky...foresaw something much more disturbing. To remove God is to eliminate the final restraint on human brutality."[145]

McGrath further adds that "whenever atheism became the establishment, it demonstrated a ruthlessness and lack of toleration that destroyed its credentials as a liberator...One of the more disturbing patterns of history is that movements that began as liberators end up becoming oppressors in their own right. It is as if the abused seems historically predetermined to become an abuser".[146] Thus, atheism has no true concern for evil—indeed, it exacerbates the problem, and it cannot contribute solutions.

Sam Harris, in his book *End of Faith*, writes: "Since propositions are so dangerous it may even be ethical to kill people for believing them. This may be seen as an extraordinary claim, but it merely enunciates an ordinary fact about the world in which we live."[147] McGrath argues that it is disingenuous for atheists to criticize adherents to any particular faith for their violence or oppression "precisely because their own recent history contains too much cruelty, oppression,

---

[144] See Ethel C. Mayne (tr.), *Letters of Fyodor Michailovitch Dostoevsky to his Family and Friends* (London: Chatto & Windus, 1914), p. 222. McGrath also states: "With precocious foresight, Nietzche declared that having lost faith in God people would now put their trust in barbaric 'brotherhoods with the aim of robbery and exploitation of the non-brothers.'" See McGrath, *The Twilight of Atheism*, p. 262.

[145] See McGrath, *The Twilight of Atheism*, pp. 148–149. Also, consider the statement of the Polish poet Czeslaw Milosz wherein he responds to Karl Marx's argument that "Religion is the opium of the people." Milosz states: "A true opium of the people is a belief in nothingness after death—the huge solace of thinking that for our betrayals, greed, cowardice, murders, we are not going to be judged." Czeslaw Milosz, "Discreet Charm of Nihilism," *The New York Review of Books* (19 November 1998).

[146] McGrath, *The Twilight of Atheism*, pp. 234–236.

[147] Sam Harris, *End of Faith*, pp. 52–53. Harris also claims: "The problem of vindicating an omnipotent and omniscient God in the face of evil is insurmountable." Ibid., p. 173.

and violence at the hands of those determined to rid the world of religions".[148]

Atheism also fails to deal with the complexities of human experience, unlike the Qur'ān and Islam. But some atheists, like Michel Onfray, claim that religion only represents a repetition of incantations but "never innovates, which solicits not the intelligence but the memory",[149] or that: "Monotheism loathes intelligence, that sublime gift defined as the art of connecting what at first and for most people seems unconnected."[150] Here, what Onfray is referring to is blind imitation (*taqlīd*), and this *is* blameworthy. Ibn al-Qayyim for instance repudiated it[151] and instead emphasized the importance of contemplation and reflection in order to gain further knowledge and insight.[152] In addition, the Qur'ān connects between many things that appear unconnected and it encourages inquiry. The Qur'ān exemplifies what is wise, and this will become more evident as the book progresses.

Now, this chapter has alluded to the most pertinent philosophies and religions and how, except for the religion of God (Glorious is He) as conveyed by His prophets, the contradictions contained within their systems of thought ultimately weaken them and reveal their incoherence, particularly if their notions are carried out to their necessary conclusions. The affairs of life are so complex that the disbelievers cannot develop a system of thought except that it will contain many definitive—not just suspected—contradictions. God

---

148 McGrath, *The Twilight of Atheism*, p. 235. McGrath states that "once in power the Bolsheviks made Utopia an extremely bloody business". Ibid., p. 234. He also argues that "Lenin, frustrated by the Russian people's obstinate refusal to espouse atheism voluntarily and naturally after the Russian revolution, enforced it arguing—in a letter in March 1922—that the 'protracted use of brutality' was the necessary means of achieving this goal." Ibid., p. 166. McGrath also states: "Communism was a 'tragedy of planetary dimensions' with a grand total of victims variously estimated...at between 85 and 100 million—far in excess of those murdered under Nazism." Ibid., p. 233.

149 See Onfray, *Atheist Manifesto*, p. 52.

150 Ibid., p. 67

151 See Abdul-Rahman Mustafa. *On Taqlīd: Ibn al-Qayyim's Critique of Authority in Islamic Law* (New York: Oxford University Press), 2013.

152 See Zeni (tr.), *Ibn Qayyim al-Jawziyya on Knowledge*, Chapter Twelve titled "The Importance of Contemplation and Reflection", pp. 269–281.

(Glorious is He) states: *Will they not then ponder on the Qur'ān? If it had been from other than God they would have found therein much incongruity.*[153]

That said, by allowing all of these various systems of disbelief to exist at one time or another, the wisdom of God in His Divine commandments is illustrated to a much greater degree. God (Exalted is He) states: *He it is Who hath sent His Messenger with the guidance and the Religion of Truth, that He may cause it to prevail over all religion.*[154] Manifesting the superiority of God's religion over all others is one of God's wise purposes for allowing all of the various religions and systems to exist, and for allowing the creation to continue until now.

The transmitted revelation of the Qur'ān and Sunna of the Prophet Muḥammad responds to all of the major ideas of other religions and philosophies—regarding both good and evil—sometimes in a clear-cut manner and at other times in a hidden fashion. The objective of the remaining chapters is to advance many of those clear-cut and hidden arguments that address the problem of suffering and evil.

Eschatological considerations

Before concluding this chapter, it is apt to cover some eschatological matters that have been raised in relation to the problem of Hellfire by a few non-Muslim thinkers.

John Hick and Marilyn McCord Adams advocate a belief in universal salvation,[155] to such an extent that the former claimed that the "doctrine of hell is morally intolerable".[156] Furthermore, Hick, in his book *Death and Eternal Life*, proposes further lives and worlds, so that

---

153 Q.IV.82.

154 This is repeated three times in the Qur'ān: Q.IX.33, Q.XLVIII.28 and Q.LXI.9.

155 Adams states: "My own view is that hell poses the principal problem of evil for Christians. Its challenge is so deep and decisive, that to spill bottles of ink defending the logical compossibility of [God's existence and being essentially omnipotent, omniscient, and perfectly good] with this-worldly evils while holding a closeted belief that (III) some created persons will be consigned to hell forever, is at best incongruous and at worst disingenuous…My own verdict is no secret: statement (III) should be rejected in favor of a doctrine of universal salvation." See Marilyn McCord Adams, "The Problem of Hell: A Problem of Evil for Christians", in Eleonore Stump (ed.), *Reasoned Faith: Essays in Philosophical Theology in Honor of Norman Kretzmann* (Ithaca and London: Cornell University Press, 1993), p. 302.

156 John Hick, *Death and Eternal Life* (London: William Collins Sons & Co., 1976), p. 456.

all of humanity may, through soul-making or spiritual development, attain salvation. This type of thinking is akin to reincarnation in Eastern thought, rather than the Christianity which he adhered to earlier in his career. To claim that there are other stages for the disbelievers in a future life or the Hereafter (other than Hellfire) is not substantiated in either the Bible or the Qur'ān.

Those Christians who adopt a position of universal salvation allude to the generality of a verse within the New Testament: "God our Saviour, Who will have all men to be saved and to come unto the knowledge of the truth."[157] However, Charles Journet interprets the verse in non-universalist terms by saying: "God wishes to save all men: if they are saved the glory is his, and if they are not, the fault is theirs."[158] Eleonore Stump also faults humankind for their failure in being saved and denies universal salvation by stating: "If men suffer because they do not heed God's warning, that is their fault. If they suffer because God failed to warn them (and when they could not have known unless God had warned them), then their suffering is God's fault."[159] Finally, Richard Swinburne rejects it by stating: "It seems to me that such a [universalist] doctrine is not that of the New Testament."[160] The Old Testament likewise does not contain what could be considered explicit verses indicating universal salvation. Furthermore, there is no discussion within the Bible of disbelievers being removed from Hellfire and placed in Paradise. On such a point, one also finds that the Qur'ān and Sunna make no pronouncements of this kind.

Hick also considers annihilation in addition to universal salvation (again preferring the latter):

---

[157] 1 Timothy 2.3–4. They also consider as proof the verse: "the kindness and love of God our Saviour toward man appeared, not by works of righteousness which we have done, but according to his mercy he saved us." Titus 3.4–5.

[158] Journet, *The Meaning of Evil*, p. 155.

[159] Eleonore Stump, "Knowledge, Freedom, and the Problem of Evil", *International Journal for Philosophy of Religion*, vol. XIV, no. 1, 1983, p. 56.

[160] Richard Swinburne, "A Theodicy of Heaven and Hell", in Alfred Freddoso (ed.), *The Existence and Nature of God* (Notre Dame: University of Notre Dame Press, 1983), pp. 37–54 (specifically p. 39).

> The needs of a Christian theodicy compel us to repudiate the idea of eternal punishment. Does this mean that we are led to universalism, in the sense of a belief in the ultimate salvation of all human souls. The rejection of the idea of a divine sentence of eternal suffering is not in itself equivalent to universalism, for there remains a third possibility of either divine annihilation or the dwindling out of existence of the finally lost. In this case there would not be eternally useless and unredeemed suffering such as is entailed by the notion of hell as unending torment; and in working out a theodicy it would perhaps be possible to stop at this point. However...God's good purpose would have failed in the case of all those souls whose fate is extinction.[161]

Marilyn McCord Adams also contemplates annihilation, but rejects it for similar reasons: "To me, it is a better theological bargain to hold the mystery that God will not give up on the wicked, will eventually somehow be able to turn them to good, than to swallow the tragic idea that created persons, finite and dependent though we are, are able to ultimately and finally defeat our Creator's purpose, the mystery of transworld final impenitence ending in the Creator's destroying His own creation."[162] Adams thus states: "My own verdict is no secret. The statement [some created persons will be consigned to hell forever] should be rejected in favor of a doctrine of universal salvation."[163]

The Christian theologian Clark Pinnock came to favour annihilation. Although he acknowledges that "classic, mainstream, traditional, and evangelical" churches all view Hellfire as an "everlasting conscious punishment", he alludes to Biblical verses mentioning that the disbelievers will "fade" and "wither", "cut off and be no more", "perish and vanish like smoke", "be altogether destroyed", and that "their destiny will be destruction" on a coming day which "will burn

---

161 Hick, *Evil and the God of Love*, p. 342. Hick states subsequently in another section: "To assert that the sufferings caused by earthly wrongdoing are eternal is, I believe, to go beyond anything warranted by either revelation or reason, and to fall into a serious perversion of the Christian Gospel." Ibid., p. 349.

162 See Marilyn McCord Adams, "The Problem of Hell: A Problem of Evil for Christians", p. 323–324.

163 Ibid., p. 302.

them up".[164] Another verse states: "Let them be blotted out of the book of the living, and not be written with the righteous."[165] And Jesus (may God bless him) is quoted according to the Synoptic Gospel: "Some will go away into eternal punishment but the righteous into eternal life."[166]

Hellfire and Paradise will be discussed further in Chapters Fourteen and Fifteen, but for now an Islamic theodicy will be advanced in depth over the next four chapters.

---

[164] See Clark H. Pinnock, "Annihilationism," in Jeremy Walls (ed.), *Oxford Handbook of Eschatology* (Oxford: Oxford University Press, 2008), pp. 462–475 (specifically 463–465). The verses include Psalm 37.2, 9–10, 20, and 38; Phil 3.19; and Malachi 4.1–2, respectively.

[165] Psalms 69.28. Also, consider Revelation 3.5: "He that overcometh, the same shall be clothed in white raiment; and I will not blot out his name out of the book of life."

[166] Matthew 25.46.

Chapter Ten

The Wisdom in Allowing Suffering

There are many causes for the manifold afflictions and sufferings witnessed in this world; however, a significant amount of them are due to the inadequate nature of humankind. Some types of suffering represent privation of the ontological. For example, privation of wealth or power represents suffering manifested as poverty or weakness, respectively. The former are blessings of God (Glorious is He), which if withheld, result in suffering but not evil per se. Other types of hardships like pain, though, are predominantly due to sinfulness.

Evil and sin, on the other hand, represent privation of the deontological, in addition to other entities beyond privation—this will be discussed in the next chapter. As a general rule, the consequence of inadequacy can be suffering or possibly harm, while that of sin is either pain or evil.

The inadequacy of humankind is manifestly evident once we consider that God's glory (Exalted is He) is infinite and that we cannot worship Him as He deserves to be worshipped. The Prophet Muḥammad (may God bless him and grant him peace) relayed that even the angels say to the Holy Lord: "Glory be to You! We have not worshipped You in a manner befitting to You."[1] That said, the angels continuously worship the Holy Lord and never disobey Him, and therefore their worship of Him can be characterized as adequate. As a result, the angels do not endure suffering or afflictions. But humankind, being unable to continuously worship Him or avoid lapses, must consequently experience privation and suffering.

---

[1] Al-Ḥākim 8739. It is "sound" according to Albānī (*Silsilat al-aḥādīth al-ṣaḥīḥa* 941). See also a similar tradition stating: "God has devout angels in the lowest heaven [who have worshipped Him] in prostration, who will not raise their heads until the Day of Judgment. On the Day of Resurrection, they will raise their heads saying: 'Our Lord, we have not worshipped You in a manner befitting to You.'" Al-Ḥākim 4502; Bayhaqī (*Shuʿab*) 164.

The hardships, misfortunes and suffering that God imposes on us, although at times very difficult, are never unjust. Rather, they represent a small degree compared to our inadequacies in worshipping and thanking Him for His many blessings as well as our sinfulness. Some of the reasons and wise purposes for the existence of suffering will now be discussed.

1. Manifestation of a greater number of Beautiful Divine Names and Glorious Attributes

As mentioned earlier in Chapter Two, God (Glorious is He) willed to manifest a spectrum of His Beautiful Names and Glorious Attributes. Some of His Names are the Most Beneficent, the Omnipotent, the Omniscient, the Most Generous and the Most Wise, while others include the One Who tests (*al-Mubtalī*), the One Who benefits, the One Who harms, as well as the One Who removes harm (*Kāshif al-ḍarr*). God's Beautiful Names also include the One Who bestows (*al-Bāsiṭ*) and the One Who constricts (*al-Qābiḍ*), and the One Who enriches (*al-Mughnī*) and the One Who bars (*al-Māniʿ*). God (Exalted is He) has determined to manifest this spectrum of His Beautiful Names in a manner concordant to His love, wisdom, holiness and justice. Injustice is not attributable to Him, and therefore God (Glorious is He) has dictated causes that permit the just manifestation of the aforementioned as well as other Names to be discussed below.

Now, the Prophet Muḥammad (may God bless him and grant him peace) said: "O God, I seek refuge in Your pleasure from Your wrath, and in Your forgiveness from Your punishment. I seek refuge in You from Yourself. I cannot praise You enough; You are as You have praised Yourself."[2] Ibn al-Qayyim explained this *ḥadīth* in part by stating:

> Some of the Sublime's Attributes and actions are superior (*afḍal*) to others. The Attribute that we seek refuge in is superior to the Attribute of His which we seek refuge from. Therefore, His Attribute of mercy is superior to wrath, and it is for that reason that the former prevails over and overcomes the latter... [S]ince His pleasure and wrath, as well

---

[2] Muslim 486/1090; Tirmidhī 3566; Abū Dāwūd 879; Ibn Māja 1179; Nasāʾī 169; Aḥmad 751.

> as forgiveness and punishment, are paired [Attributes], one should seek refuge with the former [Attribute] from the latter.[3]

Therefore, in reference to the aforementioned paired Attributes, it will be contended—and God knows best—that just as God's mercy predominates over His wrath, His benefit is greater than His harm, His bestowal is greater than His constriction, and His enrichment is greater than His withholding. This represents a key principle to understanding why the Almighty Lord has created this world in such fashion—it will be discussed again later in this chapter. Further Names and Attributes of the Holy Lord will also be discussed in Chapter Twelve.

2. *Demonstration of God's love*

God's love has also led to the creation of humanity. The Qur'ān mentions ten groups that are loved by the Holy Lord: the pious[4] (*muttaqīn*), the devout[5] (*muḥsinīn*), those who are patient[6] (*ṣābirīn*), those who repent[7] (*tawwābīn*) and purify themselves (*mutaṭahhirīn*), those who work to purify others[8] (*muṭṭahhirīn*), those who rely on God[9] (*mutawakkilīn*), those who are benevolently equitable[10] (*muqsiṭīn*),

---

[3] Zeni (tr.), *Ibn Qayyim al-Jawziyya on Divine Wisdom and the Problem of Evil*, pp. 210–211.

[4] See Q.III.76. See also Q.IX.4 and 7. Of note, Pickthall tends to translate *muttaqīn* as those who "ward off evil" or those who "keep their duty" to God.

[5] See Q.III.134. See also Q.II.195, Q.III.148, Q.V.12–13 and 93.

[6] Q.III.146: *How many of the prophets fought (in God's way), and with them (fought) large bands of godly men? They never lost heart if they met with disaster in God's way, nor did they weaken (in will) nor give in. And God loves those who are firm and steadfast* (Yusuf Ali translation).

[7] See Q.II.222.

[8] See Q.IX.108. Of note, it may be that there is no difference between *mutaṭahhirīn* and *muṭṭahhirīn*, and that both refer to purification of the self.

[9] Q.III.159: *It was by the mercy of God that thou wast lenient with them (O Muḥammad), for if thou hadst been stern and fierce of heart they would have dispersed from round about thee. So pardon them and ask forgiveness for them and consult with them upon the conduct of affairs. And when thou art resolved, then put thy trust in God. God loveth those who put their trust (in Him).*

[10] Q.LX.8: *God forbids you not, with regard to those who fight you not for (your) faith nor drive you out of your homes, from dealing kindly and justly with them: for God loveth those who are just.* Q.V.42: *If thou judgest, judge between them with equity. God loveth the equitable.* See also Q.XLIX.9.

those who follow the Prophet Muḥammad[11] (may God bless him and grant him peace), and those who fight for His sake in a unified manner.[12]

The Prophet Muḥammad also mentioned that God (Exalted is He) loves a servant "who is pious, content (*ghanī*), and hides [his piety] (*khafī*) [from others]".[13] The hiding of one's goodness from others indicates sincerity in seeking the pleasure of the Holy Lord, and the desire to avoid ostentation, boastfulness or pride. Finally, the Messenger of God said: "God loves those who are easygoing and forgiving (*samiḥ*) in selling, buying and decision-making (*qaḍā'*)."[14]

These aforementioned groups and the traits that characterize them would not have been possible in a world where suffering, disbelief and evil did not exist. For example, (1) those who are pious must avoid major sins and repent from intermediate ones; (2) those who endure calamities and hardships can only patiently do so through true reliance on God; and (3) those who seek to purify others must work to encourage them to abandon their inadequacies and sins and instead adopt goodness. Had these aforementioned groups and their traits not existed then God's love for them would have also not occurred or become manifested. Thus blameworthy or evil entities—such as inadequacy, hardships or sins—only exist ontologically so as to indirectly lead (albeit in a minority of cases) to what is beloved to the Holy Lord.

3. Demonstration of both Divine and human wisdom

Wisdom can only be truly appreciated in a finite environment with limited resources. Had humankind been created solely in Paradise, for instance, where God's grace and bounties approach infinity (for they are eternal therein), a true appreciation of God's wisdom would not have been possible. Therefore, the Holy Lord's wisdom becomes manifested more clearly in the finite environment of this earth

---

[11] Q.III.31: *Say (O Muḥammad, to humankind): If ye love God, follow me; God will love you and forgive you your sins. God is Forgiving, Merciful.*

[12] See Q.LXI.4.

[13] Muslim 2965/7432; Aḥmad 1441.

[14] Tirmidhī 1319; al-Ḥākim 2338. It is "authentic" according to Albānī (*Silsilat al-aḥādīth al-ṣaḥīḥa* 899).

wherein He has restricted a fuller manifestation of His omnipotence and magnanimity.

Moreover, if the privation of resources is great, human beings will need to act with commensurate wisdom in order to alleviate hardship. In fact, due to the degree of privation which exists, humans are unable to wisely manage it for the long-term benefit of society unless they follow God's commandments as conveyed by His prophets.

God (Exalted is He) has created more than enough sustenance for all of humankind, if wisely administered by them. However, the actions of human beings, in many instances, lead to greater poverty and afflictions. God (Glorious is He) states: *Nay, but ye (for your part) honour not the orphan, and urge not on the feeding of the poor. And ye devour heritages with devouring greed. And love wealth with abounding love.*[15] Greed and avarice as well as lack of concern for the poor and orphans lead, in part, to greater deprivation and poverty. Hoarding, injustice and evil sins of the society also lead to pain and suffering.

The story of Joseph illustrates this point further. After the king of Egypt saw a dream foretelling years of drought, none of his ministers or subjects understood the dream nor were they able to advise him on how to correctly manage the food stores. It was only Joseph's wise management and ability to interpret dreams—by the grace of God—that allowed the people to be saved from greater harm. It is only though the grace and mercy of God, and the presence of those who have been endowed with wisdom from Him, that the occurrence of harm is minimized to avoid greater afflictions or widespread death. That said, suffering will never be altogether eliminated in this worldly life as inadequacy is a necessary concomitant of the finiteness of human beings.

Therefore, the manifestation of His dazzling wisdom, as well as the wisdom of those whom He has graced, occurs more completely and clearly when privation and suffering are allowed. The above three reasons illustrate that through the allowance of suffering, some of His Names and Attributes, as well as His love and wisdom, become manifested in a just manner.

---

[15] Q.LXXXIX.15–20.

4. *SUFFERING IS A MEANS OF TRULY TESTING HUMANKIND*

The allowance of suffering is one means by which humankind is tested. God (Glorious is He) illustrates this in many verses, such as: *And He it is Who created the heavens and the earth in six days—and His Throne was upon the water—that He might try you, which of you is best in conduct,*[16] and: *We have placed all that is on the earth as an ornament thereof that We may try them: which of them is best in conduct.*[17] Indeed, such a vast array of tests exist that people cannot avoid them, no matter how hard they try.

God (Glorious is He) also states: *If God willed He could have punished them (without you) but (thus it is ordained) that He may try some of you by means of others.*[18] Thus both the good and evil of humanity are permitted to exist so as to allow the testing to occur. It is through these tests that the best ranks of humankind are elucidated. The Exalted states: *And verily We shall try you till We know those of you who strive hard (for the cause of God) and the steadfast, and till We test your record.*[19] The Holy Lord also said: *Had God willed He could have made you one community. But that He may try you by that which He hath given you (He hath made you as ye are). So vie one with another in good works.*[20]

Moreover, the Holy Lord states that He: *hath created life and death that He may try you, which of you is best in conduct.*[21] Therefore, life and death are created as part of a system that allows testing. In this regard, death will be considered as suffering—not evil. It represents a calamity (*muṣība*)[22] that is inevitable for every creature. God (Exalted is He) states: *Every soul must taste of death, and We try you with evil and with good, for ordeal. And unto Us ye will be returned.*[23] Suffering and evil are therefore allowed to ontologically exist so as to result in testing.

---

16 Q.XI.7.

17 Q.XVIII.7.

18 Q.XLVII.4.

19 Q.XLVII.31.

20 Q.V.48. See also Q.VI.165: *He it is Who hath placed you as viceroys of the earth and hath exalted some of you in rank above others, that He may try you by (the test of) that which He hath given you.*

21 Q.LXVII.2.

22 See Q.V.106.

23 Q.XXI.35.

There are a few similitudes in the Qur'ān in regards to tribulations. One of them, for example, is within God's statement (Exalted is He):

> *He sendeth down water from the sky, so that valleys flow according to their measure, and the flood beareth (on its surface) swelling foam—from that which they smelt in the fire in order to make ornaments and tools riseth a foam like unto it—thus God coineth (the similitude of) the true and the false. Then, as for the foam, it passeth away as scum upon the banks, while, as for that which is of use to humankind, it remaineth in the earth. Thus God coineth the similitudes.*[24]

This similitude represents how the believer is affected by benefits and adversity. Here water symbolizes a blessing and something beneficial, while the fire symbolizes suffering and hardships. This parable only pertains to the believer, as these inputs, whether blessings or hardships, lead to purification and a good outcome. Both blessings and hardships purify and strengthen the pious and righteous.

Verse seventeen of Sūrat al-Baqara[25] (mentioned previously) draws a parallel between the religion and fire. Although some hardships do result from following the religion and the commandments of the Holy Lord, particularly when striving against the evildoers and disbelievers, these hardships ultimately expiate and absolve the believers of their sins and lead to their purification. This is in contrast to the disbelievers and hypocrites who are burnt by the fire similar to how a dead tree or a plank of wood is.

The Prophet Muḥammad has also stated: "The greater the tribulation the greater the reward. If God loves a people, He tests them. Whoever is content with it will find God pleased [with him] and whoever is critical of it [will find] God's blame upon him."[26] So, perseverance and contentment in the face of such inevitable testing leads to a great reward from the Almighty Lord. Indeed, the Prophet (may God bless him and grant him peace) said: "Our [i.e. the

---

[24] Q.XIII.17.

[25] The verse is: *Their likeness is as the likeness of one who kindleth fire, and when it sheddeth its light around him God taketh away their light and leaveth them in darkness, where they cannot see.*

[26] Tirmidhī 2396; Ibn Māja 4031; Bayhaqī (*Sunan*) 9325. It is "authentic" according to Albānī (*Silsilat al-aḥādīth al-ṣaḥīḥa* 146). Of note, another tradition stating, "If God loves a servant He will test him so that He may hear his supplication [to Him]," is deemed to be "weak" according to Albānī (*Silsilat al-aḥādīth al-ḍaʿīfa wa'l-mawḍūʿa* 2202).

prophets'] tribulations are multiplied and our rewards for them are likewise multiplied."[27]

5. *Testing involves many factors*

There are many factors involved in testing, therefore it may be more easily considered if rendered mathematically. Testing is rendered proportional to the noted factors in the formula below. It should be noted that this only represents a framework; but consideration of these eight factors is, nonetheless, sufficient for our purposes here:

$$\text{Testing} \propto \frac{\text{Suffering (S)} \times \text{Evil (E)} \times \text{Temptation (T)} \times \text{Doubt (D)}}{\text{Blessings (B)} \times \text{Knowledge } (K_c) \times \text{Willpower } (W_f) \times \text{Piety (P)}}$$

The existence of suffering and evil are necessary for testing to occur. Furthermore, the severity of a test is dependent upon the extent of the factors in the numerator (suffering, evil, temptations or doubts).[28] The greater those factors the greater the test. Conversely, the greater one's religious knowledge, willpower, blessings and piety, then the greater one's ability to overcome trials; and in those instances the degree of testing will be less. Moreover, an experience of successfully navigating past tests and performing good deeds is important as it increases one's willpower. Such pattern recognition enables one to successfully maneuver future trials by the grace of God.

Every individual's level of testing is well known to God (Glorious is He). It was discussed above (as affirmed in the prior *ḥadīth*) that the tribulations of the prophets are the greatest. Since the prophets possess the greatest amounts of knowledge, piety, blessings (of the religious but not necessarily the material type), and the strongest willpower (whereby they are beset by the least temptations or doubts), the suffering and evil they must endure is the greatest. Undoubtedly, the Holy Lord loves the prophets as the best of His creation; however, these hardships represent a means to elevate them higher to the most

---

27 Ibn Māja 4024; Aḥmad 11,893; al-Ḥākim 119. It is "authentic" according to Albānī (*Silsilat al-aḥādīth al-ṣaḥīḥa* 144).

28 If suffering or temptations are non-existent (such as the case with the angels), then there is no testing. Furthermore, since animals lack an intellect and relevant religious knowledge, in addition to lacking a free will, they are likewise not tested.

eminent levels of Paradise. Ultimately, this is evidence of the justice of the Holy Lord as they are not granted this rank simply because the Holy Lord selected them for prophethood. Instead, it is due to their endurance of suffering as well as their true faith, devotion and striving against evil which enables them to reach the highest ranks of Paradise. As such, those who desire to attain righteousness must follow the prophets and act similarly if they are to attain exalted ranks in the next life.

We must always remember that the "extent of the afflictions and trials endured by the Prophets and Messengers of God is such that no ordinary person can complain of having suffered or [being] tested more than them".[29] They are our role models; and without them, whom would we properly emulate and how could humanity be guided?

Whilst all the prophets suffered more than the rest of creation, it should be emphasized that the suffering of the Prophet Muḥammad (may God bless him and grant him peace) was even greater—this was shown in Chapter Five and will be briefly discussed further here. His father died before he was born and his mother died in his early childhood, thus he was an orphan from the age of six. His grandfather, who took care of him thereafter, also died only a couple of years later. It was ultimately Abū Ṭālib, his uncle, who would have to care for him. Muḥammad's upbringing was also characterized by poverty.

All of the Prophet's children except Fāṭima died before him. The Prophet Muḥammad's son Abraham died young, whereupon he said: "The eye weeps and the heart is saddened, but we only say that which is pleasing to the Lord."[30] He (may God bless him and grant him peace) also witnessed the death of his beloved first wife Khadīja (may God be pleased with her).

The Messenger Muḥammad suffered years of persecution, oppression and boycott at the hands of the Meccan pagans. They

---

[29] See Saiyad Fareed Ahmad and Saiyad Salahuddin Ahmad, *God, Islam, and the Skeptic Mind*, p. 96.

[30] Muslim 2315/6025; Abū Dāwūd 3126; Ibn Māja 1589; Aḥmad 13,014.

would ridicule and deride him, call him a magician[31] or a madman,[32] and attribute evilness to him. The Prophet Muḥammad was thereafter forced to emigrate from his hometown of Mecca to Medina. He, along with his Companions, subsequently had to defend themselves from the advancing armies of the Quraysh and pagan Arabs. He also had to endure the death of seventy of his Companions in the Battle of Uḥud, and he was injured therein. This will be discussed further in Chapter Twelve, together with other events and battles the Prophet Muḥammad and his Companions endured in order to spread the message of Islam. Ultimately, the Prophet Muḥammad sacrificed everything for the Holy Lord's sake. Ibn al-Qayyim states: "No prior prophet was harmed or had to endure as much as [the Prophet Muḥammad] for God's sake."[33] May God bless the Prophet Muḥammad and grant him peace!

Again, the aforementioned equation illustrates some of the factors involved in testing. Moreover, it is proportionally related to those factors—not equivalent to them. Some are tested more while some less. Testing is utilized to elucidate and demonstrate one's sincerity to God and degrees of worship. The physical world follows God's scientific laws, whereas the religious world can be thought of as a chaotic system (in a pure scientific sense) where so many conditions and factors enter into the calculation of each individual's level of testing that it would be impossible for us to account for them all.

Finally, God (Exalted is He) has stated: *Be sure we shall test you with something of fear and hunger, some loss in goods or lives or the fruits (of your toil), but give glad tidings to those who patiently persevere. Who say, when afflicted with calamity: To God we belong, and to Him is our return. They are those on whom (descend) blessings from God, and mercy, and they are the ones that receive guidance.*[34] Therefore, those who withstand hardships for God's sake and remain steadfast will be blessed, guided further and granted mercy by God (Glorious and Most Blessed is He). Thus

---

31 See Q.X.2 and Q.XXXVIII.4. Likewise, Pharaoh and the Egyptians called Moses and Aaron magicians. See Q.XX.63 and Q.VII.109.

32 See Q.LI.52: *Even so there came no messenger unto those before them but they said: A wizard or a madman!*

33 Zeni (tr.), *Ibn Qayyim al-Jawziyya on Divine Wisdom and the Problem of Evil*, p. 260.

34 Q.II.155–157.

hardships, in such cases, have led to blessed results and consequences, which would not have occurred if good existed alone in this world.

6. THE PARADOXICAL NATURE OF SOME HARDSHIPS

Some hardships and difficulties are beneficial, but in a paradoxical manner. A paradox is defined here as something that initially appears to be implausible or impossible, but is subsequently proved to be plausible or possible by supportive arguments or data.[35] Both ontological[36] and deontological paradoxes exist.

In order to fully understand paradoxes one must have complete knowledge of all issues involved. However, since God (Exalted is He) withholds some of His knowledge for various wise purposes, we are unable to comprehend some of these paradoxes—some are never understood while others only become clear once further knowledge and a deeper perception is granted to us.

In regards to a theodicy, paradoxes can involve bringing out greater goods from suffering, hardships, and evil. These include the manifestation of higher levels of wisdom and bringing forth more beloved believers to the Holy Lord. Moreover, some types of tribulations cannot be fully realized in the absence of paradoxes. God (Exalted is He) states: *It may be that ye dislike a thing, and God brings about through it a great deal of good,*[37] and *it may happen that ye hate a thing which is good for you, and it may happen that ye love a thing which is bad for you. God knoweth, ye know not.*[38]

Most of the Divine commandments and laws are clearly good and holy, while others may involve some ambiguity. This is akin to most

---

[35] The Merriam-Webster dictionary defines a paradox as a "statement that seems contrary to common sense and yet perhaps is true". See also Roy Sorenson, *A Brief History of the Paradox: Philosophy and the Labyrinths of the Mind* (Oxford: Oxford University Press, 2003), for various approaches to defining and viewing paradoxes.

[36] For example, the universe being created from a point whereas now it is unfathomably massive is an ontological paradox. Another paradox is that the vast majority of humankind will be part of the Community of Muḥammad, although he was the last of a multitude of prophets.

[37] Q.IV.19.

[38] Q.II.216.

verses of the Qur'ān being explicit, while some are allegorical.[39] The latter commandments will ultimately be shown to also be good, but in a paradoxical and delayed manner.

One may consider God's inspiration to the mother of Moses: *Suckle him and, when thou fearest for him, then cast him into the river and fear not nor grieve. We shall bring him back unto thee and shall make him (one) of Our messengers.*[40] The commandment to cast Moses into the river is so paradoxical, yet it resulted in great good. God's wisdom in this is dazzling. Moreover, the strategy was to paradoxically have Moses brought up by Pharaoh, the enemy of the Holy Lord.[41] God (Exalted is He) states:

> *And the family of Pharaoh took him up, that he might become for them an enemy and a sorrow. Lo! Pharaoh and Haman and their hosts were ever sinning. And the wife of Pharaoh said: (He will be) a consolation for me and for thee. Kill him not. Peradventure he may be of use to us, or we may choose him for a son. And they perceived not… [And] We restored him to his mother that she might be comforted and not grieve, and that she might know that the promise of God is true. But most of them know not.*[42]

In addition, another benefit of Moses' upbringing is the recognition that God (Exalted is He) utilizes the disbelievers and evildoers for good ends, although they may be completely unaware of those greater goods or objectives.

Also consider God's statement (Exalted is He): *And if We had decreed for them: Lay down your lives or go forth from your dwellings, few of them would have done it; though if they did what they are exhorted to do it would be better for them, and more strengthening; and then We should bestow upon them from Our presence an immense reward, and should guide them unto a Straight Path.*[43] Therefore, if the Holy Lord commands something,

---

39 See Q.III.7.

40 Q.XXVIII.7.

41 See Q.XX.39: *Throw him into the ark, and throw it into the river, then the river shall throw it on to the bank, and there an enemy to Me and an enemy to him shall take him. And I endued thee with love from Me that thou mightest be trained according to My will.*

42 Q.XXVIII.8–13.

43 Q.IV.66–68.

even if it results in some individuals losing their possessions or lives,[44] its preponderant good will be for all believers in the Hereafter, and for the majority of a believing society in this world.

Moreover, privation and suffering is paradoxically beneficial to the pious. Wealth, power and material possessions may distract a person away from religious pursuits. Therefore, privation of these may result in a pious or righteous believer more sincerely pursuing religious endeavours; hence leading to a great amount of religious good.

The believers (*mu'minūn*) always derive some good from suffering. The Prophet Muḥammad (may God bless him and grant him peace) said: "The case of a believer is wonderful, since all of his affairs [ultimately] result in good. If something pleasing happens to him then he is thankful for it, and that is good for him. But if some harm afflicts him then he is patient, and that is good for him. This only applies to the believer."[45] The Prophet Muḥammad also said: "A believing man or woman continues to be afflicted in their selves, in their child, and in their wealth, such that when they return to God, they will be [expiated and] have no further sins."[46] Another narration of the *ḥadīth* states that a believer will also be afflicted in "his body"[47] and this will expiate him or her of sins. Thus suffering may be paradoxically good for the believers and a cause for their attainment of higher ranks.

God (Exalted is He) states: *No calamity befalleth save by God's leave. And whosoever believeth in God, He guideth his heart. And God is Knower of all things.*[48] Therefore, in this verse it becomes apparent that calamities

---

[44] One example of this occurred to the Israelites after they had worshipped the golden calf. Due to that major sin, the Holy Lord prescribed upon them: *And when Moses said unto his people: O my people! Ye have wronged yourselves by your choosing of the calf (for worship) so turn in penitence to your Creator, and kill (the guilty) yourselves. That will be best for you with your Creator and He will relent toward you. Lo! He is the Relenting, the Merciful.* (Q.II.54). Had the Israelites refused to do so they would not have been forgiven. See also Exodus 32.26–28 for a similar passage.

[45] Muslim 2999/7500; Aḥmad 18,934.

[46] Tirmidhī 2399; Aḥmad 7859; al-Ḥākim 1281; Bayhaqī (*Sunan*) 6543. It is "sound" according to Albānī (*Mishkāt* 1567).

[47] Aḥmad 9811; al-Ḥākim 7879. It is "sound" according to Albānī (*al-Taʿlīqāt al-ḥisān ʿalā Ṣaḥīḥ Ibn Ḥibbān* 2902).

[48] Q.LXIV.11.

afflict both believers and disbelievers; but only the believers are guided by God and derive benefit, while the disbelievers remain forsaken.

The Holy Lord, out of His mercy, has assisted the believers to overcome hardships and thereafter do good deeds. Although hardships and difficulties will not result in the disbelievers necessarily abandoning their evil ways, those same hardships will lead to the believers carrying out good actions, by the grace of God. The same incident—say, for instance, an illness—may lead a disbeliever to despair and become further from God, whereas a believer will remember God and be patient, and will thus be rewarded. So it is the response and reaction of a free-willed human being that ultimately dictates whether a hardship is beneficial or not.

Furthermore, another benefit of hardships is that the sins of Muslims are expiated by virtue of them enduring those difficulties. A Companion visited the Messenger of God while he was suffering from an illness and said: "O Messenger of God, you have a very high fever." He replied: "Yes, [the added degree of] my fever is twice as high." The Companion added: "I asked: 'Is it because you will have double the reward?' He replied: 'Yes. God will expiate the sins of any Muslim afflicted with harm. It is akin to a tree shedding its leaves.'"[49] Although the believing Muslim may not recognize that benefit in his worldly life, it occurs regardless.

When one considers altogether the high ranks that God (Glorious is He) grants the believers (*muʿminūn*) in this world and the Hereafter, one clearly perceives His omnibenevolent treatment of them. The same cannot be said in regards to the disbelievers though. Nonetheless, a believer should not seek out tribulation or afflictions, for the Prophet Muḥammad said: "A believer should not humiliate himself by subjecting himself to afflictions he cannot bear."[50] In summation, suffering tends to be disadvantageous for the majority of people, but had it not existed many paradoxical great benefits for the believers would have elapsed them.

---

49 Bukhārī 5648; Muslim 2571/6559; Aḥmad 4346.

50 Tirmidhī 2254; Ibn Māja 4016; Aḥmad 23,444; Bayhaqī (*Shuʿab*) 7028. It is "sound" according to Albānī (*Silsilat al-aḥādīth al-ṣaḥīḥa* 613).

7. *SUFFERING ELUCIDATES THOSE WHO ARE SINCERE*

One wise purpose in allowing suffering is that it allows the differentiation of those who desire this world from those who desire instead the Hereafter and are sincere to the Holy Lord. It is only through afflictions that levels of true sincerity and perseverance can be manifested.

Therefore, hardships indirectly differentiate those who are sincere from those who are easily swayed away from the true religion. The Exalted states: *And among humankind is he who worshippeth God upon a narrow marge so that if good befalleth him he is content therewith, but if a trial befalleth him, he falleth away utterly. He loseth both the world and the Hereafter. That is the sheer loss.*[51] This individual only follows the religion for its worldly benefits, instead of sincerely desiring the Holy Lord, and remaining perseverant for His sake.

The presence of hardships and failure also allows us to evaluate in-depth our intentions. A person is only rewarded if his or her intention is good: "Deeds follow intentions, and a person is only rewarded based upon his intention."[52] Had we always been successful and never failed, we would never deeply reflect upon the reality of our intentions and goals. Therefore, suffering actually leads us to purify our intentions. We might think that our intentions are pure, but with repeated and greater hardships, we must renew and further purify our sincerity to God (Glorious is He). A further consequence of hardships and suffering is that a believer perfects his or her character, speech, and action. So it is through failure and suffering that the believers may improve themselves and reflect. On the other hand, continual success hinders one from reflecting upon one's inadequacies and bad actions.

Hardships also often lead people, whether believers or disbelievers, to doubt themselves. This doubt is crucial in so far as it forces the former to contemplate that which is more correct and seek the Holy Lord. In this respect, the believers will also seek to eliminate doubts about the religion, which will result in them becoming more guided and sincere. Of course, on the other hand, it may lead some Muslims

---

[51] Q.XXII.11.

[52] Bukhārī 1; Muslim 1907/4927; Tirmidhī 1647; Abū Dāwūd 2201; Ibn Māja 4227; Nasā'ī 75; Aḥmad 168.

to disbelieve upon encountering such doubts; but such a disavowal of the religion is only because they did not take their religion seriously nor did they pursue the necessary religious knowledge: *Till, when they come (before their Lord), He will say: Did ye deny My revelations when ye could not encompass them in knowledge, or what was it that ye did?*[53] They could have corrected their ways in this world had they pursued further knowledge to allay their doubts.

In contrast to the believers, the doubts experienced by the disbelievers lead most to dive deeper into disbelief, although a few may seek true guidance. Only God (Glorious is He) knows of the disbeliever's doubts, and those doubts will ultimately be proof against them on the Day of Judgment. Such doubts that are felt during this lifetime will enable them to recognize on the Day of Judgment that Holy Lord is not unjust in punishing them. That said, the doubts experienced by the disbelievers do result in a benefit since they prevent them, in general, from becoming more arrogant.

Now, the pious will inevitably miss out on some elements of this world and suffer privation,[54] but some Muslims will chose to forgo piety and true sincerity in order gain more wealth (even if through sinful means). Therefore, these Muslims may engage in major sins like participating in interest/usury or lesser degrees of evil to acquire material possessions. These lower levels of sincerity have only become manifested due to privation.

Moreover, although some of the believers will not pursue wealth through major sins, they will wish in their hearts that they did possess it and lament missing out. In this manner, God (Exalted is He) differentiates those who truly only want the Hereafter and Paradise—not caring that they have missed out on some elements of this world—versus those who regret the loss of some pleasures and are not content with what they possess in this world. Those who are truly devout are elucidated through the privation and suffering.

One must be content with that which God (Exalted is He) has bestowed upon one. A lesson of this is seen in the example of

---

[53] Q.XXVII.84.

[54] God (Exalted is He) states: *And whosoever keepeth his duty to God, God will appoint a way out for him, and will provide for him from (a quarter) whence he hath no expectation.* Q.LXV.2–3.

Solomon (may God bless him) who was granted the greatest kingdom by God (Exalted is He), yet he did not desire anything beyond what the Almighty Lord had granted him. When the Queen of Sheba sent him a present, Solomon said: *What! Would ye help me with wealth? But that which God hath given me is better than that which He hath given you.*[55] Dhū al-Qarnayn said something similar to that when a people offered to pay him a tribute for building a dam between them and Gog and Magog: *That wherein my Lord hath established me is better (than your tribute).*[56]

Therefore, those believers who want to reach the higher ranks of Paradise must not lament the loss of any worldly wealth or possession that may occur due to their preoccupation with their religion, learning its precepts, pursuing good, and performing righteous actions. Rather, their hearts must delight in the religious knowledge and wisdom that God (Most Blessed and Exalted is He) has bestowed upon them, and must rejoice in the righteous actions He has enabled them to carry out. They must set their sights to the eternal and massive reward of Paradise.

In fact, those who are devout would not wish to trade some aspect of their religion for anything of this world. Ibn al-Qayyim related that some ascetics said: "Had the kings and their offspring known [the joy] we feel [in our hearts] they would have fought us for it with swords."[57] Although Ibn Taymiyya and many other scholars were subjected to many hardships, including being unjustly imprisoned, they never abandoned their religion nor did their joy dissipate. Indeed, the joy that the devout and truly faithful feel in their hearts counteracts the suffering that they endure in this temporary worldly life. But since those of the lesser ranks do not feel that degree of pleasure, the stress from hardships may overcome them.

Enduring hardships and suffering may also lead to and result in greater degrees of sincerity, certainty and firm resolve. If one only lives in ease and does not encounter hardships one's attainment of those noble characteristics is far reduced. For instance, had the Companions

---

55 Q.XXVII.36.

56 Q.XVIII.95.

57 Ibn al-Qayyim, *Miftāḥ dār al-saʿāda*, vol. I, pp. 96–97.

prevailed over Quraysh early in the Meccan phase without having to emigrate to Medina or endure all manner of hardships for nearly twenty years before the liberation of Mecca, then their faith, certainty and firm resolve would not have reached the high levels that they did.

Had all those hardships not occurred and bequeathed a spiritual perfection upon the Companions, which in turn improved their ability to be exemplars attracting emulation, then those who followed the Companions would have been weaker, more susceptible to corruption and deviated away from God's path within a shorter period of time. Indeed, it was because of what they had previously endured that the Companions were able to overcome the apostate (*ridda*) wars, teach and better improve the spiritual state of the Successors, and expand over vast continents within a short span of time. The Companions had to endure massive pressure, suffering and evil for what was a relatively short period of time—in comparison to the hundreds of years which the Muslims would subsequently experience with their rulership—but this indirectly led to higher degrees of true faith and righteousness than was attained by those who followed them.

In addition, those in the past who could not overcome the disbelievers except through a miracle of God (Exalted is He) possessed lower levels of faith, in general, than those who could defeat the disbelievers without miracles but with other types of God's assistance. If testing is less and miracles are greater, the faith is shorter lived than if the testing is greater and miracles are less (assuming that the society does not fail its tribulations).

In summation, a world containing much good together with suffering and evil indirectly elucidates those who are truly sincere to the Holy Lord. Privation indirectly forces the believers to purify their intentions and thus attain higher levels of faith. It also discerns those who are content with what they have been bestowed in this world from those who have doubts about the religion and are willing to perpetrate major sins in order to fulfill their desires.

8. Privation Detaches the Believers from This World Leading Them to Aspire for the Hereafter

Privation within this world serves as one means by which a believer becomes detached from this worldly life and instead aspires for the

Hereafter. The Prophet Muḥammad (may God bless him and grant him peace) said: "Whoever aspires for the Hereafter, God will organize his affairs and make his heart content, and this world will inevitably be granted to him (*rāghima*). But whoever is preoccupied with this world, then God will make him feel impoverished, will scatter his affairs, and only allow him of this world that which He has decreed for him."[58] The believer should thus aim to be content with whatever God (Glorious is He) has granted him or her in this life.

Suffering is one effective cause that allows people to recognize the lowliness of this life and its temporary nature. The Holy Lord states: *No misfortune can happen on earth or in your souls but is recorded in a decree before We bring it into existence. That is truly easy for God, in order that ye may not despair over matters that pass you by, nor exult over favours bestowed upon you. For God loveth not any vainglorious boaster.*[59] These verses illustrate that the suffering of misfortunes results in the believers adopting a mental state wherein they remain detached from this world, regardless of whether they are materially enriched or impoverished. These believers remain firm on the Straight Path, balanced, and even-keeled. Their true goal is the Hereafter, and nothing distracts them from it.

The Prophet (may God bless him and grant him peace) also said: "Live in this world as though you were a stranger or a traveller."[60] The believers recognize that this world is temporary and that one's true life is in Paradise. The good in being attached to the Hereafter leads to God's mercy and blessings. Had people only lived in luxury in this world they would have become attached to it and content with it, instead of worshipping God in a manner that He loves, or longing for His mercy and Paradise. Some living in luxury may not even wish for the Hereafter. It is thus ultimately a mercy from God that the believers experience hardships in this worldly life.

The disbelievers may also be granted more worldly goods than the believers since God, Who is the Most Just, recompenses them for anything beneficial they have done only in this worldly life. ʿUmar b. al-Khaṭṭāb once saw the Prophet Muḥammad leaning on a reed mat

---

58 Tirmidhī 2465; Ibn Māja 4105; Aḥmad 21,590. It is "authentic" according to Albānī (*Silsilat al-aḥādīth al-ṣaḥīḥa* 949).

59 Q.LVII.22–23 (Yusuf Ali translation).

60 Bukhārī 6416; Tirmidhī 2333; Ibn Māja 4114; Aḥmad 4764.

which was so hard that it left marks on his side, and there was no food in his house aside from a handful of barley. ʿUmar began to get teary-eyed, and so the Messenger asked him why he was weeping. ʿUmar said: "O Messenger of God, why should I not weep when you are the Messenger of God and His chosen one, the best of His creation, and yet you have little in your house while Chosroes and Caesar live [in luxury]." The Prophet responded: "Are you not content that they are given this world while we are granted the Hereafter?" ʿUmar said: "Yes." In another narration the Prophet responded: "Indeed, any goodness is quickened to them in this worldly life."[61]

People will inevitably become disappointed with this world at some point in their lives: some will decide that they should focus their efforts on the Hereafter rather than being attached to this life, while others will "blame God" for their troubles. These latter individuals have preferred this life over the Hereafter. May God protect us from that!

9. Suffering leads many people to achieve humility

One Divine wise purpose in allowing suffering is that it can indirectly lead to humility, which is a trait desired for itself. The Prophet Muḥammad (may God bless him and grant him peace) said: "God has inspired me that you should all be humble. That is so no one will be boastful over another and no one will transgress against another."[62]

God (Glory be to Him) is critical of arrogance and pride, and He will not enter those who are arrogant into Paradise. The Prophet Muḥammad (may God bless him and grant him peace) said: "Whoever possesses an atom's weight of arrogance (*kibr*) will not be allowed to enter Paradise... Arrogance connotes denial of the truth and looking at people condescendingly."[63] Therefore, attainment of humility is crucial. It may be that those Muslims who have some element of arrogance—but whose arrogance does not cross into disbelief—will be purified from pride in the Hellfire until the Holy Lord deems them appropriate to enter Paradise. We have no other option but to be

61 Bukhārī 4913; Muslim 3691, 3692 and 3695/1479; Ibn Māja 4153; Aḥmad 12,417.

62 Muslim 2865/7210; Abū Dāwūd 4895.

63 Muslim 91/147 and 148; Tirmidhī 1999. Of note, the first part of this *ḥadīth* was also narrated by Ibn Māja (59) and Aḥmad (3947).

humble if we want to avoid the punishment of Hellfire. And God knows best.

Suffering and the recognition of one's inadequacies leads one to realize one's humility and complete dependence on the grace of the Most Blessed Lord. Hence if one experiences bodily weakness, for example, whether due to injury or disease or otherwise, one has two options from a religious perspective. Either one can assign blame and/or become despondent, or one can supplicate to the Most Blessed Lord. In the latter case one acknowledges one's complete and utter dependence upon the Holy Lord—for nothing occurs outside of His will and all power belongs to Him. This humility and recognition, resulting from one's experience, is desired for itself. In the absence of suffering, weakness and need one would not have acknowledged the Almightiness of the Most Blessed Lord and one's humility and complete dependence upon Him. If, on the other hand, one fails to humble oneself but instead remains proud, then one is not truly a servant of the Holy Lord from a religious perspective.

One example of this in the Qur'ān is noted in the story of the brothers of Joseph. Joseph's brothers thought themselves to be better than him, but it was only after enduring hardships, poverty and suffering and seeing the harm that overcame their father Jacob—due to his separation from Joseph and Benjamin—that they recognized Joseph's religious superiority to them, acknowledged their inadequacies and admitted their sinfulness. They said to Joseph: *By God, verily God hath preferred thee above us, and we were indeed sinful!*[64] Thus, it was only then that they attained humility—the extent of which is only known by God.

One reason that God limits wealth to some and grants it to others is indicated in the verse: *If God were to enlarge the provision for His servants, they would indeed transgress beyond all bounds through the earth; but he sends (it) down in due measure as He pleases. For He is with His Servants Well-acquainted, Watchful.*[65] Therefore, transgression and haughtiness—i.e.

---

[64] Q.XII.91.

[65] Q.XLII.27 (Yusuf Ali translation). The Holy Lord also states: *God enlargeth livelihood for whom He will, and straiteneth (it for whom He will); and they rejoice in the life of the world, whereas the life of the world is but brief comfort as compared with the Hereafter*. Q.XIII.26.

the opposite of justice and humility—would have resulted had all lived in luxury.

This can be extrapolated to strength, i.e. had human beings been universally strong and not susceptible to weakness they would have likely also transgressed in the context of the free will given to them. Therefore, human suffering—whether poverty or weakness—serves to decrease the extent of transgressions for many and increase the likelihood that human beings will remain humble.

10. Suffering induces supplication to God

In times of privation or suffering one feels the need to supplicate to God (Exalted is He) for He is All-Hearing and He is the Most Generous. Had hardships and afflictions not existed, supplication to the Holy Lord would have been much less.

Remembrance of the Holy Lord and supplication to Him constitute a major part of Islam. In regards to the latter, God (Glorious is He) states: *And when My servants question thee concerning Me, then surely I am nigh. I answer the prayer of the suppliant when he crieth unto Me. So let them hear My call and let them trust in Me, in order that they may be led aright.*[66]

God (Glorious is He) loves that His servants supplicate to Him and this is an objective, in and of itself. The Prophet Muḥammad (may God bless him and grant him peace) said: "If any Muslim is afflicted with a calamity but then says: '*To God we belong and to Him is our return.*[67] O God, reward me for [enduring] my calamity, and bestow upon me something better than it,' then God will recompense him with something good."[68] Had suffering not existed then people would not have felt the need to supplicate—one should deeply reflect on the reality of this. Causes must exist, and if they do not then consequences are likewise non-existent, i.e. in this case, they would not have supplicated. Supplication to God (Exalted is He) and remembrance of Him are beloved to Him, and therefore the causes, which indirectly lead to them, must ontologically be willed to exist.

---

[66] Q.II.186.

[67] Q.II.156. The complete Qur'ānic verse is: *Who say, when afflicted with calamity: "To God we belong, and to Him is our return"; they are those on whom (descend) blessings from God and mercy, and they are the ones that receive guidance.* Q.II.156–157 (Yusuf Ali translation).

[68] Muslim 918/2126; Abū Dāwūd 3119; Ibn Māja 1598; Aḥmad 26635.

Once one's weakness and inadequacy are recognized upon being confronted by hardships and suffering, it leads one to supplicate to the Holy Lord and return to Him. If events were always good and the believers were always the strongest, they would not feel their dependence on God nor would they supplicate to Him in order to overcome their predicaments. Furthermore, by virtue of one's supplication one will become further guided, blessed by God and granted His mercy as God states: *They are those on whom (descend) blessings from God and mercy, and they are the ones that receive guidance.*[69]

We have the best example in the Prophet Muḥammad (may God bless him and grant him peace) who spent the whole night (of Friday 17 Ramadan) preceding the Battle of Badr in prayer and supplication. During the battle the Prophet continued to supplicate to God, saying: "O God, fulfill Your promise to me. Should this group of Muslims be defeated today, You will no longer be worshipped on this earth." In the end, Abū Bakr came to the Prophet and said: "O Prophet of God! Your beseeching is sufficient for He will surely fulfill what He has promised you."[70]

It is also due to the presence of hardships and afflictions, and being opposed by others, that we find greater comfort in the remembrance of the Holy Lord and supplication to Him. Surrounded by a turbulent world, we find peace in the remembrance of the Holy Lord. God (Exalted is He) describes the guided as those *who have believed and whose hearts have rest in the remembrance of God. Verily, in the remembrance of God do hearts find rest!*[71] The devout will find no peace in any other thought, state or luxury greater than that which they find by remembering the Holy Lord. Had suffering not existed, we would not appreciate that peace and comfort as significantly.

Another type of supplication is asking for forgiveness from the Holy Lord. One seeks forgiveness not only for one's sins, but also for one's inadequacies. For example, one asks for forgiveness after praying, since some deficiency will inevitably occur during one's carrying out of those prayers. The Prophet Muḥammad (may God bless him and

---

69 Q.II.157 (Yusuf Ali translation).

70 Muslim 1763/4588; Tirmidhī 3081; Aḥmad 208.

71 Q.XIII.28.

grant him peace) used to ask for forgiveness more than one hundred times a day,[72] even though he was protected from sinfulness (*maʿṣūm*). In fact, asking for forgiveness results in many religious and worldly benefits.[73]

Now, it should be mentioned that if every prayer was answered according to the wishes of every believer it would lead to many ramifications. First, it would ultimately result in laziness on the part of the believer as he or she could achieve any wish with prayer. This laziness is contrary to what God (Exalted is He) wants the believers to be, as He wants them to possess a strong willpower, which is crucial for them to walk the Straight Path to achieve proximity to Him. It would also lead to carelessness regarding one's responsibilities. Therefore, although His fulfillment of that supplication would demonstrate His omnipotence, it would lead to the occurrence of significant negative character traits amongst the believers.

Whilst one must believe that God (Glorious is He) will answer one's prayer, one must do what one can to fulfill one's need. Not doing so is called *tawākul* in Arabic and it is deemed to be religiously blameworthy. One should always rely on the Holy Lord, carry out the means (*asbāb*) that one can and which are customarily seen as necessary, and supplicate to Him—this is the true reliance (*tawakkul*) that is ordered by the religion.

Furthermore, the fact that God (Exalted is He) does not immediately satisfy all supplications prevents those who are disbelievers from joining the ranks of the believers for the sole purpose of material gain. Had God (Glorious is He) always willed that the believers would be victorious or amass more wealth, then the disbelievers—sensing the worldly benefit therein—would become believers. Although in this way many people would follow Islam, it would not be sincerely for the sake of God in many cases. In addition, although God (Exalted is He) could fulfill the supplications of all of humankind,[74] this could

---

72 See Muslim 2702/6859; Abū Dāwūd 1515; Ibn Māja 3815; Aḥmad 17,848.

73 See verses Q.VIII.33, Q.XI.3 and 52, and Q.LXXI.10–12.

74 God (Exalted is He) states in a *ḥadīth qudsī*: "If all of humankind and jinn were assembled together in one plain and I fulfilled what each one of them asked for, it would not decrease what I possess except like [the water which clings to] a needle dipped into an ocean." Muslim 2577/6572.

not be done within the limited realm of this earth, which again God has created as such in order to manifest the complex Divine wisdom.

Moreover, God (Most Blessed and Glorious is He) fulfills some prayers in this life and some He rewards in the Hereafter—no prayer of a believer goes unanswered or unrewarded. The Prophet Muḥammad (may God bless him and grant him peace) said: "If any Muslim on this earth supplicates to God with a prayer, then God will either answer it or prevent an evil of similar magnitude from harming him—as long as he does not supplicate for something sinful or that which would lead to breaking the ties of kinship."[75] Another narration states: "If any Muslim supplicates with a prayer—absent any sin or that which would break the ties of kinship—then God will grant him one of three: either He will answer his prayer [in this life], or He will save it for him until the Hereafter, or He will prevent some evil of similar magnitude."[76] Sincere supplication to the Holy Lord thus also reduces suffering and evil.

11. Privation leads to appreciating those blessings one possesses and being grateful to God

God (the Most Blessed and Almighty) loves to be thanked, and therefore the privation of a particular blessing allows people to recognize the greatness of that blessing. In the well-known tradition, God (Glory be to Him) revealed to Adam the various levels of his offspring whereupon Adam inquired: "O my Lord, why did You not make all of Your servants equal?" God replied: "I love to be thanked."[77] Due to His love of humans displaying gratitude to Him, God (Glorious is He) dictated the existence of causes which have resulted in humanity being divided into categories, with some, albeit few, being thankful for their greater blessings. There exists a bell curve for many human characteristics, and this is part of the predestination of the Almighty

---

[75] Tirmidhī 3573; Aḥmad 22,785; Bayhaqī (*Shuʿab*) 1089. It is "sound" according to Albānī (*Ṣaḥīḥ al-Targhīb wa'l-tarhīb* 1631).

[76] Al-Ḥākim 1816; Bayhaqī (*Shuʿab*) 1090. It is "sound" according to Albānī (*Ṣaḥīḥ al-Targhīb wa'l-tarhīb* 1633).

[77] Aḥmad (*Musnad*) 21,232 and (*al-Zuhd*) 256; al-Ḥākim 3255; Bayhaqī (*Shuʿab*) 4128. It is "sound" according to Albānī (*Mishkāt* 122).

Lord. The wise purposes He has dictated to manifest could not have otherwise occurred.

Often times one's blessings are not adequately recognized; but upon encountering another who is ill, paralyzed or incapacitated in some fashion, one is able to better acknowledge the Almighty Lord's great blessings upon him or her and thank Him for those favours. Although it is difficult for those actually afflicted (may God heal them), it will be more advantageous for them in the Hereafter if they believe and remain patient for God's sake (Glorious is He). The Prophet said: "On the Day of Judgment those who were healthy [in their worldly life] will wish—after seeing the reward of those who suffered—that their skin was cut up with scissors into pieces [so as to attain a similar great reward for that pain and suffering]."[78] No matter how difficult any situation or suffering is, nothing is worth disbelieving in God (Exalted is He) or failing to carry out the pillars of Islam.

God (Exalted is He) states: *And even so do We try some of them by others, that they say: Are these they whom God favoureth among us? Is not God best aware of the thanksgivers?*[79] This verse is referring to those who are favoured from a religious standpoint—not those who are given riches.[80] God (Exalted is He) is well aware of those who are most deserving of being guided and granted His mercy. In many cases, the groups that follow the prophets and religious prescripts are the poor and disadvantaged. The rich and powerful often despise those groups to such a degree that their hatred, pride, arrogance and even racism towards these groups hinder them from following the truth. Ibn al-Qayyim states that the disbelievers' statement *Are these they whom God favoureth among us?* "epitomizes their stubbornness, haughtiness and refusal to follow the truth even after fully comprehending it… This statement of theirs manifests [God's] justice, glory, power, reign and wisdom in favouring those who are suitable [for His guidance], while denying those who are not and instead deserve [to remain astray]."[81]

---

78 Tirmidhī 2402; Bayhaqī (*Sunan*) 6553. It is "sound" according to Albānī (*Silsilat al-aḥādīth al-ṣaḥīḥa* 2205).

79 Q.VI.53

80 See *Tafsīr al-Ṭabarī*, vol. XI, pp. 388–390.

81 Zeni (tr.), *Ibn Qayyim al-Jawziyya on Divine Wisdom and the Problem of Evil*, p. 46.

On the other hand, the believers are thankful to the Holy Lord as He has granted them His revelation and guidance. God (Glorious is He) advised Moses: *I have preferred thee above humankind by My messages and by My speaking (unto thee). So hold that which I have given thee, and be among the thankful.*[82] Moses had to suffer much at the hands of Pharaoh and the Egyptians as well as the Israelites, but he was advised to ignore all that and be thankful. Thus the Holy Lord is advising us to be thankful for His revelation, Scripture and faith (which He has blessed us with). If one is truly thankful for the faith and religion that God has blessed him or her with, one will not let any suffering get in the way of that gratitude. Thus, by having to undergo suffering, one's true appreciation of his Lord's blessings upon him becomes clear.

Again, the degrees of good and privation thereof result in some thanking the Holy Lord more appropriately and more completely. That said, one's good deeds do not serve as sufficient gratitude for the blessings that God (Glorious is He) has bestowed on us, such as our eyesight as well as other bodily and material powers or wealth. Those who are bestowed greater degrees of good should recognize their blessings and thank God appropriately.

Finally, the Prophet Muḥammad (may God bless him and grant him peace) continued to worship the Holy Lord to a greater degree than anyone else, and when asked about this he said: "Should I not be a thankful servant?"[83] As mentioned previously, the Prophet lived a life of material deprivation, and therefore this thankfulness is more so for his religious—but also for his ontologic—blessings. Furthermore, this *ḥadīth* also illustrates that no one can claim that they have reached such a high level of true certainty or righteousness that they are exempt from following the Holy Lord's commandments.[84] Rather, they should continue to worship the Holy Lord as prescribed and show their gratitude to Him by carrying out good, benevolent and righteous deeds.

---

[82] Q.VII.144.

[83] Bukhārī 1130; Muslim 2819/7124; Tirmidhī 412; Ibn Māja 1419; Nasā'ī 1644; Aḥmad 18,198.

[84] This is referring to those who claim Sufi antinomianism (*suqūt al-taklīf*).

12. HARDSHIPS ARE NECESSARY TO MANIFEST BENEVOLENT TRAITS
Many benevolent traits would not be manifested were it not for suffering and hardships. Principle among them is patience. God (Exalted is He) states: *And give good tidings (O Muḥammad) to the humble, whose hearts fear when God is mentioned, and the patient of whatever may befall them, and those who establish worship and who spend of that We have bestowed on them.*[85]

God advised the Prophet Muḥammad (may God bless him and grant him peace): *Messengers indeed have been denied before thee, and they were patient under the denial and the persecution till Our succour reached them.*[86] God advised the believers to be patient in many verses of the Qur'ān: *And obey God and His Messenger; and fall into no disputes, lest ye lose heart and your power depart; and be patient and persevering: For God is with those who patiently persevere.*[87] *O ye who believe! Persevere in patience and constancy; vie in such perseverance; strengthen each other; and fear God; that ye may prosper.*[88] *And We appointed, from among them, leaders, giving guidance under Our command, so long as they persevered with patience and continued to have faith in Our Signs.*[89]

Consider also that the Israelites were only saved from enslavement by Pharaoh because they remained steadfast and endured patiently. God (Glorious is He) states:

> *Said Moses to his people: "Pray for help from God, and (wait) in patience and constancy: for the earth is God's, to give as a heritage to such of His servants as He pleaseth; and the end is (best) for the righteous... And We made a people, considered weak (and of no account), inheritors of lands in both east and west, lands whereon We sent down Our blessings. The fair promise of thy Lord was fulfilled for the Children of Israel, because they had patience and constancy.*[90]

God (Exalted is He) advised the believers in the Qur'ān: *O ye who believe! Persevere in patience and constancy (iṣbirū); vie in such perseverance*

[85] Q.XXII.34–35.
[86] Q.VI.34.
[87] Q.VIII.46 (Yusuf Ali translation).
[88] Q.III.200 (Yusuf Ali translation).
[89] Q.XXXII.24 (Yusuf Ali translation).
[90] Q.VII.128 and 137 (Yusuf Ali translation).

(*ṣābirū*); *strengthen each other* (*rābiṭū*); *and fear God; that ye may prosper.*[91] The command to be patient and steadfast (*iṣbirū*) encompasses all circumstances, whereas one is advised to continue to persevere (*ṣābirū*) after one's patience and forbearance are exhausted. Therefore, this refers to exceeding and going beyond one's expected abilities—this can only be done by relying and depending on the Almighty Lord.

It seems that one is advised to endure (*rābiṭū*) in those situations which appear hopeless. Hence one must have patience and exert self-control even when one thinks that the situation, which is out of one's control, is hopeless and dire from every apparent standpoint. This is similar to the verse: *But there came to be a void in the heart of the mother of Moses: She was going almost to disclose his (case), had We not strengthened (rabaṭna) her heart (with faith), so that she might remain a (firm) believer.*[92] After having thrown him in the river, contemplating his loss and now having to endure his separation, Moses' mother persevered through a situation which appeared to be hopeless and out of her control. Her perseverance was only possible due to her faith in God's promise. God (Exalted is He) also states regarding the youth who fled to the cave due to the persecution they suffered: *And We made firm (rabaṭna) their hearts.*[93]

There are many situations, which appear hopeless—this is part of God's ontologic decree and destiny—yet the believers must endure. Although they may not be able to see the "light at the end of the tunnel", they perceive the spiritual light of the Almighty Lord and thus rely and depend on Him. The Almighty Lord states: *Or think ye that ye will enter Paradise while yet there hath not come unto you the like of (that which came to) those who passed away before you? Affliction and adversity befell them, they were shaken as with earthquake, till the messenger (of God) and those who believed along with him said: When cometh God's help? Now surely God's help is nigh.*[94] May God strengthen and guide us!

Here the story of Joseph is particularly relevant. His separation from his family, enslavement in Egypt and imprisonment thereafter would not have been thought of as being beneficial. Indeed, it is

---

[91] Q.III.200 (Yusuf Ali translation).

[92] Q.XXVIII.10 (Yusuf Ali translation).

[93] Q.XVIII.14.

[94] Q.II.214.

paradoxical that Joseph would become a minister of Egypt after being a slave and a prisoner therein. But he remained patient for decades through all of his trials; and it was his patience that allowed him to realize the good within them. Had he not been patient, he may have succumbed to despair or to a major sin. This would have led to failure, but it was his patience and reliance on God as well as God's grace that ultimately led to his success.

Again, one of the necessary requirements for fulfilling the precepts of the religion and attaining higher levels of faith and righteousness is patience, as well as certainty and a firm resolve. Those who do not possess these critical characteristics will succumb to despair or sin and ultimately fail.

Likewise, Job's patience and steadfastness in the face of the harm and evil that afflicted him resulted in his success. Job (may God bless him) is commended by the Holy Lord and all of the believers as a result of his patience: *And make mention (O Muḥammad) of Our bondman Job, when he cried unto his Lord (saying): Lo! the Devil doth afflict me with distress and torment,*[95] and in another *sūra*: *And Job, when he cried unto his Lord, (saying): Lo! adversity afflicteth me, and Thou art Most Merciful of all who show mercy.*[96]

The Almighty Lord ultimately responded to Job's supplication:

> *(And it was said unto him:) Strike the ground with thy foot. This (spring) is a cool bath and a refreshing drink. And We bestowed on him (again) his household and therewith the like thereof, a mercy from Us, and a memorial for men of understanding. And (it was said unto him): Take in thine hand a branch and smite therewith, and break not thine oath. Lo! We found him steadfast, how excellent a servant! He was ever turning in repentance (to his Lord).*[97]

God (Glorious is He) states in another set of verses: *Then We heard his prayer and removed that adversity from which he suffered, and We gave him his household (that he had lost) and the like thereof along with them, a mercy from*

---

[95] Q.XXXVIII.41.

[96] Q.XXI.83. Of note, the "adversity" mentioned in this verse is likely to be of a different nature to the "distress and torment" mentioned in the prior verse.

[97] Q.XXXVIII.42–44.

Our store, and a remembrance for the worshippers.[98] Job was steadfast (*ṣābir*) throughout his tribulation and ever repenting to the Holy Lord, and thus he was commended by God (Exalted is He). Evil is never attributable to God and here Job did not attribute his torment to God either. Adversities afflict the believers and if they remain patient, their rank will be elevated in Paradise. The Prophetic *ḥadīth*[99] in this regard was previously discussed.

In addition, Job (may God bless him) is related in the Qur'ān to have appealed to God's mercy for He is the Most Merciful—this must be the approach of the believer. Any believer who is afflicted with adversity and counters it with patience and perseverance, repents for any inadequacies (and sins), and then supplicates to the Holy Lord using His Beautiful Names and Glorious Attributes—including that He is the Most Beneficent and the Most Merciful—will be rewarded and elevated in the Hereafter.

Job never questions the Holy Lord in the Qur'ān or Sunna, unlike what is related in the Old Testament, and which led to many inappropriate conclusions by Jewish and Christian scholars—the latter will not be discussed here as they are not beneficial. Some beneficial morals though derived from the Old Testament include that Job is described as "perfect and upright, and one that feared God, and eschewed evil".[100] After Job's material possessions were all taken away, the Old Testament states: "Then Job arose, and rent his mantle, and shaved his head, and fell down upon the ground, and worshipped, And said, Naked came I out of my mother's womb, and naked shall I return thither: the Lord gave, and the Lord hath taken away; blessed be the name of the Lord."[101] And when Job was afflicted in his body, he is quoted as saying: "shall we indeed accept good from

---

98 Q.XXI.83–84.

99 The Prophet Muḥammad said: "The matter of a believer is wonderful, since all of his affairs are good: …if some harm afflicts him then he is patient, and that is good for him. This only applies to the believer." Muslim 2999/7500; Aḥmad 18,934.

100 Job 1.1.

101 Job 1.20–21.

God, and shall we not accept adversity?"[102] The Old Testament then includes Job questioning and discussing his tribulation with three acquaintances—this will not be recounted here.[103]

Now, had it not been for these tribulations and adversities, Job (may God bless him) may have not been mentioned in the Scriptures. The patience of Job and other prophets in bearing hardships and difficulties enabled them to be role models for the rest of humankind. Had they not suffered and then responded in a righteous manner, how could they be emulated? The story of Job does not, however, address why God allows suffering and evil—God (Exalted is He) withheld that knowledge for certain wise purposes.

Furthermore, one can benefit from the story of Job's tribulation from another aspect. Again, the Holy Lord restored Job with health and wealth after suffering from disease and privation. If one reflects on one's life and thinks about episodes in which some blessing was removed but then restored, one appreciates that blessing to a much higher degree after it is restored. For instance, consider one who suffered from loss of vision (whether fully or partially), but then had his or her vision restored in full. This believing individual will recognize God's great blessing of eyesight to a much higher degree than before suffering that loss. This recognition leads one to acknowledge his complete and utter dependence upon God (Glorious is He). One also realizes through this tribulation and suffering greater servitude and humility to the Almighty. The experience of this is unlike a discussion thereof, but this should suffice in allowing one to reflect either upon one's past privations or think in this fashion regarding future instances. Unfortunately, those who do not suffer temporary loss cannot appreciate that blessing to the same degree

---

[102] Job 2.10 (New King James Version). It should be mentioned here that the original King James Version (KJV) translation states instead: "shall we receive good at the hand of God, and shall we not receive evil?" Since evil is not attributable to the Holy Lord the translation is more properly rendered as "adversity". This is more consistent with what the Prophet Job would say. And God knows best. Likewise, at the conclusion in Job 42.11 it states in the New KJV that his family and acquaintances "comforted him for all the adversity that the Lord had brought upon him", while in the original KJV it states that they "comforted him over all the evil that the Lord had brought upon him".

[103] See Job 3–41.

or experience gratitude to the Lord (Exalted is He) as one who has experienced that loss. Therefore, privation and suffering becomes a necessary concomitant to such a great good.

It seems that if some (most likely only some of the truly faithful and prophets) are given much of this world, but it is subsequently taken away—yet they remain patient—then it will be granted back to them. Consider that after Solomon was severely weakened, he supplicated to God and was subsequently granted a vast kingdom: *And verily We tried Solomon, and set upon his throne a (mere) body. Then did he repent. He said: My Lord! Forgive me and bestow on me sovereignty such as shall not belong to any after me. Thou art the Bestower... And lo! he hath favour with Us, and a happy journey's end.*[104] Note here that Solomon, like Job, is mentioned in the Qur'ān to have repented. Then Solomon appealed to God's Attribute of being the One Lord Who bestows (*al-Wahhāb*), while Job appealed to His Attribute of being the Most Merciful.

Solomon (may God bless him) later said: *This is of the bounty of my Lord, that He may try me whether I give thanks or am ungrateful. Whosoever giveth thanks he only giveth thanks for (the good of) his own soul; and whosoever is ungrateful (is ungrateful only to his own soul's hurt). For my Lord is Absolute in independence, Bountiful.*[105] Therefore, both Solomon and Job were bestowed more by the Most Magnanimous after being patient upon their affliction, and both thanked Him—only the Omniscient Lord knows those who are truly sincere to Him.

The reality though is that most people who become deprived of some blessing will not have it returned to them. Nonetheless, they must remain patient and know that God, Who is the Most Magnanimous, will reward them with some other blessing in this life or ultimately in Paradise. Is there any greater way to attain a higher rank in Paradise than being patient in adversity for God's sake or carrying out righteous deeds?

Patience is incumbent upon the believers, and it cannot be proven in times of ease and luxury. Indeed, a higher level than patiently enduring hardships is accepting and being content with those difficulties. An even higher level still is to thank God for the difficulty

104 Q.XXXVIII.34–40.
105 Q.XXVII.40.

upon the realization that one's rank in Paradise can only be elevated by "traversing a bridge of hardships and tribulations".[106] These other levels will be discussed later.

Then there are the noble physical actions that are required in order to remedy a multitude of human hardships. The Prophet Muḥammad (may God bless him and grant him peace) narrated in a *ḥadīth qudsī* that God (Glorious is He) will state on the Day of Resurrection: "O son of Adam, I fell ill but you did not visit Me." An individual will reply: "O Lord, how should I visit You when You are the Lord of the Worlds?" God will respond: "Did you not know that My servant so-and-so had fallen ill, yet you did not visit him. Had you visited him, you would have found Me with him."[107] This *ḥadīth* also emphasizes in a similar manner the importance of feeding those who are hungry and quenching those who are thirsty, and that God will reward those who do such. Those who are ill, hungry or thirsty all suffer, and this *ḥadīth* affirms that the Holy Lord is with them and will reward those who work to assist them. Therefore, being proximate to the Lord in this life requires one to be at the side of those who are ill and sustain those who are hungry and thirsty.

Illnesses can be minimized through preventative medicine, medical advancements (i.e. overcoming ontological inadequacies), as well as avoidance of sin. But afflictions will never become non-existent, as God (Exalted is He) has willed that these ontologically exist so as to allow the real possibility that His religious commandments of visiting the ill and giving charity be carried out, for example.

Had diseases been absent, then doctors, nurses, hospitals, etc. would not have existed as such. The recognized good that these individuals carry out would not have been possible by extension. Fundamentally, the presence of privation results in humankind forming complex

---

106 Zeni (tr.), *Ibn Qayyim al-Jawziyya on Divine Wisdom and the Problem of Evil*, p. 261.

107 Muslim 2569/6556. Of note, this *ḥadīth qudsī* is structured in a similar fashion to the Qur'ānic verse: *Who is it that will lend unto God a goodly loan, so that He may give it increase manifold? God straiteneth and enlargeth*. See Q.II.245, and also Q.LVII.11. The Prophet Muḥammad also said: "There are five rights of a Muslim upon his brother: returning the greeting of peace, supplicating for [him] when he sneezes, accepting an invitation, visiting [him when he] is ill, and following [his or others] funeral processions." Bukhārī 1240; Muslim 2162/5650; Ibn Māja 1435; Aḥmad 10,966.

institutions to assist others in overcoming much of what afflicts them. The presence of need leads to constructive pursuits beneficial to a society. If only good existed then societal integration would be much less likely, and fewer people would work together and assist one another. Providing healthcare to the ill is one shining example of that aid and help.

Next, one of the main pillars of Islam is zakat, which has been emphasized in more than thirty verses of the Qur'ān. It has been prescribed upon all nations, as God (Exalted is He) states: *And (remember) when We made a covenant with the Children of Israel, (saying): Worship none save God (only), and be good to parents and to kindred and to orphans and the needy, and speak kindly to humankind; and establish worship and pay the zakat. Then, after that, ye slid back, save a few of you, being averse.*[108] In addition, Jesus said: *I am indeed a servant of God: He hath given me revelation and made me a prophet. And He hath made me blessed wheresoever I be, and hath enjoined on me prayer and charity as long as I live.*[109] Furthermore, the Holy Lord commanded the Muslims: *So establish regular prayer and give regular charity; and obey the Messenger; that ye may receive mercy.*[110] Zakat is contingent upon need, i.e. poverty, and it is ontologically dependent upon causes, which lead to that dearth. Thus these circumstances that afflict human beings, as well as inadequacies, are ontologically willed so as to lead to a need for zakat.

The Prophet Muḥammad (may God bless him and grant him peace) said: "Whoever fills the need of another, God will fulfill a need of his. And whoever removes a distressful ordeal (*karba*) from a Muslim, God will relieve him of one of the ordeals of the Day of Judgment."[111] Therefore, the existence of hardships allows the believers to have opportunities to benefit others in this world and benefit themselves

---

[108] Q.II.83. See also Q.V.12–13. Moreover, see Q.V.14 regarding the Christians wherein God (Exalted is He) states: *From those, too, who call themselves Christians, We did take a covenant, but they forgot a good part of the message that was sent them: so we estranged them, with enmity and hatred between the one and the other, to the Day of Judgment. And soon will God show them what it is they have done.*

[109] Q.XIX.30–31.

[110] Q.XXIV.56.

[111] Bukhārī 2442; Muslim 2580/6578; Tirmidhī 1426; Abū Dāwūd 4893; Aḥmad 5646.

by extension on the Day of Judgment in a manner that would not have otherwise occurred.

It is self-evident that giving alms and avoiding waste will minimize the incidence of hunger in the world. During the course of the famine in the year 638 CE in Medina, ʿUmar b. al-Khaṭṭāb requested aid. A caravan came from Syria; Abū ʿUbayda b. al-Jarrāḥ metaphorically said the beginning of the caravan would reach Medina while the end of it would still be in Damascus. Thus their suffering led others to assist and help them. This unity is necessary to minimize suffering, and it is a blessing from God (Glorious is He). Had that assistance been absent, though, their suffering and hardship would have been much greater.

The weakness and inadequacy of humanity requires them to work together to overcome or prevent some suffering or harm from afflicting the society in general. Human beings often need the help of others to achieve objectives, whether it is teaching knowledge to alleviate ignorance, discovering or providing remedies for ailments, giving wealth to assist in times of need, or furnishing power and strength for the benefit of others. Indeed, many local or personal cases of suffering can be reduced by supporting one another, expressing empathy, and being there to help in whatever way. Those suffering feel relief through such supportive measures even if the basis for their suffering remains. The importance of righteous actions in minimizing evil and suffering will be discussed further in upcoming chapters.

Suffering can be decreased by strength in mind and body, forbearance, diligence, industriousness, generosity, bravery, and preparing or equipping oneself for all contingencies, as well as worship of the Holy Lord and remembrance of Him. The Prophet Muḥammad (may God bless him and grant him peace) sought refuge in the Holy Lord from eight blameworthy things: "O God, I seek refuge with You from distress and grief, helplessness and laziness, miserliness and cowardice, being heavily in debt and from being overcome by men."[112] These blameworthy characteristics or states lead to suffering.

---

[112] Bukhārī 2893; Muslim 2706/6873; Tirmidhī 3484; Abū Dāwūd 1540; Nasāʾī 5464; Aḥmad 12,616.

Grief occurs as a result of past harm, while distress is due to the anticipation of a future harm. These emotions describe a negative response to harm. Feeling either of them only increases suffering going forward. Instead, one must be firm on the Straight Path and not despair. As for the second pair, Ibn al-Qayyim added that: "The [two] greatest reasons that prevent a person from goodness in this world and bliss in the Hereafter are heedlessness [i.e. ignorance], which is the opposite of knowledge, and laziness, which is the opposite of willpower and resolve. These are the origins for a person's suffering and deprivation."[113] Ultimately, humans can minimize suffering by acquiring knowledge (both spiritual and worldly) and by possessing a strong willpower.

Avoiding heedlessness and laziness are crucial. People should reflect, for instance, on how they utilize their free time. Do they engage themselves in the pursuit of religious knowledge, worship of the Holy Lord, and righteous deeds, or do they fill their time with unproductive distractions? One may seek out all types of permissible endeavours, but one must consider: are those pursued in a balanced fashion alongside religious acts or are the latter marginalized?

Miserliness leads others to suffer from privation as one does not spend appropriately to alleviate their poverty or dearth. Cowardice indicates that one fails to protect others from harm. Finally, being strained under excessive debt leads to both mental and material suffering, while being subjugated and overpowered by others is a source of great harm or evil.

In summation, the possibility of suffering and privation leads many to acquire benevolent characteristics in order to prevent or stave off their occurrence. But if hardships and afflictions do occur, other good characteristics may be indirectly engendered through them. In this manner, God's allowance of suffering and privation is wise and beneficial for some. However, since the majority of people are impatient and cannot bear hardships (especially when it comes to religious matters), they fail to realize their full potential.

If the believers do adopt the aforementioned beneficial traits and characteristics, they become ready to assume greater responsibilities.

---

113 Zeni (tr.), *Ibn Qayyim al-Jawziyya on Knowledge*, p. 140.

In this manner, they are emulating the prophets who had to be extremely patient and undergo much suffering so that they could subsequently administer their responsibilities with perfection.

On natural disasters

Natural disasters include earthquakes, floods, tidal waves, tornados, hurricanes and extensive fires, among others. Some people refer to them as "natural evil", but this term is invalid since evil is never attributable to God (Glorious is He). These disasters can obviously result in much damage and loss of life. Each of these disasters will now be examined and their fundamental natures will be elucidated.

The overarching point though is that the Holy Lord, Whose benefit preponderates over His harm, creates good entities that are predominantly beneficial, yet in a small proportion of cases that otherwise beneficial entity causes harm and suffering. Natural disasters represent an extreme manifestation of something that is otherwise predominantly beneficial. That extreme is rarely manifested and its harm is limited in comparison to the great benefit that the underlying causal entity provides. God has created all these matters in this fashion by wise and purposeful design (Glory be to Him). Had He created everything in this world to be absolutely good and beneficial, many other wise purposes, which will be discussed later, would have failed to occur.

The natural harm of earthquakes is brought about by tectonic plate movements. That said, these movements are predominately beneficial. Tectonic plate movements were critical in the formation and separation of the continents; otherwise this earth would have remained a Pangea.[114] The mountains were also subsequently formed—they did not originally exist on the earth—as a result of tectonic plate movements and earthquakes. If it were not for the mountains the earth would be less stable. God (Exalted is He) states: *And He has set up on the earth mountains standing firm, lest it should shake with you.*[115] Plate tectonics are also important for recycling, and thus

---

[114] This represents another example of one entity being separated or split apart, just like the universe was originated from a point or the formation of a human from a zygote.

[115] Q. XVI.15 (Yusuf Ali translation). See also Q. XXI.31 and Q. XXXI.10.

essential for life on earth just like water.[116] Therefore, tectonic plate movements have been predominately beneficial and essential to life on earth, far exceeding the occasional harm of earthquakes resulting from them.

Floods are, of course, extreme manifestations of the power of water. The fact that water is essential for life on earth is self-evident. The power of water has also been a source of erosion and the shaping of valleys and hills and the recycling of the earth. Although flooding may result in harm, water and the forces associated with it are predominately good. Tidal waves can be considered similarly.

Of note, the Prophet Muḥammad (may God bless him and grant him peace) asked the Holy Lord to protect the Muslim Community from natural disasters: "I asked Him not to overtake them all with flooding, and He granted me that." In another narration: "I asked Him to not overtake them all with a famine or drought (*sina*) and He granted me that."[117]

Tornados consist solely of wind and hurricanes are a combination of wind and water. Now, wind is obviously necessary and beneficial. It is necessary for driving clouds in order to allow rain to fall throughout this earth. Wind is also necessary for pollinating trees and plants so that fruits and vegetation may grow. Indeed, without it, life could not have existed. Wind only becomes harmful in an extreme manifestation of it; therefore, it is predominately beneficial and necessary for life on earth.

Although fire may result in some harm, its presence is predominately beneficial. The most obvious example of a fire is the sun, of course. Life clearly could not have existed on the earth in the absence of the sun's heat and light. The sustenance of humankind would have been quite limited had it not been for the use of fire and baking. Industrial manufacturing and modern life as we know it would not have been

---

116 Plate tectonics replenishes nutrients and recycles carbon on the earth's surface, stabilizes the atmospheric temperature through the carbon-silicate cycle, and helps to generate magnetic fields which deflect the solar winds and thus preserve life on earth. See work by Tilman Spohn and Doris Breuer at the German Institute of Planetary Research, as well as Diana Valencia, Richard O'Connell and Dimitar Sasselov at the Harvard-Smithsonian Center for Astrophysics.

117 Muslim 2890/7260; Tirmidhī 2175; Ibn Māja 3951; Aḥmad 22,125.

possible without fire. Although fire may burn people and properties, it is predominately beneficial. The presence of fire, and the fact that everyone has felt its heat or been slightly burned by it also serves to remind us of the Hellfire—one should ask the Holy Lord for His forgiveness and protection from Hell whenever that occurs.

ON DISEASE

Some of the most prevalent diseases will be briefly touched upon here. God is the best Creator, as was discussed in Chapter Three and as is clearly evidenced in the vast complexity of the human body, whether on a macroscopic or microscopic level. However, the Holy Lord has allowed alterations, inadequacies, and obstacles to occur amongst what He has created. Some of the wise purposes in allowing diseases were already mentioned earlier in this chapter. Yet, ultimately, health and well-being surpass disease and pain for all of humanity. The fundamental point of this section is that God's benefit outweighs the harm He allows to occur to humankind.

Diseases may occur due to many different causative factors: some are intrinsic/genetic, while others are extrinsic. For instance, many genetic diseases occur when an acquired change occurs to the DNA that God (Exalted is He) has created. Autosomal recessive mutations appear to be more common than autosomal dominant ones. Many diseases only occur when greater than 75% of some function is impaired, and thus two abnormal genes are necessary for the manifestation of autosomal recessive diseases. Due to this fact, the surplus capacity and reserve of our organs prevents many diseases from occurring, and this is due to the generosity of the Holy Lord and His wisdom.

Cancers represent instances in which the immune system is unable to clear the body of altered malignant cells. Genetic mutations also play a role in the genesis of many cancers. Although many cancers are deadly, some are curable as a result of advances in chemotherapy and radiation therapy. Moreover, nearly half of cancers are preventable through a modifiable healthy lifestyle and diet.[118]

---

[118] Farhad Islami MD, PhD, Ann Goding Sauer MSPH, Kimberly D. Miller MPH, et al, "Proportion and number of cancer cases attributable to potentially modifiable risk factors in the United States", *CA: A Cancer Journal for Clinicians*, vol. LXVIII, 2018, pp. 31–54.

Autoimmune diseases represent cases in which the otherwise predominantly beneficial immune system attacks some of one's tissues. Even in these diseases though, the immune system remains predominantly beneficial, and is only harmful in the manner specific to them. That said, many autoimmune disorders are becoming more manageable through medications and other treatments.

Myocardial infarctions represent an obstruction to otherwise normal blood vessels (in the vast majority of instances) either due to progressive arteriosclerosis, plaques or acute embolic events. Strokes of the brain and infarctions of other organs can be due to the same causes. That said, perfusion of an individual's organs predominates over ischemia or infarction. Moreover, advances in percutaneous and surgical revascularizations as well as medical therapies have resulted in much improved outcomes.

Diabetes mellitus occurs when the secretion of insulin is inadequate or there is peripheral resistance to its action. Individuals, through the lifestyle and dietary choices they make, can reduce the incidence of diabetes. Regardless, most are free from diabetes, while medications and treatments exist to reduce the suffering of those impacted by its wide-ranging effects on the human body.

Infectious diseases are due to bacteria or other pathogens, which are otherwise predominately beneficial when considered altogether. The bacteria living on our skin or within our intestinal tract fulfill many important functions. Furthermore, bacteria and fungi lead to recycling and many ecological benefits. Many foods, antibiotics and useful drugs are derived from fungi. Although the harm of viruses appears to far exceed their benefit, they may serve as vectors for gene therapy or cancer treatment.

Pain can represent the lesser of two harms and may prevent a greater harm, injury or affliction from occurring. For instance, the pain one experiences from appendicitis and impending rupture leads one to seek medical attention and undergo surgery before greater harm like sepsis or even death occurs. The same benefit of pain can be appreciated when ischemia occurs to an organ preceding infarction thereof. Yet, the health and blessings of all the other organs and systems, even in these instances, does predominate.

Nonetheless, it should be mentioned that diseases may occur due to sinfulness. The Prophet Muḥammad (may God bless him and grant him peace) said:

> If wickedness appears and becomes widespread amongst a society, plagues will appear as well as new types of diseases (*awjāʿ*) that were not present in prior generations. If they cheat in their weights and measures they will be stricken with famine, severe calamities and oppression by their rulers. If they withhold zakat, rain from the sky will be withheld[119]—and were it not for the animals no rain would fall. If they break their covenant with God and their covenant with His Messenger, then God will allow their enemies to overpower them, and seize what they possess. And if their rulers do not rule according to the Scripture of God and follow the goodness that God has revealed, then God will allow infighting to occur amongst them.[120]

The Muslims nowadays have suffered from all of the above consequences. A pious society that obeys His commandments (especially in the aforementioned matters) and fulfills His covenant will thus endure lesser degrees of disease and suffering accordingly. This *ḥadīth* shows, though, that the incidence of suffering is less—but not null—for the believers and Muslims when compared to the disbelievers.

On the suffering of children

The suffering of children is one of the most heartbreaking occurrences. It has led some to question the Holy Lord. This section will discuss some causes and reasons for their suffering.

First, it must be mentioned that God (Glorious is He) is never unjust, and this reality takes precedence over all other considerations. The Holy Lord does not cause any injustice whatsoever: *God is never unjust in the least degree.*[121] Therefore, God (Exalted is He) has created a system in which each individual is born sinless and innocent: *And*

---

[119] Noah (may God bless him) also said in the Qur'ān: *And I have said: Seek pardon of your Lord. Lo! He was ever Forgiving. He will let loose the sky for you in plenteous rain, and will help you with wealth and sons, and will assign unto you Gardens and will assign unto you rivers.* Q.LXXI.10–12. See also Q.LXXII.16–17.

[120] Ibn Māja 4019; Bayhaqī (*Shuʿab*) 3042. It is "authentic" according to Albānī (*Silsilat al-aḥādīth al-ṣaḥīḥa* 106).

[121] Q.IV.40 (Yusuf Ali translation).

God brought you forth from the wombs of your mothers knowing nothing, and gave you hearing and sight and hearts that haply ye might give thanks.[122] Understanding and acknowledging that the Holy Lord is absolutely just is paramount.

There is no original sin, so sinfulness cannot be a reason for the suffering of children. Furthermore, God has endowed every individual with an innate disposition (*fiṭra*), which is good, and it is our moral compass. However, since individuals are born *knowing nothing* as well as clearly weak, infants and children are by definition inadequate. Although the inadequacy of children is not sinful, any individual who is inadequate or deficient (regardless of the reason) in worshipping the Lord is rendered susceptible, ontologically, to suffering—this was discussed at the beginning of this chapter.

Now, if a good upbringing predominates then their suffering will be less. However, if their parents and society have failed to protect children or instruct them then their suffering will increase accordingly. And therein resides another reason behind the suffering of children: it is the inadequacy of those who are responsible for them. God has placed children within the responsibility of their parents, teachers, religious leaders, authority figures and the society in general, and they all must accept and fulfill such responsibility appropriately. The Prophet Muḥammad said: "Every person is responsible for their dependents/flock."[123]

Some forms of child suffering occur because of societal ills and inadequacies. God (Exalted is He) states: *Nay! but ye honour not the orphans! Nor do ye encourage one another to feed the poor! And ye devour inheritance—all with greed, and ye love wealth with inordinate love!*[124] Thus by caring for the orphans and the poor, in addition to giving alms and administering inheritance in accordance with Divine Law, poverty and the suffering of children can be lessened.

The misappropriation and inadequate support of parents, relatives, society or the international community in general is what leads to children going hungry. Children should not be dying of hunger in

[122] Q.XVI.78.

[123] Bukhārī 893; Muslim 1829/4724; Tirmidhī 1705; Abū Dāwūd 2928; Aḥmad 5167.

[124] Q.LXXXIX.15–20 (Yusuf Ali translation).

this world and if they are it is because of the inadequacy of all of the above, which should be held accountable.

Moreover, the suffering of innocent children is a clarion call for people to do their part to alleviate it; in fact, it is one of the strongest appeals to action. If societies or nations do not respond to the suffering or death of children, then they have only themselves to blame for being recompensed with suffering or evil as a consequence. They cannot rightly place the blame on God (Exalted is He), especially when one remembers that God has set this world as a test for how humans administer their responsibilities.

Here, in relation to suffering of children, the matter of Abraham and Ishmael, as well as others, will be briefly discussed. Again, death is considered to be suffering—not evil. Ibn al-Qayyim comments on this matter: "The benefit in commanding His friend Abraham to sacrifice his son was not so that the sacrifice would occur, but rather so that both the father and the son would submit firmly and completely to His commandment. Once that benefit occurred, the [actual carrying out of the] killing became harmful for them both. Therefore, God abrogated it [and commanded Abraham to sacrifice a lamb instead]. This is the true and curative answer in this matter."[125] God (Glorious is He) abrogated His command to sacrifice Ishmael and substituted him with a sacrificial lamb, because that was good and better in their case. Ishmael (may God bless him) was a great prophet and his descendants became a great nation—i.e. the Community of Muḥammad (may God bless him and grant him peace).

On the other hand, the Prophet Muḥammad's only son, whom he named Abraham, died young. Muḥammad was the Seal of the Prophets, and God (Glorious is He) dictated that he would not have any male child grow up to adulthood.[126] Nevertheless, since Muḥammad is a role model for all of humanity, those who suffer a similar loss will find a good example in him. The Messenger said: "The eye weeps and the heart is saddened, but we only say that which pleases our Lord."[127] This *ḥadīth* represents a key principle for those who suffer great loss

---

[125] Ibn al-Qayyim, *Miftāḥ dār al-saʿāda*, vol. II, p. 958.

[126] See Q.XXXIII.40: *Muḥammad is not the father of any man among you, but he is the Messenger of God and the Seal of the Prophets.*

[127] Muslim 2315/6025; Abū Dāwūd 3126; Ibn Māja 1589; Aḥmad 13,014.

by the death of their children: one must refrain from saying anything that would displease or assign blame to the Holy Lord.

Moreover, people can never know what is truly beneficial for themselves or their children. That was discussed previously in Chapter One in the case of the child with Khiḍr and Moses. Had the child grown up he would have became a disbeliever, as well as causing his parents to become disbelievers. Thus the child's death before puberty likely prevented him from becoming a denizen of Hellfire, as well as being good for his parents, who remained believers (even in the setting of his death). Although the children of believers may suffer, they all should recognize that God is benevolent with them (when this world and Paradise are both considered).

ON THE SUFFERING OF ANIMALS

The suffering of animals is due to the deficient nature of their worship of the Holy Lord. Nonetheless, all that exists in the universe (aside from many free-willed creatures) worships the Holy Lord: *Seest thou not that to God bow down in worship all things that are in the heavens and on earth, the sun, the moon, the stars; the hills, the trees, the animals; and a great number among humankind? But a great number are (also) such as are fit for punishment: and such as God shall disgrace, none can raise to honour: for God carries out all that He wills.*[128] Therefore, the animals do glorify God (Glorious is He) albeit in a restricted and inadequate fashion. This is in contrast to the angels who worship the Holy Lord continuously and adequately.

God (Exalted is He) states regarding the disbelievers: *Or deemest thou that most of them hear or understand? They are but as the cattle—nay, but they are farther astray.*[129] The Exalted also states: *Many are the jinns and men we have made for Hell: They have hearts wherewith they understand not, eyes wherewith they see not, and ears wherewith they hear not. They are like cattle, nay more misguided: for they are heedless (of warning).*[130] Had the worship of cattle or animals been adequate, then God would not have drawn a parallel between them and the disbelievers. But those of humanity

---

128 Q.XXII.18 (Yusuf Ali translation).
129 Q.XXV.44.
130 Q.VII.179 (Yusuf Ali translation).

who turn away from their intellect, follow their desires, and become seduced away from the worship of the Holy Lord are akin to animals. God (Exalted is He) also states: *God will cause those who believe and do good works to enter Gardens underneath which rivers flow; while those who disbelieve take their comfort in this life and eat even as the cattle eat, and the Fire is their habitation.*[131]

The inadequacy of animals in worshipping the Holy Lord leads to their ontological susceptibility to suffering. The notion of animal compensation in the Hereafter, as claimed by some,[132] does not appear to have any basis in revelation,[133] and will not be discussed therefore.

SUMMATION

In conclusion, God's actions are congruent and befitting to His Beautiful Names and Glorious Attributes. Suffering indirectly brings about many positive character traits, like patience, humility, reliance on God and contentment, as well as actions that are beloved to the Holy Lord. God (Exalted is He) thus put humans to the test for many wise purposes. The Holy Lord's benefit is predominant and He only allows harm to occur in a manner concordant with His justice and wisdom, and in accordance with humanity's inadequate and sinful nature. This last aspect, i.e. sins and evils, will be discussed further in the next two chapters.

---

131 Q.XLVII.12.

132 For example, the Muᶜtazila claimed that animals who suffered will be compensated in some manner in the Hereafter, or used as an instrument to torment the denizens of Hellfire. See Cüneyt M. Şimsek, 'The Problem of Animal Pain: An Introduction to Nursi's Approach', in Ibrahim M. Abu-Rabiᶜ (ed.), *Theodicy and Justice in Modern Islamic Thought: The Case of Said Nursi*, p. 113.

133 Of note, the Prophet Muḥammad mentioned that on the Day of Judgment an animal that was mistreated by its owner (or its owner did not pay zakat for it) would be resurrected to take retribution and cause pain to its owner. See Bukhārī 1460; Muslim 988/2296; Abū Dāwūd 1658; Nasāʾī 2442; Aḥmad 14,442. Note that this is in contrast to a situation wherein one human is mistreated by another. In this case, the oppressor must give away some good deeds to the victim, but if he or she no longer possesses any good deeds then the oppressor must assume some of the victim's sins—see p. 394 for further discussion in this regard. That is because humans will be rewarded or punished, while animals will neither be rewarded nor punished in the Hereafter. Thus, animals will be granted retribution but not compensation in the Hereafter. And God knows best.

Chapter Eleven

An Exposition on Evil

Five groups of evil have been forbidden by God (Glorious and Exalted is He)—they are: *indecencies [or intermediate sins] (fawāḥish), such of them as are apparent and such as are within, and [major] sins (ithm), and wrongful oppression, and that ye associate with God that for which no warrant hath been revealed, and that ye tell concerning God that which ye know not.*[1] These sins are mentioned in an increasing level of evilness, until the worst is referred to last. The worst evil is saying something about God (Glorious is He) which has no basis in the revelation. It is contended here that this predominantly entails attributing any evil to the Holy Lord[2] or saying that the Holy Lord commands any evilness: *"God never commands what is shameful: do ye say of God what ye know not?"*[3] The fact that God (Glorious is He) does not command a lesser evil, i.e. an intermediate sin (*faḥshā'* pl. *fawāḥish*), indicates by extension that He would never command any of the other four groups of sins listed in the first verse above, including major sins, oppression or idolatry. Indeed, the Holy Lord would never command any evil whatsoever.

It was already discussed in Chapter Two that evil is not attributable to the Holy Lord's Essence, Beautiful Names, Glorious Attributes nor to His purely good actions. Those who think evil of God (Glorious is He) or attribute evil to Him and do not repent will be recompensed in kind. The Exalted states that those *who think an evil thought concerning God, [for] them is the evil turn of fortune, and God is wroth against them and hath cursed them, and hath made ready for them Hell, a hapless journey's end.*[4]

---

[1] Q.VII.33.

[2] Of note, attributing evil to the Holy Lord includes denying that He will fulfill His promises: *And they say: The Fire (of punishment) will not touch us save for a certain number of days. Say: Have ye received a covenant from God—truly God will not break His covenant—or tell ye concerning God that which ye know not?* Q.II.80. Failure to fulfill a promise or covenant is due either to inability or lying. God is glorious and exalted above any deficiency or evil.

[3] Q.VII.28 (Yusuf Ali translation).

[4] Q.XLVIII.6.

We should instead affirm what the Prophet Muḥammad (may God bless him and grant him peace) said: "All goodness is in Your Hands and evil cannot be attributed to You…Blessed and exalted are You."[5] God's Names and Attributes are righteous and holy, and His actions are all characterized by wisdom, mercy, beneficence and justice.

The blasphemy of attributing evil to the Holy Lord is followed, in degree of evilness, by polytheism. God is One; He is the only Creator, and He is perfect, holy and righteous; therefore, only He deserves to be worshipped. Polytheism of any sort is punished by the Hellfire, as God (Glorious is He) states: *Verily, God does not forgive the ascribing of divinity of aught beside Him, although He forgives any lesser sin unto whomever He wills: for those who ascribe divinity to aught beside God have indeed gone far astray.*[6]

Next, it will be contended that *ithm* refers to major sins. This can be deduced from other verses, including: *And when it is said unto him: Be careful of thy duty* (*ittaqi*) *to God, pride taketh him to sin* (*ithm*). *Hell will settle his account.*[7] It has been discussed already that those who are pious avoid the major sins, so the sin referred to in the verse must be a major sin, which warrants Hellfire—not an intermediate sin. Also, consider the following verse which contains major sins: *Yet ye* [*i.e. the Children of Israel*] *it is who slay each other and drive out a party of your people from their homes, supporting one another against them by* [*major*] *sin* (*bi'l-ithm*) *and transgression?*[8]

Now, it was discussed previously that evil represents, in part, privation of the deontological. For example, not praying or not giving zakat, breaking the ties of kinship, as well as other failures to obey the Holy Lord's commandments—these are all evil. That said,

---

5 Muslim 771/1812; Tirmidhī 3422; Abū Dāwūd 760; Nasā'ī 898; Aḥmad 803.

6 Q.IV.116 (Muḥammad Asad translation).

7 Q.II.206. See verses Q.XLII.37 and Q.LIII.32 which begin as: *Those who avoid enormities of sin* (*kabā'ir al-ithm*) *and abominations* (*fawāḥish*). Also, God states in Q.XVI.90: *God enjoineth justice and kindness, and giving to kinsfolk, and forbiddeth lewdness* (*faḥshā'*) *and abomination* (*munkar*) *and wickedness* (*baghy*). Therefore, *munkar* is also synonymous with major sins. And God knows best. Of course, the righteous forbid *munkar*, i.e. major sins.

8 Q.II.85. The juxtaposition of *ithm* and transgression (*ʿudwān*) also occurs in verse: *Help ye one another in righteousness and piety, but help ye not one another in sin* (*ithm*) *and rancor* (*ʿudwān*). *Fear God, for God is strict in punishment.* Q.V.2 (Yusuf Ali translation). See also verses Q.V.62 and Q.LVIII.8–9.

it will be acknowledged that all human acts of worship to the Holy Lord are inadequate, and thus are lacking to some degree. But such worship only becomes evil when it is discordant with what God and His Messenger have commanded, does not rise to a minimum threshold of goodness, or is not done at all.

Other types of evil are due to altering or misplacing blessings (due to desires and temptations). Indeed, had blessings been maintained or placed appropriately they would have instead remained good. For instance, alcohol is derived from grapes, barley or other good things—their goodness is changed by the free will of human beings into that which God (Exalted is He) has forbidden. Satan has said: *Surely, I will command them and they will change God's creation.*[9] Alcohol is evil itself and leads to many other evils (such as murder, assaults, fornication, etc.) and is thus considered the root of evil sins (*umm al-khabā'ith*), as described in a *ḥadīth.*[10] Again, altering something from a good purpose to an evil one is the fault of human beings. Elemental entities in this world are fundamentally good, and do not become evil unless those whom God has created with a free will choose to misuse and misappropriate those entities.

Fornication can be considered as misplacing that which is good. The Prophet Muḥammad (may God bless him and grant him peace) differentiated fornication from marital relations: "If one misplaces it into that which is forbidden, would one not be blameworthy? But if one places it into that which is permissible, one will be rewarded."[11] Thus the first three types of evil are due to privation, alteration or misappropriation of good. Privation of the deontological good (below a minimum threshold) represents evil, whereas altering or misplacing the ontological or deontological good may result in evil.

Furthermore, there are other types of evil which are due to oppression and transgression against the rights of others. These can either be due to actions of the heart, such as pride, ostentatiousness and deceit, or actions of the body. Oppressive evil actions of the body

---

[9] Q.IV.119.

[10] Nasā'ī 5667; Ṭabarānī (*al-Muʿjam al-awṣaṭ*) 3667. It is "sound" according to Albānī (*Silsilat al-aḥādīth al-ṣaḥīḥa* 1854).

[11] Muslim 1006/2329; Aḥmad 21,482.

include depriving others of honour, wealth or property, and life, i.e. slandering, destroying or stealing, and killing others. Thus hidden intentions as well as apparent words and acts can all lead to injustice and oppression.

AN EXPLANATION OF THE MAJOR SINS

The Prophet Muḥammad (may God bless him and grant him peace) said: "Avoid the seven destructive major sins (*mūbiqāt*): worshipping others with God, practising magic/sorcery, killing any person that God has forbidden—as it is only [allowed] for just cause—taking usury/interest, stealing the money of an orphan, fleeing from battle, and slandering chaste believing women [of fornication]."[12]

The wickedness of the first three is clear. God (Glorious is He) states regarding the first: *Behold, whoever ascribes divinity to any being beside God, unto him will God deny Paradise.*[13] As for those who practise magic, the Holy Lord states that they will: *have no share in the happiness of the Hereafter.*[14] The great evil of murder is also self-evident: *If a man kills a believer intentionally, his recompense is Hell, to abide therein (forever): And the wrath and the curse of God are upon him, and a dreadful penalty is prepared for him.*[15] Regarding usury/interest, God (Exalted is He) states: *O ye who believe! Observe your duty to God, and give up what remaineth (due to you) from usury, if ye are (in truth) believers. And if ye do not, then be warned of war (against you) from God and His Messenger. And if ye repent, then ye have your principal (without interest). Wrong not, and ye shall not be wronged.*[16] God (Glorious is He) also advised us to take care of the orphans[17] and promised those who do injustice to them with punishment in Hellfire: *Those who unjustly eat up the property of orphans, eat up a fire into their own bodies: They will soon be enduring a Blazing Fire!*[18]

---

[12] Bukhārī 2766; Muslim 89/262; Abū Dāwūd 2874; Nasā'ī 3671.

[13] Q.V.72 (Muḥammad Asad translation).

[14] Q.II.102 (Muḥammad Asad translation).

[15] Q.IV.93 (Yusuf Ali translation).

[16] Q.II.278–279.

[17] See Q.II.83, 177 and 215; Q.IV.36; Q.VIII.41. Moreover, there is the case of Khaḍir preserving the wealth of the two orphans, as mentioned earlier in Sūrat al-Kahf (Q.XVIII.77 and 82).

[18] Q.IV.10 (Yusuf Ali translation).

Imām Dhahabī defined major sins as those "for which there is a *hadd* [i.e. legal] punishment in this world—such as murder, fornication, or theft—or any which have incurred the threat of Divine punishment, anger, or curse".[19] Tables 1 and 2 list most of the major sins as adapted from Imām Dhahabī's book *al-Kabā'ir*.[20]

Now, the Prophet (may God bless him and grant him peace) deemed the perpetration of some of the major sins to negate one from being considered a believer (*mu'min*), including fornication, theft and drinking alcohol.[21] These types are included within the first thirty major sins as listed by Dhahabī. Therefore, in general, it seems that those who have perpetrated any of the first thirty major wicked sins that Dhahabī lists[22] cannot be considered to be believers but rather only believing Muslims (*muslimūn*).[23] However, the perpetration of the latter forty (while avoiding the first thirty) may still allow one to be considered as a believer. This, again, is only a general guideline—there are some exceptions, but the point is that some major sins are more destructive and more wicked than others. And God knows best.

It was discussed previously in Chapter Seven that in order for one to be considered pious, one must avoid all of the major sins. God (Exalted is He) states in a clear-cut verse: *If you avoid the great sins, which you have been enjoined to shun, We shall efface your bad deeds (sayyi'āt), and*

---

19 Aisha Bewley (tr.), *The Major Sins* (London: Dar al-Taqwa, 2012), p. 4.

20 Most of the major sins that Dhahabī included are listed along with his numbering of each in parenthesis. The destructive major sins listed in the above *ḥadīth* are numbered 1, 3, 2, 12, 13, 15 and 21, respectively, in *The Major Sins*. Attributing evil to the Holy Lord is not listed as such in Dhahabī's scheme (although it is a form of lying against God), but is listed here in accordance with the verse mentioned at the beginning of this chapter.

21 See Bukhārī 5578; Muslim 57/202; Abū Dāwūd 4689; Ibn Māja 3936; Nasā'ī 4869; Aḥmad 8895.

22 Polytheism (1) is excluded from this discussion, as it renders one a disbeliever.

23 There may be some exceptions to the latter forty, i.e. the perpetration of some of those secondary major sins results in that person being a Muslim—not a believer. For instance, cursing the believers (particularly the Companions of the Prophet Muḥammad) is wickedness (*fusūq*) and thus renders one a wrongdoer (*ẓālim*), whereby the wrongdoers are Muslims—not believers. This will be discussed further later in this chapter.

Major Sins	Related Major Sins
Worshipping other than the Holy Lord (1)	Attributing evil to the Holy Lord
Killing unjustly (2)	Suicide (29)
Magic (3)	
Sodomy (11)	
Adultery/Fornication (10)	Lesbianism (10), Promoting sexual indecency (34)
Lying against God or His Prophet Muḥammad (14)	
Not performing prayer (4)	Neglecting the Friday prayers (65)
Withholding almsgiving (5)	
Not fasting in Ramaḍān without excuse (6)	
Not performing pilgrimage without excuse (7)	
Disobeying (*ʿuqūq*) one's parents (8)	
Breaking the ties of kinship (9)	
Usury/Interest (12)	
Stealing from orphans (13)	Stealing the spoils of war (22)
Fleeing from battle (15)	
A leader duping his followers (16)	
Arrogance/pride (17)	
Perjury (18)	Bearing false testimony (25), habitual lying (30)
Drinking alcohol (19)	
Gambling (20)	
Accusing chaste women of fornication (21)	Cursing any of the Prophet's Companions (70)
Theft (23)	Highway robbery (24), Unlawful seizure of property (28)
Perpetrating injustice (26)	
Backbiting or spreading falsehoods (43)	
Cursing a believer (44)	
Oppression (50)	

Table 1. Major Wicked Sins

Major Sins	Related Major Sins
Rendering corrupt judgments (31) Accepting bribes (32)	
Acting ostentatiously in some cases (37)	Reminding others of one's charity (40)
Learning/teaching knowledge for worldly gain (38)	
Deceit and treachery (39 and 68)	Defrauding others (62)
Denying God's determination (41)	Feeling secure from God's plan (63)
Eavesdropping and seeking out secrets (42)	
Betraying one's promises (45)	
Believing astrologers and soothsayers (46)	
Infidelity (47)	
Making images of humans or animals (48)	
Being overbearing against the weak (51)	
Harming (53) or betraying (69) the Muslims	Harming one's neighbours (52) or people in general (54)
Wearing clothing out of arrogance or pride (55)	
Men wearing gold or silk clothing (56)	
Sacrificing an animal for other than God's sake (58)	
Losing hope in God's mercy (64) Avoiding congregational prayers (66)	

Table 2. Secondary Major Sins

shall cause you to enter an abode of glory.[24] The plural (*sayyi'āt*) mentioned here therefore clearly encompasses all sins other than the major ones, i.e. they include the intermediate (*fawāḥish*) and minor (*lamam*) sins.

Another corollary from the above verse is that avoidance of major sins is paramount. God (Exalted is He) never mentions in the Qur'ān that He will forgive the major sins in general. Consider the Holy Lord's statement: *If only the People of the Book would believe and ward off (evil), surely We should remit their sins (sayyi'āt) from them and surely We should bring them into Gardens of Delight.*[25] Note, that this verse conspicuously does not mention that their major sins will be remitted—only their *sayyi'āt*.

The Prophet Muḥammad (may God bless him and grant him peace) said: "Whoever perpetrates [a major] sin and his legal punishment is quickened for him [in this worldly life], this expiates him. Otherwise, his matter is at God's discretion."[26] It seems therefore—and God knows best—that the Holy Lord will punish the vast majority of those who perpetrate major sins in accordance with His wisdom. For instance, a Jew or Christian who converts to Islam is less likely to be forgiven if he or she perpetrates fornication or thievery than a polytheist of Quraysh[27] who converted to Islam at the hand of the Prophet Muḥammad, since the former know that these are forbidden in accordance with the Old Testament (particularly the Ten Commandments) and the New Testament, whereas the latter had no such Scripture or revelation. And God knows best.

One must also repent from perpetrating intermediate and minor sins (and this is one of the traits of the pious) in order to be forgiven by the Holy Lord: *Repentance shall not be accepted from those who do evil deeds (sayyi'āt) until their dying hour and then say, "Behold, I now repent"; nor from those who die as deniers of the truth: it is these for whom We have readied*

---

[24] Q.IV.31 (Muḥammad Asad translation). This corresponds to verse Q.LXV.5: *And unto everyone who is conscious of God (yattaqi) will He pardon his bad deeds (sayyi'āt), and will grant him a vast reward* (Muḥammad Asad translation). See also Q.VIII.29: *O ye who believe! If ye keep your duty to God, He will give you discrimination (between right and wrong) and will rid you of your evil thoughts and deeds, and will forgive you. God is of Infinite Bounty.*

[25] Q.V.65.

[26] Bukhārī 7213; Muslim 1709/4463; Tirmidhī 1439; Nasā'ī 4166; Aḥmad 22,678.

[27] See the exegesis of verse Q.XXXIX.53 in Lucas (tr.), *Ṭabarī Selections*, pp. 468–474.

grievous suffering.[28] Therefore, the first group in this verse characterizes those believers who have not repented from their evil deeds—they are clearly distinguished from the disbelievers *who die as deniers of the truth*. Repentance from evil deeds during one's lifetime—the sooner the better—is therefore also necessary to avoid the possibility of punishment by the flames of Hellfire. Again, avoidance of major sins and repentance from intermediate sins is a characteristic of the pious. Listing the intermediate and minor sins is beyond the scope of this book, but outlining the major sins has been done in order to clarify what is necessary to achieve piety.

AN INTRODUCTION TO GRATUITOUS EVIL

The perpetration of major sins leads to greater levels of evil. If a society as a whole perpetrates major sins then gratuitous evils will follow. Now, it will be contended that it is not necessary that the Holy Lord must bring out some greater good out of *every* individual evil at every moment of time. Gratuitous evils will thus be defined as those that are dysteleological with consideration to direct aspects, but where there exist one or more indirect aspects by which a wise purpose can eventually be seen. The presence of evil, even the gratuitous type, and free-willed creatures who perpetrate evils does indirectly lead to the righteous believers responding in a good and positive manner to overcome the former's evil. The righteous deeds of these believers would not have been possible otherwise.

Therefore, the Holy Lord creates and utilizes evil indirectly for good ends. Evil creatures are responsible for their wickedness and will be punished—they are not commended for the good done by others in opposition to them nor the good outcomes which occur as a result. So while creatures unjustly perpetrate evil, God (Exalted is He) only allows suffering and evil to occur as a just consequence and in order for righteousness to be indirectly brought forth.

This book will contend that evil and disorder has progressively increased over time. For instance, the evil and misery of the 20th century are clearly greater than that of the 19th century and so forth back in time. It is contended that the general time frame by which

---

[28] Q.IV.18 (Muḥammad Asad translation).

the evilness of events can be compared is 100 years since the Prophet Muḥammad alluded to the fact that a "renewer" (*mujaddid*) comes every 100 years.[29] It can be deduced from this *ḥadīth* that matters return to at least the same level of evil amongst the believers as the prior century, since there is the need for that renewer of faith. But when considered more deeply, the reality is that if people require a renewer it is only because their evil has increased further than before, and because they have turned away despite the knowledge gained from the prior century's renewer. In contrast, the evilness of the disbelievers (who are the majority) and their distance from God (Glorious is He) continues to increase to an even greater degree century after century.

The Prophet Muḥammad said that as the Day of Judgment approaches "discord and trials (*fitan*) will become overwhelming (*taẓhar*), and killing (*harj*) will become widespread (*yakthur*)",[30] and "the drinking of alcohol and fornication will be widespread".[31] Thus the Prophet Muḥammad prophesized that evils will increase over time, as portrayed by these major sins, and that murder and killing will become commonplace. Indeed, oppressive injustices perpetrated on a large scale, which are considered to be satanic or demonic in type, have occurred with increasing frequency over the centuries. The worst satanic types include genocide or mass rape.

God (Exalted is He) has made it clear in the Qur'ān that He does not love many entities and groups. The Holy Lord does not love the oppressors (*muʿtadīn*),[32] the disbelievers (*kāfirīn*)[33] who perpetrate major sins (*kaffār*[in] *athīm*),[34] the transgressors (*ẓālimīn*),[35] those who

---

[29] The Prophet Muḥammad (may God bless him and grant him peace) said: "God will send for this Community someone to renew its religion every 100 years." Abū Dāwūd 4291; al-Ḥākim 8592. It is "authentic" according to Albānī (*Silsilat al-aḥādīth al-ṣaḥīḥa* 599).

[30] Bukhārī 1036; Muslim 2672/6788; Abū Dāwūd 4255; Ibn Māja 4047; Aḥmad 7488. It is also reported in some narrations that earthquakes will become more numerous and that wealth will become great—see Bukhārī 1036 and 7121; Ibn Māja 4047.

[31] Bukhārī 80; Muslim 2671/6785; Tirmidhī 2205; Ibn Māja 4045; Aḥmad 12,527.

[32] Q.II.190, Q.V.87 and Q.VII.55.

[33] Q.III.32 and Q.XXX.45.

[34] Q.II.276.

[35] Q.III.57, Q.III.140 and Q.XLII.40.

are self-conceited and boastful (*mukhtāl*[in] *fakhūr*),[36] those who betray others (*khā'inīn*)[37] in general and through the perpetration of major sins (*khawwān*[an] *athīm*)[38] in particular, those who perpetrate corruption (*mufsidīn*),[39] those who are prodigal or wasteful (*musrifīn*),[40] and those who are arrogant (*mustakbirīn*).[41] God (Glorious is He) has therefore prohibited disbelief and any evil or sinful intention, speech, or action. Ultimately, though, God's love of the prophets, truly faithful, righteous, devout and pious outweighs His hatred of the disbelievers, hypocrites and satanic types.

SATAN AND THE WISE PURPOSES IN ALLOWING HIS EXISTENCE

In regards to how evil began, the Qur'ān is clear that God (Exalted is He) created another species of creatures—beyond the angels and humans—who possess free will much like humans: they are the jinn. The evilness of the jinn preceded that of humanity. This book will maintain that all of the angels are good and follow the commandments of the Holy Lord without exception. This is in contrast to Christian belief, which states that some fallen angels rebelled against the Holy Lord.[42]

Now, the Qur'ān mentions that God (Glorious and Exalted is He) commanded a group of the angels and jinn to prostrate to Adam. All of the angels did so, while the devil Iblīs, who was a jinn, refused to do so out of pride and arrogance. The Holy Lord states: *And (remember) when We said unto the angels: Fall prostrate before Adam, and they fell prostrate, all save Iblīs. He was of the jinn, so he rebelled against his Lord's command.*[43]

---

36 Q.IV.36, Q.XXXI.18 and Q.LVII.23.

37 Q.VIII.58.

38 Q.IV.107. See also Q.XXII.38 whereby it states God does not love those who are treacherous disbelievers (*khawwān*[in] *kafūr*).

39 Q.V.64 and Q.XXVIII.77.

40 Q.VI.141 and Q.VII.31.

41 Q.XVI.23.

42 See, for instance, 2 Peter 2.4. See also Augustine, *The City of God*, Book XI, #11, 13 and 33, pp. 320–322 and 339–340.

43 Q.XVIII.50.

Satan refused to prostrate to Adam, saying: *"I am better than he: Thou didst create me from fire, and him from clay."*[44] Thus Satan not only disobeyed the commandment of the Holy Lord due to his haughtiness, but he also fundamentally misunderstood the true reality of God's wisdom. The elemental constituent of the jinn, i.e. the fire, is not better than that of humans, but rather the opposite is true. Moreover, a higher proportion of human beings (than jinn) will ultimately attain piety. Indeed, the creation should never think that their wisdom is superior to God's (Glorious and Exalted is He)—to think such is to follow in Satan's footsteps.

Fundamentally, the worst evil has already been done by Satan, as he directly disobeyed God's commandment in His Presence, and then was obstinate, haughty and proud. Furthermore, Satan obstinately refused to repent and persisted in his rebellion after being damned. He asked to be reprieved until the Day of Judgment in order to do more evil and lead humanity astray: *Reprieve me till the day when they are raised (from the dead)... Because Thou hast sent me astray, verily I shall lurk in ambush for them on Thy Right Path. Then I shall come upon them from before them and from behind them and from their right hands and from their left hands, and Thou wilt not find most of them beholden (unto Thee). [God] said: Go forth from hence, degraded, banished.*[45] Satan then said: *Then, by Thy might, I surely will beguile them every one, except Thy Servants amongst them, sincere and purified [by Thy grace].*[46] God (Glorious and Exalted is He) responded: *The Truth is, and the Truth I speak, that I shall fill Hell with thee and with such of them as follow thee, together.*[47] God (Glorious and Exalted is He) thus damned and banished Iblīs, and promised the same ultimate fate of Hellfire for those who follow him. In reality, though, no matter how repugnant the evil committed by human beings, it does not approach the aforementioned and subsequent evil of Satan to the Day of Judgment.

---

44 Q.VII.12 (Yusuf Ali translation).

45 Q.VII.14–18. See also Q.XXXVIII.71–80.

46 Q.XXXVIII.82. This was most likely stated after the Holy Lord had notified him that only those who were sincere to Him would be saved from being led astray. And God knows best.

47 Q.XXXVIII.83 (Yusuf Ali translation).

That said, there exist wise purposes in the Holy Lord allowing Satan to remain alive: one of them is to elucidate those who are sincere and have true belief amongst humankind. God (Exalted is He) states: *And [Satan] had no warrant whatsoever against them, save that We would know him who believeth in the Hereafter from him who is in doubt thereof.*[48] Had it not been for the presence of Satan, evils, temptations and doubts, then many insincere people would *appear* to be good. Only with the existence of all of the aforementioned are those who are insincere to God (Glorious is He) revealed and elucidated as such.

Ibn al-Qayyim mentions sixteen wise purposes of God (Glorious is He) in creating and allowing the devil to continue living and tempting humanity. Some of these wise purposes include:

> The Sublime made [Iblīs' disobedience] a warning to [many including] those who disobey His command, those whose pride prevents them from obeying Him, and those who persist in sinning. God likewise made the sin of the father of mankind a moral lesson for those who perpetrate a prohibition of His or disobey a commandment of His, as [Adam] then repented from and regretted [his lapse], and returned back to his Lord... [Also Satan] is a touchstone by which God tests His creation so as to differentiate those who are wicked from those who are good...
>
> Love of Him, returning to Him, depending on Him, patience [for His sake], and contentment [with His determination and decree], are the most beloved [types] of worship of God (Glory be to Him) in His sight. These types of servitude are not realized except through striving and waging battle, sacrificing oneself for God's sake, and preferring His love over everything else. Waging battle [in His path] is the apex of worship, and the most beloved to the Lord. Therefore, the creation of Iblīs and his army has [indirectly] led to the establishment of these forms of worship and their consequences. Only God can recount the wisdoms, benefits, and advantages of all that. The creation of those who oppose His messengers, deny them, and show hostility towards them leads to the complete manifestation of His signs, wondrous powers, and subtle works. The existence of those [signs] is more beloved to Him and more beneficial to His loyal supporters than their absence. Some of these signs were mentioned previously like the flood [drowning Noah's people], the staff and hand [of Moses], the parting of the [Red] sea, and the [salvation]

[48] Q.XXXIV.21.

of His friend [Abraham] after being thrown in the fire. These, in addition to many of His other signs, are proofs of His omnipotence, omniscience, and wisdom. The existence of causes leading [indirectly] to those [signs] is necessary...

One of God's Names is the Most Wise. Wisdom is one of His Attributes (Glory be to Him). His wisdom necessitates putting everything in its appropriate place. His [wisdom] dictated creating opposites and selecting rulings, characteristics, and criteria, which are fitting to each [opposite].[49]

On God accepting the repentance of Adam and Eve

Now, the Qur'ān maintains that God (Exalted is He) had decreed Adam's descent to this earth before even creating him or placing him and Eve in Paradise: *And when thy Lord said unto the angels: Lo! I am about to place a viceroy in the earth, they said: Wilt thou place therein one who will do harm and will shed blood, while we hymn Thy praise and sanctify Thee? He said: Surely I know that which ye know not.*[50] Thus the "fall" was predestined, albeit in accordance with causes, including the temptation instigated by the Devil[51] as well as the lapse of Adam and Eve with their own free will. Humanity's settlement upon earth was inevitable and could not have been avoided. Had God (Glorious is He) willed that humanity continue to live in Paradise, He could have protected Adam and Eve from ever disobeying His commandment through a variety of measures. Yet that was not His will, nor His determination.

Regardless, the Holy Lord forgave Adam and Eve after they repented from the sin they freely perpetrated. *They said: Our Lord! We have wronged ourselves. If thou forgive us not and have not mercy on us, surely we are of the lost!*[52] *Thereupon Adam received words [of guidance] from his Sustainer, and He accepted his repentance: for verily, He alone is the Acceptor of Repentance, the Dispenser of Grace.*[53] The Most Beneficent Lord accepts

---

49 See Zeni (tr.), *Ibn Qayyim al-Jawziyya on Divine Wisdom and the Problem of Evil*, pp. 130–138. These represent the 3rd, 4th, 8th, 9th and 13th wise purposes listed by Ibn al-Qayyim.

50 Q.II.30.

51 See Q.XX.120 (Yusuf Ali translation): *Satan whispered evil to him: he said, "O Adam! shall I lead thee to the Tree of Eternity and to a kingdom that never decays?*

52 Q.VII.23.

53 Q.II.37 (Muḥammad Asad translation).

the repentance of those who sincerely repent to Him and ask for His forgiveness. God (Exalted is He) also stated: *Then his Lord chose him, and relented toward him, and guided him.*[54]

The Holy Lord accepted their repentance and bestowed upon them His mercy and covenant. There was no need for humanity to be redeemed. God (Exalted is He) states: *When there come unto you from Me a guidance, then whoso followeth My guidance, he will not go astray nor come to grief.*[55] Whoever follows His guidance and fulfills His covenant will attain the Holy Lord's pleasure and Paradise. There is also no need for atonement since Adam and Eve's sin was forgiven.

Islam affirms that infants are born upon a pure innate disposition (*fiṭra*), as mentioned previously. To deny that Adam's repentance was accepted by God is to deny His vast mercy and forgiveness. Although both the vast majority of Christian and Islamic scholars affirm that Paradise will only be entered by the believers and thus deny universal salvation, to claim the doctrine of original sin and its consequences restricts further a number of God's Beautiful Names, such as the Most Beneficent, the Most Merciful and the Most Forgiving from being effective in the case of repentant believers.

Affirming God's oneness and a repudiation of the Trinity and other Christian inconsistencies

As stated earlier, the evil of worshipping other than God (Exalted is He), i.e. polytheism, is the worst and most destructive of all evils (after attributing evil to Him or to His commandments): *God forgiveth not that partners should be set up with Him; but He forgiveth anything else, to whom He pleaseth; to set up partners with God is to devise a sin most heinous indeed.*[56] The worship of any other deity is the root of disbelief, while affirming His Oneness and obeying His commandments is the basis for all good.

Worshipping God alone and affirming His Oneness is the basis of the religion. *There is no god but He: That is the witness of God, His angels, and those endued with knowledge, standing firm on justice. There is no god but*

---

[54] Q.XX.122.

[55] Q.XX.123.

[56] Q.IV.48 (Yusuf Ali translation).

He, the Exalted in Power, the Wise.[57] God's Oneness has been affirmed by all of the prophets in the Qur'ān, including Jesus (may God bless him). On the Day of Judgment God (Glorious is He) will say:

> *O Jesus, son of Mary! Didst thou say unto humankind: Take me and my mother for two deities beside God? He saith: Be glorified! It was not mine to utter that to which I had no right. If I used to say it, then Thou knewest it. Thou knowest what is in my mind, and I know not what is in Thy Mind. Thou, only Thou, art the Knower of things hidden. I spake unto them only that which Thou commandedst me, (saying): Worship God, my Lord and your Lord. I was a witness of them while I dwelt among them, and when Thou tookest me Thou wast the Watcher over them. Thou art Witness over all things.*[58]

The Prophet Muḥammad (may God bless him and grant him peace) related that the Holy Lord says:

> The son of Adam curses Me, and he should not do so; and he tells a lie against Me, and he should not do so. As for his cursing Me, it is that he says that I have a son even though: *I am the eternally besought of all, Who begetteth not nor was begotten, and there is none comparable unto Me.*[59] As for his telling a lie against Me, it is his statement that I shall not resurrect him just as I had originated him beforehand. It is just as easy for Me to resurrect him as it was to originate him.[60]

God (Exalted is He) also states:

> *Some assert, "The Most Gracious has taken unto Himself a son!" Indeed,* [*by this assertion*] *you have brought forth something monstrous, whereat the heavens might well-nigh be rent into fragments, and the earth be split asunder, and the mountains fall down into ruins! That men should ascribe a son to the Most Gracious, although it is inconceivable that the Most Gracious should take unto Himself a son! Not one of all* [*the beings*] *that are in the heavens or on earth appears before the Most Gracious other than as a servant.*[61]

The Old Testament—even the Book of Isaiah—confirms throughout that God is One: "I am God, and there is none else; I am God, and

---

57 Q.III.18 (Yusuf Ali translation).

58 Q.V.116–117.

59 See Q.CXII.1–4.

60 Bukhārī 3193; Nasā'ī 2080; Aḥmad 8220.

61 Q.XIX.88–93 (Muḥammad Asad translation).

there is none like me,"[62] and "That all the people of the earth may know that the Lord is God, and that there is none else."[63] "Know therefore this day, and consider it in thine heart, that the Lord he is God in heaven above, and upon the earth beneath: there is none else."[64] "For thou shalt worship no other god: for the Lord, whose name is Jealous, is a jealous God."[65] David (may God bless him) states in the Bible: "Wherefore thou art great, O Lord God: for there is none like thee, neither is there any God beside thee."[66]

Also consider the Biblical verse: "I am the Lord, and there is none else, there is no God beside me... I am the Lord, and there is none else. I form the light, and create darkness: I make peace, and create evil: I the Lord do all these things."[67] This verse affirms His Oneness and that God is the Creator of everything, including evil—this is also the position represented in the Qur'ān.

By worshipping Jesus in some fashion the Christians have disbelieved in the monotheism conveyed by all of the prior prophets. This topic is complex, yet it will be discussed in detail since worshipping others besides God (Glorious is He) is one of the greatest evils.

Now, God (Glorious is He) spoke directly to Adam as well as Moses, but there is nothing in Genesis or the Torah that can be alluded to in order to substantiate the Trinity. Had Jesus been a deity to be worshipped, and entry into Paradise been contingent upon it, the Holy Lord would have certainly informed the father of humanity or Moses (may God bless them both) of this. Instead, claiming that Jesus is a deity and son of God is a complete fabrication as the Holy Lord states: *Dreadful is the word that cometh out of their mouths. They speak naught but a lie.*[68]

The verses of the Old Testament affirm that only God should be worshipped. It was previously mentioned that God (Exalted is He) may withhold some of His knowledge and bestow it when He

---

62 Isaiah 46.9. See also Isaiah 45.22.

63 1 Kings 8.60.

64 Deuteronomy 4.39. See also Deuteronomy 4.35.

65 Exodus 34.14. See also Exodus 20.1–5.

66 2 Samuel 7.20–22.

67 Isaiah 45.5–7. See also Isaiah 45.18.

68 Q.XVIII.5.

wills for wise purposes. But the commandment and knowledge to worship Him alone in the proper manner is not within those types of knowledge which may be withheld. God (Glorious is He) has always commanded humanity to worship Him alone. There is no mystery in worshipping God, the Eternal and the Most Beneficent Creator. All of the prophets including Adam, Noah, Abraham, Moses, Muḥammad and Jesus (according to the Qur'ān) commanded their followers to worship God alone.

There is no definitive evidence, furthermore, in the Old Testament (or in the Qur'ān) that the prior prophets had even notified their nations about the coming of the Messenger Jesus (may God bless him) in name, much less that he should be worshipped. In contrast, the Prophet Muḥammad (may God bless him and grant him peace) states that: "All of the prophets informed their nations about the Antichrist (*al-Masīḥ al-Dajjāl*)."[69] It is self evident that knowing whom to worship is more important than knowing about the Antichrist[70]; therefore, had Jesus been a deity prior prophets would have also informed their nations similarly.

Now, Ibn Taymiyya states in *al-Jawāb al-ṣaḥīḥ*: "[God] has named others besides [Jesus] as a son [i.e. David]. Therefore, the term 'son' is not an Attribute of His [or part of the Trinity], but rather it refers to any one of His servants whom He has brought up [spiritually]."[71] David (may God bless him) received the Psalms wherein it states: "I will declare the decree: the Lord hath said unto me, Thou art my Son; this day have I begotten thee."[72] Solomon was also named His son in the Old Testament; God (Exalted is He) said to David: "And when thy days be fulfilled, and thou shalt sleep with thy fathers, I will set up thy seed after thee, which shall proceed out of thy bowels, and I will establish his kingdom. He shall build an house for my name, and I will establish the throne of his kingdom for ever. I will be his father, and

---

69 Bukhārī 3057; Muslim 2933/7363; Tirmidhī 2235; Abū Dāwūd 4316; Aḥmad 6185.

70 It could be argued that if the coming of the Antichrist was foretold then the coming of the Christ should also follow. Regardless, it still remains that the Messenger Jesus is not a deity and, therefore, should not be worshipped.

71 Ibn Taymiyya, *al-Jawāb al-ṣaḥīḥ*, vol. I, p. 814.

72 Psalms 2.7.

he shall be my son."[73] Therefore, David and Solomon (who built a temple for the Holy Lord immediately after David) were each named a "son". There is another instance in the Bible referring to the term "son", but its authenticity and interpretation is debatable.[74]

Now, stating that all of humankind are God's children is not used in Islam, in contrast to Christianity—to do so is not Islamically-sound.[75] The Prophet Muḥammad (may God bless him and grant him peace) did say though: "The prophets are brothers of different mothers, but their religion is one. Jesus, son of Mary, and I are the closest as there is no prophet in-between us."[76] At most, what could be inferred is that the Holy Lord God is the Spiritual Father of the prophets, whom He has taught His religion either by direct speech, inspiration, through Gabriel or dreams. It may be that after God speaks to the believers in Paradise, they will be considered similarly to be spiritual sons of His (Glorious and Exalted is He). And God knows best.[77]

God (Exalted is He) states: *It is not fitting for a man that God should speak to him [in this world] except by inspiration, or from behind a veil, or by the sending of a messenger to reveal, with God's permission, what God wills: for He is Most High, Most Wise.*[78] The messenger referred to here is

---

[73] 2 Samuel 7.12–14. David (may God bless him) affirmed God's Oneness in many places within the Old Testament; for instance, 2 Samuel 7.20–22: "And what can David say more unto thee? for thou, Lord GOD, knowest thy servant. For thy word's sake, and according to thine own heart, hast thou done all these great things, to make thy servant know them. Wherefore thou art great, O LORD God: for there is none like thee, neither is there any God beside thee, according to all that we have heard with our ears."

[74] See Exodus 4.22–23 where Moses told Pharaoh: "Thus saith the Lord, Israel *is* my son, even my firstborn. And I say unto thee, Let my son go, that he may serve me."

[75] An unsound tradition states: "All of the [human] creation (*khalq*) are the children (*ʿiyāl*) of God. The most beloved of His creation in His sight are those who are the most beneficial to their families." Bayhaqī (*Shuʿab*) 7045; *Ḥilya*, vol. II, p. 102. It is deemed to be "weak" according to Albānī in (*Silsilat al-aḥādīth al-ḍaʿīfa wa'l-mawḍūʿa* 1900, 3590 and 5735).

[76] Bukhārī 3442 and 3443; Muslim 2365/6130–6132; Abū Dāwūd 4675; Aḥmad 9270. See also Albānī (*Silsilat al-aḥādīth al-ṣaḥīḥa* 2182).

[77] On the other hand, God (Glorious and Exalted is He) will not speak to the disbelievers—and God knows best—for the Holy Lord states: *As for those who sell the faith they owe to God and their own plighted word for a small price, they shall have no portion in the Hereafter: Nor will God (deign to) speak to them or look at them on the Day of Judgment, nor will He cleanse them (of sin): They shall have a grievous penalty.* Q.III.77 (Yusuf Ali translation).

[78] Q.XLII.51 (Yusuf Ali translation).

Gabriel,[79] and the fact that he conveys the revelation from God to the prophets is the likely reason that Gabriel is named the Holy Spirit.[80] Of note, the Prophet Muḥammad did supplicate in the following terms: "O God, assist [Ḥassān b. Thābit] with the Holy Spirit."[81] Therefore, it was not only Jesus who was assisted by the Holy Spirit.[82]

Next, Islam maintains that Jesus is not the Word of God, but rather Jesus was created through the Word of God. Consider the verses:

> *The angels said: "O Mary! Behold God sends thee the glad tiding, through a Word [bi-kalimat[in]] from Him, [of a son] who shall become known as [ism[uhu]] the Christ Jesus, son of Mary, of great honor in this world and in the life to come, and [shall be] of those who are drawn near unto God… Thus it is: God creates what He wills; when He wills a thing to be, He but says unto it, 'Be'—and it is."*[83]

Note here that in Arabic the Word (*kalamat*) is feminine, while his name (*ism[uhu]*) is masculine—the Holy Lord (through His angels) did not say "name" in the feminine (*ism[uha]*).[84] Thus Jesus is not God's Word itself, but rather a son (*ibn* or *walad*) of Mary, who was created by the Word of the Almighty Lord.[85] Although God first formed Adam from the earth with His Hand, God breathed a spirit from Him (*min rūḥ[ihi]*) into both Adam and Jesus[86] and then said to both His Word, "Be" (*Kun*), and then they came alive fully created. Thus God (Glorious is He) states: *Verily in the sight of God, the nature of Jesus is as the nature*

---

79 See *Tafsīr al-Ṭabarī*, vol. XXI, p. 558.

80 Ibn al-Qayyim states alternatively or additionally: "Gabriel is named the Holy Spirit (*rūḥ al-qudus*) because he is pure from any faults." See Zeni (tr.), *Ibn Qayyim al-Jawziyya on Divine Wisdom and the Problem of Evil*, p. 20.

81 Bukhārī 453; Muslim 2485/6384; Nasā'ī 716; Aḥmad 21,936.

82 See Ibn Taymiyya, *al-Jawāb al-ṣaḥīḥ*, vol. I, p. 373. The assistance of the Holy Spirit is in speech.

83 Q.III.45–47 (Muḥammad Asad translation).

84 See *Tafsīr al-Ṭabarī*, vol. VI, p. 412.

85 See also Ibn Taymiyya, *al-Jawab al-ṣaḥīḥ*, vol. I, p. 270, where Qatāda states that "the Word did not become Jesus, but rather it is through the Word that Jesus came into existence", and Aḥmad b. Ḥanbal states that "Jesus is not [the Word] (*kun*); rather, he came into existence through the Word (*bi'l-kun kān*)".

86 The human being (in all cases besides Adam and Jesus) is endowed with the spirit at four months after conception—see Ibn Ḥajar, *Fatḥ al-Bārī*, vol. XI, p. 484, for instance—whereas Jesus was endowed with the spirit from conception.

of Adam, whom He created out of dust, and then said unto him, "Be"—and he is.[87]

Jesus is named the Christ, i.e. Messiah[88] (*al-Masīḥ*), because (1) he was "anointed by God (*masaḥa*[hu] *Allāh*) and purified such that he would never sin", or (2) "he was anointed and blessed",[89] or because (3) Jesus could, for instance, *heal him who was born blind, and the leper, and...raise the dead, by God's leave*,[90] by touching or wiping (*masḥ*) them.[91]

Now, as regarding the Gospels according to Matthew, Mark, Luke and John, Bart Ehrman, a New Testament scholar, states that they

> were written anonymously—the authors never identify themselves—and they circulated for decades before anyone claimed they were written by these people. The first certain attributions of these books to these authors is a century after they were produced. There are good reasons for thinking that none of these attributions is right. For one thing, the followers of Jesus, as learned from the New Testament itself, were uneducated lower-class Aramaic-speaking Jews from Palestine. These books are not written by people like that. Their authors were highly educated, Greek-speaking Christians of a later generation. They probably wrote after Jesus' disciples had all, or almost all, died. They were writing in different parts of the world, in a different language, and at a later time.[92]

Ehrman states also: "Matthew's Gospel is written completely in the third person[93]... There's not a thing in it that would make you suspect the author is talking about himself. With John it is even more clear...

---

[87] Q.III.59 (Muḥammad Asad translation).

[88] Messiah means "one who is anointed" in Hebrew while Christ is the Greek translation of Messiah. See Ehrman, *How Jesus Became God*, p. 113.

[89] See *Tafsīr al-Ṭabarī*, vol. VI, p. 414.

[90] Q.III.49.

[91] See *Tafsīr al-Rāzī*, vol. VIII, p. 222–223.

[92] Bart Ehrman, *How Jesus Became God: The Exaltation of a Jewish Preacher from Galilee* (New York: HarperOne, 2014), p. 90. Ehrman also states in another work: "their ignorance of Palestinian geography and Jewish customs suggests they composed their works somewhere else in the [Roman] empire." See Bart Ehrman, *Jesus, Interrupted: Revealing the Hidden Contradictions in the Bible (and Why We Don't Know About Them)* (New York: HarperOne, 2009), p. 106.

[93] For instance, consider Matthew 9.9: "And as Jesus passed forth from thence, he saw a man, named Matthew, sitting at the receipt of custom: and he saith unto him, Follow me. And he arose, and followed him."

[John] is not the disciple [but rather] he claims to have gotten some of his information from the disciple." Thus the apostles of Jesus, Matthew and John of Zebedee, were not the same individuals who wrote these Gospels, according to Ehrman.[94]

That said, the Synoptic Gospels (i.e. those attributed to Matthew, Mark and Luke) can be seen to be in line with much of what Jesus actually preached, if one assumes a number of factors. First, Jesus is only termed "Son of God" like David or Solomon were, as discussed previously. In addition, there are many passages in the New Testament which indicate that those who are blessed can be named as "children of God" in a spiritual sense, not literally.[95] Second, when Jesus is called "a lord" this indicates that he is a master—not a deity—much like Muḥammad was termed a "master" (*sayyid*).[96] Indeed, Jesus is reported in these Gospels to object to being called "Good Master", by replying: "Why callest thou me good? *There is* none good but one, *that is*, God."[97] But Jesus does not object here to being called a "master". In fact, each messenger is a master of his nation[98]. Also, Jesus stated that only God—not he—knows the timing of the Hour.[99] Thus the "orthodox" Christian view which considers Jesus equal to God (within the Trinity) is rendered inconsistent and is refuted by these verses of the Synoptic Gospels. Third, when Jesus is

---

94 See Ehrman, *Jesus, Interrupted,* p. 274, where he states that many of the books of the New Testament "were not written by the people to whom they are attributed".

95 See Matthew 5.9: "Blessed are the peacemakers: for they shall be called the children of God"; and Luke 20:36 regarding the inhabitants of Paradise: "Neither can they die any more: for they are equal to the angels; and are the children of God"; and John 11.52: "That also he should gather together in one the children of God that were scattered abroad"; and Paul in Galatians 3.26: "For ye are all the children of God by faith in Jesus Christ"; and 1 John 3.9–10: "Whoever is born of God doth not commit sin... In this the children of God are manifest, and the children of the devil: whosoever doeth not righteousness is not of God."

96 For instances of Jesus being named a master see Matthew 8.19 and 9.11; Mark 4.38 and 9.5; and Luke 10.25 and 17.13.

97 See Matthew 19.16–17, Mark 10.17–18 and Luke 18.18–19.

98 Of note, the Prophet Muḥammad (may God bless him and grant him peace) said: "I am the master of humanity on the Day of Judgment—[I say that] without boasting." Muslim 2278/5940; Abū Dāwūd 4673; Ibn Māja 4308; Aḥmad 10,972.

99 See Matthew 24.36.

being "worshipped"[100] it is due to his status as a king of the Jews[101] and master of the believers—not as a deity. There are also two examples of such "worship" in the New Testament: 1) the one "servant" who "fell down, and worshipped" his lord as he owed the latter a debt; and 2) Cornelius who "fell down at [the apostle Peter's] feet, and worshipped him". [102] Also, Joseph's brothers as well as Jacob, his father and a prophet, prostrated to Joseph, according to both the Old Testament and Qur'ān. Finally, let us not forget that all of the angels, every single one of them, prostrated to Adam, the father of humanity, by the commandment of the Holy Lord.[103] Fourth, when Jesus stated to a sinner who came to him, "thy sins be forgiven thee",[104] he is stating this by the allowance of the Most Forgiving. Ehrman notes that Jesus did not say "I forgive you," and is thus not claiming a divine prerogative, but rather a priestly[105] (or more correctly a prophetic) one. Indeed, God (Glorious is He) states in the Qur'ān that if a sinner were to *come unto thee [i.e. Muḥammad] and asked God's forgiveness, and the Messenger had asked forgiveness for them, they would have found God indeed Oft-Returning, Most Merciful.*[106] So if a messenger (like Jesus or Muḥammad) supplicates on behalf of a sinner[107] who seeks God's forgiveness, that believer's sin is forgiven by God (Glorious is He). Those living in a time in which a prophet is not present, on the other

---

[100] See, for instance, Matthew 2.11 and 9.18.

[101] See Matthew 2.2: "Where is he that is born King of the Jews? for we have seen his star in the east, and are come to worship him."

[102] See Matthew 18.26 and Acts 10.25, respectively. Ehrman states: "And kings were worshiped—even in the Bible (Matthew 18:26)—by veneration and obeisance, just as God was. Here, Jesus may be accepting the worship due to him as the future king." Ehrman, *How Jesus Became God*, p. 127.

[103] See verses Q.XV.29–30 and Q.XXXVIII.72–73.

[104] See, for instance, Matthew 9.2, Mark 2.5 and Luke 5.20.

[105] Ehrman, *How Jesus Became God*, p. 127.

[106] Q.IV.64 (Yusuf Ali translation).

[107] There is one exception to this rule and it involves the hypocrites, for they are insincere and do not even truly believe in the Hereafter, the Messenger, and God. God (Glorious is He) states: *And when it is said unto [the Hypocrites]: Come! The Messenger of God will ask forgiveness for you! they avert their faces and thou seest them turning away, disdainful. Whether thou ask forgiveness for them or ask not forgiveness for them is all one for them; God will not forgive them. Lo! God guideth not the evil-living folk.* Q.LXIII.5–6. See also Q.IX.80.

hand, cannot definitively know whether they are forgiven or whether their good deeds are accepted until the Day of Judgment.

There is much goodness within the Synoptic Gospels; however, there are many inconsistencies[108] therein as well as within the rest of the New Testament. One major inconsistency is that Jesus is reported to have said: "Verily I say unto you, That there be some of them that stand here, which shall not taste of death, till they have seen the kingdom of God come with power."[109] Ehrman states that Paul also "was so thoroughly entrenched in apocalyptic[110] thinking" and "was so sure that the end was coming soon that he thought he himself would be alive when judgment day arrived".[111] On the other hand, Ehrman states regarding the Gospel of John (which was written around 95 CE): "It is no accident that our final canonical Gospel, John, written after that first generation, no longer has Jesus proclaim an apocalyptic message... As time went on, the apocalyptic message came to be seen as misguided, or even dangerous. And so the traditions of Jesus' preaching were changed."[112]

---

108 Bart Ehrman points out many inconsistencies within the New Testament, the vast majority of which will not be mentioned. One prominent inconsistency though that he does mention regards when Jesus was granted the title "Son of God". Paul, according to Acts 13:32–33 (written by the same author as the Gospel of Luke), states that it occurred when Jesus was crucified. Mark 1:11 and Matthew 3.13–17 state it occurred when Jesus was baptized by the Prophet John (i.e. about 3 years before Jesus was raised). Luke 1:35 states it occurred as early as the time of Jesus' birth. Finally, John 1:1–18 locates it before this world was created for he claims that "In the beginning was the Word, and the Word was with God, and the Word was God" and the "Word was made flesh". See Ehrman, *Jesus, Interrupted*, pp. 246–249.

109 Mark 9.1. It states in Mark 13.26–30: "And then shall they see the Son of man coming in the clouds with great power and glory... Verily I say unto you, that this generation shall not pass, till all these things be done." See also Matthew 16.27–28 and Luke 9.26–27.

110 Ehrman discusses a theodicy rooted in apocalyptic thinking. However, it does not explain why God allows evil, but instead only that God "will reassert [H]is sovereignty in the future when [H]e overthrows the forces of evil and vindicates everyone who has sided with [H]im". See Bart Ehrman, *God's Problem: How the Bible Fails to Answer Our Most Important Question—Why We Suffer* (New York: HarperOne, 2008), pp. 233–260 (specifically 256 for this quote).

111 Ehrman, *How Jesus Became God*, p. 111. See 1 Thessalonians 4.17.

112 Ibid., p. 105. See also Ehrman, *Jesus, Interrupted*, pp. 81 and 157.

Moreover, the apostles and disciples of Jesus, the Messiah, expected him to be a powerful king—not a "suffering Messiah". [113] Instead of Jesus being established on the throne of David as the king of the Jews and ruling them (along with his descendants) "forever", the disciples and followers of Jesus remained few and it appeared to them that he was crucified. The apocalypse did not come, but instead they continued to be persecuted by the Roman authorities (for many generations and centuries). Later Christians were thus forced to reinterpret their understanding in accordance with those events, and develop explanations for what had instead occurred.

Now, Ehrman states that "Jesus never makes explicit divine claims about himself" in the Synoptic Gospels of Matthew, Mark and Luke.[114] Ehrman adds that Paul "never says that Jesus declared himself to be divine",[115] and he says: "Paul understood Christ to be an angel who became a human... [Consider for example] Galatians 4:14... Paul is not contrasting Christ with an angel; he is equating him with an angel. [Susan] Garrett goes a step further and argues that Galatians 4:14 indicates that Paul 'identifies [Jesus Christ] with God's chief angel'[116]."[117]

Ehrman contends that although the Gospel of John "does indeed portray him as God",[118] the reality is that: "Scholars have long held that the view of Christ in the Gospel of John was a later development in the Christian tradition. It was not something that Jesus himself actually taught, and it is not something that can be found in the other

---

[113] See also Ehrman, *Jesus, Interrupted*, pp. 88 and 228–236.

[114] Ehrman, *How Jesus Became God*, p. 4.

[115] Ibid., p. 89.

[116] See also Susan Garrett, *No Ordinary Angel: Celestial Spirits and Christian Claims About Jesus* (New Haven: Yale University Press, 2008), p. 11.

[117] Ehrman, *How Jesus Became God*, pp. 252–253. Galatians 4.13–14 states: "Ye know how through infirmity of the flesh I preached the gospel unto you at first...ye despised not, nor rejected; but received me as an angel of God, even as Jesus Christ."

[118] Ehrman, *How Jesus Became God*, p. 4. Ehrman states: "In John, Jesus is the pre-existent Word of God through whom the universe was created, who has become human (1:1–14); he is equal with God (10:30); he can claim God's name for himself (8:58); he is himself God (1:1, 20:28)." Ehrman, *Jesus, Interrupted*, p. 140. May God protect us from such heresies and blasphemous statements!

Gospels... In [John's] view, Christ was a divine being who became human...[i.e.] an incarnation Christology."[119]

Furthermore, there is no discussion of the Trinity, i.e. "three being one in substance", in the Synoptic Gospels nor the Gospel of John nor the epistles of Paul. Instead, Ehrman states that "later scribes of the New Testament [who] found this lack disturbing...inserted an explicit reference to the Trinity [in] (1 John 5:7–8). The Trinity is a later Christian invention, which was based, in the arguments of Athanasius and others... Within three hundred years Jesus went from being a Jewish apocalyptic prophet to being God himself, a member of the Trinity."[120]

This worship of "one God in Trinity" referred to in the Athanasian Creed[121] is thus in direct contradiction with the creed and monotheism

---

[119] Ehrman, *How Jesus Became God*, pp. 248–249. Ehrman also states: "If Jesus went around Galilee proclaiming himself to be a divine being sent by God—one who existed before the creation of the world, who was in fact equal with God—could anything *else* that he might say be so breathtaking and thunderously important? And yet none of [the Synoptic Gospels nor the Q, M, and L sources] say any such thing about him. Did they (all of them!) just decide not to mention the one thing that was most significant about Jesus?" Ibid., p. 125

[120] Ehrman, *Jesus, Interrupted*, p. 260. See also ibid., p. 186. Of note, the first epistle of John differs with the Gospel of John. Ehrman states regarding the epistle of John: "This book was almost certainly not written by [Jesus' disciple John, the son of Zebedee], though, and it makes no claim to be written by him... It is widely believed among scholars that 1 John was written by someone living in the same community in which the Gospel of John was written and circulated." Ibid., pp. 296–297.

[121] The Athanasian Creed can be abridged as follows: "We worship one God in Trinity and Trinity in Unity... The Godhead of the Father, of the Son, and of the Holy Ghost is all one, the Glory equal, the Majesty co-eternal... The Father uncreated, the Son uncreated, and the Holy Ghost uncreated... The Father eternal, the Son eternal, and the Holy Ghost eternal. And yet they are not three eternals but one eternal... So likewise the Father is Almighty, the Son Almighty, and the Holy Ghost Almighty. And yet there are not three Almighties, but one Almighty. So the Father is God, the Son is God, and the Holy Ghost is God; And yet there are not three Gods, but one God... So we are forbidden by the catholic religion to say; There are three Gods, or three Lords... Furthermore, it is necessary to everlasting salvation that he also believe rightly the incarnation of our Lord Jesus Christ. For the right faith is that we believe and confess that our Lord Jesus Christ, the Son of God, is God and man. God of the Substance of the Father, begotten before the worlds; and man of the substance of His mother, born in the world."

conveyed by the prophets in the Old Testament. Therefore, although the Christians affirmed prophethood, they disavowed the fundamental message and most essential article of faith enunciated by all of the prior prophets, i.e. to worship the One True and Holy God alone.

God (Glorious is He) states: *O followers of the Gospel! Do not overstep the bounds [of truth] in your religious beliefs, and do not say of God anything but the truth. The Christ Jesus, son of Mary, was but God's Messenger... Believe then in God and His Messengers, and do not say, "[God is] a trinity." Desist [from this assertion] for your own good. God is but One God; utterly remote is He, in His glory, from having a son.*[122]

Now, the later "orthodox" Christian view is that Jesus Christ was "human and divine at one and the same time and yet was one being, not two".[123] This view is contrary to reason, and it is impossible that a being be human and divine at that same time—God is glorious and exalted above any blasphemy. A being cannot be said to be fully human and angelic at the same time, much less be fully human and divine simultaneously. Now, it is true that an angel can *appear* as a human being.[124] The angel Gabriel was sent to Mary and appeared before her as a human being, and likewise Gabriel came to the Prophet Muḥammad appearing as a human being in the view of many of his Companions and taught them about submission, faith and devotion (as per the *ḥadīth* mentioned earlier). Even in that state, though, it is not reported that Gabriel ate or drank. Gabriel remained an angel and did not become a human, but only appeared in human form. On the other hand, Jesus (may God bless him) ate and drank—the New Testament and Qur'ān affirm that. Jesus was a fully human being, not an angel or a deity.

However, the believers will come to possess some angelic characteristics in the Hereafter, like being granted intrinsic light: *One day shalt thou see the believing men and the believing women—how their light runs forward before them and by their right hands.*[125] The light is theirs (*nūr*[uhum])—it is not something extrinsic. So the believers will possess

---

[122] Q.IV.171 (adapted from the Muḥammad Asad translation).

[123] Ehrman, *How Jesus Became God*, p. 286

[124] Of note, there is no example of a human being appearing as an angel in this world.

[125] Q.LVII.12.

characteristics of both humans and angels in Paradise. They will eat and drink, yet they will also possess intrinsic light and will glorify God continuously in Paradise. The believers cannot be said at that time to be human beings, as we know the meaning of that term in this world, but rather they will be created by the Holy Lord in a new form and they will be eternal.

Now, light is not matter (which is composed of atoms) but rather it can be considered as photons (which are massless and do not occupy space) or as a wave of electromagnetic radiation. Hence light is not matter and matter is not light. Furthermore, an entity cannot be said to be both light and matter at one and the same time—this is self-evident and clear-cut. In addition, both light and matter are created. On the other hand, God (Glorious and Exalted is He) is divine and uncreated. Only God knows His essence—we cannot understand His essence for there is none like Him and none comparable to Him in His essence and divinity. Therefore, claiming that Jesus was human and divine at the same time is infinitely more irrational than stating an entity can be light and matter (or fully angelic and fully human) at the same time. Indeed, it is only God (Glorious and Exalted is He) Who is divine. Now if Christians want to claim that Jesus was the Holy Lord and Father himself, then the other irrational consequences of that thinking as it relates to Jesus' existence on this earth discredits their claim. This will be discussed next.

The fundamental issue within the problem of evil regards God's omnipotence. Although most Christian theologians affirm God's omnipotence, they rarely acknowledge the incongruity of Jesus being crucified[126] (according to Christian belief) with that and with the problem of evil. In other words, if God (Glorious and Exalted

---

126 The Qur'ān maintains, of course, that Jesus (may God bless him) was not crucified, but instead raised up. God (Exalted is He) states: *That they said (in boast), "We killed Christ Jesus the son of Mary, the Messenger of God"; but they killed him not, nor crucified him, but so it was made to appear to them. And those who differ therein are full of doubts, with no (certain) knowledge, but only conjecture to follow, for of a surety they killed him not. Nay, God raised him up unto Himself; and God is Exalted in Power, Wise. And there is none of the People of the Book but must believe in him before his death; and on the Day of Judgment he will be a witness against them.* Q.IV.157–159 (Yusuf Ali translation). Jesus (may God bless him) is currently alive in proximity to the Holy Lord. See *Tafsīr al-Ṭabarī*, vol. IX, p. 379–390.

is He) has allowed suffering, evil and death to overcome a fully or partly divine being (according to Christian belief), then that would negate His omnipotence and render His allowance of evil to occur to humanity a moot point. Indeed, Christian theodicies ignore or overlook that theological fundamental flaw.

Regardless, Islam affirms that no human being can harm God (Almighty and Exalted is He) under any circumstance—the Holy Lord is established above His Throne, which is above the heavens. In a *ḥadīth qudsī*, God (Exalted is He) states: "O My servants, you cannot harm Me nor can you benefit Me."[127] God (Glory be to Him) is the Invincible (*al-Qahhār*), the Almighty (*al-ʿAzīz*), the Most High (*al-ʿAliy*) and the Irresistible (*al-Jabbār*). Therefore, blasphemously claiming that any harm or evil could occur to the Divine denies those Beautiful Names and Glorious Attributes of His.

Cursing or blaspheming the Holy Lord represents some of the greatest evils that God (Exalted is He) has ontologically permitted the disbelievers to perpetrate (whilst prohibiting it religiously), but neither causes any harm or evil to Him (Glorious is He). Instead, the evil will circle back and return upon the disbelievers who utter those falsehoods, and His wrath and punishment will overtake them in Hellfire if not beforehand in this world.

God (Glorious and Exalted is He) is omnipotent, whereas the creation are weak. Humans (including messengers and prophets) are susceptible to suffering, as was discussed in the prior chapter. The Messenger Jesus (may God bless him) likewise suffered, and that is consistent with his purely human nature—he should not be worshipped in any manner whatsoever.

Now, Plantiga argues that "any world with incarnation and atonement is a better world than any without it… [T]he value of incarnation and atonement cannot be matched by any aggregate of creaturely goods…[and] the aggregated badness would be outweighed by the goodness of incarnation and atonement… In this sense, therefore, any world with incarnation and atonement is of

---

127 Muslim 2577/6572.

infinite value."[128] Plantiga's claim is similar to Leibniz's claim that the "immense advantage by the incarnation of the Son of God"[129] is one of the reasons that this is the best possible world. Nonetheless, this notion *is* irrational.

First of all, incarnation is absolutely impossible, whether it involves Jesus or any other human being or created entity. When Moses (may God bless him) requested to see God (Glorious is He) the Qur'ān informs us: *When his Lord revealed (His) glory to the mountain He sent it crashing down. And Moses fell down senseless. And when he woke he said: Glory unto Thee! I turn unto Thee repentant, and I am the first of (true) believers.*[130] The Almighty Lord is the Greatest, and nothing can encompass Him, whether in being or in sight: *No human vision can encompass him, whereas He encompasses all human vision.*[131] To suggest that a divine being—whether partially or fully—be encompassed within the womb of a human mother is also blasphemous. Furthermore, to claim that God (Glorious and Exalted is He) has a son through the intermediary of a human mother is an even more repugnant blasphemy.

Regarding the atonement,[132] a powerful being would do everything that he could to avoid such suffering and evil; yet if the latter did

---

128 Alvin Plantiga, "Supralapsarianism or 'O Felix Culpa'", in *The Problem of Evil*, ed. Michael Peterson (Notre Dame: University of Notre Dame Press, 2017), p. 371. Plantiga previously explained "the unthinkably great good of divine incarnation and atonement. Jesus Christ, the second person of the Divine Trinity, incomparably good, holy, and sinless, was willing to empty himself, to take on our flesh and become incarnate, and to suffer and die so that we human beings can have life and be reconciled to the Father. In order to accomplish this, he was willing to undergo suffering of a depth and intensity we cannot so much as imagine, including even the shattering climax of being abandoned by God the Father himself: 'My God, my God, why have you forsaken me?'" [Mark 15.34]. Ibid., p. 368.

129 See Gottfried Leibniz, *The Theodicy*, in *The Philosophical Works of Leibniz*, tr. George Duncan, p. 195.

130 Q.VII.143.

131 Q.VI.103 (Muḥammad Asad translation). That said, Sunnis affirm the Beatific Vision for the believers in Paradise. On the other hand, the Muʿtazila and Shīʿa do not.

132 See Michael Martin, *The Case Against Christianity* (Philadelphia: Temple University Press, 1991), pp. 252–263, for various theories regarding the atonement and his rejections of them.

occur, it would indicate a deficiency in that being's power.[133] Thus to claim that such evil occurred to a fully or partly divine being would lead to the claim that the Holy Lord is not omnipotent or all-powerful in protecting Himself or a son—God is exalted above having a son!

Denial of His omnipotence is indeed heretical, blasphemous and irrational, as discussed. But to allow evil to exist amongst His servants, on the other hand, is not inconsistent with His omnipotence. It is impossible that God (Exalted is He) would ever be harmed or suffer evil at the hands of His creatures; but if such a world did exist it would be an infinitely evil world—not the best.

Now, being forgiven and brought proximate to the Almighty Lord to enjoy His love is the ultimate objective of every believer. God (Glorious is He) has allowed the believers to attain His love by following His revelation to His messengers—He is Most Praiseworthy for that. Of course, the Holy Lord is not in need of any unwise and irrational means, and He is the Most Wise. Those who completely follow His prophets (who affirmed His Oneness) and follow His commandments and Scriptures will attain His love, pleasure and Paradise.

Next, some Christians state that Jesus' death on the cross defeated the devil and rendered Satan ineffective. Gregory Boyd states:

> According to the New Testament, Jesus in principle defeated Satan and established God's kingdom. Through his ministry of exorcism and healing, and especially through his death and resurrection, he destroyed the power of the devil (1 Jn 3:8; Heb 2:14), disarmed the principalities and powers (Col 2:14–15), and put all God's enemies under his feet (Eph 1:22; Heb 1:13)[134]. But the New Testament does not on this account

[133] This is acknowledged by some Christian thinkers, most notably Process Theologians (of which Swinburne is not). See Richard Swinburne, *Divine Providence and the Problem of Evil* (Oxford: Clarendon Press, 1998), pp. 30–31.

[134] See 1 John 3.8: "He that committeth sin is of the devil; for the devil sinneth from the beginning. For this purpose the Son of God was manifested, that he might destroy the works of the devil"; Hebrews 2.14: "Forasmuch then as the children are partakers of flesh and blood, [Jesus] also himself took part the same; that through death he might destroy him that had the power of death, that is, the devil; And deliver them who through of death were all their lifetime subject to bondage"; Hebrews 1.13: "Sit on my right hand, until I make thine enemies thy footstool"; Ephesians 1.22: "And hath put all *things* under his feet, and gave him *to be* the head over all *things* to the church"; and Colossians 2.13–15: "[H]aving forgiven you all trespasses; Blotting out the handwriting

> conclude that Satan has ceased being in control of this world. This is the paradox of the already-not tension within the New Testament. While Satan has *in principle* been defeated by Christ, God's victory has not yet been fully realized on the earth... Paul understood that Satan, because of his ongoing power and inspite of his mortal wound, was able to hinder the work of the church... In sum the world of the New Testament authors was a world at war. Granted, they expressed great confidence that Jesus had in principle defeated Satan and that Satan and all those who followed him would eventually be defeated when Christ is enthroned as Lord of the cosmos. But they were just as certain that in this present fallen world order *God does not always get his way*.[135]

Now, the falsity of the notions of original sin, atonement as well as the crucifixion itself has already been alluded to. The above paragraph illustrates the contradictory situation that Christians find themselves in when trying to reconcile between the incongruence of those New Testament verses and reality. It is self-evident that evil, including gratuitous types, has only increased over the centuries since the raising of Jesus (may God bless him)—hence the effectiveness of the devil has not been become null in the slightest. Greater levels of evil have been perpetrated or allowed, particularly over the last millennia, by all religious groups (including those who are considered to be Christians). Second, worshipping other than God (in this case Jesus), as it is the principal cause for going astray and represents an unforgivable sin, has instead granted the devil the disbelief he desires to achieve from those Christians who do so. Third, when prophets were killed by the Israelites, God's wrath only increased upon them. The killing of the prophets, in addition to many other evils by the Israelites, led to the Holy Lord saying: *Thus have they drawn on themselves wrath upon wrath*.[136] The death of an individual (or even worse a prophet) is not a

---

of ordinances that was against us, which was contrary to us, and took it out of the way, nailing it to his cross; *And* having spoiled principalities and powers, he made a shew of them openly, triumphing over them in it." See also Luke 10.18–19: "And he said unto them, I beheld Satan as lightening fall from heaven. Behold, I give unto you power to tread serpents and scorpions, and over all the power of the enemy: and nothing shall by any means hurt you."

[135] Gregory A. Boyd, *Satan and the Problem of Evil: Constructing a Trinitarian Warfare Theodicy* (Downers Grove: InterVarsity Press, 2001), pp. 38–39.

[136] See Q.II.87–91, whereby the above is within verse 90.

cause of salvation for others, but rather angers the Holy Lord more. Fourth, the Old Testament and the Qur'ān never claimed that any of the prophets came and mortally wounded the devil. Although Satan will retreat, such as occurred in the Battle of Badr[137] or when a servant remembers the Holy Lord,[138] God (Exalted is He) has allowed the devil to continue to tempt and whisper evil to humankind until the Day of Judgment, as discussed previously. Finally, the Prophet Muḥammad alluded in many *ḥadīth*s that evil would increase over time, and this is what is concordant with reality.

Now, there are many reasons that the creed of Christianity deviated from that of all other prophets. One is that the "ministry" of Jesus was only one to three years in length. One can only imagine the state of the Jews or Muslims had Moses or Muḥammad, respectively, only been able to guide their followers and Companions for at most three years. In reality, a great deal of ignorance and weakness in regards to carrying out all of the Divine commandments by the early Christians occurred. Jesus is reported to have said as much in regards to the apostles in the Synoptic Gospels.[139]

A second reason for the deviance is seen by considering the case of Paul, otherwise known as Saul of Tarsus, who turned away from some commandments of God (Exalted is He) and emphasized faith in Jesus over following the Divine Law. Paul claimed: "We have believed in Jesus Christ, that we might be justified by the faith in Christ, and not by the works of the law; for by the works of the law shall no flesh be justified."[140] Bart Ehrman states: "This is Paul's teaching through both Romans (1–3) and Galatians (1–3)" and that "following the precepts and requirements of the law—getting circumcised, keeping kosher, observing Sabbath and other Jewish festivals—none of this

---

[137] See Q.VIII.48. Once Satan saw Gabriel leading the angels to aid the Prophet Muḥammad and the Companions, he retreated: *And when Satan made [the] deeds of the [disbelievers of Quraysh] seem fair to them and said: No one of humankind can conquer you this day, for I am your protector. But when the armies came in sight of one another, he took flight, saying: Lo! I am guiltless of you. Lo! I see that which ye see not.*

[138] See verse Q.CXIV.4.

[139] For instance, see Luke 12.22–40; Matthew 8.25–26 and 14.30–31; Mark 4.40; and Luke 8.24–25.

[140] Galatians 2.15.

was necessary for salvation, and if you thought (and acted) otherwise, you were is danger of losing your salvation."[141]

The author of the Gospel of Matthew, on the other hand, wrote that Christians must follow and keep the law—even better than the religious Jews. Jesus is reported to have said in the Gospel of Matthew: "Think not that I am come to destroy the law or the prophets: I am not come to destroy but to fulfill... For I say unto you, That except your righteousness shall exceed the righteousness of the scribes and Pharisees, you shall in no case enter the kingdom of heaven."[142] In addition, the author of the Epistle of James stated: "For whosoever shall keep the whole law, and yet offend in one point, he is guilty of all."[143]

Now, circumcision is part of the covenant that God (Glorious is He) gave unto Abraham: "This is my covenant, which ye shall keep, between me and you and thy seed after thee... [M]y covenant shall be in your flesh for an everlasting covenant. And the uncircumcised man child...shall be cut off from his people; he hath broken my covenant."[144] God (Glorious is He) tests those who claim to believe both in spirit and body, in inner and outer manners. The Muslims have fulfilled this commandment and His covenant. Indeed, in no verse within the Gospels does Jesus tell his disciples or followers

---

141 Ehrman, *Jesus, Interrupted*, p. 88. See Galatians 5.4. See, for instance, Paul's repeated discussions of circumcision in Romans 2.25–3.1 and Galatians 5.2–6. See also Acts 15.1–20 where dropping circumcision is traced to Peter as well as Paul and Barnabas.

142 Matthew 5.17–20. See also Matthew 19.16–22. Ehrman concludes: "Paul thought that followers of Jesus who tried to keep the law were in danger of losing their salvation. Matthew thought that followers of Jesus who did not keep the law, and do so even better than the most religious Jews, would never attain salvation." Ehrman, *Jesus, Interrupted*, p. 89.

143 James 2.10. It is unknown if the author James is the same brother of Jesus, a disciple, or another James altogether. James 2.11 continues: "For he that said, Do not commit adultery, said also, Do not kill. Now if thou commit no adultery, yet if thou kill, thou art become a transgressor of the law." The author of the Epistle of James appears furthermore to disagree with Paul in another matter regarding justification of faith as he states: "Even so faith, if it hath not works, is dead, being alone... For as the body without the spirit is dead, so faith without works is dead also." James 2.17–26. It is interesting to note that in Acts 15.13–21, a James (whether he is the same eponymous author of the Epistle of James or more likely not) sides with Peter, Paul and Barnabas in the matter of circumcision.

144 Genesis 17.10–14. See also Exodus 12.43–48 and Leviticus 5.2–9.

not to get circumcised, instead Jesus upheld it.[145] Moreover, Jesus is reported to have said: "And if thy right eye offend thee pluck it out... and if thy right hand offend thee, cut it off, and cast it from thee: for it is profitable for thee that one of thy members should perish, and not that thy whole body should be cast into hell."[146] It is self evident that an eye or a hand is more useful to a human than what is removed with circumcision, and thus those who have belittled or turned away from His covenant have acted unwisely and only achieved a trifling gain.

Although the Qur'ān does not mention Paul in name, it does state: *Do you, then, believe in some parts of the divine writ and deny the truth of other parts? What, then, could be the reward of those among you who do such things but ignominy in the life of this world and, on the Day of Resurrection, commitment to most grievous suffering.*[147] God (Glorious is He) also states that those who turn away from the Divine covenant and disobey His commandments will not attain salvation, but will instead be punished in Hellfire.[148]

Of note, Ibn Taymiyya states about Saul of Tarsus, who claimed that he saw Jesus in a vision on the road to Damascus,[149] something similar to what he said about Ibn ʿArabī.[150] Ibn Taymiyya states that if

---

[145] After some Jews objected to Jesus performing a miracle on the day of the Sabbath, Jesus is reported to have said: "I have done one work and ye all marvel. Moses therefore gave unto you circumcision; (not because it is of Moses, but of the fathers;) and ye on the sabbath circumcise a man. If a man on the sabbath day receive circumcision, that the law of Moses should not be broken; are ye angry at me, because I have made a man every whit whole on the sabbath day?" John 7.21–23.

[146] Matthew 5.29–30. See also Mark 9.43–47.

[147] Q.II.85 (Muḥammad Asad translation). Although this verse was revealed in regards to some Jews, it may concern anyone (including a Muslim) who disobeys some commandments of the Holy Lord. See ʿUmar Sulaymān al-Ashqar, *al-Maʿānī al-ḥisān fī tafsīr al-Qur'ān* (Amman: Dār al-Nafā'is, 2015), vol. I, p. 119. The Holy Lord likewise promises the punishment of Hellfire for those who believe in some prophets but disbelieve in others—see Q.IV.150–151.

[148] See Q.III.77.

[149] See Acts 9.3–9 and Galatians 1.11–16. Paul likely never met Jesus himself.

[150] Ibn Taymiyya states: "If [Ibn ʿArabī] is truthful, then it was a devil from amongst the demons that uttered [or whispered] (*alqā*[ha]) [*al-Futūḥāt al-Makkiyya*] to him." Ibn Taymiyya, *al-Radd ʿalā al-manṭiqiyyīn*, p. 489. See also Ibn Taymiyya, *al-Furqān bayna awliyā' al-Raḥmān wa awliyā' al-shayṭān*, pp. 110–111. See also Wael B. Hallaq's introduction to *Ibn Taymiyya against the Greek Logicians* (Oxford: Clarendon Press, 1993), pp. xxii–xxvii, where he discusses Ibn Taymiyya's refutation of Ibn ʿArabī.

Paul spoke the truth about having seen this vision, then he instead saw a demon pictured as Jesus speaking to him.[151] Now, this may or may not have been the case. Regardless, God (Glorious is He) may select and grant knowledge or guidance to an individual initially, but if he or she subsequently freely chooses to turn back and disobey God's commandments, then that individual will be forsaken: *And he whose sight is dim to the remembrance of the Beneficent, We assign unto him a devil who becometh his comrade; and they surely turn them from the way of God, and yet they deem that they are rightly guided.* [152] There are examples of this in the Bible and the Qur'ān. Consider, for example, the example of Saul who disobeyed a commandment of God relayed to him by the Prophet Samuel. The Bible states that God (Glorious is He) took away His mercy from Saul thereafter.[153] As for the Qur'ān, the Holy Lord states: *Relate to them the story of the man to whom We sent Our signs, but he passed them by: so Satan followed him up, and he went astray. If it had been Our will, We should have elevated him with Our signs; but he inclined to the earth, and followed his own vain desires.*[154]

A third reason that the Christian creed deviated away from that of all of the other prophets is a result of the persecution of the early Christians by the Romans and some Jews, which prevented them from being secure or establishing a polity early on. Contrast that to the early situation of the Muslims, who were able to establish a polity almost immediately. Even though a number of false prophets, like Musaylama the Liar, emerged after the Prophet Muḥammad (may God bless him and grant him peace) died, and others in the Arabian Peninsula became apostates by rejecting one or more pillars of Islam, the Companions were sufficiently empowered from their political base to coordinate campaigns to successfully destroy the unrepentant false prophets and correct the renegades. Without such political strength,

151 See Ibn Taymiyya, *al-Jawāb al-ṣaḥīḥ*, vol. I, p. 454. Ibn Taymiyya also mentioned that during his time some people in Palmyra saw an individual flying in the air claiming to be Jesus and commanding them to do some things. Ibid., p. 452.

152 Q.XLIII.36–37.

153 See 2 Samuel 7.15: "But my mercy shall not depart away from [Solomon], as I took it from Saul, whom I put away before thee [David]." See also 1 Samuel 15:1–35 and 1 Samuel 28.18.

154 Q.VII.175–176 (Yusuf Ali translation).

many more alternatives to the true Islam would have materialized, the line between truth and falsehood would have blurred over time, and many corrupt doctrines would have taken root in various parts of Arabia. But God (Glorious is He) had promised to preserve the Qur'ān and Sunna,[155] and He duly fulfilled His promise. That said, God (Glorious is He) did not promise such preservation for the prior Scriptures, in accordance with certain wise purposes.

Fourth, the Gospels according to Matthew, Mark, Luke and John were not written in the presence of Jesus. In fact, the Gospels were not written until after 70 CE, which was around 40 years after Jesus was raised—the Gospel of Mark being the first. The Gospels according to Matthew, Luke and John were written around 80, 85 and 95 CE, respectively; and Paul wrote his epistles[156] around 50–55 CE. Compare this with the fact that the Qur'ān was written on parchments in the presence of Muḥammad[157] and collected during the time of the Caliph Abū Bakr.

Therefore, with the brevity and turbulence in Jesus' ministry, the low number of his followers (certainly when compared to the larger numbers of the Companions of Muḥammad), the intense persecution that the early Christians suffered, their abandonment of some Divine commandments, and the fact that the Gospels were written decades after Jesus was raised, one can recognize some possible reasons for the fact that the Christian creed was conveyed in a manner discordant with that of all the other prophets.

It is not coincidental that God sent Jesus (may God bless him) as the last messenger of the Israelites—being preceded by a multitude of other prophets all affirming His Oneness in the Old Testament—and that the Christians themselves read the Old Testament and

---

[155] See verse Q.XV.9.

[156] Seven of the epistles were undisputedly written by Paul, and they include Romans, Corinthians, Galatians, Colossians, Philippians, 1 Thessalonians and Philemon.

[157] Pages from the oldest Qur'ān are present at the University of Birmingham in the United Kingdom. The radiocarbon dating of the parchments is between 568 and 645 CE. Muḥammad was a prophet from approximately 609 to 632 CE. See "Birmingham Qur'an manuscript dated among the oldest in the world", at www.birmingham.ac.uk/news/latest/2015/07/quran-manuscript-22-07-15.aspx. See also Muḥammad Muṣṭafā Al-Aʿẓamī, *The History of the Qur'ānic Text from Revelation to Compilation: A Comparative Study with the Old and New Testaments* (Leicester: UK Islamic Academy, 2003).

consider it part of the Bible. The doubt that Christians will inevitably experience in this world about their conception of God within a Trinity—especially in light of the incongruence in this matter of the New Testament with the Old Testament—will result in them acknowledging their disbelief and being astray on the Day of Judgment, if not in this world. They will not have a valid excuse for ignoring the clear discord in this critical and fundamental matter.

Now, God (Exalted is He) states: *O humankind! The Messenger [Muḥammad] hath come unto you with the Truth from your Lord. Therefore believe; (it is) better for you. But if ye disbelieve, still, lo! unto God belongeth whatsoever is in the heavens and the earth. God is ever Knower, Wise.*[158] By denying the Messenger Muḥammad (may God bless him and grant him peace) the Jews and Christians have denied a prophet of God and His religion, and have thus disbelieved. Disbelief in one messenger represents disbelief in all. The Messenger Muḥammad said: "If any Jew or Christian (who are both of my Community) hears about me yet dies without believing in what I have been sent with, then he will be one of the denizens of Hellfire."[159]

Dante exemplifies this disbelief when he states: "See how Mahomet is deformed and torn! In front of me and weeping, Ali walks, his face cleft from his chin up to the crown."[160] All the while, Dante placed in Limbo the prophets Noah, Abraham, Israel, Moses and David because they were not baptized and "they came before the birth of Christ [thus] they did not worship God the way one should,"[161] in addition to placing the Roman pagans and heretical philosophers there![162] Indeed, Dante followed his desires and went far astray. One

---

158 Q.IV.170.

159 Muslim 153/386; Aḥmad 8203.

160 Alighieri Dante, *The Divine Comedy Volume I: Inferno*, tr. Mark Musa (New York: Penguin Books, 1984), p. 152 .

161 Ibid., Canto IV, pp. 98–99. It is claimed that those in Limbo will not suffer physical torment, but rather mental torment. Ibid., p. 102. That Christians deem Jews to be faulty or disbelievers (despite themselves reading the Old Testament and considering it to be part of the Bible) represents another inconsistency of theirs alluded to in the Qur'ān: *And the Jews say the Christians follow nothing (true), and the Christians say the Jews follow nothing (true); yet both are readers of the Scripture.* Q.II.113.

162 Ibid., Canto IV, pp. 100–101. Examples of disbelievers placed in Limbo include: Caesar and Aristotle along with Avicenna.

runs the risk of being punished in Hellfire if one accuses a believer of disbelief; thus what about Dante who claims that the messengers before Jesus will be in Limbo (along with some pagans and heretics) and Muḥammad, a Messenger of God, will be in Hellfire?

In the end, the Prophet Muḥammad (may God bless him and grant him peace) said: "Whoever witnesses that there is no deity worthy of worship besides God alone without any partner; that Muḥammad is a servant and messenger of His; that Jesus is a servant of God and His messenger, and [that he was created through] His Word upon Mary and the [Holy] Spirit sent by Him [to her]; and that Paradise is true and Hellfire is true: God will enter him into Paradise [ultimately] no matter the extent of his deeds."[163] He also said: "If a person believes in Jesus and then believes in me, his reward will be doubled."[164]

The Israelites

Now, the Israelites, through their long history, also worshipped other deities besides God (Glorious and Exalted is He). Three cases will be discussed here: the golden calf, Baal and ʿUzayr (likely Ezra). It was this polytheism of the Israelites, as well as their unwillingness to fight against the disbelievers, that barred them from success in many instances.

After being saved by God (Exalted is He) from Pharaoh and the Egyptians, through the parting of the sea, and while Moses was away on the Mount speaking to the Holy Lord and receiving revelation and the Tablets from Him, the Israelites freely chose to worship a golden calf: *And the folk of Moses, after (he left them), chose a calf (for worship), (made) out of their ornaments, of saffron hue, which gave a lowing sound. Saw they not that it spake not unto them nor guided them to any way? They chose*

---

[163] Bukhārī 3435; Aḥmad 22675. Of note, this *ḥadīth* only affirms that an individual fulfilling the mentioned conditions will be rewarded ultimately with Paradise. It does not deny a person being punished in Hellfire if he or she has perpetrated major sins. That some will be entered into Paradise even if they have no good deeds (which were accepted or carried out) is well known, and will also be discussed in Chapters Fourteen and Fifteen.

[164] Bukhārī 3446; Aḥmad 19,532. A similar *ḥadīth* is found in Muslim 154/387, Ibn Māja 1956 and Aḥmad 19,712, whereby it states that anyone of the People of the Book who believes in his prophet (i.e. Moses or Jesus) and then believes in the Prophet Muḥammad (may God bless them all) will be recompensed with double the reward.

it, and became wrongdoers.[165] God (Exalted is He) said of Aaron: *And Aaron indeed had told them beforehand: O my people! Ye are but being seduced therewith, for lo! your Lord is the Beneficent, so follow me and obey my order.*[166] Moses said to the Israelites, according to the Old Testament:

> Remember, and forget not, how thou provokedst the LORD thy God to wrath in the wilderness: from the day that thou didst depart out of the land of Egypt, until ye came unto this place, ye have been rebellious against the LORD. Also in Horeb ye provoked the LORD to wrath, so that the LORD was angry with you to have destroyed you. When I was gone up into the mount to receive the tables of stone, even the tables of the covenant which the LORD made with you, then I abode in the mount forty days and forty nights, I neither did eat bread nor drink water: And the LORD delivered unto me two tables of stone written with the finger of God; and on them was written according to all the words, which the LORD spake with you in the mount out of the midst of the fire in the day of the assembly. And it came to pass at the end of forty days and forty nights, that the LORD gave me the two tables of stone, even the tables of the covenant. And the LORD said unto me, Arise, get thee down quickly from hence; for thy people which thou hast brought forth out of Egypt have corrupted themselves; they are quickly turned aside out of the way which I commanded them; they have made them a molten image. Furthermore the LORD spake unto me, saying, I have seen this people, and, behold, it is a stiffnecked people: Let me alone, that I may destroy them, and blot out their name from under heaven: and I will make of thee a nation mightier and greater than they. So I turned and came down from the mount, and the mount burned with fire: and the two tables of the covenant were in my two hands. And I looked, and, behold, ye had sinned against the LORD your God, and had made you a molten calf: ye had turned aside quickly out of the way which the LORD had commanded you. And I took the two tablets, and cast them

---

165 Q.VII.148. Of note, in Exodus 32.1–5, the Israelites implausibly attribute evil to the Prophet Aaron: "The people gathered themselves together unto Aaron, and said unto him, Up, make us gods, which shall go before us... And Aaron said unto them, Break off the golden earrings... And he received them at their hand, and fashioned it with a graving tool, after he had made it a molten calf: and they said, These be thy gods, O Israel, which brought thee up out of the land of Egypt. And when Aaron saw it, he built an altar before it." See also Exodus 32.35: "And the LORD plagued the people, because they made the calf, which Aaron made."

166 Q.XX.85–90.

> out of my two hands, and brake them before your eyes. And I fell down before the LORD, as at the first, forty days and forty nights: I did neither eat bread, nor drink water, because of all your sins which ye sinned, in doing wickedly in the sight of the LORD, to provoke him to anger. For I was afraid of the anger and hot displeasure, wherewith the LORD was wroth against you to destroy you. But the LORD hearkened unto me at that time also. And the LORD was very angry with Aaron to have destroyed him:[167] and I prayed for Aaron also the same time. And I took your sin, the calf which ye had made, and burnt it with fire, and stamped it, and ground it very small, even until it was as small as dust: and I cast the dust thereof into the brook that descended out of the mount. And at Taberah, and at Massah, and at Kibroth-hattaavah, ye provoked the LORD to wrath. Likewise when the LORD sent you from Kadesh-barnea, saying, Go up and possess the land which I have given you; then ye rebelled against the commandment of the LORD your God, and ye believed him not, nor hearkened to his voice. Ye have been rebellious against the LORD from the day that I knew you.[168]

Next is the issue of the Israelites worshipping Baal, which is explained in the Bible in the following verses:

> And Israel abode in Shittim, and the people began to commit whoredom with the daughters of Moab. And they called the people unto the sacrifices of their gods: and the people did eat, and bowed down to their gods. And Israel joined himself unto Baal-peor: and the anger of the LORD was kindled against Israel. And the LORD said unto Moses, Take all the heads of the people, and hang them up before the LORD against the sun, that the fierce anger of the LORD may be turned away from Israel. And

---

[167] The Qur'ān does mention Moses telling Aaron: *O Aaron! What held thee back when thou didst see them gone astray, that thou followedst me not? Hast thou then disobeyed my order? He said: O son of my mother! Clutch not my beard nor my head! I feared lest thou shouldst say: Thou hast caused division among the Children of Israel, and hast not waited for my word.* [Q.XX.92–94]. Ṭabarī states that one interpretation is that Aaron was afraid that the Israelites would divide into two groups, and thereafter would fight against one another until the monotheists would become annihilated. See *Tafsīr al-Ṭabarī*, vol. XVIII, pp. 359–360.

[168] Deuteronomy 9.7–24.

Moses said unto the judges of Israel, Slay ye every one his men that were joined unto Baal-peor.[169]

There arose another generation after them, which knew not the LORD, nor yet the works which he had done for Israel. And the children of Israel did evil in the sight of the LORD, and served Baalim: And they forsook the LORD God of their fathers, which brought them out of the land of Egypt, and followed other gods, of the gods of the people that were round about them, and bowed themselves unto them, and provoked the LORD to anger. And they forsook the LORD, and served Baal and Ashtaroth. And the anger of the LORD was hot against Israel, and he delivered them into the hands of spoilers that spoiled them, and he sold them into the hands of their enemies round about, so that they could not any longer stand before their enemies.[170]

And the children of Israel did evil again in the sight of the LORD, and served Baalim, and Ashtaroth, and the gods of Syria, and the gods of Zidon, and the gods of Moab, and the gods of the children of Ammon, and the gods of the Philistines, and forsook the LORD, and served not him. And the anger of the LORD was hot against Israel, and he sold them into the hands of the Philistines, and into the hands of the children of Ammon... And the children of Israel cried unto the LORD, saying, We have sinned against thee, both because we have forsaken our God, and also served Baalim. And the LORD said unto the children of Israel, Did not I deliver you from the Egyptians, and from the Amorites, from the children of Ammon, and from the Philistines? The Zidonians also, and the Amalekites, and the Maonites, did oppress you; and ye cried to me, and I delivered you out of their hand. Yet ye have forsaken me, and served other gods: wherefore I will deliver you no more. Go and cry unto the gods which ye have chosen; let them deliver you in the time of your tribulation.[171]

---

169 Numbers 25.1–5. See also Q.VII.138–140: *And We brought the Children of Israel across the sea, and they came unto a people who were given up to idols which they had. They said: O Moses! Make for us a god even as they have gods. He said: Lo! ye are a folk who know not. As for these, their way will be destroyed and all that they are doing is in vain. He said: "Shall I seek for you a god other than the (true) God, when it is God Who hath endowed you with gifts above the nations?"*

170 Judges 2.10–14. See also Judges 3.7–8 and Judges 8.33–34.

171 Judges 10.6–14.

The Israelite kings Ahab[172] and his son Ahaziah[173] both worshipped Baal and likewise turned away from the commandments of the Holy Lord. The Prophets Elijah (or Elias/*Ilyās*) and Elisha (*al-Yasaʿ*), among others, condemned the Israelites' worship of Baal:

> And [Elijah] said, I have been very jealous for the LORD God of hosts: because the children of Israel have forsaken thy covenant, thrown down thine altars, and slain thy prophets with the sword; and I, even I only, am left; and they seek my life, to take it away. And the LORD said unto him, Go, return on thy way to the wilderness of Damascus: and when thou comest, anoint Hazael to be king over Syria: And Jehu the son of Nimshi shalt thou anoint to be king over Israel: and Elisha the son of Shaphat of Abel-meholah shalt thou anoint to be prophet in thy room. And it shall come to pass, that him that escapeth the sword of Hazael shall Jehu slay: and him that escapeth from the sword of Jehu[174] shall Elisha slay. Yet I have left me seven thousand in Israel, all the knees which have not bowed unto Baal, and every mouth which hath not kissed him.[175]

The Qur'ān affirms the role of the Prophet Elijah (i.e. Elias) in prohibiting the Israelites from worshipping Baal: *So also was Elias among those sent (by Us). Behold, he said to his people: Will ye not fear (God)? Will ye call upon Baal and forsake the Best of Creators? God, your Lord and Cherisher and the Lord and Cherisher of your fathers of old? But they rejected*

---

[172] See 1 Kings 16.30–32: "And Ahab the son of Omri did evil in the sight of the LORD above all that were before him. And it came to pass, as if it had been a light thing for him to walk in the sins of Jeroboam the son of Nebat, that he took to wife Jezebel the daughter of Ethbaal king of the Zidonians, and went and served Baal, and worshipped him. And he reared up an altar for Baal in the house of Baal, which he had built in Samaria. And Ahab made a grove; and Ahab did more to provoke the LORD God of Israel to anger than all the kings of Israel that were before him."

[173] See 1 Kings 22.51–53 which states that Ahaziah the son of Ahab "served Baal, and worshipped him, and provoked to anger the LORD God of Israel, according to all that his father had done".

[174] See 2 Kings 10.25–28: "Jehu said to the guard and to the captains, Go in, and slay them; let none come forth. And they smote them with the edge of the sword; and the guard and the captains cast them out, and went to the city of the house of Baal. And they brought forth the images out of the house of Baal, and burned them. And they brake down the image of Baal, and brake down the house of Baal, and made it a draught house unto this day. Thus Jehu destroyed Baal out of Israel."

[175] 1 Kings 19.14–18.

him, and they will certainly be called up (for punishment), except the sincere and devoted servants of God (among them).[176]

The condition of the Israelites is further explained in the Bible:

> And the [children of Israel] rejected [the LORD's] statutes, and his covenant that he made with their fathers, and his testimonies which he testified against them; and they followed vanity, and became vain, and went after the heathen that were round about them, concerning whom the LORD had charged them, that they should not do like them. And they left all the commandments of the LORD their God, and made them molten images, even two calves, and made a grove, and worshipped all the host of heaven, and served Baal. And they caused their sons and their daughters to pass through the fire, and used divination and enchantments, and sold themselves to do evil in the sight of the LORD, to provoke him to anger. Therefore the LORD was very angry with Israel, and removed them out of his sight: there was none left but the tribe of Judah only. Also Judah kept not the commandments of the LORD their God, but walked in the statutes of Israel which they made. And the LORD rejected all the seed of Israel... So was Israel carried away out of their own land to Assyria unto this day... Unto this day they do after the former manners: they fear not the LORD, neither do they after their statutes, or after their ordinances, or after the law and commandment which the LORD commanded the children of Jacob.[177]

These Biblical verses sufficiently illustrate the manner by which the early Israelites turned away from God's commandments.

The final matter concerns some of the Israelites who considered Ezra to be the son of God, and thus preceded the Christians in claiming a son for God (Glorious is He above that): *And the Jews say: Ezra is the son of God, and the Christians say: The Messiah is the son of God. That is their saying with their mouths. They imitate the saying of those who disbelieved of old. God (Himself) fighteth against them. How perverse are they!*[178] Now, there is no authentic Prophetic narration as to how many Jews claimed that Ezra was the son of God or their false reasoning for saying so.[179] It may have only been a small group similar to "the children of Belial" who rejected Saul (*Ṭālūt*) being named a

---

176 Q.XXXVII.123–128.

177 2 Kings 17.15–34.

178 Q.IX.30.

179 See *Tafsīr al-Ṭabarī*, vol. XIV, pp. 202–205, for some opinions.

king,[180] for in the Qur'ān it states: *Their Prophet said unto them: God hath raised up Saul to be a king for you. They said: How can he have kingdom over us when we are more deserving of the kingdom than he is, since he hath not been given wealth enough?*[181] Therefore, the statement of a group may be represented in the Qur'ān as *they* without specifying whether this group is a minority or a majority—it is sufficient that it was said by some. The point is that some Jews went astray by worshipping a human as a son of God, while a majority of the Christians have done so—but, of course, God is glorious and exalted above having a son.

Moreover, rather than completely following the Divine Law and commandments, some Jews and Christians altered the Scriptures. God (Glorious is He) mentions this in the Qur'ān: *And lo! there is a party of them who distort the Scripture with their tongues, that ye may think that what they say is from the Scripture, when it is not from the Scripture. And they say: It is from God, when it is not from God; and they speak a lie concerning God knowingly.*[182] Many inconsistencies of the New Testament were discussed earlier, therefore it will be contended that a greater number of these alterations and insertions were perpetrated by the Christian writers and scribes[183]—more than those done by the Jews in the Old

[180] See 1 Samuel 10.24–27: "When [Saul] stood among the people, he was higher than any of the people from his shoulders and upward. And Samuel said to all the people, See ye him whom the LORD hath chosen, that there is none like him among all the people? And all the people shouted, and said, God save the king… But the children of Belial said, How shall this man save us? And they despised him."

[181] Q.II.247.

[182] Q.III.78. It is more probable that verse Q.III.78 refers to the Christians since God (Glorious is He) states in the following verse: *It is not (possible) for any human being unto whom God had given the Scripture and wisdom and the prophethood that he should afterwards have said unto humankind: Be servants of me instead of God; but (what he said was): Be ye faithful servants of the Lord by virtue of your constant teaching of the Scripture and of your constant study thereof* (Q.III.79). See also Q.II.79 and Q.III.71.

[183] See also Ibn Taymiyya, *al-Jawāb al-ṣaḥīḥ*, vol. I, p. 794 where he states: "The reasonable and impartial scholars have no doubt that the transmission of the text of the Torah is more authentic than the transmission of the text of the Gospel." For more examples regarding the alteration of the New Testament, see Bart Ehrman, *Misquoting Jesus: The Story Behind Who Changed the Bible and Why* (New York: HarperOne, 2005).

Testament.[184] That being said, the latter included many blasphemous statements against the prophets, as alluded to previously. And God knows best.

In addition, God (Exalted is He) states that the Israelites killed many true prophets: *We took the covenant of the Children of Israel and sent them messengers; every time, there came to them a messenger with what they themselves desired not—some (of these) they called impostors, and some they (go so far as to) slay.*[185] Although some Jews of Medina, as well as Quraysh, tried to kill the Prophet Muḥammad, God (Almighty and Most Glorious is He) protected him from their attempts.

Moreover, when the Prophet Muḥammad (may God bless him and grant him peace) conveyed the message of Islam to the Jews of Medina, some of them replied: *Our hearts are covered (ghulf)—nay, but God set a seal upon them for their disbelief.*[186] That their hearts were covered and prevented from benefitting in general is corroborated[187] by Biblical verses such as: "Circumcise therefore the foreskin of your heart, and be no more stiffnecked,"[188] and "Circumcise yourselves to the Lord, and take away the foreskins of your heart, ye men of Judah and inhabitants of Jerusalem: lest my fury come forth like fire, and burn that none can quench it, because of the evil of your doings."[189] Thus it seems—and God knows best—that the Jews were claiming to the Prophet Muḥammad that their hearts were good but covered, and therefore they could not understand the guidance. The Holy Lord's response to them—*nay, but God set a seal upon them for their disbelief*—affirmed that the hearts of those Jews were evil as well as being veiled from the truth.

Now, God (Exalted is He) mentioned two evil statements of the Israelites or Jews in the Qur'ān that will be discussed and reconciled here. It should be noted that it is not mentioned when these statements were said, how many individuals said them, or whether they will

---

184 For examples regarding the Jews see Q.II.75; Q.IV.46; Q.V.13 and 41.

185 Q.V.70. God (Exalted is He) also mentioned in Q.II.61 and Q.III.112 that the Israelites killed some of the prophets sent to them.

186 Q. IV.155. Of note, Pickthall translates *ghulf* as "hardened".

187 See also Zeni (tr.), *Ibn Qayyim al-Jawziyya on Knowledge*, pp. 113–115.

188 Deuteronomy 10.16.

189 Jeremiah 4.4.

continue to be said or thought by them[190]. Nonetheless, it appears that the consequences of these statements are lasting. And God knows best.

The first statement is mentioned as follows: *The Jews say: God's hand is shackled. It is their own hands that are shackled; and rejected [by God] are they because of this assertion. Nay, but wide are His hands stretched out: He dispenses [bounty] as He wills.*[191] Here, their evil statement against God (Glorious and Exalted is He) by attributing inadequacy and miserliness to Him was punished by the Almighty Lord in kind, i.e. by making some of the Jews miserly.

The other evil statement of some of the Jews against the Holy Lord is relayed in the verse: *God has indeed heard the saying of those who said: Behold, God is poor while we are rich. We shall record what they have said, as well as their slaying of the prophets against all right, and We shall say [unto them on Judgment Day]: Taste suffering through Fire.*[192] So in this case God (Exalted is He) did not recompense them in kind and make all of the Jews poor. The reason for this is attributable to His wisdom. The Almighty Lord states in another set of verses:

> *And We decreed for the Children of Israel in the Scripture: Ye verily will work corruption in the earth twice, and ye will become great tyrants. So when the time for the first of the two came, We roused against you servants of Ours of great might who ravaged (your) country, and it was a threat performed. Then we gave you once again your turn against them, and We aided you with wealth and children and made you more in soldiery... So, when the time for the second (of the judgments) came (We roused against you others of Our servants) to ravage you, and to enter the Temple even as they entered it the first time, and to lay waste all that they conquered with an utter wasting. It may be that your Lord will have mercy on you, but if ye repeat (the crime) We shall repeat (the punishment), and We have appointed Hell a dungeon for the disbelievers.*[193]

---

190 See *Tafsīr al-Rāzī*, vol. IX, pp. 445–448, and vol. XII, pp. 393–394. See also Ibn Taymiyya, *Minhāj al-Sunna al-Nabawiyya*, vol. I, p. 37.

191 Q.V.64 (Muḥammad Asad translation).

192 Q.III.181.

193 Q.XVII.4–8. Of note, Pickthall translates *ʿibād* as "slaves" instead of "servants". The fact that Nebuchadnezzar's army consisted of servants should be understood in the ontological—not deontological—manner. The ontological sending of Nebuchadnezzar reflects the first instance of recompense for the Israelites turning away from the Lord in accordance with the promise enunciated by Moses in Deuteronomy 31.14–30 and other Biblical verses.

Therefore, the Almighty Lord allowed many Jews to amass wealth, which allows them as a group to perpetrate greater degrees of evil, including corruption and oppression. But some of the Jews' hands being shackled and their miserliness does not hinder them from corrupting and oppressing. Thus the Holy Lord, in His wisdom, recompensed them in kind in the first instance but not in the second.

God (Exalted is He) may thus grant wealth to the wicked, in spite of their corruption, for certain wise purposes. It should also be recalled that had these Israelites and Jews not warranted the wrath of God (Exalted is He) on many occasions,[194] He would not have dealt with them as mentioned and strategized against them. Finally, this strategizing is akin to *istidrāj*, wherein the Holy Lord grants blessings to some of the disbelievers and wicked in order to delude them into thinking that they are good and prevent them from mending their evil ways—this is, again, due to God's hatred of these wicked disbelievers and His wrath upon them. This will be discussed further in the next chapter.

It is interesting to note that Ibn Taymiyya also said in this regard: "[The Christian] claim that the Lord of the cosmos was afflicted with the pain of hunger, thirst, injury and crucifixion is worse than the statement of the Jews that God is poor or that He is miserly."[195] God is glorious and exalted above these blasphemous statements! Although both statements attribute inadequacy or evil to the Almighty Lord, the Christian claim *is* worse as it attributes greater degrees thereof to Him, blatantly denies His omnipotence and Glorious Attributes, and disavows true monotheism (by claiming that Jesus was divine).

Moreover, God (Exalted is He) states towards the end of the aforementioned verses, by way of warning the Jews: *[I]f ye repeat (the crime) We shall repeat (the punishment).*[196] This principle of God recompensing them according to their misdeeds (in many cases) is affirmed in verses of the Old Testament:

---

194 God (Exalted is He) states: *Thus have they drawn on themselves wrath upon wrath.* Q.II.90 (Yusuf Ali translation). See also the many Biblical verses mentioning God's wrath upon the Israelites in this, as well as other, chapters.

195 Ibn Taymiyya, *al-Jawab al-ṣaḥīḥ*, vol. I, p. 286.

196 Q.XVII.8.

> Moses commanded the Levites, which bare the ark of the covenant of the LORD, saying, Take this book of the law, and put it in the side of the ark of the covenant of the LORD your God, that it may be there for a witness against thee. For I know thy rebellion, and thy stiff neck: behold, while I am yet alive with you this day, ye have been rebellious against the LORD; and how much more after my death? Gather unto me all the elders of your tribes, and your officers, that I may speak these words in their ears, and call heaven and earth to record against them. For I know that after my death ye will utterly corrupt yourselves, and turn aside from the way which I have commanded you; and evil will befall you in the latter days; because ye will do evil in the sight of the LORD, to provoke him to anger through the work of your hands. And Moses spake in the ears of all the congregation of Israel the words of this song, until they were ended.[197]

Thus Moses (may God bless him) informed the Israelites that "evil would befall" them in their "latter days" because of the great evil and wickedness that they would perpetrate. Subsequent prophets, according to the Old Testament, also promised the Israelites that God would punish them for their transgressions and iniquities. These prophets included Amos,[198] Hosea,[199] Isaiah[200] and Jeremiah,[201] and their warnings were mentioned in a multitude of Biblical verses.

Notwithstanding, the Prophet Muḥammad (may God bless him and grant him peace) affirmed that the early[202] Israelites and Jews would be the second largest group of believers in Paradise after the Muslims.[203] Indeed, the Holy Lord has brought forth many prophets from amongst the Israelites, as well as righteous believers, and all of them will be rewarded accordingly.

---

[197] Deuteronomy 31.14–30. See also Deuteronomy 8.18–20, 11.26–28 and 28.15–68.

[198] See Amos 2.4–16, 3.1–15, 4.6–12, 5.1–3, 7.11 and 9.1–15.

[199] See Hosea 4.1–11, 6.4–11, 7.1–16, 8.1–8, 11.12 and 13.1–16.

[200] See Isaiah 1.1–31; 5.1–30; 6.8–13.

[201] See Jeremiah 1.1–18; 3.1–25; 5.11–31; 7.1–34; 9.13–26; 11.1–14; 15.1–2; 16.5; and 20.4.

[202] Here the early Israelites are defined as those living from the time between Jacob and Jesus, while the middle are those living between Jesus and Muḥammad, and the later Jews are those living from the time of Muḥammad until the Day of Judgment.

[203] See Bukhārī 5705; Muslim 220/527; Tirmidhī 2446; Aḥmad 2448.

Finally, beyond worshipping other deities and disobeying the commandments of the Holy Lord, many of the Jews and Christians: *have taken as lords beside God their rabbis and their monks and the Messiah son of Mary, when they were bidden to worship only One God. There is no god save Him. Be He Glorified from all that they ascribe as partner (unto Him)!*[204] The Prophet Muḥammad (may God bless him and grant him peace) explained this verse: "These [Jews and Christians] did not worship [their rabbis and monks/priests in a literal sense]; but if the latter deemed something [which was prohibited instead] as permissible or something [which was permissible] as forbidden, the [people] would follow the [rabbis and monks/priests instead of the Divine Law]. That was the manner of their worship."[205]

Rabbinical Judaism—the dominant form of the Jewish religion since the destruction of the Second Temple in 70 CE (particularly since 135 CE)—is based more on the Talmud and Midrash than the Torah. It was discussed previously that much of Christian theology is derived from the teachings of Paul and the Gospel of John. Eventually, papal infallibility regarding religious matters was canonized within Catholic doctrine. August Hasler lists some of the arguments held by the proponents of papal infallibility and then points out their weaknesses.[206] It is, however, beyond the scope of this book to delve

---

204 Q.IX.31.

205 Tirmidhī 3095; Bayhaqī (*Sunan*) 20,350. It is "sound" according to Albānī (*Silsilat al-aḥādīth al-ṣaḥīḥa* 3293).

206 See August Bernhard Hasler, *How the Pope Became Infallible: Pius IX and the Politics of Persuasion*, tr. Peter Heinegg (Garden City: Doubleday & Company, 1981), pp. 150–174. See also Brian Tierney, *Origins of Papal Infallibility, 1150–1350: A Study on the Concepts of Infallibility, Sovereignty, and Tradition in the Middle Ages* (Leiden: E. J. Brill, 1972), on his tracing of the arguments for papal infallibility. The two most important Scriptural verses argued by the proponents (as they state that the Popes followed Peter) are Matthew 16.18–19: "And I say also unto thee, That thou art Peter, and upon this rock I will build my church... And I will give unto thee the keys of the kingdom of heaven: and whatsoever thou shalt bind on earth shall be bound in heaven"; and Luke 22.32: "But I have prayed for thee [i.e. Peter], that thy faith fail not: and when thou art converted, strengthen thy brethren." Of note, in regards to an Islamic parallel, the Prophet Muḥammad (as mentioned in Chapter Six) confirmed that the Rightly-Guided Caliphs would follow him, yet he did not indicate that those Caliphs were infallible. In addition, the Prophet Muḥammad confirmed that ten of his Companions would remain faithful and be entered into Paradise, yet he did not indicate that they were infallible.

deeply into those arguments or interpretations.[207] Nonetheless, those Shiite sects of Islam that deem Imams to be infallible, and thus follow their commands even if in contravention to the Qur'ān or Sunna, are susceptible to the same criticism mentioned by the Prophet Muḥammad (may God bless him and grant him peace) in the *ḥadīth*. In contrast, traditional Islam has only encouraged the following of scholars or imams if they opine in accordance with the Qur'ān and Sunna, because only the prophets are infallible.

REJECTION OF THE SHIITE DOCTRINE OF IMAMATE AND OTHER IDEOLOGIES

In that light, details of the Shiite doctrine of the imamate as well as some of their other ideologies will be rejected. First, though, the Shiite claims that ʿAlī should have followed the Prophet Muḥammad, and that Abū Bakr, ʿUmar and ʿUthmān—the Rightly-Guided Caliphs (along with ʿAlī) discussed in Chapter Six—usurped the caliphate, will be refuted.

The Shiite claim that ʿAlī should have been the first Caliph primarily begins with events surrounding the Battle of Tabuk. At that time, the Prophet Muḥammad ordered ʿAlī to stay behind in Medina while he (may God bless him and grant him peace) marched along with Abū Bakr, ʿUmar, ʿUthmān and the other Companions to Tabuk. ʿAlī said: "Are you entrusting me to remain with the women and children?" The Prophet Muḥammad replied: "Are you not content to be like Aaron was to Moses? But there will be no prophet after me."[208] Here, the Prophet was referring to Aaron remaining and being entrusted with the Israelites, while Moses went to speak with God (Glorious is He) and receive the Tablets. Thus the Prophet was emphasizing the noble rank that ʿAlī possessed in this circumstance, and that his remaining behind was not due to some deficiency. It should be noted that the

---

207 Catholic theologians themselves have interpreted papal infallibility in a variety of manners. Mark Powell investigates the views of four Catholic theologians—Henry Edward Manning, John Henry Newman and Avery Dulles, and Hans Kung—who proposed maximal, moderate and minimal papal infallibility, respectively. See Mark E. Powell, *Papal Infallibility: A Protestant Evaluation of an Ecumenical Issue* (Grand Rapids: William B. Eerdmans Publishing, 2009), pp. 49–201.

208 Bukhārī 4416; Muslim 2404/6218; Aḥmad 1532.

Prophet did not make ʿAlī the leader of the entire Community and all of the Companions in this instance,[209] as Aaron was with the Israelites.

Furthermore, this narration is not an exact comparison between ʿAlī and Aaron from all standpoints. Aaron died many decades before Moses (may God bless them both), whereas ʿAlī remained alive many decades after the Prophet Muḥammad. Moreover, the Prophet Joshua followed Moses in leading the Israelites. Therefore, no evidence exists within this *ḥadīth* for ʿAlī becoming Caliph immediately after the Prophet Muḥammad. In addition, Aaron, while remaining behind with the Israelites, did not hold accountable those who made and worshipped the golden calf for fear of dividing the Israelites.[210] It cannot be said that ʿAlī (may God be pleased with him) adopted the same approach during his caliphate in order to avoid divisions when lesser offenses than polytheism occurred. This is another manner by which the comparison of Aaron and ʿAlī is not concordant. Finally, it should be noted that the Prophet Muḥammad said: "Had there been a prophet after me it would be ʿUmar [b. al-Khaṭṭāb]."[211] There does not exist a similar sound *ḥadīth* in regards to ʿAlī.[212]

Next, the Shiites allude to two sayings of the Prophet Muḥammad (may God bless him and grant him peace) at Ghadīr Khumm. Firstly, there is the *ḥadīth* in which the Prophet Muḥammad reminded his Companions of the importance of his family and relatives (*ahl bayt*[ihi]), which includes his wives and the families of ʿAlī, ʿAqīl, Jaʿfar and al-

---

[209] In reality, just as ʿUthmān remained behind during the Battle of Badr, ʿAlī remained behind during the Battle of Tabuk—both doing so at the command of the Prophet Muḥammad.

[210] See Q.XX.94.

[211] Tirmidhī 3686; Aḥmad 14,405; al-Ḥākim 4495. It is "sound" according to Albānī (*Silsilat al-aḥādīth al-ṣaḥīḥa* 327).

[212] As for the reason that the *ḥadīth* does not specify Abū Bakr instead of ʿUmar, it may be that the greater strength of ʿUmar during his caliphate in comparison to Abū Bakr (as foretold by the Prophet in another *ḥadīth* in Bukhārī 3633; Muslim 2392/6192; Tirmidhī 2289; Aḥmad 4814) enabled ʿUmar to be distinguished in such fashion.

ᶜAbbās,[213] by saying: "I remind you (*udhakkir*^ukum^) of my relatives." He did not say "follow (*ittabiᶜū*)" my family and relatives or "follow their methodology (*sunnat*^ihim^)". On the other hand, the Prophet said: "Follow my Sunna as well as the methodology (*sunna*) of the Rightly-Guided Caliphs after me."[214] Therefore, the *ḥadīth* said at Ghadīr Khumm does not indicate that the Prophet appointed his Household for the caliphate nor does it indicate that they are infallible sources of religious knowledge. Nor is the application of the former *ḥadīth* limited to ᶜAlī, Fātima and their offspring; rather, it includes all of the wives of the Prophet, amongst them ᶜĀ'isha, as well as all of the aforementioned families.

Abū Bakr's adherence to this commandment of the Prophet Muḥammad at Ghadīr Khumm is highlighted by his following statement: "By God, it is more beloved to me to keep the ties and do good to the relatives of the Messenger of God (may God bless him and grant him peace) than to do so to my own relatives."[215] He would also say: "Preserve [the memory] of Muḥammad (may God bless him and grant him peace) by [doing good] to his family and relatives."[216] Abū Bakr's actions were emulated by those who succeeded him, including ᶜUmar.[217]

Next, consider another *ḥadīth* in which the Prophet Muḥammad states: "I have left two things: the Book of God and the Sunna of

---

[213] See Muslim 2408/6225. It should be mentioned that the Prophet Muḥammad (may God bless him and grant him peace) said: "O people, I have left among you the Book of God and my family (*ᶜitratī ahl baytī*). If you hold fast to them, you will not go astray." Tirmidhī 3786; Aḥmad 11,561. It is "authentic" according to Albānī (*Silsilat al-aḥādīth al-ṣaḥīḥa* 1761). The Prophet's wives, amongst them ᶜĀ'isha, as well as the descendants of al-ᶜAbbās are included within his family (*ᶜitratī*). The Shiites, though, have turned away from many of the Prophet's Household—this will be discussed subsequently. As for a tradition attributed to the Prophet Muḥammad in al-Ḥākim (3312) and *Ḥilya* (vol. IV, p. 306): "The similitude of my Household is like Noah's ship; whoever embarks on it is saved, whereas those who fail to do so will be drowned," it is "weak" according to Albānī (*Silsilat al-aḥādīth al-ḍaᶜīfa* 4503: vol X, pp. 5–11).

[214] Tirmidhī 2676; Ibn Māja 42; Aḥmad 17,142; Ibn Ḥibbān 5; al-Ḥākim 329; Bayhaqī (*Sunan*) 20,338. It is "authentic" according to Albānī (*Silislat al-aḥādīth al-ṣaḥīḥa* 2735).

[215] Bukhārī 3711; Muslim 1759/4580; Aḥmad 55.

[216] Bukhārī 3713.

[217] See Ibn Taymiyya, *Minhāj al-Sunna al-Nabawiyya*, vol. VI, pp. 176–177.

His Prophet. If you hold fast to them, you will not go astray."[218] But the Shiites, who have criticised the Companions and disregarded the narrations of the vast majority of them,[219] have thus turned away from almost all of the Prophetic Sunna. Love of the Companions (both the *Muhājirīn* and the *Anṣār*), who accompanied the Prophet Muḥammad in all that he accomplished by the grace of God and thereafter relayed his Sunna as per his directive, is important (as per the *ḥadīth*[220]) just as is love of the Household of the Prophet.

Following the entirety of the Prophetic Sunna is also incumbent upon every Muslim. One cannot selectively implement only parts of a *ḥadīth* or some *ḥadīth*s (or worse yet misinterpret them), while ignoring other parts or other *ḥadīth*s. Those who implement parts of the Qur'ān and Sunna, while ignoring other parts, should fear that their faith is incomplete, and that they will only be considered as Muslims—not as believers—or worse yet as corrupt individuals (*fāsiqūn*).

In addition, Ibn Taymiyya discusses and maintains that the majority of the Household of the Prophet did not follow Shiite theology.[221] For instance, they did not follow the Twelve Imām Shiite claim that the

---

218 Al-Ḥākim 318; Bayhaqī (*Sunan*) 20,336; *Muwaṭṭa' al-Imām Mālik* 46.3. It is "sound" according to Albānī (*Mishkāt* 186).

219 Etan Kohlberg explains: "For Shiʿis, the reason for excluding the Companions from the chains of transmission are twofold: first, most Companions either acquiesced in, or actively supported the usurpation of power from ʿAlī; second, the Companions lacked probity (*ʿadāla*) and cannot therefore be considered reliable transmitters." Etan Kohlberg, "Introduction" to Shiite *ḥadīth*, in Farhad Daftary and Gurdofarid Miskinzoda (eds), *The Study of Shiʿi Islam: History, Theology and Law* (London: I.B.Tauris and The Institute of Ismaili Studies, 2014), p. 168. This chapter and others upholds the unparalleled integrity and honesty of the Companions as well as their devotion to fulfilling the commands of the Prophet Muḥammad (may God bless him and grant him peace).

220 Recall, as mentioned in Chapter Six, that the Prophet Muḥammad said: "A sign of faith is love of the Medinite supporters (*Anṣār*), while a sign of hypocrisy is hatred of the supporters." Bukhārī 17; Muslim 74/235; Nasā'ī 5019; Aḥmad 12,316. It appears, and God knows best, that the Prophet specified the Medinite supporters due to the fact that they would not become the leaders of this Community—but rather the Meccan emigrants would—and thus love of the former by the later Muslims may be underdeveloped in relation to love of the Meccan emigrants. The point is that love of both the Medinite supporters as well as the Meccan emigrants is part of the faith.

221 Ibn Taymiyya, *Minhāj al-Sunna al-Nabawiyya*, vol. IV, p. 16. See also ibid, vol. I, p. 69; vol. II, pp. 46, 100, 243 and 369; vol. VII, pp. 181, 395–397 and 408; vol. VIII, p. 252.

Word of God is created nor the Shiite denial of the Beatific Vision.[222] In addition, the early Imāmī Shiite doctrine of *badā'*[223] was not held by traditional Muslims who believed that God (Glorious is He) is Omniscient and affirmed His determination (*qadar*). The Imāmī concept of *badā'* is explained by Wilferd Madelung in the following manner:

> *badā'* [indicates the] change of a decision of God in view of a change in circumstances... God's decision on human acts and human history thus must remain 'suspended' [*mawqūfa*], subject to advancement and postponement, until the autonomous choice of His creatures has occurred, when His definite decision is made... Imāmī theology rejected the concept of an eternal immutable will of God... God's will, rather, consisted of numerous ad hoc acts of will in time... The early Imāmī *kalām* theologians...accepted that God cannot know things either before they exist or before He wills them... Since God's will develops over time in multiple acts of will, His knowledge must also develop and change in time. Most Muslim theologians [therefore]...accused the Imāmī scholars of describing God as ignorant (*jāhil*) in pre-eternity.[224]

Furthermore, Ibn Taymiyya maintains that the majority of the Household of the Prophet denied the doctrine of the imamate and that the vast majority of the Household agreed that Abū Bakr and ᶜUmar should precede ᶜAlī in the caliphate.[225] Indeed, it should be mentioned that the Shiites have rejected those within the Household of the Prophet Muḥammad who are not descendants of ᶜAlī and Fāṭima, as well as those who have disagreed with their theology and doctrine.[226]

---

[222] See Abbas Muhajirani, "Twelve-Imām Shi'ite theological and philosophical thought", in Seyyed Hossein Nasr and Oliver Leaman (eds.), pp. 128–129 and 135.

[223] See Ibn Taymiyya, *Minhāj al-Sunna al-Nabawiyya*, vol. II, pp. 394–395.

[224] Wilferd Madelung, "Early Imāmī Theology as Reflected in the *Kitāb al-kāfī* of al-Kulaynī", in Daftary and Miskinzoda (eds.), *The Study of Shiᶜi Islam*, pp. 473–474. Madelung goes on to say: "The tenet of *badā'* ... lost its significance as Imāmī theology adopted Muᶜtazilī concepts"; however, in the 17th century Mullā Ṣadrā "revive[d] and reinterpret[ed] some early Imāmī tenets, in particular that of *badā'*." Ibid, pp. 459 and 474.

[225] See Ibn Taymiyya, *Minhāj al-Sunna al-Nabawiyya*, vol. VII, pp. 396–397.

[226] See Muḥammad Rashīd Riḍā, *Rasā'il al-Sunna wa'l-Shīᶜa* (Cairo: Dār al-Manār, 1947), vol I, pp. 55–56, for a list of some of the prominent individuals within the Household of the Prophet Muḥammad who have been rejected by the Shiites.

The Prophet Muḥammad said, as mentioned previously: "Follow my Sunna as well as the methodology (*sunna*) of the Rightly-Guided Caliphs after me."[227] The Prophet did not foretell that those who followed him would be illegitimate or would usurp the caliphate. Instead, the Prophet advised us to follow the methodology of each and every Rightly-Guided Caliph who followed him for those thirty years,[228] i.e. to follow that which accords with his authentic Sunna. Moreover, the Prophet Muḥammad foretold in another *ḥadīth* that the caliphates of Abū Bakr and ʿUmar would be first: "Follow the example of my two companions who will come after me: Abū Bakr and ʿUmar."[229] In addition, the Prophet Muḥammad promised that the first three generations of the Muslims, i.e. the Predecessors, would be granted victory.[230]

The second *ḥadīth* of the Prophet at Ghadīr Khumm that is relevant to our discussion is the following: "Whoever I am the guardian of (*mawlā*^hu^), ʿAlī is his guardian. May God support those who support [ʿAlī] and oppose those who oppose him."[231] It should be noted first that the believers are guardians and supporters of each other, as mentioned by God (Exalted is He): *And the believers, men and women, are protecting friends one of another; they enjoin the right and forbid the wrong, and they establish prayer and they pay zakat, and they obey God and His Messenger. As for these, God will have mercy on them.*[232] Therefore, although the aforementioned *ḥadīth* grants ʿAlī a distinguished and noble status, each and every believer is a guardian (*mawlā*) of another.

---

227 Tirmidhī 2676; Ibn Māja 42; Aḥmad 17,142; Ibn Ḥibbān 5; al-Ḥākim 329; Bayhaqī (*Sunan*) 20,338. It is "authentic" according to Albānī (*Silislat al-aḥādīth al-ṣaḥīḥa* 2735).

228 See Tirmidhī 2226; Abū Dāwūd 4646; Aḥmad 21,919; al-Ḥākim 4697; Ibn Ḥibbān 6943. It is "sound" according to Albānī (*Silsilat al-aḥādīth al-ṣaḥīḥa* 459 and *Ṣaḥīḥ al-Jāmiʿ al-ṣaghīr* 3257).

229 Tirmidhī 3805; Aḥmad 23,245; al-Ḥākim 4451; Bayhaqī (*Sunan*) 10,056. It is "authentic" according to Albānī (*Silsilat al-aḥādīth al-ṣaḥīḥa* 1233). It is noteworthy that the remainder of the *ḥadīth* states: "And follow the guidance of ʿAmmār and hold fast to the advice (*ʿahd*) of Ibn Masʿūd."

230 See Bukhārī 2897; Muslim 2532/6467.

231 Aḥmad 950; al-Ḥākim 4601; Ibn Ḥibbān 6931. It is "authentic" according to Albānī (*Silsilat al-aḥādīth al-ṣaḥīḥa* 1750). See also Tirmidhī 3713, Ibn Māja 121 and Aḥmad 641 wherein the Prophet Muḥammad states: "Whoever I am the guardian of (*mawlā*^hu^), ʿAlī is his guardian."

232 Q.IX.71.

Second, it is clear that the wording of this *ḥadīth* does not indicate that the Prophet nominated or appointed ʿAlī to be the *next* Caliph. However, it does indicate that the Prophet Muḥammad commanded and advised the believers to support ʿAlī and that he would support them. Third, the fact that the Prophet mentioned this *ḥadīth* while he was alive also affirms that he did not intend by "guardian" (*mawlā*) that ʿAlī was a Caliph, as there cannot be two Caliphs ruling the believers at the same time.[233] Fourth, it should be mentioned that there is a difference between *mawlā*, which can indicate guardian, master or supporter (or even the opposite meaning of client or protégé), and the word *walī*, which means ruler. Fifth, Nāṣir al-Dīn al-Albānī has mentioned that any claims to a prophetic tradition stating that ʿAlī "will be the Caliph after me" are fabricated. He continues by stating:

> And if we hypothesize that the Prophet (may God bless him and grant him peace) indeed said that, then it would have inevitably occurred as per his prophesy, since he is *an inspiration that is inspired* [Q.LIII.4] and God (Glory be to Him) does not betray His promise... I have also discussed many other *ḥadīths* [that have been fabricated] concerning this matter in [*Silsilat al-aḥadīth al-ḍaʿīfa wa'l-mawḍūʿa*, including numbers] 4923 and 4932.[234]

Finally, the Prophet Muḥammad said: "There will be twelve Caliphs...all of them from Quraysh."[235] Note that the Prophet did not mention that they would be from ʿAlī and his descendants nor did he mention that these twelve would arise from Banū Hāshim; rather, he mentioned that they would include Caliphs from all of Quraysh. This accords with the reality of Islamic history, whether the Rightly-Guided Caliphs, the Umayyads, the ʿAbbāsids or subsequent dynasties. Moreover, only two of the Imams claimed by the Twelver Shiites actually were Caliphs ruling over the believers, i.e. ʿAlī and

---

233 See Ibn Taymiyya, *Minhāj al-Sunna al-Nabawiyya*, vol. VII, pp. 324–325.

234 See Albānī, *Silsilat al-aḥadīth al-ṣaḥīḥa,* vol. IV, p. 344.

235 Muslim 1821/4705; Abū Dāwūd 4279; Aḥmad 20,814. See also Bukhārī 7222, Tirmidhī 2223 and Aḥmad 20,817, which describe each of the twelve as a ruler (*amīr*). This is reminiscent of the following Biblical verse: "And as for Ishmael, I have heard thee: Behold, I have blessed him, and will make him fruitful, and will multiply him exceedingly; twelve princes shall he beget, and I will make him a great nation." Genesis 17.20.

al-Ḥasan[236], while the Safavids and others were not definitively descended[237] from ʿAlī and Fātima.

Now, ʿAlī b. Abī Ṭālib assumed the caliphate at a time of great tribulation due to the martyrdom of ʿUthmān. It is important to note that the Prophet Muḥammad had prophesized that conflict would occur: "Whoever lives will see after [my death] much discord (*ikhtilāf kathīr*)."[238] However, the greatest discord did not occur until the end of ʿUthmān's caliphate, and thereafter continued into ʿAlī's caliphate (as well as thereafter). This internecine war occurred between two groups of believers: first at the Battle of al-Jamal; and the second at Ṣiffīn. These will be discussed in the next chapter.

Due to the aforementioned events, as well as others, some have resorted to maligning the Companions of the Prophet. But such people should first know that the Prophet Muḥammad (may God bless him and grant him peace) said: "Do not curse [or slander] (*tasubbū*) my Companions. By God, in Whose Hand is my soul, if any of you were to give in charity gold as much as the mountain of Uḥud, you would not be able to attain [the same reward] as them."[239] Moreover, some groups have employed the cursing of the Companions as part of their methodology. Consider the Twelver Shiites of the Safavid empire[240] who would execute any Sunni Muslim who refused to curse Abū

---

236 It should be noted that al-Ḥasan is not considered by the Ismāʿīlī Shiites to be an Imam.

237 Roger Savory mentions that great doubt exists regarding eight links of the official Safavid genealogy they trace back to Mūsā al-Kāẓim. See Roger Savory, *Iran Under the Safavids* (Cambridge: Cambridge University Press, 2007), p. 3.

238 Tirmidhī 2676; Abū Dāwūd 4607; Ibn Māja 43; Aḥmad 17,142; Ibn Ḥibbān 5; al-Ḥākim 329; Bayhaqī (*Sunan*) 20,338. It is "authentic" according to Albānī (*Silislat al-aḥādīth al-ṣaḥīḥa* 2735). The Prophet Muḥammad then states within this *ḥadīth*: "Follow my Sunna as well as the methodology (*sunna*) of the Rightly-Guided Caliphs after me."

239 Bukhārī 3673; Muslim 2540/6487; Tirmidhī 3861; Abū Dāwūd 4658; Ibn Māja 161; Aḥmad 11,516.

240 After Ismāʿīl I founded the Safavid dynasty in 1501, he ordered the killing of the Sunni scholars and forced the conversion of citizens from Sunni Islam to Shiism. See Colin P. Mitchell, *The Practice of Politics in Safavid Iran: Power, Religion and Rhetoric* (London: Tauris Academic Studies, 2009), pp. 21–35 and 72–87; Roger Savory, *Iran Under the Safavids*, pp. 27–30; Rudi Matthee, *Persian in Crisis: Safavid Decline and the Fall of Isfahan* (London: I. B. Tauris, 2012), pp. 14 and 173–176.

Bakr, ʿUmar or ʿUthmān.[241] This phenomenon has been explained by Roger Savory:

> Shīʿīs believe that Muḥammad formally designated ʿAlī as his successor (*khalīfa*) at a ceremony at Ghadīr Khumm in the year 632. Shiʿīs therefore regard the first three caliphs (Abū Bakr, ʿUmar and ʿUthmān) as usurpers, and the ritual cursing of these persons has always been a proper duty of Shīʿīs, although the emphasis placed on it varied from time to time. In the early days of the Safavid state, when revolutionary fervor was still strong, great emphasis was placed on this ritual cursing. Safavid supporters...walked through the streets and bazaars cursing not only the three "rightly-guided" caliphs mentioned above, but also all enemies of ʿAlī and the other Imāms, and Sunnīs in general. Anyone who failed to respond without delay, "May it [the cursing] be more and not less!", was liable to be put to death on the spot.[242]

How can one have a pure[243] and merciful heart if one thinks evil or curses the great Companions who spread Islam, preserved the Qur'ān and relayed the Sunna? The Prophet Muḥammad condemned cursing

---

[241] See Colin P. Mitchell, *The Practice of Politics in Safavid Iran*, pp. 75–85; Roger Savory, *Iran Under the Safavids*, pp. 27–29; Andrew Newman, *Safavid Iran: Rebirth of a Persian Empire* (London: I. B. Tauris, 2009), pp. 155–156. For further thoughts on cursing during the Safavid empire, see Rula Abisaab, *Converting Persia: Religion and Power in the Safavid Empire* (London: I. B. Tauris, 2004), pp. 26–27, 34–35 and 46–48.

[242] Savory, *Iran Under the Safavids*, pp. 27–28. It should be mentioned that this does not indicate that all Twelve-Imam Shiites curse Abū Bakr, ʿUmar and ʿUthmān. See, for example, Andrew Newman, *Safavid Iran: Rebirth of a Persian Empire*, p. 162. However, their practice of dissimulation (*taqiyya*) renders it difficult, if not impossible, to discern amongst them. See Rula Abisaab, *Converting Persia*, pp. 34–35, for an historical example of this. Of note, Shiites claim that dissimulation is based on verse Q.III.28: *Let not the believers take disbelievers for their [allies in war] in preference to believers. Whoso doeth that hath no connection with God unless (it be) that ye but guard yourselves against them, taking (as it were) security.* The reality though is that since the Shiites are a minority (being approximately 15%), they often rely on the disbelievers (except in the case of the Safavids) to empower themselves against the majority Sunnis. Therefore, the Shiites have disobeyed the principle commandment of that verse, yet have advocated dissimulation (when dealing with the Sunnis as well as others) to serve their desired ends.

[243] It is crucial to possess a pure and sound heart as God (Exalted is He) states regarding the Day of Judgment: *The Day whereon neither wealth nor sons will avail, but only he (will prosper) that brings to God a sound heart.* See Q.XXVI.88-89 (Yusuf Ali translation).

in general[244] and avoided it himself: "I have not been sent to curse others, but instead I have been sent as a mercy [to humankind],"[245] and: "Cursing another Muslim is wickedness [or lewdness] (*fusūq*)."[246] Furthermore, God (Exalted is He) said: *Bad is the name of lewdness (al-fusūq) after faith. And whoso turneth not in repentance, such are evildoers (ẓālimūn).*[247] Thus it will be contended that those who curse the Companions—the former are actually wrongdoers (*ẓālimūn*). Although those who curse may still be considered as Muslims, they will fail to reach the rank of believers (*mu'minūn*), never mind the higher ranks.

One should also take heed when God (Exalted is He) mentions that enraging the disbelievers is one objective behind the existence of the Companions: *Muḥammad is the Messenger of God. And those with him are hard against the disbelievers... that He may enrage the disbelievers.*[248] Mālik b. Anas, the eponymous founder of a Sunni school of jurisprudence, commented: "Thus anyone who feels hatred against any of the Companions of the Messenger (may God bless him and grant him peace) [should be concerned] that this verse applies to him."[249]

Moreover, there is no authentic record of the Prophet Muḥammad (may God bless him and grant him peace) criticizing Abū Bakr, ʿUmar or ʿUthmān to any significant degree during his prophethood—the same cannot be said of ʿAlī as a matter of fact.[250] Nor did the Prophet

---

244 See Muslim 2597/6608; Tirmidhī 2019; Aḥmad 8447 and 20,678; al-Ḥākim 145; Bayhaqī (*Shuʿab*) 4788. These are "authentic" according to Albānī (*Silsilat al-aḥādīth al-ṣaḥīḥa* 2635 and 2637). In some of these *ḥadīths* the Prophet says: "It is not appropriate for a truly faithful believer (*ṣiddīq*) to curse," while in others he states: "It is not appropriate for a believer (*mu'min*) to curse." As for verses Q.II.161 and Q.III.87, where all of humanity (*al-nās*) will damn and curse the disbelievers, this will occur on the Day of Judgment as indicated in Q.XXIX.25, since even the disbelievers (of the same religion) will do so to each other. See also *Tafsīr al-Rāzī* vol. IV, pp. 143; *Tafsīr al-Ṭabarī*, vol. III, p. 262.

245 Muslim 2599/6613.

246 Bukhārī 48; Muslim 64/221; Tirmidhī 1983; Ibn Māja 69; Nasā'ī 4109; Aḥmad 3647.

247 Q.XLIX.11.

248 Q.XLVIII.29.

249 Abū Nuʿaym, *Ḥilya*, vol. VI, pp. 326–327.

250 There are two instances: the first involves ʿAlī desiring to marry the daughter of Abū Jahl, wherein the Prophet Muḥammad said: "I do not give my consent. I do not give my consent. I do not give my consent except if he wishes to divorce my daughter and marry

Muḥammad ever prophesize that any of the four Rightly-Guided Caliphs would go astray. Instead, the Messenger was pleased with them and promised all four of them Paradise, but prophesized that conflict and discord would occur in general without attributing it to any one of them.

It should be acknowledged that if the Holy Lord and His prophets are pleased with any particular person then such pleasure takes precedence over all other considerations, regardless of the detractors' claims regarding the individual. God (Glorious is He) declared after the Battle of Tabuk, as mentioned previously, that the Companions have gained His pleasure, and there is nothing greater than the pleasure of God—it is what we all should seek. Those who criticize the Companions—most prominent among them being Abū Bakr, ᶜUmar, ᶜUthmān and ᶜAlī—have thought themselves to be more knowledgeable and wiser than the Holy Lord. In addition, how can one have a sound and content heart if one rejects both God's religious and ontologic decree in the ordering of the Rightly-Guided Caliphs after the Prophet? Interestingly, the Shiite principles of religion replaced belief in God's predestination[251] with belief in the imamate.[252]

As for their Imams, the Shiites hold that the imamate passed down from father to son by declaration (*naṣṣ*) in all cases. The Twelvers allowed an exception for a brother to pass it onto a brother in the case

---

[Abū Jahl's daughter]." Bukhārī 5230; Muslim 2449/6307; Tirmidhī 3867; Abū Dāwūd 2071; Ibn Māja 1998; Aḥmad 18,926. The second instance occurred after the Prophet Muḥammad advised ᶜAlī and Fāṭima to carry out the night prayers whereupon ᶜAlī responded: "Our souls are in God's Hands. If He wills to make us get up, we will rise to [pray]." The Prophet Muḥammad turned away and recited: *But man is more than anything contentious* [Q.XVIII.54]. See Bukhārī 1127; Muslim 775/1818; Nasā'ī 1611; Aḥmad 900.

251 The Prophet Muḥammad included belief in God's predestination within the pillars of faith. See Muslim 8/93; Tirmidhī 2610; Abū Dāwūd 4695; Ibn Māja 63; Nasā'ī 4993; Aḥmad 191.

252 This does not indicate that the Shiites do not believe in God's predestination—only that they dropped it from being a pillar of faith. The "five principles of religion (*uṣūl al-dīn*)" in Shiᶜism include: belief in Divine Unity, prophesy, resurrection, Imamate and Divine Justice. It should also be noted that Shiites often allude to Ibn ᶜArabī's concept of sainthood (*wilāya*) as substantiating their concept of imamate. See Sayyid Muḥammad Ḥusayn Ṭabāṭabā'ī, *Shiᶜite Islam*, ed. and tr. Seyyid Hossein Nasr (Albany: State University of New York Press, 1975), pp. 10–11 and 114–115; and Sayeh Meisami, *Mulla Sadra* (London: Oneworld Publications, 2013), pp. 2–4 and 124–125.

of al-Ḥasan and al-Ḥusayn. In no case did one of them pass it to his cousin. Divisions and new sects appeared particularly after the death of their Imam Jaᶜfar, since he originally declared his son Ismāᶜīl to be the next Imam,[253] yet Ismāᶜīl died before Jaᶜfar's death. This led some to question how an Imam could be deemed to be infallible, yet err in such an important matter and principle (*aṣl*) as to whom the imamate should be passed. A lasting split in the Shiites subsequently occurred with the Ismāᶜīlīs considering Muḥammad b. Ismāᶜīl as the next Imam, while the Twelvers considered another of Jaᶜfar's sons, Mūsā al-Kāẓim, to be their Imam. Others held that Jaᶜfar's eldest son ᶜAbd Allāh al-Aftaḥ was the next Imam, but he also died within seventy days.

In three subsequent cases, the imamate was passed on to minors: Muḥammad b. ᶜAlī al-Jawād, ᶜAlī b. Muḥammad al-Hādī (their ninth and tenth Imams respectively) and Muḥammad b. al-Ḥasan, their Twelfth Imam. This also led to questions as to how a minor could have the special religious knowledge necessary to be an Imam.

In addition, after the death of the Twelver's eleventh Imam al-Ḥasan al-ᶜAskarī in 874 CE, a period of confusion (*ḥayra*) ensued, as he did not leave a "manifest heir"; and thus they split into more than a dozen groups.[254] It was later stated by the Twelvers that al-Ḥasan al-ᶜAskarī had a child five years before his death named Muḥammad, but that the child was hidden and thereafter went into a lesser occultation (where they believed he was communicating with others via four subsequent chief emissaries) followed by a greater occultation after 941 CE (whereby he remains incommunicado). The Twelvers thus proposed that their Twelfth Imam, Muḥammad b. al-Ḥasan, will live a miraculously long life and return as a Mahdī near the end of times.

Of note, Farhad Daftary lists more than thirty different Shiite sects, which arose due to disputes regarding succession nearly each time an Imam died.[255] These sects either became marginalized or extinct or

---

[253] Farhad Daftary states: "According to the majority of the available sources, Imam al-Sadiq had originally designated his second son Ismaᶜil, the eponym of the Ismaᶜiliyya, as his successor to the imamate by the rule of the *nass*." Farhad Daftary, *A History of Shiᶜi Islam* (London: I. B. Tauris and The Institute of Ismaili Studies, 2013), p. 106.

[254] Ibid, pp. 63–64.

[255] Ibid, pp. 25–190.

led to or became grouped broadly under Twelvers, Ismāʿīlīs,[256] Zaydīs and Nuṣayrīs/ʿAlawīs.[257] It thus becomes clear that the Shiites have disputed and disagreed over the centuries regarding one of their five principles of the religion, i.e. the specifics of the imamate and the identities of their Imams.

It was alluded to earlier that kings and Caliphs are discussed in the Qur'ān and Sunna. That said, the Qur'ān never mentions infallible imams. Had the doctrine of infallible Imams been true, certainly its mention would have taken precedence over that of kings. The Qur'ān does not mention belief in the imamate as an article of faith, neither in verses 1–5, 177 or 285 of Sūrat al-Baqara, nor in any other verse within the Qur'ān.[258] Mention of infallible Imams is also absent in the statement of God (Glorious is He): *Whoso obeyeth God and the Messenger, they are with those unto whom God hath shown favour, of the prophets and the saints (al-ṣiddīqīn) and the martyrs and the righteous. The best of company are they!*[259]

Moreover, there is no mention in any Qur'ānic verse that the "Imams" should be referred to; rather, God (Glorious is He) states: *If ye have a dispute concerning any matter, refer it to God and the Messenger*

---

[256] The Ismāʿīlī doctrine holds that there were seven Imams (ʿAlī, al-Ḥusayn, ʿAlī Zayn al-ʿĀbidīn, Muḥammad, Jaʿfar, Ismāʿīl and Muḥammad b. Ismāʿīl) and that Muḥammad b. Ismāʿīl will return as a Mahdī whereby he shall "fully divulge the esoteric truths of all the preceding revelations". That said, Ismāʿīlīs currently resort to esoteric interpretations of the Qur'ān not based upon other verses of the Qur'ān nor the Sunna. They believe in the cyclical nature of history into seven eras. They incorporated an emanational cosmology and Neoplatonic philosophy into their creed. Some Ismāʿīlī scholars adopted antinomian views (*suqūt al-taklīf*). See Daftary, *A History of Shiʿi Islam*, pp. 105–144, as well as Daftary, *The Ismāʿīlīs: Their History and Doctrines* (New York: Cambridge University Press, 2007 Second Edition), pp. 223–237.

[257] The Twelvers, Ismāʿīlīs and Zaydis held that their Imams (including ʿAlī) were human, whereas the ʿAlawīs held that God incarnated (*ḥulūl*) in ʿAlī—God is exalted above such heresy! All of the groups disagreed regarding the identities of the Imams as well as a vast array of other theological and jurisprudential matters.

[258] Of note, although the Shiites agree that the Qur'ān is the infallible Word of God, they discard the vast majority of the *ḥadīth*s of the Prophet Muḥammad (may God bless him and grant him peace) as they criticize (and some of them curse) the Companions who narrated these *ḥadīth*s since the Companions accepted and gave pledge to Abū Bakr al-Ṣiddīq, ʿUmar and ʿUthmān.

[259] Q.IV.69.

if ye are (in truth) believers in God and the Last Day.[260] Finally, claiming that infallible and divinely-inspired Imams are necessary implies that the Prophet Muḥammad did not complete the message of Islam; but God (Exalted is He) states: *This day have I perfected your religion for you, completed My favour upon you, and have chosen for you Islam as your religion.*[261] In conclusion, there is no definitive proof or reference to an infallible Imam in the Qur'ān.[262]

The Prophet Muḥammad (may God bless him and grant him peace) did state: "There will always exist a group from my Community upon the truth." [263] However, there is no mention of an infallible Imam leading them or even being amongst them. Whilst some of the Shiite arguments for the need of infallible Imams are that they represent guardians of the religion for the purposes of Divine compassion/providence (*luṭf*) and to provide advantages (*maṣlaḥa*) for the believers,[264] the reality is that those they deemed to be Imams—although many of them were great religious scholars—did not empower the Muslims or have a significant impact upon the spread of Islam. Certainly their effectiveness in enjoining and promoting

---

260 Q.IV.59.

261 Q.V.3 (Yusuf Ali translation). This verse was revealed on the Day of ʿArafāt during the Farewell Pilgrimage. See Muslim 3017/7525; Nasā'ī 3002. This was nine days before Ghadīr Khumm, and therefore it cannot be claimed that ʿAlī is involved in the completion of the religion as an infallible imam.

262 See Sayyid Ṭabāṭabā'ī, *Shi'ite Islam*, pp. 173–190, for many of their arguments (most of which were addressed in the text). Some of the main Shiite references are verses addressed to Abraham, Isaac, Jacob and his righteous descendants: *I have appointed thee a leader (imam) for humankind.* [*Abraham*] *said: And of my offspring* [*will there be leaders*]*? He said: My covenant includeth not wrongdoers.* [Q.II.124]. *And We made them chiefs who guide by Our command, and We inspired in them the doing of good deeds and the right establishment of worship and the giving of alms, and they were worshippers of Us (alone).* [Q.XXI.73]. However, it is well known that prior scriptures never mentioned the presence of infallible imams, and therefore they stated that imams of prior nations/revelations remained secret, while those of the Prophet Muḥammad were known. Consider also Q.XXXII.24 and Q.XXVIII.5 wherein the weak believers were empowered to become leaders and inspired to do good deeds. Finally, consider Q.IX.12 and Q.XXVIII.41 where the plural of imam (*a'imma*) refers to the leaders of the disbelievers (both in this worldly life and in Hellfire).

263 Muslim 1920/4950; Tirmidhī 2229; Abū Dāwūd 4252; Ibn Māja 10.

264 See Sayyid Muhammad Husayn Ṭabāṭabā'ī, "The Imams and the Imamate", in Seyyed Hossein Nasr, Hamid Dabashi and Seyyed Vali Reza Nasr (eds.), *Shiʿism: Doctrines, Thought, and Spirituality* (Albany: State University of New York Press, 1988), pp. 163–165.

righteousness was less than that of the four Rightly-Guided Caliphs. Likewise, their existence did not lessen the presence of evil on a wide scale, in contrast to the successes of Abū Bakr, ʿUmar and ʿUthmān in this regard.

In addition, if such an Imam is indeed infallible then each of them should act or opine in the exact same manner, and be in agreement with the Sunna of the Prophet Muḥammad. But it is well known that al-Ḥasan acted differently than his father ʿAlī, whereby he made peace between the two groups of warring Muslims while ʿAlī fought against the other camp of Muslims. Al-Ḥasan also previously advised his father "not to leave [Medina] for Kufa", "not to ask Muʿāwiya to step down" from being governor of Syria, and "not to fight [the Battle of] Ṣiffīn".[265] Ibn Taymiyya also states: "Al-Ḥasan always used to advise [his father] ʿAlī to avoid fighting. This contradicts the creed of the Shiites, i.e. that [al-Ḥasan's] reconciliation was a calamity and source of humiliation."[266] It was previously mentioned that the Prophet Muḥammad praised al-Ḥasan's act of reconciliation and peace.

It should also be mentioned that ʿAlī burned to death those who claimed he was a deity. Many Companions, including Ibn ʿAbbās,[267] disagreed with burning them since the Prophet Muḥammad prohibited burning individuals with fire, on the basis that it is only appropriate for "God to punish using fire."[268] It should be noted that both ʿAlī and Ibn ʿAbbās are of the Household of the Prophet Muḥammad, and yet they disagreed on this matter as well as others (like temporary

---

[265] Ibn Taymiyya, *Minhāj al-Sunna al-Nabawiyya*, vol. V, p. 466.

[266] Ibid, vol. IV, pp. 40 and 535.

[267] See Bukhārī 3017; Nasāʾī 4060; Aḥmad 2551. See also Ibn Taymiyya, *Minhāj al-Sunna al-Nabawiyya*, vol. I, p. 307; vol. V, p. 495; vol. VII, p. 233; vol. VII, p. 536. Ibn Taymiyya also states that "most of the jurists" maintain that burning the apostates or heretics is incorrect. See Ibn Taymiyya, *Majmūʿ al-fatāwā*, vol. III, p. 394. Ibn Ḥajar al-ʿAsqalānī states: "The clear indication (*ẓāhir*) of the *ḥadīth* is that [burning] is forbidden and *ḥarām*, and this abrogated [the Prophet's] previous command [to the Companions he sent out]." Ibn Ḥajar, *Fatḥ al-Bārī*, vol. VI, pp. 150–151.

[268] Bukhārī 3017; Tirmidhī 1571; Abū Dāwūd 2673; Aḥmad 4018. The context of this *ḥadīth* is that the Prophet Muḥammad had originally commanded some Companions "to burn [two apostates] once they found them"; but as the Companions were leaving, the Prophet Muḥammad said: "I commanded you to burn so-and-so, but it is only appropriate for God to punish using fire. If you find those [two] then you should kill them." Bukhārī 3016; Tirmidhī 1571; Aḥmad 8068.

marriage, which will be mentioned below); thus, the Household of the Prophet is not infallible. But, most importantly, this *ḥadīth* shows that only the Prophet Muḥammad (and the other prophets) are infallible, while ʿAlī (as well as the other Rightly-Guided Caliphs and Companions) are not infallible.[269]

Moreover, the Shiites attribute many statements and opinions to their fifth and sixth Imams, Muḥammad al-Bāqir and Jaʿfar al-Ṣādiq (who were great religious scholars), which differ from their prior Imams. These differences arose, according to Ibn Taymiyya, because many of the later Shiites attributed false beliefs and fabricated statements to those two scholars.[270] This occurred mainly by a group in Kufa, Iraq and those thereafter who intentionally fabricated *ḥadīths* and traditions to them.[271] Maria Dakake alludes to Shiite attribution of statements to Muḥammad al-Bāqir and Jaʿfar al-Ṣādiq, who represent "80–90 per cent" of the traditions attributed to their Imams. Dakake states that their practices in attributing statements to them "would hardly be acceptable in Sunni *ḥadīth* methodology... In fact, *isnād* criticism as the basis for authenticating *ḥadīth* seems to emerge rather

---

269 It should not be misunderstood that negating infallibility from ʿAlī, due to this episode, thus attributes a sin to him. His juristic opinion (*ijtihād*)—whether he was unaware of the *ḥadīth* or forgot it—is rewarded as per another *ḥadīth*: "If a [judge] gives a verdict [to the best of his knowledge] yet his verdict is wrong, he will still receive a reward." Bukhārī 7352; Muslim 1716/4487; Tirmidhī 1326; Abū Dāwūd 3574; Ibn Māja 2314; Nasāʾī 5381; Aḥmad 17,774.

270 Ibn Taymiyya, *Minhāj al-Sunna al-Nabawiyya*, vol. VII, p. 534. See also Ibid, vol. VI, p. 387.

271 Ibid, vol. II, pp. 456–458 and 464–466. Ibn Taymiyya maintains that the Successors in Mecca, Medina, Syria and Basra were, on the other hand, in large part truthful. Of note, Daftary acknowledges that Iraq is "the cradle of Shiʿism". Daftary, *A History of Shiʿi Islam*, p. 98. It should also be mentioned that the Prophet Muḥammad faced and pointed towards the east and then said: "Tribulations (*fitan*) will emanate from there." Bukhārī 7093; Muslim 2905/7292; Tirmidhī 2268; Aḥmad 5109. See also Albānī's discussion in *Silsilat al-aḥādīth al-ṣaḥīḥa* no. 2494, vol. V, pp. 653–657. In another *ḥadīth* the Prophet Muḥammad supplicated: "May God bless Syria and Yemen." He was then asked multiple times to bless Najd, i.e. Iraq, but he refused, saying: "Therein will emanate earthquakes and tribulations." Bukhārī 1037. See also Albānī's discussion in *Takhrīj aḥādīth faḍāʾil al-Shām wa Dimashq li-Abī al-Ḥasan al-Rabʿī* (Riyadh: Maktabat al-Maʿārif, 2000), pp. 23–26 and 73.

belatedly in Shiʿi tradition...and even then, seems to have carried less weight and significance than it did in the Sunni tradition."[272]

As regards some of those legal differences, they include the Twelvers' permission to engage in temporary marriage, which they attributed to Muḥammad al-Bāqir and Ibn ʿAbbās.[273] This despite the fact that ʿAlī b. Abī Ṭālib himself narrated in an authentic *ḥadīth* that the Prophet Muḥammad "forbade temporary marriage after the Battle of Khaybar".[274] Likewise, later Shiites claimed that a fifth (*khums*) of the believers' money should be granted to the Imam or his deputy[275] despite the fact that ʿAlī never did so during his caliphate (nor did the Prophet Muḥammad). Instead, the Prophet and all of the Rightly-Guided Caliphs only derived this fifth from the spoils of war, i.e. from the disbelievers.[276]

Moreover, the claimed absent Twelfth Imam has not provided any benefit to the Shiites[277]—he cannot empower them nor teach them in his absence—but rather their belief in him has only harmed them. For example, the Shiites have avoided Friday prayers awaiting his

---

[272] Maria Massi Dakake, "Writing and Resistance: The Transmission of Religious Knowledge in Early Shiʿism", in Daftary and Miskinzoda (eds.), *The Study of Shiʿi Islam: History, Theology and Law*, pp. 197–200.

[273] Of note, the Zaydīs and Ismāʿīlīs forbid temporary marriage (as do the Sunnis). See Daftary, *A History of Shiʿi Islam*, pp. 155 and 187–189.

[274] See Bukhārī 4216; Muslim 1407/3431; Tirmidhī 1121; Ibn Māja 1961; Nasā'ī 4334; Aḥmad 592.

[275] Ayatollah Abu'l-Qasim Khu'i, "Diverse Religious Practices," in Nasr, Dabashi and Nasr (eds.), *Shiʿism: Doctrines, Thought, and Spirituality*, pp. 254–257.

[276] See Ibn Taymiyya, *Minhāj al-Sunna al-Nabawiyya*, vol. VI, pp. 105–106. See also verse Q.VIII.41.

[277] It should be mentioned that Sayyid Ṭabāṭabā'ī states that the "Imam also bears the function of *walayat* and the esoteric guidance of men. It is he who directs man's spiritual life and orients the inner aspect of human action toward God... The Imam watches over men inwardly and is in communion with the soul and spirit of men even if he be hidden from their physical eyes." Sayyid Ṭabāṭabā'ī, *Shiʿite Islam*, p. 214. It is sufficient to state in response that this is not even possible for a prophet as God (Glorious is He) stated to the Messenger Muḥammad: *The guiding of them is not thy duty (O Muḥammad), but God guideth whom He will; Even if thou (O Muḥammad) desirest their right guidance, still God assuredly will not guide him who misleadeth.* Q.II.272 and Q.XVI.37, respectively.

return[278] despite the fact that the Prophet Muḥammad has forbidden the abandonment of it.[279] Moreover, God (Glorious is He) did not excuse attendance at Fridays prayers due to the absence of an infallible Imam: *O ye who believe! When the call is heard for the prayer of the day of congregation, haste unto remembrance of God and leave your trading. That is better for you if ye did but know.*[280] So while the Shiites have, in general, neglected Friday and congregational prayers in the mosques, they have built shrines (or mosques) based on the tombs of many of their Imams and made visitation (*ziyāra*) or pilgrimage to them part of the religion—even though the Prophet Muḥammad forbade the Muslims from performing such deeds.[281] Further aspects related to Shiism will be discussed in the next two chapters.

---

[278] See Seyyed Hossein Nasr in Appendix II, "Ritual Practices in Shiʿism," in *Shi'ite Islam*, p. 231, who states: "In Shiʿism, although these [Friday congregational] prayers are performed in at least one mosque in every city and town, in the absence of the Imam, who according to Shiʿism is the true leader of these prayers, their importance is somewhat diminished and more emphasis is placed upon individual prescribed prayers." Rula Abisaab states: "Shiites viewed the rule of Sunnite caliphs and sultans as usurpation of the rights of their imams, the descendants of ʿAli and Fatima. Consequently, they rejected participation in Friday prayers." Abisaab also states: "Shiites have for most of their history made a half-hearted commitment to [Friday congregational] prayer during the absence of the Imam. The early Safavid Shahs understood the extent to which the convening of Friday prayer was fundamentally tied to the legitimacy and sovereignty of the ruler and attempted, for the first time in Shi'ite history, to institute it." Abisaab then goes on to investigate the viewpoints of various Safavid scholars regarding Friday prayers, i.e. whether they made it obligatory or optional, or whether they continued to consider it prohibited. See Rula Abisaab, *Converting Persia*, pp. 4, 12, 20–22, 39, 56, 71–72, 112–114, 120, 124–126 and 138.

[279] The Prophet Muḥammad said: "Whoever misses the Friday [prayer] three times out of negligence will have his heart sealed (*ṭabaʿa*)." Tirmidhī 500; Abū Dāwūd 1052; Ibn Māja 1125; Nasā'ī 1369; Aḥmad 14,559; Ibn Ḥibbān 2786; al-Ḥākim 3811; Bayhaqī (*Sunan*) 5576. It is "authentic" according to Albānī (*Ṣaḥīḥ al-Jāmiʿ al-ṣaghīr* 6143). See verses Q.IV.155, Q.VII.101, Q.IX.87, Q.X.74, Q.XVI.106–108, Q.XXX.58–59, Q.XL.35 and Q.LXIII.3 for instances where God (Exalted is He) has sealed the hearts of people. The sealing of one's heart thus puts one at risk of hypocrisy.

[280] Q.LXII.9.

[281] The Prophet Muḥammad said: "Those before you used to [build] places of worship (*masājid*) upon the graves of their prophets and the righteous believers. Do not [build] places of worship upon any grave. I forbid you from doing so." Muslim 532/1188. The Prophet Muḥammad also said that those who build a place of worship upon the grave of a righteous person are the "worst of creation in God's sight on the Day of Judgment".

Now, God (Glorious is He) praised the Companions by stating: *Ye are the best community that hath been raised up for humankind. Ye enjoin right conduct and forbid indecency; and ye believe in God. And if the People of the Scripture had believed it had been better for them. Some of them are believers; but most of them are evil-livers.*[282] It is thus prescribed upon the believers (whether they are Jews, Christians or Muslims at their respective times) to enjoin good and forbid evil. Yet, the reality is that it has been the Muslims who have best enjoined good and forbidden evil over the course of history on a societal level (even considering the discord and divisions which have also occurred). But, if the Muslims turn away from the Holy Lord's covenant or refuse to follow the Qur'ān and Sunna, they will be recompensed by being afflicted with much evil, just as occurred to the Jews and Christians when they turned away from the Divine commandments and Scriptures.

God's blessing of Islam has been described in particular by Him (Glorious and Exalted is He) as being complete (*atmam*[tu] *ʿalay*[kum] *niʿmatī*)[283] and thus it is characterized by far more knowledge than Christianity or Judaism. It is only through the Qur'ān and Sunna of the Prophet Muḥammad, as well as reason and wisdom, that the problems of evil, hypocrisy and the Hellfire can adequately be addressed. This will become clear in the next three chapters.

Bukhārī 427; Muslim 528/1181; Nasā'ī 704; Aḥmad 24,252. Certainly, the Prophet Muḥammad never made an exception for the building of places of worship or shrines upon the tombs of so-called infallible Imams.

282 Q.III.110.

283 See Q.V.3.

Chapter Twelve

The Wisdom in Allowing Evil

Now that an exposition on suffering and the major types of evils has been outlined, a detailed discussion on God's wise purposes in allowing great amounts of evil, as well as the gratuitous types, will be set out. These wise purposes will be broadly grouped under sixteen headings. The Holy Lord's construction of this world will thus be shown in this chapter, as well as the next, to be congruent with His dazzling divine wisdom.

1. Manifesting the meanings and consequences of a greater number of God's Beautiful Names

God in His glory has dictated that many of His Beautiful Names be manifested—more than Him being the Most Generous One Who is omnipotent. If evil did not exist a great number of His Names and Attributes could not have become justly and wisely manifested. This was alluded to earlier but will be expanded upon here.

The existence of evil sins, for instance, allows the manifestation of some of God's Names, like the Most Beneficent (*al-Raḥmān*), the Most Merciful (*al-Raḥīm*, *Arḥam al-rāḥimīn* and *Khayr al-rāḥimīn*), the Most Forgiving (*al-Ghafūr*, *al-Ghāfir* and *Ahl al-maghfira*), the Oft-Forgiving (*al-Ghaffār*), the Effacer [of sins] (*al-ʿAfū*), the One Who pardons (*al-Tawwāb* and *Qābil al-tawb*), the Most Compassionate (*al-Ra'ūf*) and the Most Forbearing (*al-Ḥalīm*).

As is evident here, there are many Names of God that pertain to different aspects of His mercy and forgiveness, and the Holy Lord has dictated to manifest them entirely. All of these are Eternal and Self-Subsisting Names of the Holy Lord; but they cannot become manifest unless sins exist ontologically, and God freely chooses to bestow His mercy and forgiveness upon the doers of sins.

The Prophet Muḥammad (may God bless him and grant him peace) said: "If people did not commit sins, God would dispense with them and create others who would sin [but thereafter would seek forgiveness], whereupon He would forgive them."[1] God (Glorious is He) has therefore encompassed the believers in His mercy, through all possible manners that accord with His wisdom.

But if sinners choose to persist in their evil sins and not return to God (Glorious is He), then they should know that the Holy Lord is Self-sufficient (*al-Ghanī*) and the One to Whom all praise is due (*al-Ḥamīd*).[2] God (Exalted is He) states: *And if any turns away [let him know that] God is truly Self-sufficient, the One to Whom all praise is due.*[3] Therefore, God (Glorious is He) only forsakes those who have turned away from Him; and He is not in need of anyone's worship: *It is you, who stand in need of God, whereas He alone is Self-sufficient, the One to Whom all praise is due.*[4] God is praiseworthy for all of His Beautiful Names, Glorious Attributes and righteous actions, as well as the praiseworthy objectives and wise purposes that are beloved to Him.

One should know that the Holy Lord is the Creator, the Fashioner and the Originator. He is also the Best of creators (*Aḥsan al-khāliqīn*); there being no other creator. The creation of good and evil is proof of the Holy Lord's power to create anything He wills. His creation of evil is further evidence of His omnipotence—He can create more than only that which is good. Although God (Glorious is He) hates evil, He has created it in order to utilize it to indirectly achieve wise purposes. There is nothing in existence that is absolutely evil from all aspects or whose presence cannot indirectly result in some benefit or good from at least one aspect. This will be elaborated upon later.

God is the True and Righteous King (*al-Malik al-Ḥaqq*). The Righteous King has commanded that which is good and forbidden that which is evil. Had evil not existed and everything was good, then there would be no possibility to forbid some things. The Holy Lord's commandment of good and prohibition of evil also manifests His wisdom and providence for humankind. God is the One Who tests (*al-Mubtalī*) humankind through His commandments and prohibitions. God (Exalted is He) states: *Had God so willed, He could indeed punish [the disbelievers Himself] but [He wills you to struggle] so as to test you [all] by*

---

1 Muslim 2749/6965; Tirmidhī 3539; Aḥmad 23,515.

2 See Q.XXII.64 and Q.XXXI.26.

3 Q.LX.6 (Muḥammad Asad translation). See also Q.XIV.8 and Q.LVII.24.

4 Q.XXXV.15 (Muḥammad Asad translation).

means of one another.[5] Then the Almighty Lord will judge humanity in accordance with their deeds as He is the Sovereign Lord of the Day of Religious Recompense (*Mālik yawm al-dīn*).

Furthermore, God is the Most Generous (*al-Karīm*), and what greater generosity is there than Him sustaining those who reject, curse and disbelieve in Him. Had it not been for His generosity, humankind would never have been created or originated by Him. God (Exalted is He) is omniscient and He knew all the evil that would be perpetrated, yet He brought us into existence due to His generosity and wisdom. God is the Benefactor (*al-Munʿim*) and the Bestower (*al-Wahhāb*).

Although the believers will suffer afflictions and evil in this world, God is the Most Magnanimous (*al-Jawād*). The Holy Lord knew in His eternal knowledge that He will reward them in the Hereafter with the greatest types of reward for all that they have endured. Therefore, had it not been for His perfect generosity and magnanimity, this world and the Hereafter would not have been structured as such. God (Glorious is He) has willed to manifest many more of His Beautiful Names besides being the Most Generous and the One Who is omnipotent; therefore, He has restricted the manifestation of His generosity and omnipotence in *this* world.

Although the Muslims will be temporarily overcome by the disbelievers, God is the One Who grants victory and triumph (*al-Nāṣir, al-Naṣīr* and *al-Ghālib*) to the believers. He is also the One Who humiliates the disbelievers (*Mukhzī al-kāfirīn*). Yet, these Names could not have become manifest without certain experienced circumstances being ontologically allowed. God (Glory be to Him) is the One Who assists (*al-Mu'ayyid*) and grants victory to the oppressed, weak and brokenhearted believers, and it is only He who can do so.

The Righteous Lord is also the Best Strategist (*Khayr al-mākirīn*) and He takes retribution against the evil disbelievers. In addition, the Holy Lord is the Guardian (*al-Muhaymin* and *al-Ḥafīdh*) and the Protector (*al-Walī*). The Exalted states: *If God is your helper none can overcome you, and if He withdraw His help from you, who is there who can help you after Him? In God let believers put their trust.*[6]

---

[5] Q.XLVII.4 (Muḥammad Asad translation, with a slight amendment).

[6] Q.III.160.

The Almighty Lord granted victory to the believing followers of His Messenger Noah, while drowning all of the disbelievers. He also saved Moses and the Israelites by parting the Red Sea, while drowning only Pharaoh and his army. These represent two of His greatest miracles, and they are mentioned many times in the Old Testament and the Qur'ān. Had God (Glorious is He) not permitted evil to occur nor allowed the disbelievers to temporarily overcome the Muslims (in general), the aforementioned Beautiful Names and righteous actions of His would not have become manifested.

In previous Scripture, such as the Psalms, and in the Qur'ān, God (Glorious and Exalted is He) has promised to grant victory to those believers who have amongst them a critical mass of righteous people who enjoin good and forbid the major sins: *God has promised, to those among you who believe and work righteous deeds, that He will, of a surety, grant them in the land, inheritance (of power), as He granted it to those before them.*[7] Also, consider the verses: *Before this We wrote in the Psalms, after the Message (given to Moses): My servants the righteous shall inherit the earth,*[8] and *God will most certainly succour him who succours His cause: for, verily, God is Most Powerful, Almighty, [well aware of] those who, if We firmly establish them on earth, remain constant in prayer, and give in charity, and enjoin the doing of what is right and forbid the doing of what is wrong. But with God rests the final outcome of all events.*[9]

That said, God (Glorious is He) will only grant victory when all of the purposes which He has decreed to accomplish have occurred in accordance with His wisdom—not when humans (whether believers or not) wish for it to relieve them of the evil, injustice and oppression that they are enduring. God is the Most Patient (*al-Ṣabūr*) in achieving those wise purposes. God (Exalted is He) states: *But forgive and overlook, till God accomplish His purpose; for God hath power over all things.*[10] Even when the messengers were living, victory was delayed until His wise purposes were achieved: *Till, when the messengers despaired and thought*

---

7 Q.XXIV.55.

8 Q.XXI.105.

9 Q.XXII.40–41.

10 Q.II.109.

that they were denied, then came unto them Our help, and whom We would was saved. And Our wrath cannot be warded from the guilty.[11]

One wise purpose in delaying victory is that the believers ultimately realize that no worldly cause can result in their triumph. Thus they become certain that it is only the Almighty Lord Who can grant it to them. Their victory, moreover, only occurs after they affirm their humility to the Holy Lord. The vast hardships they encountered beforehand ensure that their humility and servitude to Him will become engrained in them, and not forgotten soon after being granted victory by the Almighty Lord. It may also be that the Muslims, if granted victory before having amongst them a critical mass of pious and righteous individuals, would rule unjustly, transgress or cause greater bloodshed.

Furthermore, victory may be delayed to grant further opportunity to the disbelievers to believe, particularly if the believers have failed to adequately expose them to the true creed and faith. If one notes the events surrounding the Companions, as discussed previously, one will recognize that victory over Quraysh was very much delayed. Ultimately, the Prophet and Companions entered Mecca peacefully without bloodshed. This spared the lives of many and ultimately led to most of Quraysh believing and following the Prophet (may God bless him and grant him peace).

Now, the Righteous Lord is the One Who exalts (*al-Rāfiʿ*) and the One Who abases (*al-Khāfiḍ*), the One Who bestows honour (*al-Muʿizz*) and the One Who dishonours (*al-Mudhill*). The Holy Lord is the One Who advances (*al-Muqaddim*) the believers and the One Who blocks (*al-Mu'akhkhir*) the disbelievers from attaining His grace. Therefore, the perfect and glorious Attributes of the Lord include more than Him being holy, righteous, generous, merciful, omniscient and omnipotent—they also include paired Beautiful Names. God (Exalted is He) has dictated their manifestation in a manner consistent with His wisdom and justice for He is the Most Wise (*al-Ḥakīm*) and Most Just (*al-ʿAdl*). It is only wise and just to abase, dishonour and block those who are disbelievers or sinners—it would be unjust to do

---

[11] Q.XII.110. It should be noted that the messengers despaired of their nations believing—not of His victory. See *Tafsīr al-Ṭabarī*, vol. XVI, pp. 296– 304.

so had only a society of completely righteous believers existed. God (Glorious and Exalted is He) loves all of His Beautiful Names, which are eternal and necessary to His Essence, and loves to manifest their meanings and consequences in a wise and just manner.

In addition, God is the One Who resurrects (*al-Bāʿith*). Had all of His creation been good and adequate there would be no need to resurrect them to a Day of Judgment and hold them accountable for their actions. The Almighty Lord's resurrection of the entirety of humankind—not missing a single individual—is one of His greatest signs, and further evidence of His omnipotence. The manifestation of His Name *al-Bāʿith* as well as His creation of its necessary ontological and deontological concomitants is truly dazzling.

On the Day of Resurrection, the Holy Lord will manifest His Beautiful Names of being the Judge (*al-Ḥakam* and *al-Qāḍī*) and Reckoner (*al-Ḥasīb*) of humankind and the jinn. The Holy and Omnipotent Lord is deserving of being feared and obeyed (*Ahl al-taqwā*); however, since the disbelievers worshipped others alongside Him, blasphemed Him and mocked the believers, He will take retribution (*intiqām*) against those evildoers. His punishment will be severe (*Shadīd al-ʿiqāb*), and the disbelievers will have none to save them from Hellfire.

Although God (Glorious is He) is the Most Loving (*al-Wadūd*), He will hold accountable those who worshipped others alongside Him and violated His legal limits (particularly the major sins). The Holy Lord will bestow His love on the Day of Judgment only upon those whom He has deemed worthy of it in accordance with His wisdom. God (Exalted is He) states that He is: *The Forgiver of sin, the Accepter of repentance, the Stern in punishment, the Bountiful. There is no deity save Him. Unto Him is the journeying.*[12] All of the aforementioned Beautiful Names would not have become manifest had He not permitted evil to occur.

---

[12] Q.XL.3.

2. Bringing forth the prophets, truly faithful, martyrs and righteous believers

The Holy Lord has bestowed His greatest blessings and highest favours upon the: *prophets, the truly faithful, the martyrs and the righteous.*[13] Therefore, one of His wise purposes in creating this world is to bring forth these best possible types of righteous human beings. The absolute best of humanity are the prophets, and the Seal of them is Muḥammad (may God bless him and grant him peace).

The Holy Lord's love for the next three groups—i.e. the truly faithful, the martyrs, and the righteous—follows that of the prophets. Yet they cannot arise except in conditions where evil is allowed to predominate. The righteous, martyrs and truly faithful can only be considered as such through their forbidding of evil (and withstanding the harm of those who are evil), fighting against evil, and deeply repudiating the principles and root causes of evil, respectively. Although the Holy Lord detests wickedness and gratuitous evils, He allows them to exist because they indirectly result in the manifestation of the aforementioned groups of believers and their righteous actions. Thus gratuitous evil—as will be discussed further later—does serve a purpose. The objective of this world containing both good and evil is more than just soul-making or belief, but rather the purpose is the emergence of righteousness and higher forms of striving against evil.

The truly faithful are devout and their hearts are permeated by the truth; therefore, they recognize evil in detail and work to repudiate it using all of the above means—this was alluded to in Chapter Seven. This represents a higher level than those who fight against evil or forbid it, because true knowledge has the highest authority (*sulṭān*)[14] and the pen is mightier than the sword.[15] Ibn al-Qayyim states that the ink of the truly-faithful scholars is more valuable than the blood of the martyrs.[16] Moreover, the objective of the prophets, including the Messenger Muḥammad (whom the truly faithful emulate), is to guide people through knowledge—not to force them into submission.

---

13 Q.IV.69. Of note, Pickthall translates *al-ṣiddiqīn* as "saints".

14 Ibn al-Qayyim discussed the authoritative power of knowledge. See Zeni (tr.), *Ibn Qayyim al-Jawziyya on Knowledge*, pp. 32–34.

15 This was first said by Edward Bulwer-Lytton in 1839.

16 See Zeni (tr.), *Ibn Qayyim al-Jawziyya on Knowledge*, pp. 77–78.

The presence of hardships and evils allows for the development and existence of those who can enjoin good and forbid evil, carry out righteous deeds, strive against wickedness, and patiently assist one another to overcome evils and sins. These represent the characteristics of those who are successful as per Sūrat al-ʿAṣr.[17] The capacity to strive against evil is one of the main differentiators between humanity and all the other types of creatures, including the angels.[18]

Moreover, it may be that those time periods involving great hardships are the most beloved to the Holy Lord as they prepare the righteous and truly faithful for their great mission. Only thereafter are they able to propagate the true message and shape many others accordingly by the grace of God. These individuals are the basis for the emergence of the type of society that the Holy Lord loves—without them it could not be formed, and God's grace is infinite.

In addition, although the pious and righteous avoid major sins, they will inevitably incur some intermediate sins, and thus will try to do many good deeds to absolve themselves (through the mercy of God) and return to their prior level of faith. These include benevolent deeds, remembrance of God, supplication, sincere repentance,[19] giving charity in secret,[20] amongst many other good works. God (Exalted is He) has commended those who: *overcome evil with good*.[21] One must always seek to strengthen one's faith and persevere to achieve proximity to the Holy Lord. Recall that ʿUmar b. al-Khaṭṭāb disagreed with the Prophet Muḥammad regarding the terms of the Treaty of Ḥudaybiya, and thus he subsequently carried out, by his own admission, many good deeds seeking atonement.[22]

---

[17] Sūrat al-ʿAṣr is: *By (the token of) time (through the ages), verily man is in loss, except such as have faith, and do righteous deeds, and (join together) in the mutual teaching of truth, and of patience and constancy.* Q.CIII.1–3 (Yusuf Ali translation).

[18] Of note, the angels do not independently strive against evil, but rather only alongside the believers. Consider, for example, when Gabriel and the other angels fought alongside the Prophet Muḥammad and the Companions during the Battles of Badr and Uḥud.

[19] Q.LXVI.8: *O ye who believe, turn unto God in sincere repentance! It may be that your Lord will remit from you your evil deeds and bring you into Gardens underneath which rivers flow.*

[20] Q.II.271: *If ye publish your almsgiving, it is well, but if ye hide it and give it to the poor, it will be better for you, and will atone for some of your ill-deeds.*

[21] Q.XIII.22.

[22] This is "authentic" according to Albānī (*al-Taʿlīqāt al-ḥisān ʿalā Ṣaḥīḥ Ibn Ḥibbān* 4852).

God (Exalted is He) also advised us to: *Repel evil with that which is best*.[23] This refers to patiently enduring the harm and evil of the disbelievers (*al-ṣabr ʿalā adhā*[hum]), overlooking the ignorance of the disbelievers (*al-ṣafḥ ʿan jahl al-mushrikīn*), and controlling one's anger (*kaẓm al-ghayẓ*).[24] The enjoining of good also perpetuates further good and proves itself to be a deterrent to evil.

Now, if we assume that pious and righteous individuals represent only a small minority of the believers, then the highest levels of goodness are indeed concentrated within a very small percentage of humankind. But it is precisely this small minority of believers for whom God (Exalted is He) has declared His love and favour. In effect, the existence of evil indirectly concentrates higher levels of good within a small minority of believers. Had evil not existed then lower levels of goodness would have been present albeit within a greater number of believers.

Moreover, the greater the amount of evil, the greater the expanse and possibilities for the righteous believers to do good and strive against evil. Had evil been less then those opportunities to do good would have been less, and the differential between humans would have been less. The righteous are thus able to strive against evil in such a wide variety of manners (whether by action, speech or faith) than would have been possible in a world with less evil. God (Glorious is He) loves to be worshipped in a wide variety of manners;[25] therefore, He has created a world which allows a greater range of good to be carried out by the righteous.

This sequestering and concentration of good within the pious and righteous can also be recognized when it is considered that the reward for "a benevolent deed is multiplied 10 to 700 times".[26] The greater the deed, the more immense the reward by the Most Magnanimous Lord. Furthermore, the righteous will have their intermediate and minor sins transformed into good deeds by the Holy Lord in the Hereafter.[27] This allows them to reach much higher ranks within

---

[23] Q.XXIII.96 (Yusuf Ali translation).

[24] See *Tafsīr al-Ṭabarī*, vol. XIX, pp. 67–68.

[25] See Zeni (tr.), *Ibn Qayyim al-Jawziyya on Divine Wisdom and the Problem of Evil*, p. 146.

[26] See the Prophetic *ḥadīth* in Bukhārī 41; Ibn Māja 3823; Nasāʾī 4998; Aḥmad 9714.

[27] See Q.XXV.70. This will be discussed further in Chapter Fifteen.

Paradise and attain far greater levels of God's pleasure. God's reward for the righteous and higher ranks is truly mind-boggling.

God (Exalted is He) justly elevates the believers in Paradise according to their religious attainment in this world. The prophets endured the most hardships and afflictions, and freely strove the most against evil in all manners, and thus they are elevated to the highest levels of Paradise. The ranks of the truly faithful, martyrs and the righteous follow suit accordingly. Deeds and actions must exist to enable the pious and righteous to be elevated to the higher ranks of Paradise, as it would be unjust for them to be rewarded with the same rank as other believers who have done less. Had it not been for the existence of evil and their striving against it, the righteous could not have been ranked as such.

Indeed, the levels of Paradise would have been lower and more limited had the world not been constructed in such a fashion. Therefore, the extent of good and evil present in this world conveys the complete spectrum of religious behaviour that the Holy Lord has willed and allowed to exist, from the highest level of righteousness to the basest level of wickedness.

3. Allowing the exercise of free will

A true free will cannot be elucidated except in the presence of good and evil. First, it should be mentioned that the Prophet Muḥammad (may God bless him and grant him peace) said: "Deeds follow intentions. Therefore, each individual is recompensed according to that individual's intention."[28] Since one's intent is well known to be freely chosen, the Prophet affirmed that people's deeds are free. The will—which follows the intent, but precedes the deed—is also free by extension. In this fashion, individuals will be held accountable for all of the aforementioned and will be subject to reward or punishment.

Although good acts may exist in the absence of free will, such goodness is less than if a similar good act had been performed through a creature's free will. Moreover, the Holy Lord's reward and grace are only bestowed upon those creatures who, through their own free will and choice, worship Him alone and/or carry out good deeds for His

---

[28] Bukhārī 1; Muslim 1907/4927; Tirmidhī 1647; Abū Dāwūd 2201; Ibn Māja 4227; Nasā'ī 75; Aḥmad 168.

sake alone. The free will, which the Holy Lord has endowed human beings with, is what differentiates them from the angels.

God (Exalted is He) has constructed this world to include suffering and evil so that individuals are driven to make choices and decisions. Sometimes these choices are easier and sometimes harder, but one cannot go through this life on "cruise control". Individuals have to strive against their desires and perform good deeds so that it becomes clear and certain to them that they are only doing such good works for the Holy Lord's sake and the Hereafter—not because it coincides with their desires.

In addition, those living in this environment can no longer easily "hedge their bets", i.e. only follow God's commandments (Exalted is He) in case there is a Hereafter, or only do good because it is moral. Instead, since they must inevitably endure suffering and evil, they will only perform the best types of good deeds because of their certainty regarding God's promise of the Hereafter and in order to attain His pleasure, contentment and reward. If having faith was easier (and suffering or evil was absent), then many more people would follow the path to the Holy Lord without sincerity or true belief.

The ultimate objective of a believer is to freely render his or her will completely to the religious will of the Holy Lord, i.e. obey His commandments and prohibitions completely. Those who have experienced (*wajada*) the sweetness of faith find nothing more beloved to them than following God and His Messenger[29] by their free will. Those who achieve this are no longer distracted by their desires or temptations; and their goal is proximity to the Holy Lord: *And that thy Lord, He is the goal.*[30]

If one truly loves the Holy Lord then one will serve Him, submit oneself to Him and obey Him completely by one's own free choice. Furthermore, one will strive against evil, despite all the hardships and the enmity of others. One will freely sacrifice one's health, wealth or livelihood. One may even render oneself susceptible to imprisonment or torture, or have to sacrifice one's life for God's sake.

---

[29] See Bukhārī 6941; Muslim 43/165; Tirmidhī 2624; Ibn Māja 4032; Nasā'ī 4988; Aḥmad 12,002.

[30] Q.LIII.42.

These levels of sincerity could not have been elucidated and manifested in an environment devoid of widespread evils or one in which the disbelievers are a small minority.

It should be mentioned that although God (Glorious is He) has granted us a free will to choose whether to do good or evil, He is omniscient and has foreknowledge of all that will occur. Nothing occurs in this world except that He has allowed it (although He hates sin, wickedness and gratuitous evil). The Almighty Lord takes no risks in granting us this free will—"everything that will happen out to eternity has been written"[31] and was known to God (Exalted is He) before He originated the creation. God (Glorious is He) knows what people will freely choose to do.

The Sublime states: *Ye will not, unless God willeth. God is Knower, Wise.*[32] Thus, the free will of humankind is affirmed, and it is allowed by the Almighty Lord. The Holy Lord is omnipotent whereby He utilizes evil for good ends and ultimate objectives, while those perpetrating evil will either be punished or forgiven in accordance with His wisdom.

Finally, although the acts of free-willed creatures are predominantly evil—let us assume that the ratio of disbelievers to believers is 9:1—it should be remembered that the goodness and reward for "a benevolent deed is multiplied 10 to 700 times".[33] It may even be that the righteous deeds done purely and sincerely for His sake are rewarded more immensely. Therefore, by the grace of the Holy Lord, the multiplied goodness of the believers of humankind outweighs the evilness of the disbelievers (although the latter are much more numerous).[34] In the end, God's love of the believers, particularly the pious and higher

---

31 Tirmidhī 3319. It is "authentic" according to Albānī (*Ṣaḥīḥ al-Jāmiʿ al-ṣaghīr* 2017).

32 Q.LXXVI.30. See also Q.LXXXI.29.

33 Bukhārī 41; Ibn Māja 3823; Nasāʾī 4998; Aḥmad 9714. Some narrations allude that fasting is rewarded to an even greater degree. The reward of fasting is of a divine degree full of His grace as God (the Almighty and Most Blessed) states: "It is purely for Me and I will be the One to reward it".

34 It could be argued that the good deeds of the believers are far less than 10% of all deeds and that the pious and righteous represent a small minority of the believers—this is all true. Yet it will be maintained, even so, that the multiplied reward (up to 700 hundred times) of these good and pious deeds, as well as the reward of fasting and righteous deeds, is greater than the evil deeds. And God knows best.

ranks, who have freely chosen to obey Him and strive for His sake alone, outweighs His hatred of the disbelievers.

4. *ALLOWING THE ELUCIDATION OF TRUE SINCERITY*

God (Exalted is He) in His wisdom has willed to differentiate those who are truly sincere (*al-mukhliṣūn*) from others and grant the former high ranks in Paradise. It was discussed previously that the presence of Satan and his whispering indirectly leads to the elucidation of those who are in doubt of the Hereafter. The presence of evil, in all of its types, similarly tests people so as to differentiate those who are in doubt of the Hereafter. Only those who are sincere to the Holy Lord are able to overcome the doubts instigated by Satan or the presence of evil. Those who are insincere will ultimately turn back and be exposed as either disbelievers or hypocrites.

Indeed, the highest levels of sincerity can only become proven if one, despite being vehemently opposed by others, persists in doing righteous deeds solely for God's sake and in order to attain His pleasure and love. This can only occur in an environment with predominant or even overwhelming suffering and evil—not one devoid of or having only limited amounts of them.

For example, many of the Companions were tortured in Mecca, yet they persisted in following the Prophet Muḥammad due to their true sincerity. Bilāl b. Rabāḥ was tortured and severely beaten, yet he continued to affirm the Oneness of God[35] until he was finally set free. Khabbāb b. al-Aratt was tortured to such a great degree that he asked the Prophet (may God bless him and grant him peace): "Will you supplicate for us? Will you ask God to grant us victory?" The Prophet replied: "A man from the prior nations would be taken and thrown in a dug-up trench. Then a saw would be used to sever his head in half. Yet none of that would make him abandon the religion. Another would be tortured by ripping his muscle away from his bones and nerves. Yet that would not make him abandon the religion either.

---

[35] Ibn Māja 150; Aḥmad 3832; al-Ḥākim 5238; Bayhaqī (*Sunan*) 16,897. It is "sound" according to Albānī (*al-Taʿlīqāt al-ḥisān ʿalā Ṣaḥīḥ Ibn Ḥibbān* 7041). It states in regards to Bilāl: "He considered himself so insignificant for God's sake...Even though they dragged him through the neighborhoods of Mecca he continued to say: 'One. One.'" See also Abū Nuʿaym, *Ḥilya*, vol. I, p. 148.

God will complete this matter...but you are hasty."[36] Therefore, God (Exalted is He) allows the persecution of the believers for a certain time period—and possibly even their martyrdom—but only until His objectives have been achieved.

In addition, the believers are purified by having to endure evil. The believers are purified just as gold is purified of its impurities. This similitude, which is mentioned in the Qur'ān, was discussed earlier. Another parallel—and God knows best—is demonstrated by the heat and pressure (in addition to time) required to convert carbon into a diamond.[37] It is not coincidental that this occurs. Carbon, which represents the matter that humans are mostly made up of, becomes a diamond through pressure and heat over a significant period of time. This diamond, being the strongest material, can then shape all other types of matter accordingly. The best individual—including a prophet or a truly faithful believer—is perfect,[38] by the grace of God, and then works to perfect others (*kāmil fī dhāt*[ihi] *mukammil li-ghayr*[ihi]). The innermost aspects of a truly-faithful believer are the same as his outer, much like a diamond, which light traverses without barrier and shines brilliantly.

Ultimately, the purer and more sincere one's heart and the firmer it is on God's Straight Path, the more such a truly-faithful believer is able to strive against evil and perfect others. The sincerity and strength evident in the ranks of the righteous could not have occurred in a world devoid of evil or having lesser degrees thereof. Perseverance in the face of testing and pressure is needed to result in the higher levels of sincerity and good deeds one must exhibit in order to be accepted by God (Glorious is He) for entry into His everlasting reward.

---

36 Bukhārī 3612; Abū Dāwūd 2649; Aḥmad 21,057.

37 Indeed, Ibn al-Qayyim mentioned that Ibn Taymiyya told him: "Do not allow your heart to succumb to thoughts and doubts like a sponge. In that case, it would become saturated [with evil] only to later spew that out. Rather, consider it to be like a solid glass [diamond]: although doubts may pass by its surface, they will not become settled in it. [Then your heart] sees them for what they are due to its clarity and repels them due to its firmness." See Zeni (tr.), *Ibn Qayyim al-Jawziyya on Knowledge,* p. 196.

38 The Prophet Muḥammad (may God bless him and grant him peace) said: "Many men have attained perfection, whereas only Mary, the daughter of ʿImrān [i.e. the mother of Jesus], and Āsiya the wife of Pharaoh did so." Bukhārī 3433; Muslim 2431/6272; Tirmidhī 1834; Ibn Māja 3280; Aḥmad 19,668.

5. Allowing the elucidation of trustful dependence and reliance on God

Some of the highest acts of the heart are trustful dependence (*istiʿāna*) and reliance (*tawakkul*) on God (Glorious is He). These cannot be achieved in a setting wherein only good exists. Moreover, the real manifestations of these terms can only occur in settings where great amounts of evil exist. Even low levels of evil or the temporary existence thereof cannot indirectly lead to the manifestation of true reliance on the Holy Lord.

It will be contended that *istiʿāna* and *tawakkul* occur in separate contexts. Trustful dependence is felt and carried out when performing righteous actions and forbidding evil, striving against evil, fighting against the disbelievers, and repudiating their notions, i.e. it is displayed by the righteous and higher ranks. These acts themselves, as well as the perseverance of the righteous against the evil and injustice directed towards them for those acts, all require trustful dependence.

Reliance, on the other hand, occurs when the believers endure the harm or oppression of others. In these cases, the oppression perpetrated against them is due to factors outside of their free will or control. Reliance on God also occurs so as to carry out good deeds and pious acts or in order to avoid sins.

Trustful dependence on God is an objective of the elite: it is higher than piety because *istiʿāna* requires trusting and depending on the Holy Lord when freely choosing to carry out righteous deeds and striving against evil. On the other hand, piety only entails following a religious obligation, i.e. avoiding major sins. In addition, the righteous often anticipate and are aware that they will have to endure the injustice and evil of the wicked, and yet they still choose to strive against the latter. They continue to strive against evil and change evil to good through various actions and avenues. They persevere (*muṣābara* and *murābiṭa*) in doing so, and trustfully depend on God to aid and assist them over the evildoers. They never give up, but instead say: *God is sufficient for us! Most Excellent is He in Whom we trust!* (*hasbuna Allāh wa niʿm al-Wakīl*).[39]

Therefore, trustful dependence on the Almighty Lord can only be performed by the righteous and higher ranks. In fact, it cannot

---

[39] Q.III.173.

truly be felt or freely chosen by them unless they encounter evil, feel that they cannot independently overcome it, and therefore they turn to God Almighty, Who is Able to do all things. If lesser degrees of evil existed, then the sincere believers would be less likely to ask for assistance and aid from God (Exalted is He) or depend on Him, but would instead ask each other for help.

Although true dependence upon Him is only practised by a few elite righteous believers, since it can only be carried out in an environment containing preponderant evil, God Almighty has dictated the ontologic circumstances and causes that may permit *istiʿāna* to occur. God (Exalted is He) has said: *How many of the prophets fought (in God's way), and with them (fought) large bands of godly men? They never lost heart if they met with disaster in God's way, nor did they weaken (in will) nor give in. And God loves those who are firm and steadfast.*[40] The world is therefore constructed as such in order to allow some (albeit very few) the opportunity to manifest trustful dependence on God alone.

Consider for example the Prophet Muḥammad who repeatedly implored the Holy Lord before the Battle of Badr: "I ask You to fulfill Your promise and oath. O God, if You will [not to grant us victory] You will not be worshipped on this earth after today." Abū Bakr al-Ṣiddīq (may God be pleased with him) finally said to the Prophet: "O Messenger of God, you have beseeched your Lord sufficiently. He will surely fulfill what He has promised you."[41] The Prophet then recited the verse [which was revealed at that moment]: *Soon will their multitude be put to flight, and they will show their backs. Nay, the Hour (of Judgment) is the time promised them (for their full recompense): And that Hour will be most grievous and most bitter.*"[42] Ibn al-Qayyim states: "This beseeching [of the Prophet Muḥammad] is the essence of devoted servitude."[43] The Prophet Muḥammad was undeniably the most righteous and devoted true servant of the Holy Lord; and the Messenger (may God bless him and grant him peace) worshipped and trustfully depended on Him in the best possible manner.

---

40 Q.III.146 (Yusuf Ali translation).

41 Muslim 1763/4588; Tirmidhī 3081; Aḥmad 208.

42 Q.LIV.45–46 (Yusuf Ali translation). See Bukhārī 2915; Aḥmad 3042.

43 See Ibn al-Qayyim, *Madārij al-sālikīn*, vol. II, p. 228.

Again, trustfully depending on the Almighty Lord and supplicating to Him will only occur if one feels a great need or is encountering a dire situation that involves great suffering or evil. Injustice and oppression are therefore allowed as an indirect means to achieve that which God loves, i.e. striving against evil, praying, supplicating, beseeching, relying and trustfully depending on Him. These forms of worship all result in the believer becoming nearer and more proximate to the Holy Lord.

6. AN EXPOSITION ON THE BENEFITS OF ALLOWING THE BELIEVERS TO PERPETRATE SINS

Now, the wise purposes in allowing the believers to incur intermediate sins—not major sins—will be discussed. That said, it should be remembered that it is better to avoid intermediate sins altogether since they can have many negative consequences in this world and Hereafter. This can include becoming dispirited or feeling more distant from God (Glorious is He), for example. Also, do not forget that those believers whose sins are greater than their good deeds will be punished in the Hellfire for some time—this will be discussed later.

One wise purpose though in allowing the believers to incur intermediate sins is to allow them to repent. They will regret their sins and return to the Holy Lord, and thereafter comply with God's commandments. They will also realize their inadequacies, and thus rely on God for His protection. They will also become more humble and sincere to Him. All of these—repentance, humility, sincerity, etc.—forge a much stronger relationship between the individual and the Holy Lord than would have otherwise occurred. God (Glorious is He) states that He: *guideth unto Himself him who turneth* (*toward Him*).[44] These believers will also seek to purify themselves from those sins, and the Holy Lord loves those who seek to become pure.

Ibn al-Qayyim discussed many of these wise purposes at length. Due to the great benefit of his exposition, some of his main points will be summarized here:

> [1] God (Glory be to Him) loves the repentant believers… [R]epentance is the perfect and ultimate objective of all of humanity; and the perfection

---

[44] Q.XLII.13.

of their father [Adam] occurred through it. Note the difference between [Adam's] initial state when it was said to him, *It is (vouchsafed) unto thee that thou hungerest not therein nor art naked, And that thou thirstest not therein nor art exposed to the sun's heat,*[45] and then after [his repentance] God said, *Then his Lord chose him, and relented toward him, and guided him*[46]...

[5] [Such matters] allow the servant to recognize his need for God's protection, help and preservation...

[6] God (Glory be to Him) induces His servant to seek refuge in Him and ask for God's protection from his evil self and the plotting of his enemies. This demand represents one of the greatest causes leading to a servant's bliss.

Accordingly, the servant will begin praying and supplicating, beseeching and imploring, as well as being humble, repenting, and having love, hope, fear and other perfections that approach one hundred types. Some of these cannot be expressed verbally, but can only be experienced spiritually.

The servant's spirit is, consequently, able to reach a special proximity [to the Lord] that would not have otherwise been achieved in the absence of these causes. Then the servant will find himself at the doorstep of his Lord after being distant. This is all due to the fact that God loves and rejoices with those who repent...

The latter's heart, though, is completely humble [before the Lord]. He has no frivolities, idiocies or false images of himself. He only sees himself as sinful, and views his Lord as beneficent. He worships God with all his heart, feels himself to be completely inadequate, lowers his head, gaze and voice before his Lord with humility and submission...

[7] [...] It also necessitates such a person to be embarrassed and discount any righteous deeds he may have done, even if they are akin to the mountains, since he will require many more good deeds than even those to expiate and atone for his sins and evil deeds. He will thus deem great any little [blessing] that the Lord bestows upon him since he is not worthy or deserving of even that. He will continue to do righteous deeds and yet consider himself to be sinful. This humility and brokenness all [indirectly] result from a sin; and thus, there is nothing more beneficial for this person than this medication...

[10] God makes it known to His servants that there is no salvation except through His forgiveness and mercy, and that the servant is justly

---

45 Q.XX.118–119.

46 Q.XX.122.

held hostage by his sins. If God does not encompass him in His grace and mercy, he will inevitably be punished. None of His creation is exempt from being in need of His mercy and forgiveness, just as none is exempt from being in need of His blessings and grace...

[12] It also justifies the manifestation of God's justice upon His servant. One will recognize that God is justified to the highest degree when He allows His servant to undergo hardships. The servant will not say, 'Where did this come from?' Instead, one is not afflicted with any hardship, whether limited or great, except due to his sins. Furthermore, God has forgiven him for much more than what has befallen him...

[13] Another [benefit] is that the servant will deal with other human beings, if they harm or make mistakes with him, in a manner similar to how he asks God to treat him for his errors, mistakes and sins. Since the reward is concordant with the deed, whoever forgives others will find that God will forgive him; whoever indulges his brother if the latter harms him will find God to be merciful with him for his sins; and whoever is lenient and overlooks [others] will find that God will overlook [his errors]. But whoever probes [into the faults of others] will be dealt with likewise...

[14] [...] Also, one [who recognizes that sins and perpetrating evil are intrinsic to human beings] will give others excuses, become more merciful and accommodating of them, avoid becoming annoyed with them or seething with anger. He will desist from supplicating against them or asking God to make the earth swallow them up or send calamities upon them. He will instead ask God to bestow upon them good, repentance, and forgiveness, just as he would ask for himself, since he considers himself to be [sinful] just like them. He may even supplicate for their forgiveness and being pardoned more than he would do so for himself...

[15] Another reason is that [sinning may indirectly] remove arrogance and pride from one's heart, which may otherwise result from one being impressed with personal acts of worship. It instead replaces them with humility, brokenness, poverty and need. The Prophet (may God bless him and grant him peace) said in a *ḥadīth*, 'If you did not sin I would be afraid of something worse for you than that—pride.'[47] [...]

[16] [...] It may also be that a sin will lead a person to subsequently have fear, awe, and reverence of God, while also returning to Him, loving Him, preferring matters in accordance with His [pleasure], and taking refuge with God in a greater fashion than any of his pious deeds.

[47] Bayhaqī (*Shuʿab*) 6868; Haythamī 17,948. It is "sound" according to Albānī (*Ṣaḥīḥ al-Jāmiʿ al-ṣaghīr* 5303).

In addition, many times a sin ultimately [indirectly] leads a servant to become upright, flee to God and be distanced from his evil ways…

[19] God (Glory be to Him) loves and is greatly pleased with His servant when he repents. It has already been established that reward is concordant with the deed. One should not forget the happiness that one feels with sincere repentance. Deeply reflect on how your heart dances with joy [on such occasions], even though you may not know the exact reason for that happiness.

Only those whose hearts are [spiritually] alive feel joy when they repent. As for those whose hearts are [spiritually] dead, they only feel happiness when they fulfil their desires—they know of no other type of joy. One should weigh, therefore, between these two types of joy—the happiness that results from fulfilling one's desires is followed by a variety of emotions, including sadness, anxiety, worry and other afflictions. These people have only bought a moment's happiness, but it ultimately leads to eternal grief.

On the other hand, happiness that occurs due to obedience and after sincere repentance results in perpetual joy, bliss and a good life. Thus, you should compare the two and then select which is more appropriate for you. Ultimately, every person acts in a manner concordant with his nature.

[20] In addition, once one sees his sins, errors and negligence in fulfilling the rights of his Lord, he then appreciates his Lord's blessings more and considers them to be great, not few. He will also deem the many pious deeds that he has performed to be insufficient, because he is aware that the amount of good needed to cleanse himself of his inordinate number of filthy deeds[48] are many times greater…

There is such a vast difference between the state of the aforementioned person and the state of those who do not acknowledge the blessings of God, and feel that they should be given much more in line with their status, or feel that their Lord has not been fair with them. The latter stubbornly reject their lot due to what they feel is their perfect and virtuous nature. They feel they should have been given riches and should have been able to overpower their competition. These types are amongst those people most detested and hated people by God. The wisdom of God has dictated that these people remain abased, since they criticize the Creator and complain to Him, yet submit themselves to other creatures, serve them, and want more and more from them. Their hearts are preoccupied with serving

---

48 Q.XI.114: *Good deeds annul ill-deeds. This is a reminder for the mindful.*

rulers and people in powerful positions—they wait for the scraps and cast-offs thrown to them. Absent from their hearts is service to God, devotion to Him, delight in supplicating to Him, tranquility in remembering Him, finding consolation in fearing Him, and contentedness with Him. May God protect us from becoming bereft of His blessings and having our well-being removed away, from His retribution taking us suddenly, and from all types of His wrath...

[23] God (Glory be to Him) tests His servant with the pain of being barred and distant from Him, along with being removed from the comfort of proximity to Him. Thus, if the servant is content with this [spiritual distance] and does not miss proximity to God, but rather is content and at ease with other than God, then God will place him in a lower rank concordant with his actions as he is not worthy [of a more lofty one]. But if the servant implores and beseeches Him; seeks His aid like one who is anxious about [how he is going to get out of some calamity]; supplicates the prayer of one who is in dire need of his Lord; affirms that he has truly lost his [spiritual] life; and calls out to his Lord to return him to it; at that point he confirms that he is worthy of [a more lofty] rank, and is thus able to return to his [spiritual life], which he is in dire need of. His happiness and joy now intensify, and his pleasure and bliss become more complete. He now knows the importance [of proximity to God]; and thus, he holds fast and hard on to what he has...

[27] In addition, it becomes incumbent upon [this believer] to desist from mentioning the inadequacies of others or even thinking about them since he is preoccupied with his own faults. Blessed are those whose own faults preoccupy them from involving themselves with the inadequacies of others, and woe unto those who forget their faults and preoccupy themselves with the shortcomings of others. The latter is a sign of wretchedness while the former is one of the signs of bliss...

[30] If one contemplates the wisdom of God (Glory be to Him) it becomes clear that He has tested His servants and elite to allow them to reach the loftiest objectives and most perfect ends. They could not have reached these except by traversing a bridge composed of trials and tribulations. This bridge is so integral that they cannot reach Paradise except over it. Outwardly, this bridge involves suffering and hardship, but in reality it is a mercy, honour and blessing for us. God has bestowed upon us many great blessings and mercies as a result of these trials and tribulations.[49]

---

[49] See Zeni (tr.), *Ibn Qayyim al-Jawziyya on Divine Wisdom and the Problem of Evil*, pp. 239–257.

7. *THE WISDOM IN ALLOWING SINS TO BE PERPETRATED BY THE DISBELIEVERS*

Now, there exist many wise purposes in allowing the disbelievers to carry out sins and desires. Some of them are similar to those attained in allowing the believers to sin, like engendering regret or preventing arrogance and pride. The regret of a disbeliever may lead him or her to pursue knowledge and faith, and thus result in good for that individual. Another benefit in allowing the disbelievers to sin, from the viewpoint of the believers, will now be mentioned.

Ibn al-Qayyim mentions one wise purpose specific to the disbelievers when discussing the verse, *ye enjoy your lot awhile...and ye prate*:[50] "It is from the perfection of God's wisdom (Exalted is He) that He afflicts these [disbelievers] with distress and exhaustion in pursuing their desires and temptations so that they do not exclusively become engrossed in prating falsehood. Had they done so, these evil people would become 'leading callers to Hellfire'."[51]

These desires and temptations thus distract the disbelievers away from persecuting the believers. There are many types of these desires, including sexual temptations, drinking alcohol or abusing drugs, gambling, among many others. Although these all represent major sins and evils that are mostly done by the disbelievers, the pursuit of these desires and temptations is a lesser evil than persecuting and attacking the believers.

Many disbelievers may also be similarly distracted from pursuing major sins because they are engrossed in making a living or amassing wealth and materialistic things. The presence of these needs and desires results in them remaining insatiably preoccupied with worldly matters. Therefore, privation of the ontologic has distracted the disbelievers from pursuing worse evils.

Another wise purpose in allowing the perpetration of major sins is that they will eventually lead to disorder and weakness within the societies of the disbelievers. The occurrence of divisions and chaos can also distract the disbelievers from persecuting the believers. In conclusion, God's allowance of sins, lesser evils and privation amongst

---

50 Q.IX.69.

51 Ibn al-Qayyim, *Miftāḥ dār al-saʿāda*, vol. I, p. 110.

the disbelievers are for wise purposes. This will be further discussed later in this chapter.

8. *ALLOWING THE OCCURRENCE OF A RELIGIOUS RESURGENCE*

The Holy Lord loves repentance—this was discussed above. What follows is proof that God's love of the resurgence of the religion is even greater than His love of repentance. First, repentance only involves regretting a sin and avoiding that evil in the future. It is self-evident that carrying out righteous deeds is far superior to that avoidance (*tark*). As discussed previously, righteousness is far greater than piety (*taqwā* and *birr*).

Next, it will be contended that resurgence represents repentance followed by righteous deeds, and that the Qur'ān alludes to it by using the phrase *tāba wa aṣlaḥa*.[52] And God knows best. Repentance after a period of strangeness and distance from the Holy Lord followed by carrying out righteous deeds and forbidding others from major sins leads to that resurgence.

Righteousness and resurgence of the religion within a society are the ultimate objectives. God (Exalted is He) states in Sūrat Āl-ʿImrān: *And [that] there may spring from you a nation who invite to goodness, and enjoin right conduct and forbid indecency. Such are they who are successful.*[53] Then the Holy Lord informs the Prophet Muḥammad and the Companions: *Ye are the best community that hath been raised up for humankind. Ye enjoin right conduct and forbid indecency; and ye believe in God. And if the People of the Scripture had believed, it would have been better for them. Some of them are believers; but most of them are evil-livers.*[54] Indeed, the Prophet Muḥammad led—by the grace of God—to the guidance and resurgence of a previously disbelieving and ignorant society.

Now, the Prophet Muḥammad alluded to how God's pleasure with the repentance of His servant is greater than the relief and pleasure a

---

[52] See Q.VI.48 and 54 as well as Q.XVI.119, for instance.

[53] Q.III.104.

[54] Q.III.110.

person would experience after being saved from near-certain death.[55] Therefore, the Prophet (may God bless him and grant him peace) has described God's love of repentance in a manner understandable to our minds and extrapolatable to this world.

On the other hand, God's pleasure with righteousness has not been described in revelation similarly. It will be contended that this is because God's love of righteousness, and by extension resurgence, is far more sublime since the Holy Lord's reward for the righteous is indescribable. The Prophet Muḥammad has narrated from the Holy Lord: "I have prepared for My righteous servants (*ʿibādī al-ṣāliḥīn*) what no eye has seen, no ear has heard and no human heart has ever imagined."[56] This reward is only due to His love and pleasure with righteousness. Therefore, the love and pleasure that God (Exalted is He) has for resurgence, i.e. the combination of repentance and then carrying out righteous deeds, cannot be described fully for it is so great.

If God's love of one righteous and resurgent believer is as described above, then what about the resurgence of an entire group of righteous believers within a society? God's love of the resurgence of a society is even greater and more sublime than that of an individual. But this resurgence could not have occurred unless a whole array of causes existed leading that society to become distant from the Holy Lord followed by a critical mass of its members repenting, carrying out righteous deeds and striving against evil. In conclusion, the resurgence of a society is so beloved to the Holy Lord that He has created this world in such a manner composed of both good and evil. God's wisdom is truly dazzling.

---

[55] The Prophet Muḥammad said in a *ḥadīth*: "God is more pleased with the repentance of His servant than a man who [is forced to] encamp at a spot where his life is in jeopardy. This [individual's] riding animal carries his food and water, and he goes to rest and sleep for a short while only to wake up and find his riding animal gone. He starts looking for it and suffers from severe thirst. He then says, 'I will go back to my [initial] spot to sleep and await my death.' He lays his head down in anticipation of death, but awakes to find his riding animal standing there still laden with his provisions, food and drink. God is more pleased with the repentance of the believing servant than this person when he finds his riding animal." Bukhārī 6309; Muslim 2675/6952; Tirmidhī 2498; Ibn Māja 4249; Aḥmad 3627.

[56] Bukhārī 3244; Muslim 2824/7132; Tirmidhī 3197; Ibn Māja 4328; Aḥmad 9649.

9. Allowing gratuitous evil manifests the importance of implementing the Divine Law

It has already been discussed that disobedience of God's commandments, particularly the perpetration of major sins, is evil and deserving of punishment. Here the importance of forbidding evil, upholding the divine limits and carrying out God's legal punishments (in Muslim majority countries) for major sins will be discussed. It will be maintained that if society does not obey His prohibitions it will fall into greater evils; and if it does not carry out the legal punishments for major sins, then that represents one way for it to fall into gratuitous evils.

The Prophet Muḥammad (may God bless him and grant him peace) said: "If people witness major sins (*munkar*) [being perpetrated], but do nothing thereafter, God may punish them all."[57] The Messenger also said: "I swear by Him in Whose Hand is my soul! Either you all enjoin what is good and forbid major sins (*munkar*) or God will send upon you a punishment. Even if you supplicate to Him [to remove this punishment, He] will not answer you."[58] Many verses of the Bible also confirm these sound *ḥadīth*s. Consider, for instance:

> The house of Israel and the house of Judah have broken my covenant which I made with their fathers. Therefore thus saith the Lord, Behold, I will bring evil upon them, which they shall not be able to escape; and though they shall cry unto me, I will not hearken unto them... Therefore pray not thou for this people, neither lift up a cry or prayer for them: for I will not hear *them* in the time that they cry unto me for their trouble.[59]

---

[57] Ibn Māja 4005; Aḥmad 1; Ibn Ḥibbān 305. It is "authentic" according to Albānī (*Ṣaḥīḥ al-Jāmiᶜ al-ṣaghīr* 1974).

[58] Tirmidhī 2169; Aḥmad 23,301; Bayhaqī (*Sunan*) 20,199. It is "sound" according to Albānī (*Ṣaḥīḥ al-Jāmiᶜ al-ṣaghīr* 7070). The Prophet mentioned that this punishment may include being overpowered by one's enemies or having to endure infighting. See Ibn Māja 4019; Bayhaqī (*Shuᶜab*) 3042. It is "authentic" according to Albānī (*Silsilat al-aḥādīth al-ṣaḥīḥa*, 106). Of note, ᶜAlī b. Abī Ṭālib advised upon his deathbed: "Do not forgo enjoining good and forbidding evil. Otherwise, the most evil will lead you, and [God] will not respond to your supplications." Ibn Jarīr al-Ṭabarī, *Tārīkh al-Ṭabarī*, vol. V, p. 148; Ibn Kathīr, *al-Bidāya wa'l-nihāya*, vol. VII, p. 327.

[59] Jeremiah 11.10–14. See also Jeremiah 9.25–26: "Behold, the days come, saith the LORD, that I will punish all them which are circumcised with the uncircumcised... [for] all the house of Israel are uncircumcised in the heart." See also Jeremiah 7.9–16; 23.39–40; and 44.20–23.

Next, gratuitous evils, in the vast majority of instances, are due to the continued perpetration of major sins. Had societies worked to minimize major sins and punished those who perpetrated them accordingly, then gratuitous evils would have become either few or non-existent. If, however, the society fails to forbid and nullify widespread major sins and wickedness, then all members (including the innocent, children and weak) will be susceptible to gratuitous evils. The Prophet Muḥammad was asked: "Will we be ruined even if the righteous (*al-ṣāliḥūn*) are alive amongst us?" The Prophet (may God bless him and grant him peace) replied: "Yes, if wickedness is widespread."[60]

The responsibility of forbidding major sins and evil should be assumed by the believing society, which must be proactive and not adopt quietism or passivity. The Prophet Muḥammad (may God bless him and grant him peace) said: "If sins (*al-maʿāṣī*) are committed amongst a people, and they are able to prevent them or change them but do not, God may send a punishment upon them all."[61] These aforementioned *ḥadīths* are similar to God's statement: *And guard yourselves against a chastisement which [will not] fall exclusively on those of you who are wrongdoers, and know that God is severe in punishment.*[62]

One of the greatest evils is murder. The Almighty Lord has commanded that murderers should be punished concordantly by the death penalty. Not implementing the divine commandments or allowing murderers to be imprisoned for a limited time and later freeing them risks further unjust deaths and crimes being committed. A recent study published by the U.S. Department of Justice,[63] which

---

60 Bukhārī 3346; Muslim 2880/7235; Tirmidhī 2185; Ibn Māja 3953; Aḥmad 27,413.

61 Abū Dāwūd 4339; Ibn Māja 4009; Ibn Ḥibbān 300; Bayhaqī (*Sunan*) 20,192. It is "sound" according to Albānī (*Silsilat al-aḥādīth al-ṣaḥīḥa* 3353).

62 Q.VIII.25

63 See Matthew R. Durose, Alexia D. Cooper and Howard N. Snyder, "Recidivism of Prisoners Released in 30 States in 2005: Patterns from 2005 to 2010," Bureau of Justice Statistics, U.S. Department of Justice, April 2014. They defined violent crime as including: homicide (murder, nonnegligent manslaughter and negligent manslaughter); rape/sexual assault; robbery; and assault. Other offenses included property offenses (such as burglary, larceny/motor vehicle theft and fraud/forgery); drug offenses (such as possession or trafficking); and public order offenses (such as weapons and driving under the influence of intoxicants). The report stated that the overall recidivism rate over five years was 76.6%. However, the recidivism rate may be even higher as these criminals may perpetrate some crimes and yet go uncaught.

followed 404,638 American state prisoners, revealed that the 5-year recidivism rate for violent criminals to perpetrate another violent crime was 33.1% while it was 71.3% in total for any and all crimes. Failure to implement the Holy Lord's commandments in these cases clearly has led to further gratuitous evils.

Murder and rape should be non-existent within a society. The fact that those who have perpetrated such crimes are not deterred from doing so in the first place, and then instead of being punished appropriately are released back into society to perpetrate further violent crimes is due to the failure of society and its citizens to carry out the commandments of the Holy Lord, Who is the Most Wise. The evil and disorder caused to a society by violent crimes as well as the other property, drug and public order offences (as discussed in the aforementioned study) cannot be overstated. Furthermore, the high recidivism rates of murderers reveals that imprisonment for a limited duration fails, in the majority of cases, in its objective and only leads to a society enduring further violent crimes, encountering more death and destruction, bearing greater costs and wasting more resources.

Likewise, failure to implement the legal punishment for fornication or adultery (as prescribed in the Torah or Qur'ān) only leads to both becoming widespread. That has clearly become the case in many disbelieving societies. God (Exalted is He) states: *The adulterer and the adulteress, scourge ye each one of them (with) a hundred stripes. And let not pity for the twain withhold you from obedience to God, if ye believe in God and the Last Day.*[64] Here, God (Glorious is He) admonishes societies to fulfill His commandments, and also to avoid having pity for the perpetrators. We must avoid succumbing to claims that these legal punishments are harsh and contrary to mercy, for they are wise and result in predominant goods for the society at large. Those societies that do not uphold the Divine Law will inevitably suffer further evil, including the gratuitous type.

Preventing fornication and alcohol (or drug) use would stop or significantly decrease the incidence of yet other major sins, like rape. Had alcohol and fornication been absent within a society, then

---

64 Q.XXIV.2.

tragedies like that which occurred to Rowe's child[65] could most likely have been prevented. Gratuitous evils exist within a society due to its members perpetrating major sins and failing to carry out the divine punishments.

Let us also consider theft in this context. Theft by individuals through Ponzi schemes (like that carried out by Bernie Madoff, which involved tens of billions of dollars) or through other forms (like that by Marc Dreyer who sold fictitious promissory notes in the hundreds of million of dollars), or by corporations (like Enron, WorldCom and Tyco, among countless others) have resulted in much ruin for thousands of their victims. How many have been harmed and how many lives have these criminals knowingly ruined and destroyed? How many other thieves have gone uncaught or managed to elude accountability? How much corruption and bribery is there within corporations or bureaucracies?

Consider the Old Testament story during the conquests of Joshua when it was reported that one man named Achan stole from the spoils of war. As a result, all of the Israelites had to suffer the consequences for a period of time. It is reported that the Holy Lord said to Joshua: "Israel hath sinned, and they have also transgressed my covenant which I commanded them: for they have even taken of the accursed thing, and have also stolen... Therefore the children of Israel could not stand before their enemies, but turned their backs before their enemies, because they were accursed: neither will I be with you any more, except ye destroy the accursed from among you."[66] It was only after Joshua and the Israelites punished Achan that the "Lord turned from the fierceness of his anger" and allowed them to resume conquering their enemies. This involved only one case, so what of the ramifications when theft is widespread? It is truly a disaster for society.

It is also important to reflect upon another case, which occurred after the opening of Mecca, when a prominent woman stole an item, and one young Companion complied with a request of her tribe to

---

65 This describes a true story of a girl from Flint, Michigan who was raped and murdered by the drunken envious boyfriend of her biological mother. Rowe discusses it in many of his writings as an example of gratuitous evil. William Rowe, "Evil and Theodicy", in *Philosophical Topics*, vol. XVI, no. 2, 1988, p. 120.

66 See Joshua 7.1–26.

speak with the Prophet Muḥammad and ask that he not implement the legal punishment for it. The Prophet Muḥammad (may God bless him and grant him peace) responded: "Do you seek to plead in a matter regarding a legal punishment of God? [...] I swear by God that even if Fāṭima, the daughter of Muḥammad, had stolen I would cut off her hand."[67] This shows the importance of the legal punishment, and illustrates the fundamental significance of legal impartiality. Without the stern deterrent, theft and its harm become widespread, as we see within many societies nowadays.

The objective of upholding these legal punishments is to preserve the life, dignity and wealth of the innocent members of a society. Ultimately, the true believers whom God (Glorious is He) has praised *do not fear to be censured by anyone who might censure them*,[68] and they recognize that they must be God-fearing rather than afraid of people who are not believers or think themselves to be wiser than the Most Wise. A further illustration of the critical significance in carrying out the commandments of the Holy Lord in regards to legal punishments, and how the failure to do so is destructive, will be discussed in the next chapter.

Societies will eventually become ruined if they continue to perpetrate major sins. However, some individuals might not be ruined immediately, and some wicked individuals may even prosper. God (Exalted is He) states: *Let not the unbelievers think that our respite to them is good for themselves: We grant them respite* [*only so*] *that they may grow in their iniquity: But they will have a shameful punishment.*[69] Therefore, the Holy Lord's reprieve of the wicked results in them perpetrating further wickedness and deserving greater punishment in the Hellfire. The Prophet Muḥammad (may God bless him and grant him peace)

---

[67] See Bukhārī 4304; Muslim 1688/4411; Tirmidhī 1430; Ibn Māja 2547; Abū Dāwūd 4373; Nasā'ī 4903; Aḥmad 25,297. Of note, in Bukhārī 4304, Muslim 1688/4411 and Nasā'ī 4903, Usāma immediately asked the Prophet to supplicate for his forgiveness. In addition, ʿĀ'isha, who narrated the *ḥadīth*, stated that this woman sincerely repented (*ḥasunat tawbat*[uha]) and mended her ways thereafter, and would come to her to ask the Prophet for some requests. Finally, that which is stolen must come to what is equivalent to 1 gram of gold in order for the legal punishment to be carried out.

[68] Q.V.54 (Muḥammad Asad translation).

[69] Q.III.178 (Yusuf Ali translation).

said: "God will grant respite to an oppressor for a period of time, but once He seizes him He will not let him go."[70]

In addition to that reprieve, the Holy Lord may even grant them blessings (*niʿam*) so that they become deluded into thinking that they are good. God (Exalted is He) states: *And those who deny Our revelations—step by step We lead them on from whence they know not.*[71] Rāzī states in his exegesis: "Every time [these disbelievers] perpetrate wickedness or sins, God will grant them more types of blessings and material goods in this world. They will then become more insolent, more engrossed in wickedness, more unrestrained in wrongdoing, and perpetrate greater and greater sins—all of that is due to them being [deluded] by those blessings."[72] The Holy Lord is not unjust, and He will place the wicked in their appropriate levels of punishment in the Hereafter.

Societies are subject to complex factors—some of which take them to ruin and disorder, while others like upholding justice allow them to persist and remain ordered. Regardless, if societies continue to perpetrate major sins, do not uphold the legal punishments, and continue to oppress one another without defending justice, they face ruin. God (Exalted is He) states: *Even thus is the grasp of thy Lord when He graspeth the townships while they are doing wrong. Lo! His grasp is painful, very strong.*[73]

That said, God, Who is the Most Forgiving, treats His servants who do much wrong in a manner better than what they deserve: *If God took humankind to task by that which they deserve, He would not leave a living creature on the surface of the earth; but He reprieveth them unto an appointed term; and when their term cometh—then verily (they will know that) God is ever Seer of His servants.*[74] The Holy Lord forgives those who repent

---

[70] Bukhārī 4686; Muslim 2583/6581; Tirmidhī 3110; Ibn Māja 4018.

[71] Q.VII.182. The Prophet Muḥammad (may God bless him and grant him peace) said: "If God wills goodness for His servant, He will quicken his punishment in this world. On the other hand, if God wills evil [to overcome] him, He will delay his recompense [i.e. punishment] until the Day of Resurrection." Tirmidhī 2396; al-Ḥākim 8799. It is "authentic" according to Albānī (*Ṣaḥīḥ al-Jāmiʿ al-ṣaghīr* 308).

[72] See *Tafsīr al-Rāzī*, vol. XV, p. 418.

[73] Q.XI.102.

[74] Q.XXXV.45. See also Q.XVI.61: *If God were to take humankind to task for their wrongdoing, he would not leave hereon a living creature, but He reprieveth them to an appointed term; and when their term cometh, they cannot put (it) off an hour nor (yet) advance (it).*

and He delays, in many instances, the punishment of those who do not, giving them further chances to mend their ways.

Finally, if the legal limits of God (Exalted is He) are upheld, then it must be remembered that the punishments in this life are much less than that of the Hellfire: *And verily We make them taste the lower punishment before the greater, that haply they may return.*[75] Assuming an individual or a society rights and mends its ways in response to a punishment, then this punishment becomes paradoxically a mercy from God in reality. Of course, for those who die as disbelievers—and they are the majority—then all that they do and are afflicted with is evil and harmful.

10. Allowing gratuitous evil manifests the importance of fighting for God's sake

The second reason for the appearance of gratuitous evil, besides the failure to implement the legal punishments for major sins, is a society's failure to strive and fight against those who harbor enmity to it and attack it. The punishment resulting from the failure of a society to fight against those who oppress it is evident in the following verses: *O ye who believe, what is the matter with you, that, when ye are asked to go forth in the cause of God, ye cling heavily to the earth? Do ye prefer the life of this world to the Hereafter? But little is the comfort of this life, as compared with the Hereafter. Unless ye go forth, He will punish you with a grievous penalty, and put others in your place; but Him ye would not harm in the least. For God hath power over all things.*[76]

The Prophet Muḥammad (may God bless him and grant him peace) also alluded to this by specifically warning the Muslims that if they "forsake fighting…, God will bring humiliation upon them until they return to their religion".[77] In such a case, the society will be punished in various manners, one of which will be gratuitous evil perpetrated

---

75 Q.XXXII.21.

76 Q.IX.38–39 (Yusuf Ali translation).

77 Abū Dāwūd 3462; Aḥmad 5007; Bayhaqī (*Sunan*) 10,703. It is "authentic" according to Albānī (*Silsilat al-aḥādīth al-ṣaḥīḥa* 11). The two other things that the Prophet warned the Muslims from doing are selling through ʿīna, which is a method of taking interest through the sale of products, and being content with farming.

by the disbelievers and astray groups against it. Therefore, fighting in a pious manner for God's sake is crucial to avoiding gratuitous evils.

The Prophet Muḥammad also said specifically regarding the Muslims: "There will come a time when all nations will summon one another to descend upon you all like diners descend upon their dish."[78] The Companions asked: "Is that because our [Community] will be small in number?" The Prophet responded: "No. You will be large in number, but you will become like the scum on the surface of floodwater. God will [decree that] weakness and confusion pervade your hearts, and your enemies will no longer fear you. That is all because you will love this world and hate death."[79]

It should also be mentioned that had the majority of Muslims or a critical mass of them been believers (*mu'minūn*), they could not have been overcome by the disbelievers—God (Exalted is He) states: *God will not give the disbelievers any way (of success) against the believers.*[80] However, since the society perpetrated the wicked major sins and neglected their duties to the Holy Lord, He allowed the disbelievers to overcome the Muslims and/or sectarian infighting to occur.

The Prophet again mentioned that all nations will come together against the Muslims at that time. It appears—and God knows best—that the time we live in is what was prophesied. In past centuries attacks were limited to one or two nations waging war against the Muslims; but since 1945, most religious groups to varying degrees have oppressed, carried out genocide or perpetrated war against the Muslims. The death of Muslims in this time period approaches the six million Jews who were killed in the Holocaust.

Consider the number of Muslims who have been killed since 1945: 525,000 Algerians (from 1954–1962) and another 100,000 (in the 1990s); 1.5 million Afghanis and 60,000 Chechens (due to wars against them by the Soviets and Russians from 1979–1992 and 1996 onward, respectively); 350,000 Iraqis (by the economic sanctions of the 1990s and the 1991 war), another 300,000 (by the

---

[78] This is akin to the English idiom: "Eat you alive," meaning to overwhelm or defeat completely.

[79] Abū Dāwūd 4297; Aḥmad 22,397. It is "authentic" according to Albānī (*Silsilat al-aḥādīth al-ṣaḥīḥa* 958).

[80] Q.IV.141.

Iraqi government) and 150,000 (as a result of the 2003 war and its aftermath); 700,000 Iraqis and Iranians (due to the war between them from 1980–1988); ~74,000 Kashmiris (by the Indian government); 200,000 Bosnians and Kosovars (by the Serbians); 500,000 Somalis (as a result of starvation and war since 1991); nearly 100,000 Libyans (from 2011 until now); 600,000 Syrians (from 2011 until now, as well as the events of 1982); 200,000 Yemenis (from 2011 until now); 40,000 Rohingya (by the Buddhist government of Myanmar since 2017); and 50,000 Palestinians (from the Zionist wars and occupation since 1948).[81] These figures do not include those who were injured, raped, oppressed and displaced. Nor does it include all of the financial suffering they have endured due to loss or theft of their material possessions or destruction of their homes. These gratuitous evils and tragedies are truly monstrous.

The killing of innocent Muslims must stop. If the disbelievers are indifferent or continue to contribute to that killing then the believing Muslims must recognize that their state will only change if they take matters into their own hands and depend on the Holy Lord. The believers should remember that the Almighty Lord has advised and commanded them: *How should ye not fight for the cause of God and of the feeble among men and of the women and the children who are crying: Our Lord! Bring us forth from out this town of which the people are oppressors! Oh, give us from Thy presence some protecting friend! Oh, give us from Thy presence some*

---

[81] Figures regarding casualties occurring in Algeria, Afghanistan, Iraq, Somalia and the Arab-Israeli wars are derived from Matthew White, *Atrocities: The 100 Deadliest Episodes in Human History* (New York: W. W. Norton & Company, 2012), pp. 505–519 and 559. The Bosnian and Kosovar deaths are from Samantha Power, *"A Problem from Hell": America and the Age of Genocide*, p. 251. Some of the numbers quoted here may be lower than the real number. For example, a commonly quoted figure maintained by the Algerians is that one million were killed between 1954 and 1962, but again the figures according to Matthew White were used. The number of Kashmiri deaths is averaged between the 47,000 claimed by the Indian government and the 100,000 by many Kashmiri groups. The Syrian Observatory for Human Rights counted 570,000 Syrian deaths from 2011 to March 2019; but the true figure is likely to be much higher. Figures in other instances were based on media estimates. The aforementioned only include events wherein more than 30,000 Muslims have been killed. For instance, reliable figures do not exist regarding the number of Chinese Uyghur Muslims killed, and thus they were not mentioned within the text.

defender![82] Rāzī states that this verse represents the Exalted's criticism of the Muslims who have abandoned fighting.[83] Then God (Exalted is He) states in the following verse: *Those who believe fight in the cause of God, and those who reject faith fight in the cause of evil: So fight ye against the friends of Satan.*[84] It is incumbent upon the believers to fight against oppression and persecution, otherwise the disbelievers and deviant groups will continue to kill the Muslims or even commit genocide (as pointed out in some of the aforementioned examples).

As regards the detractors of Islam who claim that the Muslims only desire to fight wars and oppress others, the former do so simply to maintain the Muslims in a weakened state, persecuted and expelled. How many more genocides must occur before the Muslims become justified in defending themselves?

In conclusion, gratuitous evil afflicts the Muslims if they, as a society, fail to carry out the legal punishments for major sins, or if they become attached to this world and neglect fighting in His path. It is only by becoming pious and righteous that Muslims may experience the required resurgence. We must rely and trustfully depend on the Almighty Lord to achieve success: *If God is your helper none can overcome you; and if He withdraws His help from you, who is there who can help you after Him? In God let believers put their trust.*[85]

11. Blessed and Righteous Strangers can only Emerge if Strangeness and Gratutious Evil is Allowed

The Prophet (may God bless him and grant him peace) said: "Verily, Islam started as something strange (*gharīb*) and it will again revert to being strange just as it began. Blessed are the strangers (*ghurabā'*)."[86]

---

[82] Q.IV.75. Many scholars maintain that this verse was revealed regarding Mecca, and that God did answer their prayers as the Prophet Muḥammad and the Companions ultimately liberated it. See *Tafsīr al-Ṭabarī*, vol. VIII, pp. 543–546; *Tafsīr al-Rāzī*, vol. X, pp. 142–144.

[83] *Tafsīr al-Rāzī*, vol. X, p. 140.

[84] Q.IV.76 (Yusuf Ali translation).

[85] Q.III.160.

[86] Muslim 145/372; Ibn Māja 3986; Aḥmad 3784. Ibn al-Qayyim states: "Thus the believers are few when compared to all of humanity, the scholars are a small subset of the believers, and these [strangers] are only a minority of the scholars... Know that these [strangers] are the true [and elite] of humanity." See Zeni (tr.), *Ibn Qayyim al-Jawziyya on Knowledge*, p. 210.

This *ḥadīth* alludes to the ontologic willing of strangeness to occur. Moreover, it alludes to the fact that the emergence of those who have faith and carry out righteous actions in these times is desired from a deontologic perspective since they are blessed and praiseworthy. This represents a key concept in resolving the problem of gratuitous evil.

The true religion can only become strange if gratuitous evil is allowed to occur. If one reflects on the history of humanity it becomes clear that God (Exalted is He) sent the prophets and messengers only after worship of God alone or goodness became very rare or non-existent.[87] Thus had gratuitous evils not led to the conditions whereby the true religion becomes strange there would have been no need to send prophets—a righteous or truly faithful believer would have sufficed. So the presence of gratuitous evil resulting in that environment of overwhelming evil is permitted to indirectly allow for the emergence of the best of humanity.

In this regard, consider those mentioned in the Bible and Qur'ān, such as the nations of Noah, Abraham, Jonah and Muḥammad: the messenger was only sent after nearly all the people—if not all—were polytheists or worshipping other deities besides God. The fact that these disbelieving societies exhibited preponderant evil constituted a setting wherein a prophet was warranted. Thus the Holy Lord in His wisdom created the ontologic conditions wherein only a prophet could fully and completely fulfill the role of guiding the people back to God's religion. This is so because the prophets are the most blessed of humanity.

Moreover, had predominant disbelief not occurred—for instance had all of humanity believed in Noah and continued to be good generation after generation—there would have been no need for subsequent prophets. Hence Abraham, Moses, Jesus or Muḥammad (may God bless them all) would not have existed as we know them. But obviously God's determination involved the sending of these

[87] The only exception to this occurred in the case of the Israelites whereby prophets were sent in each generation to keep them on the Straight Path. Even in the case of the Israelites, God (Exalted is He) affirmed that many of them had hearts that were: *hardened and became as rocks, or worse than rocks, for hardness* [Q.II.74], that they worshipped Baal and other false deities, and that they killed some of the prophets, as mentioned previously.

great prophets, as well as a multitude of others, whom are all beloved to Him.

In essence, gratuitous evil is dysteleological from the vast majority of aspects, but not all, as some indirect goodness does eventually arise from it. Thus gratuitous evil may be dysteleological for those living at that time, but ultimately results in indirect good at a later time or a future generation.[88]

Now, since no new prophets would be sent following the death of the Messenger Muḥammad (may God bless him and grant him peace), the objective is to allow the emergence of those who strive against evil—i.e. the truly faithful, martyrs and righteous. The degree to which true belief has become rare or strange today is less than when the Prophet Muḥammad was sent since the truly faithful and righteous still possess the preserved guidance of the Qur'ān and Sunna. This is concordant to God's wisdom. The degree of strangeness in which a prophet is required to guide to the truth is necessarily worse than that which the truly faithful and righteous (through the preserved guidance of the Messenger) are required to contend with. That does not negate that the evil at this time is greater (as discussed in Chapter Eleven), but rather that only the degree of strangeness of the true religion is less now than it was before the Prophet Muḥammad was sent with his message. God (Glorious is He) in His wisdom allocates those who are appropriate for each circumstance.

The Prophet Muḥammad informed us that such a time will come. Those believers who possess certainty recognize that this time of strangeness is inevitable. Their response to it becomes like those who preceded them: *Those unto whom men said: Lo! the people have gathered against you, therefore fear them. (The threat of danger) but increased the faith of them and they cried: God is sufficient for us! Most Excellent is He in Whom we trust!*[89] Therefore, these faithful believers recognize the custom (*sunna*) of God, i.e. the inevitable occurrence of strangeness, and that it is allowed so that they may manifest their sincere loyalty to God, true faith, trustful dependence on Him and striving for His sake.

---

[88] There is one exception to this general rule and it will be discussed towards the end of Point 13.

[89] Q.III.173.

A renewal occurred, for instance, during the time of Ghazālī. His efforts in writing the *Iḥyā'* and other works taught in the Niẓāmiyya schools would ultimately lead to a "Sunni revival". This renewal then allowed Saladin to defeat the Fāṭimid Ismāᶜīlī[90] Shiite dynasty in Egypt, unite the strength of the Muslim Community and take back Jerusalem in a just and equitable manner[91] (just as ᶜUmar b. al-Khaṭṭāb took Jerusalem centuries earlier). Islamic knowledge sparked that revival, and this is the methodology of the Prophet Muḥammad (may God bless him and grant him peace), which is beloved by God (Glorious and Exalted is He).

The Prophet Muḥammad maintained that there would always remain a group of his Community upon the truth[92] and that the religion of Islam (both the Qur'ān and Sunna) would be preserved until that time. The Prophet (may God bless him and grant him peace) also said: "My Community is like the rain: it is not discernable whether the first of it is better or the last."[93] In fact, the last of this Community will become resurgent through the efforts of righteous individuals, by the grace of God. Allowing resurgence to occur amongst the followers of Muḥammad illustrates the glory of God, Who enabled and blessed them to do so, as well as the greatness of the

---

90 The Fāṭimids ruled much of North Africa from 909–1171 CE. The Nizārī Ismāᶜīlīs split away from the Fāṭimid Ismāᶜīlīs and initially settled in Alamut. The Nizārīs were later conquered by the Mongols, but some remain and are led by Aga Khan IV. The Qarmatis formed another Ismāᶜīlī sect—they are most known for stealing the Black Stone from the Holy Kaᶜba—however they are extinct. The Druze represent an offshoot of Ismāᶜīlī doctrine as they initially began by proclaiming that one of the Fāṭimid rulers was divine. See Daftary, *A History of Shiᶜi Islam*, pp. 105–144.

91 See Abdul Rahman Azzam, *Saladin: The Triumph of the Sunni Revival* (Cambridge: Islamic Texts Society, 2014), pp. 8 and 12. The holy city of Jerusalem has only been ruled by the believers when they did so with justice and tolerance. However, if a critical mass of pious believers do not exist, then the Almighty Lord has ontologically permitted Jerusalem to be ruled by disbelievers. This applies to the Muslims as it did with the early Israelites before the Messenger Jesus was sent to them.

92 This is a reference to the *ḥadīth*: "There will always exist a group from my Community upon the truth. They will not be harmed by those who have forsaken or opposed them until God's decree comes." Muslim 1920/4950; Tirmidhī 2229; Abū Dāwūd 4252; Ibn Māja 10.

93 Tirmidhī 2869; Aḥmad 12,327; Ibn Ḥibbān 7226. It is "authentic" according to Albānī (*Silsilat al-aḥādīth al-ṣaḥīḥa* 2286).

Prophet Muḥammad (may God bless him and grant him peace) and that his message has been preserved for that time of resurgence.

In conclusion, the allowance of gratuitous evil leads to times of strangeness, which then indirectly results in the emergence and manifestation of righteous believers. It is only through the ontologic decree of the existence of evil that the righteous may strive and fight against evil in a multitude of fashions, and display their sincerity and true love of the Holy Lord to the greatest of degrees.

12. An Exposition on the Fine-Tuning of Strength and Good Amongst the Muslims

Another corollary of the Prophet Muḥammad's *ḥadīth* that "Islam started as something strange (*gharīb*) and it will again revert to being strange"[94] is that the strength of the early Muslims, i.e. that of the Predecessors and caliphates (Rāshidī, Ummayad and Abbasid), was fine-tuned so that it was not so overwhelming as to result in all nations becoming Muslim. God (Exalted is He) has fine-tuned His creation from both the ontologic and deontologic aspects.

Although the Islamic empire did extend from Spain to Southeast Asia, it did not, for instance, encompass all of the Europeans. The latter chose to fight against the Muslims and reject Islam through their own free will, and the Holy Lord ontologically allowed them to do so.

The early Muslims' expansion was also limited by events, six of which will be alluded to here: the martyrdom of three of the Rightly-Guided Caliphs, the wars against the apostates, the internecine war, the Plague of ʿAmwās, the destruction wrought by al-Ḥajjāj, and the Mongolian invasion. Later events will also be mentioned briefly. Nonetheless, despite all of the above, the Islamic empire still spread to many continents and brought peace and faith to those who chose to accept Islam.

The martyrdom of ʿUmar, ʿUthmān and ʿAlī, as well as that of al-Ḥusayn (may God be pleased with them all), led to many calamities, trials and evils that resulted in discord and division. In general, the calamity that occurred to this Community due to the martyrdom of

---

[94] Muslim 145/372; Ibn Māja 3986; Aḥmad 3784.

ᶜUmar is greater than that of ᶜUthman, which is greater than that of ᶜAlī, which is greater than the martyrdom of al-Ḥusayn.[95] Those who bewail the martyrdom of al-Ḥusayn greater than that of ᶜUmar have misunderstood ᶜUmar's eminence in this Community as well as that of the other Rightly-Guided Caliphs—they should mourn the martyrdom of ᶜUmar, ᶜUthmān and ᶜAlī just as much if not more.

ᶜUthmān's martyrdom in particular precipitated the internecine wars. This, as well as the preceding wars against the apostates (which was discussed in Chapter Six), led to the death of many Companions and Successors. Furthermore, the internecine wars have resulted in much discord and division that persist to this day. Herein follows a brief discussion regarding the internecine wars: the Battle of al-Jamal and the Battle of Ṣiffīn.

As for the former battle, ᶜĀ'isha, Ṭalḥa and al-Zubayr (all of whom were promised Paradise) sought those who killed ᶜUthmān amongst the camp of ᶜAlī. Neither they nor ᶜAlī sought fighting; rather, they desired to make peace and reach an agreement. Indeed, they had come to an agreement but war was instigated thereafter by the killers of ᶜUthmān and their loyalists.[96] Unfortunately, Ṭalḥa and al-Zubayr were martyred in this battle, while ᶜĀ'isha returned back to Medina.

The second confrontation at the Battle of Ṣiffīn involved those in the camp of ᶜAlī against those following Muᶜāwiya. The latter stated that he would delay pledging to ᶜAlī until after the killers of ᶜUthmān were held accountable. Unfortunately, ᶜAlī was never able to hold the killers of ᶜUthmān accountable, whether due to his inability, the

---

95 Sunnis affirm that grave injustice was perpetrated in the killing of al-Ḥusayn, and thus mourn his martyrdom. On the other hand, the Shiites consider his martyrdom to be of "cosmic proportions," and thus hold ᶜĀshūrā' ritual processions to commemorate it. The five elements of ᶜĀshūrā' are: (1) "visitation (*ziyāra*) of Ḥusayn's shrine in Karbalā'", (2) "the mourning gathering (*majlis ḥusaynī*)", (3) "public processions (*mawkib ḥusaynī*)", (4) "practices of mortification...[such as] breast-beating...flagellation with chains (*zanjīr*) or with blades, incisions in the skull (*taṭbīr*) and other means of shedding blood", and (5) "theatrical representation of the drama of Karbalā'." See Peter Chelkowski, "Diverse Religious Practices," in Nasr, Dabashi and Nasr (eds), *Shiᶜism: Doctrines, Thought, and Spirituality*, pp. 263–268, and Sabrina Mervin, "ᶜĀshūrā' Rituals, Identity and Politics: A Comparative Approach (Lebanon and India)", in Daftary and Miskinzoda (eds.), *The Study of Shiᶜi Islam: History, Theology and Law*, pp. 511–512.

96 See Ibn Taymiyya, *Minhāj al-Sunna al-Nabawiyya*, vol. IV, pp. 316–317.

failure of his army to obey him, or for other unclear and complex reasons.[97]

Of note, Ibn Taymiyya states that had ʿAlī pursued "the killers of ʿUthmān, the harm [and number of innocent Muslims killed] would have been less than that in the Battles of al-Jamal and Ṣiffīn".[98] Ibn Taymiyya also maintains that any criticisms directed at ʿUthmān, most prominent amongst them his appointment of some of his relatives in the latter half of his caliphate, pale in comparison to the harm which occurred as a result of the fighting during the caliphate of ʿAlī.[99]

That said, the reason that Muʿāwiya and his camp were in the wrong is because pledging allegiance to the Caliph ʿAlī and following him takes precedence over holding the killers of ʿUthmān accountable (even though those killers were amongst the camp of ʿAlī). Note that the Prophet Muḥammad (may God bless him and grant him peace) prophesized years earlier that one group would be "closer to the truth"[100]—not that it was completely upon the truth, nor that the other group lacked elements of truth and goodness.

It is noteworthy that some of the prominent Companions, like Saʿd b. Abī Waqqās (one of the ten promised Paradise), Usāma b. Zayd (who was beloved to the Prophet), Muḥammad b. Maslama (who was told by the Prophet to avoid the dissension[101]), Zayd b. Thābit and Abū Hurayra, among many others,[102] refused to fight in either

---

97 Ibid, vol. IV, pp. 382–385, 410–412 and 448.

98 Ibn Taymiyya, *Minhāj al-Sunna al-Nabawiyya*, vol. V, p. 516.

99 See ibid, vol. VI, pp. 156–157.

100 Muslim 1065/2457; Aḥmad 11,018.

101 The Prophet Muḥammad (may God bless him and grant him peace) said: "There will occur dissension, division, and discord. When that happens break your sword and reside in your house until some stray hand [kills you] or you die [a nonviolent death]." Ibn Māja 3962; Aḥmad 16,029. It is "authentic" according to Albānī (*Ṣaḥīḥ al-Jāmiʿ al-ṣaghīr* 2432).

102 Ibn Taymiyya relays that Muḥammad b. Sīrīn states that no more than 30 to 100 of the Prophet's Companions (out of approximately 10,000 alive at that time) took sides or participated in those battles. Ibn Taymiyya, *Minhāj al-Sunna al-Nabawiyya*, vol. VI, pp. 236–237.

camp.[103] The Prophet Muḥammad said years earlier: "There will occur dissension (*fitna*) wherein the one who sits out is better...than one who runs to it [and participates in it]. If one can find a safe haven from it, one should take refuge therein."[104]

We should recall that God (Glorious is He) also advised in the Qur'ān, which was revealed many years prior to these events: *And if two parties of believers fall to fighting, then make peace between them. And if one party of them doeth wrong to the other, fight ye that which doeth wrong till it return unto the ordinance of God; then, if it return, make peace between them justly, and act equitably. Lo! God loveth the equitable.*[105] Therefore, God (Exalted is He) advises us first to make peace amongst those infighting.

Amongst the camp of ʿAlī was ʿAmmār b. Yāsir, and the Messenger prophesized that ʿAmmar would be killed by the party in the wrong,[106] i.e. the camp of Muʿāwiya. Nevertheless, the Holy Lord did not advise us to condemn, curse or damn the wrongdoing party; but instead He (Glorious is He) advised us to make peace and to only fight the wrongdoing party for a limited period of time, i.e. until it returns to the truth. Ibn Taymiyya states that "God (Exalted is He) did not even command us to fight every [believer] who commits injustice or does wrong, nor did He command us to fight the wrongdoers from the very beginning."[107] Also, notice that God (Exalted is He) emphasizes in three subsequent verses of Sūrat al-Ḥujurāt: (1) making peace between the believers, (2) avoiding mocking one another, and (3) avoiding thinking evil of other believers or backbiting them.[108] It should also be mentioned that a similar situation occurred when the

---

103 See Ibn Taymiyya, *Minhāj al-Sunna al-Nabawiyya*, vol. I, p. 542; vol. VII, p. 473; and vol. VIII, p. 138. Ibn Taymiyya thus states that their action, i.e. avoiding infighting between two groups of believers (who possess the correct creed), indicates that avoiding infighting is better. Ibn Taymiyya also states that if one ponders what occurred as a result of that infighting one will not see any benefit to it—instead it would have been better had they avoided it altogether. See also Ibid, vol. IV, pp. 462–464.

104 Muslim 2887/7250; Tirmidhī 2194; Aḥmad 20,490.

105 Q.XLIX.9. It should be noted that no war occurred between two groups of believers during the time of the Prophet Muḥammad.

106 See Bukhārī 447 and 2812; Tirmidhī 3800; Aḥmad 11,861.

107 Ibn Taymiyya, *Minhāj al-Sunna al-Nabawiyya*, vol. III, p.391. See also Ibid, vol. IV, pp. 390–391.

108 See Q.XLIX.10–12.

tribes of Israel fought against the tribe of Benjamin after some of the latter had committed wrongdoing.[109]

Ibn Taymiyya also states:

> The creed of Ahl al-Sunna is to desist from engaging in the disputes of the Companions as their excellence and superiority has been well established. It is instead necessary for us to love them and support them. As for what occurred between them: in some [instances] they may be excused for reasons that are hidden to us; in other matters they may have repented; and in others [God] may have forgiven them. Delving into their disputes, on the other hand, will lead to much hatred and rancour occurring in one's heart. One may be wrong or sinful in doing so, thus harming oneself. Furthermore, most of those who have delved into these matters have said things which are not pleasing to God nor His Messenger.[110]

Thus, although the Companions have made mistakes, there are many reasons for those mistakes to be forgiven by God, including them asking God for forgiveness, doing good deeds, among many others.[111] Furthermore, the Companions of the Prophet Muḥammad are more deserving of being forgiven, due to the vast preponderance of their good deeds, than those who came after them (particularly those after the first three generations of Predecessors).

Now, after the Battle of Ṣiffīn, the Khārijīs seceded from Alī's camp. ᶜAlī (may God be pleased with him) subsequently defeated them, as prophesized by the Messenger Muḥammad[112] in the Battle of Nahrawān. Therefore, out of the great harm and dissension of the Battle of Ṣiffīn indirectly came something good, i.e. the exposition of the Khārijīs and their subsequent defeat, which represented a fulfillment of the prophecy.

The fourth reason, which limited the Muslim expansion, was the Plague of ᶜAmwās. It occurred during the caliphate of ᶜUmar b. al-Khaṭṭāb and afflicted parts of newly-conquered Syria leading to the

---

[109] See Judges 20.1–48. This example is not completely concordant, though, as the tribe of Benjamin was in the wrong having harboured the wrongdoers. Here ᶜAlī and most of his camp were in the right although the wrongdoers, i.e. the killers of ᶜUthmān, were amongst them.

[110] Ibn Taymiyya, *Minhāj al-Sunna al-Nabawiyya*, vol. IV, pp. 448–449.

[111] See Ibid, vol. VI, pp. 282–293, for ten reasons mentioned by Ibn Taymiyya.

[112] See Muslim 1065/2457; Aḥmad 11,018.

death of many Companions. Amongst the dead were Abū ᶜUbayda b. al-Jarrāḥ[113] and Muᶜādh b. Jabal. Up to 25,000 people died in that plague,[114] many of whom were again Companions of the Prophet Muḥammad.

The destruction and killing wrought by al-Ḥajjāj b. Yūsuf al-Thaqafī (d. 714 CE) was also widespread. Asmā' bint Abī Bakr said to al-Ḥajjāj, after he had killed her son ᶜAbd Allāh b. al-Zubayr b. al-ᶜAwwām, that the Prophet Muḥammad had foretold: "From amongst [the tribe of] Thaqīf will emerge a liar and a destroyer. The latter will be more evil than the former." Asmā' added: "I think [that destroyer] is you [i.e. al-Ḥajjāj]."[115]

The point of the above is that had the early Muslims not been weakened by those aforementioned events their expansion would have been greater—it may have even extended throughout Europe. Had that happened, though, the time wherein true Islam would become rare and strange would have either not occurred or would have been delayed even further.

Many more causes over the last millennium, which are too numerous to list, have occurred to ultimately lead to this strangeness. Most prominent amongst them though was the destruction of Baghdad and the Abbasid caliphate wrought by the Mongolians. Hulagu and the Mongolian horde barbarically killed approximately 800,000 Muslims. They also dumped all the books into the "Tigris River, which ran black with ink and red with blood".[116] That gratuitous evil

---

113 The Prophet Muḥammad promised Abū ᶜUbayda that he would be in Paradise and also stated that he was the most trustworthy person of this Community (*amīn hādhihi al-umma*). ᶜUmar b. al-Khaṭṭāb had also considered Abū ᶜUbayda to be the best individual to succeed him as Caliph had he lived. See footnote 34 within Chapter Six. Abū Bakr was also content to pledge to Abū ᶜUbayda (as well as ᶜUmar) in Saqīfat banī Sāᶜida.

114 Of note, the Prophet Muḥammad (may God bless him and grant him peace) stated: "Any [believer] who dies from a plague is a martyr." Muslim 1915/4941; Ibn Māja 2804; Aḥmad 10,762. See also Bukhārī 3474; Aḥmad 25,212.

115 Muslim 2545/6496; Aḥmad 4790 and 26,974. The addition of Asmā' is in Muslim 2545/6496 and the commentary of Albānī (*Silsilat al-aḥādīth al-ṣaḥīḥa* 3538). Of note, the liar is al-Mukhtār b. Abī ᶜUbayd al-Thaqafī as he claimed that he received revelation from Gabriel. See Ibn Taymiyya, *Minhāj al-Sunna al-Nabawiyya*, vol. VI, pp. 340–341, and vol. VIII, p. 148.

116 See White, *Atrocities: The 100 Deadliest Episodes in Human History*, pp. 130–131.

weakened the Sunni Muslims greatly, yet it improved the condition of the Twelver Shiites.[117]

In addition, the infighting of many groups[118] against the Sunni Muslims, the perpetration of gratuitous evils by the disbelievers against the Muslims and the former's apathy or contribution toward the latter's humanitarian suffering have all resulted in the abysmal state of the Muslims today.

God (Exalted is He) could have prevented these aforementioned calamities and graced the Muslims, but He has ontologically willed that the Muslims ultimately reach a state of strangeness. This strangeness could have occurred earlier in time or have been delayed by the Almighty Lord (if He had willed by allowing other causes or barriers to exist), but the disintegration leading to this strangeness is inevitable. The Holy Lord has ontologically decreed and dictated just causes for it. It has been progressive and is deserved by the Muslims due to their inadequacies and heedlessness, perpetration of major sins and failure to uphold the legal punishments, as well as not fighting against their enemies.

It should be finally remembered that although these calamities and evils are severe, these punishments have also served to absolve and expiate the Muslims in general. Once they return to the Holy Lord and seek His help, they may be granted success and triumph: *If God helps you, none can overcome you: If He forsakes you, who is there, after that, that can help you?*[119]

13. An exposition on the fine-tuning of evil and harm amongst the disbelievers

In that same light, God (Exalted is He) has fine-tuned the varying nations of disbelievers relative to each other and to the believers.

---

[117] See Daftary, *A History of Shiʿi Islam*, pp. 74–76. The role of the Shiite Khwājah Naṣīr al-Dīn al-Ṭūṣī will be alluded to in the next chapter.

[118] For instance, the Safavid dynasty (1501–1736) under Ismāʿīl I and his son Ṭahmāsp established the Twelve Imamate Shiite religion as the state religion, killed the Sunni scholars and forcibly converted the citizens from Sunni Islam to Shiism. Of note, its eponymous founder, Safī al-Dīn Ardabīlī (d. 1334), was a Sunni Sufi. It was only later in 1399 that his descendants adopted the Twelver Shiite creed.

[119] Q.III.160 (Yusuf Ali translation).

God (Exalted is He) may strengthen or protect one disbelieving nation over another as the former may later become faithful or good. Consider the example of Quraysh and the Christian king of Yemen: the latter sought to convert the Arabs from polytheism to Christianity and demolish the Kaᶜba in 571 CE. God (Exalted is He) protected his Sacred Mosque while the people of Quraysh fled to the mountains. Although Christianity is better than polytheism, which includes idolatry, a greater goodness would ultimately arise with the emergence of Islam by sending Prophet Muḥammad (may God bless him and grant him peace), who was from Quraysh, to the entirety of humanity. Therefore, God (Exalted is He) protected Quraysh—not just His Sacred Mosque—at that time so as to allow the Prophet Muḥammad and his Companions to arise.

Consider also the wars that took place between the Romans and Persians during the time of the Prophet Muḥammad and beforehand.[120] These two warring empires suffered much reciprocal evil, death and destruction. The Almighty Lord's allowance of wars between disbelieving nations served to limit their warriors, diminish their strengths, and deplete their resources so as to prevent them from being able to overcome the believers at a later time. The Roman and Persian empires were thus subsequently defeated by the Companions and Successors (whose armies were much smaller and less equipped) due to the Holy Lord's assistance as well as His allowance of gratuitous evil to previously cause disorder and weakness among those disbelieving armies.

Since the wicked have disbelieved in the Holy Lord and His commandments, and perpetrated His prohibitions and major evils in a widespread manner, it becomes just to allow gratuitous evils to afflict them. Gratuitous or dysteleological evils thus result in greater disorder in the societies of the disbelievers, which ultimately leads to diminished strength, chaos, divisions, fragmentation or dissolution within a quicker period of time. Had gratuitous evils not been allowed the disbelievers would have remained relatively ordered for a much longer period of time.

---

120 See Q.XXX.2–6.

For the disbelievers (who are ultimately deserving of the severe punishment of Hellfire), the striking of earthquakes, plagues and other natural disasters, as well as gratuitous evils, serve to balance their populations in relation to that of the believing Muslims. This limits the number of the disbelievers in order to prevent them from overwhelming the believers (who will always be less in number and material strength) when the latter's society becomes pious and righteous.

Now, as a general rule the hardships and evils occurring to the disbelievers precede those which occur to the believers. Although the suffering endured by the believers is great it is preceded by those calamities afflicting the disbelievers. God (Glorious is He) states: *If misfortune touches you, [know that] similar misfortune has touched [other] people as well; for it is by turns that We apportion unto men such days [of fortune and misfortune]: and [this] to the end that God might mark out those who have attained to faith, and choose from among you such as [with their lives] bear witness to the truth since God does not love evildoers...and bring to nought those who deny the truth.*[121] That those calamities afflict the disbelievers first serves to strengthen, reassure and enable the believers to bear their misfortunes when they do happen to them. Although the Muslims have suffered much in the 20th and 21st centuries, the disbelievers have suffered much more in the 19th and 20th centuries.

In addition, allowing the subjugation of believers to occur at the hands of unjust disbelievers represents another reason for the Almighty Lord to justly exact retribution against the disbelievers. Consider the example of the Israelites who suffered much at the hands of Pharaoh and the Egyptians of that time. They were enslaved, suffered exceedingly and their firstborns were killed. God (Exalted is He) subsequently destroyed Pharaoh and his army in its entirety. The Holy Lord states regarding the Israelites: *And We desired to show favour unto those who were oppressed in the earth, and to make them examples and to make them the inheritors.*[122] This custom of God is relevant for all ages and all times. The Almighty Lord exacts His retribution and punishment against the disbelievers and hypocrites who have harmed and killed those who believe in Him.

---

[121] Q.III.140–141 (Muḥammad Asad translation).

[122] Q.XXVIII.5.

Therefore, not only do calamities afflicting the disbelievers precede the misfortunes of the believers, further calamities come upon the disbelievers afterwards. That is a just recompense, as the disbelievers either directly or indirectly caused the suffering of the believers or they stood by instead of relieving and assisting the latter.

Sometimes, though, God (Exalted is He) may ontologically allow the disbelievers to achieve some order and strength in their societies. Order can occur through non-religious causes (such as knowledge, technology, wealth and power) as well as upholding justice. The Holy Lord may also allow the disbelievers to overcome the Muslims if the latter perpetrate much evil or are inadequate, as previously mentioned.

God (Glorious is He) has determined how long each nation will last as a powerful actor until the disorder and chaos resulting from its evils and inadequacies overwhelm it. God (Exalted is He) has fine-tuned everything; but sometimes the wisdom thereof will not become apparent until later generations or even subsequent centuries. At the same time, God, Who is the Most Magnanimous, may sustain the disbelievers, leave them to enjoy their desires, and allow them to overcome the Muslims if the latter's society has not achieved belief, piety and righteousness to a critical level.

In conclusion, the allowance of gratuitous evils within disbelieving societies leads to their fragmentation within shorter periods of time, as opposed to the case had dysteleological evils not been permitted. This allows the revival and resurgence of the believers at the appropriate time, i.e. when they return to piety and righteousness. The occurrence of gratuitous evils amongst both the believers and disbelievers may thus serve wise purposes.

Now, there is one instance in which the presence of gratuitous evil will have no benefit and will not indirectly lead to later generations of pious and righteous believers emerging. This will occur near the end of times when no further believers will exist on this earth. At that point, only wicked disbelievers will remain for some time as dictated by the Holy Lord. It is upon these wicked disbelievers that destruction and the run-up to the Day of Judgment will occur.[123] God (Exalted is He) has dictated that destruction and punishment will

---

[123] See Muslim 2940/7381; Aḥmad 6555.

only come upon those wicked disbelievers—it would be unwise to bring that upon the believers. Therefore, the allowance of gratuitous evils during that time period prior to the end will be solely due to God's wisdom and justice. Ultimately, gratuitous evils in most cases will indirectly lead to a wise purpose realized by later generations; however, at the most fundamental level the allowance of gratuitous evils returns back to God's wisdom and justice.

14. An exposition of some of the wise purposes in allowing wars and in particular the Battle of Uḥud

Now, some of the greatest evils are perpetrated and occur in war. The destruction to life and property caused by war is indeed devastating and horrific; and innocent civilians suffer some of the greatest hardships and afflictions. That said, this section will discuss the inevitability of war and some of the wise purposes that may occur as a result of it.

God (Exalted is He) informed the angels of this inevitability[124] before creating humankind, and therefore the angels asked: "*Wilt Thou place on it such as will spread corruption thereon and shed blood—whereas it is we who extol Thy limitless glory and praise Thee, and hallow Thy Name?*" The Almighty Lord responded: "*Verily I know that which you do not know.*" [125] Although many types of corruption occur in the course of unjust wars, other types of corruption are prevented by allowing defensive wars and the just spread of God's religion. God (Exalted is He) also states: *And if God had not enabled people to defend themselves against one another, corruption would surely overwhelm the earth.*[126] Hegel states accordingly: "War is not to be regarded as an absolute evil...by war people escape the corruption which would be occasioned by a continuous or eternal peace."[127] It should be noted that the corruption alluded to in the verse occurs as a result of the oppression perpetrated by the disbelievers, whereas that alluded to by Hegel is due to peacetime leading people to become more self-centered, individualistic and determined to pursue their vain desires.

---

[124] See *Tafsīr al-Ṭabarī*, vol. I, pp. 458–471.

[125] Q.II.30 (Muḥammad Asad translation).

[126] Q.II.251 (Muḥammad Asad translation).

[127] G. W. F. Hegel, *Philosophy of Right*, tr. S. W. Dyde (Kitchener: Batoche Books, 2001), pp. 258–259.

God (Exalted is He) states: *Permission [to fight] is given to those against whom war is being wrongfully waged and, verily, God has indeed the power to succour them—those who have been driven from their homelands against all right for no other reason than their saying: "Our Sustainer is God!" For if God had not enabled people to defend themselves against one another, monasteries and churches and synagogues and mosques—in [all of] which God's Name is abundantly extolled—would surely have been destroyed [ere now].*[128]

Yet if there is no intent to spread the religion of God, humans will instead carry out war for corrupt materialistic reasons. These may include seeking out wealth, land, power, fame or any other desire, even if they claim it to be for moral reasons. Moreover, many disbelieving rulers and affluent individuals are stubbornly obstinate and seek to block the religion of God in order to maintain the status quo and preserve their power and wealth. So the only means by which it becomes possible to give those living in disbelieving societies the opportunity to follow the true religion of God is by the believers fighting against the system that those rulers and elites have set up. Thereafter, it becomes possible for each individual to have a free choice to remain as a disbeliever or to convert to the true religion—there is no compulsion in religion.

Compulsion in religion is rejected at all times (whether the Muslims are weak or strong) for the Holy Lord states: *Let there be no compulsion in religion: Truth stands out clear from error: whoever rejects evil and believes in God hath grasped the most trustworthy hand-hold, that never breaks.*[129] It is noteworthy that this verse follows immediately after the greatest verse of the Qur'ān, *āyat al-kursī*, and therefore it will receive the necessary attention it deserves.

---

[128] Q.XXII.39–40.

[129] Q.II.256 (Yusuf Ali translation). This verse prevented some of the Companions from trying to force their children and relatives (who became Jews or Christians before the advent of Islam) to become Muslims. Although it was revealed in a specific instance, its application is generalized. Ṭabarī states: "Do not force the Jews or Christians or those from whom it is permissible to take *jizya* to convert to the true religion [of Islam]. The matter of those who deviate from the guidance, after it has become clear to them, returns back to their Lord. He will take care of their punishment in the Hereafter." See *Tafsīr al-Ṭabarī*, vol. V, pp. 407–416.

Now, some have claimed that Islam was evil and spread by the sword. Consider for instance the statement of the Byzantine emperor Manuel II[130] (d. 1425): "Show me just what Muhammad brought that was new, and there you will find things only evil and inhuman, such as his command to spread by the sword the faith he preached."[131] It has been established throughout this book that the Prophet Muḥammad (may God bless him and grant him peace) only brought forth goodness and strove against evil. The spread of Islam has mostly occurred through faith and reason—not war. The Holy Lord and the Prophet Muḥammad never commanded that people should be forced into accepting Islam. As regards war, it was shown earlier in Chapter Four that Moses, Joshua, David and Solomon fought against the disbelievers in accordance with the commandment of the Holy Lord; and the Prophet Muḥammad is no different in that regard. They all fought for God's sake alone and obeyed His commandments after their victories. As for the reason that Jesus and his disciples did not engage in battle, it will be discussed below. That said, the latter's example stands in stark contrast to Christians over the ensuing centuries who have not held back from religious wars and inquisitions.

There was no compulsion when the three holy cities of Islam—Medina, Mecca and Jerusalem—came under Muslim rule. The Prophet Muḥammad (may God bless him and grant him peace) emigrated to Medina peacefully as many had already converted to Islam; and he entered Mecca victorious, without fighting, nearly eight years after his emigration. A close look at the life of the Prophet Muḥammad reveals that he never forced anyone to become Muslim. In addition, ʿUmar b. al-Khaṭṭāb entered Jerusalem peacefully[132] and

---

[130] Manuel II Palaeologus was a Byzantine emperor from 1391–1425. Manuel II travelled to many countries, including England and Hungary, so as to secure their financial and military assistance and retain his hold on power. Although Manuel II was able to fight off Ottoman attempts to take Constantinople, the latter were ultimately successful in 1453.

[131] This was originally in Manuel II Palaeologus, *Dialogue VII*, 2c, ed. Theodore Khoury, in *Sources Chretiennes,* vol. CXV (Paris: Les Editions du Cerf, 1966). See it quoted in English in Pope Benedict, "Faith, Reason and the University: Memories and Reflections," Aula Magna of the University of Regensburg, 12 September 2006.

[132] Of note, ʿUmar b. al-Khaṭṭāb never left Medina in order to travel to a conquered city or land except in the case of Jerusalem. This also illustrates the importance of Jerusalem and the Aqṣā mosque in Islam.

no inhabitants were forced to convert. The same was done by Saladin nearly five centuries later. Indeed, tolerance of other faiths is part of Islam, and the Prophetic Sunna exemplifies that.

War is only a last resort—guidance through revelation and sound religious knowledge is the primary means to spread the religion of God. God (Exalted is He) states: *Indeed [even aforetime] did We send forth Our messengers with all evidence of [this] truth; and through them We bestowed revelation from on high, and [thus gave you] a balance [wherewith to weigh right and wrong], so that men may behave with equity; and We bestowed [upon you] from on high [the ability to make use of] iron, in which there is awesome power as well as [a source of] benefits for man: and [all this was given to you] so that God might mark out those who would stand up for Him and His Messenger.*[133]

Certainly those Muslims living in Syria, Iraq, Egypt and beyond are indebted to the Prophet Muḥammad (may God bless him and grant him peace) as well as to Abū Bakr, ᶜUmar b. al-Khaṭṭāb, ᶜUthmān, ᶜAlī and Khālid b. al-Walīd, and all the other Companions and Successors who followed them and spread Islam. In fact, all Muslims around the world are indebted to them. Furthermore, it must be acknowledged that the aforementioned did not fight wars for wealth or power, but instead only in order to spread God's religion.

Just war in the name of religion is only performed because of the undeniable presence of great amounts of evil, heresy and disbelief in this world. The plethora of evil should be blamed—not religion—for such necessary combat. Moreover, fighting against the disbelievers is one mechanism to stave off persecution. Without a forceful response and a mechanism to protect themselves, the believers would be overwhelmed by the greater number of disbelievers. Nevertheless, there are rules that the believers must adhere to when engaging in such battles.

God (Exalted is He) has advised the believers to be pious throughout the Qur'ān—even in fighting: *Observe your duty (ittaqū) to God, that ye may be successful. Fight in the way of God against those who fight against you, but begin not hostilities. Lo! God loveth not aggressors. And slay them*

---

[133] Q.LVII.25 (Muḥammad Asad translation). See *Tafsīr al-Ṭabarī*, vol. XXIII, pp. 200–201.

wherever ye find them,[134] *and drive them out of the places whence they drove you out, for persecution is worse than slaughter... And fight them until persecution is no more, and religion is for God. But if they desist, then let there be no hostility except against wrongdoers... And one who attacketh you, attack him in like manner as he attacked you. Observe your duty to God, and know that God is with those who ward off [evil].*[135] Thus God has prohibited the Muslims from aggression—the pious should only wage battle in response to the aggression of the disbelievers and in equal measure. And when they do fight, the Muslims must do so in a pious manner. God (Glorious is He) grants success only to those who are pious.

Failure to defend one's community or nation against the disbelievers may result in persecution, displacement, expulsion, destruction of one's property and land, as well as death. The many instances of these types since 1945 were alluded to previously, but some examples in the Qur'ān and Sunna will be mentioned now.

During the time of Moses, the Israelites were persecuted. Despite viewing God's nine signs against Pharaoh, as well as the Almighty Lord saving them from Pharaoh and his army, the Israelites refused to fight against the disbelievers in order to enter Jerusalem. Their resultant wandering the desert, displacement and destitution was only overcome when they fought with the Prophets Moses and Joshua. Centuries later many Israelites were expelled and displaced from the holy land, and they were only able to return to it by fighting alongside the Prophet David.

The narration in Sūrat al-Kahf of the persecution of those who eventually escaped to the cave was discussed previously in Chapter One. Consider also the case of the early monotheistic Christian believers before the time of the Prophet Muḥammad who were killed by a Jewish king in Yemen.[136] God mentions in Sūrat al-Burūj the persecution and killing of these defenseless believers in a fiery ditch:

---

[134] The phrase *slay them wherever ye find them* refers to fighting against those disbelievers who have ejected and displaced the Muslims from their homes through war. In verses Q.IV.88–91, this phrase refers to fighting against those who became Hypocrites and abandoned the Community of the Muslims. See *Tafsīr al-Rāzī*, vol. X, pp. 168–173.

[135] Q.II.189–194.

[136] Other opinions exist regarding the nationality and religious affiliation of those mentioned in this *sūra*—see *Tafsīr al-Ṭabarī*, vol. XXIV, pp. 337–345.

Woe to the makers of the pit (of fire)—fire supplied (abundantly) with fuel. Behold they sat over against the (fire), and they witnessed (all) that they were doing against the believers. And they ill-treated them for no other reason than that they believed in God, Exalted in Power, Worthy of all Praise! Him to Whom belongs the dominion of the heavens and the earth! And God is Witness to all things. Those who persecute (or draw into temptation) the believers, men and women, and do not turn in repentance, will have the penalty of Hell: They will have the penalty of the Burning Fire.[137] God (Glorious is He) has dictated that some devoted servants of His become martyrs; and all of them will be rewarded immensely in the Hereafter.

Likewise, the Muslims were persecuted during the Meccan stage. Due to that persecution some fled to Ethiopia, where a just Christian ruler accepted and protected them. They found respite and were granted the freedom to worship God alone. However, many of those remaining in Mecca were tortured, harmed, ridiculed or boycotted. Yet others were martyred, including Sumayya bint Khabbāṭ, the mother of ʿAmmār b. Yāsir.

The Prophet Muḥammad, at the beginning of his ministry, remained in Mecca for thirteen years wherein he was prohibited from fighting. At this early stage, patience and perseverance in the face of persecution was incumbent. That said, it was known that at some point fighting would be prescribed since one of the earliest Meccan *sūras* states: [*God*] *knoweth that there may be (some) among you in ill-health; others travelling through the land, seeking of God bounty; yet others fighting in God's cause, read ye, therefore, as much of the Qur'an as may be easy (for you); and establish regular prayer and give regular charity; and loan to God a beautiful loan.*[138] Therefore, it was clear from the beginning of the prophethood of Muḥammad that fighting in God's cause would later be commanded upon the believers. There is no duplicity in fighting initially not being commanded, and being so commanded many years later—both commandments are wise and appropriate.

---

137 Q.LXXXV.3–10 (Yusuf Ali translation).

138 Q.LXXIII.20 (Yusuf Ali translation). Sūrat al-Muzzammil was either the third or fourth *sūra* revealed in Mecca. That said, verse 20 was revealed twelve months after verses 1–19 according to ʿĀ'isha in Muslim (746/1739); Nasā'ī (1601); and Aḥmad (24,269). Of note, prior to the twentieth verse, the night prayer was obligatory, but with its revelation that prayer became supererogatory.

The Almighty Lord fined-tuned the Prophet Muḥammad's life and commanded fighting at the appropriate time (just as He inspired him with revelation to become a messenger at the appropriate time). That commandment was only issued after the Prophet Muḥammad and the Companions had established a city-state in Medina: *Sanction is given unto those who fight because they have been wronged; and God is indeed able to give them victory.*[139] The timing of the command to fight was not only a matter of faith, numbers or having a city-state, but it was also retribution for the vast injustices previously perpetrated by the disbelievers against the believers.

The first war the Prophet Muḥammad (may God bless him and grant him peace) fought against the disbelievers was the Battle of Badr, and the Muslims were victorious therein. It was approximately two years after emigrating from Mecca to Medina. The Companions numbered 314 at the battle, which was approximately the same number of Israelites who, along with David (may God bless him), defeated Goliath and the disbelievers. It was only at that critical mass of righteous believers that God (Exalted is He) permitted and commanded the Prophet Muḥammad and the Companions to fight against the disbelievers. This is due to God's wisdom, and He is the Most Wise.

As for the early Christians during the time of Jesus (may God bless him), they were not commanded to fight against the disbelievers because they had not reached a critical mass of righteous believers, particularly when compared to the number of disbelievers. It will be contended that one factor taken into account for God's issuance of the commandment of fighting is that the number of righteous believers must be at least 10–50% in comparison to the disbelieving warriors. This contention is based on verses 65 and 66 of Sūrat al-Anfāl.[140] Had

---

139 Q.XXII.39.

140 God (Exalted is He) states: *O Prophet! Exhort the believers to fight. If there be of you twenty steadfast they shall overcome two hundred, and if there be of you a hundred (steadfast) they shall overcome a thousand of those who disbelieve, because they (the disbelievers) are a folk without intelligence. Now hath God lightened your burden, for He knoweth that there is weakness in you. So if there be of you a steadfast hundred they shall overcome two hundred, and if there be of you a thousand (steadfast) they shall overcome two thousand by permission of God. God is with the steadfast.* Q.VIII.65–66.

the Christians reached the requisite number, they would have been ordered to fight, and God knows best. However, since they were relatively weak and few, numbering only 120[141]—this being far less than 10% compared to the thousands of Roman soldiers and tens of thousands of pagans and Jews who did not follow Jesus—the early Christians were not commanded to fight. Instead, they continued to be persecuted by the disbelievers for over three centuries. This persecution ultimately led to their inability to strongly expand the number of followers and accurately preserve the religious tradition of Jesus (may God bless him)—this was discussed previously. Many were martyred. The growth of the early Christians thus remained relatively slow[142] (in contrast to that of the Muslims after the death of the Prophet Muḥammad). It was only after it was finally adopted by the Byzantine emperor Constantine that Christianity's expansion became exponential, although its theology had become corrupted (particularly with the adoption of the Trinity). Regardless, the point is that fighting was not prescribed upon the Companions of the Messenger Muḥammad until that critical mass of righteous believers was attained, both in regards to their absolute number as well as their percentage relative to the disbelieving warriors of the Quraysh and other tribes who would ultimately fight against them.

Next, nearly one year after Badr, Quraysh assembled 3000 warriors and marched to Medina to fight against the Muslims in the Battle of Uḥud. This battle and its ramifications will be discussed here as there is great wisdom and many lessons in the so-called "defeat" suffered by the Muslims. Ultimately, 700 Companions assembled against the disbelievers at the mountain of Uḥud. The Prophet Muḥammad (may God bless him and grant him peace) ordered fifty archers to protect the army from behind and to not leave their post for any reason.[143] The Companions—by God's grace—had nearly defeated Quraysh

---

141 See Acts 1.15.

142 It was estimated to be 40% per decade for the first three centuries; see Rodney Stark, *The Rise of Christianity* (San Francisco: HarperSanFrancisco, 1997), p. 7.

143 The Prophet Muḥammad said: "If you see us snatched into pieces by birds, do not leave this position of yours until I send for you. And if you see that we have defeated the enemy and trodden on them, do not desert your position till I send for you." Bukhārī 3039; Abū Dāwūd 2662; Aḥmad 18,593.

but forty of the archers, i.e. 6% of the total army, abandoned their post to claim the spoils, thus leaving the other Companions exposed from behind. Quraysh were then able to attack them from the rear and create chaos.

The Almighty Lord states: *God verily made good His promise unto you when ye routed them by His leave, until (the moment) when your courage failed you, and ye disagreed about the order and ye disobeyed, after He had shown you that for which ye long. Some of you desired the world, and some of you desired the Hereafter. Therefore He made you flee from them, that He might try you. Yet now He hath forgiven you. God is a Lord of kindness to believers.*[144] Hence this battle emphasizes the importance of the entire Community following the Prophet Muḥammad exactly as he has commanded, otherwise suffering and even death may occur.

The verse also mentions that some *desired this world*, as a reason for the suffering and evil which afflicted them. Suffering can thus occur due to the preference of this world and material gain instead of doing what is righteous and following the commandments of the Holy Lord and His Messenger. Nonetheless, the Battle of Uḥud ultimately led the Companions to further devote themselves to the Holy Lord and His cause, and become detached further from worldly matters.

The Battle of Uḥud also affirmed that suffering is inevitable in defending Islam against the disbelievers: *If ye are suffering hardships, they are suffering similar hardships; but ye have hope from God, while they have none. And God is full of knowledge and wisdom.*[145]

Another lesson from the Battle of Uḥud is mentioned by AbdulKader Thomas, who states: "When the Muslims prepared for the Battle of Uhud, they wished to use their resources to conventionally earn *riba* and be better funded in preparation for war. But the revelation came:"[146] *O ye who believe! Devour not usury, doubled and multiplied; but fear God; that ye may (really) prosper. Fear the Fire, which is prepared for those who reject Faith. And obey God and the Messenger; that ye may obtain*

144 Q.III.152. It should be noted that this verse affirms that the Holy Lord forgave all of those Companions who fled the Battle of Uḥud.

145 Q.IV.104.

146 Abdulkader Thomas, "What is *riba*?" in Abdulkader Thomas (ed.), *Interest in Islamic economics* (New York: Routledge, 2006), p. 126.

mercy.[147] As discussed previously, usury/interest is a destructive major sin (*mūbiqāt*), i.e. destructive to society as well as to the individual. Thus, even in the context of battle, which is a matter of life and death, interest (*ribā*) is prohibited.[148] No illegitimate or sinful means may be used, even if the intention is to attain a good objective and noble end.

The heroism of the Companions was also illustrated in this battle. Many Companions—including Abū Bakr, ʿUmar b. al-Khaṭṭāb, ʿAlī b. Abī Ṭālib, Abū Ṭalḥa and Saʿd b. Abī Waqqās—surrounded the Prophet Muḥammad and fervently defended him along with seven of the Medinan supporters (all of the latter seven were eventually martyred). According to Anas b. Mālik (may God be pleased with him):

> Abū Ṭalḥa defended the Prophet with his shield in front of him. Abū Ṭalḥa was a strong and experienced archer... On that day he broke two or three arrow bows. If any man passed by carrying a quiver full of arrows, the Prophet would say to him: "Give it to Abū Ṭalḥa." When the Prophet would raise his head to see the enemy, Abū Ṭalḥa would say: "O Prophet of God! Let my parents be sacrificed for your sake! Please do not raise your head and make it visible, lest an arrow of the enemy should hit you. Let my neck and chest be wounded instead of yours."[149]

The Prophet Muḥammad (may God bless him and grant him peace) was even injured; and, in fact, it was the closest he ever came to death in a battle. He said: "How can a people—who injured the face of their prophet and broke his incisor only because he calls them [to worship] God [alone]—prosper?"[150] The following verse was then revealed: *Not for thee, (but for God), is the decision: Whether He turn in mercy to them, or punish them; for they are indeed wrongdoers. To God belongeth all that is in the heavens and on earth. He forgiveth whom He pleaseth and punisheth*

---

147 Q.III.130–132.

148 See verses Q.II.275–279 and Q.IV.160–161. The Prophet Muḥammad (may God bless him and grant him peace) included usury or interest (*ribā*) as one of the seven destructive major sins. See Bukhārī 2766; Muslim 89/262; Abū Dāwūd 2874; Nasā'ī 3671.

149 Bukhārī 3811, Muslim 1811/4683.

150 Muslim 1791/4645; Aḥmad 13,657.

whom He pleaseth; but God is Oft-Forgiving, Most Merciful.[151] In fact, this verse is a further proof demonstrating that the Qur'ān is the Word of God and not an innovation of His Prophet Muḥammad. The Holy Lord affirmed that all matters and decisions return to Him: only God knows whether He will guide or punish the disbelievers, or if His punishment will overtake the disbelievers in this world or be delayed until the Hereafter. Yet it should also be mentioned here—and God knows best—that the Prophet was not supplicating for the destruction of Quraysh, but was rather concerned that God (Exalted is He) would punish and destroy them as they not only fought against him but directly injured him.[152]

Next, the Qur'ān addressed the death of the Prophet at this time as it was rumoured during the battle that the Prophet Muḥammad (may God bless him and grant him peace) had died. God (Exalted is He) stated: *Muḥammad is but a Messenger; messengers (the like of whom) have passed away before him. Will it be that, when he dieth or is slain, ye will turn back on your heels? He who turneth back on his heels doth no hurt to God, and God will reward the thankful. No soul can ever die except by God's leave and at a term appointed.*[153] So when the calamity of the death of the Prophet (may God bless him and grant him peace) actually occurred seven years later, Abū Bakr (and the Companions ultimately) were prepared and resolute in standing firm upon the Sunna of the Prophet and commandments of the Holy Lord.

As a result of the Battle of Uḥud, seventy Companions were martyred, in addition to the injuries suffered by the Prophet and other Companions. That said, the Prophet Muḥammad was given glad tidings. In that regard, after the Prophet (may God bless him and grant him peace) offered the funeral prayer for the martyrs of

---

[151] Q. III.128–129. This verse thus indicated that Quraysh would ultimately believe and follow the Prophet Muḥammad. God, in His wisdom, would subsequently guide them in 8 AH with the liberation of Mecca.

[152] The Prophet Muḥammad said: "My Lord, forgive my people for they are ignorant." Bukhārī 3477; Muslim 1792/4646; Ibn Māja 4025; Aḥmad 3611. Of note, this phrase was also said by other prophets after being injured by their nations. Moreover, the Prophet hoped that their children may become guided even if the adults of Quraysh did not become so: "I hope that God will let them beget children who will worship God alone, and will worship none besides Him." Bukhārī 3231; Muslim 1795/4653.

[153] Q.III.144–145.

Uḥud, he went up the pulpit and said: "I have been given the keys of all the treasures of the earth. By God! I am not afraid that you will worship others besides God after [my death], but I am afraid that you will compete with one another [for worldly things]."[154] Success and victory were eventually enjoyed by the majority of the believers after enduring suffering (but some were martyred).

Whilst the Quraysh inflicted heavy losses on the Muslims, the former failed to derive any significant political gains from the battle. In essence, the Battle of Uḥud did not result in a decisive victory or loss for either party in the traditional sense. Yet the Qur'ān, as argued above, provided many lessons and wise purposes that future generations of Muslims would benefit from. In conclusion, there are many wise purposes to the allowance of war, and it will be discussed further in the next chapter.

15. THE WISDOM IN ALLOWING THE ANTICHRIST TO EXIST

The Antichrist will represent the greatest tribulation and evil that will be experienced by humankind, as mentioned by the Prophet Muḥammad: "The tribulation and wickedness of the Antichrist will be the greatest experienced by the offspring of Adam."[155]

As for the wickedness of the Antichrist, it will be contended that it will be in recompense for all the evil perpetrated by humankind in this world prior to him. If one considers the evilness of the 20th and 21st centuries in particular—all the killing and genocides, all the gratuitous evils, and all the wickedness—but also all of the evil perpetrated by humankind from the beginning of creation, the Antichrist can be seen as one punishment (of many) for all that prior evil.

It will also be contended that before the coming of the Antichrist, the veracity of Islam will become certain since it will have resurged and become victorious. Thus the wise purpose in the Antichrist coming and being the greatest tribulation is that it is only in this manner that humankind can be appropriately tested at that time, and differentiated into those who truly believe from those who will

---

[154] Bukhārī 1344; Muslim 2296/5976; Aḥmad 17,344.

[155] Ibn Māja 4077; Aḥmad 16,255; al-Ḥākim 64; Ibn Ḥibbān 6650. The quoted section of the *ḥadīth* is "authentic" according to Albānī (*Ṣaḥīḥ al-Jāmiᶜ al-ṣaghīr* 7875).

only follow the religion in order to gain victory or benefit. And God knows best.

The Prophet Muḥammad (may God bless him and grant him peace) also said: "There will come a time in which the one who is resolute upon his religion [of Islam] will be like someone who is holding a burning ember."[156] It is contended that this bodily suffering will occur at the time of the Antichrist for the aforementioned reason of appropriately testing those living at that time. God (Glorious is He) has dictated that only the sincere will remain as believers to the end of their lives—the insincere will eventually turn back after tribulation or hardship.

Now, the Antichrist will initially claim that he is a prophet but thereafter will claim that he is the Lord himself. The Prophet Muḥammad said: "The [Antichrist] will claim that he is the Lord, but you will not see the [Holy Lord] until after death. Also [know that the Antichrist] is blind (*aʿwar*) in one eye, while the [Almighty] Lord is not such."[157] In addition, the Antichrist will be able to do many supernatural things—all so that he is considered the greatest tribulation. These include conquering everywhere on this earth except for Mecca and Medina, commanding the sky to rain whereupon it will rain, commanding the earth to bring forth crops whereupon it will do so,[158] and bringing back to life individuals after having killed them. Those who do not follow the Antichrist will suffer great hunger and thirst, while those who follow him will be granted food and drink. He will also have what appears to be a projection of Paradise and

---

[156] Tirmidhī 2260; Aḥmad 9073. It is "sound" according to Albānī (*Silsilat al-aḥādīth al-ṣaḥīḥa* 957). Of note, there is another tradition which states: "You will encounter days of patience. Being patient therein will be like holding onto a burning ember. Those who act as such will have fifty times the reward." Tirmidhī 3058; Ibn Māja 4014; Abū Dāwūd 4341; Ibn Ḥibbān 385; al-Ḥākim 7912; Bayhaqī (*Sunan*) 20,193. However, this tradition is "weak" according to Albānī (*Silsilat al-aḥādīth al-ḍaʿīfa wa'l-mawḍūʿa* 1025).

[157] Ibn Māja 4077; Aḥmad 22,764. The quoted section of the *ḥadīth* is "authentic" according to Albānī (*Ṣaḥīḥ al-Jāmiʿ al-ṣaghīr* 7875). This *ḥadīth* is another proof that the believers will see God (Glorious is He) in the Hereafter.

[158] See Tirmidhī 2240; Ibn Māja 4075. The quoted section of the *ḥadīth* is "authentic" according to Albānī (*Ṣaḥīḥ al-Jāmiʿ al-ṣaghīr* 7875).

Hellfire—those who do not follow him will be thrown into what appears to be Hellfire but it will instead be Paradise and vice versa.[159]

The Antichrist will remain on this earth for forty days: "One day will be like a year, another day will be like a month, another day will be like a week, and the remaining days will be ordinary days".[160] Sūrat al-Kahf will be vitally important at this junction for the Prophet Muḥammad (may God bless him and grant him peace) said: "Whoever memorizes the first [and/or last] ten verses of Sūrat al-Kahf will be protected from the Antichrist."[161]

Since the Antichrist will be the greatest evil and tribulation the world has known, victory over him will thus require a prophet. Since Muḥammad (may God bless him and grant him peace) was the Seal of the Prophets and Jesus (may God bless him) was raised up to the Holy Lord and was improperly worshipped thereafter, God (Glorious is He) has willed that Jesus will return to this earth and lead the Muslims in defeating the Antichrist. The Prophet Muḥammad said: "There will always exist a group from my Community fighting upon the truth...until the last of them fights against the Antichrist."[162] Jesus will again affirm the Oneness of the Holy Lord at that time and break the cross[163]—and Jesus will not be worshipped afterwards.

The Prophet Muḥammad (may God bless him and grant him peace) also informed us in a number of *ḥadīths*[164] that, after the Antichrist is killed, Gog and Magog will be allowed to go free such that they will kill many and cause much destruction. Jesus (may God bless him) will then supplicate to the Almighty Lord and all of Gog and Magog will die. The believers will then live in peace and prosperity for some time. Afterwards, the Holy Lord will send a wind, which will take the soul of any believer who has at least an atom's weight of faith. Subsequently, only those who are evildoers will remain on this earth.

---

159 See Bukhārī 3338; Muslim 2936/7372; Aḥmad 14,954.

160 Muslim 2937/7373; Ibn Māja 4075; Abū Dāwūd 4321.

161 Muslim 809/1883; Tirmidhī 2240; Abū Dāwūd 4323; Aḥmad 27,516.

162 Abū Dāwūd 2484; Aḥmad 19,920; al-Ḥākim 2392. It is "authentic" according to Albānī (*Silsilat al-aḥādīth al-ṣaḥīḥa* 1959).

163 See Aḥmad 7269. It is "authentic" according to Albānī (*al-Taʿlīqāt al-ḥisān ʿalā Ṣaḥīḥ Ibn Ḥibbān* 6779).

164 See Muslim 2937/7373; Tirmidhī 2240; Ibn Māja 4075; Aḥmad 6555 and 17,629.

The end of this world and the Hour will then occur only upon these wicked disbelievers (as mentioned previously).

16. Compensating the Believers for Enduring Evil and Allowing Them to Attain a Greater Reward in Paradise

It was previously discussed that one who endures for God's sake any suffering or affliction will be rewarded in the Hereafter. Nonetheless, two further evidences will be mentioned here in this regard. God (Exalted is He) states: *So those who fled and were driven forth from their homes and suffered damage for My cause, and fought and were slain, verily I shall remit their evil deeds (sayyi'āt) from them and verily I shall bring them into Gardens underneath which rivers flow—a reward from God.*[165] Some of these believers were forced from their homes and oppressed, while others were martyred. Therefore, according to this verse, these believers—even if they were not pious—will be forgiven their intermediate and minor sins in recompense for their suffering and encountering of evil. Similarly, the Holy Lord will reward pious or righteous individuals with loftier levels than they would have otherwise reached due to the suffering and evil they endured.

Also, consider the Prophetic *ḥadīth*:

> "The destitute one (*muflis*) on the Day of Resurrection is one who is part of my Community and has performed prayer, fasting and zakat but has also cursed some, slandered others, unlawfully taken the money of others, spilt the blood of others, and injured others. This [individual] must give away some of his good deeds to those [harmed] people [in recompense]. But if his good deeds become expended before he has finished recompensing them, their sins will be assumed by him and then he will be thrown into the Hellfire."[166]

So those who suffer injustice in any form will be recompensed and compensated in the Hereafter in accordance with this *ḥadīth*. This topic will be discussed further in Chapter Fifteen on Paradise.

---

165 Q.III.195.

166 Muslim 2581/6579; Tirmidhī 2418; Aḥmad 8029.

Summation

In conclusion, the presence of evil indirectly leads to many goods, such as manifesting the consequences of a greater number of God's Beautiful Names; bringing forth the best types of human beings beloved to the Holy Lord; and illustrating those who sincerely worship the Holy Lord. It also indirectly elucidates those who are patient for the sake of God; who ask forgiveness from the Most Merciful Lord; who fulfill the commandments of the Holy Lord and uphold His legal limits; who enjoin good and forbid evil; who trustfully depend on God while striving against evil; who fight in His path against the transgressing disbelievers; who repudiate with sound knowledge the arguments of the disbelievers; and who possess true faith and certainty in the Hereafter. Gratuitous evil also results in a period of strangeness, which will indirectly lead to the revival of piety and resurgence of righteousness. Had evil been non-existent, then all of these good actions in response could not have occurred.

CHAPTER THIRTEEN

Hypocrisy

Although Islamic scholars were very aware of the evil, "great harm and discord the [hypocrites perpetrate] against Islam and the Muslims,"[1] they did not expound upon it in the context of a theodicy.[2] Likewise, non-Muslim authors did not mention hypocrisy when discussing their theodicies. This chapter will seek to prove that the elucidation of hypocrisy is one of the principal wise purposes for allowing suffering and evil.

Immediately after the Opening Chapter, i.e. Sūrat al-Fātiḥa, God (Glorious and Exalted is He) divided humanity in Sūrat al-Baqara into believers, disbelievers and hypocrites. The first two groups were discussed in only four and two verses, respectively, while the hypocrites (and similitudes regarding them) were mentioned in a total of seventeen verses. These verses exposed their true natures and objectives,[3] and shall be discussed in a subsequent section.

Hypocrisy connotes the pretense of faith and virtuosity, when in reality disbelief and hatred of the believers is harboured. God (Exalted is He) states: *Evil indeed is all that they are wont to do: this, because [they profess that] they have attained to faith, whereas [inwardly] they deny the truth.*[4] The hypocrites claim to be believers, yet they betray and seek to harm the righteous. They are much more harmful than the disbelievers (except those whose evil is of a satanic nature). That is because the latter's enmity is public, so more measures can be taken

---

[1] Ibn al-Qayyim, *Madārij al-sālikīn*, vol. I, p. 355. See also Abū Rumaysah (tr.), *Characteristics of the Hypocrites* (Birmingham: Daar us-Sunnah Publishers, 2004), p. 17.

[2] Ibn al-Qayyim does not mention the hypocrites by name in his theodicy, but states that sacrificing oneself for God's sake differentiates "the truthful one from the liar (*al-kādhib*)". See Zeni (tr.), *Ibn Qayyim al-Jawziyya on Divine Wisdom and the Problem of Evil*, p. 194.

[3] Ibn al-Qayyim goes further and states: "One could almost say that the whole Quran is about the [hypocrites]." See Ibn al-Qayyim, *Madārij al-sālikīn*, vol. I, p. 364, and Abū Rumaysah (tr.), *Characteristics of the Hypocrites*, p. 44.

[4] Q.LXIII.2–3.

to protect against that enmity, while the hostility of the hypocrites is hidden and unexpected. The hypocrites represent some of the worst of humanity.

One of the fundamental reasons for their hypocrisy is that they do not truly have faith in the Hereafter—had they believed in it they would not have betrayed the Holy Lord, the Messenger Muḥammad and the Muslims. God (Glorious is He) describes the hypocrites as those who: *believe not in God and the Last Day, and whose hearts feel doubt, so in their doubt they waver.*[5] God (Exalted is He) also states: *And of humankind are some who say: We believe in God and the Last Day, when they believe not. They think to beguile God and those who believe, and they beguile none save themselves; but they perceive not.*[6]

One's ability to avoid hypocrisy is dependent upon that eschatological belief. Once one possesses true faith in the Hereafter, one should become detached (at least to some degree) from this world. Those who are truly sincere and righteous work to acquire good deeds for the sake of God and the Hereafter, and are content with whatever they possess in this life. On the other hand, the hypocrites fear that they will miss out on material things in this world if they do not join the believers, or they desire to harm the believers to a greater degree by not manifesting outwardly their disbelief and hatred.

ALLOWING SUFFERING MAY MANIFEST THE HYPOCRITES

Now, it was mentioned previously in Chapter Three that God (Exalted is He) showed Gabriel Paradise surrounded by suffering and hardships , and Hellfire surrounded by temptations and desires.[7] Whilst keeping this *ḥadīth* in mind, one should deeply reflect on the following Qur'ānic verse in which the Holy Lord describes the Day of Judgment: *The hypocrites, both men and women, [will] speak [thus] unto those who have attained to faith: Wait for us! Let us have a [ray of] light from your light! [But] they will be told: Turn back, and seek a light [of your own]! And thereupon a wall will be raised between them [and the believers], with a*

---

5 Q.IX.45.

6 Q.II.8–9.

7 See the *ḥadīth* narrated by Tirmidhī 2560; Abū Dāwūd 4744; Nasā'ī 3763; Ibn Ḥibbān 7394. It is "authentic" according to Albānī (*Ṣaḥīḥ al-Jāmiʿ al-ṣaghīr* 5210).

gate in it: within it will be grace and mercy, and against the outside thereof, suffering.[8]

This wall, which separates the hypocrites from the believers on the Day of Judgment, is similar to the suffering and hardships in this world that prevented the hypocrites from becoming believers, striving alongside them and doing the necessary good to reach Paradise. The hypocrites sought to avoid suffering in this world, but instead will be recompensed with a more severe suffering and punishment in the Hereafter. Therefore, one of the main objectives for the existence of suffering in this world is to prevent the hypocrites, whose souls are wicked, from being able to act in a manner similar to the righteous believers.

God (Glorious is He) also states: *And among humankind is he who worshippeth God upon a narrow marge so that if good befalleth him he is content therewith, but if a trial befalleth him, he falleth away utterly. He loseth both the world and the Hereafter. That is the sheer loss.*[9] When the hypocrites attain something good or desired they are happy, but when hardships arise they turn away or abandon the religion entirely. Hence this verse encompasses both those whose faith is marginal and rendered null by hardships, as well as the hypocrites. And God knows best.[10]

On the other hand, consider the early Companions of the Prophet Muḥammad (may God bless him and grant him peace) in Mecca who exemplified true faith. The Meccan Companions were subjected to great persecution, hardship, suffering and evil. They were boycotted and many went hungry. They feared for their safety as many were tortured and some were killed. At that stage, there was no significant worldly advantage to becoming a Muslim. For all these reasons, only those who were prepared to sacrifice much and endure harm and evil, in addition to truly believing, became followers of the Messenger Muḥammad. In reality, the widespread presence of suffering or persecution prevents hypocrites from existing or joining the believers. Thus hypocrisy did not exist amongst the Meccan Companions.

8 Q.LVII.13.

9 Q.XXII.11.

10 See *Tafsīr al-Ṭabarī*, vol I, p. 349.

Subsequently, the early Companions would become the leaders and rulers of the believers.

Due to this persecution (amongst other factors), the growth of the early Companions during the Meccan Period was essentially slow and linear. This is based on the assumption that there were ten Companions at three years after the beginning of Muḥammad's prophethood and approximately 100[11] after thirteen.

Now, contrast the essentially linear growth during the Meccan Period to the exponential growth that ultimately occurred after the Medinites (*Anṣār*) believed and the Meccan Companions (*Muhājirīn*) emigrated to Medina. The latter left behind their possessions, livelihoods and in some cases their families in Mecca. The Companions established a city-state in Medina and enjoyed greater levels of legitimacy. They felt more secure, and were able to freely preach their religion, which led to their numbers growing at a much faster pace. Then, within only a few years, the Prophet Muḥammad and his Companions were able, by the grace of God, to liberate Mecca and enter it peacefully. Thereafter, the majority of Quraysh and many of the inhabitants of the Arabian Peninsula became Muslim in an exponential fashion. This is based on the assumption that there were approximately 350 Companions fifteen years after Muḥammad became a Messenger, 1000 "Muslims" after sixteen years, 10,000 after twenty-one years, and 114,000 after twenty-three years.

Although a far greater number of Muslims (in name) existed during this Medinan phase, a significant number within this time period were Hypocrites. It should also be mentioned that many of those who converted to Islam in the Arabian Peninsula later became apostates after the death of the Prophet Muḥammad. The percentage of Hypocrites may have been up to 30% in 3 AH (or sixteen years after Muḥammad became a Messenger), based upon the fact that 300 Hypocrites abandoned the Prophet Muḥammad during the Battle of

---

[11] This figure is likely slightly higher, since the number of Companions who emigrated to Abyssinia (in the second emigration) was 102 (83 men and 19 women), yet this did not encompass many of the Companions who remained in Mecca. That said, by the time the Battle of Badr occurred, the Meccan emigrants who fought in it numbered approximately 86. See Safiur-Rahman al-Mubarakpuri, *The Sealed Nectar: Biography of the Noble Prophet* (Riyadh: Darussalam, 2011), pp. 148 and 296.

Uḥud, leaving only 700 Companions to fight against Quraysh. God (Glorious is He) states in this regard:

> *That which befell you, on the day when the two armies met, was by permission of God; that He might know the true believers and that He might know the Hypocrites, unto whom it was said: Come, fight in the way of God, or defend yourselves. They answered: If we knew aught of fighting we would follow you. On that day they were nearer [to] disbelief than faith. They utter with their mouths a thing which is not in their hearts. God is best aware of what they hide.*[12]

Further Hypocrites were manifest during the subsequent Battles of the Trench and Tabuk, among others. For instance, during the Battle of the Trench wherein the Companions were surrounded by 10,000 combatants, the Hypocrites abandoned and ridiculed the Muslims. God (Exalted is He) describes this difficult situation:

> *O ye who believe! Remember God's favour unto you when there came against you hosts, and We sent against them a great wind and hosts ye could not see... Then were the believers sorely tried, and shaken with a mighty shock. And when the Hypocrites, and those in whose hearts is a disease, were saying: God and His Messenger promised us naught but delusion.*[13]

On the other hand, the true believers were described by the Holy Lord: *When the believers saw the confederate forces, they said: "This is what God and His Messenger had promised us, and God and His Messenger told us what was true." And it only added to their faith and their zeal in obedience.*[14]

In essence, during times of security and relative triumph, the number or percentage of hypocrites increases significantly for they are concerned only with attaining worldly benefits and desires—not in following the commandments of the Holy Lord and His Messenger or doing good for the sake of the Hereafter. Although hypocrites may adopt or proclaim faith in the presence of security and luxury, when wars occur they manifest their true natures, abandon the devout believers or accuse the faithful of deceiving them. The importance

---

[12] Q.III.166–167.

[13] Q.XXXIII.9–12.

[14] Q.XXXIII.22 (Yusuf Ali translation). Of note, the Prophet said that he was granted victory through *ṣibā*, which is likely the wind during the Battle of the Trench. See Bukhārī 1035; Muslim 900/2087; Aḥmad 1955.

of war in elucidating the hypocrites will be discussed further later in the chapter.

In light of the fact, as mentioned above, that hypocrisy was non-existent amongst the Meccan Companions, it should be mentioned that some Shiites do not directly curse or criticize Abū Bakr, ʿUmar and ʿUthmān, but rather state that they were only good outwardly. In this fashion, some of them are insinuating that these three Rightly-Guided Caliphs were inwardly not good, i.e. were hypocrites. In claiming this (or worse) about these three Companions, the Shiites are indirectly criticizing the Prophet Muḥammad himself, as he (may God bless him and grant him peace) always associated with those three, consulted with them, and was related to them in one manner or another by marriage just as he was to ʿAlī.

Moreover, if one considers the events occurring during the caliphates of the four Rightly-Guided Caliphs (who will all be in Paradise according to the *ḥadīth*s of the Prophet Muḥammad[15]), the reality is that Abū Bakr, ʿUmar and ʿUthmān fought against the disbelievers and spread Islam, whereas ʿAlī, as a matter of fact, never fought against the disbelievers or polytheists during his caliphate, but instead only fought against the Muslims (whether the camps of ʿĀ'isha, Ṭalḥa and al-Zubayr or Muʿāwiya or the Khawārij[16]). Thus those Shiites should affirm that Abū Bakr, ʿUmar and ʿUthman were both inwardly and outwardly good, just as they do for ʿAlī.

It is quite unfortunate that many of the Shiites have continued to fight against the innocent Muslims throughout history (when able), such as during the Safavid empire, or encouraged the disbelievers to do

---

[15] See Abū Dāwūd 4649; Ibn Māja 134; Aḥmad 1638. It is "authentic" according to Albānī (*Ṣaḥīḥ al-Jāmiʿ al-ṣaghīr* 4010). See also Tirmidhī 3747; Aḥmad 1675; Ibn Ḥibbān 7002. It is "authentic" according to Albānī (*Ṣaḥīḥ al-Jāmiʿ al-ṣaghīr* 50).

[16] Of note, the Prophet Muḥammad essentially commended ʿAlī for fighting against the extremist Khawārij, as mentioned previously, whereas he (may God bless him and grant him peace) only stated that ʿAlī and his camp were "closer to the truth" in his fight against Muʿāwiya. That said, the Prophet Muḥammad abstained from mentioning the confrontation between ʿAlī and the camp of ʿĀ'isha, Ṭalḥa and al-Zubayr (regarding the killers of ʿUthmān), which indicates that both groups were justified and upon the truth. And God knows best.

so, such as during the Mongolian invasion.[17] And if a group of Shiites has fought against the disbelievers to some degree, they have fought against the Muslims to a far greater degree, as in the case of Syria during this century. The reality is that the Shiites, being a minority of approximately 15%, often rely on the disbelievers to fight against the Muslims; and likewise, the disbelievers, over the centuries as well as nowadays, have used the Shiites to serve their ends in harming the Sunnis.

Some wise purposes in allowing the possibility of hypocrisy

One may inquire: why is hypocrisy even a possibility? Now, it has already been mentioned that the devout and truly faithful do not perpetrate intermediate sins, and thus their acts are predominated by goodness. The Prophet Muḥammad (may God bless him and grant him peace) said in a *ḥadīth*: "If you did not sin I would be afraid of something worse for you than that—pride."[18] This indicates that one of the wise purposes in allowing sins is to remove, according to this *ḥadīth* and in the words of Ibn al-Qayyim, "arrogance and pride from one's heart, which would otherwise result from one being impressed with personal acts of worship".[19] But, again, those who are devout and truly faithful do not carry out those sins; therefore, it will be

---

[17] Hamid Dabashi discusses the role of Khwājah Naṣīr al-Dīn al-Ṭūṣī, a Shiite, who was a member of the entourage of the Mongolian Hūlāgū: "After consulting with Khwājah Naṣīr on the astrological timing of invading Baghdad, Hūlāgū attacked the Abbāsid capital... [Thereafter] Hūlagū was reluctant to kill the caliph, lest something terrible would happen to him and his army. Khwājah Naṣīr insisted that these were all superstitious beliefs and...suggested that the caliph be wrapped in a carpet and rolled by hand to death... There are, however, other less dramatic accounts of the caliph's execution, such as starvation, with no involvement by the Shīʿī vizier." Dabashi also states: "Khwājah Naṣīr is also credited with having converted many prominent Sunni scholars to Shiʿism, and if they refused they were executed." Hamid Dabashi, "Khwājah Naṣīr al-Dīn al-Ṭūṣī: the philosopher/vizier and the intellectual climate of his times", in Nasr and Leaman (eds.), *History of Islamic Philosophy*, pp. 531–535. See also Ibn Taymiyya, *Minhāj al-Sunna al-Nabawiyya*, vol. V, pp. 155–156, and vol. VI, pp. 374–375. Ibn Taymiyya also discusses a personal experience of his with a group of Shiites in Syria; see ibid, vol. V, pp. 158–160.

[18] Bayhaqī (*Shuʿab*) 6868; Haythamī 17,948. It is "sound" according to Albānī (*Ṣaḥīḥ al-Jāmiʿ al-ṣaghīr* 5303).

[19] See Zeni (tr.), *Ibn Qayyim al-Jawziyya on Divine Wisdom and the Problem of Evil*, p. 248.

maintained that it is their fear of hypocrisy that prevents them from being characterized by pride (*ʿujb*), arrogance (*kibr*) or haughtiness (*khaylāʾ*).

ʿAbd Allāh b. ʿUbayd Allāh b. Abī Mulayka said: "I met thirty of the Prophet's Companions (may God bless him and grant him peace) and found all of them fearing hypocrisy. Not one of them said that his faith was like the faith of [the angels] Gabriel and Michael." Ḥasan al-Baṣrī said: "No one feels safe from hypocrisy except for a hypocrite, and no one fears it save a believer."[20] It was precisely their fear of hypocrisy that made the Companions and Successors the furthest away from it, and the sincerest to God (Glorious is He). Fear of the possibility of hypocrisy also provides another mechanism for those who are righteous or pious, as well as the lower ranks, to avoid pride.

Fear of hypocrisy therefore results in the maintenance of humility for many believers. Humility is a key objective, in and of itself. Those who are arrogant will not enter Paradise as evidenced by the *ḥadīth* of the Prophet Muḥammad: "Anyone who possesses an atom's weight of arrogance will not enter Paradise... Arrogance is rejecting the truth and looking down condescendingly on other people."[21]

Second, the believers worry that their intentions are not pure enough, i.e. that they were ostentatious or hypocrites. God (Glorious is He) states regarding the righteous: *And those who dispense their charity with their hearts full of fear, because they will return to their Lord. It is these who hasten in every good work, and these who are foremost in them.*[22] The Prophet Muḥammad (may God bless him and grant him peace) said: "This [verse] describes those who fast, pray and give alms, yet are afraid that their deeds will not be accepted [by the Holy Lord on the Day of Judgment]."[23] Indeed, no one truly knows whether the Almighty Lord has accepted his or her good deeds until the Day of Judgment.

---

[20] Bukhārī mentioned these statements of Ibn Abī Mulayka and Ḥasan al-Baṣrī as an addendum to *ḥadīth* 47. See also Ibn al-Qayyim, *Madārij al-sālikīn*, vol. I, p. 365, and Abū Rumaysah (tr.), *Characteristics of the Hypocrites*, p. 45.

[21] Muslim 91/265; Tirmidhī 1999; Aḥmad 3789.

[22] Q.LX.60–61 (Yusuf Ali translation).

[23] Tirmidhī 3175; Ibn Māja 4198; Aḥmad 25,705. It is "authentic" according to Albānī (*Silsilat al-aḥādīth al-ṣaḥīḥa* 162).

In this fashion, the existence of hypocrisy adds another possibility beyond belief or disbelief. This then opens the door for individuals to examine their intentions and sincerity, and thus freely choose to not become hypocrites. In essence, true sincerity could not be elucidated had the option of hypocrisy not been a possibility. The elucidation of sincerity though is fundamental, as God (Glorious is He) states that only those who are sincere and devout will be able to avoid evilness and sinfulness, and thus will be saved from punishment in the Hereafter.[24] Ultimately, sincere faith (even if only the weight of an atom) must be achieved so as to surpass the threshold for entrance into Paradise. And God knows best.

Finally, it should be noted that the believers may attain humility and avoid arrogance due to another reason mentioned within a *ḥadīth* of the Prophet Muḥammad: "A person amongst you will act in a manner consistent with the inhabitants of Paradise such that there will only be one handbreadth between him and it; however, his [destiny noted] in the Preserved Tablet will be fulfilled. He will thus act in a manner consistent with the denizens of Hellfire and enter Hellfire."[25] Therefore, those who are wise will never feel secure about their state of goodness, but instead will always take precautions to avoid an evil ending. The devout and higher ranks are always concerned that their deeds may not be accepted by the Holy Lord or that their end will not be good.

Characteristics of the hypocrites

Lying is the first fundamental characteristic of the hypocrites. The Exalted states: *God beareth witness that the hypocrites are indeed liars*;[26] and *See, how they invent lies about God! That of itself is flagrant sin*.[27]

The Prophet Muḥammad (may God bless him and grant him peace) said: "If an individual possesses all four of these [characteristics] then he is a [true] hypocrite: [1] if he speaks, he lies; [2] if he promises,

---

[24] See Q.XII.24 and Q.XXXVII.38–40, 73–74 and 158–160. The devout will also reject attributing any inadequacy or imperfection to God (Glorious is He) based on these verses.

[25] Bukhārī 6594; Muslim 2651/6740; Aḥmad 3624.

[26] Q.LXIII.1 (Yusuf Ali translation).

[27] Q.IV.50.

he reneges; [3] if he gives an oath, he betrays; and [4] if he debates, he is obscene [or insulting] (*fajara*). If he possesses one of these four characteristics then he has that trait of hypocrisy, until he abandons it."[28] May God protect us from such a state!

After mentioning that the hypocrites are liars, the Prophet Muḥammad (may God bless him and grant him peace) declared that they renege on their promises and betray their oaths. This dishonesty is intended by the hypocrites from the beginning of such agreements. God (Glorious is He) states: *And of them is he who made a covenant with God (saying): If He give us of His bounty we will give alms and become of the righteous. Yet when He gave them of His bounty, they hoarded it and turned away, averse; so He hath made the consequence (to be) hypocrisy in their hearts until the day when they shall meet Him, because they broke their word to God that they promised Him, and because they lied.*[29] On the other hand, those unable to live up to their promises due to some inadequacies or unexpected obstacles are considered to be morally weak or incapable—not hypocrites.

The Prophet Muḥammad finally mentioned that the hypocrites stoop to using obscene words when arguing with others, as well as insulting them. The character of a believer, in contrast, should be consistently good in all states. Although some are more forbearing than others, one must not resort to indecent or offensive words, but instead should remain proper and just.

Perpetrating major sins may bring one closer to hypocrisy. Consider, for example, those who perpetrate adultery: they may exhibit all of the traits that the Prophet identified in the aforementioned *ḥadīth*. Adulterers have to lie to cover up their activities to their spouse; they will break their promises to their spouse (or to their mistress) at some point because they cannot fulfill the additional obligations; they may take an oath to their spouse that they are not having an affair; and they may become obscene and insulting when arguing with their spouse or mistress. Therefore, remaining pious and avoiding major sins is one means by which the possibility of hypocrisy may be lessened.

---

[28] Bukhārī 3178; Muslim 58/210; Tirmidhī 2632; Abū Dāwūd 4688; Nasā'ī 5020; Aḥmad 6768.

[29] Q.IX.75–77.

Second, the hypocrites follow their desires (*shahawāt*) and are plagued with doubts (*shubuhāt*). Since they are not certain of the Hereafter, they cannot avoid following their desires and temptations. The example of one who turned away from the religion and only desired this world is mentioned in the following verses: *Relate to them the story of the man*[30] *to whom We sent Our signs, but he passed them by [and sloughed them off]:*[31] *so Satan followed him up, and he went astray. If it had been Our will, We [would] have elevated him with Our signs; but he inclined to the earth, and followed his own vain desires.*[32] Thus, because this individual followed his desires, he was forsaken by God (Glorious is He).

Individuals such as this one always feel overwhelmed, whether they are asked to uphold His commandments, carry out religious obligations, and endure hardships for God's sake or are distressed just thinking about them.[33] Consequently, these hypocrites pursue their desires and turn away from the religion.

The Prophet Muḥammad (may God bless him and grant him peace) mentioned a type of person in Hellfire who will be asked by some of its denizens: "Why are you here? Did you not enjoin us to do good and forbid us from evil?" He will reply: "I used to enjoin you to do good but I would not do so myself, and I would forbid you from major sins (*munkar*) but I would perpetrate them."[34] This hypocritical individual thus followed his desires instead of the commandments of the Holy Lord.

---

[30] It was said that this man was given knowledge of God's greatest Name and his supplications were all accepted and fulfilled. There are differences of opinion as to his identity; however, it can also apply to any individual who does the same. Rāzī states that this verse is a warning to those scholars who turn away from the religion after being granted much religious knowledge and the truth. See *Tafsīr al-Rāzī,* vol. XV, pp. 403–404; *Tafsīr al-Ṭabarī*, vol. XIII, pp. 252–273.

[31] Pickthall translates *insalakha min[ha]* as "sloughed them off". This term indicates that the individual possessed religious knowledge and faith at one point but later abandoned this knowledge and turned away from the religion. Ḥasan al-Baṣrī opined that this description, in general, refers to a hypocrite. See *Tafsīr al-Ṭabarī*, vol. XIII, p. 273.

[32] Q.VII.175–176 (Yusuf Ali translation).

[33] This type of individual is compared to a dog, which pants both when active and at rest. See the remainder of verse Q.VII.176.

[34] Bukhārī 3267; Muslim 2989/7483; Aḥmad 21,784.

The hypocrite may even criticize others for perpetrating major sins, in spite of being guilty of the same. Roger Crisp and Christopher Cowton mention this as one vice of the hypocrites: they blame and criticize others for faults that they possess and perpetrate.[35]

Furthermore, the hypocrites only follow God's commandments or pursue noble religious ends if it coincides with their desires. God (Exalted is He) states: *But if right had been with them they would have come unto him willingly. Is there in their hearts a disease, or have they doubts, or fear they lest God and His Messenger should wrong them in judgment? Nay, but such are evildoers.*[36] The Holy Lord also states: *And when it is said unto them: Come unto that which God hath revealed and unto the Messenger, thou seest the hypocrites turn from thee with aversion... But no, by the Lord, they can have no (real) faith, until they make thee judge in all disputes between them, and find in their souls no resistance against thy decisions, but accept them with the fullest conviction.*[37] Those who only follow the commandments of the Holy Lord and His Prophet when it suits their desires, but abandon them otherwise, put themselves at risk of hypocrisy.

Since the hypocrites do not possess an ideology but instead only pursue that which they desire, God (Glorious and Exalted is He) has described them as blocks or planks of wood: *(They are) as though they were blocks of wood in striped cloaks.*[38] The parallel of the true believers,

---

[35] See Spiegel, *Hypocrisy*, pp. 30–32. Spiegel states therein: "Roger Crisp and Christopher Cowton offer a fourfold distinction of the vice... [1] The hypocrisy of pretense occurs when a person puts up a front of being morally better than he is... [2] the hypocrisy of blame...[entails] "moral criticism of others by someone with moral faults of their own... [3] that of inconsistency...[entails] "the uttering of some (overriding) moral requirement that does apply to oneself and then failing to live up to it"... [4] [the hypocrisy of] complacency...is to ignore the demands of morality when they become costly, to be content with one's moral status, refusing to improve or even to reflect upon it, while carrying on the pretense of virtue, blaming others for their vices, or failing to practice what one preaches." See also Roger Crisp and Christopher Cowton, "Hypocrisy and Moral Seriousness", *American Philosophical Quarterly*, vol. XXXI, no. 4, 1994, pp. 343–349.

[36] Q.XXIV.49.

[37] Q.IV.61–65.

[38] Q.LXIII.4.

on the other hand, is that of a good tree producing fruit, whereas the disbelievers are like an uprooted dead tree.[39]

The hypocrites also hedge by pledging their allegiances alternatively to both the believers or the disbelievers depending on who they feel will be victorious: *Those who wait upon occasion in regard to you and, if a victory cometh unto you from God, say: Are we not with you? and if the disbelievers meet with a success say: Had we not the mastery of you, and did we not protect you from the believers? God will judge between you at the Day of Resurrection, and God will not give the disbelievers any way (of success) against the believers.*[40] Thus they do that which is expedient for themselves and betray their oaths accordingly.

Third, many verses of the Qur'ān describe the hypocrites as being corrupt (*fāsiqīn*).[41] God (Exalted is He) explicitly states: *Surely the hypocrites are the transgressors* (*fāsiqūn*).[42] In addition, God (Exalted is He) informs us that they spread corruption and mischief: *And when it is said unto the [hypocrites]: Make not mischief in the earth, they say: We are peacemakers only. Are not they indeed the mischief-makers? But they perceive not.*[43] They think themselves to be good, but they do not truly follow the commandments of the Holy Lord and His Messenger Muḥammad (may God bless him and grant him peace). This is a characteristic of those who oppose and fight against the believers, yet claim that they are good. They will ultimately recognize—either in this world or the Hereafter—that they pursued evil and corruption.

Fourth, the hypocrites have evil intentions, including sedition. The Almighty Lord states: *If they had come out with you, they would not have added to your (strength) but only (made for) disorder, hurrying to and fro in your*

---

[39] The similitude of the believers, who affirm His Oneness, is drawn as: *Seest thou not how God coineth a similitude: A goodly saying, as a goodly tree, its root set firm, its branches reaching into heaven… Giving its fruit at every season by permission of its Lord.* The similitude of the disbelievers, who claim that others are deserving of worship besides God, is: *And the similitude of a bad saying is as a bad tree, uprooted from upon the earth, possessing no stability. God confirmeth those who believe by a firm saying in the life of the world and in the Hereafter, and God sendeth wrongdoers astray.* Q.XIV.24–27.

[40] Q.IV.141.

[41] See Q.LXIII.6. See also Q.IX.77–80 and 96, and Q.XXIV.55

[42] Q.IX.67.

[43] Q.II.11–12.

midst and sowing sedition among you.[44] They seek to sow divisions and cause harm to the Muslims, because of their extreme jealousy and hatred against the believers. Their goal is to infiltrate and destroy the believers in such a fashion that can only be achieved through their hypocrisy. These hypocrites (as well as some satanic disbelievers) are overcome with such hatred that they will destroy people's lives, families, material possessions and societies. A number of hypocritical and deviant Muslim sects (or members thereof) have even perpetrated more evil against the Muslims than some of the disbelievers.

Fifth, the hypocrites are characterized by a lazy and languid nature when it comes to carrying out the pillars of Islam. For instance, they are lazy in prayer, hesitant to give charity and are lax when fulfilling those commandments of God (Glorious is He) that they actually do carry out. The Holy Lord states: *Woe then unto those praying ones: whose hearts from their prayer are remote, those who want only to be seen and praised, and withal, deny all assistance [to their fellow men]!*[45] The Sublime also states: *The only reasons why their contributions are not accepted are: that they reject God and His Messenger; that they come to prayer without earnestness; and that they offer contributions unwillingly.*[46]

The outwardly good actions of the hypocrites are only to avoid blame or to secure praise from people—they do not act so as to attain the pleasure of the Holy Lord. And if they could achieve the praise of people without acting, they would do so: *Think not that those who exult in what they have given, and love to be praised for what they have not done—think not that they are in safety from the doom. A painful doom is theirs.*[47]

ʿAlī b. Abī Ṭālib (may God ennoble his face) said: "A hypocrite has three signs: when alone he is lazy, but when he sees people he becomes energetic; when he is praised, he increases his work; and when he is rebuked, he does less."[48] Therefore, if a hypocrite is rebuked and criticized for doing what is otherwise a good deed, he will desist from doing that goodness. In other words, he would rather please people

---

44 Q.IX.47.

45 Q.CVII.4–7 (Muḥammad Asad translation).

46 Q.IX.54.

47 Q.III.188. See *Tafsīr al-Ṭabarī*, vol. VII, pp. 465–466; *Tafsīr al-Rāzī*, vol. IX, p. 457.

48 See Muhammad Nur Abdus Salam (tr.), *Al-Ghazzali on the Treatment of Hypocrisy* (Chicago: Great Books of the Islamic World, 2002), p. 27.

than God (Glorious is He). The true believer, on the other hand, will continue to do such a good deed because he is doing it for the sake of God and His reward in Paradise.

Sixth, the hypocrites mock and deride the religion. The Holy Lord states:

> *When ye hear the revelations of God rejected and derided, sit not with them (who disbelieve and mock) until they engage in some other conversation. In that case (if ye stayed) ye would be like unto them. Lo! God will gather hypocrites and disbelievers, all together, into Hell.*[49] *The hypocrites fear lest a sūra should be revealed concerning them, proclaiming what is in their hearts. Say: Scoff (your fill)! Lo! God is disclosing what ye fear. And if thou ask them (O Muḥammad) they will say: We did but talk and jest. Say: Was it at God and His revelations and His Messenger that ye did scoff?*[50]

Seventh, the hypocrites belittle the believers and claim that they are fools: *They say: Shall we believe as the foolish believe? Are not they indeed the foolish? But they know not. And when they fall in with those who believe, they say: We believe. But when they go apart to their devils they declare: We are with you. Verily, we did but mock.*[51] The hypocrites act condescendingly towards the believers and deem them to be idiots, since the believers have faith in the Hereafter and direct their efforts to it, instead of taking advantage of worldly opportunities and gains (in ways that compromise their religious beliefs).

A FURTHER EXPOSITION OF THE HYPOCRITES

In this section some phrases used in the Qur'ān to refer to the hypocrites will be discussed. It was alluded to previously that the hypocrites are pervaded with doubts and desires, which lead their hearts to become spiritually diseased. God (Exalted is He) states when describing the hypocrites: *in their hearts is a disease.*[52] Ṭabarī mentions that this phrase refers to a "subset of the hypocrites".[53] Therefore, it will be maintained that most of the other instances, wherein that

---

49 Q.IV.140.

50 Q.IX.64–65.

51 Q.II.13–14.

52 Q.II.10.

53 See *Tafsīr al-Ṭabarī*, vol. XX, p. 327.

phrase *in their hearts is a disease* (*fī qulūb*ⁱʰⁱᵐ *maraḍ*)[54] is mentioned in the Qur'ān, refer to some of the hypocrites. These instances thus describe the hypocrites as fearing loss[55] and death,[56] disobeying some of the commandments of the Holy Lord and His Messenger,[57] not believing what God (Glorious is He) and His Prophet have promised them,[58] and harbouring rancour[59] against the believers.

Next, Sūrat al-Munāfiqūn mentions regarding the hypocrites: *That is because they believed, then disbelieved, therefore their hearts are sealed so that they understand not.*[60] Therefore, it will be maintained that the Qur'ānic phrase indicating that someone disbelieved after believing can allude to that individual being a hypocrite—not just a disbeliever or an apostate. Also, consider that one interpretation of verse 137 in Sūrat al-Nisā'—*Those who believe, then disbelieve and then (again) believe, then disbelieve, and then increase in disbelief, God will never pardon them, nor will He guide them unto a way*[61]—is that it refers to some of the hypocrites who may have believed twice but then disbelieved after each instance, and then increased in their disbelief.

Now, God (Exalted is He) states in Sūrat Āl-ʿImrān: *How shall God guide those who reject faith after they accepted it and bore witness that the Messenger was true and that clear signs had come unto them? But God guides not a people unjust. Of such the reward is that on them (rests) the damnation (laʿna) of God, of His angels, and of all humankind.*[62] The Holy Lord also states in a subsequent verse: *Those who reject faith after they accepted it, and then go on adding to their defiance of faith—never will their repentance be accepted; for*

---

54 See verses Q.V.52; Q.IX.125; Q.XXII.53; Q.XXIV.50; Q.XXXIII.12 and 60; Q.XLVII.20 and 29; Q.LXXIV.31.

55 See Q.V.52. See *Tafsīr al-Rāzī*, vol. XII, p. 375; *Tafsīr al-Ṭabarī*, vol. X, pp. 403–404.

56 See Q.XLVII.20.

57 See Q.XXIV.48–50 and Q.XLVII.26.

58 See Q.XXXIII.12. See *Tafsīr al-Rāzī*, vol. XXV, p. 161. See also Q.LXXIV.31 and *Tafsīr al-Rāzī*, vol. XXX, p. 712.

59 See Q.XLVII.29. See *Tafsīr al-Rāzī*, vol. XXVIII, p. 58; *Tafsīr al-Ṭabarī*, vol. XXII, p. 184.

60 Q.LXIII.4.

61 Q.IV.137. The other interpretation is that it refers to those who believed in Moses and the Torah but then disbelieved, believed in Jesus as a Prophet and the Gospel but then disbelieved, and finally became the worst disbelievers by denying the prophethood of Muḥammad and the Qur'ān. See *Tafsīr al-Ṭabarī*, vol. IX, pp. 314–317.

62 Q.III.86–87. Of note, Pickthall translates *laʿna* as "curse".

they are those who have (of set purpose) gone astray (al-ḍāllūn).[63] These verses thus show that those who have disbelieved after believing, which can include hypocrites, are both damned by God Almighty (which is clearly worse than His wrath being upon them[64]) and are astray.

In this fashion, it will be contended that the hypocrites of this Community are also included amongst those whom are deserving of His anger and have gone astray from the Straight Path. Therefore, when reading Sūrat al-Fātiḥa: *Show us the Straight Path, the path of those whom Thou hast favoured; not the (path) of those who earn Thine anger nor of those who go astray,*[65] we are also supplicating to God (Glorious is He) to protect us from hypocrisy. And God knows best. If what was discussed in Chapter One regarding Sūrat al-Fātiḥa is recalled, then it becomes clear that this *sūra* addresses the problem of evil from a wide variety of aspects. May the Holy Lord guide and protect us from hypocrisy, and encompass the believers in His grace and mercy!

Now, it was previously mentioned that the hypocrites are corrupt (*fāsiqūn*). God (Glorious is He) states: *Whoso judgeth not by that which God hath revealed: such are evil-livers (fāsiqūn).*[66] Therefore, those who call themselves Muslims but do not judge in accordance with God's commandments or follow the Prophet Muḥammad may, in some cases, be considered as hypocrites.

One example is a man named Dhū al-Khuwayṣira from Banī Tamīm who said to the Prophet: "O Muḥammad, be just! You have not been fair." The Prophet (may God bless him and grant him peace) said: "Woe unto you! Who will be just if I am not just? I will be in loss

---

63 Q.III.90. It should be mentioned that neither Ṭabarī nor Rāzī mention the hypocrites within the exegesis of these two verses. See *Tafsīr al-Ṭabarī*, vol VI, pp. 572–582; *Tafsīr al-Rāzī*, vol. VIII, pp. 283–285. Nonetheless, that these two verses may refer to the hypocrites is predicated upon the other verses (Q.LXIII.4 and Q.IV.137) as mentioned. And God knows best.

64 That the hypocrites are also deserving of God's wrath (*maghḍūb ʿalay*[him]) and damnation is proven within verse six of Sūrat al-Fatḥ (XLVIII): *And may punish the hypocritical men and the hypocritical women, and the idolatrous men and the idolatrous women, who think an evil thought concerning God. For them is the evil turn of fortune, and God is wroth against them and hath cursed them, and hath made ready for them Hell, a hapless journey's end.*

65 Q.I.6–7.

66 Q.V.47.

if I am not just."[67] ʿUmar (as well as other Companions like Khālid b. al-Walīd) said: "O Messenger of God, allow me to cut the neck of this Hypocrite off." The Prophet said: "God forbid that people should say that I kill my Companions. Among the progeny of this man will be people who read the Qur'ān but it will not go beyond their throats [i.e. they will have no faith in it]. They will even kill the Muslims." In another narration, the Prophet said: "You will consider your prayer insignificant in comparison to theirs and your fasting insignificant in comparison to theirs. They will read the Qur'ān, but it will not go beyond their throats."[68]

Likewise, the Prophet Muḥammad prohibited killing ʿAbd Allāh b. Ubayy b. Salūl, the leader of the Hypocrites in Medina, saying: "Leave him be, so as to prevent people from saying that [Muḥammad] kills his Companions."[69] Therefore, it is impermissible to fight against or kill the hypocrites if they do not openly fight against the believers. Instead, the hypocrites should be exposed for who they are and isolated. The Muslims should always maintain the high moral ground or retake it, and never cede it to others.

The Prophet Muḥammad (may God bless him and grant him peace) also mentioned that fanatical Muslims would exist until the Day of Judgment: "They read the Qur'ān but it does not go beyond their throats…and they will fight against Islam."[70] Thus the Prophet informed us of the coming of those who are outwardly worshippers—reading the Qur'ān and praying—but in reality are fanatics who will fight against the Muslims. The Prophet states regarding these hypocrites that "they are the most evil of the creation".[71] In this case, since these fanatics will fight against Islam, the Prophet Muḥammad commanded the Muslims to respond in kind and "fight against them".[72]

---

67 The Prophet Muḥammad (may God bless him and grant him peace) said in another *ḥadīth*: "By God, I do not bestow nor do I withhold, instead I am a distributor (*qāsim*). I only place things where I am commanded." Bukhārī 3117; Aḥmad 10,257.

68 Bukhārī 3610; Muslim 1062–1064/2447–2456; Aḥmad 11,537.

69 Bukhārī 4905; Muslim 2584/6583; Tirmidhī 3315; Aḥmad 15,223.

70 Bukhārī 3344; Tirmidhī 2188 (the text includes the first section of this *ḥadīth*).

71 See Muslim 1067/2469; Abū Dāwūd 4765; Nasā'ī 4103; Aḥmad 20,342.

72 See Bukhārī 6930; Muslim 1066/2462; Abū Dāwūd 4767; Ibn Māja 175; Nasā'ī 4102; Aḥmad 1086.

DISTINGUISHING HYPOCRISY FROM MORAL WEAKNESS AND OSTENTATIOUSNESS

Now, hypocrisy should be distinguished from moral weakness (i.e. akrasia). The latter occurs in the setting of one who "is sincerely committed to the moral standards she professes…[and] experiences genuine remorse after her [sinful] act".[73] This can be quite difficult, if not impossible, for us to discern—only God knows who is in each group. Consider, for example, the three believers who did not accompany the Prophet Muḥammad and the Companions to the Battle of Tabuk[74]: they represented the case of moral weakness, rather than hypocrisy. Nonetheless, they were punished as God (Exalted is He) commanded the Prophet Muḥammad and the Companions to avoid any communication or interaction with them—that is, until approximately the same amount of time as the Companions were away (i.e. ~ fifty days) passed by. At that point, the Holy Lord revealed: *(He turned in mercy also) to the three who were left behind; (they felt guilty) to such a degree that the earth seemed constrained to them, for all its spaciousness, and their (very) souls seemed straitened to them, and they perceived that there is no fleeing from God (and no refuge) but to Himself. Then He turned to them, that they might repent: for God is Oft-Returning, Most Merciful.*[75] Thus, the failure to fight alongside the Prophet and the other Companions rendered the probability of hypocrisy to be very high, but not absolutely so. Moral weakness can be the cause, but only in a very small minority of cases.

---

[73] Spiegel, *Hypocrisy*, p. 38.

[74] The Battle of Tabuk occurred in 8 AH. The Prophet Muḥammad (may God bless him and grant him peace) became aware of the intention of the Byzantine empire and its Arab ally, the Ghassānids, to assemble an army to attack the Muslims. The Prophet and the Muslims therefore assembled an army of 30,000 and headed for Tabuk at the northern edge of Arabia. This occurred at a time of drought, relative dearth of resources, and severe heat and therefore it was particularly difficult. Nonetheless, they arrived at Tabuk and set up camp. Although no battle occurred, many benefits did result, including the signing of treaties with a number of northern Arabian tribes. In addition, many delegations subsequently came to the Prophet and became Muslim. Of note, during the apostate wars, which occurred after the Prophet Muḥammad's death, the tribes of northern Arabia remained Muslim and did not apostate.

[75] Q.IX.118.

Ostentatiousness (*riyā'*) should also be distinguished from hypocrisy. It involves doing something good for the sake of others rather than for God's sake alone. Ostentatiousness prevents those good deeds from being accepted. If ostentatiousness pervades all of one's actions and is associated with disbelief in the Hereafter, then the individual becomes a true hypocrite. If, on the other hand, the intention is not purely for God's sake in some deeds rather than all, then the person possesses traits of hypocrisy, but this does not completely nullify his or her faith.

That said, ostentatiousness amongst the believing Muslims should not be underestimated, as it is very difficult to escape in all instances. Ibn al-Qayyim states: "A person's heart could be overflowing with [hypocrisy or ostentation] yet he may be oblivious of it due to its hidden and subtle nature."[76] Therefore, the believers should always question their motives and re-evaluate their intentions, and ensure that they are doing good deeds and striving only for God's sake alone and for the benefit of Islam. Ghazālī states in regards to some forms of ostentatiousness or minor hypocrisy:

> Know that some forms of hypocrisy are obvious, such as the person who performs the night formal prayer among people, but not when he is alone; this is obvious. More hidden than this is that one have the custom of performing formal prayer every night; but when someone else is present, he becomes more energetic and more lively...its effect will become evident at that time when people learn that he has this quality and he is pleased and finds an expansiveness in himself. This joy and expansiveness is the sign that hypocrisy is concealed in his heart. If he does not counter this delight with repugnance, it is to be feared that this hidden vein will assault his self and not demand concealment so that it manufactures a reason for people to become aware of his state... It may also be more deeply hidden than this; as it may be that he does not delight in the peoples' knowledge about him and his zeal does not increase in their presence, yet his heart is not devoid of hypocrisy. The sign of this is that when a person comes to him and does not salute (him) with peace first[, he] finds some astonishment within himself. If a person decreases his respect for him, or does not hasten to fulfill his needs, or shows no leniency in his buying and selling with him, he finds amazement in his

[76] Ibn al-Qayyim, *Madārij al-sālikīn*, vol. I, p. 354, and Abū Rumaysah (tr.), *Characteristics of the Hypocrites*, p. 16.

> heart and objects, for if that worship had not been hidden, there would not have been this amazement... When one performs an act of worship for God Most High in order to attain eternal happiness, why should one expect respect? Thus the most hidden hypocrisy is that.[77]

Thus one should not seek the respect of others nor anything greater. One must also remember that since most people are disbelievers, one will be disrespected by a greater number of people than those who confer respect. Hence, it is not advantageous to ostentatiously act out of a desire to be respected by others or to carry out good deeds for worldly reasons.

Finally, the Prophet Muḥammad (may God bless him and grant him peace) said:

> On the Day of Resurrection the first to be judged will be a man who died in battle. He will be brought forth and [God] will remind him of His blessings, and he will acknowledge them. Then [God] will say: "What did you do with them?" The man will respond: "I fought for Your sake until I was martyred." [God (Exalted is He)] will say: "You are lying; rather, you fought so that it would be said: 'He is brave,' and such was said." Then it will be commanded that this man be dragged on his face and thrown into Hellfire. Another individual who acquired knowledge and taught it, and recited the Qur'ān will be brought forth. [God] will remind him of His blessings, and he will acknowledge them. [God] will say: "What did you do with them?" This individual will respond: "I acquired knowledge and taught it, and I recited the Qur'ān for Your sake." [God (Exalted is He)] will say: "You are lying; rather, you acquired knowledge and taught it so that it would be said: 'He is a scholar,' and you read Qur'ān so that it would be said: 'He is a reciter,' and such was said." Then it will be commanded that this individual be dragged on his face and thrown into Hellfire. [Finally,] a person whom God granted many [blessings] and bestowed much wealth upon will be brought forth. [God] will remind him of His blessings, and he will acknowledge them. [God] will say: "What did you do with them?" This person will respond: "I did not leave any way in which You love wealth to be spent, except that I spent it for Your sake." [God] will say: "You are lying; rather, you did such so that it would be said: 'He is

---

77 Muḥammad Nur Abdus Salam (tr.), *Al-Ghazzali on the Treatment of Hypocrisy*, pp. 37–39.

> generous,' and it was said." Then it will be commanded that he be dragged on his face and thrown into Hellfire.[78]

The fact that these individuals were mentioned specifically in this *ḥadīth* indicates that they lacked true faith in the Hereafter, in addition to their ostentatiousness. It does not prove, however, that others who worshipped God alone and believed in the Hereafter will not go to Paradise after being punished in Hellfire for their ostentatiousness in some acts (if the Holy Lord deems them deserving of such punishment). And God knows best.

THE WISDOM IN ALLOWING OSTENTATION

Although insincere beneficial deeds will not be rewarded in the Hereafter, it is better that they are performed, even if with ostentatiousness. For example, the giving of charity by those who are acting ostentatiously is better than its absence, because it reduces the amount of suffering and evil in this world.

For example, the non-Muslims may give charity to the Muslims, but if the former do help the Muslims financially, it is an inadequate amount oftentimes—say 10% or less than what the Muslims need. And if the former do give verbal support, it is often unassociated with any tangible or meaningful action. Such superficial actions are only done so that these disbelievers or hypocrites can maintain their deceptive façade. What has occurred in Syria from 2011 until now illustrates these points well, but it is beyond the scope of this book to discuss it in detail.[79] Yet, of course, it should be reiterated explicitly that this does not apply to those non-Muslims who sincerely try to aid the innocent and helpless Muslims to the extent of their ability, and try their utmost to reduce their suffering.

Next, Jeremy Lott states that hypocrisy preserves "moral norms" without which "anarchy"[80] would result. Therefore, most people

---

78 Muslim 1905/4923; Tirmidhī 2382; Nasā'ī 3137; Aḥmad 8277.

79 Only a few books have been written on the Syrian Revolution since 2011. That said, as it relates to this chapter, one may read Nikolaos Van Dam, *Destroying a Nation: The Civil War in Syria* (London and New York: I.B. Tauris, 2017), particularly Chapter 4 titled "The ambivalent Western approach to the Syria conflict," pp. 119–137.

80 Jeremy Lott, *In Defense of Hypocrisy: Picking Sides in the War on Virtue* (Nashville: Nelson Current, 2006), p. 17.

who are disbelievers act in a generally moral and beneficial manner, even if that is sometimes simply in order to avoid appearing to be evil. In addition, hypocrisy and ostentation bring together the disbelievers (whose goals are not otherwise unified). In the absence of hypocrisy the disbelievers—particularly those who are not religious—could not work together to any large extent. Ruth Grant has stated: "In times of weakness or dependence, hypocrisy is the preferred mode of conducting politics for republics as well as principalities."[81] Hypocrisy thus serves to prop up the disbelieving societies for some time, but it is a weak means.

Grant also states: "Rulers must cultivate a reputation for virtue while doing whatever is necessary, because that reputation is itself equally necessary. Publicly cynical politics will not work."[82] Now, it could be contended that harmful conflicts would perpetually occur if the dominant politics did not involve hypocrisy. In response, it will be maintained that although conflict would be more likely to occur initially if hypocrisy was absent, over the long term politicians would better reform their policies and be more effective. In reality, hypocrisy leads to the persistence of evil and the absence of reformation.

It is only after being challenged by the pious believers that the divisions present within the disbelievers and hypocrites become clearly manifested. God (Exalted is He) states: *Thou wouldst think they were united, but their hearts are divided: that is because they are a people devoid of wisdom.*[83] Had the disbelievers and hypocrites been wise they would have abandoned their ways and followed the true religion. The order that is achieved by hypocrisy is weak and the politics employing it eventually devolves and becomes disordered. The believers, on the other hand, are held together by their certainty in and following of God's Scripture and the Prophetic Sunna. The Almighty Lord states: *If thou hadst expended all that is on the earth, thou couldst not have brought their hearts together [by thyself], but God did bring them together. Verily, He is Almighty, Wise.*[84]

---

[81] Ruth Grant, *Hypocrisy and Integrity: Machiavelli, Rousseau, and the Ethics of Politics* (Chicago: The University of Chicago Press, 1997), p. 22.

[82] Ibid., p. 27.

[83] Q.LXIX.14.

[84] Q.VIII.63 (Muḥammad Asad translation).

PREVENTION OF HYPOCRISY

Knowing the above may allow one to evaluate with greater insight one's actions and self such that one can avoid the traits of hypocrisy and ostentation. Knowing oneself, through repeated self-evaluation and introspection, although difficult, represents the beginning of the road to resolving one's inadequacies and ridding oneself of hypocrisy. Again, evaluating one's sincerity as well the complex actions of one's heart is only possible if hypocrisy is an option. Listed below are a few methods by which one may become more devoted to God (Glorious is He) and the Hereafter.

The first means to avoid hypocrisy is remembrance of the Holy Lord. God (Glorious is He) has stated regarding the hypocrites: *And when they rise to pray, they rise reluctantly, only to be seen and praised by men, remembering God but seldom.*[85] God (Exalted is He) has advised us in Sūrat al-Munāfiqūn: *O ye who believe! Let not your wealth nor your children distract you from remembrance of God. Those who do so, they are the losers.*[86]

God (Exalted is He) also said: *Obey not him whose heart We have made heedless of Our remembrance, who followeth his own lust and whose case hath been abandoned.*[87] Here, remembrance of the heart and obedience to His commandments are substituted by the hypocrites and disbelievers with heedlessness and the following of their desires. Remembrance, as per many verses of the Qur'ān, also includes praying and supplicating to the Holy Lord. The night prayers (*tahajjud*) are important in this regard, since only those who are devout and truly sincere to the Holy Lord will carry them out.

Consider also that the Messenger of God (may God bless him and grant him peace) said: "Indeed, the world is cursed; everything in it is cursed except for the remembrance of God and what is conducive to it, the scholar and the student."[88] Therefore, anyone who turns away from remembering the Holy Lord or pursuing beneficial religious knowledge is bereft of any goodness.

---

85 Q.IV.142 (Muḥammad Asad translation).

86 Q.LXIII.9.

87 Q.XVIII.28.

88 Tirmidhī 2322; Ibn Māja 4112; Bayhaqī (*Shuʿab*) 1580. It is "sound" according to Albānī (*Silsilat al-aḥādīth al-ṣaḥīḥa* 2797).

Ibn al-Qayyim proclaims that remembrance, along with knowledge and willpower, is evidence of one's loyalty to God. One who remembers the Holy Lord "becomes [spiritually] proximate [to God], whereas those who are denied it are cut off. It is the sustenance of seekers, and if one abandons it then the body [dies spiritually and] becomes like a grave".[89]

The Prophet Muḥammad also said: "Remember (*iḥfaẓ*) God and He will care for you (*yaḥfaẓ*[uka]). Acknowledge (*taʿarraf*) God in times of ease and He will show you [His providence] (*yaʿrif*[uka]) in times of hardship."[90] Ibn al-Qayyim explained this in the following terms: "When the servant acknowledges God (Exalted is He) in times of ease through remembrance of Him, the Lord will show him His providence in times of hardship."[91]

Second, God (Exalted is He) mentioned the need to give alms and charity in Sūrat al-Munāfiqūn: *And spend of that wherewith We have provided you before death cometh unto one of you and he saith: My Lord! If only thou wouldst reprieve me for a little while, then I would give alms and be among the righteous.*[92] The fact that giving charity is mentioned in this short *sūra* of only eleven verses illustrates its importance in countering hypocrisy. Through almsgiving and charity one can avoid attachment to this world (to some degree) and attain God's pleasure.

Third, Ghazālī alludes to the importance of concealing at least some of one's good and benevolent deeds to minimize the risk of hypocrisy:

> One [should] keep hidden one's good deeds and acts of devotion as one keeps hidden one's vile deeds and sins until one accustoms oneself to being content with devotion and God Most High's knowledge (of his acts). At

---

89 Ibn al-Qayyim, *Madārij al-sālikīn*, vol. II, p. 395.

90 Aḥmad 2803; al-Ḥākim 6303; *Ḥilya* vol. I, p. 314; Bayhaqī (*Shuʿab*) 1043. It is "authentic" according to Albānī (See both *Mishkāt al-maṣābīḥ* 5302 and *Ṣaḥīḥ al-Jāmiʿ al-ṣaghīr* 2961). See also Tirmidhī 2516.

91 Ibn Qayyim al-Jawziyya, *Al-Wābil al-ṣayyib wa rāfiʿ al-kalim al-ṭayyib*, ed. ʿAbd al-Raḥmān b. Ḥasan b. Qāʾid, (Mecca: Dār ʿĀlam al-Fawāʾid, 2013), p. 98. Of note, Ibn al-Qayyim mentioned one hundred benefits of the remembrance of God, whereby this was present within the twenty-second one. See also Michael Abdurrahman Fitzgerald and Moulay Youssef Slitine (tr.), *Ibn Qayyim al-Jawziyya on The Invocation of God* (Cambridge: Islamic Texts Society, 2000), p. 51.

92 Q.LXIII.10.

> the beginning this is difficult, but if one makes the effort it will become easy... Know that in concealing acts of devotion there is the benefit that one achieves liberation from hypocrisy. There is also a benefit in revealing them and that is the people's following one's example and the stimulation of their desire for goodness. It is for this that God Most High praised both of these (practices), saying: *If ye publish your almsgiving it is well, but if ye hide it and give it to the poor, it will be better for you.* (Q.2:271)... A person must not deceive himself and reveal an act of worship which he is able to conceal.[93]

Fourth, one must also always speak the truth even if against oneself, in accordance with the verse: *O ye who believe! Be ye staunch in justice, witnesses for God, even though it be against yourselves or (your) parents or (your) kindred.*[94] Truthfulness in intention, speech and acts (both of the heart and body) are the keys to avoiding hypocrisy.

Nonetheless, the aforementioned does not indicate that one should be harsh to others. The Prophet said: "God is gentle, and He loves gentleness. He assists [those believers who are gentle to be successful], whereas He does not in the case of harshness."[95] One should overlook the faults of others and not inject one's frank opinion of others at each encounter. Working with others is evidence of one's gentleness and mercy upon them—not a proof of weakness or inadequacy. One should provide unity rather than cause disunity.

Finally, if one contemplates the traits of the hypocrites outlined in the previous sections and dedicates oneself to their opposites, one will focus on being truthful and humble, fulfilling one's oaths and pledges, having strength in carrying out the pillars of Islam (particularly prayer and almsgiving) as well as the Holy Lord's commandments, remaining pious and avoiding major sins, concealing some of one's good deeds and not desiring that others respect one, speaking well of other believers and avoiding mocking or backbiting them, remaining calm and tranquil when conflicts arise, wishing the believers well, hoping that the Muslims will be granted victory, having certainty in the Hereafter, and always remembering God (Glorious is He). The Prophet Muḥammad (may God bless him and grant him peace) and

---

93 Muḥammad Nur Abdus Salam (tr.), *Al-Ghazzali on the Treatment of Hypocrisy*, pp. 46 and 50–51.

94 Q.IV.135.

95 Muslim 2593/6601; Abū Dāwūd 4807; Ibn Māja 3688; Aḥmad 902.

his Companions were the furthest away from hypocrisy, and thus they represent the best role models for true faith and sincerity to God.

ELUCIDATING THOSE WHO ARE HYPOCRITES

God (Exalted is He) has established many means to elucidate those who are hypocrites (or disbelievers). The first means is by God's abrogation (*naskh*)[96] of His commandments. Abrogation leads the hypocrites to manifest outwardly their unbelief, doubts and disobedience. God (Glorious is He) stated: *None of Our revelations do We abrogate or cause to be forgotten, but We substitute something better or similar... Would ye question your Messenger as Moses was questioned of old? But whoever changeth from faith to unbelief, hath strayed without doubt from the even way.*[97]

Consider the Holy Lord's commandment to first pray facing the Holy Mosque in Jerusalem and then His abrogation of that commandment to face the Kaᶜba in Mecca. The Holy Lord has related some statements from people at the time of this abrogation: *The foolish of the people will say: What hath turned them from the qibla which they formerly observed? Say: Unto God belong the east and the west. He guideth whom He will unto a Straight Path... And We appointed the qibla which ye formerly observed only that We might know him who followeth the Messenger, from him who turneth on his heels. In truth it was a hard (test) save for those whom God guided.*[98] The *foolish* mentioned in this verse includes the hypocrites in part, and thus the abrogation herein served to elucidate them.

Now, the wise purpose in the initial commandment was to elevate the status of Jerusalem as a place of worship within Islam. Jerusalem is the third holiest city in Islam after Mecca and Medina; but if the initial direction had been towards the Kaᶜba and not towards Jerusalem, then the latter would have never attained the esteem in the believers' hearts that is demanded by its holy and distinguished status within Islam.

---

[96] Note that the religion of God is without contradiction. Abrogation within Islam, wherein some of the Divine Laws abrogated earlier ones, are akin to the Divine Laws that were eased with Jesus, i.e. Christianity, in comparison to those of Moses, i.e. Judaism. See Q.III.50 wherein Jesus states: *And (I come) confirming that which was before me of the Torah, and to make lawful some of that which was forbidden unto you. I come unto you with a sign from your Lord, so keep your duty to God and obey me.*

[97] Q.II.105–108 (Yusuf Ali translation).

[98] Q.II.142–143.

Recall that the Holy Mosque in Jerusalem is also important for it served as the site for the Prophet Muḥammad's Night Journey (*Isrāʾ*) and Ascension (*Miʿrāj*) to Heaven. This event led to the demarcation of those who truly followed the Prophet Muḥammad at that time from those who did not. On account of Abū Bakr's faith in the event, and his statement: "If [Muḥammad] said [that this occurred], then it is true,"[99] he became thereafter known as "the truly faithful one (*al-Ṣiddīq*)".

The second means to elucidate those who are hypocrites and have doubts is through the allegorical verses of the Qurʾān. God (Exalted is He) states:

> *He it is Who hath revealed unto thee (Muḥammad) the Scripture wherein are clear revelations—they are the substance of the Book—and others (which are) allegorical. But those in whose hearts is doubt pursue, forsooth, that which is allegorical seeking (to cause) dissension by seeking to explain it. None knoweth its explanation save God. And those who are of sound instruction say: We believe therein; the whole is from our Lord; but only men of understanding really heed.*[100]

On account of this, allegorical verses serve to elucidate those who harbour doubts and have deviated from the truth. The phrase *those in whose hearts is doubt* refers to the hypocrites[101], and thus they are revealed to be amongst those who intentionally misinterpret the allegorical verses according to their desires in order to cause dissension. In contrast, one who is sincere follows the truth and clear-cut revelation, and interprets the Qurʾānic verses according to other verses, the Sunna and the exegesis of the authoritative scholars.

A third manner by which the hypocrites are manifested is through God's allowance of satanic calumnies as per the verse:

> *Never sent We a messenger or a prophet before thee but when he recited (the message) Satan proposed (opposition) in respect of that which he recited thereof. But God abolisheth that which Satan proposeth. Then God establisheth His revelations. God is Knower, Wise. That [God] may make that which the Devil proposeth*

---

99 Al-Ḥākim 4407. It is "authentic" according to Albānī (*Silsilat al-aḥādīth al-ṣaḥīḥa* 306).

100 Q.III.7.

101 For instance, Mujāhid b. Jabr al-Makhzūmī (one of the Successors) opined that *those in whose hearts is doubt* refers to the hypocrites. See *Tafsīr al-Ṭabarī*, vol. VI, p. 184.

a temptation for those in whose hearts is a disease, and those whose hearts are hardened—Lo! the evildoers are in open schism.[102]

Here, *those in whose hearts is a disease* includes the hypocrites, whereas *those whose hearts are hardened* refers to the polytheists of Quraysh, amongst others.[103] Ibn al-Qayyim states in regard to these verses: "God (Glory be to Him) has notified us that He has made that which Satan proposes—in regards to the aspirations of the Messenger—a tribulation and test for people. Thus those whose hearts are [spiritually] diseased and hardened become seduced [by those Satanic calumnies]. On the other hand, the believers are certain that the Qur'ān and the Messenger are the truth, while the proposition of Satan is falsehood."[104]

The final and most significant means to expose the hypocrites is through the allowance of war. God (Glorious is He) loves those who fight in His path since they are willing to sacrifice themselves for His sake and the Hereafter. There is no greater indicator of one's sincerity to the Holy Lord than that willingness to give up one's life. Nonetheless, it is important to remind ourselves that God (Exalted is He) has forbidden suicide, and His Prophet Muḥammad warned those who commit suicide that they will be punished with Hellfire.[105]

Now, it is impossible that the Holy Lord would create intrinsically evil humans against whom the good would fight, since He is the Most Just. It has already been discussed that God (Glorious and Exalted is He) is holy and absolutely good. His Divine commandments are absolutely good and just, and the consequences resulting from them lead to either absolute or predominately positive outcomes. Indeed, the Holy Lord does not cause any injustice.

On the one hand, had humans only been good, then the Holy Lord would not have commanded them to fight against each other, for that would be unjust and unwise. Certainly, God (Glorious is He) concordantly commands the believers to be merciful and benevolent

---

102 Q.XXII.52–53.

103 See *Tafsīr al-Ṭabarī*, vol. XVIII, p. 669; *Tafsīr al-Rāzī*, vol. XXIII, p. 241.

104 See Zeni (tr.), *Ibn Qayyim al-Jawziyya on Divine Wisdom and the Problem of Evil*, p. 47. Of note, the believers are discussed in Q.XXII.54: *And that those who have been given knowledge may know that it is the truth from thy Lord, so that they may believe therein and their hearts may submit humbly unto Him. God verily is guiding those who believe unto a right path.*

105 See Bukhārī 5778; Muslim 109/300; Tirmidhī 2043; Nasā'ī 1965; Aḥmad 7448.

with other believers. On the other hand, had intrinsically evil humans existed they would ultimately become denizens of the Hellfire, since God's wisdom dictates that He recompense each individual in accordance with his or her deeds: *Whereupon those who [in their lifetime] were bent on evildoing will be told: Taste suffering abiding! Is this requital anything but the just due for what you were wont to do?*[106] But these creatures could object to that punishment, as they were not given freedom of action. This lack of freedom amongst intrinsically evil human beings would contradict His wisdom and justice.

Furthermore, had the Holy Lord created these hypothetical people who were intrinsically evildoers but not punished them, then other evildoers would ask likewise to be exempt from His punishment. All this would be inconsistent with His wisdom, and would be vain and aimless. God is glorious and exalted above such frivolity. Instead, God (Glorious and Exalted is He) creates humans free to pursue what they will within a fine-tuned world to accord with what He wills.

Since God (Glorious is He) is just and has dictated that He will command the good to fight against the evildoers, He has created humans as being free from evil in infancy and endowed them with a sound and good innate disposition, but for disparate reasons many human beings, of their own free will, chose to become evil. No creature (not even Satan) is created evil from the outset, but instead that particular creature has freely chosen to disobey the Holy Lord or turn away from Him. The vast majority freely chose to perpetrate evil with a minority perpetrating dysteleological and gratuitous evils, such that conditions of injustice occur between humans and wickedness becomes widespread. These conditions then test and elucidate the sincerity of the believers and manifest their certainty in the Hereafter. War and fighting thus become necessary to overcome the widespread evil. God's commandment (Exalted is He) to fight in His path against the evildoers is therefore confirmed to be just and wise. God is omnipotent, and the above shows that God is the Most Just, and that His commandments are all wise, just and good.

---

106 Q.X.52. See also Q.VI.120; Q.VII.147; Q.XXVII.90; Q.XXXIV.33; Q.XLVI.20; Q.LII.16; Q.LXVI.7.

Now, human beings may think themselves to be good, but many are, in fact, insincere to the Holy Lord. Others may think that they would become good or better if their circumstances were more conducive; however, they should ask themselves if they are truly and sincerely carrying out all the good deeds that they are capable of. Instead, the majority of these individuals only want this world and to attain their desires—they are unwilling to fight or strive for God's sake. The Prophet Muḥammad (may God bless him and grant him peace), who carried out all of the commandments of his Lord (Glorious and Exalted is He), including fighting for His sake, in the best manner said: "Whoever dies without having fought, nor having even thought about doing so, dies within a division (*shuʿba*) of hypocrisy."[107] Thus only fighting or truly and sincerely thinking about doing so (which only God knows) allows one to avoid hypocrisy.

In this fashion it becomes apparent that God's allowance of evil—even gratuitous evil—results in conditions and causes which then lead to the sincere believers fighting against the disbelievers (or at least to think about doing so), while the hypocrites are manifested as not being willing to do any of these possibilities. Had these evils—even dysteleological evils—not existed then hypocrisy would not be manifested to those so deluded or arrogant to acknowledge that they harbour it. The elucidation of those who are hypocrites is thus one of the most fundamental wise purposes for God (Glorious is He) allowing dysteleological evils.

God is omniscient and knows what is in the hearts of people; but because He is the Most Just, He (Exalted is He) has dictated that He manifest to the hypocrites their deceit and hypocrisy. God, Who is omnipotent, states: *Say, (O Muḥammad): Whether ye hide that which is in your breasts or reveal it, God knoweth it. He knoweth that which is in the heavens and that which is in the earth, and God is Able to do all things.*[108] One of the consequences of God's omnipotence is that He is able to bring out the deceit and disbelief concealed in the hearts of the

[107] Muslim 1910/4931; Abū Dāwūd 2502; Nasāʾī 3099; Aḥmad 8865.

[108] Q.III.29.

hypocrites.[109] Also, recall that God (Exalted is He) states regarding the hypocrites: *They think to beguile God and those who believe, and they beguile none save themselves; but they perceive not.*[110] *The hypocrites seek to beguile God, but it is He Who beguileth them.*[111] God (Glorious and Exalted is He) has created this world in such a manner that it elucidates each and every hypocrite at all times and all places, and He will recompense them concordantly with Hellfire—it is in this manner that the Holy Lord has beguiled them. To leave one hypocrite unmanifested as such is contradictory to the wisdom of the Most Wise. God (Exalted is He) has thus fine-tuned this world from a religious standpoint to exclude anyone who is a hypocrite (or a disbeliever) from Paradise.

Again, only God (Exalted is He) knows the identities of all of the hypocrites,[112] and His justice has dictated to bring out and manifest their realities to themselves and to others. In that light, the Holy Lord did reveal the identity of some of the Hypocrites to His Prophet Muḥammad (may God bless him and grant him peace). The Prophet, in turn, informed Ḥudhayfa b. al-Yamān of the identity of some Hypocrites, and therefore he was known as "the Keeper of the Secret of the Messenger of God". The identity of the hypocrites is thus the real secret; however, this secret knowledge is not accessible to those living in a time period absent of the messengers.

God (Exalted is He) states: *Do men think that they will be left alone on saying: We believe, and that they will not be tested? We did test those before them, and God will certainly know those who are true from those who are false.*[113]

---

109 If one considers the preceding verse at Q.III.28 regarding the taking of allies in war and then considers Q.IV.144–145, which deems those "Muslims" who take some disbelievers as allies in war to be hypocrites, it can be seen that Q.III.29 alludes, in part, to bringing out the deceit and hypocrisy of the hypocrites.

110 Q.II.9.

111 Q.IV.142.

112 See, for example, Q.III.179 and its interpretation in *Tafsīr al-Ṭabarī*, vol. VII, p. 427. Ṭabarī states: "It is not God's will to reveal what is hidden within the hearts of His servants such that [humankind] knows and differentiates those who are believers from those who are hypocrites or disbelievers. Instead, [God] has differentiated them through trials and tribulations, such as the war at the [Battle] of Uḥud… That said, God revealed what He willed [regarding some of them] to His Messenger." Of note, the fact that the *khabīth* in Q.III.179 refers to a hypocrite is present in *Tafsīr al-Ṭabarī*, vol. VII, pp. 324 and 327, as well as *Tafsīr al-Rāzī*, vol. IX, p. 442.

113 Q.XXIX.2–3.

Likewise, the Old Testament affirms that the Holy Lord tests people so as to manifest those who are deceitful and excessively wicked: "The heart is deceitful above all things, and desperately wicked: who can know it? I the Lord search the heart, I try the reins, even to give every man according to his ways, and according to the fruit of his doings."[114] Each generation must be tested; hence war must be cyclical so as test humans, even though the circumstances and detailed causes leading to it will differ.

The hypocrites will avoid fighting for His sake or will do so only unwillingly if they are pressured into participation. Moreover, those hypocrites and disbelievers who are full of hatred and rancour will assist others through many means to kill the Muslims. The hypocrites and duplicitous disbelievers will betray their promises, renege on them, and fail to fulfill them. Both the disbelievers and hypocrites may claim that they are "forces for good"; but when it comes to dealing with the Muslims, they will ultimately perpetrate evil that contradicts universal principles, spread corruption, and seek to harm the Muslims. In essence, all of these types of hypocrites and disbelievers have been manifested as a result of what has occurred in Syria, Yemen and the Arab world from 2011 until now.

Although the Muslims have suffered horrific injustices, there are many wise purposes that have occurred as a result. Victory for the believers may be delayed so as to manifest and rid the Muslims of the hypocrites and deviant groups, in addition to making clear the duplicity of the disbelievers. The believers must be patient in enduring the oppression and must strive for His sake until the Holy Lord exposes the hypocrites, deviant groups and disbelievers for what they are. God's will (Exalted is He) has dictated that the truth will become manifest and triumph, but true victory always takes longer than expected. May God protect us from hypocrisy and grant victory to the pious and establish the righteous!

---

[114] Jeremiah 17.9–10. The "deceitful" may be referring to the hypocrites, while the "desperately wicked" may be referring to those who, although human, have satanic natures. And God knows best.

A CONTROVERSY REGARDING THE PROPHET MUḤAMMAD'S CONDUCT OF WAR

Now, some may criticize the Prophet Muḥammad (may God bless him and grant him peace) because he said: "War involves deception."[115] Some critics seek to imply through this that the Prophet Muḥammad was being hypocritical in the conduct of war. The fact of the matter is that war, which is a grave matter involving death,[116] is well-known by military strategists to necessarily require some element of deception.

Sun-Tzu, who is read by many military planners and held in esteem, affirmed the above, stating: "The way to war is a way of deception. When able feign inability. When deploying troops appear not to be. When near appear far. When far appear near. Lure with bait fight with chaos... If he is weak stir him to pride... If his men are harmonious split them. Attack where he is unprepared. Appear where you are unexpected."[117] Stating that war universally occurs without deception is naïve and a misrepresentation.

Consider also that the D-Day landing of the Allies who fought in World War II involved much well-planned deception. Stephen Ambrose states:

> Eisenhower, after he took command, mounted an elaborate deception plan. The code name was Fortitude; the objectives were to fool Hitler and his generals into thinking that the attack was coming where it was not, and into believing the real thing was a feint... Fortitude was a joint venture, with British and American teams working together. It made full use of the Double Cross System, of Ultra, of dummy armies, fake radio traffic, and elaborate security precautions... The Allies had to create fictitious division and landing craft on a grand scale. This was done chiefly with the Double Cross System, the talents of the American and British movie industries, and radio signals... [T]he Germans believed that the Allied force included eighty-nine divisions, when in fact the number

---

115 Bukhārī 3030; Muslm 1739; Tirmidhī 1675; Abū Dāwūd 2636; Ibn Māja 2833; Aḥmad 13,341.

116 Sun Tzu states: "War is a grave affair of state; it is a place of life and death, a road to survival and extinction, a matter to be pondered carefully." Sun Tzu, *The Art of War*, tr. John Minford (New York: Penguin Books, 2002), p. 1.

117 Sun Tzu, *The Art of War*, pp. 4–5. He repeated the premise later when he said: "War is founded on deception." Ibid., p. 42.

> was forty seven. The Germans thought the Allies had sufficient landing craft to bring twenty divisions ashore in the first wave, when they would be lucky to manage six... To check on how well Fortitude and security were working SHAEF relied on Ultra intercepts... Week after week, the summaries gave SHAEF exactly the news it hoped to receive: that the Germans were anticipating an attack on Norway, diversions in the south of France, Normandy, and the Bay of Biscay, and the main assault, with twenty or more divisions, against the Pas-de-Calais.[118]

A British double agent of Spanish descent, Juan Pujol (code-named Garbo), also deceived the Nazis into thinking that the Allies would be landing at Pas-de-Calais.[119] U.S. troops landed instead at Utah and Omaha Beaches, while British troops landed at Gold, Juno and Sword Beaches[120] in Normandy—not at Pas-de-Calais, nor any of the other locations they deceived the Germans into thinking their landing would occur at. This is but one example of deception in war. It is clear that in the absence of the D-Day landing the Allies would not have been able to defeat the Nazis on continental Europe; therefore, deception was necessary to the ultimate victory of the Allies.

Ultimately, the Prophet Muḥammad affirmed that war inevitably includes some element of deception. The Prophet (may God bless him and grant him peace) may have also been warning the Muslims that since war is like this they must not allow themselves to be deceived.[121]

Next, the Prophet Muḥammad said: "Lying is impermissible except in three instances: when a husband speaks to his wife, in war,

---

118 Stephen Ambrose, *D-Day June 6, 1944: The Climactic Battle of World War II* (New York: Simon & Schuster, 1994), pp. 80–84.

119 See Stephan Talty, *Agent Garbo: The Brilliant, Eccentric Secret Agent Who Tricked Hitler and Saved D-Day* (Boston: Houghton Mifflin Harcourt, 2012). Talty also discusses Garbo's role in another operation to deceive the Germans into thinking that D-Day would occur a year earlier, i.e. in 1943 instead of 1944. Ibid., pp. 123–131 and 141–152.

120 Stephen E. Ambrose, *D-Day*, pp. 78–79.

121 See Ibn Ḥajar, *Fatḥ al-Bārī*, vol. VI, p. 158.

and when trying to resolve [disputes] amongst people."[122] If one deeply reflects on this *ḥadīth* one will note that the objective in the first and third instances is clearly to make peace, whether amongst a married couple or people in general. Therefore, by extrapolation, the most appropriate objective of lying (or deception) in war is either to maintain the peace and avoid war altogether or to spare lives (on both sides). And God knows best.

The Prophet Muḥammad (may God bless him and grant him peace) also said: "O people, do not wish to meet the enemy [in war].[123] Instead, supplicate to God to be safeguarded from that. But if you meet them, then be patient."[124] Accordingly, the objective in Islam is to only engage in war if it is unavoidable. Maintaining the peace and ensuring justice are principle objectives within Islam; whereas unjustly pursuing wars is akin to perpetrating corruption.[125] Ultimately, the Prophetic guidance and Islam corroborate the Beatitude in the New Testament: "Blessed are the peacemakers."[126]

It should also be recalled from the last chapter that taking interest/usury is prohibited even in war. Other major sins can be considered likewise. Deception in war, therefore, should not include or involve the perpetration of any major sins. It should be emphasized again that deception may not be used outside of war.

Moreover, it is important to remember that Abraham will, out of deference, confer the intercession on the Day of Judgment to Muḥammad (may God bless them both) due to three lies that the

---

122 Tirmidhī 1939; Aḥmad 27,608. It is "sound" according to Albānī (*Ṣaḥīḥ al-Jāmiʿ al-ṣaghīr* 7723). The only other exception is when a person is certain or nearly certain that he or she will be killed otherwise, as in the case of ʿAmmār b. Yāsir. See Q.XVI.106. That said, it is best to follow the Prophetic guidance: "Whoever sees a major sin (*munkar*) being perpetrated should change it with his hands. If he cannot then with his tongue. If he cannot then with his heart, and that is the weakest of faith." Muslim 49/177; Tirmidhī 2172; Abū Dāwūd 4340; Ibn Māja 1275; Nasāʾī 5009; Aḥmad 9231. Therefore, in cases where death is not a near certainty, lying is forbidden.

123 Sun Tzu said something similar: "Ultimate excellence lies not in winning every battle but in defeating the enemy without ever fighting." Sun Tzu, *The Art of War*, p.12.

124 Bukhārī 2966; Muslim 1742/4542; Abū Dāwūd 2631.

125 See Q.V.64 where the pursuit of warfare is spoken of in a negative light.

126 Matthew 5.9.

former spoke.[127] Those three lies[128] refer to Abraham saying: [1] *I feel sick,*[129] [2] *But this, their chief hath done it. So question them, if they can speak,*[130] and [3] saying that his wife, Sarah, was instead his sister when confronted by a pharaoh of Egypt. If one notes the nature of these three cases (which were designed to allow him to destroy the idols, protect himself from blame, or possibly—but not certainly—to protect himself from being killed), they do not fall within the three criteria that the Holy Lord permitted, as mentioned by the Prophet Muḥammad. Consequently, Abraham (may God bless him) will consider those instances to be lapses, and God knows best.

In conclusion, deception and lying are to be avoided in all cases except for what was permitted above.

A case study of hypocrisy

Now, the hypocrites may uncommonly fight alongside the believers against the disbelievers, but only for worldly reasons. In one instance, the Companions of the Prophet Muḥammad had deemed someone amongst them to be a brave fighter, but the Prophet (may God bless him and grant him peace) told them: "He is amongst the denizens of Hellfire." So, one of the Companions followed this man until the latter was wounded gravely. At that point, the wounded man hastened death and killed himself with his own sword. The Companion then went back to the Prophet Muḥammad and said: "I bear witness that you are the Messenger of God." The Prophet said: "What has reaffirmed that to you?" The Companion then told him the story of that man, and the Prophet Muḥammad said: "A person will carry out deeds consistent with those in Paradise as it appears to people, but he will be amongst the denizens of Hellfire. And an individual will initially perpetrate actions that are consistent with the denizens of Hellfire, such that people will think [that he will ultimately be one of the denizens], but [he will later do good and] his end will

127 See Bukhārī 4712; Muslim 194/481; Tirmidhī 2434; Aḥmad 2692.

128 See Bukhārī 3358; Muslim 2371/6145; Aḥmad 2546.

129 Q.XXXVII.63. Abraham said this in order to turn the polytheists away from him so that he could then destroy their idols.

130 Q.XXI.63. Abraham said this after breaking the idols of the polytheists.

be in Paradise."[131] We should therefore avoid judging others (unless revelation in their matter exists) for only God, the Omniscient Lord, knows what is hidden in people's hearts and what their end will be.

In light of the above, an ambiguous matter concerning Ṭālūt, or Saul, will be investigated, together with a discussion of other beneficial religious matters. The contention will be that, based on proofs from revelation, his end was not as a believer.

First, God (Glorious is He) states: *Bethink thee of the leaders of the Children of Israel after Moses, how they said unto a Prophet whom they had: Set up for us a king and we will fight in God's way... Their Prophet said unto them: God hath raised up Saul to be a king for you.*[132] The Bible describes the inappropriateness of the Israelites' request:

> Now make us a king to judge us like all the nations. But the thing displeased Samuel, when they said, Give us a king to judge us. And Samuel prayed unto the LORD. And the LORD said unto Samuel, Hearken unto the voice of the people in all that they say unto thee: for they have not rejected thee, but they have rejected me, that I should not reign over them. According to all the works which they have done since the day that I brought them up out of Egypt even unto this day, wherewith they have forsaken me, and served other gods, so do they also unto thee.[133]
>
> And Samuel called the people together unto the LORD to Mizpeh; And said unto the children of Israel, Thus saith the LORD God of Israel, I brought up Israel out of Egypt, and delivered you out of the hand of the Egyptians, and out of the hand of all kingdoms, and of them that oppressed you: And ye have this day rejected your God, who himself saved you out of all your adversities and your tribulations; and ye have said unto him, Nay, but set a king over us.[134]
>
> And when ye saw that Nahash the king of the children of Ammon came against you, ye said unto me, Nay; but a king shall reign over us: when the LORD your God was your king. Now therefore behold the king whom ye have chosen, and whom ye have desired! And, behold,

---

131 Bukhārī 2898; Muslim 112/306. In another *ḥadīth* the Prophet said: "Only those who have [sincerely] submitted themselves [to the Lord] will enter Paradise. Indeed, God will use some who are wicked to aid this religion." See Bukhārī 3062; Muslim 111/305; Aḥmad 8090.

132 Q.II.246–247.

133 2 Samuel 8.5–8.

134 2 Samuel 9.17–19.

> the LORD hath set a king over you. If ye will fear the LORD, and serve him, and obey his voice, and not rebel against the commandment of the LORD, then shall both ye and also the king that reigneth over you continue following the LORD your God: But if ye will not obey the voice of the LORD, but rebel against the commandment of the LORD, then shall the hand of the LORD be against you, as it was against your fathers... And all the people said unto Samuel, Pray for thy servants unto the LORD thy God, that we die not: for we have added unto all our sins this evil, to ask us a king.[135]

As represented in these Biblical verses, it is inappropriate to ask the Almighty Lord for a king as it reflects a desire to turn away from His commandments as well as the commandments of His prophets and messengers.[136] It may then be asked: For what were the Israelites to beseech God (Exalted is He) since they were oppressed, driven from their homes and humiliated? The answer is that they should have requested a messenger. It was previously pointed out in Chapter Four that the messenger is granted victory while this is not necessarily the case with a prophet. And the Qur'ānic verse explicitly mentions that a prophet, not a messenger, was amongst them at that time. Therefore, had they been knowledgeable and pious they would have supplicated for a messenger (or that Samuel be granted that status). And God knows best.

The Almighty Lord was critical of their request but obliged them. God (Exalted is He) grants his kingdom to whomever He wills: *Say: O God! Owner of Sovereignty! Thou givest sovereignty unto whom Thou wilt, and Thou withdrawest sovereignty from whom Thou wilt. Thou exaltest whom Thou wilt, and Thou abasest whom Thou wilt. In Thy hand is the good. Thou*

---

[135] 1 Samuel 12.12–19.

[136] See also Lawrence Freedman, *Strategy: A History* (Oxford: Oxford University Press, 2013), p. 20, who states that it reflected "the Israelites' desire to be led in the same way as other nations".

art Able to do all things.[137] Ultimately, God (Glorious is He) has created everything and placed everyone in his or her appropriate place.

As investigated previously in Chapter Six, when the phrase "God grants His sovereignty/kingdom (*yu'ti al-mulk*) to whom He will" is used this connotes that the recipient and owner of that kingdom is good. However, when God (Exalted is He) describes someone as being a king (*malik*), then that characterization indicates that this individual is a disbeliever or hypocrite. For instance, God never describes the Messenger David (may God bless him) as being a king; but instead the Almighty Lord states that He granted him sovereignty (*ātā*[hu] *Allāh al-mulk*)[138] and made him a Caliph (*khalīfa*). On the other hand, Saul is termed a king in the Qur'ān: *God hath appointed Ṭālūt as king over you.*[139]

Next is the issue of his name, Ṭālūt. There are four individuals in this story; three of them are named in the Qur'ān while one is not. The three named ones are Ṭālūt, David and Jālūt, while Samuel is instead simply titled as a "prophet". David (*Dāwūd*) is one of the greatest messengers of God, as was discussed before. Goliath (*Jālūt*) is an evil disbeliever who fought against the believers and was killed, by the grace of God, by David. The naming here of Ṭalūt is similar to that of Jālūt, and thus it suggests that they are associated with one another. One explanation for that is that both Jālūt and Ṭālūt fought against David (may God bless him) in this world—Jālūt's story being mentioned in the Qur'ān, while Saul's enmity is mentioned in the Bible and will be discussed below. The other explanation being that they are in the same abode in the Hereafter, i.e. Hellfire.

As for the disparity in name, i.e. Saul in the Bible and Ṭālūt in the Qur'ān, it may be that God (Exalted is He) changed his name from Saul to Ṭālūt after he deviated. And God knows best. Similarly, the Devil's

---

137 Q.III.26. The Biblical verses in Daniel 2.19–23 are similar: "Daniel blessed the God of heaven… Blessed be the name of God for ever and ever: for wisdom and might are his: And he changeth the times and the seasons: he removeth kings, and setteth up kings: he giveth wisdom unto the wise, and knowledge to them that know understanding: He revealeth the deep and secret things: he knoweth what is in the darkness, and the light dwelleth with him. I thank thee, and praise thee, O thou God of my fathers, who hast given me wisdom and might, and hast made known unto me now what we desired of thee: for thou hast now made known unto us the king's matter."

138 Q.II.251.

139 Q.II.247 (Yusuf Ali translation).

former name (also not mentioned in the Qur'ān) was subsequently changed to Iblīs[140] or Shayṭān (Satan) after he rebelled and disobeyed the commandments of the Almighty Lord. On the other hand, the Prophet Jacob (*Yaʿqūb*) (may God bless him) was bestowed another name due to his righteousness, i.e. Israel (*Isrā'īl*)—both of these names were mentioned in the Qur'ān.

Next, God states: *Their Prophet said to them: "God hath appointed Ṭālūt as king over you." They said: "How can he exercise authority over us when we are better fitted than he to exercise authority, and he is not even gifted with wealth in abundance?" He said: "God hath chosen him above you, and hath gifted him abundantly with knowledge and bodily prowess: God granteth His authority to whom He pleaseth. God careth for all, and He knoweth all things."*[141] Now, God (Glorious is He) explains the manner in which He has chosen (*iṣṭafā*) Ṭālūt: it is that He has granted him knowledge (*ʿilm*) and bodily prowess (*jism*). As for knowledge, it is well known that it does not necessarily result in guidance. Ibn al-Qayyim discusses ten reasons for why one may not become guided despite being knowledgeable.[142] Some reasons include wanting to maintain one's power, desiring to attain or remain in a leadership position, pursuing one's temptations, retaining or further pursuing wealth, fearing the loss of one's fame or status, being proud and arrogant, among others. These reasons may also explain why some become hypocrites and others choose to continue to be astray and perpetrate evil.

On the other hand, God (Glorious is He) states that He bestowed wisdom upon David (may God bless him): *So they routed them by God's leave and David slew Goliath; and God gave him the kingdom and wisdom, and taught him of that which He willeth.*[143] God (Glorious is He) also states regarding David: *We made his kingdom strong and gave him wisdom and decisive speech.*[144] Before being granted wisdom one must pursue and attain the truth and carry out good deeds, and David (may God bless him) did so. One must know the truth and differentiate it from

---

140 Iblīs is derived from the Arabic word *ablasa*, which means "to despair of all hope and goodness".

141 Q.II.247 (Yusuf Ali translation).

142 See Zeni (tr.), *Ibn Qayyim al-Jawziyya on Knowledge*, Chapter Five, pp. 108–122.

143 Q.II.251.

144 Q.XXXVIII.20.

falsehood in order to know the appropriate place for things and display wisdom. A hypocrite or one who is known to be a habitual liar can never possess true wisdom.

In fact, wisdom is juxtaposed to the Book or Scripture of God in the vast majority of instances it is mentioned. For example, God (Glorious is He) states: *God verily hath shown grace to the believers by sending unto them a messenger of their own who reciteth unto them His revelations, and causeth them to grow, and teacheth them the Scripture and wisdom; although before (he came to them) they were in flagrant error.*[145] God never states in the Qur'ān that He has granted wisdom (*ḥikma*) to the disbelievers or hypocrites, but they may be given knowledge.

Thereafter, God (Exalted is He) stated that He granted Ṭālūt bodily prowess (*jism*). The Bible likewise affirms that "from his shoulders and upward he was higher than any of the people".[146] Now there is only one other verse in the Qur'ān which mentions the word *jism*—in the plural (*ajsām*)—and it characterizes the hypocrites: *And when thou seest them their figures (ajsām) please thee; and if they speak thou givest ear unto their speech. (They are) as though they were blocks of wood in striped cloaks.*[147] On the other hand, God characterizes the prophets by saying: *And commemorate Our Servants Abraham, Isaac, and Jacob, possessors of power and vision;*[148] and: *apostles, endowed with firmness of heart.*[149] Therefore, God's characterization of Saul as being endowed with bodily prowess is another indication that he is amongst the hypocrites.

Some may say though that the Holy Lord chose Saul, and therefore we should not criticize him. But it is important to differentiate, as do Ibn Taymiyya and Ibn al-Qayyim among other scholars, between God's ontologic and deontologic/religious will.[150] For instance, they differentiate between God's ontologic sending (*baʿth*)

---

145 Q.III.164. See also Q.LXII.2, Q.II.129, Q.II.151, Q.III.48, Q.V.110, among many other verses.

146 1 Samuel 9.2.

147 Q.LXIII.4

148 Q.XXXVIII.45 (Yusuf Ali translation).

149 Q.XLVI.35 (Muḥammad Asad translation).

150 See Zeni (tr.), *Ibn al-Qayyim al-Jawziyya on Divine Wisdom and the Problem of Evil*, Chapter Fourteen. See also Ibn Taymiyya, *al-Jawāb al-ṣaḥīḥ*, vol I, pp. 117–120. Of note, Ibn al-Qayyim and Ibn Taymiyya do not discuss choosing (*iṣṭafā*) amongst the terms.

of Nebuchadnezzar and his army against the Israelites: *We sent against you Our servants given to terrible warfare: They entered the very inmost parts of your homes; and it was a warning (completely) fulfilled;*[151] and between His religious sending of the messengers: *For We assuredly sent amongst every people a messenger, (with the command), "Serve God, and eschew evil." Of the people were some whom God guided, and some on whom error became inevitably (established).*[152]

One of the most explicit examples in the Qur'ān of an ontologic versus deontologic term can be appreciated in regards to His "choosing (*iṣṭafā*)". God (Glorious is He) states: *Behold! the angels said: "O Mary! God hath chosen thee and purified thee and chosen thee above the women of all nations."*[153] God (Glorious is He) thus repeats "chosen (*iṣṭafa*)" twice in this verse. It is contended that one of them indicates the religious selection, i.e. Mary was chosen to be a truly faithful woman (*ṣiddīqa*) and the mother of a Messenger, while the other indicates the ontologic selection in that she was chosen to give birth to Jesus (may God bless him) without being touched by a man as well as being chosen for other material favours. There are other examples of ontologic choosing in the Qur'ān.[154] The contention here is that God's choosing of Ṭālūt is not from a religious standpoint, but rather only from an ontologic standpoint. The manner by which Saul was ontologically chosen was by being granted bodily prowess and knowledge, but not wisdom or religious faith (at least not at the time of his death).

Next, after the Israelites had traversed the river, God (Glorious is He) states: *And after he had crossed (the river), he and those who believed with him, they said: We have no power this day against Goliath and his hosts. But those who knew that they would meet God exclaimed: How many a little company hath overcome a mighty host by God's leave! God is with the steadfast.*[155] Therefore, God mentioned the believers in this verse separately from Ṭālūt (*he and those who believed*); and this is another evidence pointing to the fact that at some point beforehand Ṭālūt ceased to be a believer.

---

151 Q.XVII.5 (Yusuf Ali translation).

152 Q.XVI.36 (Yusuf Ali translation).

153 Q.III.42 (Yusuf Ali translation).

154 See verses Q.XXXIX.4 and Q.XXXVII.153.

155 Q.II.249.

Moreover, this is the last mention of Saul. The story then turns to those who are devout and to David (may God bless him). The Holy Lord states: *And David slew Goliath; and God gave him the kingdom and wisdom, and taught him of that which He willeth.*[156] The Almighty Lord graced David, while He neglected Ṭālūt. God (Exalted is He) mentions in another *sūra* that David *enjoyed, indeed, a near approach to Us, and a beautiful place of (Final) Return,*[157] whereas there is no mention of a good end for Ṭālūt.

Now, the Old Testament does discuss Saul in more depth, and a further understanding can be gained of four potential reasons for him being forsaken. May God protect us! First, according to the Old Testament, Saul disobeyed a direct commandment of the Lord as conveyed by Samuel, the Prophet of God:

> Samuel also said unto Saul, The LORD sent me to anoint thee to be king over his people, over Israel: now therefore hearken thou unto the voice of the words of the LORD. Thus saith the LORD of hosts, I remember that which Amalek did to Israel, how he laid wait for him in the way, when he came up from Egypt. Now go and smite Amalek, and utterly destroy all that they have, and spare them not; but slay both man and woman, infant and suckling, ox and sheep, camel and ass... And Saul smote the Amalekites from Havilah until thou comest to Shur, that is over against Egypt. And he took Agag the king of the Amalekites alive, and utterly destroyed all the people with the edge of the sword. But Saul and the people spared Agag, and the best of the sheep, and of the oxen, and of the fatlings, and the lambs, and all that was good, and would not utterly destroy them: but every thing that was vile and refuse, that they destroyed utterly. Then came the word of the LORD unto Samuel, saying, It repenteth me that I have set up Saul to be king: for he is turned back from following me, and hath not performed my commandments.[158] And it grieved Samuel; and he cried unto the LORD all night. And

---

[156] Q.II.251.

[157] Q.XXXVIII.25.

[158] Contrary to the apparent Biblical portrayal, where it stated: "It repenteth [M]e that I have set up Saul to be king", in Islam God (Glorious and Exalted is He) knows all that will transpire from before the creation of this world until the Day of Judgment. God was well aware that Saul would disobey His commandments, and therefore He obliged the Israelites only to make him a king—nothing more. Saul thereafter disobeyed God's commandments through his own free choice.

when Samuel rose early to meet Saul in the morning, it was told Samuel, saying, Saul came to Carmel, and, behold, he set him up a place, and is gone about, and passed on, and gone down to Gilgal. And Samuel came to Saul: and Saul said unto him, Blessed be thou of the LORD: I have performed the commandment of the LORD. And Samuel said, What meaneth then this bleating of the sheep in mine ears, and the lowing of the oxen which I hear? And Saul said, They have brought them from the Amalekites: for the people spared the best of the sheep and of the oxen, to sacrifice unto the LORD thy God;[159] and the rest we have utterly destroyed. Then Samuel said unto Saul, Stay, and I will tell thee what the LORD hath said to me this night. And he said unto him, Say on. And Samuel said, When thou wast little in thine own sight, wast thou not made the head of the tribes of Israel, and the LORD anointed thee king over Israel? And the LORD sent thee on a journey, and said, Go and utterly destroy the sinners the Amalekites, and fight against them until they be consumed. Wherefore then didst thou not obey the voice of the LORD, but didst fly upon the spoil, and didst evil in the sight of the LORD? And Saul said unto Samuel, Yea, I have obeyed the voice of the LORD, and have gone the way which the LORD sent me, and have brought Agag the king of Amalek, and have utterly destroyed the Amalekites. But the people took of the spoil, sheep and oxen, the chief of the things which should have been utterly destroyed, to sacrifice unto the LORD thy God in Gilgal. And Samuel said, Hath the LORD as great delight in burnt offerings and sacrifices, as in obeying the voice of the LORD? Behold, to obey is better than sacrifice, and to hearken than the fat of rams. For rebellion is as the sin of witchcraft, and stubbornness is as iniquity and idolatry. Because thou hast rejected the word of the LORD, he hath also rejected thee from being king. And Saul said unto Samuel, I have sinned: for I have transgressed the commandment of the LORD, and thy words: because I feared the people, and obeyed their voice.[160] Now therefore, I pray thee, pardon my sin, and turn again with me, that I may worship the LORD. And Samuel said unto Saul, I will not return

[159] Here Saul and some of the Israelites, in essence, deemed their wisdom to be greater than that of the Most Wise. Again, one must follow the commandments of the Holy Lord Who is Omniscient and take into account all complexities and details.

[160] Of note, it was ultimately Samuel who did kill Agag: "Then said Samuel, Bring ye hither to me Agag the king of the Amalekites. And Agag came unto him delicately. And Agag said, Surely the bitterness of death is past. And Samuel said, As thy sword hath made women childless, so shall thy mother be childless among women. And Samuel hewed Agag in pieces before the LORD in Gilgal." 1 Samuel 15.32–33.

> with thee: for thou hast rejected the word of the LORD, and the LORD hath rejected thee from being king over Israel. And as Samuel turned about to go away, he laid hold upon the skirt of his mantle, and it rent. And Samuel said unto him, The LORD hath rent the kingdom of Israel from thee this day, and hath given it to a neighbour of thine, that is better than thou.[161]

Again, this reveals the critical importance of following God's commandments. Turning away from implementing God's commandments leads to being forsaken by the Holy Lord.

Second, according to the Old Testament, Saul was jealous of David and sought to kill him,[162] despite knowing with certainty that the Holy Lord had graced David. Ultimately, David (may God bless him) told Saul:

> [K]now thou and see that there is neither evil nor transgression in mine hand, and I have not sinned against thee; yet thou huntest my soul to take it. The LORD judge between me and thee, and the LORD avenge me of thee: but mine hand shall not be upon thee...The LORD therefore be judge, and judge between me and thee, and see, and plead my cause, and deliver me out of thine hand.[163]

Third, according to the Old Testament, Saul ordered that the priests of the Lord be killed:

> And the king [Saul] said unto the footmen that stood about him, Turn, and slay the priests of the LORD; because their hand also is with David, and because they knew when he fled, and did not shew it to me. But the servants of the king would not put forth their hand to fall upon the priests of the LORD. And the king said to Doeg, Turn thou, and fall upon the priests. And Doeg the Edomite turned, and he fell upon the priests, and slew on that day fourscore and five persons that did wear a linen ephod. And Nob, the city of the priests, smote he with the edge of the sword, both men and women, children and sucklings, and oxen, and asses, and sheep, with the edge of the sword. And one of the sons of Ahimelech

---

[161] 1 Samuel 15:1–28. This is also mentioned in 1 Samuel 28.18. See also 2 Samuel 7.15: "But my mercy shall not depart away from [Solomon], as I took it from Saul, whom I put away before thee [David]."

[162] See 1 Samuel 23.14–29 and 1 Samuel 24.1–15.

[163] 1 Samuel 24.11–15.

> the son of Ahitub, named Abiathar, escaped, and fled after David. And Abiathar shewed David that Saul had slain the LORD's priests.[164]

Fourth, according to the Old Testament, Saul would meet his end by committing suicide:

> Now the Philistines fought against Israel: and the men of Israel fled from before the Philistines, and fell down slain in mount Gilboa. And the Philistines followed hard upon Saul and upon his sons; and the Philistines slew Jonathan, and Abinadab, and Malchi-shua, Saul's sons. And the battle went sore against Saul, and the archers hit him; and he was sore wounded of the archers. Then said Saul unto his armourbearer, Draw thy sword, and thrust me through therewith; lest these uncircumcised come and thrust me through, and abuse me. But his armourbearer would not; for he was sore afraid. Therefore Saul took a sword, and fell upon it. And when his armourbearer saw that Saul was dead, he fell likewise upon his sword, and died with him. So Saul died, and his three sons, and his armourbearer, and all his men, that same day together.[165]

Thus, according to the Old Testament, Saul committed suicide after sustaining a wound in battle just like the hypocrite mentioned in the *ḥadīth* at the beginning of this section did. Therefore, just as the Prophet Muḥammad (may God bless him and grant him peace) foretold the evilness of the aforementioned hypocrite and that his end would be Hellfire, Samuel—according to the Old Testament—foretold of Saul being forsaken by the Almighty Lord. Nathan also confirmed this in the Old Testament when he relayed to David that God informed him: "But my mercy shall not depart away from [David], as I took it from Saul, whom I put away before thee."[166]

God (Exalted is He) selected Ṭālūt to be a king, and that was appropriate to him; but the Most Wise and Most Just did not select him to be a king-prophet or a messenger. On the other hand, the Holy

---

[164] 1 Samuel 22.17–21. Saul also broke a covenant and killed the Gibeonites, according to 2 Samuel 21.1: "Then there was a famine in the days of David three years, year after year; and David inquired of the LORD. And the LORD answered, It is for Saul, and for his bloody house, because he slew the Gibeonites."

[165] 1 Samuel 31.1–6.

[166] 2 Samuel 7.15–17.

Lord granted David (may God bless him) a kingdom and established him as a Messenger and Caliph—that was from His wisdom and grace.

God (Glorious is He) knows what is in the hearts of men and He is able to manifest their true selves and what they hide: *Say, (O Muḥammad): Whether ye hide that which is in your breasts or reveal it, God knoweth it. He knoweth that which is in the heavens and that which is in the earth, and God is Able to do all things.*[167] If an individual possesses any religious goodness, the Holy Lord will guide him or her to become a believer, worship Him alone, and ultimately grant that individual a share in Paradise. As for those who turn away from God's commandments and do not implement the Divine Law, i.e. they are corrupt, they will be forsaken by the Holy Lord, afflicted with gratuitous evils in this world and punished with Hellfire in the Hereafter. In that regard, one should avoid following in the footsteps of king Saul or Saul of Tarsus.

God (Exalted is He) states: *As for that abode of the Hereafter* [*i.e. Paradise*] *We assign it unto those who seek not oppression* [*nor seek to exalt themselves*[168]] (*ʿuluwwᵃⁿ*) *in the earth, nor yet corruption.*[169] Some may deviate from the Divine commandments or true theology of Islam so as to empower themselves or attain a leadership position, while others innovate novel (but corrupt) systems of thought seeking to attain glory and exalt themselves above those who would follow them. Some of these may even claim that they have dreamt about the Prophet Muḥammad and fabricate traditions to him so as to develop their innovations—those fabricators should fear the punishment of Hellfire. Others may attribute false statements to great religious scholars so as to gain credibility in leading those who would follow them astray.

Ultimately, the true nature of each person is elucidated as a result of the construct of this world and the presence of tribulations and evil within it. In that light, each will be accorded his or her appropriate position in the Hereafter by the One Who is Omniscient, Omnipotent and Most Wise.

---

167 Q.III.29.

168 See Muḥammad Asad's translation wherein Paradise is granted only to: *those who do not seek to exalt themselves on earth, nor yet to spread corruption.*

169 Q.XXVIII.83. The hypocrites are noted to be corrupt in verses Q.II.11–12. It was also noted in Chapter Four that those whom the Holy Lord has named "king(s)" (*malik* or *mulūk*) in the Qurʾān are corrupt.

Now that it has been shown that one significant objective and wise purpose behind the existence of evil is to manifest those who are hypocrites, a question can be asked: Is it concordant with God's justice to subject all of humanity to suffering and evil for that objective (as well as the other wise objectives mentioned in the previous chapters)? The answer is in the affirmative and the next chapter seeks to prove it.

PART THREE

Chapter Fourteen

Hellfire

This chapter will deal with a number of issues relevant to the severe punishment of Hellfire. First, it was mentioned earlier that this chapter would advance the contention that the punishment of Hellfire will end for most of the disbelievers. Second, it will be contended that it is just for the Holy Lord to test the vast majority of humanity through the occurrence of suffering and evils, even the gratuitous type, so as to discern the disbelievers and hypocrites from those who are truly believers, and to achieve other wise purposes. This is so because the vast majority of humanity—even after being afflicted with all those occurrences—will still be deserving of a greater punishment, i.e. that of Hellfire. Keeping those objectives in mind, the chapter will begin by addressing the status of the believers, i.e. those who will either immediately or ultimately enter Paradise.

Now, God (Glorious is He) has repeatedly advised us throughout the Qur'ān to be pious (*muttaqūn*), as mentioned previously. His advice is from His providence, and the achievement of such a noble pious state is from His grace. The Holy Lord states: *Observe your duty* (*ittaqū*) *to God, and know that God is severe in punishment.*[1] This chapter will maintain that only the pious will be saved from Hellfire and entered into Paradise immediately, while all other believing Muslims will be punished by the Hellfire (to some degree) before being entered into Paradise.

God (Exalted is He) states: *Those who kept their duty* (*muttaqīn*) *dwell in gardens and delight, happy because of what their Lord hath given them, and* [*because*] *their Lord hath warded off from them the torment of Hellfire.*[2] The Holy Lord also states: *Those who kept their duty* (*muttaqīn*) *will be in a place secured. Amid gardens and watersprings… And He hath saved them* (*waqā*^{hum})

---

1 Q.II.196.

2 Q.LII.17–18.

from the doom of Hell.[3] *And God delivereth those who ward off evil… Evil toucheth them not, nor do they grieve.*[4] *But We shall save those who guarded against evil (alladhīna attaqaw), and We shall leave the wrongdoers therein, [humbled] to their knees.*[5] Likewise, the pious (*abrār*) are described by God (Exalted is He) in the following terms: *God hath warded off from them the evil of that day, and hath made them find brightness and joy; and hath awarded them for all that they endured: a Garden and silk attire.*[6] Ultimately, all of the aforementioned verses illustrate that the pious are singled out for absolute salvation from any punishment of Hellfire.

Furthermore, many verses in the Qur'ān specify that Paradise will be brought near to the pious. Consider, for example, the verses: *And the Garden is brought nigh for those who kept from evil (li'l-muttaqīn), no longer distant. [And it is said]: This is that which ye were promised. [It is] for every penitent and heedful one, who feareth the Beneficent in secret and cometh with a contrite heart.*[7] *And the Garden will be brought nigh for those who ward off [evil] (muttaqīn).*[8] Another verse of the Qur'ān specifies that the Hereafter will be better for those who are pious: *And the reward of the Hereafter is better, for those who believe and ward off [evil].*[9] Again, the reason for this is that only the pious (and higher ranks) will enter Paradise immediately, thus avoiding altogether the punishment of Hellfire.

God (Exalted is He) also states:

> *And a generation hath succeeded them who inherited the scriptures. They grasp the goods of this low life [as the price of evil-doing] and say: It will be forgiven us… Hath not the covenant of the Scripture been taken on their behalf that they should not speak aught concerning God save the truth? And they have studied that which*

---

[3] Q.XLIV.51–56.

[4] Q.XXXIX.61 (Muḥammad Asad translation). See also Q.LXLII.14–17: *So I warn you of the raging (talaẓẓā) Fire… Distant from it shall remain he who is truly conscious of God (al-atqā).*

[5] Q.XIX.72.

[6] Q.LXXVI.11–12. It was contended before in Chapter Seven that *abrār* is another term for the pious.

[7] Q.L.31–33. See also Q.XXXIX.73: *And those who feared (ittaqaw) their Lord will be led to the Garden in crowds: until behold, they arrive there; its gates will be opened; and its keepers will say: "Peace be upon you! well have ye done! enter ye here, to dwell therein"* (Yusuf Ali translation).

[8] Q.XXVI.90.

[9] Q.XII.57.

is therein. And the abode of the Hereafter is better, for those who ward off [*evil*] (*yattaqūn*). *Have ye then no sense?*[10]

This verse indicates that those who expect that they can perpetrate any evil and be forgiven because of their faith alone are deluded. Only the pious, i.e. those who avoid the major sins and regret their intermediate and minor sins, will be forgiven of the latter and be saved from Hellfire.

God (Glorious is He) also states: *O ye that believe! Fear* (*ittaqū*) *God and believe in His Messenger, and He will bestow on you a double portion of His mercy.*[11] So, this verse mentions two matters: belief and piety, whereby these two together result in a *double portion* of God's mercy. Now, it is well known that Paradise represents God's mercy, and it is reserved for those who believe in God and His messengers, including Muḥammad, and worship the Holy Lord alone. The contention herein is that being saved from the Hellfire is another mercy of God, and it is reserved for those who are characterized by piety.[12] The pious fear God (Glorious and Exalted is He) and Hellfire, and that fear leads them to avoid major sins and carry out greater good and benevolent deeds (*birr*).

That being saved from Hellfire is a consequence of God's mercy is also substantiated by other verses: *He hath inscribed for Himself (the rule of) mercy... On that day, if the penalty is averted from any, it is due to God's mercy.*[13] The Holy Lord has also specified and selected His mercy for the pious, as He states: *And when those who believe in Our revelations come unto thee, say: Peace be unto you! Your Lord hath prescribed for Himself mercy, that whoso of you doeth evil* (*sū'*) *through ignorance and repenteth afterward thereof and doeth right,* (*for him*) *lo! He is Forgiving, Merciful.*[14] Note that this verse specifies the sin as an intermediate one (*sū'*), not a major

---

[10] Q.VII.169. See also Q.VI.32 and Q.XII.109: *Verily the abode of the Hereafter, for those who ward off (evil), is best.*

[11] Q.LVII.28.

[12] Ibn Taymiyya and Ibn al-Qayyim (among others) contend that this double portion refers to the fact that the reward of the Muslims is double that of the monotheistic Christian and early Jewish believers as per the *ḥadīth* of the Prophet in Bukhārī 7533; Tirmidhī 2871; Aḥmad 4508. See Ibn Taymiyya, *al-Jawāb al-ṣaḥīḥ*, vol. I, pp. 76–77, and Zeni (tr.), *Ibn Qayyim al-Jawziyya on Divine Wisdom and the Problem of Evil*, p. 85.

[13] Q.VI.12 and Q.VI.16 (Yusuf Ali translation).

[14] Q.VI.54. Note that this verse specifies the evil as *sū'* (the singular of *sayyi'āt*) and it was previously discussed that this refers to any sin aside from a major one.

one (*kabīra* or *munkar*). Therefore, only the pious have been protected from Hellfire—the lower ranks of believers are not selected for such protection.

Moreover, consider the threefold division that God (Exalted is He) mentions in the following verse: *Then We have given the Book for inheritance to such of Our servants as We have chosen: but there are among them some who wrong their own souls* (*ẓālim li-nafs*^{ihi}); *some who follow a middle course* (*muqtaṣid*); *and some who are, by God's leave, foremost* (*sābiq*) *in good deeds; that is the highest grace.*[15] It will be contended that those who have wronged themselves (*ẓālimūn*) include: (1) those believing Muslims who perpetrated the most wicked major sins[16] (and were not punished for them in this world), as well as (2) the believers who had perpetrated some of the secondary major sins[17] and whose evil deeds were more numerous than their good ones.[18] Next, it will be contended that the term *muqtaṣidūn* represents those believers whose good deeds at least balance (or are greater than) their evil deeds, and they will be discussed later in this chapter as well as the next. Finally, it will be contended that those who are foremost in good deeds (*sābiqūn*) are the pious and higher ranks—they will be discussed further in the next chapter.

Now, the Prophet Muḥammad (may God bless him and grant him peace) stated that on the Day of Judgment the Holy Lord will inform Adam that the portion of humanity to be punished by Hellfire (*baʿth al-nār*) will be "999 out of every 1,000".[19] The Companions wept after they heard the Messenger tell them that. May God protect us through His mercy from Hellfire and enter us into His mercy of Paradise! In another *ḥadīth*, the Prophet Muḥammad relays that it will be said: "Take ninety-nine out of every one hundred." The Companions then

---

15 Q.XXXV.32 (Yusuf Ali translation).

16 See Table 1 in Chapter Eleven.

17 See Table 2 in Chapter Eleven.

18 Of note, Ṭabarī and Rāzī both opine that the term *ẓālimūn* refers to believing Muslims, and that they will be granted salvation ultimately—see *Tafsīr al-Ṭabarī*, vol. XX, pp. 465–471 and *Tafsīr al-Rāzī*, vol. XXVI, pp. 238–240. It should be mentioned that in other instances within the Qur'ān those who worship others alongside the Holy Lord are also termed *ẓālimūn*. Thus, it will be contended that injustice (*ẓulm*) in the Qur'ān can refer to: (a) polytheism or (b) perpetration of a major sin.

19 Bukhārī 6530; Muslim 222/532; Tirmidhī 3169; Aḥmad 6555.

asked, "O God's Messenger! If ninety-nine out of every one hundred of us are taken away, what will remain of us?"[20]

These two authentic *ḥadīth*s will be reconciled by contending that the first is general to all of humanity, while the latter only involves the believing Muslims from the Community of Muḥammad (as well as those who believed in God from past nations). Now, if we apply what was mentioned previously, i.e. that the pious are saved from being punished by Hellfire, we may then contend that the one individual out of a thousand refers to the pious one. Thus, only one out of a thousand is pious and completely avoids Hellfire, while ninety-nine others (out of a thousand) on average will go to Paradise after being punished.[21]

This is, indeed, a very frightening thought, to say the least. The Prophet Muḥammad (may God bless him and grant him peace) said: "If you knew what I knew you would weep much and laugh only rarely."[22] Some narrations include the Prophet Muḥammad saying: "You would go out in the streets beseeching God."[23] One should always beseech God (Glorious and Exalted is He) for salvation from Hellfire, since as contended above, the vast majority, unfortunately, will be punished in Hellfire.

The above is also consistent with the *ḥadīth* mentioned earlier in Chapter Three wherein the angel Gabriel states (after being shown Hellfire surrounded by temptations): "By Your might, I fear that no one will be saved [from Hellfire], but instead all will enter it.'[24] In that regard, God (Exalted is He) could have punished anyone who

---

20 Bukhārī 6529; Aḥmad 3677.

21 Of note, this is mentioned as one possible solution by Ibn Ḥajar al-ʿAsqalānī in *Fatḥ al-Bārī*, vol. XI, p. 390.

22 Bukhārī 6631; Muslim 901/2089; Tirmidhī 2313; Ibn Māja 4191; Nasā'ī 1475; Aḥmad 24,520.

23 Tirmidhī 2312; Ibn Māja 4190; al-Ḥākim 7905; Bayhaqī (*Sunan*) 13,337. The quoted portions of the *ḥadīth* are "sound" according to Albānī (*Silsilat al-aḥādīth al-ṣaḥīḥa* 1722).

24 Tirmidhī 2560; Abū Dāwūd 4744; Nasā'ī 3763; Ibn Ḥibbān 7394. It is "authentic" according to Albānī (*Ṣaḥīḥ al-Jāmiʿ al-ṣaghīr* 5210).

perpetrated any sin,[25] but He has dictated to forgive and have mercy upon the pious who have repented from intermediate and minor sins.

The pious will race on the bridge (*ṣirāṭ*) over Hellfire, such that they will be entered into Paradise untouched by its flames and unharmed. On the other hand, it will be contended—and God knows best—that some of the believers, i.e. *muqtaṣidūn*, will have only parts of their body touched by the flames of Hellfire as they pass on the bridge, but that they will not be immersed in Hellfire. This will be discussed further in the next chapter. However, other believers who have perpetrated greater sins and the believing Muslims (collectively *ẓālimūn*) will fall into the Hellfire and be punished therein before being entered into Paradise.

Every believer will face the consequences of his or her actions. The Prophet Muḥammad (may God bless him and grant him peace) said:

> Do you know who the destitute one (*muflis*) is? [...] The destitute one on the Day of Resurrection is one who is part of my Community and has performed prayer, fasting and almsgiving but has also cursed some, slandered others, unlawfully taken the money of others, spilt the blood of others [but not killed them], and injured others. This [individual] must give away some of his good deeds to those [harmed] people [in recompense]. But if his good deeds become expended before he has finished recompensing them, their sins will be assumed by him and then he will be thrown into Hellfire.[26]

This *ḥadīth* therefore describes the predicament of some of the believing Muslims who have perpetrated these injustices. They will

---

[25] See the Prophetic *ḥadīth*: "Had God [willed to] punish all in the heavens and all on the earth, He could punish them without being unjust to them." Abū Dāwūd 4699; Ibn Māja 77; Aḥmad 21,589; Ibn Ḥibbān 727; Bayhaqī (*Sunan*) 20,874. It is "authentic" according to Albānī (*Ṣaḥīḥ al-Jāmiʿ al-ṣaghīr* 5244).

[26] Muslim 2581/6579; Tirmidhī 2418; Aḥmad 8029. Note that the Prophet Muḥammad mentioned cursing others in the *ḥadīth* before the major sins of slandering, stealing, or injuring others. The predicament of the believing Muslims in Hellfire is also corroborated by another *ḥadīth* of the Prophet Muḥammad: "Once some of the believers are rescued (*khalaṣa*) from Hellfire...they will [supplicate] for their brothers who remain in Hellfire, saying: 'They used to fast, pray and perform pilgrimage with us.'" Muslim 183/454; Ibn Māja 60; Aḥmad 11,898.

be punished in Hellfire and entered into Paradise only after being recompensed for the harm and evil they had inflicted upon others.

Now, in regards to the aggregate ninety-nine out of a hundred believing Muslims, it may be impossible to know the selection factor between the pious, believers and believing Muslims (regardless of whether that factor is the same or variable), as no definite proof from the Qur'ān or Sunna exists (unlike the percentage who will completely avoid the punishment of Hellfire, i.e. the pious 0.1% as contended above). That said, in order to provide a framework based on the different ranks of those who have faith (as discussed in Chapter Seven) it will be hypothesized, based on reason and experience, that the number of the believers (*mu'minūn*) is nine-fold that of the pious, and that the number of the believing Muslims (*muslimūn*) is nine-fold that of the believers.[27] A further framework regarding the elite ranks (*sābiqūn*) will be discussed in the next chapter.

Based upon this hypothesis, though, which appears concordant with reality, for every hundred (out of a thousand) there is, on average, one who is pious (which also includes the higher ranks of those who are devout, righteous, truly faithful as well as the prophets); nine who are believers (but do not reach the rank of piety); and ninety who are believing Muslims (but do not reach the rank of the believers). Finally, the denizens of Hellfire are nine-fold the number of the ultimate inhabitants of Paradise, i.e. nine hundred, on average, out of every thousand human beings. The main point, however, is that the inhabitants of Paradise will be one hundred out of a thousand on average, regardless of whether the proportion of believers (including the pious) relative to the believing Muslims is one-ninth or greater.

Next, if it is assumed that the number of Muslims is roughly 20% of humanity or 200 out of every 1,000 on average, then it would appear that approximately one half of the 'Muslims' in name will never go to Paradise (and God knows best) either because they were extremists or fanatics, fought against the religion, or disbelieved in the

---

[27] This also represents an average throughout the ages: the percentage of believing Muslims, believers, and pious will increase (above a critical mass) and decrease depending on their faith and actions over different generations.

Almighty Lord and were completely ignorant of Islam.[28] Thus, the pious (*muttaqūn*) and believers (*mu'minūn*), who are 10% of the Muslim inhabitants of Paradise (on average), represent 5% of those who are 'Muslims' in name only. If one deeply reflects on these percentages one will find them to be plausible and concordant with reality.

Now, the Prophet Muḥammad said: "My Community (*ummatī*) will divide into seventy-three groups. All of them are in Hellfire except for one—that which follows myself and my Companions."[29] Ibn Taymiyya states regarding this *ḥadīth* that the Prophet Muḥammad (may God bless him and grant him peace) did not say all of those other seventy-two groups would be punished in Hellfire forever or eternally.[30] Thus, it is possible that the punishment of some of those groups will be for a temporary period, and that some within these groups will be considered as believing Muslims.

A corollary of all of the above is that a minority group of the Muslims, which, for instance, comprises 15% or less of the total number of 'Muslims' in name, cannot claim that it alone will enter Paradise to the exclusion of the Sunnis, i.e. Ahl al-Sunna wa'l-Jamāᶜa, who are the majority. Of note, for a group representing 15% of the Muslims to be the one hundred believing Muslims out of a thousand who will ultimately enter Paradise on average (to the exclusion of all other groups of Muslims), the Muslims would need to represent nearly 70% of humanity,[31] but that is clearly not the case. Since the

---

[28] The Prophet Muḥammad said: "This knowledge [inherited from the Prophet] will be conveyed by the successors [of this Community] who are upright and trustworthy. They will repudiate the distortions of the extremists, those who attempt to break-up [the religion] by negating [its precepts], and the misinterpretations of those who are ignorant." Bayhaqī (*Sunan*) 20,911; Ibn Kathīr, *al-Bidāya wa'l-nihāya*, vol. X, p. 337. It is "authentic" according to Albānī (*Mishkāt* 248). Of note, a discussion of this *ḥadīth* and its authenticity is present in Zeni (tr.), *Ibn Qayyim al-Jawziyya on Knowledge*, pp. 237–238.

[29] Tirmidhī 2641; al-Ḥākim 444. It is "sound" according to Albānī (*Ṣaḥīḥ al-Jāmiᶜ al-ṣaghīr* 5343). In another narration, the saved are those who are from his "Community (*al-jamāᶜa*)", i.e. they follow the traditions of the Prophet and the Rightly-Guided Caliphs. See Abū Dāwūd 4597; Ibn Māja 3992; Aḥmad 16,937; al-Ḥākim 443. It is "authentic" according to Albānī (*Silsilat al-aḥādīth al-ṣaḥīḥa* 204).

[30] Ibn Taymiyya, *Minhāj al-Sunna al-Nabawiyya*, vol. V, p. 241.

[31] In addition, this assumes that all members of that group would enter Paradise; however, if the fraction is only half (as maintained above in the text), it would be *impossible* for that minority group to be the sole group (to the exclusion of the Sunnis) to enter Paradise.

Sunnis most correctly follow the Prophet Muḥammad (may God bless him and grant him peace) and all of his Companions (may God be pleased with them), and since they represent the majority of Muslims, those believers amongst the Sunnis will be the primary ones to enter Paradise by the mercy and grace of the Holy Lord. It may be that some of the minority groups who are close to the Sunnis in creed[32]—but are not hypocrites, extremists or fanatics, nor are they amongst those who have fought against the believers out of rancour, nor are completely ignorant of Islam—will enter Paradise ultimately. And God knows best. Nonetheless, in conclusion, the Sunnis will represent the overwhelming majority of the Muslim believers in Paradise.

ON THOSE DISBELIEVERS WHOSE PUNISHMENT IN HELLFIRE WILL END

The disbelievers will now be discussed. God (Glorious is He) has stated: *God forgiveth not that a partner should be ascribed unto Him.*[33] The Holy Lord then states in Sūrat al-Mā'ida: *Whoso ascribeth partners unto God, for him God hath forbidden Paradise. His abode is the Fire.*[34] Thus, the One God (*al-Wāḥid al-Aḥad*) has promised those who worship any other thing or being alongside him—whether idols or Jesus or otherwise—will never enter Paradise.

God (Glorious is He) will also say to the denizens of Hellfire on the Day of Judgment: "If you owned everything on earth would you have given it up to save yourself [from Hellfire]?" They will reply in the affirmative and God will say to them: "I asked you much less than that: only that you not worship anyone else but Me. But you refused [to worship Me alone] and instead worshipped others."[35] Thus, worshipping the Holy Lord alone and affirming His Oneness is a necessary requisite for salvation.

Now, universal salvation was alluded to in Chapter Eight. Although it has little basis in revelation, some of the arguments of its proponents include: (1) that all of humanity is endowed with a good innate disposition (*fiṭra*), which will inevitably manifest itself

---

32 Salvation is therefore not predicated upon any claimed notion absent from the Sunni creed.

33 See Q. IV.48 and 116.

34 Q.V.72.

35 Bukhārī 6557; Aḥmad 12,289.

once all other sins are expiated through punishment in Hellfire for a long (but temporary) duration; (2) that God's wrath on the Day of Judgment will eventually completely subside, hence the disbelievers will eventually be bestowed His pleasure; and (3) that since God's mercy is infinite, it will eventually encompass all of humanity in the Hereafter (just as His mercy has encompassed them in this world).

The first argument will not be dealt with here as it was adequately discussed in the translator's introduction to *Ibn Qayyim al-Jawziyya on Divine Wisdom and the Problem of Evil.*[36] As for the second argument, the proponents base it loosely on the *ḥadīth* of the Prophet Muḥammad (may God bless him and grant him peace): "My Lord is angry today [i.e. the Day of Judgment] in a way that He has never been before. And He will never be as angry as that again."[37] In fact, though, this *ḥadīth* only affirms that God's wrath will never be the same as it is on the Day of Judgment—not that it will subside completely. God's wrath will decrease after the Day of Judgment, but it is incorrect to derive from this *ḥadīth* that His wrath will become null or that the punishment will end for all disbelievers as a consequence. And God knows best.

As for the third argument, the Prophet Muḥammad (may God bless him and grant him peace) said: "When God decreed that He would create [this world], He inscribed in His Book (that is present above the Throne): 'My mercy prevails (*ghalabat*) over My wrath.'"[38] In another *ḥadīth*, the wording is: "My mercy precedes (*sabaqat*) My wrath."[39] These *ḥadīth*s affirm that God's wrath—although existent and not null—will be preceded and prevailed over by His mercy. It is

---

[36] See Zeni (tr.), *Ibn Qayyim al-Jawziyya on Divine Wisdom and the Problem of Evil*, pp. XXV–XXVII.

[37] Bukhārī 4712; Muslim 194/480; Tirmidhī 2434; Aḥmad 9623. Ibn al-Qayyim explains that this *ḥadīth* "explicitly states that this [His] wrath [on the Day of Judgment] will be great, but that it will not remain as such. It is well known that the denizens of Hellfire will enter it due to that wrath. Had that wrath perpetuated, then their punishment would have been eternal likewise as it is a consequence of that wrath. But when the Lord (Most Blessed and Exalted is He) becomes content and that wrath wanes, then its consequences also dissipate." See Zeni (tr.), *Ibn Qayyim al-Jawziyya on Divine Wisdom and the Problem of Evil*, p. 190.

[38] Bukhārī 3194; Tirmidhī 3543; Aḥmad 7500.

[39] Bukhārī 7422; Muslim 2751/6970; Ibn Māja 189; Aḥmad 9159.

self-evident that the disbelievers have experienced God's mercy in this world, in some fashion or another and to varying degrees; thus, His mercy has preceded His wrath of the Hellfire. In addition, it should be recalled, as was mentioned previously according to a *ḥadīth*, that God's punishment could have encompassed all.[40] God (Glorious and Exalted is He) manifests the consequences of each of His Beautiful and infinitely perfect Names in a manner consistent with His wisdom, mercy and justice. Therefore, in so far as a solution to the problem of Hellfire affirms that the consequences of His mercy predominate or prevail over His wrath then that solution is concordant.

What follows are arguments contending that the punishment of the majority of the disbelievers will end, and that these disbelievers will be annihilated in Hellfire. More specifically, as long as a solution contends that ninety-nine or less (of the 900 disbelievers condemned to Hellfire) will be punished eternally, then God's mercy (which is ultimately bestowed to one hundred out of a thousand who are eternal inhabitants of Paradise) prevails over His wrath as per the *ḥadīth*.

Now, it was mentioned above that God (Exalted is He) will punish most of the Muslims before entering the believers into Paradise. The Prophet Muḥammad mentioned that some of these believing Muslims "will have half of their lower leg consumed by the Hellfire and in some it will be up to their knees... They will then be placed in a River of Life."[41] This and other *ḥadīth*s prove that some bodily parts of Muslims being punished in Hellfire will be annihilated, and it is only after submersion into the River of Life that they will become regenerated.

---

40 The Prophet Muḥammad (may God bless him and grant him peace) said: "Had God [willed to] punish all in the heavens and all on the earth, He could punish them without being unjust to them." Abū Dāwūd 4699; Ibn Māja 77; Aḥmad 21,589; Ibn Ḥibbān 727; Bayhaqī (*Sunan*) 20,874. It is "authentic" according to Albānī (*Ṣaḥīḥ al-Jāmiʿ al-ṣaghīr* 5244).

41 Bukhārī 6560; Muslim 184/457; Aḥmad 11,533. The Prophet then mentions in this *ḥadīth* that three further levels of believing Muslims will later be removed from Hellfire. The goodness of these believing Muslims was minimal, as it was described as being a dinar's weight, then half of a dinar, and finally the weight of an atom. Thus, God will remove those who affirmed His Oneness, but never performed any good deeds. For a similar *ḥadīth*, which mentions that parts of the believing Muslims' bodies will be consumed by the Hellfire, see Bukhārī 7439; Ibn Māja 60; Nasā'ī 5010; Aḥmad 11,081.

The Prophet Muḥammad (may God bless him and grant him peace), on the other hand, excluded the bodily parts of a believing Muslim involved in prostration[42] from being consumed, i.e. annihilated, by Hellfire. It is self-evident that a disbeliever (either because he never worshipped the Holy Lord or because it was never accepted) possesses no such part of his body. Thus, the Hellfire may then, by extrapolation, be able to annihilate the disbelievers' bodies in their entirety.

Next, consider that the Prophet Muḥammad stated: "The Hellfire complained to its Lord saying: 'My Lord, some of my parts have consumed [i.e. annihilated] others.'"[43] Thus, it is necessary for a believer to affirm, in accordance with this *ḥadīth*, that parts of Hellfire have already been annihilated. Another *ḥadīth* states that on the Day of Judgment there will continue to be space in Hellfire until: "God (Most Blessed and Exalted is He) places His Foot on it, which leads it to contract (*yanzawī*) and become completely full."[44] This indicates that further parts of Hellfire will become annihilated on the Day of Judgment.

The above authentic *ḥadīth*s confirm that parts of Hellfire have been and will be annihilated, and that the bodily parts of some of those being punished in Hellfire will become annihilated. The aforementioned may thus hint and suggest that annihilation will occur to other parts of the Hellfire after the Day of Judgment. Therefore, it is not impermissible to contend that *part* of the Hellfire will be annihilated after the disbelievers enter it.

Next, God (Glorious is He) states in the Qur'ān: *And [the word] will be spoken: "Today We shall be oblivious of you as you were oblivious of the coming of this your Day [of Judgment]; and so your goal is the fire, and you shall have none to succor you.*[45] The Holy Lord will also say to the disbelievers: *"Taste, then, [the recompense] for your having been oblivious of the coming of this your Day [of Judgment]—for verily We are now oblivious of you: taste, then, [this] abiding (khuld) suffering for all [the evil] that you were wont to do!"*[46] The word *nasīnā* (or *nansā*) is translated above as

42 See Bukhārī 6573; Muslim 182/451; Ibn Māja 4326; Nasā'ī 1140; Aḥmad 7717.

43 Bukhārī 3260; Muslim 617/1401; Tirmidhī 2592; Ibn Māja 4319; Aḥmad 7247.

44 Muslim 2846/7173; Aḥmad 12,440.

45 Q.XLV.34 (Muḥammad Asad translation).

46 Q.XXXII.14 (Muḥammad Asad translation).

oblivious, and one meaning of *nasiya* is to render into oblivion[47] or annihilation. It will thus be contended that God (Glorious is He) will neglect and ignore them for some time in Hellfire, but will annihilate them at a later time in accordance with His wisdom. Note also that God (Exalted is He) did not say that they would be punished eternally (*abad*^{an}) in this verse, but instead He mentioned that the punishment would be abiding for a long period of time (*khuld*)—the significance of this will be explained below.

Now, God (Exalted is He) has stated in three verses of the Qur'ān that the disbelievers will be punished eternally in Hellfire (*khālid*^{īna} *fīhā abad*^{an}). Thirty-four verses of the Qur'ān, however, state that the disbelievers will be in Hellfire for a long period of time (with variations on the verb *kh-l-d*),[48] but do not mention eternity (*abad*^{an}). As for those aforementioned three verses, the first is: *Whoso disobeyeth God and His Messenger, lo! his is fire of Hell, wherein such dwell forever* [*eternally*].[49] The second verse is: *God hath cursed the disbelievers, and hath prepared for them a flaming fire, wherein they will abide forever* [eternally]. *They will find (then) no protecting friend nor helper. On the day when their faces are turned over in the Fire, they say: Oh, would that we had obeyed God and had obeyed His messenger!*[50] The third verse is: *But God (Himself) testifieth concerning that which He hath revealeth unto thee; in His knowledge hath He revealed it; and the angels also testify. And God is sufficient Witness. Lo! those who disbelieve and hinder (others) from the way of God, they verily have wandered far astray. Lo! those who disbelieve and deal in wrong, God will never forgive them, neither will He guide them unto a road, except the road of Hell, wherein they will abide forever* [eternally].[51]

Therefore, it will be affirmed that some of the disbelievers, in accordance with these verses, will be punished eternally in Hellfire. In that regard, it will be contended that there exists a wise purpose

---

47 See *The Hans Wehr Dictionary of Modern Written Arabic*, ed. J. M. Cowan (Urbana: Spoken Language Services, 1994), under the entry of *na-si-ya*, p. 1130.

48 These verses utilize the terms: *khālid*^{īna}, *khālid*^{ūna}, *al-khuld*, *yakhlud*, among other similar terms derived from the root *kh–l–d*. A long period of time is also suggested by the phrase *lābith*^{īna} *fīha aḥqābā* in verse Q.LXXVIII.23.

49 Q.LXXII.23.

50 Q.XXXIII.64–66.

51 Q.IV.166–170.

in the Holy Lord mentioning that the punishment is eternal in only the aforementioned three verses: these three verses correspond to three (out of the seven) respective gates of Hellfire designated for eternal punishment. So, the denizens who enter those three gates of Hellfire will be punished eternally. On the other hand, those denizens entering the other four gates to Hellfire will ultimately be annihilated (as shall be discussed below).[52]

Since it is contended that only some disbelievers will be annihilated, calculating the proportion who will suffer eternal punishment could be postulated in the following terms: (1) three sevenths, in accordance with the number of the gates of Hellfire; (2) the proportion of verses discussing eternality in Hellfire versus those mentioning only a lasting punishment (based on *kh-l-d*); or (3) it may be unattainable for us to know. The first option is not concordant with God's mercy prevailing and preponderating over His wrath; therefore, it will not be pursued. The middle option, however, will be advanced; consequently, by calculating the proportion of verses stating that the punishment will be eternal (*khālid*^*īna* *fīha abad*^*an*) versus those stating it will be forever (based on *kh-l-d*), i.e. three out of thirty-seven verses, it alludes to 73 out of the 900 denizens of Hellfire being punished eternally.[53] The other denizens (827 of 900 disbelievers on average) will be annihilated after a long duration of punishment, and thus for them the punishment will end. In light of the above arguments, part of Hellfire will be annihilated, and along with its annihilation will be the disbelievers therein. The point is that less than ninety-nine out of a thousand (on average) will be eternally punished, and thus this solution affirms that God's mercy will prevail over His wrath.

Now, some may maintain that the Qur'ān states that the denizens of Hellfire will not die—God (Glorious is He) states: *Whoso cometh guilty (mujrim*^*an*) *unto his Lord, verily for him is Hell. There he will neither die*

---

[52] There are seven gates to Hellfire—see Q.XV.44. Of note, there are eight gates to Paradise—see Bukhārī 3257. This will be discussed in the next chapter.

[53] Alternatively, if only the verses containing *khālid*^*ūna* or *khālid*^*īna*, i.e. twenty-nine verses, are considered (thus excluding the other eight derivatives of *kh-l-d*), then 93 rather than 73 out of the 900 denizens will be eternally punished. In that case, 807 disbelievers will be annihilated.

nor live.[54] However, it will be contended that the term 'truly wicked' (*mujrim*) refers to those who will be eternally punished in Hellfire, and it is affirmed in the aforementioned solution that some will never die nor be annihilated. God (Exalted is He) also states: *The guilty (mujrimīn) are immortal in Hell's torment... And they cry: O master! Let thy Lord make an end of us. He saith: Lo! here ye must remain.*[55] It may even be that the truly wicked will be informed that others have been annihilated, and therefore they will request it, but they will be denied—and God knows best. Of note, this verse also proves that the denizens of Hellfire would prefer annihilation over eternal torment. Thus, the claim[56] that the denizens would prefer to remain in Hellfire rather than be annihilated[57] is untrue.

Another response to this issue is that death (*mawt*) is different than annihilation (*fanā'*). If one deeply reflects on the former term, one will find that every instance of *mawt* mentioned in the Qur'ān is necessarily followed by life or resurrection. For instance, God (Glorious is He) states: *How disbelieve ye in God when ye were dead and He gave life to you! Then He will give you death, then life again, and then unto Him ye will return.*[58] Hence, life and death are inextricably linked. Therefore, negating the occurrence of death connotes that the disbelievers will never be resurrected after their punishment in Hellfire. Thus, Hellfire is the final abode and destination of the disbelievers,[59] whether they are annihilated or remain therein to be punished eternally. They

---

54 Q.XX.74.

55 Q.XLIII.74–77.

56 For example, Ibn ʿArabī claims that the denizens will find Hellfire pleasing because of the nature of their constitutions: "No one will desire to leave his domicile, and each will be happy with it." See Chittick, *Ibn ʿArabī: Heir to the Prophets*, pp. 136–141.

57 Of note, had God (Exalted is He) only created (1) the believers in Paradise and (2) the denizens who are to be eternally punished, the world would have appeared much different. The polarization in society would either result in the wicked criminals continually fighting against the believers or in each group completely isolating itself from the other. Many of the wise purposes that are achieved in this world as discussed in Chapters Twelve and Thirteen, in particular, would not have occurred. Thus, the existence of (3) those denizens who will ultimately be annihilated is a necessary requisite to the occurrence of many wise purposes.

58 Q.II.28.

59 That Hellfire is the final abode for its denizens is affirmed in Q.XIV.29 and Q.XXXVIII.60.

will never "die" to be resurrected again to live in another abode. As a result, it is affirmed that none of the disbelievers will ever enter Paradise; hence, universal salvation is rejected. And God knows best.

As for those who are eternally punished, it will be contended that three groups (corresponding to the three verses and three eternal gates) are likely to be included therein. The first group includes those who encountered the messengers directly yet disbelieved. This is based on the aforementioned verses, which state that the punishment of Hellfire will be eternal (*khālid*^{īna} *fīhā abad*^{an}) when addressing the disbelievers who directly encountered the messengers. It is also established in the Qur'ān that those who directly encountered the messengers (or had the ability to do so), yet disbelieved in them, were destroyed.[60] That is because those who disbelieved after directly encountering the messengers are far more evil, in general, than those who disbelieved yet did not live in a time in which a messenger existed. Since the majority of humanity lived after the Messenger Muḥammad, yet never directly encountered him (may God bless him and grant him peace),[61] they will not be punished eternally in Hellfire unless they fall within the two below groups—and God knows best.

---

[60] See Q.XXVIII.59: *And never did thy Lord destroy the townships, till He had raised up in their mother(-town) a messenger reciting unto them Our revelations. And never did We destroy the townships unless the folk thereof were evil-doers*, as well as Q.XVII.15: *We never punish until we have sent a messenger.* This punishment refers to the destruction of those disbelievers in this world, such as what occurred to those who disbelieved in Noah and some of the other messengers. See a discussion of this by Ibn al-Qayyim in *Miftāḥ dār al-saʿāda*, vol. II, pp. 955–957. In Q.II.101, the Holy Lord also states to those living during the time of Muḥammad (may God bless him and grant him peace): *How can ye disbelieve, when it is ye unto whom God's revelations are recited, and His Messenger is in your midst?*

[61] For instance, the Holy Lord states in Q.XXXII.3: *It is the Truth from thy Lord, that thou mayst warn a folk to whom no warner came before thee, that haply they may walk aright*; Q.XXXVIII.47: *If (We had) not (sent thee to the Quraysh), in case a calamity should seize them for (the deeds) that their hands have sent forth, they might say: Our Lord! why didst Thou not sent us a messenger? We should then have followed Thy signs and been amongst those who believe!* Also, Q.XX.134: *And if we had destroyed them with some punishment before it, they would assuredly have said: Our Lord! If only Thou hadst sent unto us a messenger, so that we might have followed Thy revelations before we were (thus) humbled and disgraced!* The point is that God (Exalted is He) affirms in these verses that some have not encountered the prophets and messengers. Since the Prophet Muḥammad is the Seal of the Prophets, this indicates that those who

The second group to be punished eternally includes the hypocrites, as God (Glorious is He) informed us: *The hypocrites will be in the lowest depths (al-dark al-asfal) of the Fire.*[62] The hypocrites were discussed at length in the prior chapter, and they (along with those who possess satanic natures) harbour the greatest enmity and rancour against the believers.

Here it should be mentioned that the Prophet Muḥammad (may God bless him and grant him peace) said regarding his uncle Abū Ṭālib, who remained a disbeliever: "[Abū Ṭālib] is in a shallow part of Hellfire, and were it not for me he would have been in the lowest depths (*al-dark al-asfal*) of Hellfire."[63] It is clear that Abū Ṭālib was never a hypocrite, nor did he fight against the Prophet. Instead, Abū Ṭālib defended and protected his nephew, although he remained and died as a disbeliever. Abū Ṭālib did, however, encounter the Messenger Muḥammad, of course, and as aforementioned those disbelievers who encountered the messengers directly will be punished eternally, as a general rule. But the Most Wise Lord exempted Abū Ṭālib from eternal punishment due to the great benefit he provided to the Prophet Muḥammad. This *ḥadīth* also adds further proof to this grouping scheme in that those who encountered the messengers are eternally punished in the lowest depths of Hellfire. Finally, that Abū Ṭālib is in a shallow part of Hellfire indicates that he will eventually be annihilated, and therefore his punishment will end. And God knows best.

The third group, which will be punished eternally, includes those whose natures are satanic. The Holy Lord has affirmed that some humans possess satanic natures: *Thus have We appointed unto every prophet an adversary—devils of humankind and jinn who inspire in one another plausible discourse through guile.*[64] The Prophet Muḥammad also mentioned that some humans possess satanic natures.[65] It is self evident

---

have lived since the time of his death until now have never encountered a prophet—that is self-evident. That said, they have the message of Islam, preserved in the Qur'ān and Sunna, so that they may believe, and they will thus be held accountable.

62 Q.IV.145.

63 Bukhārī 3883; Muslim 209/510; Aḥmad 1763.

64 Q.VI.112.

65 See Tirmidhī 3691. It is "sound" according to Albānī (*Ṣaḥīḥ al-Jāmiʿ al-ṣaghīr* 2496).

that Satan's eternal punishment will be the worst; and those human beings whose natures are satanic will follow suit in being eternally punished.[66] And God knows best.

As for these three groups, which will be punished eternally in Hellfire, those who encountered and directly met a messenger[67] and disbelieved are a very small percentage of humankind—not even 0.1%. The vast majority of humanity came after the Messenger Muḥammad (may God bless him and grant him peace) yet have never met him, and therefore they will not be eternally punished unless they are amongst the last two groups. Finally, the hypocrites and those who have satanic natures are a minority amongst the disbelievers—certainly in the single digit percentage. Thus, reason and experience, which suggests that they represent less than 10% of humanity, is concordant to these three groups being 9.3% or less.

Now that the elucidation of those disbelievers who will be annihilated and those who will be eternally punished has occurred, the following Qur'ānic verse can be understood: *As for those who will be wretched (on that day) they will be in the Fire; sighing and wailing will be their portion therein. Abiding there so long as the heavens and the earth endure save for that which thy Lord willeth. Thy Lord is Doer of what He will.*[68] God (Exalted is He) will, in accordance with His wisdom, end the punishment for the majority of the denizens of Hellfire by annihilating them along with those parts of Hellfire (this explains *save*

---

[66] Of note, the Prophet Muḥammad has affirmed that those who commit suicide will be punished in Hellfire by repetitively committing the act that led to his or her suicide in this world (in addition to the multitude of other punishments in Hellfire). In some *ḥadīths* the punishment of those who have committed suicide will be eternal (*khālid^{an} mukhallad^{an} fīhā abad^{an}*), while in other *ḥadīths* it does not specify an eternal punishment. See Bukhārī 5778; Muslim 109/300; Tirmidhī 2043; Nasā'ī 1965; Aḥmad 7448 for the former *ḥadīths*, while the latter can be found in Bukhārī 6047; Muslim 110/302–304; Tirmidhī 2636; Abū Dāwūd 3257; Nasā'ī 3770; Aḥmad 16,389. It will thus be maintained that if the disbeliever who committed suicide had encountered a messenger, was a hypocrite or had a satanic nature, then that individual will be punished eternally in Hellfire. And God knows best the ultimate fate of the others who have committed suicide (whether Muslim or non-Muslim) after being punished in Hellfire (whether to annihilation versus salvation or to annihilation, respectively).

[67] As discussed in the text, there may be exceptions to eternal punishment for the denizens within this group (which directly met the messengers and yet disbelieved).

[68] Q.XI.106–107.

for that which thy Lord willeth), but a minority will be punished eternally (and this explains the threat encompassed within: *Thy Lord is Doer of what He will*). And God knows best.

At this point it has become clear that the vast majority of humanity—nearly all—will be punished in the Hellfire[69] due to their sins and what they deserve (may God protect us!). In lieu of that reality, the Holy Lord's allowance of widespread suffering and evil in this worldly life is justified, and concordant to the unjust, sinful and disobedient nature of humanity. Any suffering or evil in this world that leads a person to right their ways represents a lesser harm and evil relative to the greater harm of Hellfire. God (Glorious is He) states: *And verily We make them taste the lower punishment before the greater, that haply they may return.*[70]

Unfortunately, 90% of humanity will suffer in this life and be punished in the Hereafter—never to be entered into God's mercy of Paradise. God (Exalted is He) states about the denizens of Hellfire: *Even if they see all the signs, they will not believe in them; and if they see the way of right conduct, they will not adopt it as the way; but if they see the way of error, that is the way they will adopt. For they have rejected our signs, and failed to take warning from them.*[71] Ultimately, the denizens of Hellfire have only themselves to blame for their disbelief, arrogance, corruption and evil actions—each individual is ultimately solely responsible for the evil and major sins he or she perpetrates. The denizens freely chose to turn away from the Holy Lord, rather than worshipping Him alone, loving Him, and obeying His commandments, and thus God (Glorious and Exalted is He) has determined that they are deserving of Hellfire.

Considering all that has been mentioned, we can also now comprehend more deeply the verse: *We did indeed offer the Trust to the*

---

[69] Of note, it should be mentioned that had it not been for Divine hiddenness, then any human being who sinned (i.e. all of humanity) would have either been punished immediately or in Hellfire. Therefore, due to the construct of this world and what was discussed above, the pious and righteous will be allowed to continue to carry out good deeds and not be punished in the Hereafter despite the fact that they have incurred intermediate sins.

[70] Q.XXXII.21.

[71] Q.VII.146.

heavens and the earth and the mountains; but they refused to undertake it, being afraid thereof: but man undertook it. He was indeed unjust and foolish.[72] Humanity is indeed characterized as sinful and foolish since 99.9% will be punished by Hellfire in some fashion, while 90% are disbelievers who will never exit Hellfire.

This chapter has definitively proven that the Holy Lord has informed the Muslims of far more regarding the Day of Judgment and the Hereafter in the Qur'ān and Sunna than that which was revealed to the Jews and Christians in the Old and New Testaments. In addition, by reconciling all that is present in the authentic and sound Islamic revelation, the complex wisdom of the Almighty Lord has become more apparent. The next chapter will elucidate God's mercy and grace which He has ordained and specified to the believers in a manner concordant to His wisdom: *I smite with My punishment whom I will, and My mercy embraceth all things, therefore I shall ordain it for those who ward off (evil) and pay zakat, and those who believe Our revelations.*[73]

---

[72] Q.XXXIII.72 (Yusuf Ali translation).

[73] Q.VII.156.

Chapter Fifteen

Paradise

God (Glorious is He) has promised to bestow His love and pleasure, as well as His infinite mercy and grace upon the inhabitants of Paradise. The Holy Lord will bestow upon the believers spiritual, intellectual and bodily pleasures, which He has not granted to any other creature.[1] Indeed, even the believer in the lowest level of Paradise will be rewarded with ten times what the richest individual in this world possessed.[2] Moreover, God (Glorious is He) has created Paradise so sublime and majestic that the pleasures of this world will be incomparable to its everlasting joy and perpetual bliss.

Now, it is incumbent to know that it is only due to the grace and mercy of the Holy Lord that He will enter the believers into Paradise. Salvation is essentially predicated upon God's grace. The Prophet Muḥammad (may God bless him and grant him peace) informed us: "No one will enter Paradise solely due to their [good] deeds." The Companions inquired: "Not even you, O Messenger of God?" The Prophet replied: "Not even I, until God encompasses me in His grace and mercy."[3] The true believers are always *seeking grace from God and [His] good pleasure*.[4]

Therefore, the goods deeds of the believers—no matter how great or numerous—are insignificant when compared to what is befitting to God (Glorious and Exalted is He), nor can they ever suffice in appreciation of His vast and innumerable blessings upon them. Moreover, upon entering the eminent Paradise, the believers will recognize that they are not deserving of it as it will be far beyond their wildest dreams. Nonetheless, whilst entry of the believers into Paradise will only occur due to the grace and magnanimity of God,

---

1 See Bukhārī 6571 and 7511; Muslim 187–189/463–465; Aḥmad 3899.

2 See Bukhārī 6549; Muslim 2829/7140; Tirmidhī 2555; Aḥmad 11,835.

3 Bukhārī 5673; Muslim 2816/7116; Aḥmad 7587.

4 Q.XLVIII.29 (Yusuf Ali translation).

the Most Generous will rank them therein according to their good deeds.

The Holy Lord knew in His eternal knowledge that He would reward the believers, and it will be contended that He created Paradise before creating humanity as evidence of that knowledge. This world was only created so as to be a theatre in which the faithful believers could perform good acts that enable them, by the grace and mercy of God, to be entered into Paradise. God (Exalted is He) states: *What is the life of this world but amusement and play? But verily the home in the Hereafter, that is life indeed, if they but knew.*[5]

The pleasures of Paradise are spiritual, intellectual and bodily

The pleasures enjoyed by the believers in Paradise will be spiritual, intellectual and bodily. The greatest pleasure will be the spiritual pleasure attained by virtue of the Beatific Vision: *Some faces, that Day, will beam (in brightness and beauty); looking towards their Lord.*[6] God (Exalted is He) has dictated that only those who had faith in this world will see Him in the Hereafter. The Prophet Muḥammad (may God bless him and grant him peace) stated that there will be "nothing more beloved to the [believers] than seeing their Lord (Almighty and Most Glorious is He)",[7] and their faces will become more radiant after every time they see Him.

That said, it should be noted that their sight cannot completely encompass the Exalted Lord: *No human vision can encompass Him, whereas He encompasses all human vision.*[8] The believers will see Him from a viewpoint that He will allow (much like how people see the sun and the moon according to a *ḥadīth*[9]), and the Holy Lord is glorious and exalted above any similitudes to His creation.

---

[5] Q.XXIX.64 (Yusuf Ali translation).

[6] Q.LXXV.22–23 (Yusuf Ali translation).

[7] See Muslim 181/449; Tirmidhī 2552; Ibn Māja 187; Aḥmad 18,935.

[8] Q.VI.103 (Muḥammad Asad translation). For an extended discussion of the Beatific Vision, the relevant verses and *ḥadīths*, and statements of the Companions, Successors and scholars, see Ibn Qayyim al-Jawziyya, *Ḥādī al-arwāḥ ila bilād al-afrāḥ*, ed. Zā'id b. Aḥmad al-Nushayrī (Mecca: Dār ʿĀlam al-Fawā'id, 2007), pp. 618–712.

[9] See, for instance, the *ḥādīths* of the Prophet Muḥammad as relayed in Bukhārī 554;

The Prophet Muḥammad (may God bless him and grant him peace) also relayed that the Holy Lord will be pleased with the believers once they enter Paradise,[10] and God (Glorious is He) has confirmed that His pleasure, contentment and favour (*riḍwān*) are greater than the pleasures within Paradise itself.[11] The Holy Lord will speak to the believers and it may be that He will teach them or allow them to learn from His infinite knowledge, such that they will never tire thereof—and God knows best. Therefore, the greatest pleasures are the spiritual and intellectual ones: seeing God (Glorious is He) at regular intervals in Paradise, enjoying His pleasure and favour, delighting in His presence, and speaking with Him.

The pleasure of God (Glorious is He) and entry into Paradise are the ultimate goals of those who have faith in Him, are devoted to Him and hope for His reward. Just as seeing the Holy Lord is more pleasing to the believers than their bodily enjoyment in Paradise, striving for His sake alone and being devoted to Him takes precedence over hoping for His reward of Paradise: *And that thy Lord, He is the goal.*[12]

Now, God (Glorious is He) has stated: *Race one with another for forgiveness from your Lord and a Paradise whereof the breadth is as the breadth of the heaven (samā') and the earth, which is in store for those who believe in God and His messengers.*[13] God (Exalted is He) also stated: *And vie one with another for forgiveness from your Lord, and for a Paradise as wide as are the heavens (samāwāt) and the earth, prepared for those who ward off (evil).*[14] Therefore, it seems—and God knows best—that there are two massive Gardens, which together come to form Paradise. The Garden of Paradise designated for the believing Muslims (*muslimūn*) and the believers (*mu'minūn*) may be as large as this universe, whereas the Garden of Paradise (including the *Firdaws*) to be settled by the true

---

Muslim 633/1434; Tirmidhī 2551; Abū Dāwūd 4729; Ibn Māja 177; Aḥmad 19,205 as well as in Muslim 182/451; Tirmidhī 2554; Abū Dāwūd 4730; Ibn Māja 179; Aḥmad 9058.

[10] See Bukhārī 6549; Muslim 2829/7140; Tirmidhī 2555; Aḥmad 11,835.

[11] See Q.IX.72.

[12] Q.LIII.42.

[13] Q.LVII.21.

[14] Q.III.133. Part of the second Garden is named *Firdaws*, and it is specified for the righteous and higher ranks, as per verse 107 of Sūrat al-Kahf. And God knows best.

elite, i.e. the prophets, truly faithful, martyrs, righteous, devout and pious, may be as large as the multiverse.[15]

Similar to the aforementioned division, God (Exalted is He) divided the inhabitants of Paradise into two groups in Sūrat al-Wāqiᶜa: first, He distinguished the foremost (*sābiqūn*), who are the most proximate and the nearest (*muqarrabūn*) to the Holy Lord: *And those foremost (in faith) will be foremost (in the Hereafter), these will be those nearest (to God).*[16] The Holy Lord then mentioned the other group as being those who are on the right (*aṣḥāb al-yamīn*).[17] It is contended that those who are proximate to the Holy Lord are the pious and higher ranks, since the pious (*abrār*) are mentioned as being proximate (*muqarrabūn*) in Sūrat al-Muṭaffifīn[18], while the believers and believing Muslims are those who are on the right.

Now, since the *Firdaws* part of Paradise exists just below the Throne of the Holy Lord, according to a *ḥadīth*,[19] the messengers, prophets, truly faithful, martyrs and righteous who will occupy it[20] will live in the closest proximity to God (Glorious is He), Who has established Himself above His Mighty Throne. Thus, it appears to be the case that the messengers and prophets as well as the truly faithful, martyrs and righteous are, and will forever be, the best of God's creation—anteriorly and posteriorly—not just the best of humanity. More specifically, God (Glorious is He) has taken Muḥammad and Abraham (may God bless them both) as friends[21]—this being such an eminent honour and supreme distinction for them. And God (Exalted is He) will settle Muḥammad and Abraham in the closest proximity to Him

---

[15] As per verse 21 of Sūrat al-Ḥadīd, the width of the first Garden is the same as the heaven (*samā'*), which may indicate a galaxy of this universe or the universe itself. Verse 133 of Sūrat Āl-ᶜImrān states that the width of the second Garden is the same as the heavens (*samāwāt*), which may indicate that it is the size of this universe or all that God has created besides Paradise itself, i.e. the multiverse. And God knows best.

[16] Q.LVI.10–11. The pious are foremost in attaining good deeds in this world and also precede other believers in entering Paradise. These two reasons may explain the repetition of *sābiqūn* in these verses. And God knows best.

[17] See Q.LVI.27.

[18] See Q.LXXXIII.18–28.

[19] See Bukhārī 2790; Tirmidhī 2530; Aḥmad 8419.

[20] See Q.XVIII.107.

[21] See Q.IV.125, as well as Bukhārī 3654; Aḥmad 11,134.

within the two highest stations of Paradise. Jesus, Moses and Noah (may God bless them all) will follow the both of them in the highest stations of Paradise. It is only due to God's love of the messengers, prophets, truly faithful, martyrs and righteous and their acts that He (Glory be to Him) has created this world as we know it, including both good and evil, for that has indirectly enabled them to reach the *Firdaws* and live in the closest possible proximity to Him (Exalted is He). All praise and glory is due to the Most Loving, Most Wise and Most Magnanimous Holy Lord.

Next, consider the *ḥadīth qudsī* in which the Prophet Muḥammad related that God (Exalted is He) has said: "I have prepared for My righteous servants (*ʿibādī al-ṣāliḥīn*) what no eye has seen, no ear has heard, and no human heart has ever imagined."[22] The righteous will enjoy pleasures so sublime in *Firdaws* that they can never be imagined by any human being who has ever lived or will ever live in this world, regardless of future technological advancements. This represents another distinction and favour enjoyed by the righteous and higher ranks for their striving against evil, enjoining good and changing things for the better.

As for the levels (*darajāt*) within Paradise, it will be contended that the Garden designated for the believers and believing Muslims will contain 100 major levels, in accordance with the *ḥadīth* of the Prophet Muḥammad (may God bless him and grant him peace): "Verily in Paradise there are 100 levels, wherein [the distance] between one level and that which is above it is [the distance] between the heaven (*samāʾ*) and the earth."[23]

On the other hand, it will be contended that only God knows the number of levels within the Garden prepared for the pious and higher ranks, since the Prophet Muḥammad only singled out those who

---

[22] Bukhārī 3244; Muslim 2824/7132; Tirmidhī 3197; Ibn Māja 4328; Aḥmad 9649. See also Bukhārī 4779; Muslim 2825/7135; Tirmidhī 3292; Aḥmad 22,826.

[23] Tirmidhī 2530; Ibn Māja 4331; Aḥmad 22,738; Ibn Ḥibbān 4612; al-Ḥākim 267; Bayhaqī (*Sunan*) 18,494. It is "authentic" according to Albānī (*Silsilat al-aḥādīth al-ṣaḥīḥa* 1913). Another *ḥadīth* states that the distance between "two levels is [the distance traversed] over 100 years," but it does not specify the method by which that distance is travelled. Tirmidhī 2529; Aḥmad 7923. It is "authentic" according to Albānī (*Silsilat al-aḥādīth al-ṣaḥīḥa* 922).

strive or fight against evil (*mujāhidūn*) for 100 levels,[24] while leaving out the number of levels for the best of humanity, i.e. the prophets and the truly faithful. For example, the Prophet Muḥammad (may God bless him and grant him peace) is alone within the highest level (*al-maqām al-maḥmūd*) wherein he will be granted intercession by God's permission on the Day of Judgment.[25] Thereafter, there are 124,314 prophets and messengers[26] who are greatly beloved to the Holy Lord and will be ranked in the highest levels of Paradise.

Next, depending on whether *jihād* is interpreted as striving against one's desires, or as striving against evil and forbidding it, or as fighting and battling against evil, *mujāhidūn* may connote the pious and devout, the righteous, or the fighters in God's Path, respectively. Most likely, it is the third interpretation, thus leaving undefined the levels of the other elite types.

In addition, the ranks of the elite, i.e. the pious, devout, righteous, martyrs and truly faithful, would be expected to be greater than the 100 levels designated for the believers and believing Muslims,[27] especially since their Garden could be as large as the multiverse. God (Exalted is He) states: *Verily the Hereafter will be greater in degrees and greater in preferment*.[28] For these reasons, it is again contended that only God (Glory be to Him) knows the number of major levels within Paradise. This will become clearer below.

It will also be contended that there are minor levels within the major ones. The Prophet Muḥammad mentioned that an individual will be granted a higher level for each prostration that he or she

---

[24] See Bukhārī 7423; Muslim 1884/4879; Nasā'ī 3134.

[25] See Bukhārī 614; Tirmidhī 211; Abū Dāwūd 529; Ibn Māja 722; Aḥmad 14,817. See also Muslim 384/849; Tirmidhī 3614; Abū Dāwūd 523; Nasā'ī 678; Aḥmad 6568.

[26] This number was discussed in Chapter Four. See Aḥmad 22,288; Ibn Ḥibbān 361. It is "authentic" according to Albānī (*Silsilat al-aḥādīth al-ṣaḥīḥa* 2668 and *Mishkāt al-maṣābīḥ* 5737).

[27] Some have opined that the levels of Paradise are the same number as the number of Qur'ānic verses, according to the *ḥadīth*: "Your level will be concordant to the last verse you read." Tirmidhī 2914; Abū Dāwūd 1464; Aḥmad 6799; al-Ḥākim 2030; Ibn Ḥibbān 766; Bayhaqī (*Shuʿab*) 1840. It is "authentic" according to Albānī (*Silsilat al-aḥādīth al-ṣaḥīḥa* 2240 and vol. V, pp. 281–284). But here this will be contended to reflect the minor levels within each of the major levels.

[28] Q.XVII.21.

performed[29] and for each verse of Qur'ān that he or she memorized and recited.[30] In addition, a believer will be raised to a higher level due to the supplication of his or her offspring.[31] That said, it may be that the extent of these deeds and supplications are sufficient to raise one to a higher major level. And God knows best.

Now, the pious will live in *lofty mansions, one above another...beneath them flow rivers (of delight): (such is) the promise of God: never doth God fail in (His) promise.*[32] Their mansions will be made of bricks of gold and silver.[33] The believers (*mu'minūn*) will reside in homes 60 miles in length made of pearl,[34] and their homes will overlook the rivers of Paradise. If those are the sizes of the residences of the believers and pious in Paradise, then one cannot imagine the palaces of the righteous and higher ranks. It is significant that no Qur'ānic verse or *ḥadīth* exists describing the palaces of the righteous, since they are unimaginable. Accordingly, although the Prophet Muḥammad did, for instance, see the palace of ᶜUmar b. al-Khaṭṭāb in Paradise, he did not describe it.[35] That said, the residences of the righteous will be seen by the believers (in levels lower than theirs) as stars are seen in this world in the (night) sky[36]—even though darkness is non-existent in Paradise, and only various degrees of light and brightness exist therein. Finally, since the length of the greatest palace in this world is only a small fraction of 60 miles, this represents one evidence that the names of entities in Paradise are incomparable to those of this world.

Moreover, a *ḥadīth* of the Prophet Muḥammad affirms the fact that the entities within Paradise are necessarily of sublime quiddities and essences: "[The area of] one foot in Paradise is better than this world

---

[29] Muslim 488/1093; Tirmidhī 388; Ibn Māja 1422; Nasā'ī 1139; Aḥmad 22,377.

[30] Ibn Māja 3780; Aḥmad 11,360. It is "authentic" according to Albānī (*Ṣaḥīḥ al-Jāmiᶜ al-ṣaghīr* 8121).

[31] Ibn Māja 3660; Aḥmad 10,610; Bayhaqī (*Sunan*) 13,459. It is "sound" according to Albānī (*Silsilat al-aḥādīth al-ṣaḥīḥa* 1598). See also Muslim 1631/4223; Abū Dāwūd 2880; Ibn Māja 241; Aḥmad 8844.

[32] Q.XXXIX.20 (Yusuf Ali translation).

[33] See Tirmidhī 2526; Aḥmad 8043; Ibn Ḥibbān 7387; Bayhaqī (*Shuᶜab*) 6699. It is "authentic" according to Albānī (*Silsilat al-aḥādīth al-ṣaḥīḥa* 2662).

[34] See Bukhārī 4879; Muslim 2838/7158; Tirmidhī 2528; Aḥmad 19,576.

[35] See Bukhārī 3242; Tirmidhī 3688; Aḥmad 8470.

[36] See Muslim 2830/7141; Tirmidhī 2556; Aḥmad 22,876.

and all that it contains."[37] Even the most stunning palaces and vistas of this world will be insignificant relative to the surreal and idyllic beauty of Paradise.

It should be mentioned here that the Prophet Muḥammad informed us that those who prayed twelve supererogatory units of prayer will be granted another home in Paradise for each day they did so.[38] Likewise, those who participated in the building of a mosque will be bestowed a palace in Paradise.[39] And for each separate utterance in which God (Glorious is He) is praised or glorified, the believer will have a tree planted; thus expanding further his or her vast garden within Paradise.[40]

As for the bodily pleasures,[41] suffice it to say that the good pleasures, which the Holy Lord has permitted the believers in this world, must be present in Paradise. Had that not been the case they would wish, while living in Paradise, for some good pleasure of this world, and the Hereafter would therefore entail (in some aspects) less bliss for them than this lesser world. That said, the good pleasures of this world when compared to those of Paradise are similar only in name. The rapture, ecstasy and bliss that the believers will experience in Paradise are sublime and far beyond those of this world: *No person knows what delights of the eye are kept hidden (in reserve) for them—as a reward for their (good) deeds.*[42] In reality, the pleasures of Paradise include the good ones of this world, in addition to further ones specific to the Hereafter that God (Glorious is He) has delayed until then. Those pleasures

---

[37] Bukhārī 6568; Aḥmad 13,780. Even the "pebbles" on the ground that the believers tread upon are instead pearls and rubies. See Tirmidhī 2526; Aḥmad 1075; Ibn Ḥibbān 7387. It is "authentic" according to Albānī (*Ṣaḥīḥ al-Jāmiᶜ al-ṣaghīr* 3116).

[38] See Muslim 728/1694; Tirmidhī 415; Nasā'ī 1797; Aḥmad 26,774.

[39] See Bukhārī 450; Muslim 533/1189; Tirmidhī 318; Ibn Māja 735; Nasā'ī 688; Aḥmad 19,440.

[40] See Tirmidhī 3464; Ibn Ḥibbān 826; al-Ḥākim 1847 and Ibn Māja 3807 for two *ḥadīths* in this matter. They are both "authentic" according to Albānī (*Ṣaḥīḥ al-Jāmiᶜ al-ṣaghīr* 6424 and 2613, respectively).

[41] The bodily pleasures enjoyed by the believers in Paradise are affirmed in many verses of the Qur'ān, such as Q.LVI.10–40. For a *ḥadīth* of the Prophet Muḥammad in this regard, see Aḥmad 19,268 and Ibn Ḥibbān 7424, which is deemed to be "authentic" by Albānī (*Ṣaḥīḥ al-Jāmiᶜ al-ṣaghīr* 1623).

[42] Q.XXXII.17 (Yusuf Ali translation).

are exclusively good and pure—they are devoid of any evilness, deficiency or inadequacy.

The body will be resurrected along with the spirit to live in Paradise. The believers will all be the height of Adam (may God bless him),[43] and they will remain forever young and never age.[44] Their faces will be radiant and they will be granted light: *Their light will run before them and on their right hands; they will say: Our Lord! Perfect our light for us, and forgive us! Thou art Able to do all things*.[45] They will continue to glorify and praise God (Exalted is He) just as one breathes involuntarily.[46] Their hearts will be pure and free from any envy.[47] They will never sleep nor suffer fatigue,[48] and they will never fall ill.[49] All will be clothed in the finest silk[50] and adorned with luxury, and they will enjoy Paradise perpetually and eternally.

God (Exalted is He) has destined that the believers inhabiting Paradise will never suffer nor encounter evil. Suffering is present in this world, the Hellfire and "surrounding Paradise"[51]—but not within Paradise. After entering Paradise, the believers will immediately forget all of the suffering and evil they endured in this world, and it will be as if they never experienced them.[52] That said, Paradise and God's pleasure can only be attained by overcoming the hardships and suffering of this world as well as enduring its trials and evils. Moreover, the believers

---

43 The Prophet Muḥammad said: "God created Adam in his image, 60 cubits tall... Everyone who enters Paradise will be in the image of Adam... That said, humankind has continued to decrease [in height] until now." Bukhārī 6227; Muslim 2841/7163; Aḥmad 8171. One cubit is equivalent to one-and-a-half feet.

44 See Muslim 2837/7157; Tirmidhī 3246; Aḥmad 8258.

45 Q.LXVI.8.

46 See Muslim 2835/7152; Aḥmad 14,769.

47 See Q.XV.47. See also Bukhārī 3254; Muslim 2834/7147; Tirmidhī 2537; Aḥmad 8198.

48 See Q.XXXV.35.

49 See Muslim 2837/7157; Tirmidhī 3246; Aḥmad 8258.

50 See Q.XXII.23 and Q.XXXV.33 as well as Q.XVIII.31; Q.XLIV.53; and Q.LXXVI.21.

51 See Muslim 2822/7130; Tirmidhī 2559; Nasā'ī 3763; Aḥmad 7530.

52 See Muslim 2807/7088; Aḥmad 13,112.

will be compensated with a variety of rewards for their suffering in this world.[53]

GOD'S PLEASURE AND FAVOUR

Now, the Holy Lord states: *And in the Hereafter there is grievous punishment, and (also) forgiveness from God and His good pleasure.*[54] Thus, there are three initial possibilities in the Hereafter: punishment, God's forgiveness and/or His pleasure. The punishment in Hellfire will be inflicted upon the hypocrites, disbelievers and sinful believers (*ẓālimūn*), whereby only the last group will be removed from Hellfire. As regards God's forgiveness, a verse specific to the pious and devout states: *For such the reward is forgiveness from their Lord, and Gardens with rivers flowing underneath—an eternal dwelling: How excellent a recompense for those who work (and strive)!*[55] God's forgiveness thus allows the pious and devout to enter His Paradise without being punished in Hellfire. As for the third possibility, i.e. those granted His good pleasure, it will be contended that they are specifically the prophets and messengers, as well as the truly faithful, martyrs and the righteous (*ṣāliḥīn*): *God hath shown favour [unto] the prophets and the saints and the martyrs and the righteous.*[56] It will be further asserted that these favoured groups, while still living in this world, are granted the Holy Lord's good pleasure.

In that regard, the Holy Lord was, according to many verses of the Qur'ān, pleased with the Companions of the Prophet Muḥammad in this world, i.e. before the Day of Judgment: *The [Meccan] Muhājirīn and the [Medinite] Anṣār, and those who followed them in goodness—God is well pleased with them.*[57] Another verse distinguishes those who pledged before the Treaty of Ḥudaybiya: *God was well pleased with the believers when they swore allegiance unto thee beneath the tree.*[58] God (Glorious is

---

[53] For example, the believers who suffered poverty and dearth will enter Paradise before the wealthy in most cases. See Tirmidhī 2354; Ibn Māja 4123; Aḥmad 8521; Ibn Ḥibbān 676. It is "sound" according to Albānī (*Ṣaḥīḥ al-Jāmiʿ al-ṣaghīr* 8076).

[54] Q.LVII.20.

[55] Q.III.136. It was previously mentioned that Q.III.133–135 discusses the characteristics of the pious as well as the devout, and thus Q.III.136 discusses their reward.

[56] Q.IV.69.

[57] Q.IX.100.

[58] Q.XLVIII.18.

He) was also pleased with the Companions who fought in the Battle of Badr to such a degree that the Prophet Muḥammad (may God bless him and grant him peace) said regarding Ḥāṭib b. Abī Baltaʿa: "It may be that God has said about those who participated in the Battle of Badr: 'Do whatever you will—I have forgiven you.'"[59] Another narration states: "Do whatever you will since you have already deserved (*wajabat*) Paradise."[60] Since Ḥāṭib had already attained the pleasure of God—whereby only God knows those who are righteous and have attained His pleasure—the Holy Lord graced him and exempted him from His anger and from any punishment.[61] Thus, the foremost Companions were granted God's pleasure in this world.

In that light, it will be asserted that the righteous and higher ranks are included amongst those whom God is well pleased in this world due to His favouring them, as per the aforementioned Qur'ānic verse.[62] Consider that the Prophet Muḥammad (may God bless him and grant him peace) said: "The greater the tribulation, the greater the reward. If God loves a people, He will test them. Whoever is pleased with [tribulation] will attain the pleasure [of God], and whoever is angry with it will be subject to the anger [of God]."[63] In that light, the Prophet Muḥammad went further in another *ḥadīth* and informed us that the righteous, in particular, are pleased to undergo tribulations: "The righteous...are pleased to undergo tribulation [or afflictions] (*balā'*)."[64] One reason that the righteous may be pleased with tribulation and content with the ontologic will of God is their recognition that

---

[59] Bukhārī 3007; Muslim 2494/6401; Tirmidhī 3305; Abū Dāwūd 2650; Aḥmad 600.

[60] Bukhārī 3983.

[61] Ḥāṭib b. Abī Baltaʿa had betrayed the Prophet Muḥammad and the Companions by sending a letter to Quraysh in 8 AH so as to inform them that the Muslim army would be advancing towards Mecca to liberate it. That letter was subsequently found and retrieved by ʿAlī b. Abī Ṭālib, al-Zubayr and al-Miqdād before reaching Quraysh. See the aforementioned *ḥadīth* references as well as Safiur-Rahman al-Mubarakpuri, *The Sealed Nectar*, p. 523 and Zeni (tr.), *Ibn Qayyim al-Jawziyya on Knowledge*, p. 262.

[62] See Q.IV.69.

[63] Tirmidhī 2396; Ibn Māja 4031; *Ḥilya*, vol. VII, p. 10; Bayhaqī (*Shuʿab*) 9325. It is "sound" according to Albānī (*Silsilat al-aḥādīth al-ṣaḥīḥa* 146).

[64] Ibn Māja 4024; Aḥmad 11,893; al-Ḥākim 119. It is "authentic" according to Albānī (*Silsilat al-aḥādīth al-ṣaḥīḥa* 144).

the presence of evil has indirectly enabled them to strive against it, and thus attain a great reward. Regardless, by reconciling these two *ḥadīths*, the righteous, in particular, are distinguished and favoured with the pleasure of God.

Now, it will be contended that one consequence of God (Glorious is He) being well pleased with the righteous and higher ranks, and favouring them, is that they will not be questioned regarding their intermediate or minor sins on the Day of Judgment.[65] This becomes more evident if one considers the statement of God (Exalted is He): *[Those] who repenteth and believeth and doeth righteous work; as for such, God will change their evil deeds (sayyi'āt) to good deeds. God is ever Forgiving, Merciful.*[66] In this fashion, all of the deeds of the righteous will either be good or transformed into good. It will be contended that the reason the Holy Lord will reward the righteous by transforming all their sins into good deeds is because they strove to forbid wickedness and transform the actions of others from evil to good. Regardless, since all of the deeds of the righteous are ultimately good nothing will remain for them to be questioned about. God's grace, love and favour[67] upon the righteous is indeed great.

On the other hand, the intermediate and minor sins of the pious will only be ultimately forgiven and pardoned[68]—but not transformed into good deeds. Therefore, in contrast to the righteous, God (Glorious is He) delays His pleasure for the pious until after questioning them on the Day of Judgment and forgiving them. That

---

[65] See Ibn Māja 4286; Aḥmad 2241. It is "authentic" according to Albānī (*Silsilat al-aḥādīth al-ṣaḥīḥa*, 2179). Of note, the Prophet Muḥammad (may God bless him and grant him peace) said: "Whoever is questioned [suffers a form] of punishment." Bukhārī 6536; Muslim 2876/7225; Tirmidhī 3338; Abū Dāwūd 3093; Aḥmad 24,200. That said, all will be asked about the manner by which they utilized the blessings of God (like safety, health, wealth, and food or drink). See Q.CII.8 and *Tafsīr al-Ṭabarī*, vol. XXIV, pp. 581–586.

[66] Q.XXV.70.

[67] This also indicates that a righteous person need not necessarily be devout, but only pious, i.e. avoid major sins and repent from others and regret them, if he or she strives against evil and forbids the major sins. And God knows best.

[68] See the prior discussion in Chapters Seven and Eleven, as well as the verse Q. LXV.5: *And unto everyone who is conscious of God (yattaqi) will He pardon his bad deeds (sayyi'āt) [i.e. intermediate sins].*

said, the pious, like the righteous, will not grieve nor experience fear on the Day of Judgment.[69]

We can also better understand here Sūrat al-ᶜAṣr wherein God (Glorious is He) states: *By (the token of) time (through the ages), verily [humankind] is in loss, except such as have faith, and do righteous deeds, and (join together) in the mutual teaching of truth, and of patience and constancy.*[70] Here all of humankind has lost out in some fashion except those who are righteous. The loss of the disbelievers is absolutely the greatest since they will never enter Paradise nor will they see the Exalted Lord. However, even most of the believers will experience loss,[71] since those believers below the rank of the righteous will have lost out on the opportunity for God's reward for all the time that they failed to fill with good deeds, as well as losing out on having their sins transformed into good. On the other hand, since God (Glorious is He) will transform the sins—and by extension those acts which are permissible (*mubāḥ*) but not necessarily otherwise rewarded—into good deeds, all of the time spent by the righteous in this world is rewarded with good. The degree and extent of the reward for the righteous is indeed unfathomable and unimaginable, and therefore the levels and ranks they occupy must likewise be incomprehensibly great and vast. God's grace (Glorious and Exalted is He) is infinite, and He is the Most Beneficent and Most Generous.

On the Believers Who Are on the Heights (al-Aᶜrāf)

Now, God (Exalted is He) states: *And on the Heights are men who [will]... call unto the dwellers of the Garden: Peace be unto you! They enter it not [yet] although they hope (to enter). And when their eyes are turned toward the dwellers of the Fire, they say: Our Lord! Place us not with the wrong-doing folk (ẓālimīn)... (Unto the [believers on the Heights it will be] said): Enter the Garden. No [further] fear shall come upon you nor is it ye who will grieve.*[72]

It has been discussed already that the polytheists and wrongdoers will enter Hellfire before the pious enter Paradise. The above verse

69 See Q.VII.35 (Muḥammad Asad translation).

70 Q.CIII.1–3 (Yusuf Ali translation).

71 Note that God (Glorious is He) states loss (*khusr*), not total and absolute loss (*al-khusr*).

72 Q.VII.46–49.

mentions that those who are on the Heights (*al-Aʿrāf*) will not be punished in Hellfire itself, but will be delayed in entering Paradise. Therefore, it will be contended that these people on the Heights represent some of the believers (*muqtaṣidūn*) who are punished by flames from Hellfire as they pass on the bridge (*ṣirāṭ*) over it, and are thereafter delayed on the Heights before entering Paradise. They have perpetrated some of the secondary major sins (and for that they are punished by the flames of Hellfire), but otherwise have done more good deeds than (or at least an equal amount to) their intermediate and minor sins (*sayyi'āt*); hence, they are not entered into Hellfire itself to be punished.[73] Those believers, on the other hand, whose sins are greater than their good deeds, as well as the believing Muslims who have perpetrated the major wicked sins, will be punished in Hellfire. God's pleasure will only be bestowed upon the sinful believers after they are questioned, forgiven for some sins and punished accordingly for others, as discussed, and entered into Paradise by His grace. And God knows best.

On the last believing Muslim to enter Paradise

The last of the inhabitants of Paradise to be entered into the eternal abode of peace and everlasting bliss will be one who says (according to the *ḥadīth*): "Exalted is He Who has rescued me from [Hellfire]. God has granted me something which He has not given anyone else from the first or last nations..." God (Almighty and Most Glorious is He) will say to him: "Would you be content if I granted you that which one of the kings of the world had?" The man will then say to the Holy Lord: "I would be pleased." Then after the Holy Lord grants him ten times what is in this world, this individual will say: "Are you joking with me even though You are the Lord of the Worlds?" At this point, the Prophet Muḥammad (may God bless him and grant him peace) laughed and said that the God (Almighty and Most Glorious is He) will laugh and say: "I am not joking (*lā astahzi'u*) with you, but instead I am capable of anything I will."[74]

---

[73] This is also concordant with verse Q.XI.114: *good deeds annul ill-deeds* (*sayyi'āt*).

[74] See Bukhārī 6571 and 7511; Muslim 187–189/463–465; Aḥmad 3899.

Therefore, God (Glorious is He) has determined that the believer in the lowest level of Paradise will be granted ten times what the richest person in this world had. Again, it is not because the faith of the lowest-ranked believer in Paradise "deserves" this reward; rather, it is because God (Exalted is He), out of His grace and generosity, has determined this to be the minimum reward for a believer entering Paradise. Those believers within all of the higher ranks will be placed in Paradise with degrees of reward that are far greater.

In addition, as mentioned previously, the believers who will ultimately be rewarded in Paradise are only 10% of humanity—this is not due to any miserliness from the Holy and Almighty Lord nor any incapability. Had God willed, He (Glory be to Him) could have placed all of humanity in Paradise. The fact that the believer occupying the lowest rank will be bestowed at least ten fold what the wealthiest human being in this world temporarily possessed confirms that. But since 90% of humankind did not worship the Holy Lord alone in accordance with His commandments, His wisdom and justice rejected their entry into the abode of peace, bliss and reward.

Next, God (Glorious and Exalted is He) will ask the believers in Paradise: "Are you satisfied?" They will respond: "How can we not be satisfied when You have bestowed upon us that which You have not granted anyone else of Your creation?" Then God will state: "I will grant you something greater than that: My pleasure, and I will never be angry (*lā askhaṭu*) with you again."[75] In another *ḥadīth*, God (Glorious is He) will then remove the veil and they will be able to see their Lord (Almighty and Most Glorious is He)—this will be the most beloved [blessing granted] to them.[76] This *ḥadīth* again affirms the Beatific Vision, and that this spiritual pleasure will be the greatest one the believers will experience in Paradise.

Now, although the majority of the believers will initially be punished in Hellfire, since they will ultimately enter Paradise and see the Holy Lord, the experience of punishment will fade away and pale in comparison. The believers will consider all of the hardships and difficulties they encountered as worthwhile in order to see and speak

---

75 Bukhārī 6549; Muslim 2829/7140; Tirmidhī 2555; Aḥmad 11,835.

76 Muslim 181/449; Tirmidhī 2552; Ibn Māja 187; Aḥmad 18,935.

with God (Glorious and Exalted is He). That said, the believer must make a choice whether he or she would rather experience difficulty in this world[77] or in the Hereafter. Either one chooses the path of piety and righteousness, or the believer will be forced to endure an even more difficult path in the Hereafter on his or her way to Paradise. Although the path is difficult, the reality is that no one aside from the believers will be permitted to meet the Almighty Lord, see Him, speak to Him, and be loved by Him (Glorious and Exalted is He). Although this path is difficult, God (Glorious and Exalted is He) has determined it to be necessary to attain His love and pleasure.

On the number of inhabitants in Paradise

The number of prophets and messengers is 124,315, according to a previously-mentioned *ḥadīth*.[78] Let us assume for the purposes of this discussion, and so as to provide a framework, that there is a selection factor amongst the elite ranks within Paradise. It will be hypothesized that this selection factor is less than that between the believers and believing Muslims, which was discussed in the last chapter to be a factor of nine, since here it describes the ranks of the elite 1% of the inhabitants of Paradise.[79] The number of the next rank, i.e. the truly faithful, would thus be in the hundreds of thousands.

Of note, we will not include the martyrs in this framework for the principal reason that the martyrs may occupy a varying spectrum, i.e. they may have been prophets or they can be any of the spiritual ranks from the truly faithful down to the believing Muslims. But because they sacrificed themselves and were killed in His path, God (Glorious is He) favours and graces them by granting them a higher rank than they would otherwise occupy (assuming their rank was that of the righteous or lower). It should also be noted that the spirits of the martyrs are already in Paradise living in proximity to the Holy Lord.

---

77 See Q.III.42 and Q.II.214.

78 See Aḥmad 22,288; Ibn Ḥibbān 361. It is "authentic" according to Albānī (*Silsilat al-aḥādīth al-ṣaḥīḥa* 2668 and *Mishkāt al-maṣābīḥ* 5737).

79 The selection factor could be the same between the different ranks of truly faithful, righteous, devout and pious or it may vary. However, the objective is to provide a framework along which the noted religious concepts may be understood. Only God knows the number of each rank.

God (Exalted is He) has stated: *Think not of those, who are slain in the way of God, as dead. Nay, they are living. With their Lord they have provision.*[80] The Prophet Muḥammad (may God bless him and grant him peace) stated that their spirits are within birds, which fly from lamps hanging (within the *Firdaws* part of Paradise) from the Throne of the Almighty Lord.[81] The Holy Lord has greatly graced the martyrs by allowing their spirits to enter Paradise before the Day of Judgment. And since the spirits of the martyrs already exist within Paradise, they do not necessarily enter Paradise through one of its eight gates.[82] Therefore, their matter is different than the rest of the believers; thus, they will not be included in this framework.

On another note, there are nine verses in the Qur'ān, which mention that the inhabitants of Paradise will be rewarded eternally (*abad*[an]).[83] It was discussed in the last chapter that there are only three such verses regarding the denizens of Hellfire, and it was contended that only those denizens who enter through the three respective gates will be punished eternally in Hellfire. It will be contended here that these nine verses correspond to the nine manners by which Paradise will be entered, and they are the eight gates of Paradise[84], as well as the manner by which the martyrs enter it before the Day of Judgment—and God knows best. This maintains the consensus belief that all of the believers entering Paradise will be rewarded eternally therein, as well as representing further evidence to strengthen the basis of the

---

80 Q.III.169.

81 Muslim 1887/4585; Tirmidhī 3011; Abū Dāwūd 2520; Ibn Māja 2801.

82 Those who strove or fought (*jāhada*) will have a specific gate, but the Prophet Muḥammad did not name one for the martyrs—this being concordant with their spirits already being in Paradise and not needing, therefore, to enter via a gate to Paradise.

83 These verses are Q.IV.57 and 122; Q.V.119; Q.IX.22 and 100; Q.XVIII.3; Q.LXIV.9; Q.LXV.11; Q.XCVIII.8. God's love and favour (Glorious is He) for the righteous and higher ranks (who have striven against evil) is distinguished, while He has encompassed the remaining believers in His eternal reward due to His magnanimity, grace and mercy.

84 It should be noted here that the Prophet Muḥammad (may God bless him and grant him peace) supplicated on behalf of Abū Bakr (may God be pleased with him) that he enter from all eight gates of Paradise. See Bukhārī 1897; Muslim 1027/2371; Tirmidhī 3674; Nasā'ī 2238; Aḥmad 9800.

contention within the last chapter that only some of the denizens will be eternally punished.

To continue, the number of the next rank—for the purpose of this framework—i.e. the righteous, will be in the millions. The Prophet Muḥammad (may God bless him and grant him peace) said: "My Lord (Glorious is He) promised me that [the first] of my Community to enter Paradise will be seventy thousand, who will not be questioned nor punished; accompanying each thousand will be another seventy thousand."[85] Therefore, the number of those entering Paradise from amongst the Community of the Prophet Muḥammad who are not questioned will be 4.9 million according to this *ḥadīth*. This is consistent with what was mentioned and contended in a prior section, i.e. that the righteous and truly faithful ranks who trustfully depend on the Holy Lord in striving against evil will not be questioned.

The devout will be in the tens of millions, while the pious will number in the hundred(s) of millions. In aggregate, the numbers of these elite ranks will be in the hundred(s) of millions. Added to these will be an unspecified number of martyrs. Therefore, according to this hypothetical framework, the total number of humanity to live (being 1000 times the aggregated number of the pious and higher ranks) will be in the hundred(s) of billions. And God knows best.

God has fine-tuned matters, and He is omnipotent and omniscient (Glory be to Him). Although only 10% of all of humanity will be entered into Paradise by the Holy Lord, the believers will still represent many ten(s) of billions, and thus a massive number. In this fashion, it can be seen that the number of major and minor levels they will reside in must be massive as well—this was alluded to previously.

God (Glorious is He) has created all of humanity and has selected human beings for each of the aforementioned ranks and levels. The Holy Lord could have created many hundreds of billions of human beings who, out of their free will worshipped Him alone and only did good, i.e. were devout individuals, but being human their worship would be intermittent and inferior to the continuous worship of the angels, and thus their creation as such would be pointless. God is

---

[85] Ibn Māja 4286; Aḥmad 2241. It is "authentic" according to Albānī (*Silsilat al-aḥādīth al-ṣaḥīḥa*, 2179).

the One Holy Lord Who is sublime and exalted above any frivolity, evilness, injustice, deficiency or fault.

God (Exalted is He) has instead brought about what He loves in accordance with His wisdom and justice: manifestation of His Beautiful Names and Glorious Attributes; creation of the messengers, prophets, truly faithful, martyrs and righteous as well as the devout and pious (all of whom are beloved to Him); and many wise purposes, as mentioned previously. Those beloved and favoured by God (Exalted is He) freely chose to carry out good deeds, strive against evil, change things for the better and patiently endure hardship for His sake alone. Even though these righteous believers may be relatively few, they represent the best types of humanity, and they will live in the highest levels of Paradise in close proximity to Him (Glorious is He). What the Holy Lord has willed has occurred in a manner concordant with His love, wisdom, mercy, beneficence, glory and justice.

ON THE HIGHEST AND MOST BLESSED STATION IN PARADISE

The Prophet Muḥammad (may God bless him and grant him peace) occupies the absolute highest and most sublime level in Paradise—it is the most blessed and most glorious station (*al-maqām al-maḥmūd*). Therefore, the Prophet Muḥammad (may God bless him and grant him peace) will be the best from amongst millions of righteous believers, the best of ten(s) of billions of believers, and the best of hundred(s) of billions of human beings. God (Glorious is He) has stated: *And arise* [*O Muḥammad*] *from thy sleep and pray during part of the night* [*as well*]*, as a free offering from thee, and thy Sustainer may well raise thee to a glorious station* [*in the life to come*].[86] The Prophet Muḥammad also said: "Whoever says upon hearing the call [to prayer], 'O Lord of this perfect call and established prayer, grant Muḥammad the [ability] to intercede (*al-waṣīla*), [Your] ultimate grace (*al-faḍīla*), and raise him to the blessed station (*al-maqām al-maḥmūd*), which You have promised him,' then it is permissible for me to intercede for him on the Day of Judgment."[87] Thus, God (Glorious is He) has promised the Prophet Muḥammad to

[86] Q.XVII.79.

[87] Bukhārī 614; Tirmidhī 211; Abū Dāwūd 529; Ibn Māja 722; Aḥmad 14,817. See also Muslim 384/849; Tirmidhī 3614; Abū Dāwūd 523; Nasā'ī 678; Aḥmad 6568.

place him in the highest level and most blessed station in Paradise, *al-maqām al-maḥmūd*.

Furthermore, the Prophet Muḥammad said: "I will be the leader of all of humankind on the Day of Judgment—[I say that] without boasting. I will carry the flag of praiseworthiness—[I say that] without boasting. On that Day, all prophets, whether Adam or those after him, will be under my flag. I will be the first granted intercession and the first to intercede—[I say that] without boasting."[88] Therefore, the Prophet Muḥammad (may God bless him and grant him peace) will intercede for a vast number of his Community (who are at least half and possibly even two thirds of the inhabitants of Paradise).[89] And the Holy Lord promised the Prophet Muḥammad, who wept while supplicating on behalf of his Community, that he would be pleased with their state in the Hereafter.[90]

Since the majority of the inhabitants of Paradise will be followers of the Prophet Muḥammad (amongst other reasons alluded to in this book), his existence is truly a mercy unto humankind: *We sent thee not save as a mercy for the peoples*.[91] The Prophet Muḥammad will be the first to enter Paradise,[92] and his Community will precede others in doing so.[93] Moreover, he (may God bless him and grant him peace) will be granted the River of *Kawthar*[94] in Paradise, which flows into a Pool (*ḥawḍ*)—those of his Community who drink from this Pool will never thirst again.[95]

---

88 Tirmidhī 3148; Ibn Māja 4308; Aḥmad 2546. It is "authentic" according to Albānī (*Ṣaḥīḥ al-Jāmiʿ al-ṣaghīr* 1468).

89 See Bukhārī 6528; Muslim 221/529; Tirmidhī 3168; Ibn Māja 4283; Aḥmad 3661. It may be that the Community of Muḥammad represents more than half of the inhabitants, and thus are two thirds. This hypothesis is based loosely on the *ḥadīth*: "The inhabitants of Paradise will be 120 rows (*ṣaff*) wherein 80 will be from this Community." Tirmidhī 2546; Ibn Māja 4289; Aḥmad 23,002; Ibn Ḥibbān 7459; al-Ḥākim 273. It is "authentic" according to Albānī (*Ṣaḥīḥ al-Jāmiʿ al-ṣaghīr* 2526). It is unclear though whether each row includes the same number of believers.

90 See Muslim 202/499.

91 Q.XXI.107.

92 See Muslim 197/486. See also Aḥmad 12,469. It is "authentic" according to Albānī (*Silsilat al-aḥādīth al-ṣaḥīḥa* 2411 and *Ṣaḥīḥ al-Jāmiʿ al-ṣaghīr* 7118).

93 Muslim 855–856/1978–1982.

94 See Q.CVIII.1.

95 See Bukhārī 6583; Muslim 2290/5968; Tirmidhī 2445; Ibn Māja 4303; Aḥmad 22,822.

May the Holy Lord allow the Prophet Muḥammad to intercede for us on the Day of Judgment and allow us to drink from the Pool! May the Holy Lord protect us from Hellfire and enter us into Paradise, His eternal mercy and grace and the everlasting abode of bliss! And may the Holy Lord allow us to see Him, speak to Him, and reside in close proximity to Him (Glorious and Exalted is He) within the higher levels of Paradise! Amen!

Epilogue

It is now clear that the Almighty and Holy Lord has structured this world, Hellfire and Paradise congruent to His love, wisdom, mercy, grace and justice. The Holy Lord has only allowed suffering and evil, even the gratuitous type, so as to allow the manifestation of many wise purposes.

Now, the Holy Lord mentioned four stories in Sūrat al-Kahf (as discussed in Chapter One)—the first three stories discussed the importance of youth believing in the Holy Lord, the importance of wealth and possessions in addition to belief, and the importance of knowledge (the last being illustrated in the story of Khiḍr and Moses). It will be contended that since Dhū al-Qarnayn (who was mentioned in the fourth story) possessed all three of these elements, God (Exalted is He) granted him sovereignty, power and victory.[1] It will also be asserted that the type of religious knowledge necessary to being granted sovereignty by the Almighty Lord, particularly in this time of strangeness (*ghurba*), is specifically that which concerns a theodicy (as illustrated by Khiḍr) and that which counters evil (as illustrated by Dhū al-Qarnayn).

Therefore, and God knows best, any efforts to counter evil and any books or writings, which propose a theodicy and elucidate God's many wise purposes[2], may spark a revival of piety and resurgence of righteousness and Islam by God's grace. The Holy Lord has decreed to bring about the resurgence of this Community of the Prophet Muḥammad in times of strangeness through religious and theodicean knowledge, as well as a critical mass of society acting righteously and trustfully depending on Him—not through direct miraculous interventions by Him (Almighty and Most Glorious is He), as He provided to prior nations. If this resurgence is actively pursued as exemplified by the Companions of the Prophet Muḥammad (may

---

[1] I would like to thank Aḥmad Mabrūk for this thought.

[2] It should be emphasized again that only God (Glorious is He) knows all of His wise purposes in detail, just as only He knows the complete interpretation of His Scripture, the Qur'ān. See Q.III.7.

God bless him and grant him peace), it may occur within 20 years. On the other hand, if a passive approach is adopted or if the believers are few and incapable (as illustrated in Sūrat al-Kahf), it may take a total of 300 years. Regardless, it *will* occur. In this fashion, it can be contended that the Holy Lord bestows knowledge and a deeper understanding for certain wise purposes after having withheld it for other wise purposes—one of them being to allow the occurrence of a resurgence after a period of strangeness.

A further dimension to the wisdom behind God withholding knowledge of His wise purposes is that it has allowed for debate and intellectual activity. This is alluded to in the Qur'ānic verse:

> *And had thy Sustainer so willed, He could have surely made all humankind one single community: but [He willed it otherwise, and so] they continue to hold divergent views [all of them] save those upon whom thy Sustainer has bestowed His grace. And to this end has He created them all. But [as for those who refuse to avail themselves of Divine guidance,] that Word of thy Sustainer shall be fulfilled: "Most certainly will I fill Hell with jinn as well as with humans, all together."*[3]

Had knowledge been absolutely complete and preserved from the time of Adam, debate and intellectual activity could not have occurred, and therefore God (Glorious is He) withheld some of His infinite knowledge.

One may think of this similar to how God (Exalted is He) withheld knowledge from the prior Jews and Christians, but then perfected Islam. The Holy Lord has graced the believers following the Prophet Muḥammad (may God bless him and grant him peace) by guiding them to the whole truth. God (Exalted is He) states: *This day have I perfected your religion for you and completed My favour unto you, and have chosen Islam as your religion.*[4] The theodicy outlined throughout this book shows the perfection and strength of Islam and its superiority over all other religions, including Judaism and Christianity.

Moreover, had our knowledge and understanding been almost complete from the beginning, the suffering and evil that humanity had to experience would have been greater in order to allow for an

---

[3] Q.XI.118-119 (Muḥammad Asad translation).

[4] Q.V.3. The above translation is edited slightly from Pickthall's where he instead states: *and have chosen for you as religion al-Islam.*

appropriate degree of testing to occur. It was discussed previously that the coming of the Antichrist is in part to appropriately test humanity, since the understanding and knowledge of the believers will be far deeper and more certain, and they will have attained victory beforehand. May God guide and strengthen the believers who are alive at that time! And may God bless Jesus and those Muslims who will fight with him against the Antichrist!

The current oppression against the Muslims will end by the support and providence of the Almighty Lord, and the resurgence of Islam will occur. God is the One Who allows events to occur, which expiate and absolve the Muslims of their sins, and it is He Who thereafter grants victory to the believers—even if they are weak and oppressed. Granting victory and a resurgence to the believers through religious and theodicean knowledge illustrates His holiness, omniscience and wisdom to a far greater degree than through miracles. Although miracles demonstrate His omnipotence, they have already occurred multiple times in the past, whereas resurgence in the absence of a messenger during a time of widespread and abject strangeness has yet to occur. And God knows best.

God (Glorious is He) has willed the occurrence of many wise purposes, not because He is in need of them, but because He loves their manifestation and fulfillment. These wise and beloved purposes again include manifesting the consequences of a greater number of His Beautiful Names and Glorious Attributes, as well as the emergence of the best of humanity, i.e. the messengers, the prophets, the truly faithful, the martyrs and the righteous, who will live in the closest proximity within Paradise to the Almighty Lord Who has established Himself above His Throne. Furthermore, suffering and evil indirectly bring about many positive character traits and actions of the heart, like patience, humility, devotion, reliance and trustful dependence on God as well as many righteous actions, such as fulfilling the commandments of the Holy Lord and enjoining good, forbidding evil and striving against it, fighting in His path against the transgressing disbelievers, and repudiating false arguments and notions with sound religious knowledge. Due to the structure of this world, the believers can carry out, by their free choice, the widest possible spectrum of pious and righteous deeds with the hope of attaining the Holy Lord's mercy, grace and pleasure. Finally, one of the wise purposes is differentiating the true believers from those who are hypocrites. As a consequence of the nature of this world, those who are disbelievers, hypocrites and satanic are manifested as such. Ultimately, the Holy Lord's love of the believers and particularly the righteous is greater than His hatred of the denizens of Hellfire.

Thus, the question becomes whether one is willing to endure the suffering and evil of this world while being pious and carrying out greater degrees of good deeds, so as to attain what the Holy Lord loves and is pleased with? If one is willing to do so, it can only be accomplished through true and sincere love of God (Glorious and Exalted is He) and by following His Messenger Muḥammad (may God bless him and grant him peace). We must also constantly remind ourselves when facing hardships, tribulations and evil that the glory and exaltedness of the Holy Lord is far beyond what we can sacrifice and perform for His sake. We cannot worship the Holy Lord as is befitting to Him (Glorious and Exalted is He) nor show sufficient gratitude to Him for all of His blessings. This will become clear to all of humankind on the Day of Judgment—if not in this world—and particularly all the more to the believers after they enter Paradise and see and speak to the Holy Lord.

May God (Almighty and Most Glorious is He) save us from Hellfire through His mercy and enter us into Paradise by His mercy and grace! Indeed, the Holy Lord is the Most Beneficent, Most Merciful, Most Praiseworthy, Most Wise and Most Just. On the Day of Judgment: *The [pious] will exclaim: "All praise is due to God, Who has made His promise to us come true, and has bestowed upon us this expanse [of bliss] as our portion, so that we may dwell in Paradise as we please!"* [...] *And thou wilt see the angels surrounding the Throne of [God], extolling their Lord's glory and praise. And judgment will have been passed in justice on all, and the word will be spoken: "All praise is due to God, the Lord of the Worlds!"*[5]

[5] Q.XXXIX.74-75 (adapted from Muḥammad Asad's translation).

Bibliography

Abdul Aziz (tr.), Suraqah. *A Refined Explanation of the Sanusi Creed The Foundational Proofs*. Rotterdam: Sunni Publications, 2013. [=Foudah, Saᶜīd. *Tahdhīb sharḥ al-Sanūsiyya*.]

Abdus Salam (tr.), Muhammad Nur. *Al-Ghazzali on the Treatment of Hypocrisy* from the *Alchemy of Happiness*. Chicago: Great Books of the Islamic World, 2002.

Abisaab, Rula. *Converting Persia: Religion and Power in the Safavid Empire*. London: I. B. Tauris, 2004.

Abrahamov (tr.), Binyamin. *Ibn al-ᶜArabī's Fuṣūṣ al-Ḥikam: An Annotated Translation of 'The Bezels of Wisdom'*. London and New York: Routledge, 2015.

Abū Khaliyl (tr.). *English Translation of Jāmiᶜ at-Tirmidhī*. Riyadh: Darussalam Publications, 2007. [=Tirmidhī, Abū ᶜĪsā Muḥammad b. ᶜĪsā al-Sulamī al-. *Jāmiᶜ al-Tirmidhī*]

Abu-Rabiᶜ (ed.), Ibrahim M. *Theodicy and Justice in Modern Islamic Thought: The Case of Said Nursi*. Farnham: Ashgate Publishing, 2010.

Abū Rumaysah (tr.). *Characteristics of the Hypocrites*. Birmingham: Daar us-Sunnah Publishers, 2004. [=Ibn Qayyim al-Jawziyya, Abū ᶜAbd Allāh Shams al-Dīn Muḥammad b. Abī Bakr. *Madārij al-sālikīn bayn manāzil iyyāka naᶜbudu wa-iyyāka nastaᶜīn* (extract)]

Abū Zayd, Bakr b. ᶜAbd Allāh. *Ibn Qayyim al-Jawziyya: ḥayātuh āthāruh mawāriduh*. Riyadh: Dār al-ᶜĀṣimah, 1995.

Adams, Marilyn McCord. "The Problem of Hell: A Problem of Evil for Christians," in Eleonore Stump (ed.), *Reasoned Faith: Essays in Philosophical Theology in Honor of Norman Kretzmann*. Ithaca and London: Cornell University Press, 1993, pp. 301–327.

Adams, Marilyn McCord and Adams, Robert Merrihew (eds.). *The Problem of Evil*. Oxford: Oxford University Press, 1990.

Adams, Robert M. "Must God Create the Best?" *The Philosophical Review*, vol. LXXXI, no. 3, 1972, pp. 317–332.

Ahmad, Saiyad Fareed and Ahmad, Saiyad Salahuddin. *God, Islam, and the Skeptic Mind: A Study on Faith, Religious Diversity, Ethics, and the Problem of Evil*. Kuala Lampur: Blue Nile Publishing, 2004.

Akbas, Muhsin. *The Problem of Evil and Theodicy in Jewish, Christian and Islamic Thoughts*. Saarbrücken: Scholar's Press, 1999.

Aᶜẓamī, Muḥammad Muṣṭafā al-. *The History of the Qur'ānic Text from Revelation to Compilation: A Comparative Study with the Old and New Testaments*. Leicester: UK Islamic Academy, 2003.

Albānī, Muḥammad Nāṣir al-Dīn al-. *Silsilat al-aḥādīth al-ḍaᶜīfa wa'l-mawḍūᶜa wa-atharuhā al-sayyi' fi'l-umma*. Riyadh: Maktabat al-Maᶜārif, 1992.

———. *Silsilat al-aḥādīth al-ṣaḥīḥa wa-shay' min-fiqhhihā wa-fawā'idihā*. Riyadh: Maktabat al-Maᶜārif, 1995.

———. *Takhrīj aḥādīth faḍā'il al-Shām wa Dimashq li-Abī al-Haṣan al-Rabᶜī*. Riyadh: Maktabat al-Maᶜārif, 2000.

Ali, Abdullah Yusuf. *The Holy Qur'an: Text, Translation, and Commentary*. Lahore: Sheikh Muḥammad Ashraf Publishers, 1938.

ᶜAlī b. Abī Ṭalḥa. *Tafsīr Ibn ᶜAbbās al-musamma ṣaḥīfat ᶜAlī b. Abī Ṭalḥa*. Ed. Rāshid ᶜAbd al-Munᶜim al-Rajjāl. Beirut: Mu'assasat al-Kutub al-Thaqāfiyya, 1991.

Aligheri, Dante. *The Divine Comedy, Volume I: Inferno*. Tr. and ed. Mark Musa. New York: Penguin Books, 1984.

Ambrose, Stephen. *D-Day June 6, 1944: The Climactic Battle of World War II*. New York: Simon & Schuster, 1994.

ᶜĀmirī, Sāmī. *Mushkilat al-sharr wa wujūd Allāh: al-radd ᶜalā abraz shubhat min shubuhāt al-malāḥida*. London: Takween Studies and Research, 2016.

Anjum, Ovamir. "Sufism without Mysticism? Ibn Qayyim al-Ǧawziyyah's Objectives in *Madāriǧ al-Sālikīn*", in Caterina Bori and Livnat Holtzman (eds.), *A Scholar in the Shadow: Essays in the Legal and Theological Thought of Ibn al-Qayyim al-Ǧawziyyah* (Oriente Moderno XC, no. 1. Rome: Istituto per l'Oriente C. A. Nallino, 2010), pp. 161–188.

Aquinas, Thomas. *On Evil*. Tr. Richard Regan and ed. Brian Davies. Oxford: Oxford University Press, 2003.

Asad (tr.), Muḥammad. *The Message of the Qur'ān*. Bristol: The Book Foundation, 2003.

Aṣbahānī, Abū Nuᶜaym Aḥmad b. ᶜAbd Allāh al-. *Ḥilyat al-awliyā' wa-ṭabaqāt al-aṣfiyā'*. Beirut: Dār al-Kutub al-ᶜIlmiyyah, 1988.

Ashqar, ʿUmar Sulaymān ʿAbd Allāh al-. *Al-Maʿānī al-ḥisān fī tafsīr al-Qur'ān*. Amman: Dār al-Nafā'is, 2015.

ʿAsqalānī, Ibn Ḥajar al-. *Fatḥ al-Bārī sharḥ Ṣaḥīḥ al-Bukhārī*. Ed. Muḥibb al-Dīn al-Khaṭīb. Beirut: Dār al-Maʿrifa, 1960.

Augustine. *The City of God*. Tr. Marcus Dods. Peabody: Hendrickson Publishers, 2014.

Azami (tr.), Rashad Ahmad. *Stories of the Prophets*, Riyadh: Darussalam, 2003. [=Ibn Kathīr, Abū al-Fidā' Ismāʿīl ʿImād al-Dīn b. ʿUmar. *Al-Bidāya wa'l-nihāya* (extract)]

Azzam, Abdul Rahman. *Saladin: The Triumph of the Sunni Revival*. Cambridge: Islamic Texts Society, 2014.

ʿAbd al-Bāqī, Muḥammad Fu'ād. *Al-Muʿjam al-mufahras li-alfāẓ al-Qur'ān al-Karīm*. Beirut: Mu'assasat al-'Aʿlamī lil-Maṭbūʿāt, 1999.

Baghawī, al-Husayn b. Masʿūd b. Muḥammad al-Farrā' al-. *Tafsīr al-Baghawī*. Ed. ʿAbd al-Razzāq al-Mahdī. Beirut: Dār Iḥyā' al-Turāth al-ʿArabī, 1999.

Bayhaqī, Abū Bakr Aḥmad b. al-Ḥusayn al-. *Al-Asmā' wa'l-ṣifāt*. Ed. ʿAbd Allāh b. Muḥammad al-Ḥāshidī. Jeddah: Maktabat al-Suwādī, 1999.

———. *Shuʿab al-īmān*. Ed. ʿAbd al-ʿAliy ʿAbd al-Ḥamīd Ḥāmid. Riyadh: Maktabat al-Rushd, 2003.

———. *Al-Sunan al-kubrā li'l-Bayhaqī*. Ed. Muḥammad ʿAbd al-Qādir ʿAṭā'. Beirut: Dār al-Kutub al-ʿIlmiyyah, 2003.

Bell, Joseph N. *Love Theory in Later Ḥanbalite Islam*. Albany: State University of New York Press, 1979.

Bergmann, Michael. "Skeptical Theism and Rowe's New Evidential Argument from Evil", *Nous*, vol. XXXV, no. 2, 2001, pp. 278–296.

Bewley (tr.), Aisha. *Good and Evil*. London: Dar Al Taqwa, 1994. [=a work by Muḥammad Mitwallī al-Shaʿrāwī]

———(tr.). *Muhammad Messenger of Allah: Ash-Shifa of Qadi 'Iyad*, 2nd edition. Granada: Madinah Press, 1992.

———(tr.). *The Major Sins*. London: Dar Al Taqwa, 2012. [=Dhahabī, Shams al-Dīn al-. *Al-Kabā'ir*]

Buchman (tr.), David. *Al-Ghazālī: The Niche of Lights*. Provo: Brigham Young University Press, 1998. [=Ghazālī, Abū Ḥāmid Muḥammad b. Muḥammad al-. *Mishkāt al-anwār*]

Burrell, David B. *Deconstructing Theodicy: Why Job Has Nothing to Say to the Puzzle of Suffering*. Grand Rapids: Brazos Press, 2008.

Burrell, David B., and Daher, Nazih, (tr.) *The Ninety-Nine Beautiful Names of God*. Cambridge: Islamic Texts Society, 1995. [=Ghazālī, Abū Ḥāmid Muḥammad b. Muḥammad al-. *Al-Maqṣad al-asnā fī sharḥ asmā' Allāh al-ḥusnā*]

Chittick, William. *Ibn ʿArabī: Heir to the Prophets*. Oxford: Oneworld, 2007.

———. "Ibn ʿArabī", in Seyyed Hossein Nasr and Oliver Leaman (eds.), *History of Islamic Philosophy*. London: Routledge, 1996, pp. 497–509.

———. "Rūmī and *waḥdat al-wujūd*", in Amin Banani, Richard Hovannisian and Georges Sabagh (eds.), *The Heritage of Rumi*. New York: Cambridge University Press, 1994.

———. *The Self-Disclosure of God: Principles of Ibn al-ʿArabī's Cosmology*. Albany: State University of New York Press, 1998.

———. *The Sufi Path of Knowledge: Ibn Al-ʿArabi's Metaphysics of Imagination*. Albany: State University of New York Press, 1989.

Clarke (tr.), Abdassamad. *The History of the Khalifahs who took the right way*. London: Ta-Ha Publishers, 1995. [=Suyūṭī, Jalal al-Dīn al-. *Tārīkh al-Khulafā'* (extract)]

Coban, Izzet. "Nursi on Theodicy: A New Theological Perspective", in Anna-Teresa Tymieniecka and Nazif Muhtaroglu (eds.), *Classical Issues in Islamic Philosophy and Theology Today*. New York: Springer, 2010.

Confucius. *The Analects*. Tr. D. C. Lau. New York: Penguin Books, 1979.

Cowan (ed.), J. M. *The Hans Wehr Dictionary of Modern Written Arabic*. Urbana: Spoken Language Services, 1994.

Crisp, Roger and Cowton, Christopher. "Hypocrisy and Moral Seriousness", *American Philosophical Quarterly*, vol. XXXI, no. 4, 1994, pp. 343–349.

Dabashi, Hamid. "Khwājah Naṣīr al-Dīn al-Ṭūṣī: the philosopher/vizier and the intellectual climate of his times", in Seyyed Hossein Nasr and Oliver Leaman (eds.), *History of Islamic Philosophy*. London and New York: Routledge, 1996.

Daftary, Farhad. *A History of Shiʿi Islam*. London: I. B. Tauris and The Institute of Ismaili Studies, 2013.

———. *The Ismāʿīlīs: Their History and Doctrines*. New York: Cambridge University Press, 2007.

Daftary, Farhad and Miskinzoda, Gurdofarid, (eds.). *The Study of Shiʿi Islam: History, Theology and Law*. London: I. B. Tauris and The Institute of Ismaili Studies, 2014.

Dakake, Maria Massi. "Writing and Resistance: The Transmission of Religious Knowledge in Early Shiʿism", in Farhad Daftary and Gurdofarid Miskinzoda (eds.), *The Study of Shiʿi Islam: History, Theology and Law*. London: I. B. Tauris and The Institute of Ismaili Studies, 2014.

Dārimī, Abū Muḥammad ʿAbd Allāh b. ʿAbd al-Raḥmān al-. *Sunan al-Dārimī*. Ed. Ḥusayn Salīm Asad al-Dārānī. Riyadh: Dār al-Mughnī, 2000.

Dawkins, Richard. *The God Delusion*. New York: Houghton Mifflin, 2006.

Dhahabī, Abū ʿAbd Allāh Shams al-Dīn Muḥammad b. Aḥmad al. *Siyar aʿlām al-nubalā'*. Editor-in-Chief Shuʿayb al-Arna'ūṭ. Beirut: Mu'assasat al-Risāla, 1985.

Dostoevsky, Fyodor. *The Brothers Karamazov*. Tr. Pevear, Richard and Volokhonsky, Larissa. New York: Farrar, Straus and Giroux, 1990.

Ehrman, Bart. *God's Problem: How the Bible Fails to Answer Our Most Important Question—Why We Suffer*. New York: HarperOne, 2008.

———. *How Jesus Became God: The Exaltation of a Jewish Preacher from Galilee*. New York: HarperOne, 2014.

———. *Jesus, Interrupted: Revealing the Hidden Contradictions in the Bible (and Why We Don't Know About Them)*. New York: HarperOne, 2009.

———. *Misquoting Jesus: The Story Behind Who Changed the Bible and Why*. New York: HarperOne, 2005.

Elkaisy-Firemuth, Maha. *God and Humans in Islamic Thought: ʿAbd al-Jabbār, Ibn Sīna, and al-Ghazālī*. New York: Routledge, 2006.

Evans, Gillian R. *Augustine on Evil*. Cambridge: Cambridge University Press, 1982.

Fitzgerald, Michael Abdurrahman, and Slitine, Moulay Youssef, (tr.) *Ibn Qayyim al-Jawziyya on The Invocation of God*. Cambridge: Islamic

Texts Society, 2000. [=Ibn Qayyim al-Jawziyya, Abū ʿAbd Allāh Shams al-Dīn Muḥammad b. Abī Bakr. *al-Wābil al-ṣayyib min al-kalim al-ṭayyib* (extract)]

Flew, Antony and Varhese, Roy Abraham. *There is a God: How the World's Most Notorious Atheist Changed His Mind*. New York: Harper One, 2007.

Freedman, Lawrence. *Strategy: A History*. Oxford: Oxford University Press, 2013.

Ghazālī, Abū Ḥāmid Muḥammad b. Muḥammad al-. *Iḥyā' ʿulūm al-dīn*. Beirut: Dār Ṣādir, 2010.

Gleick, James. *Chaos: Making a New Science*. New York: Penguin Books, 1987.

Grant, Ruth W. *Hypocrisy and Integrity: Machiavelli, Rousseau, and the Ethics of Politics*. Chicago: The University of Chicago Press, 1997.

Greene, Brian. *The Elegant Universe: Superstrings, Hidden Dimensions, and the Quest for the Ultimate Theory*. New York: Vintage Books, 2000.

Griffin, David Ray. *God, Power, and Evil: A Process Theodicy*. Philadelphia: Westminster Press, 1976.

Ḥākim, Abū ʿAbd Allāh Muḥammad b. ʿAbd Allāh al-. *Al-Mustadrak ʿalā al-Ṣaḥīḥayn li'l-Ḥākim*. Ed. Muṣṭafā ʿAbd al-Qādir ʿAṭā'. Beirut: Dār al-Kutub al-ʿIlmiyyah, 1990.

Hallaq, Wael. *Ibn Taymiyya against the Greek Logicians*. Oxford: Clarendon Press, 1993.

Harris, Sam. *The End of Faith: Religion, Terror, and the Future of Reason*. New York: W. W. Norton & Company, 2004.

Hart, Michael H. *The 100: A Ranking of the Most Influential Persons in History*. New York: Citadel Press, 1978.

Hasker, William. "God and Gratuitous Evil", in Michael Peterson (ed.), *The Problem of Evil*. Notre Dame: University of Notre Dame Press, 2017, pp. 473–487.

Hasler, August Bernhard. *How the Pope Became Infallible: Pius IX and the Politics of Persuasion*. Tr. Peter Heinegg. Garden City: Doubleday & Company, 1981.

Haythamī, Abū al-Ḥasan Nūr al-Dīn ʿAlī al-. *Majmaʿ al-zawā'id wa-manbaʿ al-fawā'id*. Ed. Ḥusām al-Dīn al-Qudsī. Cairo: Maktabat al-Qudsī, 1994.

Hecht, Jennifer Michael. *Doubt: A History: The Great Doubters and Their Legacy of Innovation from Socrates and Jesus to Thomas Jefferson and Emily Dickinson*. New York: Harper One, 2003.

Hegel, G. W. F. *Philosophy of Right*. Tr. S. W. Dyde. Kitchener: Batoche Books, 2001.

Herman, Arthur L. *The Problem of Evil and Indian Thought*. Delhi: Motilal Banarsidass, 1976.

Hick, John. *Death and Eternal Life*. London: William Collins Sons & Co., 1976.

———. *Evil and the God of Love*. New York: Palgrave Macmillan, 2010 (First Edition 1966).

———. "An Irenaean Theodicy", in Stephen T. David (ed.), *Encountering Evil: Live Options in Theodicy*. Louisville: Westminster John Knox Press, 2001, pp. 38–72.

———. "Soul-Making and Suffering", in Marilyn McCord Adams and Robert Merrihew Adams (eds.), *The Problem of Evil*. Oxford: Oxford University Press, 1990.

Holtzman, Livnat. "Ibn Qayyim al-Jawziyyah", in Joseph E. Lowery and Devin Stewart (eds.), *Essays in Arabic Literary Biography II:* 1350–1850. Wiesbaden: Harrassowitz Verlag, 2009, pp. 202–222.

Hoover, Jon. *Ibn Taymiyya's Theodicy of Perpetual Optimism*. Leiden: Brill, 2007.

———. "Against Islamic Universalism", in Birgit Krawietz and Georges Tamer (eds.) *Islamic Theology, Philosophy and Law: Debating Ibn Taymiyya and Ibn Qayyim al-Jawziyya*. Berlin: De Gruyter, 2013.

———. "A Typology of Responses to the Philosophical Problem of Evil in the Islamic and Christian Traditions", *The Conrad Grebel Review*, vol. XXI, no. 3, 2003(Fall), pp. 81–96.

———. "God's Wise Purposes in Creating Iblīs: Ibn Qayyim al-Ǧawziyyah's Theodicy of God's Names and Attributes", in Caterina Bori and Livnat Holtzman (eds.), *A Scholar in the Shadow: Essays in the Legal and Theological Thought of Ibn al-Qayyim al-Ǧawziyyah* (Oriente Moderno XC, no. 1. Rome: Istituto per l'Oriente C. A. Nallino, 2010), pp. 113–134.

Hourani, George. "Averroes on Good and Evil", *Studia Islamica*, vol. XVI, 1962, pp. 13–40.

Hume, David. *Dialogues Concerning Natural Religion*. Ed. Richard H. Popkin. Indianapolis/Cambridge: Hackett Publishing Company, 1980.

Ibn ʿAbd al-Barr, Abū ʿUmar Yūsuf b. ʿAbd Allāh b. Muḥammad. *Jāmiʿ bayān al-ʿilm wa-faḍlih*. Ed. Abū al-Ashbāl al-Zuhayrī. Dammam: Dār Ibn al-Jawzī, 1994.

Ibn ʿArabī, Muḥyī al-Dīn Muḥammad b. ʿAlī. *Al-Futūḥāt al-Makkiyya*. Ed. Aḥmad Shams al-Dīn. Beirut: Dār al-Kutub al-ʿIlmiyya, 1999.

Ibn Ḥanbal, Abū ʿAbd Allāh Aḥmad b. Muḥammad. *Musnad al-Imam Aḥmad*. Eds. Shuʿayb al-Arna'ūṭ and ʿĀdil Murshid. Beirut: Mu'assasat al-Risāla, 2001.

———. *Al-Radd ʿalā'l-zanādiqa wa'l-Jahmiyya*. Ed. Daghash b. Shabīb al-ʿAjamī. Kuwait City: Ghirās, 2005.

Ibn Ḥazm, Abū Muḥammad ʿAlī b. Aḥmad b. ʿAbd Allāh b. Saʿīd. *Asmā' al-Ṣaḥāba al-ruwāt wa-ma li-kulli waḥid min al-ʿadad*. Beirut: Dār al-Kutub al-ʿIlmiyya, 1992.

Ibn Ḥibbān, Abū Ḥātim Muḥammad. *Ṣaḥīḥ Ibn Ḥibbān*. Ed. Shuʿayb al-Arna'ūṭ. Beirut: Mu'assasat al-Risāla, 1988.

Ibn Ḥibbān, Abū Ḥātim Muḥammad, and Albānī, Muḥammad Nāṣir al-Dīn al-. *Al-Taʿlīqāt al-ḥisan ʿalā Ṣaḥīḥ Ibn Ḥibbān*. Jeddah: Dār Bawzīr, 2003.

Ibn Kathīr, Abū al-Fidā' Ismāʿīl ʿImād al-Dīn b. ʿUmar. *Al-Bidāya wa'l-nihāya*. Damascus: Dār al-Fikr, 1986.

Ibn Māja, Abū ʿAbd Allāh Muḥammad b. Yazīd, and Albānī, Muḥammad Nāṣir al-Dīn al-. *Ṣaḥīḥ Sunan Ibn Māja/Ḍaʿīf Sunan Ibn Māja*. Riyadh: Maktabat al-Maʿārif, 1997.

Ibn Qayyim al-Jawziyya, Abū ʿAbd Allāh Shams al-Dīn Muḥammad b. Abī Bakr. *Badā'ʿ al-fawā'id*. Beirut: Dār al-Kutub al-ʿArabī, 2010.

———. *Ḥādī al-arwāḥ ilā-bilād al-afrāḥ*. Ed. Zā'id b. Aḥmad al-Nushayrī. Mecca: Dār ʿĀlam al-Fawā'id, 2007.

———. *Ighāthat al-lahfān min maṣāyid al-Shayṭān*. Ed. Muḥammad ʿUzayr Shams and Muṣṭafā b. Saʿīd Ītīm. Mecca: Dār ʿĀlam al-Fawā'id, 2011.

———. *Ijtimāʿ al-juyūsh al-Islāmiyya ʿalā ḥarb al-Muʿaṭṭila wa'l-Jahmiyya*. Ed. Zā'id b. Aḥmad al-Nushayrī. Mecca: Dār ʿĀlam al-Fawā'id, 2009.

———. *Iʿlām al-muwaqqiʿīn ʿan-Rabb al-ʿĀlamīn*. Beirut: Dār al-Kitāb al-ʿArabī, 2006.

———. *Madārij al-sālikīn bayn manāzil iyyāka naʿbudu wa-iyyāka nastaʿīn*. Beirut: Dār al-Kitāb al-ʿArabī, 1996.

———. *Miftāḥ dār al-saʿāda wa-manshūr wilāyat al-ʿilm wa'l-irāda*. Ed. ʿAbd al-Raḥmān b. Ḥasan b. Qā'id. Mecca: Dār ʿĀlam al-Fawā'id, 2015.

———. *Miftāḥ dār al-saʿāda wa-manshūr wilāyat al-ʿilm wa'l-irāda*. Ed. Sayyid b. Ibrāhīm b. Ṣādiq ʿImrān and ʿAlī Muḥammad. Cairo: Dār al-Ḥadīth, 1994.

———. *Mukhtaṣar al-Ṣawāʿiq al-mursala ʿalā'l-Jahmiyya wa'l-Muʿaṭṭila*, abridged by al-Mawṣilī, Muḥammad. Ed. al-ʿAlawī, al-Ḥasan b. ʿAbd al-Raḥmān. Beirut: Dār al-Kutub al-ʿIlmiyyah, 1993.

———. *Shifā' al-ʿalīl fi-masā'il al-qaḍā' wa'l-qadar wa'l-ḥikma wa'l-taʿlīl*. Ed. Aḥmad b. Ṣāliḥ b. ʿAlī al-Ṣamʿānī and ʿAlī b. Muḥammad b. ʿAbd Allāh al-ʿAjlān. Riyadh: Dār al-Ṣamayʿī, 2013.

———. *Ṭarīq al-hijratayn wa-bāb al-saʿādatayn*. Ed. Muḥammad Ajmal al-Iṣlāḥī. Mecca: Dār ʿĀlam al-Fawā'id, 2008.

———. *Al-Wābil al-ṣayyib wa rāfiʿ al-kalim al-ṭayyib*. Ed. ʿAbd al-Raḥmān b. Ḥasan b. Qā'id. Mecca: Dār ʿĀlam al-Fawā'id, 2013.

———. *Zād al-maʿād fī hady khayr al-ʿibād*. Beirut: Mu'assasat al-Risāla, 1994.

Ibn Rajab, Zayn al-Dīn ʿAbd al-Raḥmān. *Dhayl ṭabaqāt al-Ḥanābila*. Ed. ʿAbd al-Raḥmān b. Sulaymān al-ʿUthaymīn. Riyadh: Maktabat al-ʿUbaykān, 2005.

Ibn Taymiyya, Taqī al-Dīn Aḥmad b. ʿAbd al-Ḥalīm. *Majmūʿ al-fatāwā*. Ed. ʿAbd al-Raḥmān b. Muḥammad b. Qāsim. Medina: Mujammaʿ al-Malik Fahd li-Ṭibāʿat al-Muṣḥaf al-Sharīf, 1995.

———. *Dar' taʿāruḍ al-ʿaql wa'l-naql*. Ed. ʿAbd al-Laṭīf ʿAbd al-Raḥmān. Beirut: Dār al-Kutub al-ʿIlmiyyah, 2009.

———. *Al-Furqān bayna awliyā' al-Raḥmān wa awliyā' al-Shayṭān*. Ed. ʿAbd al-Qādir Arna'ūṭ. Damascus: Makatibat Dār al-Bayān, 1985.

———. *Al-Jawāb al-ṣaḥīḥ li-man baddala dīn al-Masīḥ*. Ed. Safar b. ʿAbd al-Raḥmān al-Ḥawālī. Riyadh: Maktabat al-Malik Fahd al-Waṭaniyya, 2011.

———. *Majmūʿat al-rasā'il wa'l-masā'il li-Ibn Taymiyya*. Ed. Rashīd Riḍā. Cairo: Lajnat al-Turāth al-ʿArabī, 1976.

———. *Minhāj al-Sunna al-Nabawiyya fī naqd kalām al-Shīʿa wa'l-Qadariyya*. Ed. Muḥammad Rashād Salām. Riyadh: Jāmiʿat al-Imām Muḥammad b Saʿūd al-Islāmiyya, 1986.

———. *Al-Radd ʿalā'l-manṭiqiyyīn*. Beirut: Dār al-Maʿrifa, 2010.

———. *Al-Radd ʿalā man qāl bi-fanā' al-janna wa'l-nār*. Ed. Muḥammad b. ʿAbd Allāh al-Samharī. Riyadh: Dār Balancia, 1995.

———. *Risāla fī maʿnā kawn al-Rabb ʿādilan wa fī tanzīhihi ʿan al-ẓulm* in *Jāmiʿ al-rasā'il li-Ibn Taymiyya*. Ed. Muḥammad Rashād Sālim. Riyadh: Dār al-ʿAṭā', 2001.

Ibn Warraq. *Why I am not a Muslim*. Amherst: Prometheus Books, 2003.

Inati, Shams. *The Problem of Evil: Ibn Sīna's Theodicy*. Binghampton: Globe Publications, 2000.

Inwagen, Peter van. *The Problem of Evil: The Gifford Lectures delivered in the University of St. Andrews in 2003*. Oxford: Oxford University Press, 2006.

———. "The Problem of Evil, the Problem of Air, and the Problem of Silence", in James E. Tomberlin (ed.), *Philosophical Perspectives: vol. 5, Philosophy of Religion*. Atascadero: Ridgeview, 1991, pp. 135-65.

ʿIzz, Ṣadr al-Dīn Muḥammad b. Abī al-. *Sharḥ al-ʿAqīda al-Ṭaḥāwiyya*. Beirut: al-Maktab al-Islāmī, 1984.

Jackson, Sherman. *Islam and the Problem of Black Suffering*. Oxford: Oxford University Press, 2009.

Jayatilleke, K. N. *The Message of the Buddha*. Ed. Ninian Smart. New York: The Free Press, 1975.

Journet, Charles. *The Meaning of Evil*. Tr. Michael Barry. London: Geoffrey Chapman, 1963.

Kalin, Ibrahim. "Mullā Ṣadrā on Theodicy and the Best of All Possible Worlds", *Journal of Islamic Studies*, vol. XVIII, no. 2, 2007, pp. 183–201.

Karmānī, Ḥarb b. Ismāʿīl b. Khalaf al-. *Masā'il Ḥarb: al-nikāḥ ila niyāyat al-kitāb*. Ed. Fāyiz Aḥmad b. Ḥāmid Ḥābis. Mecca: Jāmiʿat Umm al-Qurā, 2001.

Kates, Carol A. "A Nietzschean Theodicy", *International Journal for Philosophy of Religion*, vol. LV, 2004, pp. 69–82.

Keller (tr.), Nuh Ha Mim. *The Reliance of the Traveller: A Classic Manual of Islamic Sacred Law*. Beltsville: Amana Publications, 1994. [=Ahmad ibn Naqib al-Misri, *ʿUmdat al-sālik*]

Khalil, Mohammad. *Islam and the Fate of Others: The Salvation Question*. Oxford: Oxford University Press, 2012.

Khān (tr.), Muḥammad Muḥsin. *The Translation of the Meaning of Ṣaḥīḥ al-Bukhārī*. Riyadh: Darussalam Publications, 1997. [=Bukhārī, Abū ʿAbd Allāh Muḥammad b. Ismāʿīl al-. *Ṣaḥīḥ al-Bukhārī*]

Khaṭṭāb (tr.), Nāṣiruddīn, al-. *Ali ibn Abi Tālib*. Riyadh: International Islamic Publishing House, 2010. [=a work by Ali M. Sallabi]

——— (tr.). *English Translation of Ṣaḥīḥ Muslim*. Riyadh: Darussalam Publications, 2007. [=Naysāpūrī, Abū al-Ḥusayn Muslim b. al-Ḥajjāj, al-. *Ṣaḥīḥ Muslim*]

——— (tr.). *English Translation of Sunan Abu Dawud*. Riyadh: Darussalam Publications, 2008. [=Sijistānī, Abū Dāwūd Sulaymān b. al-Ashʿath al-Azdī al-. *Sunan Abī Dāwūd*]

———(tr.). *English Translation of Sunan Ibn Mājah*. Riyadh: Darussalam Publications, 2007. [=Ibn Māja, Abū ʿAbd Allāh Muḥammad b. Yazīd. *Sunan Ibn Māja*]

———(tr.). *English Translation of Sunan an-Nasā'ī*. Riyadh: Darussalam Publications, 2007. [=Nasā'ī, Abū ʿAbd al-Raḥmān Aḥmad b. Shuʿayb al-. *Sunan al-Nasā'ī*]

——— (tr.). *The Biography of ʿUthman ibn ʿAffān Dhun-Noorayn*. Riyadh: International Islamic Publishing House, 2007.

King, William. *Essay on the Origin of Evil*. New York: Garland Publishing, 1978.

Knysh, Alexander D. *Ibn ʿArabi in the Later Islamic Traditions: The Making of a Polemical Image in Medieval Islam*. New York: SUNY Press, 1998.

Koslowski (ed.), Peter. *The Origin and the Overcoming of Evil and Suffering in the World Religions*. Dordrecht: Kluwer Academic Publishers, 2001.

Krawietz, Birgit, and Tamer, Georges, (eds.). *Islamic Theology, Philosophy and Law: Debating Ibn Taymiyya and Ibn Qayyim al-Jawziyya*. Berlin: De Gruyter, 2013.

Leaman, Oliver. *Evil and Suffering in Jewish Philosophy*. Cambridge: Cambridge University Press, 1995.

Leibniz, Gottfried. *The Theodicy*, in George Duncan (tr.), *The Philosophical Works of Leibniz*. New Haven: Tuttle, Morehouse, & Taylor, 1890, pp. 194–204.

———. *Discourse on Metaphysics: Correspondence with Arnauld and Monadology*. Tr. George Montgomery. Chicago: The Open Court Publishing Company, 1902.

Lott, Jeremy. *In Defense of Hypocrisy: Picking Sides in the War on Virtue*. Nashville: Nelson Current, 2006.

Lucas (tr.), Scott. *Ṭabarī Selections from The Comprehensive Exposition of the Interpretation of the Verses of the Qur'ān*. Cambridge: The Royal Aal Al-Bayt Institute for Islamic Thought and Islamic Texts Society, 2017.

Mackie, J. L. "Evil and Omnipotence", *Mind*, vol. LXIV, no. 254, 1955 (April), pp. 200–212.

Madelung, Wilferd. "Early Imāmī Theology as Reflected in the *Kitāb al-kāfī* of al-Kulaynī", in Farhad Daftary and Gurdofarid Miskinzoda (eds.), *The Study of Shiʿi Islam: History, Theology and Law*. London: I. B. Tauris and The Institute of Ismaili Studies, 2014.

Mālik b. Anas. *Muwaṭṭa' al-Imām Mālik*. Ed. Muḥammad Fu'ād ʿAbd al-Bāqī. Beirut: Dār Iḥyā' al-Turāth al-ʿArabī, 1985.

Maqsood, Ruqaiyyah Waris. *The Problem of Evil* (*A Study of Evil, Fate, Freewill and Predestination, Forgiveness, and Love*). New Delhi: Adam Publishers and Distributors, 2003.

Marmura, Michael E. *The Metaphysics of the Healing*. Provo: Brigham Young University Press, 2005.

———(tr.). *The Incoherence of the Philosophers*. Provo: Brigham Young University Press, 2000. [=Ghazālī, Abū Ḥāmid Muḥammad b. Muḥammad al-. *Tahāfut al-falāsifa*.]

Martin, Michael. *The Case Against Christianity*. Philadelphia: Temple University Press, 1991.

Matthee, Rudi. *Persian in Crisis: Safavid Decline and the Fall of Isfahan*. London: I. B. Tauris, 2012.

Mayne (tr.), Ethel C. *Letters of Fyodor Michailovitch Dostoevsky to his Family and Friends*. London: Chatto & Windus, 1914.

McCarthy (tr.), Richard Joseph. *Deliverance from Error: An Annotated Translation of al-Munqidh min al-ḍalāl and other Relevant Works of Al-Ghazālī*. Louisville: Fons Vitae, 1980.

McGrath, Alister. *The Twilight of Atheism: The Rise and Fall of Disbelief in the Modern World*. New York: Galilee and Doubleday, 2006.

Meisami, Sayeh. *Mulla Sadra*. London: Oneworld Publications, 2013.

Meister, Chad. *Evil: A Guide for the Perplexed*. New York: Bloomsbury, 2018.

Meister, Chad and Moser, Paul K., (eds.). *The Cambridge Companion to the Problem of Evil*. New York: Cambridge University Press, 2017.

Mervin, Sabrina. "ᶜĀshūrā' Rituals, Identity and Politics: A Comparative Approach (Lebanon and India)", in Farhad Daftary and Gurdofarid Miskinzoda (eds.), *The Study of Shiᶜi Islam: History, Theology and Law*. London: I. B. Tauris and The Institute of Ismaili Studies, 2014.

Mill, John Stuart. "The Philosophy of the Conditioned as Applied by Mr. Mansel to the Limits of Religious Thought", in J. M. Robson (ed.), *Collected Works of John Stuart Mill.* Toronto: University of Toronto Press, 1979.

Mitchell, Colin P. *The Practice of Politics in Safavid Iran: Power, Religion and Rhetoric.* London: Tauris Academic Studies, 2009.

Mohammadi (tr.), Mohammad. *The History of the Four Caliphs*. London: Turath Publishing, 2012. [=a work by Muḥammad al-Khuḍrī Bak al-Bājūrī]

Muhajirani, Abbas. "Twelve-Imām Shi'ite theological and philosophical thought", in Seyyed Hossein Nasr and Oliver Leaman (eds.), *History of Islamic Philosophy*. London and New York: Routledge, 1996.

Mundhirī, Abū Muḥammad ᶜAbd al-ᶜAẓīm b. ᶜAbd al-Qawī al-. *Al-Targhīb wa'l-tarhīb min al-Ḥadīth al-sharīf.* Ed. Ibrāhīm Shams al-Dīn. Beirut: Dār al-Kutub al-ᶜIlmiyyah, 1996.

Mundhirī, Abū Muḥammad ᶜAbd al-ᶜAẓīm b. ᶜAbd al-Qawī al-, and Albānī, Muḥammad Nāṣir al-Dīn al-. *Ṣaḥīḥ al-Targhīb wa'l-tarhīb/ Ḍaᶜīf al-Targhīb wa'l-tarhīb*. Riyadh: Maktabat al-Maᶜārif, 2000.

Mustafa, Abdul-Rahman. *On Taqlīd: Ibn al-Qayyim's Critique of Authority in Islamic Law*. New York: Oxford University Press, 2013.

Nadler, Steven. *The Best of All Possible Worlds: A Story of Philosophers, God, and Evil in the Age of Reason*. Princeton: Princeton University Press, 2010 (First Edition 2008).

Nasā'ī, Abū ᶜAbd al-Raḥmān Aḥmad b. Shuᶜayb al-, and Albānī, Muḥammad Nāṣir al-Dīn al-. *Ṣaḥīḥ Sunan al-Nasā'ī/Ḍaᶜīf Sunan al-Nasā'ī*. Riyadh: Maktabat al-Maᶜārif, 1999.

Nasr (tr.), Seyyed Hossein. *Shi'ite Islam*. Albany: State University of New York Press, 1975. [=a work by Sayyid Muḥammad Ḥusayn Ṭabāṭabā'ī]

Nasr, Seyyed Hossein and Dabashi, Hamid and Nasr, Seyyid Vali Reza, (eds.). *Shiʿism: Doctrines, Thought, and Spirituality*. Albany: State University of New York Press, 1988.

Newman, Andrew. *Safavid Iran: Rebirth of a Persian Empire*. London: I. B. Tauris, 2009.

Nietzsche, Friedrich. *Beyond Good and Evil: Prelude to a Philosophy of the Future*. Tr. Marion Faber. Oxford: Oxford University Press, 1998.

Onfray, Michel. *Atheist Manifesto: The Case Against Christianity, Judaism, and Islam*. Tr. Jeremy Leggatt. New York: Arcade Publishing, 2007.

Ormsby, Eric. *Theodicy in Islamic Thought: The Dispute over al-Ghazālī's "Best of All Possible Worlds"*. Princeton: Princeton University Press, 1984.

Outler (tr.), Albert C. *Augustine: Confessions and Enchiridion*. Philadelphia: The Westminster Press, 1955.

Ozkan, Tubanur Yesilhark. *A Muslim Response to Evil: Said Nursi on the Theodicy*. Farnham: Ashgate Publishing, 2015.

Paine, Thomas, *The Age of Reason*. London: Freethought Publishing, 1880.

Pavlin, James. "Sunni *Kalām* and Theological Controversies", in Seyyed Hossein Nasr and Oliver Leaman (eds.), *History of Islamic Philosophy*. London: Routledge, 1996, pp. 105–118.

Peterson, Michael L. *God and Evil: An Introduction to the Issues*. Boulder: Westview Press, 1998.

——— (ed.). *The Problem of Evil*. Notre Dame: University of Notre Dame Press, 2017.

Peterson, Michael L and VanArragon, Raymond J (eds.). *Contemporary Debates in the Philosophy of Religion*. Malden: Blackwell Publishing, 2004.

Pickthall (tr.), Muḥammad Marmaduke. *The Meaning of the Glorious Qur'an*. London: Allen & Unwin, 1976.

Plantiga, Alvin. *God, Freedom, and Evil*. Grand Rapids: William B. Eerdmans Publishing, 1974.

———. "Self Profile", in James E. Tomberlin and Peter van Inwagen (eds.), *Profiles: Alvin Plantiga*. Dordrecht: D. Reidel Publishing, 1985.

———. "Supralapsarianism, or 'O Felix Culpa'", in Peter van Inwagen (ed.), *Christian Faith and the Problem of Evil*. Grand Rapids: Eerdmans, 2004, pp. 1-25.

Pope, Alexander. *Alexander Pope: The Major Works*. Ed. Pat Rogers. Oxford: Oxford University Press, 2006.

Powell, Mark E. *Papal Infallibility: A Protestant Evaluation of an Ecumenical Issue*. Grand Rapids: William B. Eerdmans Publishing, 2009.

Power, Samantha. *"A Problem from Hell": America and the Age of Genocide*. New York: Harper Perennial, 2002.

Publisher (ed. and tr.) *Provisions for the Hereafter* (*Mukhtaṣar Zād al-Maᶜād*). Riyadh: Darussalam, 2003. [Ibn Qayyim al-Jawziyya and At-Tamimi, Muḥammad ibn Abdul Wahhab. *Zād al-maᶜād*]

Publisher (tr.) *The Names and Attributes of God According to the Doctrine of Ahl-us-Sunnah wal Jamaᶜah*. Suffolk: Jamᶜiat Ihyaa' Minhaaj Al-Sunnah, 1999. [=a work by ᶜUmar Sulaiman al-Ashqar]

Publisher (tr.). *The Sealed Nectar: Biography of the Noble Prophet*. Riyadh: Darussalam, 2011. [=Mubarakpuri, Safiur-Rahman al-. *Al-Raḥīq al-makhtūm*]

Qadhi, Yasir. "The *'Unleashed Thunderbolts'* of Ibn Qayyim al-Ǧawziyyah: An Introductory Essay", in Caterina Bori and Livnat Holtzman (eds.), *A Scholar in the Shadow: Essays in the Legal and Theological Thought of Ibn al-Qayyim al-Ǧawziyyah* (Oriente Moderno XC, no. 1. Rome: Istituto per l'Oriente C. A. Nallino, 2010), pp. 135–149.

Quinn, Philip L. "God, Moral Perfection, and Possible Worlds", in Frederick Sontag and M. Darrol Bryant (eds.), *God: A Contemporary Discussion*. New York: Rose of Sharon Press, 1982, pp. 199–215.

Ratzinger, Joseph. *Eschatology: Death and Eternal Life*. Tr. Michael Waldstein and ed. Aidan Nickols. Washington, D.C.: The Catholic University of American Press, 1988.

Rāzī, Muḥammad b. ᶜUmar Fakhr al-Dīn al-. *Al-Arbaᶜīn fī uṣūl al-dīn*. Beirut: Dār al-Kutub al-ᶜIlmiyyah, 2009.

———. *al-Mubāḥith al-mashriqiyya fī ᶜilm al-ilāhiyyāt wa'l-ṭabīᶜiyyāt*. Qom: Intishārāt Bīdār, 1950.

———. *Tafsīr al-Rāzī* or *al-Tafsīr al-kabīr* or *Mafātīḥ al-ghayb*. Beirut: Dār Iḥyā' al-Turāth al-ᶜArabī, 1999.

Rapoport, Yossef and Ahmed, Shahab, (eds.). *Ibn Taymiyya and his Times*. Karachi: Oxford University Press, 2010.

Rees, Martin. *Just Six Numbers: The Deep Forces That Shape the Universe*. New York: Basic Books, 2001.

Riḍā, Muḥammad Rashīd. *Rasā'il al-Sunna wa'l-Shīᶜa*. Cairo: Dār al-Manār, 1947.

Rowe (ed.), William. *God and the Problem of Evil*. Maiden: Blackwell Publishing, 2001.

Rowe, William L. "Evil and Theodicy", *Philosophical Topics*, vol. XVI, no. 2, 1988, pp. 119–132.

———. "The Problem of Evil and Some Varieties of Atheism", *American Philosophical Quarterly*, vol. XVI, no. 4, 1979 (Oct.), pp. 335–341.

Rudolph, Ulrich. "Occasionalism", in Sabine Schmidtke (ed.), *The Oxford Handbook of Islamic Theology*. Oxford: Oxford University Press, 2016, pp. 347–363.

Saᶜdī, ᶜAbd al-Raḥmān b. Nāṣir b. ᶜAbd Allāh al-. *Tafsīr al-Saᶜdī: Taysīr al-Karīm al-Raḥmān fī Tafsīr kalām al-Mannān*. Cairo: Dār Ibn Ḥazm, 2012.

Ṣanᶜānī, Muḥammad al-. *Rafᶜ al-astār li-ibṭāl adillat al-qā'ilīn bi-fanā' al-nār*. Ed. Muḥammad Nāṣir al-Dīn al-Albānī. Beirut: al-Maktab al-Islāmī, 1984.

Schmidtke (ed.), Sabine. *The Oxford Handbook of Islamic Theology*. Oxford: Oxford University Press, 2016.

Schniedewind, William M. *How the Bible Became a Book: The Textualization of Ancient Israel*. Cambridge: Cambridge University Press, 2004.

Scott, Mark S.M. *Pathways in Theodicy*. Minneapolis: Fortress Press, 2015.

Shah, Muhammad Maroof. *Problem of Evil in Muslim Philosophy: A Case Study of Iqbal*. Delhi: Indian Publishers' Distributors, 2007.

Shihadeh, Ayman. "Avicenna's Theodicy and Rāzī's Anti-Theodicy", *Intellectual History of the Islamicate World*, vol. VII, 2019 (Jan.), pp. 61–84.

———. "Theories of Ethical Value in Kalām: A New Interpretation", in Sabine Schmidtke (ed.), *The Oxford Handbook of Islamic Theology*. Oxford: Oxford University Press, 2016, pp. 384–407.

———. *The Teleological Ethics of Fakhr al-Dīn al-Rāzī*. Leiden: Brill, 2006.

Sijistānī, Abū Dāwūd Sulaymān b. al-Ashʿath al-Azdī al-, and Albānī, Muḥammad Nāṣir al-Dīn al-. *Ṣaḥīḥ Sunan Abī Dāwūd/Ḍaʿīf Sunan Abī Dāwūd*. Riyadh: Maktabat al-Maʿārif, 1998.

Sorensen, Roy. *A Brief History of the Paradox: Philosophy and the Labyrinths of the Mind*. Oxford: Oxford University Press, 2003.

Speak, Daniel. *The Problem of Evil*. Malden: Polity Press, 2015.

Spencer, Robert. *The Truth about Muhammad: Founder of the World's Most Intolerant Religion*. Washington, DC: Regnery Publishing, 2006.

Spiegel, James S. *Hypocrisy: Moral Fraud and Other Vices*. Grand Rapids: Baker Books, 1999.

Stark, Rodney. *The Rise of Christianity: How the Obscure, Marginal Jesus Movement Became the Dominant Religious Force in the Western World in a Few Centuries*. San Francisco: HarperSanFrancisco, 1997.

Stump, Eleonore. "Knowledge, Freedom, and the Problem of Evil", *International Journal for Philosophy of Religion*, vol. XIV, no. 1, 1983, pp. 49–58.

———. *Wandering in Darkness: Narrative and the Problem of Suffering*. Oxford: Clarendon Press, 2010.

——— (ed.). *Reasoned Faith: Essays in Philosophical Theology in Honor of Norman Kretzmann*. Ithaca and London: Cornell University Press, 1993.

Subkī, Taqī al-Dīn ʿAlī b. ʿAbd al-Kāfī al-. *Al-Iʿtibār bi-baqā' al-janna wa'l-nār* in *al-Durra al-maḍiyya fī al-radd ʿalā Ibn Taymiyya*. Damascus: Maṭbaʿat al-Taraqqī, 1928.

Sun-Tzu. *The Art of War*. Tr. John Minford. New York: Penguin Books, 2002.

Suyūṭī, ʿAbd al-Raḥmān Jalāl al-Dīn b. Abū Bakr al-, and Albānī, Muḥammad Nāṣir al-Dīn al-. *Ṣaḥīḥ al-Jāmiʿ al-ṣaghīr wa-ziyādatih/Ḍaʿīf al-Jāmiʿ al-ṣaghīr wa-ziyādatih*. Beirut: al-Maktab al-Islāmī, 1988.

———. *Tashyīd al-arkān fī laysa fi'l-imkān abdaʿ mimmā kān*, addendum to *Iḥyā' ʿulūm al-dīn*. Beirut: Dār Ṣādir, 2010.

Swinburne, Richard. *Providence and the Problem of Evil*. Oxford: Clarendon Press, 1998.

———. "A Theodicy of Heaven and Hell", in Alfred Freddoso (ed.), *The Existence and Nature of God*. Notre Dame: University of Notre Dame Press, 1983, pp. 37–54.

Ṭabarānī, Sulaymān b. Aḥmad al-. *Al-Muʿjam al-kabīr*. Ed. Ḥamdī b. ʿAbd al-Majīd al-Salafī. Cairo: Maktabat Ibn Taymiyya, 1994.

———. *Al-Muʿjam al-awṣaṭ*. Eds. Ṭāriq b. ʿAwaḍ Allāh b. Muḥammad and ʿAbd al-Muḥsin b. Ibrāhīm al-Ḥusaynī. Cairo: Dār al-Ḥaramayn, 1995.

Ṭabarī, Abū Jaʿfar Muḥammad b. Jarīr b. Yazīd al-. *Tafsīr al-Ṭabarī* or *Jāmiʿ al-bayān fī ta'wīl al-Qur'ān*. Ed. Aḥmad Muḥammad Shākir. Beirut: Mu'assasat al-Risāla, 2000.

Tabrīzī, Muḥammad b. ʿAbd Allāh al-Khaṭīb al-. *Mishkāt al-maṣābīḥ*. Ed. Muḥammad Nāṣir al-Dīn al-Albānī. Beirut: al-Maktab al-Islāmī, 1985.

Talty, Stephan. *Agent Garbo: The Brilliant, Eccentric Secret Agent Who Tricked Hitler and Saved D-Day*. Boston: Houghton Mifflin Harcourt, 2012.

Tewes, Kevin. *Answering Christianity's Most Difficult Question: Why God Allows us to Suffer*. Chapel Hill: Triune Publishing, 2015.

Thomas (ed.), AbdulKader. *Interest in Islamic Economics: Understanding riba*. New York: Routledge, 2006.

Tierney, Brian. *Origins of Papal Infallibility, 1150–1350: A Study on the Concepts of Infallibility, Sovereignty, and Tradition in the Middle Ages*. Leiden: E. J. Brill, 1972.

Tirmidhī, Abū ʿĪsā Muḥammad b. ʿĪsā al-Sulamī al-, and Albānī, Muḥammad Nāṣir al-Dīn al-. *Ṣaḥīḥ Sunan al-Tirmidhī/Ḍaʿīf Sunan al-Tirmidhī*. Riyadh: Maktabat al-Maʿārif, 1998.

Tzu, Lao. *The Tao Te Ching*. Tr. Ralph Alan Dale. London: Watkins Publishing, 2006.

Van Dam, Nikolaos. *Destroying a Nation: The Civil War in Syria*. London and New York: I.B. Tauris, 2017.

Voltaire. "The Lisbon Earthquake: An Inquiry into the Maxim, 'Whatever Is, Is Right'", in Voltaire, *From the Works of Voltaire: A Contemporary Version*. Tr. William F. Fleming. New York: E.R. DuMont, 1901, Volume X, Part II, pp. 8–18.

———. *Candide, Zadig, and Selected Stories*. Tr. Daniel M. Frame. New York: Signet Classic, 2001.

Watt, Montgomery. "Suffering in Sunnite Islam", *Studia Islamica*, No. 50, 1979, pp. 5–19.

Walls (ed.), Jeremy. *The Oxford Handbook of Eschatology*. Oxford: Oxford University Press, 2008.

Williams (tr.), Khalid. *The Principles of the Creed: Book 2 of The Revival of the Religious Sciences*. Louisville: Fons Vitae, 2016. [=Ghazālī, Abū Ḥāmid Muḥammad b. Muḥammad al-. *Iḥyā' ʿulūm al-dīn* (Book II)]

Winter, Timothy. "Islam and the Problem of Evil", in Chad Meister and Paul K. Moser (eds.). *The Cambridge Companion to the Problem of Evil*. New York: Cambridge University Press, 2017.

Wright, N. T. *Evil and the Justice of God*. Downers Grove: InterVarsity Press, 2006.

Yaqub (tr.), Aladdin M. *Al-Ghazālī's Moderation in Belief*. Chicago: The University of Chicago Press, 2013. [=Ghazālī, Abū Ḥāmid Muḥammad b. Muḥammad al-. *Iqtiṣād fi'l-iʿtiqād*]

Zajjāj, Ibrāhīm b. Sahl b. al-Sārī al-. *Maʿānī al-Qur'ān wa iʿrābuh*. Ed. ʿAbd al-Jalīl Shalabī. Beirut: ʿĀlam al-Kutub, 1988.

Zeni (tr.), Tallal. *Ibn Qayyim al-Jawziyya on Divine Wisdom and the Problem of Evil*. Cambridge: Islamic Texts Society, 2017. [=Ibn Qayyim al-Jawziyya, Abū ʿAbd Allāh Shams al-Dīn Muḥammad b. Abī Bakr. *Miftāḥ dār al-saʿāda wa-manshūr wilāyat al-ʿilm wa'l-irāda* (extract) and *Shifā' al-ʿalīl fī masā'il al-qaḍā' wa'l-qadar wa'l-ḥikma wa'l-taʿlīl* (extract)]

———(tr.). *Ibn Qayyim al-Jawziyya on Knowledge*. Cambridge: Islamic Texts Society, 2016. [=Ibn Qayyim al-Jawziyya, Abū ʿAbd Allāh Shams al-Dīn Muḥammad b. Abī Bakr. *Miftāḥ dār al-saʿāda wa-manshūr wilāyat al-ʿilm wa'l-irāda* (extract)]

Zimbardo, Philip. *The Lucifer Effect: Understanding How Good People Turn Evil*. New York: Random House, 2007.

Index

Footnotes are indicated by 'n' after the page number; '*t*' indicates tables.

A

Aaron, 39, 49, 96, 132, 134, 303
ʿAlī/Aaron comparison, 314–15
prophethood, 58
Abbasid caliphate, 320, 370, 375, 402n17
ʿAbd Allāh b. Rawāḥa, 90
ʿAbd Allāh b. Salām, 76, 86
ʿAbd Allāh b. Ubayy b. Salūl, 101, 117n60, 413
ʿAbd Allāh b. ʿUmar, 100, 117, 120
ʿAbd Allāh b. al-Zubayr, 121n74
ʿAbd al-Raḥmān b. ʿAwf, 104, 109, 118, 119
ʿAbd al-Raḥmān b. al-Ḥārith b. Hishām, 121n74
Abisaab, Rula, 331n277
ablution, 94, 95
  dry ablution (*tayammum*), 101
Abraham, 46, 49, 52–54, 74, 117, 367, 431–32
  honours bestowed upon him by God, 52
  one of the greatest messengers, 64, 470
  prophethood lineage, 52, 53, 55
  sacrifice of Ishmael, 54–55, 261
Abraham (Prophet Muḥammad's son), 226, 261
Abrahamov, Binjamin, 166n76, 168nn85–86, 175n120

Abū Bakr al-Ṣiddīq, 14, 86, 92, 109–16
  Abū Bakr/ʿUmar comparison, 114
  appointed by the Prophet Muḥammad as his successor, 113–14
  Badr, Battle of, 94, 110, 240, 348
  buried alongside the Prophet Muḥammad, 116
  caliphate of, 90, 112, 113–15, 117, 319
  Companion most beloved to the Prophet, 111, 115
  eminent status of, 111–12, 120, 136, 401
  Ḥudaybiya Treaty, 110
  leader after the Prophet Muḥammad, 112–14
  migration from Mecca to Medina, 81, 81n32, 110
  Paradise and, 104, 109, 111, 121n76, 483n84
  pilgrimage, leading of, 112–13
  pledging allegiance to, 115
  prayer, leading of, 113
  Prophet's Household and, 316
  proselytizing, 109
  Qur'ān, manuscript of, 115, 121, 300
  a truly faithful servant (*ṣiddīq*), 114
  Uḥud, Battle of, 110, 389

wealth, 109, 110
see also Rightly-Guided Caliphs
Abū Hurayra, 100, 372–73
Abū Jahl, 89, 323–24n249
Abū Lahab, 89
Abū Musā al-Ashʿarī, 121n76
Abū Saʿīd al-Khudrī, 92
Abū Ṭalḥa, 389
Abū Ṭālib, 80n29, 122, 226, 463
Abū ʿUbayda b. al-Jarrāḥ, 104, 111, 253, 375
Adam, viii, 8, 9, 49, 166n76, 242
creation of, 283–84
disobedience and punishment, 25n43, 51
'Everyone who enters Paradise will be in the image of Adam…', 475n43
the fall, 51, 180n22, 277
the fall, wise purposes of, 147, 180
felix culpa, 184, 198n85
forgetfulness as reason for his sin, 51n23
God 'taught Adam all the names', 35, 50
God's acceptance of Adam's repentance, 51, 277–78
honours bestowed upon him by God, 50
Satan and, 50, 51, 148, 274–75
Adams, Marilyn McCord, 197, 214, 216
Adams, Robert M., 188–89
ʿadl, *see* justice
adultery/fornication, 126n5, 266, 273, 297n143
accusing chaste women of, 269*t*
major sin, 97–98, 142, 267, 268, 269*t*, 405
punishment of, 359
Ahl Bayt, *see* Household of the Prophet
Ahl al-Sunna, 374
ʿĀ'isha bint Abī Bakr, 99–101, 103, 111, 316
Battle of Banū Muṣṭaliq, 100
Battle of al-Jamal, 101, 371
ḥadīths narrated by, 100
ʿAlawīs, 326
Albānī, Nāṣir al-Dīn al-, 320
alcohol, 266
drinking alcohol, 142, 268, 269*t*, 273, 354, 359–60
ʿAlī b. Abī Ṭālib, 81n31, 86, 119, 122–24, 357n58, 401, 409
advised by al-Ḥasan, 328
ʿAlī/Aaron comparison, 314–15
caliphate of, 90, 123–24, 315, 320, 321
delay in pledging allegiance to Abū Bakr, 115
divisions and discord during ʿAlī's caliphate, 123–24, 321, 372, 374
eminent status of, 319
ḥadīth transmission, 169
Jamal, Battle of al-, 371–72
Khārijīs, 123–24
Khaybar, Battle of, 122
martyrdom of, 124, 370–71
migration from Mecca to Medina, 122
Muʿāwiyya, delay in pledging allegiance to ʿAlī, 371
Nahrawān, Battle of, 124, 374
Paradise and, 104, 109, 119
Ṣiffīn, Battle of, 371–74
Tabuk, Battle of, 122, 123, 314, 315n209

Uḥud, Battle of, 389
see also Rightly-Guided Caliphs
alms/almsgiving, 33, 51, 143, 253, 260, 327n261, 403, 405, 452
benefits of, 36, 142, 420
hiding it from public view, 340, 421
ostentation and, 417
the pious, 127
reminding others of one's charity, 270*t*
withholding almsgiving, 269*t*
see also zakat
ʿAmmār b. Yāsir, 319n229, 373, 385, 431n122
Amos, 312
ʿAmr b. al-ʿĀṣ, 111
Anas b. Mālik, 100, 102, 138, 389
anbiyāʾ, *see* prophets
angels, 4, 25, 26, 27, 35, 50n18, 78, 274
Badr, Battle of, 94, 296n137, 340n18
belief in, 34
created from light, 33, 36
free will and, 36, 343
striving against evil, 340n18
suffering, absence of, 218
Uḥud, Battle of, 340n18
worship of God by, 9, 33–34, 218, 262
see also Gabriel
anger, 341, 477
animals
making images of, 270*t*
sacrificing an animal for other than God's sake, 270*t*
suffering of, 262–63
annihilation (*fanāʾ*), 458–61, 464n66
death/annihilation distinction, 461
of desires 156, 209
in Hellfire, 458–61, 463–64
of parts of Hellfire, 458, 460, 464
annihilationism, 215–17
Anṣār, *see* Medinite supporters
Antichrist (*al-Masīḥ al-Dajjāl*), 88, 281
ḥadīths on, 393
Jesus and Muslims' fight against, 87, 89, 393, 491
Sūrat al-Kahf as protection against, 393
wisdom in allowing the existence of, 391–94
anti-theodicy
Ashʿarī anti-theodicy, 152–53
Hume, David, 190–91
Mackie, J.L., 194–96
Rāzī, Fakhr al-Dīn al-, 164n67
Rowe, William, 198–99, 201, 360n65
antinomianism, 209, 244n84, 326n255
apocalyptic thinking, theodicy rooted in, 287n110
apostasy, 91, 112, 115, 235, 299, 399
ʿAqaba Pledge, 81
Arabian Peninsula, 69, 83, 86, 88, 91, 117, 299, 399
arbitrariness, 20, 154, 186, 187, 188
Aristotle, 29, 202, 301n162
Arnaldez, R., 154
Arnauld, Antoine, 185, 186–87
arrogance/pride, 173, 221, 237, 269*t*, 270*t*, 402–403, 404
Hellfire and, 465
Satan, 9, 274

sinning and, 351, 354
asceticism, 133–34, 156, 234
devout asceticism (*wara*ʿ), 133–34
Ashʿarī, Abū al-Ḥasan al-, 20n11, 151
Ashʿarīs, 20, 164n67, 175, 202n100
anti-theodicy, 152–53
approach to the problem of evil, 151–55
divine voluntarism and occasionalism, 42n56, 187, 188
Āsiya, 136, 346n38
aṣlaḥa (reform), 131, 132–33
Asmā' bint Abī Bakr, 375
Athanasian creed, 289n121
atheism, 210–13
amoral atheism, 210
Buddhism, 207–208
consequences of, 211–12
Harris, Sam, 212
Mackie, J.L., 194–96
materialistic atheism, 208n126
Onfray, Michel, 210n140, 213
Paine, Thomas, 211
Rowe, William, 199
Augustine of Hippo, 178, 180
evil as non-being, 181
evil as privation of good, 178
the fall, 180n22
free-will theodicy, 178–79
Averroes, *see* Ibn Rushd
Avicenna, *see* Ibn Sīnā
awliyā', *see* saints

B

Badr, Battle of, 37n37, 82, 89, 119, 386
Abū Bakr al-Ṣiddīq, 94, 110, 240, 348
angels at, 94, 296n137, 340n18
Companions of the Prophet, 94, 386, 399n11, 477
Gabriel, 296n137, 340n18
Muḥammad, the Prophet, 240, 348
non-Muslim prisoners, 117
Satan's retreat, 296
Bājūrī, Ibrāhīm al-, 151
Banū Hāshim, 80n29
Banū Muṣṭaliq, Battle of, 100
Banū Muṭṭalib, 80n29
Beatific Vision, 293n131, 318, 468, 481
beauty
Beautiful Names of God, 18, 19, 22, 27, 44
Creation, 43, 44, 158
Muḥammad, the Prophet, 86
Paradise, 474
belief, 9, 11, 20, 34, 87, 148, 276, 368, 379, 410, 449, 489
eschatological belief, 397
in the pillars of faith, 34
believers (*mu'minūn*), 141, 453
avoiding major wicked sins, 142, 268
believer/Muslim distinction, 114, 143, 268, 317
benefits of allowing believers to incur intermediate sins, 349–53
cursing a believer, 269*t*
differentiated from disbelievers and hypocrites, ix, 492
Paradise, 394, 472, 473, 484
Paradise: on the Heights (*al-Aʿrāf*), 479–80
Straight Path, 6
suffering as paradoxically

beneficial for, 230–31
traits of, 37, 268
victory over evil and disbelievers, 335–37
believing Muslims (*muslimūn*), 141–42, 453
believer/Muslim distinction, 114, 143, 268, 317
Paradise, 471, 480–82
Benedict, Pope, 154
'the best of all possible worlds', 41–45, 160–63
Adams, Robert M., 188–89
Arnauld, Antoine, 185, 186–87
Divine wise purposes, 44
Ghazālī, Abū Ḥāmid al-, 160–61, 163, 171n102
Hume, David, 190–91
Ibn ʿArabī, 171
Ibn al-Qayyim, 41, 161–63
Ibn Taymiyya, 41
incarnation and atonement, 292–93
Islamic perspective on, 41–44, 160–63, 197
Journet, Charles, 188
Leibniz, Gottfried, 185–86, 188, 293
Malebranche, Nicholas, 185–87
Nadler, Steven, 185–87, 189–90, 203
not the best possible world, 44, 163, 186, 188–91
Nursī, Saʿīd, 158
opposition to Leibniz's optimism, 188–91, 196
Plantiga: Felix Culpa Theodicy, 198, 292–93
Voltaire, 189
see also Creation; world
Bible
see Gospels; New Testament; Old Testament
Bilāl b. Rabāḥ, 345
blameworthy characteristics, 213, 241, 253
blasphemy, 72, 290, 292–94
attribution of evil to God, vii, 23, 148, 262, 264–65, 269*t*
blessing
blessed strangers, allowing the emergence of, 366–70
decreasing testing, 225
evil due to altering or misplacing blessings, 266
granted to the disbelievers so as to lead to them becoming deluded (*istidrāj*), 311, 362
gratitude for His blessings, 5, 11, 67, 219, 242–44, 249–50, 352–53, 492
greatest blessings bestowed upon the prophets, truly faithful, martyrs, and righteous 339
withheld by God, 14–15
bliss, 9, 25, 161–62, 467, 474
Boyd, Gregory, 294–95
bribery, 270*t*, 360
Buddhism, 207–209
Dhammapada, 208
Bukhārī, Abū ʿAbd Allāh Muḥammad, 78
Ṣaḥīḥ al-Bukhārī, 78n15

C

causality, 33, 51, 152
charity, *see* alms/almsgiving
children
born sinless and innocent, 259–60, 278, 425

death of, 261–62
disobedience of parents (ʿuqūq) as major sin, 269t
inadequacy of, 260
suffering of, 192–93, 201, 259–62, 360n65
supplication for parents by, 143
see also orphans
Chittick, William, 166–67, 167n82, 172, 175n120, 461n56
Christianity, 23, 49, 73, 177, 210, 377
alteration of New Testament, 308
attributing inadequacy to God, 311
Christian theology, 313
Christians of Najrān, 122
disbelief in Muḥammad, the Prophet, 301
expansion of, 387
following monks/priests instead of the Divine Law, 313–14
gone astray, 6–7, 8, 295, 296–301, 387
humankind as God's children, 282, 285
love for God, 137–38
papal infallibility, 313, 314n207
persecution of Christians, 299, 300, 384, 387
universal salvation, 215–16, 278
worship of Jesus within Trinity, 72–73, 280-81, 285, 288-90, 293n128, 301
circumcision, 296–98, 357n59
commandments, 5, 14, 28, 72
deontological commandments, 33
disobeying God's commandments, 296, 298–99
divine command ethics, 20n11, 32, 151–52, 153
evil as abandonment of God's commandments, 149
free will and Divine commandments, 33
God's wise purposes in His commandments, 15
importance of following God's commandments, 49, 359, 361, 440n159, 441
paradoxical commandments 228–30
Ten Commandments, 39, 271
Companions of the Prophet, 77, 84, 85n49, 332, 337
Badr, Battle of, 94, 386, 399n11, 477
'the best generation of Adam's offspring', 104
cursed by Shiites, 321–23, 326n257
God's pleasure with, 105, 476–77
ḥadīth transmission, 169
Ḥudaybiya Treaty, 105
impermissibility of criticizing them, 112, 153n27, 317, 323–24, 374
love for, 124, 317
Meccan Companions (*Muhājirīn*), 81, 105, 317n220, 385, 398–99, 401, 476
Medinite supporters (*Anṣār*), 81, 105, 123, 317n220, 389, 399, 476
migration to Medina, 81, 235, 399
Paradise and, 104, 105, 119, 476–77

persecution and torture of, 80, 345, 398–99
Plague of ʿAmwās, 374–75
Trench, Battle of the, 95
true faith and righteousness of, 235
Uḥud, Battle of, 227, 389, 390, 400
Confucianism, 206, 209
Confucius, 206
consensus (*ijmāʿ*), 16, 105, 167, 174, 483
contentment (*riḍā*), 140, 156, 224, 263, 276, 343, 469
contentment during hardship, 250
corruption (*fasād*), 41, 317, 360
hypocrites and, 408, 412
kings and, 106–107, 108
war and, 380, 381
cowardice, 253, 254
fleeing from battle, 267, 269*t*
Cowton, Christopher, 407n35
Creation, 19, 28, 174
beauty of, 43, 44, 158
as cause for good, 33
Divine wise purposes in, 15, 35, 41, 42, 44, 162, 193
falaq/split apart, 16, 29
Ibn al-Qayyim: three abodes, 161
paired opposites in, 29, 158, 161
symmetry, 31
see also Divine Names
creation (process of), vii–viii, 28–29
angels, creation of, 33
by accident, argument of, 30n12
Divine fine-tuning, 29–32, 41, 42, 44, 370
Divine love, 19
Divine will, 21–22, 186–87
God is eternally creating, 28n4
humankind, creation of, 25, 35, 36, 180, 182, 220, 484
necessity, argument of, 30n12
ontological creation, 29, 32, 33
the pen, 19n9
Creator (*al-Khāliq*), 5, 28–29, 33, 43, 334
Allāh, 23
the Best of creators (*Aḥsan al-khāliqīn*), 334
God as Creator of good and evil, 16, 29, 32, 41, 42n56, 43, 147, 156, 174, 334
God as perfect Creator, 41, 43, 44
see also Divine Names
Crisp, Roger, 407n35

D

Dabashi, Hamid, 402n17
Daftary, Farhad, 325, 325n252, 329n270
Dajjāl, al-Masīḥ al-, *see* Antichrist
Dakake, Maria, 329–30
Dante, Alighieri, 301–302
David (*Dāwūd*), viii, 49, 107, 280, 281, 386
affirming God's Oneness, 282n73
as a Caliph, 108, 443
David/Muḥammad comparison, viii, 64–65, 97–103
graced by God, 439, 441, 443
'the greatest worshipper of humankind', 64
ḥadīth, 63–64, 67
king-prophet, 108
marriage of, 97–98, 99, 102

one of the greatest messengers, 63, 435, 443
resurgence of religion, 11
Saul and, 98, 439, 441, 442
wisdom, 66–67, 436
Day of Judgment, 5, 11, 42, 45, 338, 478–79, 492
Divine wrath on, 163, 456
intercession in, 472, 485, 486
Muḥammad, the Prophet on, 91, 93, 95, 163, 273, 450, 472, 485, 486
signs of the proximity of, 273
death, 115, 143
death/annihilation distinction, 461
dying as a disbeliever, 363
as suffering, not evil, 223, 261
Sūrat al-Fātiḥa, recitation at time of death, 7
death penalty, 358
debt, 253–54, 286
deceit and treachery, 266, 270*t*, 426
deficiency, 240, 294
God is infallible above any deficiency, 22, 23, 165, 195, 201, 264n2, 485
deism, 30–31, 205, 211n142
deontology
deontological commandments, 33
deontological paradox, 228
evil and sin as privation of the deontological, 218, 265, 266
ontology/deontology differentiation, 28, 437–38
pairing in the deontological realm, 29
dependence (*istiʿāna*), ix, 6
trustful dependence on God, 6, 347–49, 368, 491
Devil, *see* Satan
devotion (*iḥsān*), 127, 133, 137, 226, 491
the devout (*muḥsinūn*), viii, 220, 234, 402, 404
characteristics of, 126–27, 133
devout ascetics, 133–34
fear of God, 126
incurring minor sins (*lamam*), 126, 137
Paradise, 470, 472, 476, 484
the pious/the devout distinction, 125–30
Satan and, 126–27
Dhahabī, Shams al-Dīn, 268
Dhāt al-Riqāʿ, 120
Dhū al-Khuwayṣira, 412–13
Dhū al-Qarnayn, 12, 14, 234, 489
disbelief, vii, 35, 99, 174, 214
disbelief in Muḥammad, the Prophet, 301, 309
disbelief in prophets and messengers, 46–47, 49, 301, 462, 463, 464
forbidden by God, 274
disbelievers, 9, 12, 44, 89, 224, 492
darkness, immersed in, 40n49
deception of the believers, 417, 428
disobedience, 9
dying as, 363
fine-tuning of evil and harm amongst, 376–80
gratuitous evils and, 377, 379–80
harbouring ill or evil thoughts of the Holy Lord, 5, 292
Hellfire, 174–76, 378, 455–66, 476

natural disasters and, 378
persecution of the believers 10–11, 354, 364–66, 378, 384–85
polytheism, 268n22
punishment, 379–80
will never enter Paradise, 461–62, 479
disease/illness 251–52, 257–59
assisting/visiting the ill, 251
causes of, 257–59
Divine decree, correct approach to, 118
Job, 249
Muḥammad, the Prophet, 113
pain, 258
sinfulness and, 259
Sūrat al-Fātiḥa, 7
see also plague
disobedience, 269*t*
disbeliever, 9
disobeying God's commandments, 296, 298–99
Satan, 25n43, 275, 436
Saul, 299
Divine Attributes, vii, 4–5, 6, 18, 23, 24, 78, 139, 153, 157, 219–20
beneficence, 3–4,148, 150n20, 265, 485
everything is linked to, 157–58
forgiveness, 20, 21, 333–34
generosity, 335
holiness, 108, 148, 219
Immanence, 25, 140
infallibility, 22–23, 29, 164, 165, 195, 201, 264n2, 485
justice, 8, 21, 23, 148, 424
knowledge, 13, 19, 22, 27, 31, 165
manifestation of, vii–viii, 147–48, 162, 179, 193, 219–20, 333–38, 491
no Attribute of God is fully manifested, 196
omnibenevolence, 150, 151, 155, 231
omnipotence, 19, 30, 33, 148, 155, 196, 291–92, 294, 335, 338, 426
omniscience, 14, 19–21, 24, 30, 31, 44, 148, 196
paired Attributes, 219–20
perfection, 23, 28n4
praiseworthiness, 5, 20, 22, 148, 188, 204n110, 294, 334, 492
sovereignty, 109
Transcendence, 25, 154
see also Divine grace; Divine love; Divine mercy; Divine Names; Divine wisdom; Divine wrath; Oneness
Divine commandments, *see* commandments
Divine decree, 118
ontological decree, 246, 324, 370, 376
Divine Essence, 174
Beautiful Names of God and, 18, 22, 338
divine and uncreated, 24
Divine grace, 342–43, 351, 480, 487
David, graced by God, 435, 439, 441, 443
Joseph, graced by God, 247
Muḥammad, the Prophet, graced by God, 317, 399, 485

Paradise, 221, 467, 468, 480, 492
salvation and, 455, 467–68
upon the pious and righteous, 447, 478
Divine hiddenness, 26, 140, 195n70, 201, 465n69
Divine Law, 38, 47
abrogation, 422
following rabbis, monks/priests instead of the Divine Law, 313–14
gratuitous evils and the importance of implementing the Divine Law, 357–63
Jesus and, 297–98
kings and pharaohs, 107
Muḥammad, the Prophet, 85
Divine love, 19, 20, 22, 274, 294
God's will is concordant with His wisdom and love, 22
of the believers predominates over His hatred of the disbelievers and hypocrites, viii, 274, 492
of goodness and belief, 20, 32
of manifesting the consequences of His Beautiful Names, 24, 338, 485, 491
of repentance 355–56
of the resurgence of a society 356
those beloved to God, 220–21
Divine mercy, 4, 19, 20, 21, 219–20, 333–34
God's mercy precedes His wrath, 174, 175, 456–57
God's mercy prevails and preponderates over His wrath 220, 460
Paradise and, 449, 467, 468, 492
salvation from Hellfire and, 449
Divine Names
the All Cognizant (*al-Khabīr*), 19
Allāh, 23
the Almighty (*al-ʿAzīz*), 19, 22, 292
the Benefactor (*al-Munʿim*), 26, 335
the Best Strategist (*Khayr al-mākirīn*), 335
the Bestower (*al-Wahhāb*), 18, 250, 335
the Determiner (*al-Muqaddir*), 158
the Doer of Good (*al-Barr*), 18
the Effacer [of sins] (*al-ʿAfū*), 24, 333
the Ever-Forgiving (*al-Ghaffār*), 24
the Ever-Living (*al-Ḥayy*), 18
the Ever-Relenting (*al-Tawwāb*), 24
the Fashioner (*al-Muṣawwir*), 28, 334
the Forbearing (*al-Ḥalīm*), 24, 333
the Guardian (*al-Muhaymin, al-Ḥafīdh*), 335
the Guide (*al-Hādī*), 23
Healer (*Shāfī*), 157
the Holy (*al-Quddūs*), 22
the Holy King (*al-Malik al-Quddūs*), 108
the Invincible (*al-Qahhār*), 292
the Irresistible (*al-Jabbār*), 18n3, 292
the Judge (*al-Ḥakam, al-Qāḍī*), 23, 338

King of the Day of Religious Recompense (*Malik Yawm al-Dīn*), 7, 108
Lord of the Worlds, 5, 28, 46, 52, 251, 480
the Loving/the Most Loving (*al-Wadūd*), 24, 338
the Most Beneficent (*al-Raḥmān*), 4, 18, 333
the Most Compassionate (*al-Ra'ūf*), 333
the Most Forgiving (*al-Ghafūr, al-Ghāfir, Ahl al-maghfira*), 24, 333
the Most Generous (*al-Karīm*), 335
the Most High (*al-ʿAliy*), 19n7, 22, 174, 292
the Most Just (*al-ʿAdl*), 23, 26, 337
the Most Magnanimous (*al-Jawād*), 335
the Most Merciful (*al-Raḥīm, Arḥam al-rāḥimīn, Khayr al-rāḥimīn*), 4, 24, 25, 250, 333
the Most Patient (*al-Ṣabūr*), 336
the Most Wise/All Wise (*al-Ḥakīm*), 19, 20, 25, 157, 161, 219, 337
the Oft-Forgiving (*al-Ghaffār*), 333
the Omniscient (*al-ʿAlīm*), 19, 219
the Omnipotent, viii, 19, 219
the One God (*al-Wāḥid al-Aḥad*), 455
the One Who abases (*al-Khāfiḍ*), 26, 27, 29, 337
the One Who advances (*al-Muqaddim*), 337
the One Who answers supplications (*al-Mujīb*), 25
the One Who assists (*al-Mu'ayyid*), 335
the One Who bars (*al-Māniʿ*), 26, 219
the One Who bestows (*al-Bāsiṭ*), 26, 219
the One Who bestows honour (*al-Muʿizz*), 26, 27, 337
the One Who blocks (*al-Mu'akhkhir*), 337
the One Who constricts (*al-Qābiḍ*), 26, 219
the One Who dishonours (*al-Mudhill*), 26, 27, 337
the One Who enriches (*al-Mughnī*), 26, 219
the One Who exalts (*al-Rāfiʿ*), 26, 27, 29, 337
the One Who is faultless and bestows peace (*al-Salām*), 22
the One Who grants repentance (*al-Tawwāb*), 19n7
the One Who grants victory and triumph (*al-Nāṣir, al-Naṣīr, al-Ghālib*), 335
the One Who harms (*al-Ḍārr*), 26
the One Who humiliates the disbelievers (*Mukhzī al-kāfirīn*), 335
the One Who knows the Unseen (*ʿĀlim al-ghayb*), 14
the One Who is near (*al-Qarīb*), 25
the One Who pardons (*al-Tawwāb, Qābil al-tawb*), 333
the One Who removes harm (*Kāshif al-ḍarr*), 219

the One Who resurrects (*al-Bāʿith*), 338
the One Who tests (*al-Mubtalī*), 219, 334
the One to Whom all praise is due (*al-Ḥamīd*), 19n7, 22, 334
the Originator (*al-Bāri'*), 28, 334
the Protector (*al-Walī*), 26, 335
the Reckoner (*al-Ḥasīb*), 23, 338
the Righteous King (*al-Malik al-Ḥaqq*), 108, 334
the Self-Sufficient (*al-Ghanī*), 334
the Self-Sustaining (*al-Qayyūm*), 18
Sovereign Lord of the Day of Judgment (*Malik yawm al-dīn*), 5, 335
the Subtly Kind (*al-Laṭīf*), 24
the Trustee (*al-Wakīl*), 26
the Truth (*al-Ḥaqq*), x, 23
the Vast (*al-Wāsiʿ*), 19n7
see also Creator; Divine Attributes; Divine Names, general issues on

Divine Names, general issues on, 18–27, 78, 139, 153
Beautiful Names of God, 18, 19, 22, 27, 44
everything is linked to, 157–58
infallibility and Divine Names, 22–23
manifesting the consequences of, vii–viii, 147–48, 162, 219, 333–38, 491
paired Beautiful Names, 29, 158
see also Divine Names

Divine providence, 170, 186, 202–203, 327, 334, 420, 447

Divine silence, rejection of, 201

Divine voluntarism, 42n56, 152, 187–88
Ibn al-Qayyim's rejection of, 188n51
see also Divine will

Divine will, 20, 21–22, 28n4, 437–38
as absolute will, 20n11, 151
Arnauld, Antoine on, 186–87
Augustine: two divine 'wills', 179
as concordant with God's wisdom and love, 22
creation and, 21–22, 186–87
ontological will, 148, 179, 252, 367, 376
religious will, 140, 179, 343

Divine wisdom, 19–20, 21, 186, 187, 221–22, 277, 466
Ibn al-Qayyim on, 161–63
as justification for God's acts, 151
see also theodicy: Islamic theodicean solutions

Divine wise purposes, 19, 21, 22, 333, 491
in Creation, 15, 35, 41, 42, 44, 162, 193
existence of evil allows the manifestation of many Divine wise purposes, 156, 202, 334
the fall, wise purposes of, 147, 180
negation of, 151
see also theodicy: Islamic theodicean solutions

Divine wrath, 6, 173, 219–20
Day of Judgment, 163, 456
God's mercy precedes His wrath, 174, 175, 456–57

God's mercy prevails and preponderates over His wrath 220, 460
Hellfire and, 174–75, 456–57, 460
hypocrites, 412
Israelites, 303–304, 311
Jews, 6–7
upon those who attribute evil to Him, 6, 264
Dostoevsky, Fyodor, 192–94
The Brothers Karamazov, 192–93
consequences of atheism, 211–12
suffering of children, 192–93
doubt, 232–33, 345, 346n37
hypocrites, 406, 410, 422
Draper, Paul, 191n59
drug offence, 354, 358n63, 359
Druze, 369n90
dysteleology
dysteleological evil, 198, 200, 272, 368, 377, 425
dysteleological suffering, 182
see also gratuitous evil

E

ego/lower self (*nafs*), 148
Ehrman, Bart, 284–89, 296–97
Elias/Elijah (*Ilyās*), 49, 71n110, 74, 93, 306
Elisha (*al-Yasaʿ*), 49, 71n110, 306
emanation, 30, 163–64
enacting (*mufʿūl*), 163, 172, 174
difference between God's acts and what He enacts, 148, 161
enemy, 65, 135, 190, 350, 360, 364, 376, 431
being overpowered by, 91, 259, 357n58
Satan, 9, 50–51
victory over, 65
see also war
Enoch (Idrīs), 49
eschatology
Islamic approaches to, 174–76
non-Muslim approaches to, 214–17
see also Hellfire; Paradise; salvation
eternity, 19, 344, 459
eternal punishment in Hellfire, 459–65, 483
eternal reward of Paradise, 467–68, 475–76, 483
God is eternally creating, 28n4
Ethiopia, 80, 83, 119, 385
Eve, 50–51, 147, 195n70, 277–78
Satan and, 50, 148
evil (*sharr*), vii, ix, 197
alcohol as the root of many evil sins (*umm al-khabā'ith*), 266
attribution of evil to God, vii, 23, 148, 262, 264–65, 269*t*
avoidance of, 4, 6, 36, 200
Devil as source of, 4, 17, 149
essential evil, 164
evil as misplacing the ontological or deontological good, 266
existence of evil allows the manifestation of many Divine wise purposes, 156, 202, 334
existence of evil may indirectly lead to greater goods, 12, 149, 272
five groups of evil forbidden by God, 264–67
free will and, 43, 164, 165, 342–45

humanity and, 35
increases over time, 272–73, 296
necessity of evil for the greater good, 158, 198n85, 205
non-existence of, claims of, 149, 171, 173, 181, 206
religious system and, 177
transformation into good, 10, 115, 131
see also the entry below related to evil; gratuitous evils; privation; sin; theodicy; theodicy: Islamic theodicean solutions

evil, striving against and forbidding it (*jihād*), ix, 10, 17, 32, 137, 339, 347, 472, 491
as distinction between humanity and other creatures, 340
Islamic obligation to forbid evil, 132
mujāhidūn, 472, 483n82
repudiation of evil, ix, 137, 339, 347, 491
striving/fighting against disbelievers in a pious and righteous manner, 11, 384

extremism, 134, 137, 453, 454n28, 455

F

faith (*īmān*), 6, 14, 127
actions resulting from, 38
definition of, 34
higher levels of, 12, 140, 235, 247
sincere faith, 147, 404
Straight Path and, 6
true faith, 38, 136, 226, 235, 368, 395, 397, 398, 422

faith, experiencing the sweetness of, 139, 343

family and kinship, 85
breaking the ties of kinship, 269*t*
parents, 13–14, 201

fanā', *see* annihilation

fanaticism, 413, 453, 455

fasād, *see* corruption

fasting, 141
benefits of, 142
David and, 64
Muḥammad, the Prophet and, 87
not fasting in Ramaḍān without excuse, 269*t*
reward for, 344nn33–34

Fāṭima bint Muḥammad, 89n72, 92, 122, 226

Fāṭimids, 369n90

fawāḥish, *see* intermediate sins

fear of God, 125
the devout, 126
the pious, 126, 127, 449

fine-tuning, 31–32, 386, 484
Divine fine-tuning in creation, 29–32, 41, 42, 44, 370
of evil and harm amongst the disbelievers, 376–80
free will and, 32
of strength and good amongst the Muslims, 370–76

fiṭra, *see* innate disposition

forgetfulness, 13n46
Adam, forgetfulness as reason for his sin, 51n23
of good deeds, 13

forgiveness, 51
asking for God's forgiveness, 240–41, 286
Divine Attribute, 20, 21, 333–34

Muḥammad, the Prophet, 85, 286
fornication, *see* adultery/fornication
free will, 26, 195, 425, 491
affirmed and allowed by God, 344
angels, 36, 343
Divine commandments and, 33
Divine fine-tuning and, 32
evil and, 43, 164, 165, 342–45
God's determination and, 51
good deeds and, 342, 491
hardship and, 231
Hellfire and, 465
importance of, 36
free will theodicy 184
Augustine of Hippo, 178–79
Islamic free-will theodicy, 150, 173
King, William, 179
Mackie, J.L.: opposition to free will theodicy, 194–96
Plantiga, Alvin: free will defense, 196–98
Rowe, William opposition to free will theodicy, 199

G

Gabriel, 34, 290
Badr, Battle of, 296n137, 340n18
being shown Paradise and Hellfire, 34–35, 397
Holy Spirit (*al-rūḥ al-qudus*), 34, 283
as a messenger, 34, 282–83
Revelation and, 34–35, 79, 397
see also angels
gambling, 269*t*, 354
genocide against the Muslims, 205, 273, 364–66, 391
Ghazālī, Abū Ḥāmid al-, 160n50, 165
'the best of all possible worlds', 160–61, 163, 171n102
concealing one's good deeds, 420–21
on Hellfire, 175–75
on hypocrisy, 415–16
Iḥyā' ʿulūm al-dīn, 137, 369
on mystical unveiling, 157n38
'Sunni revival', 369
theodicy, 160–61, 163
the truly faithful, 137
on universal salvation, 175
God (Allāh), *see* Divine Attributes; Divine Essence; Divine grace; Divine love; Divine mercy; Divine Names; Divine providence; Divine wisdom; Divine wise purposes; Oneness
Gog and Magog, 12, 102, 234, 393
Goliath (*Jālūt*), 64, 107, 386, 435–36, 438–39
good deeds, 6, 142–43, 340, 449
to absolve sins, 340
assisting the hungry and thirsty, 251
assisting/visiting the ill, 251
concealing one's good deeds, 420–21
doing good without expecting reward, 15
free will and, 342, 491
fruit of beneficial knowledge, 129
muqtaṣidūn (believers with good/evil deeds in balance), 450, 452, 480

Paradise and, 467–68
reward for, 341, 342, 344
sābiqūn (foremost in good deeds), 450, 453, 470
suffering and, 11
goodness/the good
Creation as cause for good, 33
God as Creator of good and evil, 16, 29, 32, 41, 42n56, 43, 147, 156, 174, 334
God's love and command of, 32
greater good, 14, 149, 156, 158, 185, 196, 200, 228–29, 239, 272
Islam, obligation to enjoin good and forbid evil, 132
light as pure good and source of all goodness, 40
unsurpassable moral goodness, 183
Gospels, 39, 79, 284–89
Christian theology, 313
inconsistencies of, 287–88
love for God, 138
Synoptic Gospels, 138, 217, 285, 287, 288–89, 296
transmission of the text of, 308n183
writing of, 284, 300
see also Jesus; New Testament
Grant, Ruth, 418
gratitude, 5, 242–44, 249–50, 492
during hardship, 250–51
God loves to be thanked, 242
Moses, 244
Muḥammad, the Prophet, 85, 244
gratuitous evil, ix, 184, 198–201, 272–74
Antichrist and, 391
definition, 272
disbelievers and, 377, 379–80
dysteleological evil, 198, 200, 272, 368, 377, 425
karma and reincarnation, 207
Hasker, William, 199–200
Hick, John, 199
Ibn al-Qayyim on, 150
importance of fighting for God's sake and, 363–66
importance of implementing the Divine Law and, 357–63
justification for, 150, 339, 357–66, 368, 380, 489
major sins and, 272, 358, 360
open theists on, 184
Rowe, William, 198–99, 201, 360n65
strangeness and, 366–70
graves
places of worship upon graves, 331–32n280
visitation of (*ziyāra*), 331, 371n95
Greene, Brian, 31n15
grief, 253, 254, 352
Griffin, David Ray, 179
guidance, 436
divine guidance, 6, 20, 23–24, 49
messengers and prophets, 20, 47, 339
Revelation and, 31
Straight Path and, 6, 23, 49
ʿUmar b. al-Khaṭṭāb, inspired with divine guidance, 114, 116–17, 169

H

ḥadīth, 100, 106, 317, 492
ʿĀ'isha bint Abī Bakr, 100

ʿAlī b. Abī Ṭālib, 169
angels, 33
Antichrist, 393
Companions of the Prophet, 169
David, 63–64
the destitute, 394, 452
Divine Attributes, 219–20
fabricated *ḥadīth*, 167–68, 168n86, 171n99, 320, 329, 443
Ghadīr Khumm *ḥadīths*, 315–16, 319–20, 322
Ḥadīth collections, 167, 168, 171n99
ḥadīth qudsī, 23, 148, 241n74, 251, 292, 471
Ḥadīth scholars, 78, 171n99
Hellfire, 174, 450–51, 456–58
innate disposition (*fiṭra*), 148
isnād criticism, 329–30
love for God, 138
Shiʿi Islam, 326n257, 329–30
transmission of, 169
Zaynab bint Jaḥsh, 102–103
Ḥafṣa, 115–16, 121
Hagar, 53–54
Ḥajj, *see under* pilgrimage
Ḥajjāj, al-, 370, 375
Hallaq, Wael, 298n150
hardship, 340
free will and, 231
Muḥammad, the Prophet and, 226–27, 236–37
Paradise surrounded by, 35, 147, 250–51, 353, 397, 475–76, 477
paradoxical nature of some hardships, 228–31
perfection and, 158
prophets' tribulations, 225–26
purification and, 224, 230, 231, 235
religion and, 38
reward and, 224–25, 231
see also suffering
harm
due to human inadequacy, 218
lesser harm, 13, 465
harming the Muslims as major sin, 270*t*
hypocrites, harmfulness of, 396–97
suffering and evil as means to a lesser harm in the Hereafter, 465
Harris, Sam, 212
Hart, Michael, 73n117, 86, 117n62
Ḥasan b. ʿAlī al-, 92, 122, 321n236, 324–25
caliphate of, 90, 106n12, 124, 321
reconciliation and peace, 328
Ḥasan al-ʿAskarī, al-, 325
Ḥasan al-Baṣrī, 403, 406n31
Hasler, August, 313
Ḥassān b. Thābit, 283
Ḥāṭib b. Abī Baltaʿa, 477
heart, 346n37, 352
light in the heart of the believer, 36–38
permeated by the truth in the truly faithful, 339
sealing of the heart, 331n278
spiritually diseased in the hypocrites, 400, 410–11, 424
Hellfire, ix, 174–76, 489
annihilation in, 458, 460, 461, 463, 464
annihilation of parts of Hellfire, 458, 460, 464

arrogance/pride, 465
the destitute one (*al-muflis*), 452–53
disbelievers, 174–76, 378, 455–66, 476
Divine wrath and, 174, 175, 456–57, 460
eternal punishment, 459–65, 483
free will and, 465
Gabriel being shown the Hellfire, 34–35, 451
gates to Hellfire, 460, 483
Ghazālī, Abū Ḥāmid al-, on, 174–75
ḥadīths, 174, 450–51, 456–58
hypocrites, 406, 427, 463, 464, 476
Ibn ʿArabī on, 175, 461n56
Ibn al-Qayyim on, 175–76
Ibn Taymiyya on, 175
muqtaṣidūn, 452
Muslims in, 453–54, 457–58, 480
the pious: salvation from any punishment of Hellfire, 447–50, 451–52, 465n69, 476
polytheism and, 265, 455, 479
portion of humanity to be punished by, 450–51, 453, 465–66
punishment, 362, 363
punishment before entering Paradise, 447, 451, 452–53
punishment will end for most of the disbelievers, 176, 447
ṣirāṭ (bridge over Hellfire), 452, 480
temptations and, 35, 397
ẓālimūn, 452, 476, 479
see also universal salvation
Helm, Paul, 184
Hereafter, *see* Hellfire; Paradise
heresy, 164–65, 168n85, 172, 173, 203, 294
Hick, John, 177
Death and Eternal Life, 214–15
gratuitous evil, 199
soul-making theodicy, 179–83, 191, 198–99
universal salvation, 214–16
ḥikma, *see* wisdom
Hinduism, 206–207, 209
Advaita Vendanta, 207
karma, 206–207, 209
reincarnation, 206–207
Holocaust, 203–205, 364
Berkovitz, Eliezer, 203
Cohen, Arthur, 204
Jewish theodicy, 203–205
Leaman, Oliver, 203–205
Maybaum, Ignaz, 203
Rubinstein, Richard, 204
Weisel, Elie, 203–204
see also Jews; Judaism
homosexuality, 57–58, 269*t*
Hoover, Jon, 22, 28n4, 150, 152, 171–72, 174n116
Hosea, 312
Household of the Prophet (*Ahl Bayt*), 315–18, 328–29
Hūd, 49, 73, 74
Ḥudaybiya Treaty, 82–83, 95, 105, 476
Abū Bakr al-Ṣiddīq, 110
ʿUmar b. al-Khaṭṭāb, 340
ʿUthmān b. ʿAffān, 120
Ḥudhayfa b. al-Yamān, 92, 118, 427
humankind
'the best of humankind', viii, 104, 339
created from earth, 36

created to fulfil a purpose, 44
creation of, 25, 35, 180, 182, 220, 484
as divine viceroys on Earth, 50
evil and, 35
inadequacy of, 218, 240, 253, 260, 266
ontological characteristics of, 25, 26
Hume, David, 190–91, 210
humility, 245
attaining humility as wise purpose of suffering and evil, 237–39, 337, 349, 350, 402
fear of hypocrisy and, 403
perfect humility, 139
Ḥunayn, Battle of, 85n49
hunger, 80n29, 95, 227, 253, 311, 392
assisting the hungry and thirsty, 251, 253
children's hunger, 260–61
famine, 68, 91, 253, 259, 442n164
see also poverty
Ḥusayn, b. ʿAlī al-, 122, 324–25
ʿĀshūrāʾ rituals, 371n95
martyrdom of, 370–71
hypocrisy, ix
definition of, 396
elucidation of hypocrisy as wise purpose for allowing suffering and evil, 345, 396, 397–404, 422–28, 444, 447, 492
fear of, 403
Ghazālī, Abū Ḥāmid al-, on, 415–16
Ibn al-Qayyim on, 415
moral weakness/hypocrisy distinction, 414
ostentation/hypocrisy distinction, 415
prevention of, 419–22
reasons for, 397
Saul (*Ṭālūt*) as case study of, 433–43
war, elucidation of hypocrisy as wise purpose of, 400–401, 424–28
see also hypocrites; ostentation
hypocrites, 38n40, 224
Divine wrath upon, 412
eternal punishment for, 463, 464
fanatical Muslims, 413
harmfulness of, 396–97
Hellfire, 406, 427, 463, 464, 476
identity of some Hypocrites, 427
impermissibility to fight against/kill the hypocrites, 413
Medinan phase, 399
prayers for, 117
Qurʾān on, 396, 410–13, 423, 427n109
Tabuk, Battle of, 400
Trench, Battle of the, 400
Uḥud, Battle of, 399–400, 427n112
see also hypocrites, characteristics of
hypocrites, characteristics of, 404–17, 421
betraying oaths, 405, 408, 428
condescending towards the believers, 410
corruption, 408, 412
disbelieving after believing, 411–12

dishonesty, 405
doubts, 406, 410, 422
evil intentions and sedition, 408–409
harbouring rancor or hatred, 396, 428, 463
harming the believers 396, 409, 413
laziness regarding the pillars of Islam, 409
lying, 404–405
major sins, 405, 407
mocking and deriding religion, 410
moral criticism of others, 407
obscene/insulting when debating, 405
spiritual disease of their hearts, 400, 410–11, 424
worldly attachments and desires, 397, 400, 406, 407, 432
see also hypocrisy; hypocrites

I

Iblīs, *see* Satan
Ibn ʿAbbās, 81n31, 328, 330
Ibn Abī Mulayka, 403
Ibn ʿArabī, Muḥyī al-Dīn, 165–72, 324n251
on 'the best of all possible worlds', 171
confusion/bewilderment (*ḥayra*), 170–71
critique of, 167–70, 298n150
on evil, 171–72
Fuṣūṣ al-ḥikam, 166, 167, 168n85
al-Futūḥāt al-Makkiyya, 166, 167, 298n150
ḥadīth, approach to, 167–68, 171n99
on Hellfire, 175, 461n56
monism, 165–68, 170, 172, 173
on mystical unveiling, 165, 168–70
'the Seal of the Saints', 169
Ibn ʿAṭā' Allāh al-Iskandarī, 156
Ibn Ḥanbal, Aḥmad, 283n85
Ibn Ḥazm, 154–55, 155n31
Ibn Kathīr, 14, 68, 73n118, 401n16
Ibn Masʿūd, ʿAbd Allāh, 37n37, 89n72, 92, 116, 319n229
Ibn Qayyim al-Jawziyya, vii, 5n10, 213, 234, 261
on 'the best of all possible worlds', 41, 161–63
on Divine Attributes, 219–20
on Divine Names, 22
divine voluntarism, rejection of, 188n51
falaq, meaning of, 16
on Hellfire, 175–76
on hypocrisy, 415
Ibn Qayyim al-Jawziyya on Divine Wisdom and the Problem of Evil, 147, 161, 456
on innate disposition, 148,
on intermediate sins, 349–53
light in the heart of the believer, 37–38
love for God, 139
Madārij al-sālikīn, 135
on Muḥammad, the Prophet, 77, 227
pious and righteous traits, 129–30
remembrance of God, 420
on repentance, 349–50, 352
on sacrifice of Ishmael, 54–55
on Satan, 150, 276–77
al-Ṣawāʿiq al-mursala, 176

Shifā' al-ʿalīl, 175
on sins, benefits of allowing to incur in, 349–53, 354
on Solomon, 66–67n90
on the strangers, 366n86
Ṭarīq al-hijratayn, 149
traditionalist theodicy, 147–50, 154
on the truly faithful, 136, 137
on universal salvation, 175–76
on the upright and trustworthy, 134–35
Zād al-maʿād, 176
Ibn Rushd, 165
Ibn Sabʿīn, 172
Ibn Sīnā (Avicenna), 29, 160n50, 172n103, 301n162
critique of, 164–65
necessity, argument of, 30n12
theodicy of, 163–65
Ibn Taymiyya, 234, 308n183, 311, 329
on 'the best of all possible worlds', 41
critique of Ibn ʿArabī, 167, 171n99, 298
critique of Paul (Saul of Tarsus), 298–99
on Divine Names and Attributes, 22, 28n4
on Divine will being concordant with the Divine love and wisdom, 22, 41
on doubts, 346n37
on Hellfire, 175
on Muḥammad, the Prophet, 77, 79n26, 84, 91, 93
on Muslim infighting, 372, 373n103, 374
on the approach of the Prophet's Household to the Shiites, 317–18
on the Rightly-Guided Caliphs, 105, 318
on the truly faithful, 136
Ibn Warraq, 210
idolatry, 9, 51, 155, 210
forbidden by God, 264
tribe of ʿĀd, 73n118
ignorance, 341
evil as, 149
iḥsān, *see* devotion
ijmāʿ, *see* consensus
illness, *see* disease/illness
īmān, *see* faith
Inati, Shams, 164
Indifferent Deity Hypothesis, 191n59, 199, 201
infallibility, 117, 313n206
Divine Attribute, 22–23, 29, 164, 165, 195, 201, 264n2, 485
Imams' infallibility, claims of, 314, 325, 326–29
papal infallibility, claims of, 313, 314n207
prophets, 98, 99, 314, 329
injustice, 155n33, 219, 267
evil as, 149
large scale of, 273
major sin, 269*t*
ẓulm, 450n18
innate disposition (*fiṭra*), 38, 148, 176, 260, 278, 425, 455–56
innovation in religion, 443
intercession, 286–87, 431, 472, 485–86
intermediary, 46, 152
intermediate sins (*fawāḥish*), 126, 142, 264, 272

avoidance of, 127, 349
benefits of allowing believers to incur, 349–55
forbidden by God, 264
forgiven in reward for suffering, 394
Ibn al-Qayyim on, 349–53
minimizing intermediate sins, 133
the pious and, 126, 128, 271, 272, 340, 449, 465n69, 478
repentance, 271, 349–50
the righteous, 135, 340, 465n69, 478
see also sin
Inwagen, Peter von, 195n70, 199
Iqbal, Muhammad, 173
Irenaeus: Irenaean theodicy, 180–81
Isaac, 47n7, 49, 54, 55, 56n48, 327n261, 437
Isaiah (Dhū al-Kifl), 49, 68, 312
Ishmael, 47n7, 49, 53–55, 88n66, 261, 320n235
Islam, ix, 38n40, 177, 210, 369
a complete revelation, 79, 327, 332, 490
five pillars of, 87, 115, 141, 143, 243, 252, 409
as God's religion, 49
holy cities of, 94, 382, 422
Islamic empire, 120, 370
love for God, 138
no compulsion in Islam, 382–83
obligation to enjoin good and forbid evil, 132
as Revelation, 49
reviving/resurgence of Islam, 137, 369, 489–90, 491
spread of, 86, 91, 117–18, 120, 227, 370, 375, 382–83, 399
strangeness/'Islam started as something strange…', 366–67, 370, 375, 376, 489
see also Muslims
Ismāʿīl I, 321n240, 376n118
Ismāʿīlīs, 325, 326, 326n255, 330n272, 369n90
Israelites, 60–62, 116, 230n44, 245, 302–14, 384
alteration of the Scriptures, 308–309
attributing inadequacy and miserliness to God, 310, 311
Baal, worship of, 302, 304–307, 367n87
enslaved by Pharaoh and the Egyptians, 58, 378, 384
evil statements of, 309–11
Ezra (ʿUzayr), 302, 307–308
golden calf, worship of, 302–304, 315
killing of prophets, 309, 367n87
the promised land, 62
scattering of, 69
the second largest group of believers in Paradise, 312
strategizing against (*istidrāj*), 311
wrath of God upon, 311
see also Jews; Judaism; Moses
istiʿāna, *see* dependence

J

Jābir b. ʿAbd Allāh, 95
Jackson, Sherman, 155–56
Jacob (*Yaʿqūb*), 47n7, 49, 238, 286, 312n202, 327n261, 436
Isrāʾīl, 436
Jacob's sons, 55n47

knowledge and gnosis, 55–57
Jaʿfar b. Abī Ṭālib, 90
Jaʿfar al-Ṣādiq, 315, 325, 326n255, 329
Jamal, Battle of al-, 101, 123, 321, 371, 372
Jayatilleke, K. N., 207–208, 209
Jeremiah (Armiyā'), 68–69, 312
Jerusalem, 94, 369, 382, 422
Aqṣā Mosque, 55, 93, 382n132, 423
destruction by Nebuchadnezzar armies, 69
Jesuits, 194n69, 195n70
Jesus, viii, 8, 10, 39, 46, 93, 302
affirming God's Oneness, 72, 279, 393
created through the Word of God, 283–84
crucifixion of, claims of, 48, 71, 288, 291–92, 311
disciples of, 105–106, 284, 288, 297, 382
divine and human nature, claims of, 290, 291
Divine Law and, 297–98
divine nature, claims of, 288–89
faith in Christ, 296
fighting against the Antichrist, 87, 89, 393, 491
incarnation and atonement, claims of, 292–94
messenger and prophet, 47n8, 48, 70–72, 74, 292, 300
miracles by, 70–71
Muḥammad, the Prophet and, 282
one of the greatest messengers, 64, 471
Satan, defeated by Jesus, 294–96
as 'son' of God, 281, 285
worship of, 8–9, 73n117, 280, 281, 285–86, 292, 295, 455
see also Gospels; Messiah
Jews
disbelief in Muḥammad, the Prophet, 301, 309
Divine wrath upon, 6–7
following the rabbis instead of the Divine Law, 313
Jewish philosophers on the problem of evil, 202–205
Jews of Medina, 76n10, 77n11, 80n30, 309
see also Holocaust; Israelites; Judaism
jihād, *see* evil, striving against and forbidding it
jinn, 262, 274
Satan, 9, 274
Sūrat al-Nās, 17
Job, 49, 203, 247–50
John (*Yaḥyā*), 49, 70
Jonah, 49, 367
Joseph, 13n46, 49, 55–56, 58, 222, 238, 286
paradox, 246–47
patience, 247
Joshua, 12–13, 60, 61–62, 68, 315, 360, 382, 384
Journet, Charles, 188, 215
Judaism, 49, 177, 210
love for God, 137–38
Rabbinical Judaism, 313
see also Holocaust; Israelites; Jews
Judgment, 335
see also Day of Judgment
justice (*ʿadl*), 128, 134
Divine Attribute, 8, 21, 23, 148, 424

K

Kaʿba, 55, 112, 116, 377, 422
  Black Stone, 369n90
  circumambulation (*ṭawāf*), 82
  Muḥammad's prayer in, 89n72, 109
  prayer, 116, 422
  see also pilgrimage
Khabbāb b. al-Aratt, 345
Khadīja, 79, 80n29, 226
Khālid b. al-Walīd, 90
Khalil, Mohammad, 174–75
Khan, Saiyad, 77n13
Khārijīs, 123–24, 374, 401n16
Khaybar, 48n12
  Battle of Khaybar, 112, 122, 330
Khiḍr, 12, 13–15, 262, 267n17, 489
Khoury, Theodore, 154
killing (unjustly), 267, 269*t*, 273, 375, 384–85, 391
  genocide, 194n68, 205, 273, 364, 365, 366
  of innocent Muslims, 364–66
  murder as one of the greatest evils, 358
  of prophets, 295–96, 309, 367n87
  punishment for, 358–59
  recidivism, 359
king/kings (*malik/mulūk*), 106–107, 326, 434–35
  caliph/king distinction, 108
  corruption of, 106–107, 108
  Divine Law and, 107
  inappropriateness of asking for a king, 433–34
  king/Pharaoh distinction, 107
  king-prophet, 107–108, 442
  Saul, 308, 433–35, 436, 442
King, William, 179
knowledge, 143
  believer's knowledge, 37–38
  Divine knowledge, 13, 19, 22, 27, 31, 165
  God's withholding of knowledge, 22, 79, 228, 280–81, 490–91
  human knowledge as evidence of God's favour, 35–36, 50
  messengers and prophets' knowledge, 56–57
  mystical unveiling, 157, 165, 168–70
  religious knowledge, 25, 35, 142, 234, 489
  scientific knowledge, 31
  theodicean knowledge, 13, 489, 491
Kohlberg, Etan, 317n218
Kuspinar, Bilal, 159

L

lamam, *see* minor sins
laziness, 241, 253, 254
Leaman, Oliver, 202–203, 204–205
Leibniz, Gottfried, 185n39
  'the best of all possible worlds', 185–86, 188–90, 293
  rejection of divine voluntarism, 188
light, 36–40, 291
  angels, created from light, 33, 36
  believers' angelic characteristics in the Hereafter, 290–91
  ḍiyā', 39
  God is the Spiritual Light of the heavens and the earth, 39–40
  light in the heart of the believer, 36–38

light upon light, 37–38
material light, 36–37
Muḥammad, the Prophet, 39–40
nūr, 39
as pure good and source of all goodness, 40
Qur'ān, 37–40
Revelation, 39
Scriptures, 39
spiritual light, 36–37, 40
Lot, 49, 53, 57, 74
Lott, Jeremy, 417
love, 140
love for the Medinite supporters (*Anṣār*), 123, 317
love for Muḥammad, the Prophet, 76, 138
sacrifice and, 140–41, 149–50
suffering as means towards love and moral goodness, 183
see also Divine love; love for God
love for God, 127, 137–41, 492
love and obedience to God, 138
perfect love for God, 139–41, 149–50
in time of suffering and evil, 139
the truly faithful, 137
lying, 404–405, 430–32

M

McGrath, Alister, 211, 212–13
Mackie, J.L., 194–96
Madelung, Wilferd, 318
magic/sorcery, 68, 267, 269*t*
Maimonides, Moses, 202–203
major sins, 142–43, 267–72, 338
avoidance of, 142, 271, 336, 340
definition, 268
destructive major sins, 267, 268n20, 278, 389
forbidden and disliked by God, 264, 271, 273–74
gratuitous evils and, 272, 358, 360
hypocrites, 405, 407
ithm, 264, 265
kabā'ir, 126
munkar, 142, 265n7
punishment for, 338, 357, 360
secondary major sins, 270*t*, 450
society: major sins, gratuitous evils and legal punishment, 358–62, 366
wicked major sins, 143, 268, 269*t*, 450
ẓulm, 450n18
see also sin
Malebranche, Nicholas, 185–87
Mālik b. Anas, 323
Manichaeism, 179
Manuel II Palaeologus, 382
Marmura, Michael, 163–64
marriage
marriage of prophets, 96–103
temporary marriage, 328–29, 330
martyr, 6, 90, 339, 385, 386, 389, 390
ʿAlī's martyrdom, 124, 370–71
Christians, 387
al-Ḥusayn's martyrdom, 370–71
martyrdom, 346
Paradise, martyrs in, 342, 470, 472, 476, 482–84
ʿUmar's martyrdom, 115, 118, 370–71

ʿUthmān's martyrdom, 118, 121, 123, 321, 370–72
Marx, Karl, 212n145
Mary, mother of Jesus, 69–70, 283, 302
perfection of, 136, 346n38
a truly faithful woman (*ṣiddīqa*), 70, 136, 438
Māturīdī, Abū Manṣūr Muḥammad al-, 155, 158
Māturīdīs, 155–56
Mecca, 53, 55n45, 337, 382
liberation of, 390n151, 399
Muḥammad, the Prophet, 65, 80, 81n31, 83, 94, 385
see also Kaʿba; pilgrimage
Meccan Companions (*Muhājirīn*), 81, 105, 317n220, 385, 398–99, 401, 476
Medina, 76, 80, 94, 382, 386
Jews of Medina, 76n10, 77n11, 80n30, 309
Meccan Companions, migration to Medina, 81, 235, 399
Muḥammad's migration from Mecca to, 65, 80n29, 81, 81n32, 110, 122, 227, 382
Medinite supporters (*Anṣār*), 81, 105, 123, 317n220, 389, 399, 476
mercy, 4, 126
decreases evil in the world, 4
Divine Attribute, 4, 19, 20, 21, 219–20, 333–34, 449, 456
see also Divine Attributes
messengers (*rusul*), viii, 46, 282–83
belief in, 34, 46–47
best of humankind, viii
chosen by God, 21
disbelief in, 462, 463, 464
guidance by, 20, 47
number of, 48–49, 482
prophet/messenger distinction, 47–48
victory granted by God, 47–49, 83, 434
see also prophets
Messiah, 48, 70, 72, 84, 288, 307, 313
Christ, 284n88
see also Jesus
Michel, Thomas, 158–59
Mill, John Stuart, 193n66
Milosz, Czeslaw, 212n145
minor sins (*lamam*), 126, 272
the devout, 126, 137
forgiven in reward for suffering, 394
the pious, 126, 271, 449, 478
repentance and, 271
the righteous, 135
the truly faithful, 137
see also sin
miserliness, 160, 253, 254, 310, 311, 481
Mongols, 369n90, 370, 375, 402
monism, 172, 207
Ibn ʿArabī, 165–68, 170, 172, 173
Oneness of existence (*waḥdat al-wujūd*), 166–67
monotheism, 10, 73, 210, 213, 280, 289–90, 304n167, 311
moon
light/*nūr*, 39n46
splitting of, 92–93
Moses, 46, 49, 58–61, 134, 293, 312, 336
Israelites' polytheism, 302–305
marriage of, 96–97

one of the greatest messengers, 64, 471
paradoxical commandments 228–29
patience, 15n55, 244, 245
the promised land, 62
Revelation, 79
Sūrat al-Kahf, 12–13, 14, 15, 489
Tablets, 132, 302–304, 314
Muʿādh b. Jabal, 37n37, 375
Muʿāwiya, 124, 328, 371–72, 373, 401
mufʿūl, *see* enacting
Muhājirīn, *see* Meccan Companions
Muḥammad, the Prophet, viii, 3nn1–3, 49, 74, 77n13, 367
Ascension to Heaven (*Miʿrāj*), 93, 423
call to God, 79–83
characteristics and legacy, 83–87, 348
death, 81n31, 92, 100, 114, 390
distinction from other prophets, 74n2
faith, 34
fasting, 87
following the Prophet, 221, 492
hardship, 226–27, 236–37
illiterate prophet, 75n4
illness, 113
as illuminating lamp, 39–40
intercession by, 94, 95, 286, 431
leadership, 86
love for, 76, 138
marriage of, 99–103
mentioned in prior Scriptures, 76
migration from Mecca to Medina, 65, 80n29, 81, 81n32, 110, 122, 227, 382
miracles by, 92–95
Night Journey (*Isrāʾ*), 93–94, 423
obedience to, 6, 76
Paradise, granted the most blessed station in, 485–86
pilgrimage, 87
poverty, 236–37, 244
prayer, 85, 87, 89n72, 93, 94, 109
prohibited cursing, 323
prophesies by, 87–92, 95, 103, 106n11, 118, 121–22, 124, 273, 319, 321, 372–75, 392–93, 432, 442
prophethood, proofs of, 77–79, 86, 87, 95, 103, 124
Qurʾān and, 84–85
Ramaḍān, 85
resurgence of religion, 11
Seal of the Prophets (*khātam al-nabiyyīn*), viii, 8, 75, 79n26, 169–70, 261, 339, 462n61
sent to all of humankind, 75, 76
supplication before the Battle of Badr, 94, 240, 348
Uḥud, Battle of, 389
victory over the disbelievers, 82, 83, 86
zakat, 87
Muḥammad al-Bāqir, 329, 330
Muḥammad b. al-Ḥasan, 325
Muḥammad b. Ismāʿīl, 325, 326n255
Muḥammad b. Maslama, 372–73
Muḥammad b. Sīrīn, 372n102
muḥsinūn, *see* the devout
Mujāhid b. Jabr al-Makhzūmī, 423n101
muʾminūn, *see* believers

muqtaṣidūn (believers with good/ evil deeds in balance), 450, 452, 480
Mūsā al-Kāẓīm, 321n237, 325
Muslim, Abū al-Ḥusayn, 78
  Ṣaḥīḥ Muslim, ixn1, 78n16
Muslims, 332, 399
  evil perpetrated against Muslims, 205, 364–66, 428, 491
  fine-tuning of strength and good amongst, 370–76
  five rights of a Muslim upon his brother, 251n107
  genocide against, 205, 273, 364–66, 391
  harming/betraying the Muslims as major sin, 270*t*
  infighting, 364, 373n103, 376, 401–402
  see also believing Muslims
muslimūn, *see* believing Muslims
Mu'tah, Battle of, 90
Muʿtazilīs, 42n56, 150–51, 202n100
muttaqūn, *see* the pious

N

Nadler, Steven, 185–87, 189–90, 203
nafs, *see* ego/lower self
Nahrawān, Battle of, 124, 374
Najāshī, al-, 89–90
natural disasters, 158–59, 189, 255–57, 273n30, 378
necessary concomitant, 162, 222, 250
need, 238, 241, 253, 349
  for God's assistance and protection, 4, 350, 353
  zakat and, 252
Neoplatonism, 163, 181, 326n255
  plenitude, principle of, 158, 172n103, 181, 202
New Testament, 215
  alteration of, 308n183
  inconsistencies of, 287, 295, 301, 308
  on major sins, 271
  on Satan, 294–95
  see also Gospels; Jesus
Nietzsche, Friedrich W., 212n144
Nizārīs, 369n90
Noah, 46, 49, 51–52, 74, 259n119, 281, 301, 336, 367, 462n60
  Noah's ship, 52, 316n213
  one of the greatest messengers, 64, 471
non-Muslims, 154
  approaches to the problem of evil, 177–214
  eschatology, 214–17
Nursī, Saʿīd, 157–60
Nuṣayrīs, 326

O

obedience
  to God, 6, 138
  to Muḥammad, the Prophet, 6, 76
  to the prophets, 74
occasionalism, 20n11, 33n20, 187
Old Testament, 6–7, 53, 300–301, 308–309, 428
  Abraham, 53n38, 54n42
  Adam, 50nn20–21, 51n22
    affirming God's establishment of this world by His wisdom, 19

affirming God's Oneness, 279–80, 282n73, 300
Daniel, Book of, 435n137
David, 97–98, 99
Deuteronomy, 63n74, 88, 137, 303–304
Exodus, 59n63
Genesis, 50n20, 51n22, 52n28, 53n38, 54n42, 56nn48–51, 320n235
on the Israelites, 304, 306–307, 357, 433–34
Isaiah, Book of, 279–80
Jacob, 55–56
Jeremiah, Book of, 19, 357, 428
Job, 248–49
Joseph, 56n48
Joshua, Book of, 61–62
Judges, Book of, 305
Kings, Book of, 98–99, 306nn172–74, 307
Lot, 57n54
love for God, 137–38
marriages of Moses, David, and Solomon, 96–99, 102
on monotheism, 19, 280, 300–301
Moses, 58, 59n63, 60–61, 96
Noah, 52n28
Numbers, Book of 60–61, 96, 304–305
prophetic predictions, 88
prophets viii, 68
prophets not mentioned in, 73
Samuel, Book of, 97, 98n115, 433–34, 439–42
on Saul, 439–42
Solomon, 66, 67n91, 98–99
on the spiritual 'sons' of God, 281–82
Ten Commandments, 39, 271
on turning away from the Divine commandments, 299
omnipotence, *see under* Divine Attributes
omniscience, *see under* Divine Attributes
Oneness (Divine Oneness), viii, 18
affirming God's Oneness, 278–82, 393
affirming God's Oneness as requisite for salvation, 455, 457n41
Old Testament, 279–80, 282n73, 300
Qur'ān 8, 49, 74
Sūrat al-Fātiḥa, 8
Sūrat al-Kahf, 8
Onfray, Michel, 210n140, 213
ontology, 51
evil as misplacing the ontological good, 266
ontological characteristics of humanity, 25, 26
ontological creation, 32, 33
ontological decree, 246, 324, 370, 376
ontological existence of sins, 333
ontological paradox, 228
ontological predestination, 14, 246
ontological will, 148, 179, 252, 367, 376
ontology/deontology differentiation, 28, 437–38
pairing in the material ontological creation, 29

suffering/evil as privation of the ontological, 218, 354
oppression, 266–67, 269*t*
forbidden by God, 264
optimism, *see* 'the best of all possible worlds'
Ormsby, Eric, 160
orphans, 14n54, 128, 222, 226, 267
ostentation (*riyā'*), 221, 270*t*, 415–16, 419
ostentation/hypocrisy distinction, 415
wisdom in allowing ostentation, 417–18
see also hypocrisy
Ozkan, Tubanur, 157–58

P

pain, 258
sinfulness and, 219
see also disease/illness; grief
panentheism, 173
pantheism, 172, 205
Paradise, 161–62, 468, 489
Beatific Vision, 293n131, 468, 481
beauty of, 474
believers, 394, 472, 473, 484
believers' angelic characteristics in the Hereafter, 290–91
believers who are on the Heights (*al-Aʿrāf*), 479–80
believing Muslims, 471, 480–82
bliss, 467, 474
Companions of the Prophet, 104, 105, 119
the devout, 470, 472, 476, 484
disbelievers will never enter Paradise, 461–62, 479
Divine grace and, 221, 467, 468, 480, 492
Divine mercy and, 449, 467, 468, 492
entering Paradise, 76–77, 302, 404, 447
Firdaws, 469, 470, 471, 483
Gabriel and, 34–35, 397
Gardens of, 469–70, 471, 472
gates to, 460n52, 482
God's pleasure and favour, 476–79
good deeds and, 467–68
hardship and, 35, 147, 250–51, 353, 397, 475–76, 477
Israelites/Jews, 312
levels of, 342, 345, 471–73
martyrs, 342, 470, 472, 476, 482–83, 484
Muḥammad, the Prophet: the most blessed station (*al-maqām al-maḥmūd*), 485–87
Muslims in, 454–55, 486
nearness to God in, 470–71, 491
perfection of, 41
the pious, 447, 448, 452, 470, 472, 473, 476, 478–79
pleasures in: spiritual, intellectual, bodily pleasures, 467, 468–76, 481
portion of humanity to be in, 481, 482–84
prayers and, 472–73, 474
prophets and messengers, 342, 470–72, 476, 482, 486
reward in, 394, 467, 476, 477, 479, 483
the righteous, 10n34, 342, 470, 471, 472, 473, 476, 477–78, 479, 484, 485

Throne of God, being the roof of, 130, 292, 470, 483, 491
the truly faithful, 342, 470, 472, 472, 482
paradox, 228
deontological paradox, 228
ontological paradox, 228
paradoxical commandments 228–30
paradoxical nature of some hardships, 228–31
paradoxical prediction, 88
patience, ix, 129–30, 245, 385, 491
in the face of persecution, 385, 392n156
Job, 247–50
Joseph, 247
Moses, 15n55, 244, 245
need of, 15, 245–47, 250, 341
the patient (*ṣābirīn*), 220
Solomon, 250
Paul, (Saul of Tarsus), 73, 287, 288, 295, 296–97, 298–99, 443
Christian theology, 313
epistles written by, 300n156
People of the Book, 39–40, 75, 105n10, 271n126, 291, 302n164
see also Christianity; Judaism; Jews
perfection
achieving perfection, 41, 127, 346n38
Creation, 42–43
Divine Attribute, 23, 28n4
hardship and, 158
of Islam, 170, 327, 490
Paradise, 41
perfect humility, 139
perfect love for God, 139–40, 149–50
perfect worship, 139
soul-making theodicy and human perfection, 182
the truly faithful, 136, 346
persecution, 10, 11, 226, 346, 354, 383–85
of Christians, 299, 300, 384, 387
of Companions of the Prophet, 80, 345, 398–99
of the seven believers in *Sūrat al-Kahf*, 10, 246, 384
Peterson, Michael, 177
Pharaoh, 46, 58–60, 107, 245, 336, 378
piety (*taqwā*), viii, 3, 74, 133, 225, 379
importance of, 125–30, 449, 482
revival of, ix, 395, 489
righteousness is superior to piety when confronting evil, 10, 347, 355
see also the pious
pilgrimage, 141
Abū Bakr al-Ṣiddīq and, 112–13
benefits of, 142
Farewell Pilgrimage, 83, 113, 327n260
Ḥajj, 142n76
Muḥammad, the Prophet, 87
not performing pilgrimage without excuse, 269*t*
Shiʿi Islam, 331
ʿUmra, 82, 120, 142n76
Pinnock, Clark, 216–17
the pious (*muttaqūn*), viii, 125–30, 141, 447, 453
advising others to be pious, 74

birr (pl. *abrār*), 128
characteristics of, 127–30, 133
fear of God, 126, 127, 449
God's grace and, 447
God's love for, 220, 221
Hellfire, salvation from any punishment of, 447–52, 465n69, 476
intermediate sins, 126, 128, 271, 272, 340, 449, 465n69, 478
major sins, avoidance of, 126, 128, 135, 272, 340, 449
manifestation of the pious as Divine wise purpose, viii, 44
minor sins, 126, 271, 449, 478
Paradise, 447–48, 452, 470, 472–73, 476, 478–79
the pious/the devout distinction, 125–30
Qur'ān, 7
plague, 118, 259, 378
Plague of ʿAmwās, 370, 374–75
see also disease/illness
Plantiga, Alvin, 154n29, 195n70
critique of Mackie, 195n74, 197
Felix Culpa Theodicy, 198, 293n128
free will defense, 196–98
incarnation and atonement, 292–93
on theodicies, 197–98n84
'transworld depravity', 196–97, 197n82
plenitude, principle of, 158, 172, 181, 202
polytheism, 10, 57, 80n29, 98, 113, 210, 265, 268n22, 367
Buddhism, 207
Confucianism, 206
fight against, 62, 65
Hellfire and, 265, 455, 479
Hinduism, 206, 207
worshipping other than God, 269*t*, 278, 295
ẓulm, 450n18
Pope, Alexander, 186n44
poverty, 222, 476n53
good qualities of the poor, 243
striving to resolve poverty, 32–33
see also hunger
Power, Samantha, 193–94n67, 365n81
praiseworthiness, 41, 153, 367
Divine Attribute, 5, 20, 22, 148, 188, 204n110, 294, 334, 492
praiseworthy characteristics, 130, 133
praising God, 7n20, 188n50, 474
God glorified Himself, 8n21
a means of inoculating one from ill thoughts of God, 5, 7
Sūrat al-Fātiḥa, 5, 7
Sūrat al-Kahf, 7–8
prayer
Abū Bakr al-Ṣiddīq, 113
avoidance of sins and, 142
avoiding congregational prayers, 270*t*
benefits of, 5, 142
David, 64
ʿ*Eīd* prayers, 93
five obligatory daily prayers, 3, 5, 93, 141
Friday prayer, 93, 331
Friday prayers, neglect of 269*t*, 330–31, 331nn277–78
Kaʿba, 89n72, 109, 116, 422
leading the, 113

Muḥammad, the Prophet, 85, 87, 89n72, 93, 94, 109
night prayers, 77, 85, 324n249, 419
not performing prayer, 269*t*
Paradise and, 472–73, 474
prostration, 86, 89n72, 109, 142, 458, 472–73
Rightly-Guided Caliphs, 109
supererogatory prayers, 142, 385n138, 474
Sūrat al-Fātiḥa, 3
see also remembrance of God; supplication
Predecessors (*salaf*), 147, 150, 319, 370, 374
predestination (*qadar*), 44, 153–54, 324
Adam's fall, 277
ontological predestination, 14, 246
pride, *see* arrogance/pride
privation
evil as privation, 171, 172, 180
evil and sin as privation of the deontological, 218, 265, 266
privation boni theory, 158
suffering as privation of the ontological, 218, 354
prophets (*anbiyā'*), viii, 3, 6, 28, 147, 282
arising from Abraham's lineage, 52, 53, 55
belief in, 46–47, 49
the best of humanity, viii, 339
characteristics of, 46, 255
criticism of, 97
false prophets, 86–87, 115, 299
guidance by, 339
hardship, 225–26
infallibility, 98, 99, 314, 329
killing of, 295–96, 309, 367n87
king-prophet, 107–108, 442
manifestation of prophets as Divine wise purpose, 44
marriage of, 96–103
number of, 48, 482
prophet/messenger distinction, 47–48
Qur'ān, 49, 73–74
religion, 46
see also messenger
Protestantism, 180n21, 181
Providence, *see* Divine providence
Psalms, 39, 64, 79, 217, 281
the righteous, 131n32, 336
punishment, 12, 25, 357–62
adultery, 359
death penalty, 358
disbelievers, 379–80
God's punishment, 21, 338, 361–62
killing, punishment for, 358–59
legal punishment, 268, 271, 359–61
Lot's people, 57
major sins, punishment for, 338, 357, 360
Satan, 25n43, 464
see also Hellfire
purification, 220, 224, 346
hardship and, 224, 230, 231, 235
religion and, 38
suffering and, 232

Q

qadar, *see* predestination
Qadarīs, 150–51
Qatāda, 283n85
Queen of Sheba, 68, 106, 107, 234

Quinn, Philip, 183
Qur'ān, ixn1, 4, 213, 214, 316–17
allegorical verses of, 423
Beautiful Names of God, 18
exegesis, 37n37
as final revelation to humanity, 74
light, 37–39
manuscript of, 115, 121, 300
memorization of, 473
the pious, 7
recitation of, 142, 473
revelation of, 7–8, 34, 78, 81n31, 95
supremacy of, 78–79
theodicy, vii, 3, 17
see also individual *sūras*
the Quraysh, 80n29, 81n31, 122, 337, 377, 390
caliphs from, 320
claim to religious leadership of Arabia, 83
conversion to Islam, 83, 399
opposition and wars against Muslims, 82–83
Uḥud, Battle of, 387–88, 390, 391

R

Rabīʿa al-Aslamī, 112
Ramaḍān, 85, 141
rape, 267, 273, 358n63, 359, 360n65
Rāshidī caliphate, 370
Rāzī, Fakhr al-Dīn al-, 8n21, 164n67, 362, 366, 450n18
God as Creator, 42n56
reason, 153, 206, 208, 332
Islam and, 382
truth and, 38
reincarnation, 206–207, 215
reliance on God (*tawakkul*), ix, 220, 241, 347–49
religion, 46, 177, 214
hardship and, 38
perfection in religious affairs, 127
religious knowledge, 25, 35, 142, 234, 489
religious resurgence, 11, 355–57, 366, 369–70, 489
religious will, 140, 179, 343
There is no compulsion in religion, 193, 381–82
remembrance of God, 156, 163, 239, 253
benefits of, 419–20
neglect of, 13
peace in, 240
repentance, 132–33, 250, 271, 349–50, 355
God's acceptance of Adam's repentance, 51, 277–78
God's love for, 349–50, 355–56
Ibn al-Qayyim on, 349–50, 352
Satan, refusing to repent, 275
those who repent (*tawwābīn*), 220
resurrection, 11, 79n26, 338, 461
Day of Resurrection, 251, 338
Revelation, 25
Gabriel and, 34–35, 79
guidance and, 31
Islam, 49
as 'light', 39
reward, xn2, 335
doing good without expecting reward, 15
free will and, 36

good deeds and, 341–42, 344
hardship and, 224–25, 231
Paradise, 394, 467, 476–77, 479, 483
the righteous, 341–42, 479
ribā, *see* usury/interest
riḍā, *see* contentment
the righteous (*ṣāliḥūn*), viii, 141, 201, 336, 339, 389, 471
characteristics of, 130–32, 134, 339
critical mass of righteous, 489
depending on God, 6
God's favour upon, 476–79
God's love for, 22, 356, 478, 492
importance of, viii, 10
intermediate and minor sins, 135, 340, 465n69, 478
major sins, avoidance of, 135, 340
manifestation of the righteous as Divine wise purpose, 44
Paradise, 10n34, 342, 470–73, 476, 477–79, 484–85
Psalms on, 131n32, 336
reward for, 341–42, 479
righteous scholars, 132, 135
Straight Path, 6
striving against evil, 133–35, 341, 370
Sūrat al-Kahf, 10
righteousness, viii, 9–10, 17, 132, 339
God's love for, 356
resurgence of, ix, 395, 489
righteousness is greater than piety, 128, 355, 449
as ultimate objective in society, 355
Rightly-Guided Caliphs, 105–106, 124, 323–24, 330, 401
duration of caliphates, 90, 106
following the methodology (*sunna*) of, 106, 114, 316, 319, 321n238, 454n29
following the Prophetic Sunna, 108
not infallible, 313n206, 329
prayer, 109
zakat, 109
see also Abū Bakr al-Ṣiddīq; ʿAlī b. Abī Ṭālib; ʿUmar b. al-Khaṭṭāb; ʿUthmān b. ʿAffān
riyāʾ, *see* ostentation
Rowe, William, 198–99, 201, 360n65
Rūmī, Jalāl al-Dīn al-, 156
Ruqayya bint Muḥammad, 119
rusul, *see* messengers

S
Saadya ben Joseph/Saadya Gaon, 202
sābiqūn (foremost in good deeds), 450, 453, 470
Saʿd b. Mālik (Saʿd b. Abī Waqqāṣ), 104, 109, 119, 372–73, 389
Saʿd b. Muʿādh, 80
Saʿd b. ʿUbāda, 114–15
Saʿdī, ʿAbd al-Raḥmān al-, 41
Safavid dynasty, 321–22, 321n240, 322n241, 331n277, 376n118, 401
Safī al-Dīn Ardabīlī, 376n118
Saʿīd b. al-ʿĀṣ, 121n74
Saʿīd b. Zayd, 104, 109
saints (*awliyāʾ*), 6, 141
not necessarily perfect, 135n50
Saladin, 369, 383

salaf, *see* Predecessors
Ṣāliḥ, 49, 73, 74
ṣāliḥūn, *see* the righteous
salvation, 350
  affirming God's Oneness as requisite for salvation, 455, 457n41
  Divine grace and, 467
Samuel, 65, 68, 299, 308n180, 433–34, 435, 439–41, 442
Satan, 274–77
  arrogance, 9, 274
  disobedience and punishment, 25n43, 275, 436
  Iblīs, 9n29, 436
  Ibn al-Qayyim on, 149, 150, 276–77
  a jinn, 9, 274
  Nursī, Saʿīd on, 159
  punishment of, 25n43, 464
  refusing to repent, 275
  Shayṭān, 9n29, 436
  as source of evil, 4, 17, 149
  Sūrat al-Kahf, 9
  Sūrat al-Nās, 17
  tempting Adam, 50, 51, 148
  wise purposes in allowing the existence of, 149, 276–77, 345
satanic calumnies, 423–24
satanic nature, 396, 463–64, 492
Saul (*Ṭālūt*), 98, 437, 433–43
  disobedience, 299
  as king, 308, 433–35, 436, 442
  suicide, 442
Saul of Tarsus, *see* Paul
Savory, Roger, 321n237, 322
scholars
  Ḥadīth scholars, 78, 171n99
  righteous scholars, 132, 135
  theodicy, Islamic theological schools and scholars on, 147–74
  truly faithful scholars, 136, 339
Scott, Martin, 177n3
Scriptures, viii, 25, 79
  alteration of, 308–309
  as 'light', 39
  see also Gospels; Qur'ān; Torah
Shah, Muhammad Maroof, 173nn108–10
sharr, *see* evil
Shihadeh, Ayman, 153n26, 164n67
Shiʿi Islam, 314–32, 401–402
  absent Twelfth Imam, 330–31
  ʿĀshūrā' rituals, 371n95
  badā', doctrine of, 318
  Beatific Vision, denial of, 318
  claim of ʿAlī as first caliph, 123, 314–16, 318, 320, 322
  criticism of the Companions by, 317, 321, 326n256, 401
  dissimulation, 322n242
  divisions and sects, 325–26
  five principles of religion (*uṣūl al-dīn*), 324n251, 326
  ḥadīth methodology, 326n257, 329–30
  ḥadīths said at Ghadīr Khumm, 315–16, 319–20, 322
  Household of the Prophet as descendants of ʿAlī and Fāṭima, 318
  imamate, doctrine of, 314, 318, 324–26, 330, 330n276
  Imams' infallibility, claims of, 314, 325, 326–29
  Iraq, 329n270
  a minority, 322n242, 402, 454–55

pilgrimage, 331
on pledging allegiance to Abū Bakr, 115n51
sainthood (*wilāya*), 324n251, 330n276
Sunna, 317, 326n255
Sunni/Shiʿi conflict, 321–22, 376n118, 402
see also ʿAlawīs; Ismāʿīlīs; Twelver Shiites; Zaydīs
Shuʿayb, 24n36, 49, 73–74, 132
ṣiddiqūn, *see* the truly faithful
Ṣiffīn, Battle of, 123, 321, 328, 371–72, 374
sin, 19
benefits of allowing disbelievers to incur, 354–55
consequences of, 51, 349
expiation of, 230, 231, 456
ontological existence of, 333
original sin, 260, 278, 295
prayer as means to avoid sins, 142
as privation of the deontological, 218
secondary major sins, 270*t*, 450
wicked major sins, 143, 268, 269*t*, 450
see also intermediate sins; major sins; minor sins
sincerity, 221
suffering/evil and the elucidation of sincerity, 232–35, 276, 344, 345–46, 392
testing and, 227
society
atheism: deconstructive effect upon societies, 211
failure to fight against oppression, 363–66
general wrongdoing, 158–59
major sins, gratuitous evils and legal punishment, 358–62, 366
reformation of, 133
righteousness as ultimate objective in society, 355
striving and fighting against evil, 133
working together to overcome or prevent suffering, 253
sodomy, 58, 126n5, 269*t*
Solomon, 49, 65–68, 96, 107, 234, 281–82, 285, 299n153, 382, 441n161
marriages of, 98–99
patience, 250
repentance, 250
son of David and Bath-sheba, 97n114
wisdom and sovereignty, 65–67, 250
worshipping God alone, 99
soul, 137–38, 167
soul-making theodicy, 181–82
Hick, John, 179–83, 191, 198–99
human perfection as aim of, 182
Irenaeus, 180–81
Schleiermacher, Friedrich, 180n21
Speak, Daniel, 183
Spiegel, James S., 98n116, 407n35
Spinoza, 202, 203
stealing, 142, 358n63, 365
from orphans, 267, 268, 269*t*
legal punishment for, 360–61
stealing the spoils of war, 269*t*, 360
Straight Path, 3, 236
divine guidance to, 6, 23, 49
elucidated by the Prophet Muḥammad, 171

those who are not on, 6
Sūrat al-Fātiḥa, 6, 412
Stump, Eleonore, 215
Successors, 134, 235, 329n270, 403
as 'the best of humankind', 104
suffering, ix, 161, 218–63, 272
absence of rule of law as cause of, 15
animal suffering, 262–63
blameworthy characteristics as source of, 253–54
children's suffering, 192–93, 201, 259–62, 360n65
the greater good, suffering as means to, 149, 156, 239
human inadequacy as cause of suffering, 15, 218–19
Ibn al-Qayyim on, 149
love and moral goodness, suffering as means towards, 183
neglecting the suffering of the weak and innocent, 193–94
as privation of the ontological, 218
purification and, 232
striving to resolve suffering, 32, 253
working together to overcome or prevent suffering, 253
see also hardship; theodicy: Islamic theodicean solutions
Sufism, 156–57, 160n50
mystical unveiling, 157, 165, 168–70
Sufi antinomianism, 244n84
suicide, 269*t*, 424, 442, 464n66
Sumayya bint Khabbāṭ, 385
Sun-Tzu, 429
Sunna of the Prophet Muḥammad, ixn1, 20–21, 77–78, 95, 100, 214, 316–17
following the Sunna, 91, 106, 114, 317, 319, 321n238
necessary for a theodicy, vii, 17, 125
Shiʿi Islam and, 317, 326n255
Sunni Islam, 16, 154, 174
Ahl al-Sunna wa'l-Jamāʿa, 454
infighting against Sunni Muslims, 376
Paradise, 454–55
'Sunni revival', 369
Sunni/Shiʿi conflict, 321–22, 376n118, 402
supplication, 94, 142–43
asking for God's forgiveness, 240–41
God's answer to, 241–42
Muḥammad, the Prophet, 240
sincere supplication to God reduces suffering and evil, 242
suffering as motivation for, 239–42, 349
see also prayer
Sūrat al-Aḥzāb, 102
Sūrat Āl-ʿImrān, 74, 125, 136, 355, 411, 470n15
Sūrat al-Anʿām, 49
Sūrat al-Anfāl, 386
Sūrat al-ʿAnkabūt, 74
Sūrat al-ʿAṣr, 340, 479
Sūrat al-Baqara, 7, 224, 326, 396
Sūrat al-Burūj, 384–85
Sūrat al-Falaq, 3, 16, 17
Sūrat al-Fatḥ, 83, 412n64
Sūrat al-Fātiḥa, 3–7, 8, 17, 108, 412
praising God, 5, 7
prayer, 3

Straight Path, 6, 412
Sūrat al-Ḥadīd, 470n15
Sūrat al-Ḥujurāt, 124, 373
Sūrat al-Ikhlāṣ, 3n3, 16
Sūrat al-Isrāʾ, 8n21, 78n20
Sūrat al-Kahf, 3, 7–15, 17, 469n14, 489, 490
Dhū al-Qarnayn, 12, 14, 489
Khiḍr, 12–15, 262, 267n17, 489
Moses, 12–15, 489
Muḥammad, the Prophet, 3n2
Oneness of God, 8
praising God, 7–8
protection against the Antichrist, 393
regarding Satan, 9
revealed in Mecca, 15n55
the righteous, 10
story of the believer and the disbeliever, 11–12
story of the seven believers, 10–11, 384
worship, 8–9, 11
Sūrat al-Māʾida, 39, 455
Sūrat al-Munāfiqūn, 411, 419, 420
Sūrat al-Muṭaffifīn, 470
Sūrat al-Muzzammil, 385n138
Sūrat al-Nās, 3, 8n23, 16, 17
Sūrat al-Nisāʾ, 411
Sūrat al-Nūr, 37–40, 101
Sūrat al-Ṣāffāt, 74
Sūrat al-Shuʿarāʾ, 74
Sūrat al-Wāqiʿa, 470
Sūrat al-Zukhruf, 74
Suyūṭī, Jalāl al-Dīn al-, 160–61
Swinburne, Richard, 182n27, 215
Syria, 84, 117, 365, 374–75, 402, 417, 428

T

Ṭabarī, Muḥammad b. Jarīr al-, 41, 42, 112, 410
falaq, meaning of, 16
on hypocrisy, 427n112
on Solomon, 66n90
Tafsīr al-Ṭabarī, 66n90, 381n129, 427n112, 450n18
Ṭabāṭabāʾī, Sayyid, 330n276
Tablets, 39, 132, 302–304, 314
Tabuk, Battle of, 109, 112, 324, 414n74
ʿAlī b. Abī Ṭālib, 122, 123, 314, 315n209
hypocrites, 400
moral weakness, 414
Muḥammad's miracles, 95
ʿUthmān b. ʿAffān, 120
Ṭāʾif, 80n29
Ṭalḥa, 104, 109, 119, 371, 401
Taoism, 205–206
taqwā, *see* piety
tawakkul, *see* reliance
temptation, 35, 276, 397
testing
factors involved in, 225–28, 235
sincerity and, 227, 346
suffering as means of testing humankind, 223–28, 392, 447, 491
Tewes, Kevin, 183
thankfulness, *see* gratitude
theism, 171n102, 172, 177, 195n70, 196
theodicy, vii–ix
demands upon a theodicy hypothesis, 177, 177n3
importance of, 153
justification for pursuing a theodicy, 153–54

Qur'ān, vii, 3, 17
Sunna, vii, 17
theodicean knowledge, 13, 489, 491
see also the entries below for theodicy
theodicy: Islamic theodicean solutions, 489, 490
benevolent traits, allowing the manifestation of, 245–55, 263, 491
blessed and righteous strangers, allowing the emergence of, 366–70
bringing forth the best of humanity, viii, 104n5, 122, 223, 225, 339, 367, 395, 470, 485, 491
bringing forth those most favoured by God, 272, 339–42, 491
dependence and reliance on God, allowing the occurrence of, 347–49
Divine Attributes and Names, manifesting the consequences of a greater number of, 219–20, 333–38, 491
free will, allowing the exercise of, 342–45
God's love, allowing the demonstration of, 220–21
gratitude to God, suffering as incentive for, 242–44, 249–50
gratuitous evils and the importance of fighting for God's sake, 363–66
gratuitous evils and the importance of implementing the Divine Law, 357–63
heroism, allowing the manifestation of, 389
humility, allowing the attainment of, 237–39, 337, 349, 350, 402
hypocrisy, elucidation of, 345, 396, 397–404, 422–28, 444, 447, 492
Paradise, allowing the believers to attain a greater reward in, 394
punishment of those who disobey the Divine Law and perpetrate major sins, 357–62
religious resurgence, allowing the occurrence of, 355–57
sincerity, allowing the elucidation of, 232–35, 276, 344, 345–46, 392
suffering and evil as means to a lesser harm in the Hereafter, 465
supplication to God, suffering and evil as incentive for, 239–42, 349
testing humankind, suffering as means of, 223–28, 447
wisdom, allowing the demonstration of, 221–22
worldly detachment and desire for the Hereafter, 235–37, 388
theodicy, Islamic theological schools and scholars on, 147–74
Ashʿarīs, 151–55
Ghazālī, Abū Ḥāmid al-, 160–61, 163
Ibn ʿArabī, 165–72
Ibn ʿAṭā' Allāh al-Iskandarī, 156

Ibn al-Qayyim, 147–50, 154, 162–63
Ibn Rushd, 165
Ibn Sabʿīn, 172
Ibn Sīnā, 163–65
Iqbal, Muhammad, 173
Māturīdīs, 155–56
Muʿtazilīs, 150–51
Nursī, Saʿīd, 157–60
Qadarīs, 150–51
Sufism, 156–57
traditionalist doctrine, 147–50, 154, 155
see also 'the best of all possible worlds'
Thomas, Abdulkader, 388
Torah, 39, 47n8, 71, 79, 105n10, 280, 313, 359, 411n61, 422n96
Muḥammad, the Prophet, 76
transmission of the text of, 308n183
Toynbee, Arnold, 77n13
Trench, Battle of the, 82, 95, 400
tribulations, *see* hardship
Trinity, 8, 73, 280–81, 285, 289, 290, 293n128, 301, 387
Athanasian Creed, 289n121
see also Christianity
the truly faithful (*ṣiddiqūn*), viii, 37–38, 234, 339
Āsiya, 136, 346n38
characteristics of, 135–37, 339, 346
manifestation of the truly faithful as Divine wise purpose, 44
Mary, mother of Jesus, 70, 136, 438
minor sins, 137
Paradise, 342, 470, 472, 472, 482
perfection, 136, 346
recognizing evil, 137
religious truth and 38
striving against evil, 135, 346
truly faithful scholars, 136, 339
Ṭūṣī, Naṣīr al-Dīn al-, 402n17
Twelver Shiites, 317–18, 320–21, 325, 326, 376
cursing the Companions, 321–23, 326n256
imamate, doctrine of, 324–25
occultation, 325
temporary marriage, 330
Twelve Imamate Shiite religion as state religion, 376n118
see also Shiʿi Islam

U

Ubayy b. Kaʿb, 37
ʿudūl, *see* upright and trustworthy
Uḥud, Battle of, 82, 85n49, 90, 387–90
Abū Bakr al-Ṣiddīq, 110, 389
ʿAlī b. Abī Ṭālib, 389
angels at, 340n18
Companions of the Prophet, 227, 389, 390, 400
defeat at, 387, 391
hypocrites, 399–400, 427n112
lessons from, 388–91
Muḥammad, the Prophet, 227, 389–90
the Quraysh, 387–88, 390, 391
ʿUmar b. al-Khaṭṭāb, 389
ʿUmar b. al-Khaṭṭāb, 86, 101, 111–12, 116–19, 236–37, 253, 382
Abū Bakr/ʿUmar comparison, 114

appointed by Abū Bakr as successor, 116
buried alongside the Prophet Muḥammad, 116
caliphate of, 90, 117–18, 319
eminent status of, 116–17, 120, 136, 315, 401
al-fārūq, 116
ḥadīths on, 116
Ḥudaybiya Treaty, 340
inspired with divine guidance (*muḥaddath*), 114, 116–17, 169
Islam, spread of, 117–18
martyrdom of, 115, 118, 370–71
Paradise and, 104, 109, 121n76, 473
Prophet's Household, 316
Uḥud, Battle of, 389
wealth, 109n27
see also Rightly-Guided Caliphs
Umayyad caliphate, 320, 370
Umm Kulthūm bint Muḥammad, 119
ʿUmra, *see under* pilgrimage
universal salvation, 176, 216, 455–57
Adams, Marilyn McCord, 214, 216
Christianity, 215–16, 278
Ghazālī, Abū Ḥāmid al-, 175
Hick, John 214–16
Ibn al-Qayyim, 175–76
rejection of, 215, 278, 462
Scriptures on, 215
upright and trustworthy (*ʿudūl*), 134–35
ʿUqba b. Abī Muʿayṭ, 89, 109–10, 110n28
Usāma b. Zayd, 115, 361n67, 372–73
usury/interest (*ribā*), 142, 233, 267, 269*t*, 363n77, 388–89, 431
ʿUthmān b. ʿAffān, 86, 109, 118, 119–22, 123, 315n209
caliphate of, 90, 120–21
dhū al-nūrayn, 119
eminent status of, 120, 121, 401
Ḥudaybiya Treaty, 120
Islam, spread of, 120
martyrdom of, 118, 121, 123, 321, 370–72
nomination as caliph, 119
Paradise and, 104, 109, 120, 121n76
pledging allegiance to, 119
Qur'ān, manuscript of, 121
refusal to shed the blood of the Muslims, 121
Tabuk, Battle of, 120
see also Rightly-Guided Caliphs

V

virtue, 134
Voltaire, 189, 211n141

W

waḥdat al-wujūd, *see* monism
war, 190, 377
commandment to fight piously for God's cause, 383–87, 425
corruption and, 380–81
deception in war: controversy on, 429–32
elucidation of hypocrisy as wise purpose of, 400–401, 424–28

fleeing from battle, 267, 269*t*
heroism, allowing the manifestation of, 389
inevitability of, 380
internecine wars, 123, 370, 371–73
just war, 383–84
justification of war, 380–91, 424–28
as last resort in spreading God's religion, 383
stealing the spoils of war, 269*t*, 360
unjust war, 205, 380
war against Muslims, 364–65
Waraqa b. Nawfal, 79
Watt, Montgomery, 157
wealth, 109, 110, 233–34, 238–39, 243, 273n30
will, *see* Divine will; free will
Winter, Timothy, 152, 156
wisdom (*ḥikma*), 25, 136, 210, 275, 437
definition, 155
suffering and the demonstration of divine and human wisdom, 221–22
see also Divine wisdom
wise purpose, *see* Divine wise purposes
world (this world), 489
decay, inadequacy and deficiencies of, 44
detachment from this world and desire for the Hereafter, 235–37, 388, 397
hypocrites, worldly attachments and desires, 397, 400, 406, 407, 432
other worlds, 27
temporality of, 236
as trial and tribulation, 9
see also 'the best of all possible worlds'
worship, viii, 3
angels' worship of God, 9, 33–34, 218, 262
inadequacy of human worship, 266, 492
Sūrat al-Fātiḥa, 5–6
Sūrat al-Kahf, 8–9, 11
worshipping God alone, 11, 18, 72–73, 74, 141, 278, 281, 290
worshipping other than God, 269*t*, 278, 295, 455, 465
wrath, *see* Divine wrath
wrongdoers (*ẓālimūn*), 323, 450, 452, 476

Z

Zachariah, 49, 69–70
Ẓāhirī, Dāwūd al-, 155n31
Ẓāhirī school, 154n30, 155n31
zakat, 141, 252
importance of, 252, 420
Muḥammad, the Prophet, 87
Rightly-Guided Caliphs, 109
withholding zakat, 259
see also alms/almsgiving
Zamzam, 53
Zayd b. Ḥāritha, 90, 101, 102, 119
Zayd b. Thābit, 121, 372–73
Zaydīs, 326, 330n272
Zaynab bint Jaḥsh, 101–103
Zoroastrians, 150n17
Zubayr b. al-ʿAwwām al-, 104, 109, 119, 371, 375

www.ingramcontent.com/pod-product-compliance
Lightning Source LLC
Chambersburg PA
CBHW032012230426
43671CB00005B/55
* 9 7 8 1 7 3 4 6 3 6 2 7 7 *